STUDIES IN MUSIC HISTORY

STUDIES IN
MUSIC HISTORY

ESSAYS
FOR OLIVER STRUNK

EDITED BY HAROLD POWERS

EDITORIAL COMMITTEE
JOSEPH KERMAN, KENNETH LEVY, LEWIS LOCKWOOD,
ARTHUR MENDEL, NINO PIRROTTA

PRINCETON, NEW JERSEY
PRINCETON UNIVERSITY PRESS
1968

Copyright © 1968 by Princeton University Press
ALL RIGHTS RESERVED
L.C. Card: 67-21028
Publication of this book has been aided by the
Elsie and Walter W. Naumburg Fund
in the Department of Music, Princeton University
and by the Presser Foundation

Printed in the United States of America
by Princeton University Press

Music examples by Music-Book Associates,
New York, New York

This book has been composed
in Linotype Granjon

FOREWORD

IN the late summer of 1964 a small group of Oliver Strunk's former students and colleagues met in Cambridge and initiated discussions whose final outcome is this volume. The group constituted itself an Editorial Committee; in the end, the bulk of the work became the responsibility of Professor Powers, but all members of the committee have fully shared in the tasks of revision, each in his own areas of interest.

No overall plan for the volume was formed, but there was one decision made at the outset: invitations to participate were sent only to former students of Professor Strunk, present and former colleagues of the Princeton University Music Department, and certain other long-term colleagues of Professor Strunk whose scholarly careers are in some special sense bound in with his own. Not all those who were invited could participate, but from those who are represented here has come forth a variety of approaches—philosophical, documentary, analytical, critical, biographical, not to mention compositional—whose historical and systematic range as a whole seems to reflect that of the distinguished scholar to whom they are individually dedicated.

The Editorial Committee acknowledges most gratefully the generous gifts from the Presser Foundation of Philadelphia and the Elsie and Walter Naumburg Fund in the Department of Music at Princeton University, which have helped make this publication possible. Thanks are due as well to Mrs. Eve Hanle of the Princeton University Press for her expert editorial guidance.

HAROLD POWERS

CONTENTS

CONTENTS

STUDIES IN MUSIC HISTORY

SCHOLAR AND TEACHER

OLIVER STRUNK'S remarkable intellectual and personal capacities are activated by a love of music and an insatiable curiosity about its phenomena. Even where music-historical inquisitiveness has necessarily taken control—as in his work in Byzantine music, now of many years' standing—both the goal and the method are a connoisseur's knowledge of the music itself.

> Only too obviously, if we are ever to deal with this part of the music at all, we must begin by learning to read the early sources directly, just as they were read by the scribes who wrote them and the singers for whom they were written. And we can succeed in this only if we bring to the task some part of the familiarity with the conventions of Byzantine melody that these scribes and singers must have possessed.

This observation appears in "The Notation of the Chartres Fragment" àpropos of the problems in Byzantine sources before 1100, but its spirit informs all of Strunk's work, not only in research but also in the transmission of learning. The first dissertation supervised by him opens with acknowledgment

> first and foremost to Professor Oliver Strunk—not even (from this vantage point) so much for his guidance on the dissertation, as for his teaching and his example of scholarship over a longer period. Teaching and scholarship come to the same thing with him, as indeed will have to be said of anyone who can still embody, in our time, the idea of "professor."

Thus a review of Strunk's career must take into account, however briefly, all aspects of his activities as a most distinguished member of the community of scholars. The account finds itself shifting from the *Monumenta Musicae Byzantinae* known to the specialist, to the *Source Readings in Music History* known to every student; from the journal articles to the significant footnotes in other people's publications acknowledging his help, and from the archives all over the world to the small study in Firestone Library next to the seminar room and the student carrels.

The notebooks which have been gathered together in that study are extensive and meticulous. Included in them are great quantities of polyphonic music which Strunk has transcribed over the years, analyses and orderings of various bodies of repertory from Notre Dame and Trent church music to Handel and Wagner operas, lengthy passages of primary source material, and of course innumerable references to scholarly literature in each of the areas in which he has interested himself. His own publication, however, is quite restricted. In the areas of Western chant, opera history (especially Wagner), and medieval polyphony, he has published nothing of his considerable work. In Haydn research and Renaissance music, what he has published represents only a small fraction of what he has done. In what might be called general music history, as represented by the *Source Readings in Music History*, and in Byzantine music research, his publication is monumental in more than one sense.

Many students have benefited from Strunk's deep and always current knowledge of Western chant, its literature, and its problems and byways; some have pursued the subject with distinction. His studies of seventeenth- and eighteenth-century opera are bearing fruit through the stimulus provided students who have profited from his knowledge of the repertory and its supporting literature, and from his direct perception of its central problems. The enormous collection of material devolving from his lifelong enthusiasm for Wagner is only now beginning to be exploited. In all of these areas former students have on occasion made quite specific use of items from the Strunk notebooks.

In studies in early polyphonic music, as well as in secular medieval monophony, his relationships with scholars active in such research is of some significance. Still more significant probably is the fact that many scholars now working other veins received their initiation into the profession of musical scholarship in his "Proseminar in Medieval Musicology," the rough equivalent of courses elsewhere called "Notation" or "Musical Paleography." Even as beginning students they were not presented with a textbook or a method, but rather were shown directly to the primary sources, the essential bibliographical aids, and the important existing scholarship. They were not given mere puzzles in musical decoding; rather, they were led to examine source relationships and interpretation as well as problems of notation. Transcription was just one phase of research in medieval musicology, and students as a matter of course worked on material which had not been published. Strunk has always been available with unstinting assistance, but one soon came to feel it was improper to take advantage of his willingness to be consulted until other avenues had been exhausted, in the expectation that then meetings with him would not be wasted on trivia but would bring forth the kind of observation, suggestion, or correlation that only he could make. Partly for this reason, and partly because of the example he set in his own participation, students at the very outset of their studies came to expect of themselves the same thoroughly professional attitude toward scholarship which is a hallmark of Strunk's own work.

In the areas of sixteenth-century music and Haydn research the bulk of his work has remained unpublished, though it has played a role in work done by colleagues as well as in that done by his own students; he has always been ready to give his material freely to whomever wished to make good use of it. In Gustave Reese's *Music in the Renaissance* (pp. 469-72) appears a well-known list and classification of Palestrina's masses, with annotations of basic type and for pre-existing material where relevant; it was "compiled in the main by Oliver Strunk," and the typology is his. Reese's gigantic work makes fullest use of Renaissance music published by his colleagues and predecessors; in his Preface he also acknowledges unpublished transcriptions provided by Dragan Plamenac, Charles Warren Fox, and Oliver Strunk.

On page 23 of the September 1948 *Bulletin of the American Musicological Society*, one reads that Strunk's talk at the New York Public Library on "The London Symphonies of Haydn: a New Chronology" was "to be published in *The Musical Quarterly*." It never appeared, but one can only hope that more of his materials will find as good a home as this did. In Rosemary Hughes's *Haydn*, the author recalls Strunk's talk in a footnote on page 71, and gracefully alludes to his "allowing me to make use of his notes on this point." In her Foreword as well she expresses thanks for his "generously allowing me to make use of his unpublished material on Haydn, and for his constant readiness to help me with advice and information."

In the years just before the Second World War a number of European musicologists came to the United States to make their homes, and in so doing, to help immeasurably in the establishment of music history as an important aspect of American academic and musical life. Strunk was among the most active of those Americans who took part in encouraging and assisting brilliant scholars to find a home and feel at home here. Among those who came was Alfred Einstein, bringing with him vast quantities of transcriptions and text which eventually became *The Italian Madrigal*, published by Princeton University Press. Several persons played important roles in bringing this publication to fruition. Strunk's role, which occupied him during the early years of the war period, is described by Einstein (in *The Italian Madrigal*, p. vii) as follows:

> The entire manuscript was thoroughly revised by Professor Oliver Strunk of Princeton University—a task so ungrateful that I can never be sufficiently grateful for it.

Strunk's own articles and reviews in the fields of Renaissance music and Haydn provide interesting comparisons and contrasts. In each case a new interpretation or construction is provided for a historically significant composition or repertory, or a novel feature hidden in the sources or in the music itself is brought to light. As often as not, what comes forth results not simply from new evidence but from a right understanding of known material, buttressed by a wide familiarity with unpublished as well as published sources relevant to the matter at hand. In each case one is struck by two things: how much lies beneath the surface in the way of comprehensive grasp of the general area, and how each problem calls forth a particular approach stemming from the particular nature of the evidence.

In the paper "Some Motet-Types of the 16th Century," for example, motets of Palestrina are examined from the point of view of "the general character and extent of the relationship between liturgical situation and musical style." Many casual but revealing side glimpses at the practice of other composers, such as Josquin, Byrd, and de Monte, are included. The paper concludes, in part:

> To deal effectively with any large body of evidence the historian must begin by putting it in order. . . . Which [means of ordering] he begins with may in the end make very little difference; before he has finished he will probably have used them all. . . . [But] a means in keeping with the spirit and intention of the works themselves is the logical first step and, in any event, an essential one.

To be sure, it is rare for Strunk to expound any philosophy of humane scholarship in such formal terms. A somewhat similar expression, in a colloquial vein perhaps more familiar to his students and friends, happens to have been frozen in print in the report of a discussion:

> When you look for a needle in a haystack, perhaps you may turn it up by system, but often you find it simply by kicking the straws around.[1]

The article "Haydn's Divertimenti for Baryton, Viola, and Bass," though parallel to the paper on motet-types in dealing with a consistent repertory of works, stands in contrast to it in several ways. Here Strunk had to deal with a body of music known to be incomplete, and with an ordering of the material partly given by the composer himself. Manuscript copies of a good portion of the repertory (acquired by the Library of Congress in 1906) and Haydn's catalogue of the year 1805 (at the time of Strunk's study still unpublished) are considered together with other kinds of sources—arrangements published in Haydn's lifetime, Pohl's study, and so on. From these an overall survey emerges of the sources for the repertory and of its nature and significance. Interspersed with discussions of sources are many instances and examples of those "laboratory experiments" in which, in one way or another, the inception or development of some of Haydn's most characteristic compositional procedures are pointed out and examined.

An even more striking parallel and contrast can be drawn from two other articles, one from each of these same fields. "Notes on a Haydn Autograph" is a well-known detective story about Haydn's late keyboard compositions, centered on the last three sonatas for piano. It begins with the acquisition by the Library of Congress of the autograph of the late E♭ Sonata, dated 1794, and "composta per la celebre signora Teresa di Janson." To the one completely new fact—the date—is added a precise establishment of the identity of the dedicatee and an account of certain events of her life, taken from existing but hardly well-known biographies of her daughter and her father-in-law, from contemporary reports, and from archival documents. These are combined with whatever is relevant from primary and secondary sources on Haydn himself. The result of sur-

---

[1] David Hughes (ed.), *Instrumental Music*, Cambridge, Mass. 1959, p. 53.

rounding the newly learned date with hitherto unrelated evidences is a chronology of Haydn's last works for the piano (including of course "trios" and "violin sonatas"): the given work is placed in its musical context.

The article "Guglielmo Gonzaga and Palestrina's *Missa Dominicalis*" shows, as it were, an inversion of this process. Here a circumstantial context, in the form of letters from Palestrina to the Duke of Mantua, was known; the letters deal with masses that Palestrina was to set to "reform" plainsongs to be supplied by the Duke. From Palestrina's letters the nature of the Duke's part of the correspondence is induced and a suggestion is provided for the type of plainsong that must have been involved. In the end, Strunk was able to propose a particular surviving composition which just fits the peculiar characteristics implied by the letters: from the given circumstantial context the work is inferred.

As in Haydn research and in the study of sixteenth-century music, so also in fifteenth-century music it is probably only Strunk's students and directly concerned colleagues who are aware of the depth of knowledge which he can bring to bear on a particular problem or composition. His discovery that certain compositions in the Old Hall manuscript contained unspecified canons ("The Music of the Old Hall Manuscript: A Postscript") demanded not only an intimate acquaintance with the sources and compositional techniques of the period but a lively imagination, scholarly as well as musical. Taking a hint from a realization by H. B. Collins of another unspecified canon in the manuscript, and from Collins' observation that at several points the written cantus part has a "telescoped" double text, Strunk says: ". . . the rest is easy and the surprising thing is that the obvious conclusions were not drawn long ago." To which one might add a comment inserted by Manfred Bukofzer in a footnote of his own, appended when the "Postscript" was included in the reprint of Collins' original article:[2] "We have here again an object-lesson of the well-known fact that certain hints escape detection so long as the point they hint at is not understood."

In Strunk's review of Father Feininger's edition of the Power *Alma Redemptoris* Mass, a number of significant aspects of this important and till then virtually unknown work are set forth in very short order: its position at the beginning of the tenor-mass

---

[2] *Studies in Medieval and Renaissance Music*, ed. Manfred Bukofzer, p. 81.

development along with its "companion" the *Rex Saeculorum* Mass, and its importance as evidence for the English influence, as well as internal features such as the "scholastic" layout of the tenor itself and the peculiarly significant disposition of the metric signatures. Strunk's use of every available secondary source, from the then newly published description of the Aosta manuscript down to the incipits in the catalogue of the Trent manuscripts in the Austrian *Denkmäler* series, is a valuable lesson in how to work with what one can get.

If one can conclude that research work ought to have some *raison d'être* beyond publication for its own sake, it should not surprise anyone that in those of Strunk's publications that stand forth as major landmarks in musicology there is an explicit or implicit motive for the amount of energy and effort that lies behind them. There are two fields in the history of music in which his work has had and will have a lasting impact through its appearance in print, not only for what it shows but for what it is. Paradoxically, one of these fields is the history of music itself.

The *Source Readings in Music History* "has, at bottom, a practical purpose—to make conveniently accessible to the teacher or student of the history of music those things which he must eventually read." The quality of the work thus intended shows not only in the translations (most of which were new, and all of which are admirably suited to their particular purposes) but even more in the criteria for inclusion and in the annotations, both of which are discussed in the Foreword. As a reminder of the utility of the work, a utility which goes far beyond what appears on the surface, one might consider two items in areas not hitherto touched upon in these pages; many more could be adduced along similar lines.

One of the most difficult and controversial aspects of "The Greek View of Music" is the relationship of Plato's *harmoniai* with the writings of the theorists. In a single footnote to his excerpt from the *Republic*, Strunk provides a translation of the one specifically relevant later passage, from Aristides Quintilianus, and a three column-inch bibliography of modern opinion, with succinct but sufficient hints to its use. In the passages from Rameau's *Traité* a similar manner of selection and annotation is apparent. The selection of the Preface permits the presentation of two threads which constantly recur in Rameau's writings: his Cartesian reliance on derivation "from a self-evident principle," and his skipping back over a century and a half to Zarlino as his one worthy predecessor. The particular passage which Strunk selected from Book Two, through the addition of a number of ingeniously strategic footnotes quoting from and occasionally illustrating Rameau's own *table des termes*, allows for the introduction and definition of every important concept developed by Rameau, as a "continuous, self-contained, and independently intelligible passage," to quote one of the criteria adumbrated in the Foreword.

It is through the *Source Readings* that Strunk's name has reached large numbers of students and teachers of music history. But during the period in which he was bringing this work to completion, he was actively engaged in fundamental work in what to most musical scholars is still an esoteric branch of musicology. That the particularly challenging problems and difficulty of the sources in Byzantine music play a role in Strunk's interest cannot be gainsaid. Yet the impetus seems not so much that there is a wealth of unfamiliar material to be found and explored, but even more that the study of Byzantine music is inescapably bound in with the complexities of the early Christian music of the West which Strunk knows so well. Thus it is ultimately an integral part of the wellsprings of other and more directly accessible manifestations of musical creativity in Western musical history. Since this generally little-known area has occupied the major part of Strunk's energies for many years, it seems appropriate to survey his labors in this field a little more extensively, and for convenience, under topical headings.

His attention was drawn to this study in the middle 1930's, when the field was in an early stage of development. A handful of older scholars had produced work of increasing refinement since the beginning of the century. One result of their activity was the formation in 1931 of the *Monumenta Musicae Byzantinae* (*MMB*), an international organization for the publication of Byzantine musical monuments, founded by three senior Europeans (Tillyard, Wellesz, and Høeg) under the auspices of the Union académique internationale. But the first fruits of their corporate enterprise appeared only in 1935, and in the United States there were no specialists in the subject. When Strunk began his studies, he was more or less isolated from contact with scholarly tradition and from nearly all manuscript sources; he was further isolated from the latest literature by the war in 1939. Nonetheless, he made rapid progress with the limited materials at hand.

Basic theory. First results of his work were taken up in Gustave Reese's *Music in the Middle Ages* (1940), and a first article appeared in 1942: "The Tonal System of Byzantine Music." One central problem of Byzantine chant is that no adequate description of the intervals that make up the tonal system is provided, either in the discussions by Byzantine theorists or in the nature of the notation itself. A working approximation of the system had been reached by trial and error, but it was Strunk's considerable service to show—through careful observation and a few imaginative deductions—what the precise disposition of the tonal system was. By doing this he gave a solid basis to all future transcriptions of Byzantine melodies. The article also contains an analysis of Byzantine melodic procedures that has become classic. With the problem of tonal system settled, Strunk turned to the one equally puzzling obstacle to authoritative melodic transcriptions. In "Intonations and Signatures of the Byzantine Modes" (1945), he explained the system of preparatory formulas and starting tones that govern the openings of the hymns. Again, earlier studies had arrived at experimental solutions, but Strunk provided the theoretical proof, and with it corrected errors, filled gaps, and further insured the soundness of transcriptions.

New sources. In the first paragraph of "The Tonal System" (1942), Strunk announced three separate studies. The first two appeared as his articles of 1942 and 1945, but the third, which was to discuss the psalm-tones of the Eastern Church, was not published. With the resumption of international activity after the war, and the expanded possibilities for research, the project was evidently set aside to await a broader view of the materials. In the summer of 1950 Strunk returned to Europe on the first of several journeys which in the next ten years took him to most of the important centers for Byzantine manuscripts in Western Europe and the Christian Near East. In quick order he explored the sources at Paris, Milan, Rome, Grottaferrata, Messina, and Athens, and the monasteries at Grottaferrata and on Mount Athos, Patmos, and Mount Sinai. From this time on, the major portion of his creative energies was devoted to problems in Byzantine chant, and his phenomenal knowledge of the sources soon set the pace for all others in the field.

Melismatic chants. Results of his new studies are evident first in "S. Salvatore di Messina and the Musical Tradition of Magna Graecia" (1953). Behind the modest precision of this title lies the identification of the highly important soloist's book (the Psaltikon) and the choirbook (the Asmatikon) used at Constantinople and cathedral churches throughout the Empire from about the tenth through thirteenth centuries. The combined repertories of melismatic chants in these two books correspond roughly in function and significance to those in the Graduale and Responsoriale in the Western Church. In "The Alleluia-Cycle in Byzantine Chant," a paper delivered at New York in January 1955, Strunk described the Byzantine counterparts of the Western Alleluia verses at Mass. Ten years of additional study produced little to improve this treatment, but the paper remains unpublished; many of its findings, however, have been put to use in a recent dissertation by the Danish Byzantinist, C. Thodberg. In an extensive chapter drafted in 1953 or 1954, Strunk examined the Byzantine counterparts of the Western Gradual Responds, the Prokeimena; again this material remains unpublished, as does a paper on the Kontakia in the recension of the Psaltikon, first delivered at Copenhagen in 1958. In effect, Strunk's discussions of the Alleluia verses and Prokeimena, both of which break fresh ground, offer the full picture of the Byzantine chants that are counterparts to the Responsorial Mass chants in the West.

Cathedral and monastic practice. With his "The Byzantine Office of Hagia Sophia" (1956), Strunk turned to another central problem. Here he examined musical and liturgical differences between the cathedral and monastic rites from the ninth through fifteenth centuries. The subject has major importance for the history of music, but a good deal of its substance lies within the competence of historians of the liturgy. Strunk's authoritative contribution filled an obvious gap and was quickly taken into the standard literature of Byzantine liturgiology.

Pre-history. For the historian of musical liturgy, the central problem is, in Strunk's words, "How can we control the evidence of our oldest manuscripts? To what extent does their melodic tradition reflect that of earlier times?" In a unique argument, "St. Gregory Nazianzus and the Proper Hymns for Easter" (1956), Strunk shows that two Easter hymns found with notation only in considerably later sources were likely to have been sung in much the same way by the middle of the sixth century. With this he established the historical authority of the musical style found in both the Sticherarion and the Hirmologian, the two principal collections of Byzantine syllabic hymns (they correspond roughly to the Western Antiphonale and Hymnary), which are preserved with musical notation only from the tenth century onward.

Byzantium and the West. In 1957 Strunk contributed a short article, "L'Influsso del canto liturgico orientale su quello della chiesa occidentale," to a collective volume on the occasion of Pius XII's encyclical letter "Musicae sacrae disciplina." Here he discussed musical relations between Byzantium and the West, showing that the fundamental division into modes, and the psalmodic procedures that accompany it, were related in the two churches during the early ninth century. It is characteristic that although Strunk has published nothing restricted to the subject of Western chant, his knowledge of it, demonstrated by authoritative touches in his articles, runs as deep as it does for the East. He returned to the question of East-West relationships in "The Latin Antiphons for the Octave of the Epiphany" (1963), in which positive musical and liturgical answers are supplied for questions connected with the celebrated Carolingian borrowing of the antiphon-series *Veterem hominem.* In quite a different spirit, his "A Cypriote in Venice" (1962), a genial compliment to his friend Knud Jeppesen, explores "a strange meeting between the music that interests (Jeppesen), the music of sixteenth-century Italy, and the music of Byzantium."

Psalmody. The study of Byzantine psalmody, first projected in 1942, and touched briefly in "L'Influsso" in 1957, received full-dress treatment in "The Antiphons of the Oktoechos" (1960). The unassuming title and economy of presentation (eighteen pages) mask a contribution of major importance. The Byzantine system of syllabic psalm-tones and cadences is synthesized from thirteenth- and fourteenth-century sources, and its melodic stability and historical authority are traced to the late eighth century, in part with the support of Slavic sources of the twelfth century. In effect this demonstration supplies for Byzantine psalmody what the *Commemoratio brevis* and the earliest tonaries supply for our knowledge of psalmody in the West from the ninth through eleventh centuries.

Early Byzantine notations. Although Byzantine manuscripts with melodic notation go as far back as the middle of the tenth century, their notation becomes fully decipherable only in the late twelfth century. Earlier notations, like the staffless neumes in the West, provided only part of the information necessary for transcription, and they have generally been considered impossible to transcribe without a later control. Strunk's first contribution to the problem was his "The Classification and Development of the Early Byzantine Notations" (1950). This was followed in 1955 by "The Notation of the Chartres Fragment," which offers, again under a heading of deceptive modesty, the precise classification and the method for transcription of a broad range of early Byzantine notations. This result had much more than simple methodological importance since a considerable number of Byzantine chants are preserved only in earlier manuscripts that employ the less complete notations. Strunk would return to this problem in his studies of early Slavic chants, again in the introduction to his paleographical album, *Specimina notationum antiquiorum* (1966), and eventually in a projected full-scale handbook to the early notations.

Slavic chant. During a trip to Mount Athos in 1955, Strunk took the occasion to examine, along with the Greek manuscripts, two twelfth/thirteenth century Slavic manuscripts with musical notation in the library of the Chilander monastery. His report to the Dumbarton Oaks Research Library on these manuscripts, one a Sticherarion, the other a Hirmologion, was incorporated in Professor Roman Jakobson's important facsimile editions of both manuscripts (Copenhagen, 1957). This first exposure to Slavic musical sources led Strunk to a remarkable penetration of the literary, liturgical, and musical history of the early Slavic chants. In 1964, for the annual symposium at Dumbarton Oaks, his paper "Two Chilandari Choir-Books" clarified the relationship of the medieval Slavic chants to their Byzantine originals, and provided the first scientific transcriptions from the previously enigmatic Slavic notations.

The MMB and the RISM. Strunk's distinguished contributions to Byzantine studies received official recognition in 1958 with an invitation from the three founding members of the *MMB* to join them as a fourth member of the board. In 1961, following the death of C. Høeg, he was called to the directorship of the entire enterprise, with responsibility for all of its research and publication projects. One of his first steps as director was to speed plans for the inventory of Byzantine musical and theoretical manuscripts before 1500, which was to be carried out by an international team of scholars under the joint auspices of the *MMB* and the *Répertoire international des sources musicales*. Within two years Strunk assembled the full materials for three of the most important deposits of manuscripts (Mount Sinai, Grottaferrata, and Messina), and laid the groundwork for extension of the inventory to other major centers. At the same time he was assuring the expansion of the *MMB* by recruiting young scholars, by promoting its publication projects, and, most significantly, by the continuing example of his own creative research.

It is in considerable measure through Strunk's contributions during the past three decades that the field of Byzantine music has reached the level of professional maturity it enjoys. His keen intelligence, always seeking out the essential questions, has illuminated one dark corner after another. Much of what must eventually be done within the field will be a filling-in of developments to which his mind first gave structure. Yet outweighing even the breadth and substance of his discoveries is the standard of craftsmanship he has set. His accurate and elegant contributions, so carefully understated in presentation, are as nearly faultless distillations from the available evidence as musicology and Byzantine studies have known. Little of what he has committed to print will be budged by further discoveries; not a line adds to the "muddying of waters" he scorns. Those who know his work may recognize in a tribute by a founding member of the *MMB*, a scholar a generation his senior, something of the nature of their own respect. As this colleague completed proofs for an important publication he received recent works by Strunk that cut across the same material. He sent this postscript to the printer:

> The learned articles by Professor Strunk reached me too late for use . . . but I am glad to say that our views are in general agreement. Where differences appear, all readers will understand that his more recent conclusions, based on far ampler material and fortified by fuller experience, are likely to be nearer the truth.

On March 22, 1966, Oliver Strunk completed his sixty-fifth year. This same spring saw his retirement from formal teaching as Professor of Music at Princeton University, after nearly thirty years at that institution. Actually, his scholarly activities might be said to have begun in 1928, when he returned from his Berlin studies with

Wolf, Schering, Sachs, and Blume to take up duties at the Library of Congress. He left the Library, of whose Music Division he had become chief, to go to Princeton in 1937, at a critical point in the history of the discipline he had surveyed in 1932 in his influential *State and Resources of Musicology in the United States.* In the three decades since that period, musical scholarship in America has grown from a trickle to a cataract. Insofar as this growth has been guided by men and minds rather than by impersonal mechanical social forces, his has been a major influence: there is no stream of *kleine Beiträge,* no five-foot shelf of *Grundlagen.* But if the American Musicological Society has played a role in the growth of scholarly studies in music here, he was one of its half-dozen founding fathers, and the first editor of its journal. If the influx of distinguished European scholars both before and after the war has stimulated musical scholarship in America, he has often been instrumental in their settling on this side of the water. If the Eighth Congress of the International Musicological Society in New York in 1961 marked the coming of age of American musicology and the augury of its primacy, his was a guiding hand. It is typical that he agreed to accept nomination and to serve as President of the American Musicological Society not at the time of the Congress to which it was host but for the term just preceding, when the organization had to be drawn up, funds found, invitations issued, and arrangements made. His reputation as a scholar and as a man among leaders of the profession, both here and abroad, eminently fitted him for such a task.

That a man of few public appearances, with a relatively modest bibliography except in one recondite specialty, can command the respect and affection of his most distinguished colleagues as well as of his students bespeaks a very special combination of qualities of mind, heart, and character. Indeed, his wide learning and shrewd intelligence, his constant preoccupation with striking to the heart of the matter from the closest sources, his distrust of system for its own sake, his intense and painstaking labors in the collection of large amounts of material, his generosity with colleagues and students alike, and his release for publication of only certain results he considers of significance—all of these characteristics are of a piece inseparable. In a time of new reflection about the aims and methods of musicology, his work and his influence is toward the opening, not the closing of questions: new discoveries lead not to conclusions but to new tasks. And in a time of endless discussion of teaching versus research, his implicit values for musical scholarship and attitudes about the transmission of learning are an all too rare amalgam: the research of scholars and the informing of students are aspects of the same thing, directed not merely toward mastery of materials and techniques but toward sensitization to problems. In Oliver Strunk the teacher, the scholar, and the man are indivisible: musical insight, intellectual *virtuosismo*, immense learning, generous tolerance, and courtesy are permeated with humane sensibility and moral responsibility.

FOUR CANONS

MILTON BABBITT

* The verbal and note quotations are from the *Birthday Canons* to Carl Engel **by** Arnold Schoenberg.
© 1943, by G. Schirmer, New York.

Je - - dem geht es so;

dem geht es so; Kei - ner

Kei - ner bleibt bei zwan - zig e - wig steh'n."

bleibt bei zwan-zig e - - wig steh'n."

(♩ = 84)

Je - - dem geht es so;

"Je - - dem geht es so; Kei-ner bleibt bei zwan -

Kei - ner bleibt bei zwan - zig e - wig

zig e - wig stehn." "Kei - ner bleibt

steh'n." "Kei - ner bleibt bei

bei zwan - zig e - wig steh'n."

zwan - zig e - wig steh'n." "Je - dem geht es__ so."

"Je - dem geht es__ so."

(♩ =96)

Je - dem geht es so; Kei - ner__

Je - dem geht es so; Kei - ner__

bleibt bei zwan - zig e - wig steh'n."

bleibt bei zwan - zig e - wig steh'n."

"Je - dem geht es so; Kei - ner bleibt__

"Je - dem geht es so; Kei - ner bleibt__

bei zwan - zig e - wig steh'n."

bei zwan - zig e - wig steh'n.'

I. MUSIC HISTORY

CURRENT HISTORIOGRAPHY
AND MUSIC HISTORY

DONALD JAY GROUT

RECENT English and American studies in the philosophy of history,[1] in contrast to most earlier work in this field, are primarily analytical, reflecting current interest in the nature of scientific explanation. For the most part, they seem to have grown out of "the challenge posed by the existence of historical knowledge, with its imprecisions and particularity, to the conclusions reached about the nature of scientific method and objectivity won by an analysis of the logic of the natural sciences."[2] Although the discussion is carried on most often with reference only to general history, much of it is clearly applicable to specialized historical fields. The present essay is an attempt to outline some of the main issues and arguments, together with some thoughts they suggest which may be relevant to historical studies in music.[3]

[1] *History and Theory,* 1 (1960-61)—, with bibliographies in Supplements Nos. 1 and 3; William Dray, *Philosophy of History* (Englewood Cliffs, N.J.: Prentice-Hall, 1964); W. H. Walsh, *Philosophy of History* (New York: Harper, 1960); R. G. Collingwood, *The Idea of History* (New York: Oxford University Press, 1956); Maurice H. Mandelbaum, *The Problem of Historical Knowledge* (New York: Liveright, 1938); Marc Bloch, *The Historian's Craft* (New York: Knopf, 1953); Sidney Hook, *The Hero in History* (New York: John Day, 1943); Raymond Aron, *Introduction to the Philosophy of History* (Boston: Beacon Press, 1961); Patrick Gardiner, *The Nature of Historical Explanation* (London: Oxford University Press, 1952); Leo Strauss, *Natural Right and History* (Chicago: University of Chicago Press, 1953); Sir Isaiah Berlin, *Historical Inevitability* (London: Oxford University Press, 1954); William Dray, *Laws and Explanation in History* (Oxford: Oxford University Press, 1957); Jacques Maritain, *On the Philosophy of History* (New York: Scribner, 1957); Arnold Hauser, *The Philosophy of Art History* (New York: Knopf, 1959); E. H. Carr, *What Is History?* (New York: Knopf, 1962); Karl R. Popper, *The Poverty of Historicism* (London: Routledge & Kegan Paul, 1961). Collected readings: Herbert Feigl, ed., *Readings in the Philosophy of Science* (New York: Appleton-Century-Crofts, 1953); Fritz Stern, ed., *The Varieties of History* (Cleveland and New York: World Publishing Co., 1956); Patrick Gardiner, ed., *Theories of History* (Glencoe, Ill.: The Free Press, 1959); Hans Meyerhoff, ed., *The Philosophy of History in Our Time* (Garden City: Doubleday, 1959); H. P. R. Finberg, ed., *Approaches to History* (London: Routledge & Kegan Paul, 1962); Sidney Hook, ed., *Philosophy and History* (New York: New York University Press, 1963); Alan Donagan, ed., *Philosophy of History* (New York: Macmillan, 1965).

[2] Hook, *Philosophy and History,* p. x.

[3] A notable step in this direction, and one to which I gladly acknowledge indebtedness, is Arthur Mendel's "Evidence and Explanation," published in International

Unquestionably a great deal of excellent history, musical and other, has been and is being written without benefit of express philosophical analysis of such matters as the possibility of objective historical knowledge or the nature of historical explanation. Yet presuppositions about these matters underlie all historical writing, and their analyses may serve to clarify the historian's task and perhaps suggest new lines of investigation in particular cases. While it is true that the discipline of historical musicology is still in the relatively early stage of assembling material, the constantly increasing specialization within the field makes it desirable from time to time to consider general questions of common concern.

The word "history" denotes (1) past events, considered in their chronological order; or (2) a record of past events. History in the second sense has two distinguishing characteristics: its form is narrative and its subject matter is past events which involve human agency. History differs from other types of narrative in being "tethered to reality."[4] Restriction to human agency excludes the genetic sciences and the "historical" aspects of the physical sciences, particularly astronomy and geology. Natural events (as earthquakes) become subject matter of history insofar as they affect human actions or enter into the explanation of human actions. Findings of the natural and social sciences may be used in historical explanations, their methods may be applied in historical studies, and their development may be the subject of special branches of history.

Music history has the distinguishing characteristics of history as above defined, together with the limitation that its subject matter is confined to (1) musical events and (2) other events insofar as they affect musical ones or are affected by them. The relationships between music history and the systematic branches of musicology (as acoustics, psychology, aesthetics, music theory, ethnomusicology) are analogous to those between general history and the natural and social sciences as indicated in the preceding paragraph. Systematic studies of music may make use of historical conclusions and may also contain historical statements.

Musicological Society, *Report of the Eighth Congress, New York 1961* (Kassel [etc.]: Bärenreiter, 1962), II, 3-18. See also the chapter "The Philosophy of Music History" in Glen Haydon, *Introduction to Musicology* (New York: Prentice-Hall, 1941) for an account of some of the issues in earlier literature on this subject.

[4] Sir Isaiah Berlin, "History and Theory," in *History and Theory*, 1 (1960-61), 25.

Although there is no "clearly marked group of philosophical problems peculiar to history,"[5] contemporary analysis has tended to focus on certain questions, all interrelated but conveniently divisible into questions about (respectively) *objectivity* and *explanation*.

Objectivity

The fundamental question might be phrased thus: Is it possible to give a true account of the past?

Apparently not. In the first place, most of "the past" is unknown, while the remainder is known only by inference from such evidence as is available to us in the present—evidence which we can never be sure is complete. Moreover, since even the known past events are too numerous to be recorded practicably and since some of them seem more important than others, people who write history always select certain events to write about. They then impose on these selected events a pattern, a structure or "meaning," which is something different from the events themselves. At either or both these stages of his activity a historian's judgment is bound to be affected by his personal opinions or prejudices, or by those of his nation or his social class, or by the general "climate of opinion" prevailing at the time and place of his life. "The historian, before he begins to write history, is a product of history."[6] Therefore, no historian can either know the past in its entirety or write about any part of it objectively; therefore, it is impossible to give a true account of the past; therefore, all history is false. This absurd conclusion suggests that we might do well to rephrase the original question, narrowing its scope and eliminating some of the ambiguous terms.

Can history be objective in the sense of "value free"? Or are judgments of value logically, necessarily inherent in the nature of historical investigation?

Some would deny that they are: true, a historian elects to study a certain range of facts because he finds them interesting or significant; but if choice at this level is evaluative, it is at any rate not peculiar to history, since comparable choices are made for like reasons by natural scientists too. The peculiar task of history, it is argued, is to establish facts about the past and explain them. Disagreement about either verification or explanation, if these have

[5] Gardiner, *Theories of History*, p. 273.
[6] Carr, *What Is History?*, p. 48.

been properly carried out, will be due to differences of judgment about the adequacy of our knowledge of the relevant laws and conditions; but such judgments are not judgments of value. Still, what about the facts a historian chooses to mention in his narrative? Are they not chosen on a basis of value? No, because such choices are dictated by the requirements of the subject he is investigating; they are determined by judgments of relevance, not value; and facts may be relevant for other reasons than being among the causal conditions of an event. Furthermore, although two historians may give different accounts of the same period, selecting or emphasizing different facts, it does not necessarily follow that either account is false or that one is better than the other; the facts stated in both may be equally true and the conclusions supplementary, not contradictory.

The full strength of this position cannot be appreciated until we have examined the model of causal explanation which many philosophers believe to be essential in historical investigation. Meanwhile, let us try to summarize the arguments of the opposing school—which apparently includes most of the historians who have taken part in the current debate.

History, they remind us, is about human actions; these involve motives and choices, which in turn imply value judgments. One cannot claim to understand historical events, therefore, without taking values into account. Moreover history, unlike mathematics or symbolic logic or the natural sciences, has no technical vocabulary of specially defined terms, but is written in ordinary language, which reflects the structure of human thinking in being permeated with expressions that imply judgments of value. Elimination of all such expressions would reduce any historical account to a narration of "facts" viewed from the outside. Such an account is conceivable; but if "history is what historians do" and not what some philosophers tell them they ought to do, such an account would not be history. Not merely a historian's choice of topic but also his choice of which facts are relevant (even of those included on the minimal basis of "memorability"), the direction in which he points the facts (the "sense" he gives them), and the language in which he recounts them, are all tied to judgments of values of one kind or another. This does not mean that there are no public criteria in such matters but only that the appropriate kind of criticism with respect to them is more like criticism of a work of art than of a demonstration in geometry.

Of course, values in history are those of the time studied. Part of a historian's task is to understand the values of the past; but he is able to understand them only as they have some relation to his own values, only through his own knowledge as a human being of how human beings think and act. While he does not commit the anachronism of judging the past by standards of the present, he can illuminate the past by the light of the present: showing the past as it looks to us while recognizing that this was not how it looked to itself.

It seems to be agreed by most historians and defended by many philosophers that, while value judgments are to be admitted in historical studies, there are nonetheless certain rough but generally satisfactory criteria of objectivity (in the broader sense of the word) which a historian's professional colleagues and other informed readers can apply: criteria such as respect for truth, no blinking of awkward facts, no gratuitous moralizing, no ulterior interest (as in propaganda). So the question "Can history be objective?" turns out to be like "Can stories be interesting?" The answer is yes, but that some histories are more objective than others.[7]

Most of the foregoing applies, *mutatis mutandis*, to the writing of music history; but the special range of aesthetic values has also to be considered here.[8] What is the place of judgments about the aesthetic value of individual works, composers, or styles in music-historical studies? There can be no doubt that such judgments legitimately influence the choice of a particular field of work. We study music history because (among other reasons) we are interested in music, and we study particular works or composers or schools because we are particularly interested in them. True, our motives need not be purely aesthetic. We can choose to study some music of the remote or recent past which we may think neither great nor perhaps even very "good" music, with a view to showing its role in a certain cultural configuration, or because it helps us to understand some other music, or for innumerable other reasons. There is no

[7] See Christopher Blake, "Can History Be Objective?" in *Mind*, LXIV (1955), 61-78; reprinted in Gardiner, *Theories of History*, pp. 329-43.

[8] I leave aside as immaterial to the present discussion the general philosophical problems of the objectivity of values and the nature of aesthetic values; also, I am not distinguishing between "judgments" and "verdicts" in aesthetics. It is to be expected that a historian, like a critic, will try to justify his judgments and present them persuasively enough to induce his readers to accept them, at any rate temporarily.

need to indulge in reproaches or moral directives about such choices, though there are some general desiderata that might be kept in mind.[9] The question is, once a choice has been made, does any historical treatment of music necessarily involve judgments about the aesthetic value of the music under consideration? Most music historians would probably agree with Professor Arthur Mendel that "anyone who has never experienced this baffling, aesthetic interest in a work has not even begun to understand it."[10] As a general historian understands the actions of human beings in the past by virtue of being himself human, so a music historian understands music of the past by virtue of being himself a musician. Even while one is examining a work of music as a means toward understanding something else, it is difficult to see how he can appraise its significance without reference to its aesthetic qualities.

Just as it is possible to describe human actions in language that contains no evaluative words, so it is possible to describe a work of music, or a group of works, in such a way. It may be that Sir Isaiah Berlin has in mind descriptions of this sort as appropriate in historical monographs within "an artificially delimited field . . . noting only what, say . . . methods of composing music have in common and constructing [a] model solely out of these common characteristics, however much of general interest [one] may be leaving out."[11] It seems unlikely, however, that one could produce exclusively on this principle a history of music that would define the technical elements precisely enough and at the same time include a sufficient number of separate instances to provide a basis for deriving empirical "laws" of succession in music history. For certain steps in musical analysis and historical study—if one may for the moment speak of the two as if they were separable—non-evaluative descriptions are probably indispensable; but whatever improvements may eventually be made in the technique of purely objective description of music, its final purpose is to suggest and support more inclusive modes of insight.[12]

[9] See Bernard Bailyn, "The Problems of the Working Historian," in Hook, *Philosophy and History*, pp. 92-97.

[10] Mendel, "Evidence and Explanation," p. 16.

[11] Berlin, "History and Theory," p. 16. See also Max Weber, "Der Sinn der 'Wertfreiheit' der soziologischen und ökonomischen Wissenschaften," in *Gesammelte Aufsätze zur Wissenschaftslehre*, 2nd edn. (Tübingen: J. C. B. Mohr, 1951), pp. 505ff.

[12] See, for example, Joseph Kerman, "On William Byrd's *Emendemus in melius*," *The Musical Quarterly*, XLIX (1963), 431-49.

Some further considerations are relevant to the question of aesthetic values in music-historical study. Events become significant for general history usually not because of what they were in themselves but because of their effect on later events. The creation of any work of music is a unique event which may or may not have had important historical consequences; yet the work itself, regardless of the degree of its historical effectiveness, may become significant in music history because we now regard it as having aesthetic value.[13] However, it seems obvious that works or groups of works that have produced much effect on the subsequent development of the art of music (at least as far as Western music is concerned) have done so because in the first place people simply found them pleasant, interesting, stimulating, or uplifting to hear, apart from any other reasons. A music historian will try to explain why certain works are historically significant and his explanation will probably involve showing why they were regarded as good music in their time. With the help of the available evidence, a historian will enter into the thought of the time, if possible to a point where he sympathetically comprehends its standards of judgment; but he may describe these, if he likes, by comparing them with standards of the present.

Still, history of music consists of more than listing individual works and describing past norms of aesthetic judgment. Music history purports to show certain kinds of connections among musical events that have occurred within a definite period of time and between these and other musical or non-musical events. The existence of the specified connections is the historian's thesis and the events he narrates are his supporting evidence. Whether in a given case the facts have been properly established, whether the evidence adequately sustains the thesis, whether all relevant evidence has been considered and reasonably interpreted, and whether the facts chosen have received attention in proportion to their importance, are questions which can be decided only by using the same practical criteria of objectivity that apply to any historical writing. Specifically, these criteria need to be invoked when it appears that music history is being slanted for narrowly nationalistic purposes or being used to set up exclusive claims for one particular type of musical composition.

Judgments of objectivity are of course complicated by the fact

---

[13] More generally: the historical significance of an event does not exhaust its significance.

that musical as well as general historians come to their work with differing and often irreconcilable beliefs about such fundamentals as the ultimate meaning and goal of the historical process, the nature and order of values, the possibility of free choice in human action, the social functions of art, and so on. Such beliefs, and with them conceptions of the proper aims and objects of historical study, differ not only from place to place but also from time to time. It may be remarked that a historian is the less likely to be at the mercy of his own particular situation the more he is aware of it.[14] Absolute objectivity, in musical as in general history, is out of the question; relative objectivity (if the oxymoron may be allowed) is precariously achievable.

Explanation

In current literature on the philosophy of history a large share of attention is given to the theory of historical explanation. One body of philosophical opinion[15] holds that a valid historical explanation is one which asserts a relation of cause and effect between two real events and shows that what is asserted is an instance of an empirically confirmable general hypothesis of the form "Whenever A then B" or "Whenever A then probably (to a more or less closely ascertainable degree) B," in which A and B stand for certain classes or properties of events. This type of explanation, which allows B to be predicted, is characteristic of the natural sciences; it is practicable for situations in which the preconditions (A) can be exactly specified and in which they recur or can be duplicated so that the result (B) can be observed often enough to justify the "whenever" (or "whenever . . . probably") of the hypothesis. Unfortunately, situations of this kind seldom exist in history. Either the preconditions cannot be exactly specified, or if they can they neither recur nor can be duplicated; or else, if the stipulated requirements can in some measure be met, they come out to "laws" that are either so vague or so commonplace ("all power corrupts") as to be of little use for explaining events of any complexity, or so circumstantial and complicated that they apply to only a single instance and thus are not "general."

[14] Carr, *What Is History?*, p. 163.

[15] The classical statement of this position is Carl G. Hempel, "The Function of General Laws in History," in *The Journal of Philosophy*, xxxix (1942), 35-48; reprinted in Gardiner, *Theories of History*, pp. 344-56. See also Hempel, "Reasons and Covering Laws in Historical Explanation," in Hook, *Philosophy and History*, pp. 143-63.

Insofar as historians explain by reference to general laws of human behavior (as distinct from citing, in the course of an explanation, laws tentatively established in the natural sciences), they are using "explanation sketches," that is, making imperfect explanations based on "laws" of some such form as "Whenever *A*-sort-of-things then probably *B*-sort-of-things." Although explanation sketches do not really explain, they may be useful as partial explanations and for suggesting directions in which to search for new evidence or for calling attention to possibly new significance of evidence already known; but that the sketches in principle can ever be filled out so as to become usable for predictive explanations in general history— for example, through the establishment of laws of human behavior by psychology or the other social sciences—appears doubtful. The "covering law" formula can always be applied to analyze particular historical propositions and to expose for criticism the general presuppositions that may lurk in the background of such propositions. By and large, however, explanation by subsumption under general laws is not characteristic of historical investigation or of history as historians actually write it.

This situation has led to philosophical attempts to validate other types of historical explanation. Explanations by the covering-law model belong to a class that may be called "linear," that is, explanations of one event (or complex of events) by reference to earlier ones. Another kind of linear explanation may consist of showing that a given outcome, although it could not have been certainly predicted, was nevertheless "what might have been expected": the preconditions were necessary but not by themselves sufficient to produce the result.[16] Such explanations are often found in other kinds of narrative writing, for instance in novels and dramas. Thus the ending of *Othello* is sufficiently explained by showing that, given Othello's jealous disposition, the events represented were such as could plausibly have brought him to the point of murdering Desdemona. A related kind of linear explanation, more characteristic of history, might be called "explaining how," in contrast to "explaining why." This depends on narrating events with a certain fullness and con-

---

[16] See Gilbert Ryle, *The Concept of Mind* (London: Hutchinson, 1949), pp. 43-45, 120-25, for analysis of this type of quasi-causal explanation. Such explanations can possibly be regarded as coming under the "probability" feature of the covering law theory: see Hempel, "Reasons and Covering Laws," pp. 144-49.

creteness, showing each as unique but at the same time showing how all, in varying degrees of importance, interact to form "patterns which satisfy us because they accord with life as we know it and can imagine it."[17] On this view, a good historical explanation is not one which compels us to accept it as logically entailed by premises but rather one which persuades us, as a work of art may persuade us, to see it as the "right," the "inevitable" way of structuring the given elements. These two kinds of linear explanation of course involve incidental, often implicit, reference to vague general maxims about how human beings act, as well as overt reference to the dispositions of particular individuals; but the explanation remains valid for the purpose of history even though the maxims may not be empirically fully verifiable or the postulated dispositions be sufficient for predicting particular actions.

Another class of explanations may be called "configurational." These explain historical events or situations in a "horizontal" rather than a "vertical" (linear) way, by showing them to be similar in certain discernible and important respects to other contemporary events or situations, so that they form an integral part of a total contemporary pattern. Still another kind of historical explanation is "explaining what,"[18] showing a certain conjunction of events as a member of a class of such conjunctions of which there are other examples in history, such as revolutions or processes of response to environmental change.

It need not be assumed that the various types of explanation are mutually exclusive. All types may converge.

> Historians will continue to employ characteristically historical explanations side by side with others of predictive pattern so long as history continues to be written. . . . It is perfectly possible for the intelligibility or rationality of an action to be explained, without any claim being made as to its actual or theoretical predictability.[19]

Save to those who are spellbound by dichotomies, there is nothing

[17] Berlin, "History and Theory," p. 24.

[18] See William Dray, " 'Explaining What' in History," in Gardiner, *Theories of History*, pp. 403-408 (not published previously).

[19] W. B. Gallie, "Explanation in History and in the Genetic Sciences," in *Mind*, LXIV (1955), 160-80; reprinted in Gardiner, *Theories of History*, pp. 386-402. The quotation is in Gardiner, p. 399.

scandalous in the idea that a statement . . . may be at once narra-tive, explanatory and conditionally predictive, without being a conjunctive assemblage of detachable sub-statements.[20]

The central events which music history aims to explain are those having to do with the creation of individual works of music.

I use the more general word "creation" in order to avoid the implications of "composition," a concept not applicable to all musics; also as intending to include works not notated or notated only partially or notated only at a time distinctly later than that of their creation (as with folksongs). The creation of a work of art is an "event" which, like all events in history, has to be inferred from evidence; commonly, the principal evidence is the present existence of the work.

These events are "central" simply because all other musical events depend on them. Biographical facts and facts about the diffusion of musical works may enter into historical explanations of other musi-cal and non-musical events. Insofar as studies of theory, aesthetics, and the like are historical, their subject matter is not music but ideas about music. Analysis and criticism, though often utilizing historical data, deal with a work of music primarily as a present object of inquiry. Naturally, the various approaches continually intermingle in actual writing and speaking about music.

The historian's first task is to establish, by examining and inter-preting the evidence, the actual occurrence of the events he proposes to explain—namely that certain works of music were created at certain times and places by perhaps identifiable individuals. His evidence may be indirect (as remains of musical instruments or allusions in written records) or direct (as a performance or a score). From indirect evidence he can establish no more than the creation of certain *kinds* of music; from direct evidence, that of particular works. With a score, he must not only establish its authenticity as a record of the composer's intention but also interpret that intention in terms of sound. What he then seeks to explain is the creation of the work, in the particular form in which he has it.

The need for explanation arises from the desire to ease mental tension caused by puzzlement.[21] Doubtless no explanation of the

---

[20] Ryle, *The Concept of Mind*, p. 141.

[21] John Passmore, "Explanation in Everyday Life, in Science, and in History," in *History and Theory*, II (1962-63), 105-23.

creation of a work of music, any more than of any other human action, can be exhaustive. The special kind of explanation called "historical" characteristically begins by observing those features which a particular work shares (as shown by examination) with other works that were created around the same time and place, and by constructing from these common features a provisional concept of a musical style. The usefulness of such a historical style-concept depends on the existence, within the defined limits, of a significant number of musical works having significant common characteristics.[22] The temporal boundaries extend from the moment when the common characteristics can be discerned to the moment when they no longer can be. The style-concept will evolve as new facts are taken into account; eventually it may cover a longer or shorter period, a smaller or larger geographical area, or be more or less detailed, include sub-styles, and so on, according to the amount of detail required by the historian's particular purpose. The essential is that a style-concept delineate a historical entity, a definite segment of time and space within which works of music are created having a structure that "differs in certain respects from their structure at earlier or later periods"[23] or at other places.

The practical difficulty about periodization in music history is not so much that the boundaries are hard to define as long as the works under consideration belong to one fairly homogeneous tradition (for example, Western art music), as that several types or "layers" of music may exist simultaneously in one region and, in addition, quite different types or even different systems of music in other regions. As a consequence, revision of the boundaries, or multiple sets of boundaries, may be required when the historian's attention expands to take into account music from more than a single tradition.

Style-concepts serve to establish convenient units for historical study and also as "ideal-type" concepts[24] for normative description

---

[22] What is "significant" obviously depends on the situation. As a rule the length of the period and the number of common characteristics will vary inversely; the more detailed the description of common characteristics the fewer the individual examples, etc.

[23] "It is possible to delineate time periods within which human events have a *structure* which differs in certain respects from their structure at earlier or later periods." Carey B. Joint and Nicholas Rescher, "The Problem of Uniqueness in History," in *History and Theory*, 1 (1960-61), 160.

[24] Max Weber, "Die 'Objektivität' sozialwissenschaftlicher und sozialpolitischer

of individual works. Also, they are explanatory: to ascribe a work to a style—that is, to say that it is like other works that were being created around the same time and place—is already to say something more about its creation than could be said by a mere description of its characteristics.[25]

Having thus begun by means of style-concepts, music history may continue by seeking explanations of the several styles themselves and of their succession. One way of doing this is to point to contemporary conditions that can reasonably be supposed to have affected the way in which new works within a given style were shaped. Among such contemporary conditions may have been: music already known, particularly that taken as exemplary; ideas about the nature, functions, and structure of music in general; musical notation and instruments; ideals and techniques of performance; the kinds of occasions on which music was performed; acoustical properties of places where music was heard; the kinds of music approved by various social groups; the social and economic status of musicians; relations between producers and consumers of music; and so on. Explanations of this sort are causal in that, first, they show the limitations, technical and ideological, within which creators of music worked;[26] and second, they indicate what conditions were relatively favorable or unfavorable to the creation of certain kinds of music and show how the creation of individual works was affected by those conditions. Such explanations are also configurational, in that they show connections between a given work or works and the contemporary situation both in the relatively autonomous sphere of music and in other, non-musical spheres.

The configurational approach may be extended to explain a musical style by comparing it with contemporary styles in literature and other arts and in contemporary technology, science, philosophy, and

---

Erkenntnis," in *Gesammelte Aufsätze*, pp. 191ff; *Wirtschaft und Gesellschaft*, 4th edn. (Tübingen: Mohr, 1956), pp. 1, 2, 10; J. W. N. Watkins, "Ideal Types and Historical Explanation," in Feigl, *Readings in the Philosophy of Science*, pp. 723-43 (revised and expanded version of a paper first published in *The British Journal for the Philosophy of Science*, III [1952-53], 22-43).

[25] Ryle (p. 142) contrasts the two statements "The bird is flying south" and "The bird is migrating"; the latter "describes a flying process in terms which are partly anecdotal, but are also partly predictive and explanatory."

[26] Compare Wölfflin's well-known remark, "Not everything is possible at all times" (*Principles of Art History*, Introduction).

history. The aim then is to show that the music of a given period, since it is like these other cultural manifestations in certain important respects, "fits"—is congruous with and helps to illuminate—the total culture of the time. Explanations of this sort frequently involve metaphor, which itself may have explanatory value.[27] Also, a historian sometimes may posit a single source or cause for a particular cultural configuration, or try to comprehend it under one unifying idea.

Configurational explanations may be combined with or incorporated into explanations of a more distinctly linear type. Successive changes in musical style may be explained by placing them in the framework of larger patterns of change (for example, "evolution" either within a limited period or through the history of a civilization); or by showing them as instances of a recurrent pattern of change (for example, alternations of "ethic" and "pathic" styles); or by showing that style changes regularly occur in a certain way (for example, by processes analogous to those of "adaptation" in biology). More strictly linear are explanations which assume certain kinds of change (for example, in the social structure as determined by methods of production) as basic and attempt to show how changes in musical style are related to these.[28] Other "covering laws" are sometimes advanced as explanations in music history: for example, that every known innovation has unknown antecedents; or that the most flourishing historical periods are those in which there is a lively interchange between art music and folk music. These and similar generalizations are explanation sketches, serviceable but under the same restrictions that apply to their kind in any historical investigation.

It must be remembered that even in the "exact" sciences causal explanations do not serve to predict particular events but only classes or properties of events, and that in history even this much prediction is uncertain. Music history can assert that, since a certain style is known to have existed, the necessary preconditions must also have

[27] Max Black, *Models and Metaphors* (Ithaca, N.Y.: Cornell University Press, 1962), Chapter iii ("Metaphor"), pp. 25-47 and 236; Monroe C. Beardsley, *Aesthetics* (New York: Harcourt Brace [1958]), pp. 134-54, 159-62. Compare also C. M. Turbayne, *The Myth of Metaphor* (New Haven: Yale University Press, 1962) and George Kubler, *The Shape of Time* (New Haven: Yale University Press, 1962).

[28] See Georg Knepler, "Musikgeschichte und Geschichte," in *Beiträge zur Musikwissenschaft*, v, 4 (1963), 291-98.

existed; and the music historian can then try to find and describe these preconditions. Supposing he succeeds, however, he cannot conclude that anyone knowing only the preconditions could, or probably could, have predicted the rise of that particular style, let alone of any particular work. "Pre-dated predictions" are really post-dated predictions.[29] But post-dated predictions are still valuable as historical explanations: they show that a certain outcome, known to have occurred, was "what might have been expected" in that particular case.

What further explanation of an individual work of music can history offer, beyond placing it in a certain category of style and explaining that style? It seems that at least two distinct types of historical explanation are possible at this point. Each uses the method of comparison but in a different way. In the first type, certain technical features of a work—for example, the means of achieving melodic continuity or formal coherence—may be compared with the means employed for the same ends in other works from quite different periods and styles.[30] The second type of explanation proceeds within the context of a single style. The historian begins by isolating those characteristics in virtue of which a given work exemplifies the style within which he has located it. He can then go on, moving his camera (so to speak) closer to the object, drawing more tightly the meshes of his style-concept, until he arrives at characteristics which are peculiar to this one work and which cannot be accounted for by adducing more evidence about the circumstances under which it was created. At that point, history has no more to say in explanation of that particular event. Its uniqueness, the mystery at its heart, has been isolated by identifying and thereby removing everything it had in common with other events.

But history deals with consequences as well as antecedents. History can enlarge the understanding of a work of music by showing what effects it had on subsequent events, musical and other. Moreover, a great work not only markedly affects the future but also, in a strange way, alters the past: that is, its existence makes everyone—contemporaries and later generations—see all that had come before

---

[29] Mendel, "Evidence and Explanation," p. 14. See analysis in Arthur C. Danto, "Narrative Sentences," in *History and Theory*, II (1962-63), 146-79.

[30] In the language of a common metaphor this might be described as comparing different "solutions" of the same "problem"; it is a form of "explaining what" in the sense defined above.

differently from the way they would have seen it had the work in question never been created. This partly explains why the history of music has to be written anew in each generation: new works do not supersede old ones but take their place among them in the whole array of the past, subtly modifying all former relationships. Bach's music, we say, has not changed; but we hear it otherwise than we would if it were not for Beethoven, Wagner, Debussy, and Schoenberg. One of the historian's most necessary and most difficult tasks is to reconstruct in imagination the sound of past music not simply "as it was" but "as it seemed" to its creator and his contemporaries.

Some Miscellaneous Observations

Progress. The notion of progress, so conspicuous in nineteenth-century historical writing, is fundamental to one important general music history, C. H. H. Parry's *The Evolution of the Art of Music*, written around 1893.[31] Parry conceives of progress as a historical process extending over a long time, not necessarily involving "improvement" but unitary because consisting of successive realizations of one dominating goal or purpose: "The long story of the development of music is a continuous and unbroken record of human efforts to extend and enhance the possibilities of effects of sound upon human sensibilities." Such comprehensive, grandiose conceptions of the whole sweep of history are foreign to most modern historians; indeed, the subject of progress receives little attention in contemporary English and American philosophy of history. As far as the history of any art is concerned, it seems an accepted principle to restrict the concept of progress to improvement in technique, in the means of accomplishing a certain artistic result, and not apply it in the form of comparative judgments about artistic goals. Thus construed, "progress" is likely to be found only within a limited historical context and there only when the properties of one work (or group of works) are such that a historian can reasonably view certain earlier works as less successful attempts to realize an artistic purpose which the later work first adequately defined. Thus one might speak of progress in opera from Peri to Monteverdi, but not from Monteverdi to Mozart.

[31] First published as *The Art of Music* (London: Kegan Paul, 1893); revised as *The Evolution of the Art of Music* (London: Kegan Paul, 1896; numerous later editions). The quotation is from the edition published by D. Appleton, New York and London: 1912, p. 333.

History and Music History. The history of music is, among other things, the history of successive ways of articulating the passage of time. Musical rhythm and the rhythm of history tend to be felt in similar ways at any given period. If this hypothesis is correct, then it can hardly be mere coincidence that Hegel was writing his lectures on the philosophy of history at the same time that Beethoven was working on the *Missa solemnis.* Here is one way of approach to a relationship between music and general history that might repay further investigation.

Historical Inevitability. The question of determinism or "inevitability" in history has been endlessly debated and the end is not yet. In a crude form, historical determinism would say of a past event not that it was about what might have been expected under the circumstances but that it, or something very like it, was inevitable, "decreed by the inexorable march of history," or some such expression. Applied to the past, this doctrine amounts in effect to no more than a claim to prove the impossibility of events that never occurred. Applied to the present, it has an unfortunate proclivity to turn into a concealed statement of the form "This is occurring, therefore it is inevitable," and then to be used for justifying anything from forms of political organization to atonality and the twelve-tone technique, on the ground that they are fulfilling historical necessity. In more reputable formulations the issue arises in music history as soon as we begin to observe uniformities among unique events. How did the uniformities come about? Given that a certain musical style or a certain work was created at a certain time, it is probably meaningless to ask whether it "was inevitable," but it is not meaningless to ask more practical questions, and among these are some questions with which Western historians of music will probably have to deal much more explicitly in the future than they have usually done in the past. In what sense, and to what extent, were creators of music at any specified time and place "free"? In what respects were they bound by limiting physical conditions? What possibilities were open to them? In what ways and by what means were their artistic intentions shaped by their economic status and by their social and intellectual environment? How much were they and other people aware of such influences? What kind of originality, if any, was rewarded? Was the "rebel" an admired figure? More generally, to what extent has the history of music been shaped by outstanding individuals?

How much of the greatness of a "great" composer was due to genius, how much to favorable circumstances, and how much to the luck of having "made his entry" into history at the right moment? Is there any objective sense in which his music (apart from a verbal text) can be said to "represent" or "embody" collective attitudes or aspirations of his time? And if so, what is the relation between any values so embodied and the aesthetic value of the music? That these and similar questions are seldom neatly answerable lies partly in the nature of the complex issues of freedom and determinism that envelop the understanding of all human action.

II. WORDS AND MUSIC IN CHRISTIAN LITURGY

THREE BYZANTINE ACCLAMATIONS

KENNETH LEVY

MEDIEVAL liturgical chants preserved by one or two sources claim a larger measure of interest than their share of the manuscript tradition suggests. Some of them turn out to be oddities which, like the *unica* of medieval secular monody and art-polyphony, owe their isolation among known sources to the narrowness of their original diffusion. Others reflect a more promising set of conditions, for the impulse to preserve a melody in notation diminished as it was simple or well known. Numbers of the most popular chants were as a matter of course excluded from manuscripts by economy-minded scribes, and on occasion a unique chant represents a main line of music that otherwise was purposely ignored. The number of Byzantine hymns that are found with notation by the tenth century runs into the thousands, yet the melodies for the *stichera automela*—the handful of model tunes that ranked with the most familiar of all proper hymns—were copied only in the rarest circumstances before the fall of the Empire.[1] In much the same way, the melodic traditions for the widely used chants of the ordinary are first preserved in isolated sources no earlier than the thirteenth century, while some of the commonest of them continue to be transmitted solely through oral tradition for centuries more. The three liturgical acclamations published here are all chants of the ordinary. Each is preserved by a single manuscript, and each will be a candidate for the elusive company of chants that would have been best known to the Byzantine congregation. The first, Σοφία (*sapientia*), is a deacon's monition; the second, Εἰς πολλὰ ἔτη, δέσποτα (*ad multos annos, domine*), and the third, Αἰωνία ἡ μνήμη (*memoria aeterna*), are choral or congregational acclamations.

I. Σοφία—*sapientia*

Ex. 1

---

[1] An *automelon* is reconstructed after two eleventh-century sources by Oliver Strunk, "The Notation of the Chartres Fragment," *Annales musicologiques*, III (1955), 26-31.

At several points in the Divine Liturgy—the Byzantine Mass—it is the custom for a deacon to call out the name of Sophia, or Holy Wisdom. With this he draws the attention of the congregation to the presence of the Incarnate Word, and he enjoins them to receive the forthcoming gifts of the Holy Spirit. In the modern rite this monition is heard among the opening ceremonies of the Liturgy, at the Little Entrance, as the Gospel-book is carried in procession into the church; it is heard again as the appointed reader prepares to recite the Epistle and the Gospel; and it is heard again as an introduction to the First and Second Prayers of the Faithful, which precede the processional entry of the Gifts at the offertory. Each of these usages reaches well back in the medieval tradition.[2] In the earlier Greek rite the monition had still wider applications. It is found in the oldest copy of the Euchologion, the standard prayer-book, which contains the text and rubrics for the Mass-ordinary and some other services, and which corresponds roughly to a sacramentary and pontifical combined. While the Barberini Euchology (Barb. gr. 336), a manuscript of the eighth/ninth century, has only occasional rubrics for the ordinary Liturgies of Saint Basil and Saint John Chrysostom, its directions are fuller for the Lenten Liturgy of the Presanctified where the Σοφία is used to introduce the Old Testament lessons.[3] No less remarkable than the Barberini manuscript is a Palestinian (?) Greek missal of the ninth century (Leningrad gr. xliv) which preserves a layer of unique liturgical practice. The manuscript served as a memorandum for the lessons and chants of the Mass-proper, but a few ordinary texts are entered systematically as points of reference, and among these the Σοφία is assigned to a deacon, evidently before the recitation of the Creed.[4] In the well-documented tradition of the Constantinopolitan Typikon, the collection of liturgical *ordines* of the ninth and tenth century, this monition, again an obligation of the deacon, is heard as the prepa-

---

[2] *Hieratikon* (Rome, 1950), pp. 113, 115, 117, 121, 122; P. N. Trempelas, Αἱ τρεῖς Λειτουργίαι (Athens, 1935), pp. 46ff, 52, 65, 67n16; J. M. Hanssens, *Institutiones liturgicae de ritibus orientalibus*, iii (Rome, 1932), 174ff, 201, 209, 215. The use of the term "acclamation" for short liturgical formulas is discussed by Dom Cabrol in *Dictionnaire d'archéologie chrétienne et de liturgie*, i¹ (1903), cols. 244ff, 260.

[3] Vat.Barb. gr. 336, f. 261.

[4] J.-B. Thibaut, *Monuments de la notation ekphonétique et hagiopolite de l'église grecque* (St.-Pétersbourg, 1913), p. 18, and appendix, pp. 3*ff.

ration for a wide range of liturgical functions: before a lesson, canticle, troparion, prayer, and litany.[5]

A short and presumably simple chant like Σοφία was not apt to be notated very often. For earlier times there is little indication that it was sung at all rather than just recited. In the liturgical commentary by pseudo-Sophronios of Jerusalem, a compilation that cannot be dated before the twelfth or thirteenth century, the instruction is, εἶτα φωνεῖ (literally, *intones*) ὁ διάκονος, "Σοφία";[6] the same term is used in the twelfth/thirteenth century description of the Liturgy in Athens MS 662,[7] and it is echoed by Symeon, archbishop of Thessalonica (d. 1429), when he discusses the monition at the Little Entrance (καὶ μεγαλοφώνως ἐκβοῶν, "Σοφία, ὀρθοί") and at the Gospel (καὶ ἡ φωνὴ δὲ τοῦ διακόνου, τὸ "Σοφία, ὀρθοί").[8] The commentators might have used λέγει if they had speech or recitative in mind; or perhaps ψάλλει or ᾄδει for a chant in more florid style; instead they used φωνεῖ, which may indicate a relatively simple chant for the monition they knew.[9]

The single source that preserves a musical setting is not from the Empire itself but from Magna Graecia, the Graeco-Byzantine area of south Italy. The Euchologion Vat. Borg. gr. 7, whose principal content is a rubricated text of the Liturgy of Saint John Chrysostom, was copied, according to its colophon, in the year 1353 by the deacon John at the town of Soleto, near the tip of the Italian heel.[10] In the

---

[5] J. Mateos, *Le Typicon de la grande église*, II (*Orientalia christiana analecta*, Vol. 166; Rome, 1963), p. 319. There are four Byzantine formulations with this text: Σοφία; Σοφία, ὀρθοί; Ἐν σοφίᾳ προσχῶμεν; Ἐν σοφίᾳ Θεοῦ προσχῶμεν (the formula in Leningrad gr. XLIV).

[6] Migne, *PG* 87, col. 4000; on the sources of the commentary see F. E. Brightman in *Journal of Theological Studies*, IX (1907-08), 249-50 and H.-G. Beck, *Kirche und theologische Literatur im byzantinischen Reich* (Munich, 1959), pp. 436, 645.

[7] Trempelas, Αἱ τρεῖς Λειτουργίαι, pp. 6-7.

[8] Migne, *PG* 155, cols. 720, 292.

[9] The use of φωνή in the tenth-century *Book of Ceremonies* is discussed by A. Vogt, *Constantin VII Porphyrogénète: Le Livre des cérémonies, Commentaire*, I (Paris, 1935), 81; Vogt's conclusion ("il ne s'agit que de chants") is refined by J. Handschin, *Das Zeremonienwerk Kaiser Konstantins und die sangbare Dichtung* (Basel, 1942), pp. 9, 155ff, and by F. Dölger, "Zur Ausführung weltlicher Musik am byzantinischen Kaiserhof," *Byzantinische Zeitschrift*, XLII (1943: ergänzter Band, Neudruck, 1959), 218-19.

[10] Vat. Borg. gr. 7, f. 30; P. Franchi de' Cavalieri, *Codices graeci Chisiani et Borgiani* (Rome, 1927), pp. 118-20; R. Devreesse, *Les Manuscrits grecs de l'Italie méridionale* (*Studi e testi*, tom. 183; Rome, 1955), p. 51.

usual plan of an Euchologion there is no provision for music; the content, restricted essentially to the prayers (εὐχαί) for which it is named, regularly excludes texts that require notation. The deacon John, however, ignored the rule at one point. As he prepared to enter the monition Σοφία at the Second Prayer of the Faithful, he was evidently overcome with pious enthusiasm. He solemnized this moment in copying the text of the Mass by figuratively breaking into song and adding neumes for the monition which he as a deacon would have sung countless times. As the occasion for this musical excursion, he chose a high point in the deacon's ministry. The Σοφία at the Second Prayer of the Faithful is the last and most portentous of the exhortations to Wisdom, and it is followed directly by the congregational chant of the Cherubic Hymn at the offertory: in effect, the body of Christ is at hand, and here above all the deacon is his herald. It is at the same point in the Liturgy that the commentary by pseudo-Sophronios mentions Σοφία.[11] And the fourteenth-century mystic theologian Nicholas Cabasilas takes some pains to connect the function of the monition with a specific phrase of the Cherubic Hymn ("let us lay aside all earthly cares—πᾶσαν τὴν βιωτικὴν ἀποθώμεθα μέριμναν").[12]

The melody in the Borgia manuscript is as simple as one would expect; it covers a descending fourth from C to G in stepwise curves (see Ex. 1).[13] As it stands, however, it is an isolated phenomenon and there is no way to assess its authority. It is too much to see a patent of authority in its melodic simplicity. And while the deacon John probably copied the deacon's chant as it was sung at Soleto during the middle of the fourteenth century, there is no direct indication of how the same text was sung at another time or place.

II. Εἰς πολλὰ ἔτη, δέσποτα—ad multos annos, domine

Ex. 2

[11] Migne, *PG* 87, col. 4000.

[12] Migne, *PG* 150, col. 413. An apparent counterpart to this monition in the Mozarabic rite occurs in the Leon antiphoner, f. 41; L. Brou and J. Vives, *Antifonario visigótico mozárabe de la catedral de Léon (Monumenta hispaniae sacra, serie liturgica*; Vol. v, 1 [Barcelona-Madrid, 1959]), 39; the monition (?) *sapientiam* here precedes the proper Sacrificium for the feast of St. Andrew; in function the Mozarabic Sacrificium corresponds to the Byzantine Cherubic Hymn at the Great Entrance.

[13] Vat. Borg. gr. 7, f. 14v.

Among the opening ceremonies of the Divine Liturgy, at the Little Entrance with the Gospel-book, before the Kontakion and Trisagion are sung, it is the Byzantine custom to address chanted acclamations to the secular and ecclesiastical officials of the day. Although no firm evidence for the practice is found earlier than the thirteenth or fourteenth century, it is probably much older, and something about its age may be inferred from the corresponding position of the *laudes regiae* and episcopal *laudes*, between the Gloria and Epistle, in the Frankish Mass of the eighth and ninth centuries.[14] In the Byzantine pontifical Liturgy there is an elaborate and widely copied set of imperial acclamations in the authentic G-mode, with intentions for the royal family, the patriarch, and on occasion the local archbishop.[15] In the less solemn form of the Liturgy there is a shorter ordinary or episcopal acclamation (it precedes the imperial acclamations in the pontifical Liturgy) addressed to the bishop or the celebrant, with a chant in the authentic E-mode that is preserved by a single source. The manuscript (Vienna theol. gr. 185),[16] probably copied at Thessalonica between 1385 and 1391, is an outstanding example of the musical anthology called *Akolouthiai*, or *Orders of Service*, for Vespers, Lauds, and the three Liturgies. The collection was originally compiled at Constantinople or Thessalonica in about 1300 by the composer Joannes Koukouzeles; but despite this late date, the *Akolouthiai* preserve the best and earliest traditions for many of the Byzantine psalmodic and ordinary chants.[17] Their basic content, reflecting in part an early Palestinian (?) monastic

[14] M. Andrieu, *Les Ordines romani du haut moyen-âge*, IV (*Spicilegium sacrum lovaniense, Études et documents*, fasc. 28; Louvain, 1956), pp. 162ff. E. H. Kantorowicz, *Laudes regiae* (Berkeley, 1943 [1958]), pp. 87ff.

[15] A. A. Dmitrievskii, *Opisanie liturgicheskich rukopisei*, II (Kiev, 1901), p. 307; Trempelas, Αἱ τρεῖς Λειτουργίαι, p. 39. The music was first published in transcription by H. J. W. Tillyard, "The Acclamation of Emperors in Byzantine Ritual," *Annual of the British School at Athens*, XVIII (1911-12), 239-60, and reprinted several times, most recently by E. Wellesz, *A History of Byzantine Music and Hymnography*, 2nd edn. (Oxford, 1961), pp. 115-16; the transcription is better taken a fifth higher and without the flat signature. The earliest dated appearance of the same acclamation has been pointed out by Professor Strunk in a musical manuscript of the year 1336, "The Byzantine Office at Hagia Sophia," *Dumbarton Oaks Papers*, IX/X (1956), 180n21.

[16] A facsimile of f. 9 of this manuscript, showing the beginning of the Vesper-Psalms, is published by Wellesz, *Byzantinische Musik* (Breslau, 1927), p. 93.

[17] The first demonstration of their importance was by Professor Strunk, "The Antiphons of the Oktoechos," *Journal of the American Musicological Society*, XIII (1960), 53ff.

practice, is relatively stable, but the scribes were free to add or omit, particularly when dealing with the florid "kalophonic" elaborations of standard melodies that make up the bulk of each copy. With unparalleled scrupulousness, however, the scribe of Vienna 185 entered the music for the ordinary acclamation Εἰς πολλὰ ἔτη, δέσποτα at its regular place among the opening ceremonies of the Liturgy (see Ex. 2).[18]

Like the chant for Σοφία, this unique acclamation covers the fourth, G to C, but here the melody rises first to the C, then completes a nearly symmetrical curve by falling again to the G. While a single embellishing tone at the cadence reaches F, the line never drops to the nominal final of the mode on E. The Vienna manuscript assigns the chant to a *domestikos*, or choir-leader, yet it is likely that the choirs or the congregation themselves repeated the same music or a simpler form of it. An instruction for congregational repetition sometimes accompanies the imperial acclamations.[19]

The question again is whether the unique melody was restricted to the time and place of its appearance. In this case a provisional answer can be drawn from a series of melodic parallels that connect the ordinary acclamation in Ex. 2 with a widely based musical tradition for the Mass-ordinary. In Exx. 3a-3f what may be a single melodic pattern is accommodated to eight texts of the ordinary that occupy positions from the Introit through the Canon of the Byzantine Mass: Ex. 3a (= Ex. 2) is the acclamation at the Little Entrance; Ex. 3b is the Amen that introduces the Trisagion;[20] Ex.

[18] Vienna theol. gr. 185, f. 236. In the monastic Liturgy described in Vat. gr. 573 (fourteenth/fifteenth century) the acclamation is addressed by the deacon to the officiating priest as the Little Entrance begins; it follows the *Sophia* and precedes the congregational chant of the *Eisodikon* (f. 66v). In the fourteenth-century patriarchal Liturgy it is assigned first to the *episkopianoi*, then repeated individually by the *psaltai*; Dmitrievskii, *Opisanie*, II, 305, after Jerusalem, Saba 607; the wording of the Saba manuscript is incorporated in the description of the ceremonies of ordination at the patriarchal Liturgy by the *protonotarios* Demetrios Gemistos (*ca.* 1360-70), in Vat. gr. 721, f. 185v.

[19] Athens 2062 (before 1385; on the date see Strunk in *Dumbarton Oaks Papers*, IX/X [1956], 199), f. 56; Mt. Athos, Lavra E. 173 (A.D. 1436), f. 97v; in the Athos MS it is the *protopsaltes* who alternates with the congregation, in Athens it is the *domestikos*; also Sinai 1251, f. 113v, and Sinai 1584, f. 198 (both manuscripts, copies of the Kalophonic Sticherarion, date between A.D. 1427 and *ca.* 1440).

[20] Mt. Athos, Koutloumousi 457 (*ca.* A.D. 1360 to 1385), f. 194; I should like to express thanks to Abbé M. Richard, to Father G. Nowack, and to the Institut de Recherche et d'Histoire des Textes at Paris for the opportunity to consult photographs of this manuscript.

3c is the exclamation Δύναμις heard with the Trisagion;[21] Ex. 3d is the most authoritative melodic tradition for the triple Alleluia that precedes the Gospel;[22] Ex. 3e is the monition at the dismissal of the catechumens and beginning of the *missa fidelium*;[23] Ex. 3f is the chant for the Sanctus within the Byzantine Canon;[24] Ex. 3g is the opening of the hymn, Σὲ ὑμνοῦμεν, σὲ εὐλογοῦμεν, sung following the Commemoration, and Ex. 3h is the Amen heard twice at the Words of Institution (it differs from the Amen before the Trisagion [Ex. 3b] only in the underlay of text).[25]

It seems that an unusual dignity was attached to the music in Ex. 3 since a number of the most solemn chants of the Mass-ordinary are represented there: the Trisagion, the Alleluia before the Gospel, the Sanctus, and the ordinary Amen.[26] In effect, these are the nucleus of the musical ordinary as it existed in the later fifth century.[27] The chants in Ex. 3, which reach us in solo and choral versions of the thirteenth and fourteenth centuries, were sung originally either by or on behalf of the congregation; for reference they will be called the "congregational" ordinary, or "ordinary A." The acclamation in Ex. 2 (=Ex. 3a) would be the first of several applications of this material in the course of the Liturgy, and though the scribe of the Vienna manuscript took the trouble to write it down, it was surely too familiar to have needed the support of notation. Of the chants in Ex. 3, all but one are from the *Akolouthiai*. The Δύναμις (Ex. 3c) is from the *Asmatikon*, a thirteenth-century collection that transmits

[21] Mt. Athos, Lavra Γ.3 (an *Asmatikon* of the 13th[?] century), f. 51.

[22] Milano, Ambrosiana L. 36 *sup.* (A.D. 1341 to *ca.* 1360), ff. 242, 252. The triple Alleluia is assigned to the congregation as late as the sixteenth-century Euchologion, Vat. gr. 1213, f. 11v; the rubric is published by N. Krasnoseltsev, *Svedenia o nekotorich liturgicheskich rukopisiach vatikanskoi biblioteki* (Kazan, 1885), p. 133.

[23] Sinai 1527 (middle-fifteenth century), f. 375; a related melodic version sung at the end of the Liturgy is in Athens 2837 (A.D. 1457), f. 192; I am greatly obliged to Mr. Michael Adamis for a transcription of this version.

[24] Athens 2458 (A.D. 1336), f. 167v.

[25] Ex. 3g: Athens 2458, f. 168; Ex. 3h: Ambrosiana L. 36 *sup.*, f. 261v.

[26] Nearly all Byzantine melodies for the Trisagion through the early fourteenth century are members of a single melodic family to which the 'Αμήν (Ex. 3b) and Δύναμις (Ex. 3c) belong. I have discussed the chants in Exx. 3e-3h and some others related to them in "The Byzantine Sanctus," *Annales musicologiques*, VI (1958-63), 7ff.

[27] *Dictionnaire d'archéologie chrétienne et de liturgie*, VI, cols. 1610-1614; A. Raes, *Introductio in liturgiam orientalem* (Rome, 1947), pp. 43ff. Omitted are only the ordinary communion-chants, on which see n. 48 below.

Ex. 3

music for the choir of *psaltai* of Hagia Sophia at Constantinople.[28] It appears, therefore, that the melodic practice of the chants in Ex. 3 can claim roots in both the Constantinopolitan and monastic traditions.

Two other settings of Εἰς πολλὰ ἔτη, δέσποτα will be of some interest now. The first of these (Ex. 4a) is sung at the ordination of a metropolitan or bishop. Again a unique chant, it is preserved by a source of the middle-fifteenth century that provides music for nine repetitions of the text; all are variants of a single underlying pattern whose simplest state appears in Ex. 4a.[29]

The second (Ex. 4b.1) is an acclamation at the vigil of the Exaltation (September 14), with music that represents the late-fourteenth-century cathedral usage of Thessalonica.[30] A comparison of Ex. 4b.1 with Ex. 4a suggests a possibility of common origin to which there will be occasion to return.[31]

The distinguishing element in Ex. 4b.1 is the cadential formula that is identified as formula Z. Further applications of this cadence can be observed in half a dozen other chants of the fourteenth-century repertory: Ex. 4b.2 is a petition that follows the first vespers of the Exaltation;[32] Ex. 4c is the same petition as it is sung at the

---

[28] The date of the *Asmatikon* is set back nearly two centuries by the existence of Slavic copies of the late eleventh and early twelfth centuries; see my paper "The Byzantine Communion-Cycle and its Slavic Counterpart," in *Actes du XIIe Congrès International des études byzantines*, II (Belgrade, 1964), 571ff. The earliest preserved melody for the Trisagion, representing the main tradition (see n. 26 above), is in a twelfth-century Slavic manuscript, the so-called Blagoveshchensky Kondakar (Leningrad Public Library, MS Q. I. No. 32), f. 104.

[29] Sinai 1527, f. 374v; see P. N. Trempelas, Μικρὸν Εὐχολόγιον, I (Athens, 1950), 192ff.

[30] Athens 2061 (between A.D. 1391 and 1425), f. 73; on this manuscript and its tradition see the article by Professor Strunk cited in n. 15 above.

[31] Of the four liturgical positions for the acclamation Εἰς πολλὰ ἔτη in the Byzantine rite, the music for three has now appeared: 1) in Ex. 2; 2) in Ex. 4a; 3) in Ex. 4b.1. The fourth is at the end of the Liturgy, as a conclusion to the texts Πολυχρόνιον ποιῆσαι ὁ Θεὸς and Τὸν δεσπότην καὶ ἀρχιερέα ἡμῶν, which follow the Εἴη τὸ ὄνομα Κυρίου (*Sit nomen Domini*); see Athens 2837, f. 193v, and Wellesz, *A History of Byzantine Music and Hymnography*, 2nd edn.; pp. 116ff. Western liturgical parallels with music are preserved for usages 1), 2), and 4); a consideration of their music belongs with a re-examination of the music of the *Laudes regiae*; recent contributions to this subject are listed in H. Hucke's "Eine unbekannte Melodie zu den *Laudes regiae*," *Kirchenmusikalisches Jahrbuch*, 42 (1958), p. 32.

[32] Vienna, theol. gr. 185, f. 286.

Ex. 4

opening of the service on the next morning;[33] Ex. 4d is the standard introduction to the Prokeimenon, the Byzantine counterpart of the Gradual-Respond, before the Epistle at the Divine Liturgy, and at Sunday Lauds;[34] Ex. 4e is the standard introduction to the Alleluia of the Liturgy (the continuation has been seen in Ex. 3d);[35] Ex. 4f is a petition at the close of the imperial acclamations;[36] Ex. 4g is a chant for Amen at the cathedral vespers of the Exaltation.[37] Three modes (authentic D, plagal F, and plagal G) and four ways of beginning are represented among these seven chants, but the cadential formula is the same each time. Like some other Byzantine formulas, its attachment is to a position in the tonal system rather than to a particular mode or group of modes: it is restricted to the identically constructed fourths that descend from F and C.

In Ex. 4 there is a second series of ordinary chants whose widely spaced liturgical assignments are linked by related—in this case identical—musical materials. There is again a musical continuity within the ordinary, but now the unified stratum runs through both the Mass and office, and the texts, which serve as preparations, announcements, and petitions, are essentially the province of clerical assistants: they are sung by the soloist (*domestikos, protopsaltes,* or *monophonarios*) or by the reader. Where the musical tradition in Ex. 3 has been called a "congregational" ordinary ("A"), the one in Ex. 4 can provisionally be called a "collateral" ordinary, or "ordinary B." One other chant has been examined whose function may place it with "ordinary B," though its delivery by the deacon sets it apart somewhat. This is the Σοφία of Ex. 1. That its music may also belong here is suggested by comparing Ex. 4h (= Ex. 1) with Exx. 4b-4g. It seems possible that the chant for Σοφία (Ex. 4h) represents a south Italian musical variant of formula Z, with the stylized cadential figure modified in a way that is found in other chants that are comparable between the south Italian-Greek and Byzantine repertories. An independent variant of this material within the properly Byzantine tradition may perhaps be recognized in the comparison that has been proposed between Exx. 4a and 4b.1, which would indicate something of the range allowed when recasting the material.

[33] Athens 2062, f. 56.
[34] Liturgy: Athens 2458, f. 146v. Lauds: Ambrosiana L. 36 *sup.*, f. 104v.
[35] Athens 2458, f. 147v.   [36] *Ibid.*, f. 144.   [37] Athens 2061, f. 73.

With the melodic connections in Exx. 4b-4g, and with the possible additions to these of Exx. 4a and 4h (= Ex. 1), the ordinary "B" can take a place beside the ordinary "A" of Ex. 3 as a second basic element of the Byzantine chanted service. Once again a functional layer of the ordinary has a musical identity of its own. The significance of this can scarcely be ignored, for though it is possible that musical uniformity was imposed at a relatively late stage in the development of the service, it is at least as likely that it reflects quite an early practice. Within the Western ordinary, the relatively late choral chants that have come down through the Latin tropers seem on the whole to be independent compositions, yet the possibility of underlying musical connections will have to be considered within this repertory in the light of the Byzantine practice—particularly the melodic practice in Ex. 3. It may not be unreasonable to suppose that similar techniques would have prevailed in an early state of the Western ordinary.

III. Αἰωνία ἡ μνήμη—*memoria aeterna*

Ex. 5

One of the most remarkable ceremonies of the Eastern church is the public cursing of heretics and blessing of the pious that accompanies the liturgical recitation of synodal acts. Until about the thirteenth century, half a dozen church councils were commemorated in yearly offices at which epitomes of their acta and acclamations were read.[38] Later the number of these services was reduced, and eventually only the Synodikon for the Council in Constantinople of 843, which settled the fate of the iconoclastic party and restored the icons, continued as a reminder of the custom. The office for this

[38] G. Engberg, "Les Credos du synodicon," *Classica et mediaevalia*, XXIII (1962), 293-95.

council, with its acclamations, is still published in modern service-books at Sunday of Orthodoxy, the first Sunday in Lent.[39] The origins of the conciliar acclamations can probably be traced to the acclamations addressed by the Roman senate to the Emperor.[40] In the Byzantine liturgical practice they may at first have been spontaneous and only later formalized, since no two councils arrange this part of their Synodikon in quite the same way. There are, however, three more or less stable acclamatory elements among the conciliar services: the Cursings, or *anathemas*; the Blessings, with the refrain Αἰωνία ἡ μνήμη (*memoria aeterna*); and the Polychronismoi, or *multos annos* hails, with the refrain, πολλὰ τὰ ἔτη. A melodic tradition is preserved only for the Blessing, Αἰωνία ἡ μνήμη. It is found in a manuscript of the middle-fifteenth century, Sinai 1527, a relatively poor copy of the *Akolouthiai* which nevertheless contains some unusual chants (see Ex. 5).[41] The melody is in the authentic E-mode and is assigned "for the *synodikon*" at a time when only the Synodikon of Orthodoxy can be intended. There are three repetitions; the formula that appears the third time (Σ′) is probably related to the familiar *synagma* that is found in the melodic styles of the Sticherarion and Asmatikon.[42] Apart from the melismatic flourish at the end of each line the chant is syllabic, and as it stands it must be close to a congregational form. For the *anathemas* and the Polychronismoi that accompany the Blessings no comparable music is known. However, something more about the music for the councils can be learned from an earlier source, Bodleian MS Holkham 6, which contains a set of six conciliar offices provided throughout with ekphonetic neumes. The manuscript was copied shortly after 1050 at Antioch, but it probably reflects an archetype compiled between 843 and 920.[43] To judge from the space reserved for each line of text, the neumes were part of the original plan. They

[39] *Triodion* (Athens: Apostolic Diaconate, 1960), pp. 144ff; N. Nilles, *Kalendarium manuale*, II (Innsbruck, 1897), 101-18.

[40] Kantorowicz, *Laudes regiae*, p. 68.

[41] Sinai 1527, f. 375; this MS has supplied Exx. 3e and 4a; it is also a source for the liturgical drama published by M. M. Velimirović, "Liturgical Drama in Byzantium and Russia," *Dumbarton Oaks Papers*, XVI (1962), 354ff.

[42] G. Dévai, "The Musical Study of Koukouzeles in a 14th-century Manuscript," *Acta antiqua academiae scientiarum Hungaricae*, VI (1958), 226.

[43] R. J. H. Jenkins and C. Mango, "A Synodikon of Antioch and Lacedaemonia," *Dumbarton Oaks Papers*, XV (1961), 225-33. V. Laurent, "La Liste épiscopale du synodicon de la métropole de Lacédémone," *Revue des études byzantines*, XIX (1961), 210n5.

show that each of the three acclamatory elements received constant music at each synod where it appeared. The *anathema* is always introduced by the ekphonetic pair *kathistai . . . kathistai,* and is itself sung to the pair *bareia . . . bareia.*[44] The Blessing and the Polychronismos receive identical music: again the pair *kathistai . . . kathistai* as preparation, but now the *oxeia . . . teleia* for the acclamations.[45]

Until the present there has been no key to the ekphonetic notation. Neither a parallel setting, combining the ekphonetic and later melodic notations, nor an explanation of the notation from the side of Byzantine theory has appeared. It would be tempting to suppose that the melody for Αἰωνία ἡ μνήμη transmitted by the fifteenth-century Sinai manuscript is in fact related to the traditional music for the ekphonetic pair *oxeia . . . teleia* as it was sung from the eleventh-century Holkham manuscript, and that it may also represent the melodic transcription for the same ekphonetic pair when it is found throughout the liturgical lectionaries. The evidence is not conclusive but it seems to point the other way. Our best control of the ekphonetic notation may be through the unique table of signs added to a final leaf of Sinai MS 8, an eleventh-century copy of the prophetic lectionary.[46] Many of the standard ekphonetic pairs are apparently transcribed here into an early-Byzantine melodic notation of the eleventh/twelfth century, whose primitive state does not indicate exact pitch though it allows general melodic comparison. On examination it seems unlikely that this table's "resolution" for *oxeia . . . teleia* is in fact related to the melodic formula in Sinai 1527. To judge from the testimony of Sinai 8, the melodic formula for Αἰωνία ἡ μνήμη in Sinai 1527 would not be the one indicated for that text by the neumes of the Holkham Synodikon.[47]

With this final acclamation our opening rule about unique chants

[44] The ekphonetic signs are identified and discussed by C. Höeg, *La Notation ekphonétique* (*Monumenta musicae byzantinae, Subsidia,* Vol. I, fasc. 2; Copenhagen, 1935). A diplomatic copy after the Holkham MS, showing the noted *anathemas,* is published by Wellesz, *A History of Byzantine Music and Hymnography,* 2nd edn., p. 260.

[45] The Blessing occurs for the Sixth and Seventh Councils and the *horos* of the Council of 920 (Holkham MS 6, ff. 17, 18f, 117v, 130, 131, 141v-47, 150-51v). A related form, Αἰωνία μνήμη, with identical neumation, appears for the Council "in trullo" (f. 91v).

[46] Höeg, *La Notation ekphonétique,* pp. 20-22, 24ff, and pl. III.

[47] Along with the interpretation of the Sinai table, the entire question of the ekphonetic notation needs review.

seems to have failed. Yet for the first two of our three ordinary acclamations, the unique chants may in fact have had the wide circulation that their isolated transmission leads one to suspect. It seems reasonably clear that the acclamation Εἰς πολλὰ ἔτη, δέσποτα, in Ex. 2, is an element of the Mass-ordinary "A" that is represented in Ex. 3. It is less clear whether the chant for Σοφία, in Ex. 1, is actually a south Italian derivative of the characteristic formula of ordinary "B," represented in Ex. 4; nor can the possibility be dismissed that the Σοφία is related to the layer of chants in Ex. 3. Yet by focusing attention on the two musical layers within the Byzantine ordinary, the unique acclamations have illuminated developments that are decidedly more important than themselves. The chants of ordinaries "A" and "B" supplied the musical continuity for much of the Byzantine Mass and for part of the office. It must be determined how widely diffused and deeply rooted these traditions were, how likely there were to have been complementary or competitive traditions, and—in the final analysis—how significant the melodic distinctions between the traditions really were: for on the one hand, the melodic layers within the ordinary may be (as they are presented here) wholly independent musical phenomena; but on the other, they may simply have been melodic variants subordinate to a comprehensive modal area (related in some way to the modes on E and plagal G) from which most or even all the melodic material of the Byzantine ordinary was customarily drawn.[48] This final possibility raises questions that are at the root of the musical contribution to the early Christian service. In a limited space they cannot be adequately stated, much less have their implications explored.

For the moment it is worth observing that since a number of examples that represent ordinary traditions—"A" (Ex. 3) and "B" (Ex. 4)—are themselves preserved only in rare copies, the rule about unique chants may be invoked a final time. It can be argued that the likelihood implied by each isolated appearance should be compounded, and that the result is a persuasive, cumulative warrant of authority for each of the traditions.

[48] A third melodic layer within the ordinary (in the E-modes) appears among the offertory hymns and ordinary communions; it is discussed in my "A Hymn for Thursday in Holy Week," *Journal of the American Musicological Society*, xvi (1963), 157ff. This ordinary "C" might be called the "communicant's" ordinary; until the functions of these layers of chants are understood more fully it seems best to use simply the letters "A," "B," and "C."

ON THE STRUCTURE
OF THE ALLELUIA MELISMA:
A WESTERN TENDENCY IN WESTERN CHANT

IT has been a central concern of the literature on the Gregorian Alleluia to pursue that genre from early Judeo-Christian beginnings to Byzantine prototypes, and thence through a uniquely long period of composition that was marked as well by major changes of style as by a steady growth of the repertory.

In a study that is memorable for its display of critical sensitivity, Peter Wagner read meaning in those style changes for the growth of an indigenous Western—as opposed to an inherited Oriental—compositional tradition. Contrasting the melismas of the Alleluias with those of the Mass responsories and the tracts, he wrote

> We have recognized the organic course of the series of notes as the most prominent characteristic of melisma structure in the Mass responsories and in the tracts. Less often they constitute a symmetrical pattern, effected principally through the repetition of note groups. However the situation in the Alleluia chants is quite the reverse. In only a very few instances do the melismas proceed without regularity or plan, without disposition in groups that are immediately and clearly recognizable. Most of the others are models of transparent structure, with all the parts organized in a symmetrical configuration. In this the former group shows itself to be the older, the latter as more recent and as the product of aesthetic deliberation. . . . The older group foregoes any symmetrical arrangement of its parts; in the more recent Alleluia chants the melismas are always clearly constructed and of a manifest order. The former are reminiscent of the melismatic melody of the Orient, which still today undulates in unregulated fashion. The latter display in their clear structure Latin, Roman traits.[1]

To represent the older group, Wagner quoted this melody:

---

[1] *Gregorianische Formenlehre* (Leipzig, 1921), p. 398 (translation mine).

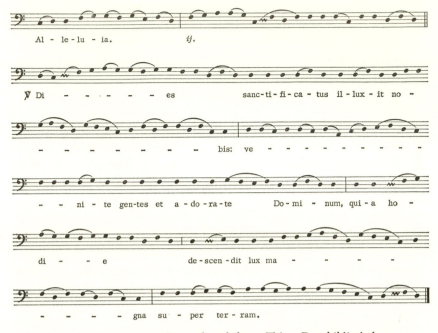

Ex. 1. Wagner, p. 399. Reproduced from Trier, Dombibliothek 153.

It grows out of the repeated intonation of a limited number of short, characteristic melodic turns and a frequent pausing on the two tones of choice, F and especially D. These circumstances can indeed result in the near identity of extended passages, as in the first and third phrases of the verse. But it seems fundamentally different from the invention of a longer line which is repeated as a matter of structural principle. Such is clearly the case in Ex. 2.

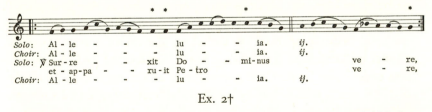

Ex. 2†

† The melody is quoted as an extreme case of the repetition scheme by Friedrich Gennrich, in *Grundriss Einer Formenlehre des Mittelalterlichen Liedes* (Halle, 1932), p. 108.
* These notes are sung in the verse only.

This chant incorporates all three of the features by which Wagner characterized his later group: the repetition of the Alleluia melisma after the verse to give an overall ABA form, the adaptation of the

Alleluia melody for the verse itself, and the repetition of melodic groups within the verse.[2]

I should like to show, now, three Alleluia melismas that reflect still a further stride in the direction of change that Wagner observed between the types of Exx. 1 and 2.

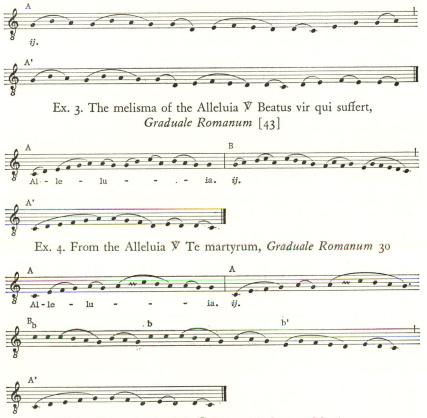

Ex. 3. The melisma of the Alleluia ℣ Beatus vir qui suffert, *Graduale Romanum* [43]

Ex. 4. From the Alleluia ℣ Te martyrum, *Graduale Romanum* 30

Ex. 5. From the Alleluia ℣ Beatus vir Sanctus Martinus, *Graduale Romanum* 652

[2] Wagner proposed this style contrast as an internal criterion for chronology among the Alleluias. Specifically, he proposed the year 608 as a watershed separating the types represented above, on the following argument: The Alleluia *Adorabo* (*Graduale Romanum* [73]) shows a tendency to symmetry in the verse but it does not repeat the Alleluia melisma after the verse, hence it is to be considered transitional. The melody is unique to the *Adorabo* text, so that it must be original to that text and its ritual function—the consecration of a church. The first known occasion of that ritual—the dedication of the Roman Pantheon in 608—fixes that year as the approximate time of separation between the two Alleluia types. Wagner executed this series of deductions in a speculative way, and we must still regard it with the greatest suspicion, for more is assumed than is demonstrated about the transitional role, and especially the age, of the *Adorabo* melody.

Like the melody of Ex. 2, these involve repetitions of one sort or another, but unlike the latter, the repetitions are not literal. The differentiation of the matched phrases is at the cadence, and in each case it is a differentiation of endings on the confinalis and finalis, respectively. This has the effect of polarizing each of the passages, of imposing on it a direction on the phrase-to-phrase—over and above the note-to-note—level. A serial construction of literal repetitions is potentially open ended, for it involves no process that is directed toward a goal. In contrast, repetitions like those of Ex. 3-5 function in closed, integrated musical configurations. The difference is critical, for it is just toward structures of the sort which these examples represent in miniature that much of the subsequent musical practice of the West has aimed.

In the Middle Ages, directed musical structures of this sort, depending then principally on matched but differentiated phrases, were the counterparts in music of the symmetries of rhymed, accentual Latin verse. Earliest in the sacred, non-liturgical songs,[3] later in the tropes and proses, phrases of equal length matched isosyllabic lines, masculine and feminine cadences matched the alternation of full with catalectic lines, and rhyme schemes were reflected in range and cadence differentiations that depended upon the structure of the modal octave. For a single representative specimen I offer the following.[4]

Ex. 6. From Misset and Aubry, *Les Proses d'Adam de St. Victor*
(Paris, 1900), p. 238

[3] Songs, for example, by the St. Gall poets Ratpert (*ca.* 890), Hartmann the Younger (925), and Waldram (active *ca.* 900), preserved in such sources as St. Gall 360 and 381. The real vogue of musical settings of accentual verse waited until the eleventh and especially the twelfth century.

[4] This review of the characteristics of the musical settings of accentual verse is necessarily brief. For a detailed study I refer the reader to my "Musical Syntax in the Middle Ages: Background to an Aesthetic Problem" in PERSPECTIVES OF NEW MUSIC, Vol. 4, No. 1 (1965), pp. 75-85.

This manner of organizing music was widely adopted in the later Middle Ages and after: in monody and polyphony, in vocal and instrumental music, in sacred and secular music. On the face of it, and especially on Wagner's criteria, it would appear to be a rather sharp departure from the core of plainsong practice. If it was to count at all in chant composition, it is reasonable that it should have been substantially confined to melismatic writing, for this sort of structure applied to a prose text would constitute a crude misalliance of words and music.[5] But that it should occur at all in chant poses some interesting questions regarding the bearing of chant composition and non-liturgical practice upon one another.

One wonders whether structuring techniques developed to support chant melismas suggested ways of setting the new poetry without obscuring its form; or whether the composers of new chant imitated the song writers in the only place where it was feasible for them to do so, in the melisma; or, indeed, whether both were not pursuing the same ideals of symmetry—but with the song writer, like the instrumental musician, working in a field more fertile for their realization. Very likely this is a chicken-egg question, and it makes little sense to hope to choose one answer over another. But it is a matter worth considering in any case, for it offers a way of holding liturgical and non-liturgical music up to the same light. Specifically, one would like to know how widely represented those structures are in the chant, and when in the history of chant they entered the repertory. I propose to make an approach to these questions through the Alleluias of the *Graduale Romanum*.

As a beginning I should like to refer back to Exx. 3-5 and recapitulate the essential features of those forms that distinguish them from the simple repetition schemes represented by Ex. 2. The elements of the form are phrases matched minimally in length and contour. They are arranged in a closed configuration, either contiguously or with intervening phrase or phrases, and closure is a matter of the differentiation of phrases on the basis of the structure of the modal octave. Usually the antecedent phrase ends on some tone other than the final, while the consequent ends on the final. On occasion, as we shall see, both may end on the final, but they lie in the tetrachord and pentachord, respectively, of the modal octave (see No. 14 in

[5] Such a case is melody No. 14 in Table 1, below.

Table 1, below). The effect in either case is a structure that combines the quality of symmetry—shared with the simple repetition schemes—with that of direction, something which the latter lack. It is a matter of dynamic, as opposed to static, form.

The *Graduale Romanum* contains 296 Alleluia texts set to a number of melodies which—taking into account the multiple use of some melodies—is something less than that. If we project on to the repertory in the *Graduale* the ratio of texts to melodies which Apel reported for the *Liber Usualis*[6]—3:2—we can expect approximately two hundred melodies, more or less. Among those, seventeen contain melismas which answer to the criteria which I have outlined above. In this simple statistic, crude as it is, there is the suggestion of an answer to one of our questions: the sort of order that became common in non-liturgical music of all kinds is to be found in the melismas of less than 10 per cent of the Alleluia melodies. The clarity and symmetry of the remainder of that majority of the Alleluias of which Wagner wrote is a matter of simple repetition schemes. There remains the question, when in its history did this notion of order enter the chant? Two sorts of evidence will be relevant here: that bearing on the age of the seventeen melodies, and variant versions of some of the melismas that suggest change in the direction of the form which they ultimately assumed.

Of the seventeen melodies of this study, only five are associated with texts that occur in the graduals of the eighth and ninth centuries included in Hesbert's *Antiphonale Missarum Sextuplex*.[7] It is reasonable, then, to judge the approximate age of the remainder according to their earliest appearance in subsequent graduals. Lacking, still, the concordances for the Gradual, we shall have to rely on sources for which inventories are already available—apart from the *Sextuplex* sources, principally the publications of the *Paléographie musicale* and, to a limited extent, some isolated single publications. The obvious hazard here is that we may miss an earlier source for this or that melody. How decisive that hazard is, we may judge after we have considered the evidence.

The seventeen melodies reproduced in Table 1, most of them melismas, are cast in four groups according to the earliest occurrence of a text with which each is associated in the *Graduale Romanum*.[8]

---

[6] *Gregorian Chant* (Bloomington, 1958), p. 383.   [7] (Bruxelles, 1935).

[8] This cautious wording merely reflects the obvious: we cannot presume to have found the oldest source for a melody if we can read only its text.

Those groups are constituted as follows:

Group I, earliest occurrence in a source with texts only—the *Sextuplex* sources, eighth/ninth centuries.

Group II, earliest occurrence in a musical source showing the direction, but not the magnitude of melodic intervals, ninth/tenth centuries.

Group III, earliest occurrence in a musical source showing both direction and magnitude of melodic intervals, eleventh/thirteenth centuries.

Melodies reported in Group IV do not occur in any of the published sources and are presumed to be of later origin than those of I, II, and III.

TABLE 1

SEVENTEEN ALLELUIA MELODY-FRAGMENTS
FROM THE *Graduale Romanum*†

Group I

1.

GR 286, closing melisma of the verse. Graduals of Monza, Rheinau, Mont-Blandin, Compiègne, Corbie, Senlis. ℣ Dominus in Sina. Mode 8.

2.

GR [49], beginning of the Alleluia melisma. Graduals of Compiègne, Corbie, Senlis. ℣ Justus ut palma. Mode 1.

3.

GR 378, beginning of the Alleluia melisma. Graduals of Compiègne, Corbie, Senlis. ℣ Paratum cor meum. Mode 3.

† Each fragment is accompanied by the following information: its location in the *Graduale Romanum* (GR) and—where this is not apparent—within the chant, the oldest sources, and the incipit of a verse text with which it is associated in the latter, and the mode assignment. In general I have quoted only that portion of the melody which is involved in the formal procedures to which I have reference in the text. However in some instances I have thought it instructive to show the context in which that portion falls. Thus in No. 10, I mean primarily to show the bar-like arrangement of the phrases bbb', but also to show the order of the full Alleluia section in which this fits.

(TABLE 1—Continued)

GR [30]. Graduals of Compiègne and Corbie. ℣ Te martyrum. Mode 5.

GR 351, end of the Alleluia melisma. Graduals of Compiègne, Corbie, Senlis. ℣ Domine Deus salutis. Mode 3.

GR 343. St. Gall 359 and 339, Laon 239, Chartres 47. ℣ Eripe me. Mode 2.

GR [43]. St. Gall 359 and 339, Einsiedeln 121, Laon 239. ℣ Beatus vir qui suffert. Mode 1.

GR [19], within the verse. Montpellier H 159. ℣ Sancti tui Domine florebunt. Mode 8.

(TABLE 1—Continued)

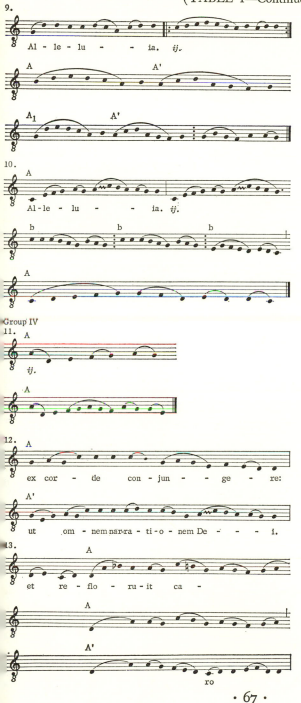

9.
Al - le - lu - - ia. *ij.*

A A'

A₁ A'

GR 340. Gradual of St. Yrieix. ℣ Magnus Dominus. Mode 7. (This melody has been cited by Bruno Stäblein as a fully developed specimen of Wagner's second category, in the article "Alleluia," *MGG*, i, col. 345.)

10.
A
Al - le - lu - - ia. *ij.*

b b b

A

GR 652. Sarum Gradual. ℣ Beatus vir Sanctus Martinus. Mode 5.

Group IV
11. A
ij.

·A

GR 39**. ℣ Gloriosus Deus. Mode 4.

12. A
ex cor - de con - jun - - ge - re:

A'
ut om - nem nar-ra - ti-o - nem De - - - i.

GR 528, within the verse. ℣ In multitudine. Mode 8.

13. A
et re - flo - ru - it ca -

A

A'
ro

GR [146], within the verse. ℣ In Deo speravit. Mode 1.

· 67 ·

(TABLE 1—Continued)

14.

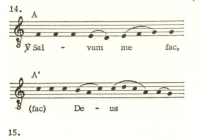

GR [139], within the verse. ℣ Sal-
vum me fac. Mode 3 (sic).

15.

GR 510, the end of the Alleluia melisma. ℣ Videbitis. Mode 8.

16.

GR 59**, within the verse. ℣ Dominus dabit. Mode 6.

17.

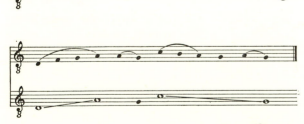

GR 609. ℣ Sancte Michael Archan-
gele. Mode 8.

With regard to formal principle, the melodies constitute five types. Three of these are founded on the antecedent-consequent principle: the simple AA′ (Nos. 1-3, 5-8, 11, 12, 14), the rounded ABA′ (No. 4), and the bar-like AAA′ or AA′A″ (Nos. 10 and 13). The fourth is the principle of the melodic sequence (No. 9). The last three melodies (Nos. 15-17) embody a principle that is perhaps even more modern. Each involves an embellished linear motion—expressed in an arrangement of short motives—that is directed toward the final. In No. 17 the motion is first to the confinalis, then to the finalis. I have underlaid all three melodies with reductions showing their outlines. While these melodies are not built in matched phrases, they share with the others a forward motion toward a goal and a sure sense of the tonality.

The table suggests a tentative answer to our second question, regarding the location of the seventeen melodies, and the way of organizing music which they manifest, in the long history of the Alleluia. Five melodies are represented in sources of the eighth/ninth centuries (but only the first of these in the very oldest sources). Two melodies were introduced into the repertory in the ninth/tenth centuries, and three additional ones made their earliest appearance in the eleventh/thirteenth centuries. The remaining seven melodies evidently had their origins, in any case, after the eleventh century. That this is not too conservative an impression is confirmed by another circumstance.

While the melodies of Group II cannot be read precisely with regard to the magnitude of their intervals, their parallel construction would be reflected in parallel neumatic groups, as in Fig. 1a, a facsimile of a source for melody No. 5. However early sources for melodies 1, 6, and 7 (Figs. 1b-d) show neumatic patterns which suggest something other than the clearly parallel construction of the *Graduale Romanum* versions. In all three cases a reduction of the line, with a resulting sharpening of the form, seems to have taken place sometime after these early versions were recorded. In one case, melody No. 6, we can see the difference quite clearly, for the melody had not yet assumed its final form when it was included in the eleventh-century Gradual of St. Yrieix. Example 7 compares that version with the final one as it appears, for instance, in the thirteenth-century Sarum Gradual.

Fig. 1*

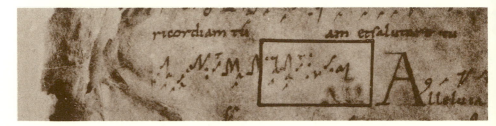

a. Alleluia V Domine Deus salutis. St. Gall 339, p. 128

b. Alleluia V Ostende Nobis. Laon 239, p. 166

c. Alleluia V Eripe me. St. Gall 339, p. 127

d. Alleluia V Beatus vir qui suffert. St. Gall 339, p. 130

* The reproductions are from the following published sources: a, c, and d, *Paléographie Musicale*, Series 1, Vol. 1 (Solesmes, 1889); b, *Paléographie Musicale*, Series 1, Vol. 10 (Tournai, 1909).

Ex. 7. The melisma from the Alleluia ℣ Eripe me, *Graduale Romanum* 34

* Paris, Bibliothèque Nationale, fonds latin 903, published as Volume XIII of the *Paléographie Musicale* (Tournai, 1925), p. 242.
† W. H. Frere, ed., *Graduale Sarisburiensis* (London, 1894), p. 147.

We must presume from this that in the period of the Group II sources the structures of Table 1 had even less currency than the table itself would suggest. And of course it underlines, too, the caution I have already expressed, that we cannot assume that the Group I melodies were sung in their final form at the time of the *Sextuplex* sources. To our conclusions regarding the relatively minor role played by goal-oriented structures among the Alleluias, we must add the high probability that they entered the repertory gradually, and relatively late in its history. It seems fair to say, then, that composers who employed them widely elsewhere did not in any case take their models from plainsong.

But perhaps one can read even further meaning from this apparently tentative introduction of a new way of organizing melodies in an era just preceding the invention of diastematic notations.

Notations which represent the direction but not the magnitude of melodic intervals function largely as mnemonics. As such they are especially well suited to music in which standard melodic turns and patterns, already known to the singer, play a significant role. But as composers turned away from variation and mosaic as the principal means of making melodies, in favor of constructions founded in the modal scales and their pitch hierarchies, those notations would have lost their effectiveness. A pattern of neumes repeated very nearly to the last detail is really a poor representation for a phrase structure that depends for its functioning upon cadential variations. The taste for such constructions may well have constituted one of the pressures that resulted in notations which represented the magnitude of intervals precisely.[9] Underlying, and

[9] Another, clearly, was the interest in a counterpoint of such a complexity that it could not be improvised.

coinciding with this fundamental difference in the manner of composing melodies is a sharp turn in the Western conception of mode, from Aurelian's collections of formulas to the ordered pitch systems earliest discussed in the *Alia Musica*. The change in the aims of notation of which I have spoken followed just on the heels of the new modal doctrine. In short, melodic style, its theoretical wellspring, and its graphic representation appear to have undergone fundamental modification in closely coordinated fashion.

THE *TROPI AD SEQUENTIAM*

PAUL EVANS

MEDIEVAL church composers continued to seek new opportunities for their musical activity within the framework of the Mass even after the Carolingian standardization of the liturgy brought the main period of Gregorian chant composition to a close. A particularly important outlet for new musical creation was the Alleluia of the Mass. Not only were a certain number of new Alleluia melodies composed during the later Middle Ages, but there were also various types of additions and interpolations which were developed in connection with the Alleluia and which were used to embellish its performance.

These additions to the Alleluia form a significant repertory of medieval monody and include all the basic categories of liturgical interpolation found in the music of the Western church. There were, for example, purely melodic additions to the chant. These were the well-known *sequentiae*, which were the long, elaborate melismas sung at the repetition of the Alleluia after the verse. There were also purely textual additions. These included not only the familiar *prosae*, which were the texts added to the *sequentiae*, but also the smaller-scaled Alleluia *prosulae*, which were texts added to the melismas of the official chant itself.

Interpolations of this kind accounted for most of the unofficial embellishment of the Alleluia in the Middle Ages; and the *sequentiae* and *prosae*, at least, have received intensive study. But one other category of addition to the Alleluia is much less well known. This is the trope itself, in which both text and music were added simultaneously to a pre-existent chant. Admittedly, troping in this sense was very rare in connection with the Alleluia, but it does exist in one rather special category, that of the *tropus ad sequentiam*.[1] Here, in a striking way, the basic techniques of medieval interpolation were combined.

As its name implies, the *tropus ad sequentiam* was a brief introductory trope performed before the singing of the melismatic

---

[1] Some of the texts of the *tropi ad sequentiam* have been published in the *Analecta Hymnica*, Vol. 49, "Tropen zum Proprium Missarum," ed. Clemens Blume (Leipzig, 1906), pp. 268-70. See also Léon Gautier, *Histoire de la Poésie Liturgique au Moyen Age: Les Tropes* (Paris, 1886), p. 154n, for a brief description.

sequentia or its corresponding *prosa*.[2] Its use was apparently not widespread in medieval Europe, since it is found almost exclusively in the Aquitainian monasteries centering around Saint-Martial de Limoges in southwest France.[3] It was probably introduced in the early decades of the tenth century, since the earliest Aquitainian troper, Paris BN lat. 1240, dating from around 930,[4] already contains *sequentia* tropes, although largely as marginal additions—a circumstance which suggests that the tropes were being created at about the same time as the troper itself was being copied. Certain *sequentia* tropes continued to be sung for a time in the eleventh century, and even an occasional new one was composed; but their use declined with that of the other tropes for the proper of the Mass, and examples are not found after the eleventh century.

The function of the *tropus ad sequentiam* was to introduce the singing of the *sequentia* on the greatest feast days of the Christian year and to express the joy of the Church on the occasion of these great festivals. "Christ has arisen from the dead, having broken the chains of death," begins the *sequentia* trope for Easter, "and the angels rejoicing call out in the highest, saying: *Alleluia*. . . ." And at this point, the singing of the great Easter *sequentia Fulgens preclara* commences.[5]

The repertory of *sequentia* tropes is small, and their use was apparently limited to feasts of the greatest solemnity. There are *sequentia* tropes for Christmas and the Epiphany, and for Easter, Ascension Day, and Pentecost. The only saints honored with *sequentia* tropes are Stephen, John the Evangelist, John the Baptist,

[2] The rubric "ad sequentiam" is the most common form, although one also finds "ante prosam," etc. The incipits of the following chant are usually given simply with the word "Alleluia," implying the *sequentia*, although occasionally the opening words of the *prosa* are also found.

[3] Even though the principle of the *sequentia* trope was known in the Germanic area of troping, it was not widely cultivated there. *Analecta Hymnica*, Vol. 49, p. 269, quotes a Christmas trope from St. Gall MS 484 as the only extant example of a *sequentia* trope from a non-French source. Actually, the area can be more strictly limited even than that, since the French sources involved are all Aquitainian. The St. Martial tropers which contain *sequentia* tropes are listed in the Index below.

[4] Heinrich Husmann, in his volume for RISM, *Tropen- und Sequenzenhandschriften* (Munich, 1964), pp. 137-38, favors a date later than that usually assigned to Paris BN lat. 1240, although he gives no direct evidence for it. It would seem to be difficult to maintain such a late date considering the notation and the repertory of the troper.

[5] This is trope No. 16 in the Index below. Each trope discussed will be referred to by its Index number.

Martin, and, as we would expect, Martial. There are also tropes for the Nativity of the Blessed Virgin and for the Dedication of a Church.

The texts of the *sequentia* tropes tend to be brief and are usually in prose. Those few texts which are poetic use the quantitative verse forms of the regular trope repertory. For example, the following trope for the feast of St. Martial is in dactyllic hexameters:

> Xpistus apostolico Marcialem culmine compsit;
> Laudibus angelicis nos inde canamus ovanter:
> *Alleluia.*[6]

There is even a use of the elegiac distich in the following trope for the Dedication of a Church:

> Regi inmortali laudes nunc dicite celsas,
> Alleluia canens nostra caterva sonet:
> *Alleluia.*[7]

On the whole, however, the style of the tropes tends to be very simple, suggesting at least a partial recognition on the part of the trope writer of the already extremely elaborate nature of the Gradual-Alleluia-Prosa complex.[8]

Like the other tropes of the Mass, the texts of the *sequentia* tropes are specifically related to the feasts which they embellish. However, unlike the other tropes, the individual *sequentia* trope texts are quite frequently adapted to fit various feasts—a very uncommon practice in terms of the trope repertory as a whole. For example, the fairly widespread Epiphany trope *O dux magorum*:

> O dux magorum, tibi sit laus, gloria, iocunditas sempiterna;
> nos quoque omnes dicamus, eia: *Alleluia.*

is found adapted for the Nativity of the Blessed Virgin in Paris BN lat. 1120 and Paris BN lat. 887:

[6] Trope No. 15. The reference to Martial as an Apostle indicates that *sequentia* tropes were still being written in the early decades of the eleventh century, when the question of the Apostolacy of St. Martial was the subject of fervent debate. See, for example, Paul Hooreman, "Saint-Martial de Limoges au Temps de l'Abbé Odolric (1025-1040)," *Revue Belge de Musicologie*, III (1949), 5-36.

[7] Trope No. 9.

[8] The extreme limits which the embellishment of this section of the Mass could reach are seen in Paris BN lat. 887, for example, where for Easter the Gradual *Haec dies* is preceded by the trope *Preclara adest dies*, the Alleluia *Pascha nostrum* is furnished with the prosula *Iam redeunt*, and the *sequentia* is introduced by the usual *sequentia* trope *Xpistus surrexit*.

O virgo gloriosa, tibi sit laus . . . etc.

and for the feast of St. Martial in Paris BN lat. 887:

O sacer gloriose, tibi sit laus . . . etc.[9]

The Dedication trope *Regi inmortali laudes*, mentioned above, has a relatively neutral text which allowed it to be used unaltered for various feasts, including St. Martial and St. Martin in Paris BN lat. 1240. However, its text was also adapted as follows in Paris BN lat. 1118 in order to make explicit its relationship to St. Martial:

Sancto Marciali laudes nunc promite celsas . . . etc.[10]

Again in Paris BN lat. 1118, a single trope is used for three major feasts of Our Lord. The following Christmas trope:

Filius Dei te nascente, rex adorande pastor bone, gregem conservare dignaris precamur: *Alleluia.*

is adapted as follows for Easter:

Salvator mundi te resurgente, rex . . . etc.

and for the Ascension:

Salvator mundi te ascendente, rex . . . etc.[11]

In Paris BN lat. 1084, the trope *Sancte Iohannes precursor* for St. John the Baptist is adapted to *Sancte Martine confessor* for the feast of St. Martin, although in this case, quite untypically, the melody is also altered.[12]

This process of text adaptation suggests that the basic impetus to the creation of *sequentia* tropes must have been remarkably brief. One sees, for example, that five of the seven most widely disseminated tropes—Nos. 4, 5, 9, 12, and 16 in the Index below—are found already in the earliest of the tropers, Paris BN lat. 1240. As other *sequentia* tropes were needed, it apparently became the practice simply to adapt old texts to new uses rather than compose new tropes. The process even went so far that occasionally introductory tropes from other Mass chants were used as *sequentia* tropes. Thus,

---

[9] Tropes Nos. 6, 8, and 7.
[10] Tropes Nos. 9 and 14.
[11] Tropes Nos. 1, 11, and 10.
[12] Tropes Nos. 12 and 13.

the Introit trope *Gaudeamus omnes* for the feast of St. Stephen is used as a *sequentia* trope for the same feast in Paris BN lat. 887, the Easter Introit trope *Inmortalis filius Dei* occurs as a *sequentia* trope for Monday in Easter Week in Paris BN lat. 1118, and the Introit trope *Pastor orbis claviger* for St. Peter is used in a slightly varied form as a *sequentia* trope in Paris BN lat. 1084.[13]

Among the few newly composed tropes from a later period are the two eleventh-century tropes written to recognize the Apostolacy of St. Martial;[14] but the obvious importance of this event for the Abbey of St. Martial, as well as the propagandistic ends which these new texts might serve, would justify the creation of new works.

From a musical point of view, the adaptation of texts to different uses suggests a very uncharacteristic casualness on the part of the trope writer to the music of the trope and its relationship to the chant which it embellished. With only the single exception mentioned above, the textual adaptation was not accompanied by a comparable melodic alteration, and the music of the trope remains the same, even though the *sequentiae* which it introduces are different in terms of mode, melodic idiom, and so forth. Musically as well as textually, therefore, the *sequentia* tropes quickly began to display a loss of creative vitality which only gradually came to affect the process of troping as a whole.

The music of the *sequentia* tropes is quite unassuming, as we would expect from the preceding discussion of the texts. The melodies are usually simple, being in the neumatic style of the regular trope repertory. They thus maintain a stylistic independence from the *prosa* or *sequentia* which they introduce, avoiding both the syllabic style of the former and the pure melismatic writing of the latter. Since they are introductory tropes, the problem of adapting the melody to the chant which is being embellished is not a particularly crucial one. Some effort is made to accommodate the final cadence of the trope to the opening of the *sequentia*. But beyond that, the tropes appear to be brief, self-contained compositions, which could, at least in some cases, be sung before various *sequentiae* without too much concern for melodic propriety.

---

[13] In at least one case, this process was reversed. The *sequentia* trope for St. Martial *O sacer gloriose* (No. 7), which is itself, as we have seen, an adaptation of the Epiphany trope *O dux magorum*, occurs in a shortened form as a Communion trope in Paris BN lat. n.a. 1871.

[14] Nos. 15 and 3. Cf. n. 6 above.

The *tropi ad sequentiam* make up a small part of the total repertory of troping, but nonetheless they furnish a fine example of the
excessive lengths to which the medieval process of interpolation
could go. They are, indeed, like the *Regnum prosulae*, essentially
additions to additions within the liturgy; and considering this basic
redundancy, it is perhaps not surprising that their distribution was
not widespread. The limitations of troping as a creative process
appear in especially sharp outline in the *sequentia* tropes. But this
weakness was inherent in the trope repertory as a whole and helps
to account for the gradual loss of favor experienced by troping in
the course of the eleventh and twelfth centuries.

The following is a complete index of the St. Martial *sequentia*
tropes, with an indication of the manuscripts in which each occurs.[15]
The folio on which the trope appears is given for each troper, an
asterisk signifies an occurrence of the text without music.

The index is followed by a transcription of the principal tropes
arranged according to the church year. Each trope is preceded by
an indication of its feast, its number in the index, and the specific
troper used for the transcription. Textual variants will be found
in the index.

The *sequentiae* or *prosae* for which the tropes were intended are
not invariably indicated in the manuscripts. Where they are known,
their titles are given in the index following the feast designation.

---

[15] For a description of the manuscripts, see Husmann, *Tropen- und Sequenzenhandschriften*, pp. 117-48.

Index

Paris Bibliothèque Nationale
fonds Latin

	887	903	909	1084	1118	1119	1120	1121	1240	n.a. 1871
Filius Dei te nascente (Nat Dom) ADEST UNA					15					
Hodie replevit Dominus (Pentecost)			*45v			*46, 175	*37v	24		
Marcialis primus fidei (Martial) CONCELEBREMUS			46v			61				
Natus est altissimi (Nat Dom)	11		*11			*6			*19	
Nobile triumphum decoremus (Stephen)			*14v						*20	
) dux magorum (Epiph) EPIPHANIAM DOMINO	17		19v	*41				9v		
) sacer gloriose (= No. 6) (Martial) VALDE LUMEN	34									
) virgo gloriosa (= No. 6) (Nat BMV)	37						*56v			
Regi inmortali laudes (Ded Eccl; Martial; Martin; Ioh Ev; Ascen) AD TEMPLI HUIUS	15, 23v		33v	122		39	33	20v	*36v, *37v	
Salvator mundi te ascendente (= No. 1) (Ascen) REX OMNIPOTENS DEI					59					
Salvator mundi te resurgente (= No. 1) (Pasch)					45v					
Sancte Iohannes precursor (Ioh Bapt)	29						*40v		(*)35v	
Sancte Martine confessor (Text = No. 12) (Martin)					121v					
Sancto Marciali laudes (= No. 9) (Martial) CONCELEBREMUS						79v				
pistus apostolico Marcialem (Martial) ALLELUIA Non vos me			46			60v				
pistus surrexit ex mortuis (Pasch) FULGENS PRECLARA	20v	153	24	66v	45v, 52v	24	22v	13v	31	15

Ex. 1. In Nativitate Domini—*Natus est altissimi* (No. 4; Paris 887, f. 11)

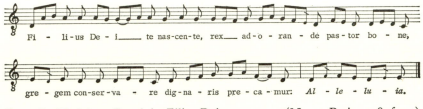

Ex. 2. In Nativitate Domini—*Filius Dei te nascente* (No. 1; Paris 1118, f. 15)

Nobile triumphum decoremus laudibus protho Stephani eximii: *Alleluia*

Ex. 3. In Natale S. Stephani—*Nobile triumphum decoremus*
(No. 5; Paris 909, f. 14v)

Ex. 4. In Epiphania Domini—*O dux magorum* (No. 6; Paris 1121, f. 9v)

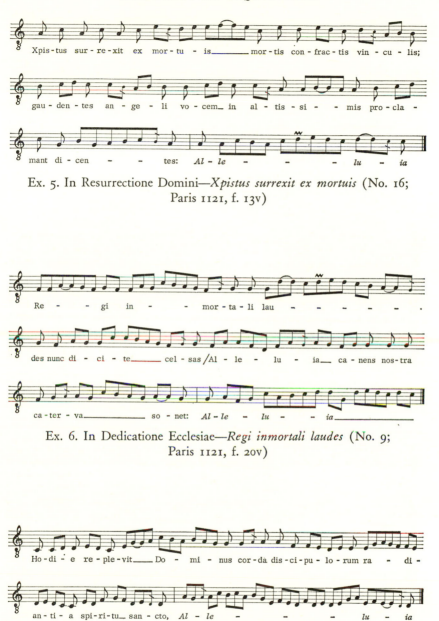

Ex. 5. In Resurrectione Domini—*Xpistus surrexit ex mortuis* (No. 16;
Paris 1121, f. 13v)

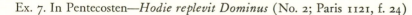

Ex. 6. In Dedicatione Ecclesiae—*Regi inmortali laudes* (No. 9;
Paris 1121, f. 20v)

Ex. 7. In Pentecosten—*Hodie replevit Dominus* (No. 2; Paris 1121, f. 24)

Ex. 8. In Natale S. Iohannis Baptistae—*Sancte Iohannes precursor*
(No. 12; Paris 887, f. 29)

Ex. 9. In Natale S. Martialis—*Xpistus apostolico Marcialem* (No. 15;
Paris 909, f. 46)

Ex. 10. In Natale S. Martialis—*Marcialis primus fidei* (No. 3;
Paris 909, f. 46v)

III. SOURCES, PROBLEMS: ARS NOVA
AND RENAISSANCE

SOME DATES FOR
BARTOLINO DA PADOVA

PIERLUIGI PETROBELLI[*]

ALTHOUGH Bartolino da Padova, after Francesco Landini and Nicolò da Perugia, is the composer from the Italian "Ars Nova"[†] of whom the largest number of works have survived—thirty-eight madrigali and ballate—very little attention has been devoted to this musician. We have an edition in modern notation of all but one of his compositions,[1] since they occur all together in the Squarcialupi Codex[2] (even though this is an edition which

---

[*] The author expresses his thanks to Professor Gianfranco Folena, and to his friends Alberto Limentani and Enzo Mengaldo, for their kind and authoritative help in solving certain problems of textual criticism and linguistic interpretation that appear in the course of this essay; and to Lewis Lockwood for translating the essay into English.

[†] In spite of the many discussions on the subject, I am still convinced that there are reasons for using this term in connection with Italian polyphonic music of the fourteenth century.

[1] The ballata "Serva çiaschuno chom' è facto a luy," preserved in the Lucca Codex (Mn), fol. 2a.

[2] Florence, Bibl. Laurenziana MS Pal. 87, fols. 101v-120v. A complete list of the works of Bartolino and a substantial bibliography of writings about him will be found in the *Dizionario Biografico degli Italiani* (Rome: Istituto dell' Enciclopedia Italiana), VI, 634-36 (available also in offprint); the article is by the present writer.

We give here the list of manuscripts containing compositions by Bartolino together with their conventional sigla and the numbers and types of compositions they contain:

Firenze, Biblioteca Nazionale Centrale, MS Panciatichi 26 (FP) (1 madrigale, 1 ballata)

Paris, Bibliothèque Nationale, Fonds Italien 568 (P) (3 madrigali, 1 ballata)

Paris, Bibliothèque Nationale, Nouv. acq. franç. 6771 (Reina) (PR) (9 madrigali, 16 ballate)

London, British Museum, MS Add. 29987 (Lo) (5 madrigali, 1 ballata)

Lucca, Archivo di Stato, codice Mancini (Mn) (4 madrigali, 9 ballate)

Firenze, Bibl. Laurenziana, MS Palatino 87 (Squarcialupi) (FL) (11 madrigali, 26 ballate)

Modena, Biblioteca Estense, MS Lat. acq. 568 (Mod a) (2 madrigali, 1 ballata)

Paris, Bibliothèque Nationale, Nouv. franç. 4917 (PZ) (1 ballata)

Faenza, Biblioteca Comunale, MS 117, transcription for keyboard instruments (Fa) (3 madrigali)

The concordances for these compositions, together with many valuable bibliographical references for the individual works, will be found in K. von Fischer, *Studien zur italienischen Musik des Trecento und frühen Quattrocento, Publikationen der*

has the limitations to be expected of a publication based on a single manuscript printed after the death of its editor, and without his final revision).[3] Yet what has been written about Bartolino so far, even by specialists of this period, has been limited to brief references, included in descriptions of codices containing works by him, or in studies and reviews dealing with the period as a whole.[4] Only just recently has there appeared a study of the composer himself written with care and devotion, which contains a useful description of the circumstances in which Bartolino most probably lived and worked.[5] But since this study lacks a certain rigor in its presentation and mode of argument, certain of its conclusions may be open to question.

The main reason for uncertainty about Bartolino is the absence of documents—apart from the compositions and some literary references[6]—concerning the specific facts of his career. At the end of this essay we shall propose some cautious hypotheses based on documentary evidence that is probably contemporary with the musical and poetic texts set by Bartolino; but these can be put forward only as hypotheses, and must be regarded as such.

The only certain element of evidence for the figure of Bartolino is provided by the texts on which his compositions are based; through the study of their content, we will be able to delimit our observations to a specific environment, circle of individuals, and historical period.

The first datum that can be established with reasonable certainty is the order to which our "Frater" belonged. From the habit in which he is portrayed in the Squarcialupi Codex, fol. 101v, and from the

Schweizerischen Musikforschenden Gesellschaft, Ser. ii, Vol. 5 (Berne, 1956); p. 78 of this study gives all the compositions of Bartolino according to the numerical listing adopted by the author.

When this article was in the proof stage, I was kindly informed of an essay which had previously escaped my attention: K. von Fischer, "Drei unbekannte Werke von Jacobo da Bologna und Bartolino da Padua," Miscelánea en homenaje a monseñor Higinio Anglés, I (Barcelona, 1958-61), 265-81, where the author convincingly proposes the attribution to Bartolino of the madrigal "La bianca selva" (PR, fol. 19v).

[3] J. Wolf, Der Squarcialupi Codex (Lippstadt, 1955), pp. 159-94.

[4] For this bibliography see the above-mentioned article in the Dizionario Biografico degli Italiani.

[5] N. Goldine, "Fra Bartolino da Padova, Musicien de Cour," Acta Musicologica, xxxiv (1962), 142-55.

[6] For the reference to Bartolino in Il Paradiso degli Alberti by Giovanni da Prato and in the Liber Saporecti by Simone Prudenzani, see, among others, N. Goldine, "Fra Bartolino da Padova," pp. 142-44.

indication, "Frater Carmelitus," which heads the ballata "I bei sembianti," fol. 121r, of Mod a, we can be sure that Bartolino belonged to the order of Carmelites.

Another established fact, and one essential to the determination of Bartolino's circle of activity, is provided by the fact that the text of the ballata "La sacrosanta carità d'amore" is the work of Giovanni Dondi dall'Orologio. The identification of Dondi's poem with the text set by Bartolino is by Levi,[7] who nevertheless doubts Dondi's authorship, holding that the text of the ballata (which in the Marciana Codex containing this author's works bears the ascription "Balata Florentie") is only a reworking of a popular Florentine text collected by Dondi during his sojourn in Florence between 1368 and 1371. Levi's doubts are connected with his interpretation of a sonnet by Dondi, "La donna che te sembra cordogliosa"; this is an answer to a sonnet by Francesco di Vannozzo, "Nuovamente una donna assai pietosa," which in this same Marciana Codex bears the significant attribution, "Franciscus Vanocij Magistro Johanni pro balata quam nuper didicerat."[8] In this sonnet,[9] Vannozzo speaks allegorically of the ballata (which appears in the guise of a beautiful woman), asking Dondi to come to hear it now that he, Francesco di Vannozzo, has learned it, and before he forgets it ("Dunque, fin che

[7] E. Levi, *Francesco di Vannozzo e la lirica nelle corti lombarde durante la seconda metà del secolo XIV* (Florence, 1908), p. 335.

[8] Venice, Bibl. Marciana MS Cl. XIV, lat. 223, fol. 35a.

[9] We give here the text of the sonnet from the edition published by Medin, *Le Rime di Francesco di Vannozzo*, a cura di Antonio Medin, in *Collezione di opere inedite o rare* (Bologna, Commissione per i testi di lingua, Casa Carducci, 1928), p. 90, No. 68 of the collection:

> *Idem F. V. ad Magistrum Johannem [Dondi]*
>
> Nuovamente una donna assai pietosa,
> con atti begli e d'angelica forma,
> per grazia sua dignata è de por l'orma
> nel mio piccol albergo e li riposa.
> Ma duolmi chè mi par melanconosa,
> sì che talor nel viso si disforma,
> e parmi che piangendo se conforma
> con voler dir che carità è nascosa.
> Ond'io de lei, ch'oggi da noi si sfanta,
> dolìame forte e domandai del nome:
> subito ella rispose: "Sacrosanta,"
> dicendo dolcemente el perché e 'l come.
> Dunque, fin che fermato ha qui la pianta,
> piacciave de veder so' dolce chiome.

fermato ha qui la pianta / piacciave de veder so' dolce chiome"). Levi interprets Dondi's reply[10] as a return invitation to Vannozzo to set to music the ballata, "La sacrosanta carità d'amore," which he had transcribed at Florence from popular sources.[11] Levi's interpretation of the meaning of the sonnet is opposed by Medin, in a review of Levi's book; Medin's view, much more persuasive than that of Levi, is that the ballata, when sent to Vannozzo to be inserted into his repertoire, had already been set to music. On the basis of this view, one ought to attribute to Dondi alone the text of the ballata, and the expression "vesta graciosa" would refer not to the poetic form but to the musical setting already in existence.[12] This

[10] *Responsio magistri Johanis*

La donna che ti sembra cordogliosa
    perchè si lagna, ma del ver t'informa,
    dicendo ch'oggi al mondo par che dorma
    quella virtù che tanto è preziosa,
Venuta è a te con vesta graciosa,
    tanto che se agradir vorrai sua norma
    comparer pò con lode ne la torma
    de l'altre, e più se la torai per sposa.
E se ver' lei tuo grazia fie cotanta
    spesso porrò qui le tediose some,
    odendo come questo donna canta.
So ben che l'altre ch'èn del suo cognome
    de dolce e bel piacer tutte s'avanta,
    ma tu li aquisterai nuovo prenome.

(*Le Rime di Francesco di Vannozzo*, a cura di Antonio Medin, p. 91, No. 69).

[11] E. Levi, *Francesco di Vannozzo*, p. 337.

[12] A. Medin, review of the volume by E. Levi (see n. 7), in *Giornale Storico della Letterature Italiana*, LV (1910), 401-402: "A chi ben guardi, le cose vanno rimesse sicuramente a posto così: la ballata *La sacrosanta* è veramente del Dondi, che la scrisse a Firenze, onde il suo nome di fiorentina, e venne musicata (*veste graziosa*) da Frate Bartolino da Padova. Il Dondi prega il V. di gradirla e preferirla a tutte le altre dolci ballate (non accenna alle sue) che egli conosceva; e se io, continua il Dondi, l'udrò cantare da te con la usata tua soavità, allieverò la noia della mia vita. So bene che tutte le altre ballate (non quelle del Dondi) sono superiori a questa mia [. . .] ma questa avrà da te nuovo splendore, ossia rifulgerà per merito tuo." This interpretation is repeated by Medin in *Le Rime di Francesco di Vannozzo*, edited by him, as a note to the sonnet, "La donna che ti sembra cordogliosa," given as No. 10. For the use of the term *veste* (or *vesta*) with the exact meaning, "musical setting," see also, in the *Rime* of Dante Alighieri (ed. G. F. Contini, 3rd edn. Einaudi: Torino, 1963), the ballata *Per una ghirlandetta* (pp. 38-39), at line 21: "Le parolette mie novelle,/. . ./ per leggiadria ci hanno tolt'elle/ una *vesta* ch'altrui fu data" (and see also Contini's note). See as well, the sonnet *Se Lippo amico* (pp. 22-23), lines 13-16: ". . . esta pulcella nuda,/ che ven di dietro a me sì vergognosa/ ch'a torto gir non osa/ perch'ella non ha *vesta* in che si chiuda."

conclusion leads to two considerations of fundamental importance to our problem. The first concerns the dating of the ballata. Both Levi and Medin agree that it was written (or transcribed) by Dondi between the years 1368 and 1371, the period of his sojourn at Florence. Since Dondi died in 1389,[13] one is compelled to conclude that the ballata was sent by the poet to Francesco di Vannozzo with "vesta graciosa"—i.e., accompanied by a musical setting—and that it was set by Bartolino some time between this three-year period (1368-71) and 1389.

Of greater importance is the second conclusion. Giovanni Dondi dall'Orologio occupies a singular position in the cultural history of the second half of the fourteenth century. Dondi was born in Chioggia around 1330 and was awarded the laureate in medicine in Padua in 1354. He was a member of the Council of Doctors at Padua and in a short time became so well known as a physician, philosopher, and astronomer that he was invited to Florence to teach during the period between 1368 and 1371. As a friend and confidant of Petrarch, Giovanni Dondi is the most conspicuous figure among a group of poets (some more able than he, but less versatile and less well known) active in the region of Italy of which Padua was the center.[14] It was in Padua that in all probability Giovanni lived until 1383, the year in which he transferred to Pavia as a physician in the service of Gian Galeazzo Visconti. His residence at Padua thus embraced the greater part of his active life. These indications, and above all the numerous affinities of style, speech, and even content which exist between the poetry of Giovanni Dondi and the texts set to music by Bartolino, give us a firm orientation toward Padua as a place in which Bartolino lived and worked. As we shall see, this thesis is confirmed by the analysis of some of the poetic texts themselves.

In Bartolino's madrigals it is sometimes possible to discover the name of the lady to whom the work is addressed hidden among the words of the ritornello; this practice was much in vogue among Ars Nova composers.[15] The content of such madrigals, and especially

[13] V. Bellemo, *Jacopo e Giovanni De' Dondi dall' Orologio*, note critiche con le rime edite e inedite di Giovanni Dondi e altre aggiunte (Chioggia, 1894), p. 119.

[14] *Ibid.*, pp. 109ff. See also *Le Rime di Giovanni Dondi Dall'Orologio*, per cura di A. Medin (Padova, 1895), p. [v], which essentially summarizes the information given by Bellemo.

[15] See for example the madrigals by Johannes de Florentia, "Apres'un fiume

the allegorical language used in them, rich in allusions, suggests that each was addressed to a particular lady, an identifiable individual and that each was written on a specific occasion, and thus should be datable within fair limits. On this basis, N. Goldine has proposed the identification of "CATARINA," the name found hidden in the ritornello of the madrigal, "Le aurate chiome," with Caterina da Carrara, daughter of Francesco il Vecchio, lord of Padua, who married Stefano, Count of Veglia, in 1372. Goldine attributes the composition to that occasion, suggesting that it was written as a wedding piece; yet the text of the madrigal contains no allusion that would corroborate this thesis.[16]

Nor is this the only madrigal by Bartolino containing the name of a woman in the first verse of its ritornello. The madrigal "Quel sole che nutrica" introduces a new name, "ORSOLINA," hidden in the same portion of the poem. The text was published earlier by Carducci[17] and Goldine.[18] In this diplomatic transcription a number of emendations needed for the meter are suggested; it is taken from the one manuscript in which the work is preserved:

> Quel sole che nutrica 'l gentil fiore
> discende talor giù per veder quello,
> c'a·llui di lui par esser[e] più bello.
> Poï ch'alquanto seco à contemplato
> ritorna su e riferisce ally dei
> l'amirabil belleça di costei.
> HOR SOL IN Alto ciel di tuo biltate
> laudano gli a(n)gel la som(m)' onestade.[19]

---

chiaro," "O perlaro gentil, che dispogliato," "Più non mi curo della tua compagna" (ANNA); those of Magister Piero, "All' ombra d'un perlaro," "Sovra un fiume regale" (ANNA); "Si come al canto della bella Iguana" (MARGHERITA). Nino Pirrotta, ed., *The Music of Fourteenth-Century Italy, Corpus Mensurabilis Musicae 8*, I (Amsterdam, 1954), and II (1960).

[16] The name was identified in the ritornello of the madrigal for the first time by Ettore LiGotti (N. Pirrotta and E. LiGotti, "Il codice di Lucca," in *Musica Disciplina*, IV [1950], p. 116).

[17] G. Carducci, *Musica e Poesia nel mondo elegante del sec. XIV*, in *Opere di Giosuè Carducci*, VIII, 380. Not "reading" the hidden name, Carducci feels the need to propose for lines 7 and 8 the reading: "Or su in alto ciel di tuo' biltate/ Gli angioli laudan la somma onestade."

[18] N. Goldine, "Fra Bartolino da Padova," p. 119. Goldine omits the third verse, however.

[19] FL, fols. 106v-107r. The text of line 7 appears in the manuscript (part of the

Taken as a whole, this text might well suggest the visit of a father, a personage of high position ("Quel sole") to a daughter ("che nutrica 'l gentil fiore"), a young lady named "Orsolina," or "Orsola," who is at a distance from the place in which the father habitually resides ("discende talor giù per veder quello"). This place of residence is not just anywhere, it is a place of some importance in which people of high rank live ("ritorna su e riferisce ally dei"); it is, in short, a court.

From his marriage with Giovanna dalle Calze in 1354, Giovanni Dondi had a son, Jacopo, and four daughters; the oldest daughter, Orsola, married Jacopo da Camposampiero in 1378,[20] and was still alive after 1390.[21] And as we have pointed out, in 1383 Giovanni Dondi moved to Pavia, where he was received with due honor by the court of Gian Galeazzo Visconti as the physician of the duke and the ducal family. These and other facts are transmitted to us by the "Epistulae" of Dondi's that are preserved; and from them we also learn that in August of a certain year (not precisely determined, but between 1383—the year of his departure from Padua—and 1389, the year of his death at Genoa) the famous physician and astronomer returned temporarily to Padua.[22] If we look once again at the text set by Bartolino, we see that there are striking similarities between its content and these events. The name "Orsola" is the same; so is the figure of the father, a man of elevated social and cultural position, and his residence at a court, to which he must return—all these elements suggest that the madrigal had been set by Bartolino on the occasion of a (or the) visit of Giovanni Dondi to his daughter Orsola, who had remained at Padua, between 1383

---

tenor) in this significant form: "Ho hor sol in al hor sol in alto ciel di tuo biltate." The repetition of the syllables in performance doubtless revealed the name of the lady to whom the piece was addressed.

Variants in the cantus part: line 7, "Laudan gli angioli, onestate."

[20] V. Bellemo, *Jacopo e Giovanni De' Dondi*, p. 100. A. Gloria, *Monumenti dell' Università di Padova*, II (Padova, 1888), p. 133, Document No. 1454: this is the gift contract, according to which Jacopo da Camposampiero receives 500 gold ducats from Giovanni Dondi, "dotante nomine honeste et sap. d. d. Ursule eius filie sponse et uxoris legiptime dicti Jacobi."

[21] Orsola Dondi, daughter of Giovanni, is one of the heirs of Benedetto Dondi, Giovanni's brother. This is seen from the will drawn up after 1390 and published by Bellemo, *Jacopo e Giovanni De' Dondi*, pp. 345ff.

[22] *Ibid.*, pp. 116ff. Bellemo proposes the year 1384, without much evidence.

and 1389.[23] The occasional character of the piece fits well into the taste and practice of the Venetian-Lombard poetic circle of the late fourteenth century, of which Giovanni Dondi was the best known, if not the most gifted, representative. It is significant that we find among his poems some that are similar to texts set by Bartolino, including a "Mandriale pro Domino C.", which is followed in the manuscript by a "Balata pro eodem," a "Balata pro Agnola," and the madrigal, "Ne l'aspra selva, tra grande animali," which repeats exactly the metrical scheme and rhyme scheme that is typical of all the madrigals set by Bartolino.[24]

Given the relationship of Dondi and Bartolino, and the characteristic musical style of Bartolino's work, we are not surprised to find in the inventory of Giovanni Dondi's very extensive library, among texts on medicine, philosophy, astronomy, Latin classics, and the works of his friend Petrarch, a volume described by the compiler of the inventory as "Cantiones in lingua gallica."[25] Bartolino's compositions, although written in the musical notation of the Italian Ars Nova, show no more than feeble resistance to the preponderant French influence of the period, especially in rhythmic features.[26] The presence of a volume containing French songs in the library of one of the authors of Bartolino's texts may well be a valuable hint which could help us reconstruct the paths by which French influence reached the composer's work.

It was Friedrich Ludwig who first said that Bartolino should be reckoned among the second generation of Ars Nova composers, the

[23] It is rather less likely that the lady, to whom this work is addressed, was Orsola Contarini (wife of Pietro da Carrara, natural son of Francesco il Vecchio and of Maria di Curtarolo), who died at Padua in 1405. Cf. J. Salomonio, *Urbis Patavinae Inscriptiones sacrae, et prophanae* . . . (Padua, 1701), p. 65, No. 123; P. Litta, *Famiglie Celebri Italiane,* "Carraresi di Padova," Tav. V; Galeazzo e Bartolomeo Gatari, *Cronaca Carrarese,* a cura di A. Medin e G. Tolomei, in *Rerum Italicarum Scriptores,* nuova edizione a cura dell'Istituto Storico Italiano (Città di Castello, 1909), Tomo XVII, 1, 1, p. 472 n 8.

[24] *Le Rime di Giovanni Dondi Dall'Orologio,* per cura di A. Medin, pp. 43ff.

[25] V. Lazzarini, "I libri, gli argenti, le vesti di Giovanni Dondi dall' Orologio," *Bollettino del Museo Civico di Padova,* N. S., 1 (1925), 11-36 (also as offprint). The reference is found as No. 113 of the inventory, p. 29 of the article, p. 21 of the offprint.

[26] N. Pirrotta, "L'Ars Nova Italienne," in *Histoire de la Musique,* ed. Roland-Manuel, 1 (Paris, 1960), 799. Notable too is the fact that this characteristic is especially clear in the madrigal with French text, "La douce çere," which will be discussed later in this article.

generation of Francesco Landini in the second half of the fourteenth century. Ludwig's starting point was his observation that the text of the ballata "Chi tempo à"[27] can be attributed to Matteo Griffoni, who lived from 1351 to 1426.[28] The text of the ballata was published for the first time by Giusto Grion, who derived it from Codex IV of the Biblioteca del Seminario in Padua;[29] and it was later published by Carducci.[30] To Ludwig's observations we can now add a few new points.

The critical edition of Matteo Griffoni's major work, the *Memoriale Historicum de Rebus Bononiensium*, is preceded by an extensive and well-documented biography of him.[31] Bolognese by birth, and the descendant of one of the most famous local families, Matteo Griffoni was a poet only in the most incidental sense, devoting himself instead to the reconstruction of his family genealogy (of his reconstruction only brief fragments remain), and above all to the writing of a chronicle of the principal events of his time, the *Memoriale*. Matteo's trip to Venice from July to October 1373[32] offers small support for the theory of a meeting with Bartolino at Padua, since Matteo had left Bologna at this time in flight from a plague that had struck the city; and it seems reasonable to suppose that he would have been avoiding, rather than seeking, any personal contacts.

Matteo Griffoni played an important role in the public life of Bologna at the end of the fourteenth and beginning of the fifteenth century. At the age of 22 he was already notary of the Curia Vescovile, and in 1387 he was made Cancelliere of the Society of Notaries.[33] In 1391 he assumed his first diplomatic tasks; the second of these, in December of this year, brought him to Padua as ambassador of the city of Bologna. Bologna, a confederated city, was sending one hundred lances to Francesco Novello da Carrara, Lord of Padua. Matteo himself tells us about his embassy in these terms:

[27] FL, fol. 112r; PR, fol. 16r. Modern transcription: J. Wolf, *Der Squarcialupi Codex*, pp. 178-79.

[28] F. Ludwig, "Geschichte der Mensuralnotation von 1250-1460: Besprechung des gleichnamigen Buches von J. Wolf," in *SIMG*, VI (1904/05), 636.

[29] *Delle rime volgari. Trattato di Antonio da Tempo . . .* , a cura di Giusto Grion, *Collezione di opere inedite o rare* (Bologna, 1869), p. 361.

[30] *Cantilene e Ballate, Strambotti e Madrigali nei secoli XIII e XIV*, a cura di G. Carducci (Pisa, 1871), p. 327.

[31] *Matthaei de Griffonibus Memoriale Historicum de Rebus Bononiensium* in *Rerum Italicarum Scriptores*, nuova ed., a cura dell'Istituto Storico Italiano, Tom. XVIII, Parte II, a cura di L. Frati e A. Sorbelli (Città di Castello, 1902), pp. ivff.

[32] *Ibid.*, p. v.   [33] *Ibid.*

M.CCCLXXXXI

[. . .]

Eodem anno, de mense decembris. Comune Bononiae misit Paduam in auxilium domini Paduae, sui colligati, centum lanceas equitum armorum et miserunt Matthaeum de Griffonibus ambaxiatorem cum dictis gentibus.[34]

From the preface provided by the editors of the *Memoriale*, it appears wholly probable that Matteo Griffoni left Bologna, or was disengaged from his Bolognese interests, only for official reasons attached to his duties, and what we have reported is the only proof that he was in Padua. In short, his presence there was neither a private nor accidental matter, but was entirely determined by his role as ambassador of the city of Bologna. This sojourn bore fruit shortly thereafter; four months later a treaty was signed linking Padua and Bologna, to which other principalities and cities were added.[35] It does not, then, seem too adventurous to propose the period toward the end of 1391 (the period of Matteo's embassy) as the date of composition of the music for the ballata "Chi tempo à"; this appears more plausible still if one considers the "tone" to which the Carraresi aspired for their court. Culture and politics, art and diplomacy were joined together in the lives of a group of individuals who exercised each of these activities in turn, and among whom the most famous was Francesco Petrarca.[36]

Imperial[37]

Imperial sedendo fra più stelle
dal ciel disces'un carro d'onor degno
sotto signor d'ogn'altro più benigno;

---

[34] *Ibid.*, p. 84.

[35] "M. CCCLXXXXII . . . Eodem anno, de mense aprelis, die xj aprelis. Fuit bandita et publicata liga facta inter comune Bononiae, comune Florentiae, marchionem Ferrariae, dominum Paduanum, dominos de Ravenna, dominum de Faventia et dominum Imolae ad defensionem statuum omnium praedictorum colligatorum et contra quoscumque alios volentes eos offendere." *Ibid.* See also p. vii.

[36] For a useful and documented description of the palace and court of the last Carraresi, see especially the book by E. Levi, *Francesco di Vannozzo*, Ch. 3: "Francesco di Vannozzo a Padova e la coltura nella corte dei Carraresi," pp. 59ff.

[37] Although this and the following texts have been published by other writers, I have thought it useful to present them once again, since the analysis of textual details requires the reader's close attention to the poems. In addition, the previous editions contain but few of the variants in the sources. In establishing the text of a

Le rote soy guidavan quatro done,
Iusticia e temperancia cum forteça
et an' prudença tra cotanta alteça.
Nel meç'un saracin con l'ale d'oro
tene 'l fabricator de so tesoro.[38]

The content of this poem has been discussed several times and has been variously interpreted. Nino Pirrotta has pointed out its exact allusion to the arms of the Carraresi, the lords of Padua, whose emblem was the red chariot on a white field ("un carro d'onor degno");[39] Mlle Goldine, incorrectly attributing the composition to Giovanni da Ravenna, but justly emphasizing the first words of the

---

poem the present procedure has been that of following as closely as possible the version of one manuscript, chosen for its linguistic authority and for the value of the reading it offers, corrected however by means of the other manuscripts in those details in which the principal source is clearly in error. In the texts all the linguistic peculiarities are preserved, adapted to modern spelling (np=mp, etc.). All the variants, including the purely graphic ones, found in the various sources, are given in the critical apparatus. This is done not out of an excess of philological zeal, but in order to put the largest amount of material possible at the disposition of the student who may wish to deal, even on the linguistic level, with the problem of filiation of the codices of the Ars Nova. For sigla, etc., see n. 2 above; superscript letters refer to parts.

[38] P, fols. 47v-48r; PR, fols. 22v-23r (on fol. 13r the tenor repeated); Mn, fols. 19a^v-21a^r; FL, fols. 109v-110r; Mod a, fols. 29v-30r; Fa, fols. 73v-76. The complete text is found only in PR^c and Mn^c; Mod a lacks line 6; lines 1-2-3-7-8 are found in P^c and P^t; PR^t; FL^c and FL^t; Mod a^t; Mn^t. Attributions: Mod a^c: "Dactalus de padua fecit"; FL: "Magister Frater Bartolinus de Padua."
For this text, PR^c has been used as principal source.
Line 1. All manuscripts give the form: *Inperial*, with the exception of PR^c (⟨*I*⟩*nperialle*), Mn^c (*Inperiale*), Mn^t and Mn^{ct} (*Imperiale*); PR^t: *stele*.
Line 2. This line is written twice in identical form for each manuscript (PR^t: once only). PR, Mn, Mod a: *Dal*; PR^c: *desese*; Mn: *descese*; PR^t: *caro*; Mod a: *dingno*.
Line 3. P^c: *Sotto sotto segno*; P^t: *Sott'un*; PR^c: *Sotto soto*; PR^t: *Sotto segnor*; Mn^c: *Sotto sotto un*; Mn^t: *Sotto sotto un segnor*; FL^c: *Sotto sotto*; FL^t: *Sott'un*; Mod a: *Socto socto*; PR, Mn: *via*; Mod a: *ma*; Mn: *benegno*; Mod a: *benin⟨gno⟩*.
Line 4. Mn: *soe*; Mod a: *sue*; PR: *guranian*; Mn: *quattro*; Mod a: *quactro*.
Line 5. Mod a: *Iustitia et temperança con forteçça*; Mn: *Iustitia et temperantia con forteçça*.
Line 6. Mn: *et am prudentia con cotanta alteçça*.
Line 7. PR^c: *Nel meço saracin*; Mod a: *sarayn*; Mn: *Nel meço un*; P^c: *coll'ale*; PR^t: *cum l'alle*.
Line 8. P^c: *Tenea 'l*; P^c: *de suo*; Mn: *del so thesoro*; FL: *di suo*; Mod a^c: *del so thexoro*; Mod a^t: *del so tesoro*.

[39] N. Pirrotta, "Il Codice di Lucca," *Musica Disciplina*, v (1951), 119ff.

poem, thinks the madrigal was written for Francesco da Carrara il Vecchio, thus attributing the piece to the period between 1364 and 1367.[40]

A close analysis of the entire meaning of the madrigal and the exact sense of some of its terms suggests another dating. The text contains two heraldic allusions: the chariot with four wheels ("Le rote soy guidavan quatro done") and the Saracen with golden wings ("Nel meç'un saracin con l'ale d'oro"). This last emblem, the head of a Moor with two small horns, flanked by two large golden wings, is a symbol typical for the family of the Carrara but is not characteristic for any single member; we find it as an emblem for Ubertino da Carrara,[41] for Francesco il Vecchio,[42] for Francesco Novello.[43] The two emblems, taken alone, can therefore provide us no help in our problem of dating. Nor can the coins minted by the Carraresi help to solve the problem, even though the ritornello of the madrigal

[40] N. Goldine, "Bartolino da Padova," pp. 150-51. The attribution to Giovanni da Ravenna is untenable. It is based on the assertion (p. 151 n 50) that the text of the madrigal is contained in Padova, Bibl. del Seminario Cod. LIX. A complete description of the contents of this manuscript and the identification of the authors of the texts found in it is given in Antonio Medin's preface to *Le Rime di Francesco di Vannozzo*, p. xxiii. The name of Giovanni da Ravenna does not appear. An examination of the manuscript has confirmed the absence of the text of *Imperial*.

[41] Padua, Bibl. del Museo Civico, Cod. BP 124 xxii ("Liber cimeriorum dominorum de Carraria"), a parchment manuscript of the late fourteenth century, fol. 16. The six lines inserted into the manuscript below the figure are found in G. and B. Gatari, *Cronaca carrarese*, p. 25.

[42] Padua, Bibl. del Museo Civico, Cod. BP 124 xxii, fol. 20. The lines below the heraldic figure which permit identification of the lord to whom the emblem belongs are the following:

> Heros septenus Franciscus Marte gerebat
> Carriger hunc comuni Patavi dum sceptra tenebat.
> Omnis in hoc virtus domino fuit. Omnia gessit
> Librate. Rigidus sibi queque rebellio pressit.
> Armis consilio, nulli fuit iste secundus
> Incubuit quotiens belli discrimine pondus.

[43] Padua, Bibl. del Museo Civico, Cod. BP 124 xxii, fol. 21. On this page, which follows the one on which we find the crest of Francesco il Vecchio, there appears an emblem with a red chariot with four wheels in a field of silver, and above it the crest of the Saracen with golden wings. It is not, however, accompanied by the lines (as the preceding emblems are) which would permit identification of the personage to whom the emblem refers. The most plausible hypothesis by which the absence of the lines may be explained is that the manuscript was written during the hegemony of Francesco Novello, in whose honor such laudatory verses would not have been included, owing to the well-known tragic end of his *signorìa*.

makes explicit allusion to the fact that they bear the device of the Saracen ("Nel meç'un saracin con l'ale d'oro / tene 'l fabricator dey so tesoro"). The only known examples of Carrarese coins bearing this emblem are three cited by Litta, which according to him are preserved in the "Museo di Milano."[44] That the "Saracen with golden wings" mentioned in the madrigal is actually the emblem used in Carrarese coins, is confirmed, however, by one of the sources of *Imperial*, Mod a, which contains on folio 30^r the cantus of this madrigal. The fascicle containing this composition is characterized by illuminated initials in gold and other colors. As distinct from the others, the miniature which adorns the "I" of "Imperial" is not composed merely of decorative designs (whorls, stylized leaves, drops of gold). In this initial, two figures are clearly recognizable: around the letter, there is blue sky in which is depicted the constellation of the Chariot (Auriga), and below it, the head of a Moor with two wings of gold, and with the banderoles descending to form the figure of a crest. Pirrotta, who has described this manuscript more completely and exhaustively than anyone else, made it clear that the compositions of Bartolino transmitted in this manuscript are preserved "in a tradition so slovenly that the name of the composer is given in three different forms, one for each composition, and, in one case, deformed into 'Dactalus' ";[45] this estrangement from the original version is confirmed by the fact that the maker of the decoration has misinterpreted the allusion to the "carro d'onor degno," interpreting it as an allusion to the constellation rather than to the heraldic symbol. This error did not, however, prevent his understanding the "sarayn con l'ale d'oro" as an exact allusion to the

---

[44] P. Litta, *Famiglie celebri italiane*, Carraresi di Padova, Table 1, figs. 1, 2, and 13. The coin represented in Fig. 13 bears on its verso the inscription, "Francisschus de Carraria. Sptimus dux Paduae." The coin thus refers to Francesco il Vecchio (see the verses given in n. 42). The other two coins contain no details that would permit our attributing them to the period of his rule, nor to that of Ubertino or that of Francesco Novello. It is also interesting to note that none of the three examples reproduced by Litta is included in the numismatic collection of the Museo Bottacin attached to the Museo Civico of Padua, doubtless the largest collection of Carrarese coins. This collection does include, however, a number of "tessere" bearing the figure of the crest with the Saracen (yet unfortunately these too contain no internal element that would offer a firm dating). These "tessere" are in the form of coins and functioned as a "permit," a sign of recognition.

[45] N. Pirrotta, "Il Codice Estense Lat. 568 e la musica francese in Italia al principio del '400" (Palermo, 1946), p. 28.

Carrarese coins, since the lower part of the miniature repeats in remarkable fashion the heraldic emblem as we know it from the numismatic design described by Litta.

If we pass from numismatics to the closely related field of sphragistics we can find further points useful to our purpose. It has long been known that Francesco Novello da Carrara used the figure of the Saracen for his own seal during certain well-established periods of his tenure. He adopted this emblem for the first time during his brief *signorìa* of 1388: indeed, it is found in documents dated between September 1 and November 1 of that year.[46] In the period of his second and greater hegemony (which began in 1390), Francesco Novello used for a period of ten years the seal which contained only the chariot. Still, "at the beginning of the 15th century a change occurred in Carrarese seals that has not yet been explained. On the 5th of February, 1400, Francesco da Carrara wrote to the ruler of Este, telling him to consider authentic letters sealed with the symbol of the Saracen, and not with that of the chariot, and to consider this a fixed arrangement until it should be altered."[47] And so far as can be discerned from surviving documents, it seems that this seal, thereafter replaced by others of a different form, was not valid beyond August 15, 1402.[48]

If we reread closely the entire text of Bartolino's madrigal, and consider its meaning as a whole, we can conclude that it was written in praise of a Carrarese lord (that praise is involved is evident from the explicit reference to the four cardinal virtues in the second tercet) at the moment in which he is being invested with imperial authority (the opening words of the text), and for an occasion on which he rises to a level equal to that of princes and personages of the highest rank ("sedendo fra più stelle"); the text also tells us that the title and the imperial office are being conferred on the Carrarese lord by an Emperor who shows him respect and regard ("sotto signor d'ogn'altro più benigno").

[46] A. Gloria, *Intorno ai diplomi dei principi da Carrara* (Padua: Prosperini, 1859), pp. 18-22; V. Lazzarini, *Due sigilli di Francesco Novello da Carrara* (Padua, 1900; an offering for the wedding Rimbaldi-Marinelli, p. 7).

[47] V. Lazzarini, *Due sigilli di Francesco Novello*, p. 9. The author, after having reproduced the letter from Francesco Novello to the Podestà of Este (n. 5) *in extenso*, says that the documents dated April 6, August 3, and September 3, 1400, are sealed with the figure of the Saracen, indicated by the words "sub meo Cimeriali sigillo."

[48] *Ibid.*, p. 12.

In August and September of 1401, the newly elected Emperor, Robert of Bavaria, decided to travel to Italy, ostensibly and officially to be crowned in Rome, but in actuality to put an end to the territorial ambitions of Gian Galeazzo Visconti, who now threatened to extend his dominion to include all of mid-northern and central Italy. It was only natural that those military and political forces in Italy that had traditionally been linked to the Empire should be associated with this undertaking; also included were those that had to be concerned about Gian Galeazzo's territorial expansion, and these included the lord of Padua and the community of Florence. These facts form the immediate background to what we learn from Gatari's *Cronaca carrarese,* written in a lively and vigorous style:

Quando el signor misser Francesco da Carara se partì da Padoa per andare a Trento a lo 'nperadore. M°CC C C° I°

On the Departure of Messer Francesco da Carrara from Padua to go to Trent to the Emperor. 1401.

Venuto el giorno del termene dato dinanzio, che fu a dì xxviii del mexe de setenbre MCCCCI°, fecie il magnifico Signore misser Francesco da Carara intonare sua tronbeta, per la quale ognuno suo citadino comandato s'apresentò cum sue arme alla gran corte, soto le gieneralle bandiere chararexe: per che, adunate loro giente tuta, montò il signor su(o) uno suo corsieri grosso de pello leardo, e con mollti strumenti usì de sua citade de Padoa con cercha doa millia cavalli, omeny notabelly e bataglioxi, e andò per la via de Trevixo, e tanto cavalcò per sue giornate, che arivò alla citade de Trento, dove li atrovo lo 'nperadore, e da luy e da tuti i baroni d'Alemagna, fu onoratamente ricieuto. E, stato più dì a gran consigli lo 'nperadore e' Fiorentini e 'l signor de Padoa e i baroni d'Alemagna, e fate le sue mostre de loro giente d'arme, trovossi aver cercha XXXII millia persone da cavallo e da piè. Fata la richa mostra, deliberò lo 'nperador de far uno capi-

On the day that had been determined beforehand, which was on the 28th of the month of September 1401, the great lord messer Francesco da Carrara ordered that the trumpet be sounded, at which signal all the citizens appeared with their arms at the great court, under the flag of the Carrarese. And when all the troops had gathered, the lord himself mounted one of his grey chargers, and, to the sound of instruments he issued forth from the city of Padua with about two thousand horsemen— good and battleworthy men—and went by way of Treviso, and pressed his journey until he arrived at the city of Trent, where the Emperor was, and was honorably received by him and by all the barons of Germany. Now, the Emperor was for several days in council with the Florentines and the lord of Padua and the barons of Germany; and, having a review of their men-at-arms, they found themselves to have about 32 thousand men,

tano gieneralle, e fu con suoi baroni, e deliberarono fare per gienerale capitano de tuta l'oste de lo 'nperio misser Francesco da Carara; e a luy dato l'onorato bastone e la inperialle bandiera dell'aquila, gli disse, che comandasse tuto suo volere, che chadauno signore, grande e picolo, l'ubidirebe. Alora misser Francesco da Carara, inperiale capitano, fecie comandamento fare che tuta giente fusse in ordene per seguitar le 'nperiale bandiere e 'l capitano per cavalcare per l'altro giorno versso la cittade de Bressa in Lonbardia a' danni del ducha de Milano (. . . .)[49]

on horse and foot. After this excellent review, the Emperor determined to create one captain-general, and he conferred with his barons, and determined to make Francesco da Carrara captain-general of the entire army of the Emperor. And thus they gave him the baton of office and the imperial flag, of the eagle, saying that he should command in full power, and that every lord great and minor would obey him. Then Francesco da Carrara, imperial captain, gave orders, saying that the whole army should make ready to follow the imperial flag, and they rode towards the city of Brescia in Lombardy to war on the Duke of Milan. . . .

We can scarcely overlook the coincidence between the historical events narrated in this remarkable piece of prose, and the content of the text set by Bartolino. What is most striking in the text of the chronicle is the repetition of the adjective "imperial,"[50] used with undoubted local pride (understandable in Gatari, who witnessed and took part in the last events in the rule of the Carraresi); it is this adjective which, significantly, opens the madrigal text and characterizes its content.

We are thus inclined to suppose that Bartolino set this madrigal in honor of the naming of Francesco da Carrara as captain-general of the Imperial army, and we would accordingly date the composition in the second half of 1401.

"La douce çere" is another madrigal text set by Bartolino in which heraldic symbolism plays an important role in the meaning of the entire piece. Those who have so far attempted to set a date for the composition have generally been in agreement concerning the heraldic figures involved; their attempts have been based on the fact that the opening line presents apparent analogies of meaning with the first line of another madrigal by Bartolino which is traditionally

---

[49] G. and B. Gatari, *Cronaca carrarese*, p. 471.

[50] Note, among other things, the reading "inperiale," which is supported by the great majority of the musical manuscripts containing the setting by Bartolino.

associated with the Visconti;[51] it has long been thought that the text of "La douce çere" was written in honor of a member of the ruling family of Milan, and that the "fier animal" must be the serpent of the Visconti, from whose mouth a boy emerges. On this assumption, and on the basis of the short tenure of Gian Galeazzo Visconti in Padua, from the end of 1388 to June 1390, both these madrigals have been attributed to that period.[52] Now, however, the examination of certain historical documents enables us to clarify the meaning of this text, and thus to fix its date of composition with a fair degree of certainty.

> La douce çere d'un fier animal
> se poyt intendre per signifians:
> "Grant ardimant et humile senblans."
> Le vis human, le bust d'un lion
> intresegiés d'un brief allegier
> que dit: "Lialmant sans doctier."
> A son col port un scut tout blans
> Che d'engonbrier il fet tout garans.[53]

[51] The two lines are: "La douce çere d'un fier animal" and "La fiera testa che d'uman si ciba." "This one [La fiera testa] seems to me to refer to the serpent of the Visconti, to the 'emblem in which the naked boy emerges from the mouth of the snake'" (G. Carducci, *Musica e Poesia nel mondo elegante del sec. XIV*; in *Opere di G. Carducci*, VIII, 389); "Some connection exists between Nicolò [del Preposto] and Bartolino. To be more exact: the well-known trilingual text 'La fiera testa' attributed to Petrarch, was set by Nicolò and by Bartolino (and perhaps by Scappuccia, if he was a musician and not a poet). It is the mate to a setting by Bartolino of a French text, *La douce çere*, and refers to the Visconti." (E. LiGotti, *La poesia musicale italiana del sec. XIV* [Palermo, 1944], p. 66 n 103); F. Ghisi, in *MGG*, I, 1349-50, erroneously describes the two texts as belonging to a single poem.

[52] N. Goldine, "Bartolino da Padova," pp. 153-54.

[53] FP, fols. 108v-109v; P, fols. 41v-42r; PR, fols. 13v-14r; Mn, fol. 1a (tenor and ct only); Lo, fols. 15v-16r; FL, fols. 101v-102r; Fa, fols. 70-71. The complete text of the madrigal is found only in FL^c and P^c; lines 1-2-3-7-8 in FL^t, FL^ct, PR^c (only the first word of the third line), PR^t, FP^c, Lo^c (in an Italianized version which clearly shows that the scribe understood nothing of the meaning of the text; the version of Lo is given at the end of this note), Mn^t and P^t. Fa gives the beginning of the poem. As basis we have used the manuscript P. Attributions: FP: "Fra bartolino da p(er)ugia"; P^c: "F(ra)t(er) Bartholin(us)"; FL: "Magister Frater Bartolinus de Padua"; Mn: "de Padua"; Lo: "Fratre Bartolini de Padoua."

Line 1. FP: *doulse*; PR^c, FP: *cere*; PR^ct, Mn: *ciere*; Fa: *La dolce sere* and *La dolze sire*; Lo^t: *La doce cerra*; Lo^ct: *La dolce cerra*.

Line 2. FP, Mn: *poit*; PR^c: *puit*; PR^t: *en puit*; FP: *entendre*; PR^c: *Intende*; PR^t: *entende*; FP, PR: *por*; Mn, FL^ct: *pour*; FP, PR, Mn: *sanefiance*.

Line 3. P^c: *gran*; FP: *umble*; P^t: *umile*; PR: *humele*; Mn: *hu(n)ble*; FP: *semblance*; Pr, Mn: *senblance*.

Taken as whole, "La douce çere" does not appear to refer to any specific historical fact, in sharp contrast to "La fiera testa." The eight lines of the text must instead be understood as a general encomium of a noble personage, who is referred to in specific heraldic terms ("se poyt intendre per signifians").

The structure of the text will be of help in interpreting the meaning. The two tercets are constructed in parallel form: each closes with a kind of motto, a "heraldic device," which explains the verbal meaning to be attributed to the figure or emblem depicted in the preceding lines. The second tercet is simply a more explicit reference to the heraldic symbols already mentioned in the first tercet:

Tercet I: "The pleasing appearance of a wild animal can be understood to mean: 'great daring and humble appearance' ";[54]

Tercet II: "The human face, the bust of a lion, crossed (?) by an attached blazon, which reads: 'loyally without doubting.'"

The ritornello contains a further illustration of the details ornamenting the heraldic figure described in the tercets, and especially

---

Line 4. P: *lo buste*; FL: *lyon.*

Line 5. FL: *Intre figies.*

Line 6. FL: *Lyamant; dottier.*

Line 7. Pc: *Et an su col*; Pt: *Et a suo col*; PR: *A sol col*; FL: *An su col*; FP, Mn, PR: *porta*; FP, Mn: *un escu*; PR: *u scu*; Pc *tut*; PR, Mn: *tot.*

Line 8. FP: *que*; FP, PR: *de go(n)brier*; Mn, FLc, FLct: *d'engon(n)brer.*; FP: *feit*; Pc: *fect*; PR: *fiet*; Pc: *tut*, PR, Mn: *tot grans.*

This is the version in Lo:

> La dolce cera d'u fer animale
> Se pot' e(n)te(n)der por sinasiance
> Grand ardime(n)t et humele seblance
> a so quel porta un escuter brans
> che di glon bien le fort tot gl . . . mis.

[54] It is worth noting that the expression, "la douce çere," in Italianized form, is found in a sonnet by Francesco di Vannozzo, in the second poem in the series entitled, "Cantillena Francisci V. pro Comite Virtutum," in which, figuratively, various Italian cities address themselves to Gian Galeazzo Visconti, asking him to be their lord (note too that the city which speaks in the second poem is Padua itself):

> Corona santa, ch'èi da Dio mostrata
> per pace dar a l'italica gente,
> *con dolce ciera* e con allegra mente
> ti priego ch'io ti sia raccomandata.

(*Le Rime di Francesco di Vannozzo*, p. 268).

of the lion: "On his neck he carries a white shield, which guards him from all danger." Even with the uncertainties attendant on this text,[55] the overall meaning is evident; and beyond any doubt the heraldic figure is that of a lion bearing a white shield.

The second lord of Padua was Marsilio Papafava da Carrara, whose coat of arms was the customary red chariot with four wheels, but whose special crest was formed by a lion with a cloak adorned with small golden wheels.[56] Indeed, the lion is not only characteristic of the crest of the second lord of Padua, but it also appears in the crests of his descendants, and particularly among those bearing the family name Papafava. At the beginning of their chronicle, the Gatari give a useful explanation of this:

È a dichiarare, per consolacione di letore e di chiunche aldirà legiere, perchè i predetti Papafava portava l'arma del lione com el caro insembremente; è da savere, che per la dita pestilenzia innanzo ditta era rimaxa una garzona sola, senza padre e madre ed ogni parentado; ed esendo rimaxa tra le mani d'alchuni suo' comesari, cresendo adunque la garzona e fattasi bella si de persona come di visso, e non esendo, come si po' credere, da molti richiesta per ispossa, e a niuno per sua volontà non consentire, pure aspetando la inspiracione divina, (per) la quale non tardò niente a venire, ch'el garzone inanzo ditto Papafava, esendo richisimo e fatto bello di la persona, e pro' e ardito e costumato e sagio, fe' richiedere questa donna per ispossa, al(la) quale ella, si come astuta e vertuosa e savia consentì, con condicione che sempre lui e suo' desendenti dovesse portare l'arma sua d'ella; la quale era un lione

Now we shall explain, for the benefit of the reader and of anyone to whom it may be read, why the aforesaid Papafava bore the arms of the lion with the chariot; it should be known that because of the plague described earlier there remained alone a certain young girl, without father or mother or any other relative. And remaining alone among some of her retainers, the girl grew up, and became fair in person as well as in visage. But not being requested by many as a bride, as one can well imagine, and not consenting to anyone of her own will, but rather waiting for divine inspiration—it was not long in coming to pass that the aforesaid young man, named Papafava, being very rich and very handsome, and brave and robust, and virtuous and wise, asked the hand of this lady in marriage. To which she consented, being clever and virtuous and wise, on the condition that he and his descendants should always

[55] The most difficult passage is that in line 5, in which the expression "brief allegier" must be interpreted as "brief allegie(r)"="letter attached." In short, it should refer to a scroll that would cross the figure of the lion.

[56] See the miniature associated with him in the above-mentioned "Liber cimeriorum dominorum de Carraria," Padua, Bibl. del Museo Civico, BP 124 xxii, fol. 15. The lines found below the miniature are given in G. and B. Gatari, *Cronaca carrarese*, p. 23.

rampante azuro nel canpo bianco: a la quale volontà il preditto Papafava promesse di portare; e cosi sempre atexe sua promessa: si che senpre i predeti sucedenti Papafava portava el lione azuro ne la targa bianca, e al collo del predetto lione portava uno schudo bianco e in quello un carro rosso; e per sto muodo il portarono longo tempo, cioè perfino al tempo del signore misser Francesco giovene da Carara, nel quale qui adrieto di lui tractaremo: sì che il preditto misser Francesco il remosse per lo muodo il quale qui di sotto il discriveremo. Portava il detto signore misser Marsilietto Papafava da Charara una testa e 'l petto d'uno lione azuro per cimiero serenatto tuto di peluzzi d'oro, e per simile seguia tutta la banda de l'elmo; e ne la targha sua bianca portava una croxe vermiglia, e ne i due quarti di quella era due chari rossi, e negli altri due, due lioni azuri ranpanti.[57]

bear her arms: on which was an azure lion rampant in a white field. Papafava promised to bear these arms, and held to his promise. And thus the aforesaid descendants of Papafava have always borne the arms of a lion, azure, in a white shield, and with a white emblem on the neck of the lion, with a red chariot in it. This coat of arms they bore for a long time, that is, down to the time of lord messer Francesco da Carrara the Younger, of whom we will say more in what follows; for messer Francesco caused it to be removed in a way that we will describe presently. Messer Marsilietto Papafava da Carrara bore the crest of the head and breast of an azure lion, adorned with a mane of gold which similarly continued around the shield from the crest. And on his white shield a vermilion cross, and on two quarters of it were two red chariots, and, in the other two, two azure lions rampant.

It is needless to emphasize that this description of the coat of arms and crest of Marsilio Papafava da Carrara corresponds in its essential components to the heraldic figure on which "La douce çere" is based: the lion with a white shield on its neck. Despite the French text (as we have seen, a rather debased French and probably written in Italy), the madrigal is thus written in honor of one of the descendants of the second lord of Padua.[58] Unfortunately, the Gatari, in their chronicle, do not keep their promise to reveal when Francesco Novello suppressed the coat of arms bearing the blue lion with a white shield on his neck; we can, however, regard the terminal dates of his *signorìa* (1390-1405) as the chronological limits for the madrigal set to music by Bartolino.

Both the musical and literary components of this work furnish evidence of the slow but certain infiltration of the French musical style into the area of the Italian Ars Nova. And the French influence in the musical style of Bartolino should be considered alongside the

[57] *Ibid.*, p. 26.

[58] One can exclude the theory that the madrigal was written in honor of Marsilio, since he died on March 21, 1338 (*ibid.*, p. 23).

actual presence in Padua, at the same period, of certain musicians of
Franco-Flemish origin. The most important of these is Johannes
Ciconia: on July 31, 1401, the Liégeois musician, then at the height
of his maturity, was invested with the prebend of S. Biagio di Roncaglia, which was under the control of the arch-priest of the Cathedral of Padua, Francesco Zabarella.[59] Ciconia was not yet in Padua
when this investiture took place; his presence there is not attested
to before April 26 and 27, 1403, on which dates he is named as
witness to the drawing up of two legal documents.[60] But from April
of 1403 until his death at the very end of 1411, Johannes Ciconia
lived at Padua as canon of the cathedral.

In addition, Codex Mn, one of the manuscripts most abundant in
works by Bartolino, is the only source known for the madrigal "Per
quella strada lactea del cielo"[61] explicitly attributed to Ciconia, and
its text undoubtedly refers to the red chariot of the Carrarese coat
of arms, supplying exact parallels in meaning to the text of *Imperial*.

Alba Columba

Alba columba con soa verde rama,
   in nobile çardino nutrichata,
   "Pax, pax" nunciando su l'al' è montata.
Posò suo vuolo suso un verde scoglio
   per riposars' e, mirando in çoso,
   prese argumento de volar più soso;
perché gustava çà i boni odori
   ch'era là su tra fronde et altri fiori.[62]

---

[59] S. Clercx, *Johannes Ciconia, Un musicien liégeois et son temps* (Brussels, 1960),
Vol. 1, p. 39.

[60] *Ibid.*, p. 40.   [61] *Ibid.*, Vol. 2, pp. 7, 43-45.

[62] PR, fols. 14v-15r; Lo, fols. 12v-13r; FL, fols. 105v-106r. The complete text is in
PR^t, Lo^c and FL^t; the lines 1-2-3-7-8 in PR^c, Lo^t, FL^c; in PR^{ct} the lines 1 and 7.
For this text PR^t has been used as principal source.

Line 1. PR^c: *colunba*; Lo^c: *cholumba*; FL: *colonba, suo.*

Line 2. Lo^t; *nobele, nutrica(n)ta*; FL: *giardino nutricata.*

Line 3. PR^c: *mu(n)tata*; Lo^c: *nunzando sull'al'è*; Lo^t: *Nu(n)tzian(n)do*; FL.
nu(n)tiando in su.

Line 4. PR^c: *Posso; vollo*; Lo^c: *so volo su l'un, schoglio.* FL^t: *volo, in verde.*

Line 5. Lo^c: *susso*; FL^t: *riposarsi et rimirando in giuso.*

Line 6. Lo^c: *arghumento del*; FL^t: *argomento di*; all MSS: *suso.*

Line 7. Lo^c: *y boni oduri*; Lo^t: *gu(n)stava, i(n)*; FL^c *gusta gia i bon'odori*; FL^t:
gia.

Line 8. Lo^c: *iran, fiuri*; FL^c: *eran lassu tra frond' ed altri*; FL^t: *eran lassu tra
fro(n)di.*

This madrigal has also been considered heretofore to be a general occasional composition, lacking specific reference to persons and events; the image of the dove has been interpreted as an allusion to a recently deceased wife[63] or as a general symbol of peace, the most obvious interpretation of the symbol of the dove.[64]

If we analyze the text according to the same criteria we have applied to the preceding poems, seeking to discern in it precise allusions to heraldic symbols and to historical events, not only will the resultant interpretations of this madrigal be more convincing, but a more concrete dating for it will be possible. That the dove ought to be considered a heraldic symbol is specified by the adjective "nobile" in line two; this entire line seems to have the function of underscoring the allusive and heraldic character of the figure. Nor do I think that doubts can seriously be entertained as to the identification of the emblem described in the madrigal with that of Gian Galeazzo Visconti, who, as Count of Virtù, had as his emblem a white dove with the motto "à bon droit," created for him by Petrarch.[65] This identification is in perfect agreement with other poetic texts written expressly to celebrate the emblem with the white dove, such as the "Canzona morale fatta per la divisa del Conte di Virtù" by Francesco di Vannozzo[66] and the sonnet by Giovanni

---

[63] G. Carducci, *Musica e Poesia nel mondo elegante italiano del XIV. secolo*, in *Opere complete*, VIII, 363: "A finer symbol is the dove in this third [madrigal]: was it by chance a noble bride, the pledge of peace between two families, recently lost?"

[64] E. LiGotti, *La poesia musicale italiana del sec. XIV* (Palermo, 1944), p. 87: "In one madrigal, indeed, peace is invoked, almost as Sacchetti did when he wrote some twelve sonnets on the peace of 1396 (cf. the madrigal "Alba colomba" by Bartolino . . . and the twelve sonnets of Sacchetti, on pp. 332-39 of his *Libro delle Rime*, published by Laterza) when the war against the Visconti made the desire for peace real indeed. . . ." Following this theory of LiGotti's, Ghisi (*MGG*, I, 1349-50) places the madrigal in 1396; Goldine, "Bartolino da Padova," pp. 154-55, proposes instead the date 1392.

[65] Cf. F. Novati, *Il Petrarca e i Visconti*, in *F. Petrarca e la Lombardia* (Milan, 1904), pp. 73ff.

[66] *Le Rime di Francesco di Vannozzo*, p. 4. Medin proposes the date "1389 or thereabouts" for this canzone. In this poem lines 174-82 are especially noteworthy in connection with the works of Bartolino (these lines are given by the author to Petrarch), not only because they mention the "alba tortorella," but particularly because the characterization of the virtues is accomplished in a manner wholly analogous to that of the second tercet of *Imperial*.

> Lice di parte in parte a l'uom posare:
> l'una t'ho detto e a l'altra ora t'invito,

Dondi which bears the title "Pro Domino Comite."[67] It establishes
with fair certainty the chronological limits within which the poem
must be dated: Gian Galeazzo became Count of Virtù in 1368, and
he died on September 3, 1402. The madrigal must therefore fall
between these extremes. The text also contains more than one reference to a well-defined historical and political situation: it is evidently
composed for an occasion on which Gian Galeazzo Visconti has
reached a higher level of power ("su l'al' è montata"), announcing
proposals for peace ("'Pax, pax' nunciando" and "con soa verde
rama"; this last expression may be understood to refer to the "green
olive branch," and in this way the author of the text plays on the
double meaning of the expression, which is emblematic and allegorical at the same time, in reference to the dove). The first tercet,
taken alone, suggests either of two events: that of Gian Galeazzo's
rise to power in becoming lord of Milan after having fraudulently
overthrown his uncle, Bernabò Visconti, in May of 1385; or the
occasion of his investiture by the Emperor as Duke of Milan, which
occurred in September 1395. Accepting the thesis that Bartolino was
a "court musician" (of the court of the Carraresi, that is), one might
be able to support either of these hypotheses. Immediately after his
rise to power, at a time when he did not yet feel entirely secure in
his position "because some of the sons of Bernabò were still at liberty,"[68] Gian Galeazzo determined to forge an alliance with Nicolò
and Alberto d'Este, with Francesco il Vecchio of Carrara, lord of
Padua, and with Francesco I Gonzaga, lord of Mantua. For his part,
Francesco da Carrara "sent ambassadors to the Count of Virtù to
wish him well in his [new] power,"[69] in order to ingratiate himself
with Gian Galeazzo. It would seem reasonable, therefore, to suppose
that the madrigal set by Bartolino could have been sent to the Vi-

---

> dimostrandoti a dito
> ziò che comprende l'alba tortorella,
> la quale con Umeltà s'inbella,
> a Purità conzonta e Castitate;
> ché se con lui legate
> seran queste tre donne,
> ferme colonne fieno a mantenere
> al tuo signore magnanimo volere.

[67] *Le Rime di Giovanni Dondi*, p. 18, No. 16.

[68] L. A. Muratori, *Delle Antichità Estensi*, Parte Seconda, in *Raccolta delle opere minori di L. A. Muratori*, T. xvi (Naples, 1741), 139.

[69] G. Cittadella, *Storia della dominazione carrarese in Padova* . . . (Padova, 1842), ii, 33.

sconti court, to celebrate the reconciliation of the two houses.[70] No less possible would be another thesis, namely that the madrigal was set by Bartolino at the order of Francesco Novello da Carrara, to be brought, with other rich gifts, by the Paduan embassy on the occasion of the imperial investiture of Gian Galeazzo.[71]

The second tercet, however, contradicts both of these theories; it defines more clearly the character of Gian Galeazzo's newly acquired power. At the time when the madrigal was written, the Count of Virtù had recently made a new territorial conquest ("Posò suo vuolo suso un verde scoglio"), by means of which he would extend his own domain ("prese argumento de volar più soso"); this, then, is what is celebrated by the author of the madrigal text. This interpretation clearly contradicts the theory that the text was composed by order of the Carraresi; they certainly would not have sought to celebrate (as the madrigal clearly does) the latest territorial conquests made by the Count of Virtù.

On November 21, 1388, Gian Galeazzo Visconti signed an armistice with Francesco Novello da Carrara, who had been lord of Padua for just a few months as a result of the renunciation of the

---

[70] I proposed this thesis earlier in the above-mentioned article in the *Dizionario Biografico degli Italiani*; cf. n. 2.

[71] "*Quando fu fatto ducha de Millan el Conte de Vertù a dì XIII de setenbre.* Anno dominy MCCCLXXXXV, à dì XIII del mexe de setenbre fu nela egregia citade de Millan misser Zuane Galiazo conte de Vertù fatto ducha de Millan e de la Lonbardia per li anbasadori dello nperadore; e a quela cotal festa fu in Milano tute le signorie e anbasarie di Franza, d'Inghilterra, d'Ispagna, de Alemagna e de tuta Italia, e a tute fu fato magnifici onori, secondo la qualità loro; e tra l'altre signorie d'Italia, el Conte de Vertù, per pagificarsi col signor de Padoa, el mandò a invidare, che li piacesse dover eser a Milano a la sua festa. Ale qual cose il signor rispoxe non poderli eser, ma li faria eser i figliuoli; e così li mandò misser Francesco Terzo da Carara e Jacomo da Carara fradelly, e per sua conpagnia andò con costoro misser Francesco Buzacarin, misser Michiele da Rabata, misser Morando da Porcile, Pollo da Lion, misser Redolfo da Cara[ra], Piero da Carara, Albrigo Lion Papafava da Carara, ed oltra li mandò cercha LX^{ta} torniadori e zostradori xii, i quali dovesono onorare l'andata di sora detti e la festa del ducha; era in tuto la cometiva da costoro cavali VI^c; e più li mandò il signore misser Francesco da Carara a donare al ducha de Milan siey belisimy destrery oltra misura grandy e poderosi, tra' quali due ne fu coverti d'uno veluto de grana con l'arme del charro suso. Azonti dunque i deti Chararexi a Milano, el duca de Milan, per più amorevoleza mostrarli, li andò incontro a piede una grandeta via fuora dela corte soa; e prima li avea mandado incontro molta quantità de gentilomeni. Venia avanti costoro con strumenti, prima tuti i cimiri dal torniero con pulide e bele divise [. . .]" (G. and B. Gatari, *Cronaca carrarese*, pp. 449-50).

title by his father, Francesco il Vecchio. This renunciation had been a final attempt to save the Carrarese hegemony in Padua, but it did not succeed. Indeed, the house of Carrara found itself in a position of clear disadvantage not only in a military sense but also because of the hostility within the city—a hostility that it had brought upon itself, owing to its marked favoritisms and, above all, to its willful policy of confiscation and economic plunder. Gian Galeazzo, perfectly aware of this state of affairs, was able to take advantage of it in an exceptionally able way. Instead of entering the city like a conqueror immediately after the armistice, he was clever enough to wait until his presence in Padua should be requested by the city itself, so that he might thus assume the role of "liberator"; ". . . the exclusion of the many who were opposed to the new state of affairs from the Council General, an exclusion freely desired by the provisional government, signaled the triumph of the shrewd policies of Gian Galeazzo. Padua itself came to him, invited him, acclaimed him as its leader, received with festivities the army of Dal Verme, who, at the head of the entire force, entering the city on the 18th of December and receiving the flag of the community, initiated the new government."[72] The gradual triumph of the forces within the provisional government favorable to the Visconti is reflected fairly clearly in the sections of the chronicle of the Gatari relevant to this period; and especially clear, on the part of the city's representatives, is their wish to deal with the Count of Virtù in such a way that the city, while granting him the most honored treatment, should lose none of its own dignity.[73] In this framework of civic decorum, which gives minute descriptions of the meeting of the representatives of Padua with the Visconti—extending even to details concerning the clothes worn by the ambassadors and their retinue—we might well place the madrigal by Bartolino too. Thus, its date of composition would in all likelihood be toward the end of 1388.

[72] E. Pastorello, *Nuove ricerche sulla storia di Padova e dei Principi da Carrara al tempo di Gian Galeazzo Visconti* (Padova, 1908), p. 40.

[73] "Eletti i sovrascritti citadini, fu per la università di Padoa a lor detto, che fuseno coi signori e podestà a fare la 'lecione degli anbasadori e a formare i capitolli e diliberare le vestimente e la spessa che avesse a fare gli anbasadori, e che guardasse a fare per sifatta maniera che non gli fusse di vergogna, e che ogni cosa fusse magnamente fatta a ciò che fusse senpre d'onore dela città di Padoa, e che al Conte di Virtù paresse anbasata reale, a ciò che lui l'avesse a grata; i quali tutti promisse di fare iusta sua possa" (G. and B. Gatari, *Cronaca carrarese*, p. 345).

Although the hypotheses advanced thus far may neither in themselves nor as a group constitute a complete and convincing account,
the facts assembled nevertheless permit us to assert, with a high degree of probability, that Bartolino lived in his native city during at
least the period in which he composed the works discussed. Although
it has been thought that he was in Florence during the exile of the
Carraresi between 1388 and 1390/91 (a hypothesis closely linked to
the narrow interpretation of Bartolino as "court musician"), there
is evidence against this in the relationships of various kinds established by Bartolino, not only with the Carrara family but also with
Giovanni Dondi, with Matteo Griffoni, and with many others.
Evidence even more valuable than that furnished by Giovanni da
Prato in his *Paradiso degli Alberti*, who says of the madrigals of
Bartolino, "di quelli fatti a Padova."[74]

If this, then, is true, it would be in the Carmelite monastery in
Padua that one might find evidence of Bartolino's presence. Yet
the documents remaining from that establishment, both published
and unpublished, contain no reference to a "Frater Bartolinus de
Padua." If, however, one realizes that "Bartolinus" is only a diminu-
tive for "Bartolomeus" (and it is doubtful that the form "Bartolinus"
would have appeared in official documents), the possibility of identifying him becomes a little more likely.

One, who must be mentioned but then excluded because the dates
connected with him are too late, is a "frater bartholomeus ab omnibus
sanctis de padua," whose name appears for the first time in the

---

[74] On the basis of a detailed analysis of historical and political events in Florence
around 1390, Hans Baron concludes that the ideas expressed by the characters in the
Paradiso (whose actual presence in Florence at that time is demonstrated by Wesse-
lowski in the introductory volume of his edition of the narrative), should in fact
be considered as reflecting the political situation; consequently these ideas reflect an
attitude of thought not contemporary with the personages themselves but rather
of the time at which the narrative was written, i.e., about 1425/26. Hans Baron,
*Humanistic and Political Literature in Florence and Venice at the beginning of the
Quattrocento* (Cambridge, Mass., 1955), Ch. 1. From this conclusion follows the
deduction that the reference to "madriali," and especially to "quelli fatti a Padova
per Frate Bartolino," can be considered a bit of precise testimony to musical activity
of about 1425. "Whatever, as a result of our criticism, the *Paradiso* has lost as a
source of information on the late Trecento, it has gained as a literary work reflecting
Florentine ideals and attitudes characteristic of the period in which it was written."
H. Baron, *ibid.*, p. 34. This point of view is in agreement with the proposed "late"
dating of the manuscripts containing Bartolino's works.

membership of the monastery in a document dated April 10, 1421,[75] and who held the duty of "sacrista" (responsible for the sacristy) from May 22, 1426, until September 11, 1430.[76] There remains, however, the name of the prior of the monastery in the years around 1380, "Frater bartolomeus de santa cruce de padua," who, according to the thorough research of dott. Gasparotto, may be identified with the "Frater Bartolomeus de Sata," who appears in the Roll of the Carmelites of the Sacred College of the Theologians of Padua. This Bartolomeus in turn might well be that "Frater Bartolameus patavinus sacrarum litterarum magister," who, in 1376 "in Conventu Padue" had made at his own expense the *Obituarium* of the monastery itself, which is still preserved in the Archiepiscopal Library at Osimo.[77]

The coincidence of these dates with those proposed for the musical settings is certainly surprising, but in the hope of avoiding dangerous deductions and conclusions in the future, I submit this identification only as a plausible hypothesis, nothing more. If it were verified (and it cannot now be excluded) we would have another indication of the out-of-the-way character of musical activity among Italian composers of the fourteenth century vis-à-vis their daily occupations.

[75] Padua, Sezione di Archivio di Stato, Conventi Soppressi. S. Maria del Carmine, busta 163, No. 30. In this document, containing the list of the brothers comprising the Carmelite community of Padua in that year, "frater Bartholomeus ab omnibus sanctis" is indicated as "subprior dicti Conventus." His name appears as well in the documents dated June 12, 1424; August 11, 1425; October 29, 1426; December 10, 1426; May 10, 1427; and probably later (Padova, Sezione di Archivio di Stato, Conventi Soppressi. S. Maria del Carmine, busta 163, Nos. 35, 36, 40, and 41). The document No. 25 of the same collection, dated December 31, 1419, contains the list of all the members of the community, but not the name of "frater Bartholomeus ab omnibus sanctis."

[76] Padua, Sezione di Archivio di Stato, Conventi Soppressi. S. Maria del Carmine, No. 15: "Anno domini m̊ccccxiiij die xxvj mensis madij. Hoc est inventarium sacrastie conventus padue ordinis fratrum sancte dei genitricis marie de monte carmeli vissum (?) tempore prioratus fratris petronii de ferarie. Et tempore sacristie fratris jacobi de padua . . ." (fol. 114).

"–1426– Die mercurij 22° madij omnia suprascripta exeunte fratre jachobo de padua et eodem die intrante fratre bartolomeo ab omnibus sanctis de padua tempore fratris petronij de feraria prior dicti conventus recepta fuerunt."

"1430– Die lune .xj. septenbris omnia suprascripta fuerunt revisa tempore prioratus fratris johannis andree de padua sacre theologie bachalarij et corepta exeunte fratre bertholameo ab omnibus sanctis de padua et eodem die intrante fratre Jacobo de padua. Anno domini M.cccc.xxx." (fol. 122v).

[77] C. Gasparotto, *S. Maria del Carmine di Padova* (Padua, 1955), p. 109 and Documents ix and x.

Through such observations it may be hoped that the "island" of
the Italian "Ars Nova" may take on increasingly concrete and specific
features, not only as a large-scale historical phenomenon but in relation to the lives and affairs of individual composers.[78]

[78] To complete the picture supplied by the documents, we transcribe here the
section of the inventory containing the list of musical liturgical books existing in
the sacristy of the church of the Carmine of Padua on the date at which the inven-
tory was made (May 26, 1414; cf. n. 76):
". . .
Item octo antiphonaria per totum annum valde pulchra.
Item quinque gradualia per totum annum valde pulchra.
Item duo lectionaria unum de tempore aliud de sanctis.
Item duo ordinalia unum de nova rubrica.aliud de antiqua.
Item duo salteria.
Item unum martillogium [sic!]
Item tria processionaria.
Item unum colectarium.
Item unum proserium.

[Later addition]
Item unum allium [sic] proserium novum. . . .
Item unum librum cum multis officijs beate marie et de corpore xpisti et Kyrie-
leison. et cum ymnis. . . ."
(Padua, Sezione di Archivio di Stato, Conventi Soppressi. S. Maria del Carmine,
No. 15, fols. 121v-122r).

CHURCH POLYPHONY APROPOS OF A NEW FRAGMENT AT FOLIGNO

NINO PIRROTTA

A S A VETERAN in the field of Ars Nova studies, and one who
has spent most of his life among old documents and parchment leaves (or their photographic reproductions), I have
occasionally complained to myself that I never had the chance to
discover the tiniest fragment of Ars Nova music. It is unfair of me
to do so, however. I may not possess the invisible feelers that alert
and guide the born discoverer, but I have the good fortune of having
many friends, and I have been gratified a number of times by the
kindness and generosity shown by one or another of them in bringing to my attention his own discoveries. The late Professor Hans
David, of the University of Michigan at Ann Arbor, provided an
instance of such generosity, which I can repay only in kind by turning the modest results I have derived from it into a joint act of
homage to a common friend to whom I am indebted for many
things, primarily for the gift of his friendship.

I have benefited, too, from the prestige surrounding every kind of
specialization. How weak my kind is, however, must have become
apparent to Professor David; for I have done nothing, at least
ostensibly, by way of commenting on two photographs he gave to
me several years ago, reproducing a new fragment with polyphonic
music he had found in my own country, namely, in Foligno. I have
not, indeed, kept them under cover for some thunderous release at
a favorable moment. On the contrary, I have shared the information
they provide with other scholars and have given duplicates of the
photographs whenever asked to do so. The sheer truth is that the
contents of Professor David's gift have challenged, intrigued, and to
a certain extent baffled my specialist's wit. I am reminded, in fact,
of a story by Edgar Allan Poe, involving a murder investigation in
which witnesses of different nationalities can agree only to the extent
that the voice of the murderer, which they have all heard, spoke a
language different from their own. In the case under consideration
here, I am the sleuth and also the first witness. To me, the Foligno
fragment, although found in an Italian library and presenting some

features that are usually connected with Italian notation, does not suggest the familiar associations of an Italian manuscript.

Whether my reaction be justified or not, the *fauxbourdon* style of one of the pieces in the fragment, combined with some suspicion I have always had of notational collusions between mediaeval Italy and England, prompted me to seek advice from an acknowledged expert in mediaeval, and particularly English music; my second witness was Professor Frank Ll. Harrison, then visiting at Princeton. When he left Princeton for England, Professor Harrison took the photographs with him. Later on, he kindly told me that in his opinion, supported by others who had also seen the photographs, the Foligno fragment had nothing to do with England.

My next step was to mail the photographs to a friend in Italy and have them submitted to Professor Renato Piattoli, of the University of Florence. The latter's judgment as a paleographer confirmed my specialist's arrogance in denying an Italian origin; he added the suggestion that the fragment might be French. Thus the photographs, mailed back to me, once more crossed the Atlantic, this time headed for Paris, where Dr. François Lesure, well-known editor of the *Répertoire international des sources musicales*, expressed the opinion that the fragment might be German, especially if the illuminated capitals in it were of the *sang-de-boeuf* shade of red. At this point, being unable for the moment to verify the shade of the colored initials, and knowing that I would soon have the opportunity to go to Italy, I decided to postpone any announcement of the results—or non-results—of this very cooperative venture[1] until I had seen the fragment myself.

The fragment is presently kept in a box containing "Frammenti di pergamene antiche" in Sala A of the Biblioteca Comunale of Foligno. It is a vellum double leaf—four pages, that is, each measuring about 252 by 170 millimeters, or 10 by 6¾ inches. According to information provided by Signor Feliciano Baldaccini of the Foligno library, it was formerly the cover of a volume which came to the library from one of the religious institutions suppressed in 1860 by the then new Italian government. This is confirmed by the inscription "Theophilact. ī E . . ."[2] running across one of its sides at

---

[1] I would like to express my gratitude here to all the friends I have consulted for their interest in the Foligno puzzle.

[2] It must read "Theophilactus in Euang[elia]," but the abbreviation signs are

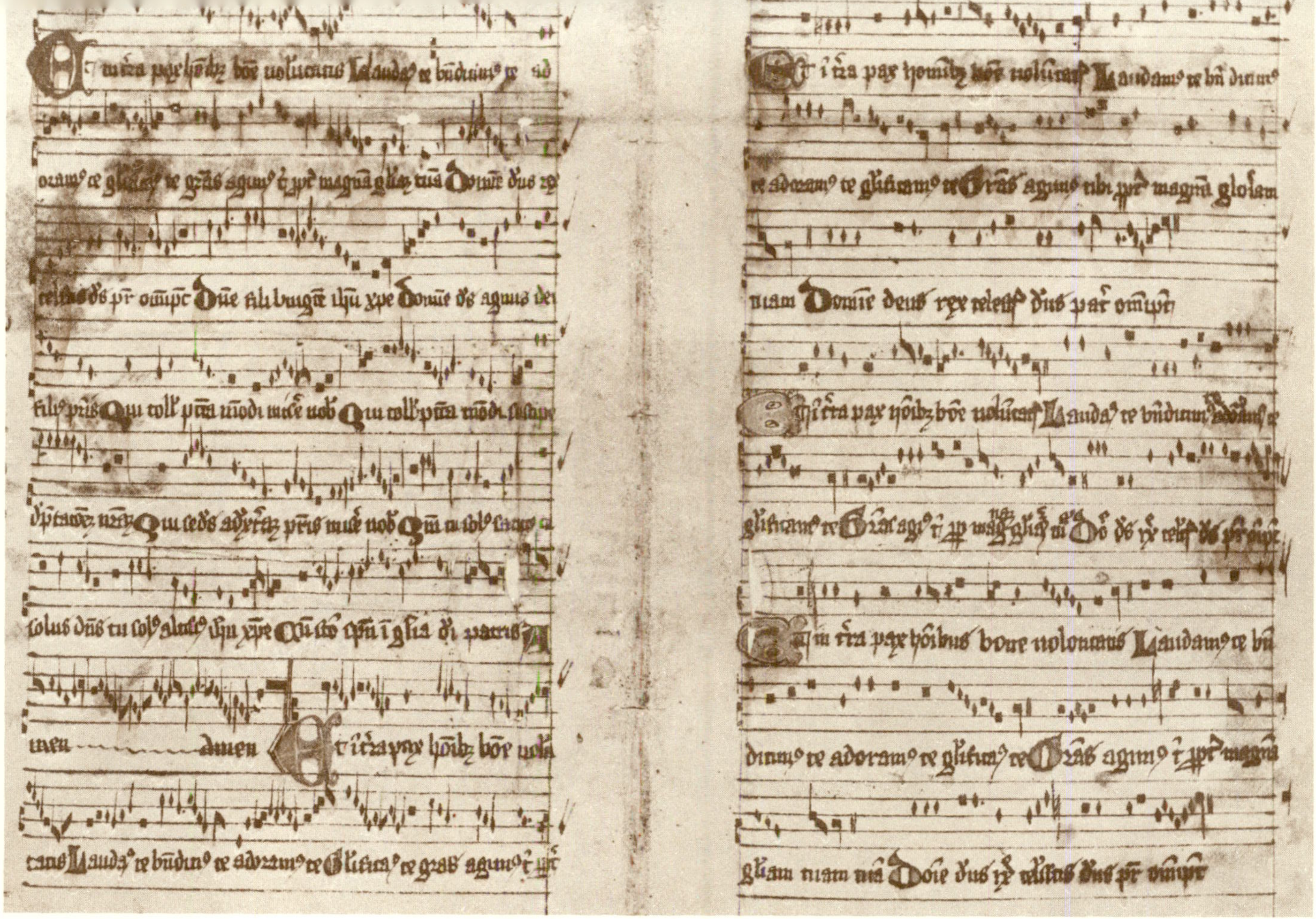

Fig. I. The Foligno Fragment, Side One, ff. 2v and 1r

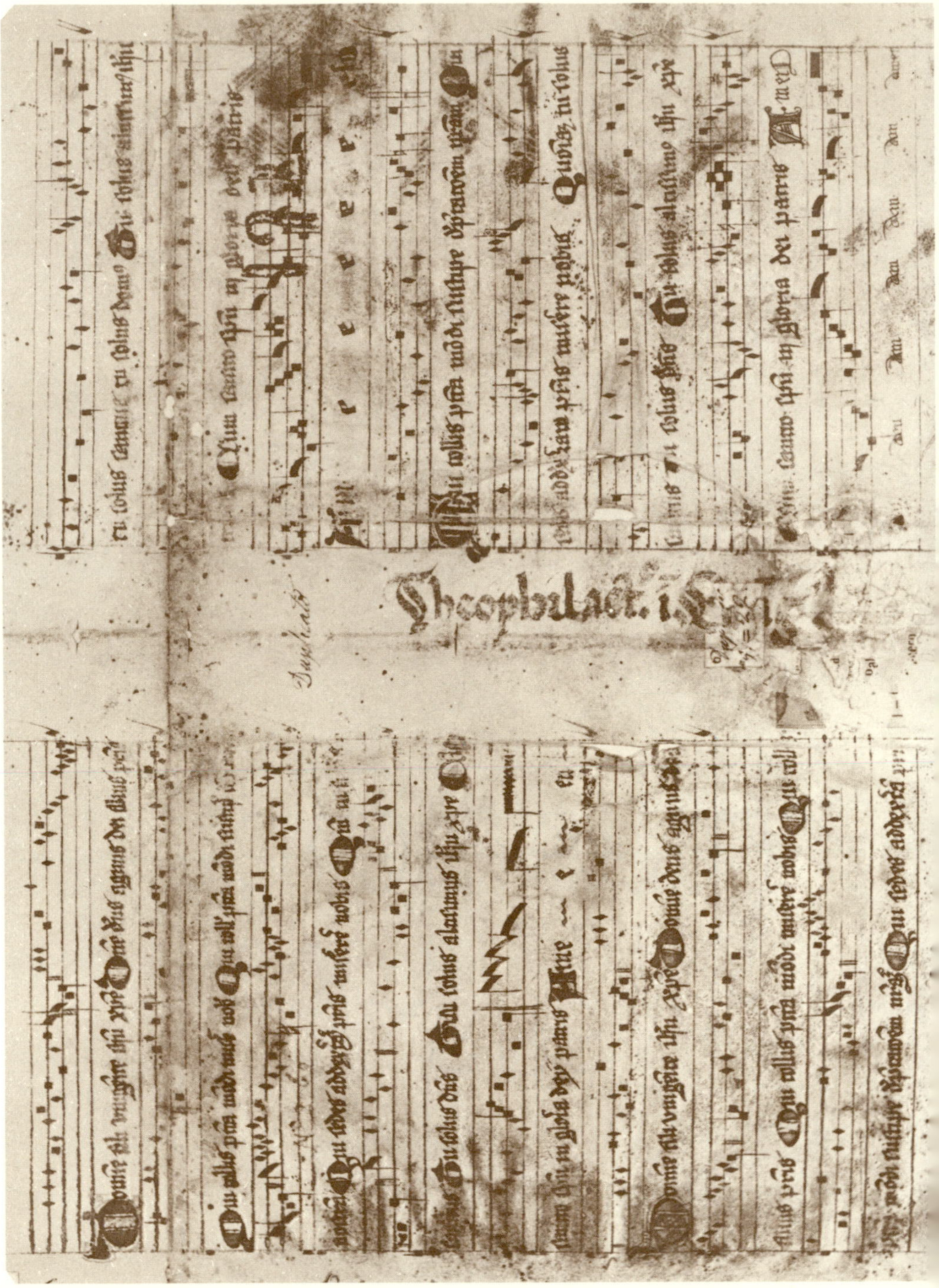

the place which evidently corresponded with the back of the volume. None of the pages preserves any trace of foliation figures (those appearing on the facsimiles are my addition *to the photographs*); on each of them two vertical lines frame eight pentagrams, leaving rather narrow margins on either side, as well as above and below the staves.

The narrow margins, plus the fact that the staves are completely filled with music and underlined with text (the latter in a rather heavy handwriting full of abbreviations), give the pages a quite crowded appearance. A modest, but painstaking decorative effort—including larger and smaller illuminated capitals and touches of red added without any notational significance to the vertical strokes indicating rests in the music—does not overcome the sense of dullness due to the lack of any balanced arrangement on the page. For the record, only a few of the initials are red, and they are much brighter than the *sang-de-boeuf* shade; the others are blue, green, and faded Havana brown, and are so distributed as to mark each individual part of a polyphonic piece with initials all of the same color. The brown ink used for text and music is also faded.

Some figures on the page to the right of the "Theophilact." inscription—probably a library number for the volume—indicate that this page was at some time considered as the front page. In spite of this, I have preferred to call f. 1r the page on the right of the other side of the fragment, on which the text and music of three voices of an *Et in terra* run from a miniated initial to the words "deus omnipotens." To me this seems to indicate the beginning of a fascicle, the proper place from which to start the description of the fragment's contents. In fact, the superius part of the same piece continues to its end on f. 1v, followed by the continuation of the tenor part up to the words "Qui sedes ad dexteram patris." The rest of the tenor must have appeared on the upper part of the next page, now lost, followed by the completely missing second section of the contratenor.

---

unclear, and a recent label partially covers the last word. The book protected by the double leaf was therefore by the eleventh-century theologian Theophylact; the work is better known in a Latin translation by Johannes Oecolampadius as *In quatuor evangelia Enarrationes*. Neither the early editions of the Latin version (Basel, 1524 and 1554; Cologne, 1528 and 1541), nor the print of the Greek original (Rome, 1542) match the size of the Foligno fragment, since they are all large, thick folio volumes. That the work in the Foligno library was not a manuscript is indicated by the recent inscription "Duplicato"; it must then have been a more recent (partial?) edition, which I have not been able to identify.

A proof in favor of this arrangement, and a counterpart to it, is found, after a gap of undetermined width, on f. 2r, where the three upper staves are filled with the end of a tenor part going from "Tu solus sanctus" to "Amen" (again a Gloria text), and the remaining five staves, with the second half of the contratenor of the same piece, from "Qui tollis . . . suscipe" to "Amen." Once more a complete superius part, and once more a Gloria text, fill six and a half staves on f. 2v (the last page of the fascicle beginning on f. 1r). They are followed on the remaining one and a half staves by another part running from "Et in terra" to "gratias agimus tibi propter . . . ," whose precise relationship to the preceding I would like to leave undecided for the moment.

As far as we can see, f. 1r was probably not only the front page of a fascicle, but also the beginning of a section of Gloria settings continued on the next fascicle. The arrangement, grouping together settings of each single text of the Mass ordinary, places our fragment in a category with the well-known manuscript of the Chapter Library at Apt, dating from the second or third decade of the fifteenth century.[3] Dates are not easily assigned on the basis of the rather formal writing in which sacred texts are often cast, and the difficulty is increased in the case of the Foligno fragment by our inability to determine its geographical provenance; yet, it seems to me a fair guess to date it also within the first third of the fifteenth century.

This by no means provides a date for the music in the fragment. If we examine the notation of its Gloria No. 1 (ff. 1r-1v), we shall find that Philippe de Vitry might well never have existed for its composer, were it not for an isolated figure of a minim at its very beginning. As I understand it, the single upward tail applied to a note following two unsigned semibreves indicates, once and for all, the rhythmic meaning of every following group of three, or occasionally four, undifferentiated semibreves in a frame of minor *tempus* and major prolation—that is, ♩. ♩ ♪ or ♩ ♪ ♩ ♪, respectively. Other rhythmic interpretations might be possible; this, however, seems most plausible to me because it is in agreement with the prevailing rhythm of most Mass music of this time, representing, after all, a survival, in sound if not in notation, of the old, relaxed first mode. Combined with the use of *puncti* (*divisionis* as well as *perfectionis*),

---

[3] See Amedée Gastoué, *Le Manuscrit de musique du Trésor d'Apt* (Paris, 1936), and the review by Guillaume de Van in *Acta musicologica*, XII (1940), 64-69.

it is consistent with the notational stage of the *Roman de Fauvel*[4] and with the rules given by Marchettus de Padua when he comes to speak "de tempore imperfecto modo gallico."[5] It would place the date of the piece—at least its notational date—at about one century earlier than the fragment itself.

Imperfect *tempus* and major prolation are also omnipresent on the remaining two pages of the Foligno fragment. They are fully spelled out in what survives of the two lower parts of Gloria No. 2 (f. 2r), by means of upward tails for the semibreves *minimae*. Upward tails alternate on the last page (f. 2v) with downward ones applied to perfect semibreves whenever there might be some doubt about their being perfect. These features suggest a slightly later date for the music on ff. 2r-2v than for the first Gloria, and for the music on f. 2v, some analogy with Italian notation.[6]

One consistent feature of the Foligno fragment is that all the parts in all its pieces are texted. In Gloria No. 1—the only one to provide a sample of complete three-voice texture—the three parts move in almost absolute simultaneity (Ex. 1). Even a few measures suffice to identify the piece as the one to which I was referring when I mentioned the presence of some *fauxbourdon* style. They also give immediate evidence of the lack of accuracy of the version given in the fragment (see the passages marked by asterisks in Ex. 1).

I must stress that I do not consider *fauxbourdon* style as being exclusively, or even typically English. Nor does Professor Harrison, if I correctly interpret his views.[7] Many pages of *Fourteenth-Century Mass Music in France*, recently edited by Hanna Stäblein-Harder,[8]

---

[4] See the facsimile, ed. Pierre Aubry (Paris, 1907), especially the motet *Quare fremuerunt*, f. 1r.

[5] The full title of the chapter (the sixth of *Pomerium*, Liber II, Tractatus III) is "De nominibus et proportionibus semibrevium de tempore imperfecto modo Gallico et Italico." See also the preceding chapter, "De distantia et differentia modi cantandi de tempore imperfecto inter Gallicos et Italicos. . . ." Both appear in Martin Gerbert, *Scriptores ecclesiastici de musica* (St. Blaise, 1784), Vol. III, 175-78, and, in a much improved version, in Marchetus de Padua, *Pomerium*, ed. Giuseppe Vecchi (American Institute of Musicology, Corpus Scriptorum de Musica 6 [Rome], 1961), pp. 172-80.

[6] It should be considered, however, in connection with both the date and possible provenance of the piece, that both features appear in an unmistakably French manuscript, the *Roman de Fauvel* (see n. 4), for instance, on ff. 3 and 6.

[7] I refer here to verbal exchange of opinions with Professor Harrison apropos the Foligno fragment.

[8] The music was published in 1962 by the American Institute of Musicology as a

Ex. 1. Gloria Foligno No. 1, f. 1r

one-volume item of the series "Corpus Mensurabilis Musicae." A "Companion Volume" to this, having the same title, publisher, and date, is included in the series "Musicological Studies and Documents," and contains comments and critical notes. For the sake of a clearer distinction the two works will be referred to henceforth as CMM, 29 (i.e., "Corpus Mensurabilis Musicae," 29) and MSD, 7 ("Musical Studies and Documents," 7).

indicate how common it also was on the Continent, although only the Gloria Apt No. 37[9] approaches the insistence on *fauxbourdon* successions displayed in Foligno No. 1. These successions are the result of one of many different *punctus-contra-punctum* techniques, all aimed—whether they were improvised or written down—at obtaining a rich choral sound. This one, that of repeated 6/3 chords, represents a particularly easy way of getting the desired result in melismatic passages. If anything needs to be said here about English polyphony, it is, I think, that its most characteristic feature is not to be seen in *fauxbourdon* procedures, but rather in the fact that even its most refined manifestations always preserved a feeling for a *choral* sound, to which only improvised, or very simple written polyphony remained faithful on the Continent.

When I speak of choral sound, I do not necessarily mean the sound produced by more than one singer to a part[10]—we find, after all,

[9] Attributed in the manuscript to a certain Susay; see Stäblein-Harder, CMM, 29, pp. 57-58, and MSD, 7, p. 48. In the latter, the view is expressed that the author may have been the same Johannes (or Jehan) Susay (or Suzoy) who composed three pieces in the MS Chantilly, Musée Condé 1047. Were this true, the fact that a sophisticated composer should have made his style simple and plain when writing "cathedral" music would provide additional evidence for the discussion of sacred polyphony in the last part of the present study. I suspect, however, that Apt No. 37 may be older than "the beginning of the 15th century," and therefore be by a different Susay despite the parallel sixth chords in the piece—"Quite a *modern* effect" (italics replace the quotation marks of the original) according to Stäblein-Harder, but probably quite modern only because we have officially recognized *fauxbourdon* as a new technique originating not earlier than *ca.* 1430.

[10] I shall never tire of insisting that normal polyphonic performance required one singer to a part, with occasional doubling only of the superius (not to consider possible instrumental doublings). Evidence for this is given, for instance, by Frank D'Accone, "The Singers of San Giovanni in Florence during the 15th Century," *Journal of the American Musicological Society*, xiv (1961), 307-58, and more extensively in his unpublished "A Documentary History of Music at the Florentine Cathedral and Baptistry during the Fifteenth Century" (Harvard University Dissertation, 1960). Precious information on the number and names of church singers has often been given (by Haberl for St. Peter's in Rome, by Casimiri for Padua, by Sartori for Milan, and by many others for various churches) under the mistaken impression that such singers formed a "chapel." In the papal, as in princely chapels, the number of singers tended to increase during the second half of the fifteenth century, yet even here one must take into account the many leaves of absence granted to singers, as well as their justified or unjustified absences. Even when there is evidence that twelve or fifteen were present, this does not mean that they all sang in the same polyphonic pieces, and the continuing need for a plainchant choir must also be considered. The doubling of superius parts performed by boys, which became more and more frequent during the sixteenth century, also

that even up to the seventeenth century a group of soloists could still be called a chorus.[11] At the time under consideration, shortly before the beginning of the so-called choral polyphony, the concept of chorus may have been that of a polyphony in which the element of harmonic, vertical *concordia* prevailed over that of contrapuntal (the meaning of the words "contra punctum" has been completely reversed) individualization of lines.[12] Most particularly, this concern for simultaneity and vertical concordance must have been typical of all kinds of improvised *choral* polyphony—and here I use this adjective with still another implication, i.e., to indicate performance not by virtuoso singers, but rather by regular members of a monastic or chapter choir.[13]

---

increased the need for someone to guide their performance and pull them together. It thus happened that the *magister puerorum*, originally a teacher of grammar and musical theory, gradually became the *magister capellae* or conductor. I suspect that the habit of choral singing may have originated in the imperial Hapsburg court, and later spread, becoming a baroque form of expression.

[11] Choruses in early operas are usually performed by characters who have already appeared as soloists, if only for the roles of "una Ninfa" or "un Pastore." (I do not refer, of course, to such gigantic choruses as those of Caccini's *Rapimento di Cefalo*, which are wholly in the tradition of the previous *intermedi*.) In later operas, choruses often provide songs or sound effects backstage, to which all the characters whose presence was not needed on stage were called to contribute. (I have in mind the choral description of a hunt in Cavalli's *Didone*; but often it was merely a short interjection of "Guerra, guerra!" or "Morte, morte!") Finally, the concluding, often moralizing comments, on which most seventeenth-century operas end, are usually cast in the form of short choruses performed by the four principal characters. Slightly different, but also pertinent, is the case of polychoral church performances in which "choruses" including the Caccini girls and other famous soloists of the Medicean court were pitted against other vocal or instrumental groups (see Angelo Solerti, *Musica, ballo e drammatica alla corte Medicea dal 1600 al 1637* [Florence, 1905], pp. 58, 64, 85, 106, 129-30, 144, *et passim*).

[12] It seems to me that most of the so-called choral polyphony (see Manfred Bukofzer, "The Beginnings of Choral Polyphony" in *Studies in Medieval and Renaissance Music* [New York, 1950], pp. 176-89) could be explained as an alternation between contrapuntal sections performed by two or three unaccompanied soloists and portions in which the voices of the same performers come together in a more chordal texture supported by instrumental parts. It is true, however, that there are instances in which a superius part, supported by untexted (i.e., probably instrumental) parts, is inscribed "Chorus," possibly suggesting a unison performance by two or three singers.

[13] In keeping with all that has been said in the preceding notes, I do not think that the whole chapter took part in the performance, but only two, three, or possibly four of its members designated *ad hoc*.

Coming back to the Gloria Foligno No. 1, the only reason we can produce for not considering it an example of written-down improvisation is that none of its parts has the nature of a pre-existing melody on which the *cantus ad librum*, as improvisation was sometimes called, may have been based. It is, then, a truly composed piece, only reminiscent of the sound of improvised polyphony.

While the three voices of Gloria No. 1 are always kept close together, with the contratenor constantly in a middle position, the tenor and contratenor of Gloria No. 2 (its only extant parts) are more widely spaced, and eventually cross each other in the Amen.[14] Of the missing superius we can only guess that it may have started in a *duodecima* position, occasionally risen to the double octave above the tenor, and stayed always at some distance from the latter, even when contrary motion produced a mutual reapproaching. The general style of the setting, although basically harmonic, and with simultaneous recitation of the text in all the parts, must have given a little more contrapuntal and rhythmic freedom to the voices than did the preceding piece. Short connecting passages, the usual size being two breves in length, appear occasionally either in the tenor or in the contratenor, marking the conclusion of some section of the text. Similar connecting passages can be seen in the Gloria and Credo of Machaut's Mass, in Apt No. 8 and in Ivrea Nos. 62 and 63, to mention only a few Gloria settings.[15]

The nature and possible relationship of the two Gloria parts appearing on f. 2v of the Foligno fragment have been left undecided up to this moment because I thought that a more precise knowledge of what preceded might have helped to determine them. At first glance, the two parts, both notated with a C clef on the second line, seem to belong to two different settings, since they both begin with a *longa*, the first on G, and the second on F. The starting of two new pieces on f. 2v, however, would be in sharp contrast with the pattern we have found in the preceding pages, on which the voice-

---

[14] The only intervention of a possibly, but not necessarily, different hand in the Foligno fragment occurs at the end of this contratenor part, where, after the usual illuminated *A*, someone has added (in a lighter and smaller script than that of the other texts) first the syllable "men," then several repetitions of the letters "Am," and a final "Amen."

[15] See Stäblein-Harder, CMM, 29, Nos. 34 (pp. 57-58), 37 (pp. 60-62), and 38 (pp. 63-65).

parts of one piece (or of a section of it) followed each other, first on the same page, then on the next, beginning from the top. It can also be recalled that the two *Et in terra* beginning on f. 2v share a detail of notation that does not appear in the preceding pieces, namely, the downward tails indicating perfect semibreves. An attempt to combine the two parts in spite of the strident clash of their initial *longae* produces a result in which further clashes alternate with surprising consonances and combine in even more surprising rhythmic parallelism (Ex. 2). Having already seen from No. 1 that

Ex. 2. Beginning of Gloria Foligno No. 3, f. 2v

the notation of the fragment is far from being flawlessly accurate, I am inclined to consider the music on f. 2v a badly corrupt version of one single Gloria No. 3.

If this hypothesis is correct,[16] Foligno No. 3 must have been a setting in which a duet of high-pitched voices was supported by one lower voice, probably without text, or by a tenor-contratenor duo. One might be tempted to call it a setting in motet style—even more so if the lower part, or parts, had applied isorhythmic techniques. If the missing tenor also had a text, and had the modest rhythmic activity of the tenors in the previous pieces, instead of the holding of notes that often characterizes isorhythmic tenors, the piece would have assumed a more *conductus*-like appearance than most ordinary settings that are so labeled.[17] In either case, what survives of the piece seems to indicate a rather early date, at about the middle of the fourteenth century.

Conjectural as the dates of both the fragment and the music it contains are—not to speak of the fact that no plausible conclusion has been reached in regard to their provenance—an assessment of them is more in the nature of a tentative opinion than a reasoned conclusion (although many a reasoned conclusion is nothing more than a reasonable opinion). I am inclined to think that the Foligno manuscript originated in the chapter of a provincial monastic, collegiate, or cathedral church, either in Italy (probably north of Rome) or in southern Germany. Its provincial origin would account for the lack of characteristics on which a more determined geographical assignment could be made. As a *church* manuscript, it would belong in the same category in which the already mentioned Apt manuscript, or the fragment[18] containing the Sorbonne (more properly Besançon) Mass—to name only the most obvious examples—belong. Heinrich Besseler once described the Apt manuscript as "ein kirch-

[16] In a private letter, Professor Kurt von Fischer, to whom I sent duplicates of the Foligno photographs, expressed the opinion that the two parts belong to two different settings. I hope to convince even him that we are faced with a single, badly corrupted piece.

[17] I am not at ease with any of the recently proposed classifications and terminologies which have been variously used and interpreted. The confusion produced in my mind by any proposal of a radical revision or refinement of an already accepted terminology (almost inevitably followed by even subtler counterproposals) leads me to avoid any such attempt and simply describe what I see in the music. I agree that this is easily done when one is dealing with only three (incomplete) pieces.

[18] See the description, discussion, and facsimile reproduction by Jacques Chailley, "La Messe de Besançon et un compositeur inconnu du XIVᵉ siècle: Jean Lambelet," *Annales musicologiques*, II (1954), 90-103.

liches Gegenstück"—a churchly counterpart—of the secular collections of the time.[19] I would not extend that description to the Foligno
manuscript without some additional qualifications. One has to do
with the secular nature of the counterparts; for only a few of the
secular collections are secular from every point of view; while many
are secular in content, but may have been assembled by and for
ecclesiastics. On the other hand, the concept I have of the church
manuscripts is, I suspect, somewhat more defined than Besseler's
vague "kirchliches." In keeping with my *choral* conception, I think
they were created, as I have already stated, as polyphonic choirbooks
for either monastic, collegiate, or cathedral churches. As such, they
should be set apart from those sources in which the selection and
arrangement of sacred pieces, and occasionally the mixture of sacred
and secular, reflect the more sophisticated, more up-to-date, and also
the more mundane taste of clerics exerting their musical skills in
private chapels.[20]

If my distinction is correct, the artistic polyphony contained in
the latter sources deserves our attention because of its extraordinary
significance, not because it represents the common or general practice
of that period. It was recorded and preserved with particular care
because of its refinement, as a model not easy to imitate and fit into
daily common practice, yet inspiring and rewarding. As for the
mainstream of church music in the strict sense of the word, it is
difficult to make generalizations. First of all it involves the activity
of hundreds or thousands of churches of different types, locations,
and importance. Secondly, our attention having been focused until
now on the other type of activity, the available evidence has to be
unraveled out of passing remarks or devious footnotes and imple-
mented with new and better focused information.

As I see it in my hypothetical generalization, church practice still
considered plainchant as its basic element. This by itself would require some kind of re-focused attention, since the performance of
plainchant was undergoing considerable change in the direction of

---

[19] "Studien zur Musik des Mittelalters: I. Neue Quellen des 14. und beginnenden
15. Jahrhunderts," *Archiv für Musikwissenschaft*, VII (1925), 202.

[20] For this reason we should reconsider to what extent the arrangement of some
manuscripts in which polyphonic settings of the Ordinary are grouped by category
(Kyries, Glorias, etc.) depends on their origin as church (polyphonic) choirbooks,
rather than on their date. Manuscripts containing one single Mass-cycle formed by
evidently unrelated pieces can also be placed in the same category. They probably
represent all the written-down ordinary polyphony included in the chapter's repertory
at the time.

rhythmization, occasionally, but not too often recorded in a curious kind of half-mensural, figured, plainchant notation. To this one should add a certain amount of creative activity, mainly concerned, as far as I know, with newly composed ordinarium settings.[21]

Polyphony—either written down or unwritten—naturally grew out of that frame as a more elaborate way of fulfilling the liturgical requirements in regard to music. Unwritten polyphony added one or two, seldom more, simple lines to the plainchant, either in its unmeasured version, or, more likely, in its more recent rhythmization. It was called *cantus ad librum* on the assumption that the singers assembled around a choirbook and performed their different parts while reading (or "sighting") the basic melody from it. How much this was the real procedure we shall reconsider after having examined the case of the written-down polyphony. In principle, the writing of a polyphonic sacred setting should indicate that the piece had no plainchant foundation, as in the case of the Gloria Foligno No. 1, or that its construction on a plainchant melody was of such an elaborate nature that the piece could not be memorized easily. In fact, some of the pieces thus preserved are pure reflections of improvisational techniques, often of a more elementary kind than the procedures described in most *artes contrapuncti*. Others belong to either of the two categories for which notation seems to be more

[21] Evidence of such practices has not often been brought to the attention of scholars. I can begin by mentioning the passages on performance of plainchant by Hieronymus de Moravia, *Tractatus de musica*, ed. Simon M. Cserba (Regensburg, 1935), pp. 179-87, and then add the occurrence of figural plainchant notation in some of the Cividale manuscripts, the most conspicuous example being the four Passions—all in the hand of one Comucius de la Campagnolla, a canon and imperial notary at Cividale in the first half of the fifteenth century—which form the contents of Codex XXIV. How long the practice survived (along with the usual and more common neumatic notation, to which we do not know what rhythmic interpretation was given) is shown in the MS St. Gall, Stiftsbibliothek 546, from the first quarter of the sixteenth century, described by Otto Marxer, *Zur spätmittelalterlichen Choralgeschichte St. Gallens* (St. Gall, 1908). The latter source is of great interest not only for its figural notation, but also for the new melodies it gives (particularly Credo melodies, often beginning with the usual formula of Credos I, II, and IV of the *Liber Usualis*, then going their own way), and finally for the inscriptions specifying alternation between an evidently homophonic "Chorus" and "Organum" (Marxer, pp. 149-51, 163-65, 167-68, 175-76, *et passim*) or "Organista" (*ibid.*, pp. 159-60, 161-63, 166). Whether the latter refer to the organ and its player or to improvised (so to speak) polyphony cannot easily be determined. At any rate, it is worth noting that the performer at times is required to "hold" some notes (*ibid.*, Credo on pp. 163-66, where the "Organum" inscription later becomes, on p. 166, "Organista tenet"), as if some kind of *symphonia basilica* was meant.

justified, but they have reached us in bad versions, which would have needed revision if the sources had really been used in performance.

In this connection the clash of G against F at the beginning of Foligno No. 3 (if my interpretation of the two parts as belonging to the same Gloria is correct) is a joy to my musicologist's eye, if not to my ear, as evidence that the writing down of the piece had nothing to do with the requirements of its performance. So are the mistakes in Foligno No. 1 and in many of the Apt readings, as well as in those of other manuscripts. They convey to me the impression that the writing down was, in the type of sources I am trying to describe, a sort of gratuitous gesture in most cases, dictated by a *religio* for the written book, and by an almost ritual habit of assembling around a lectern for the singing. It certainly represents a gift from the usually anonymous ecclesiastical scribe to his unknown, musicologically oriented descendants. Once a piece had been accepted in the repertory of a chapter choir—whatever the ways of and reasons for that acceptance may have been—it was rapidly memorized, so that the written version was soon reduced to the status of a symbol or a vague mnemonic aid, and oral tradition took over. This may also have applied to the so-called improvisations, agreed upon just once (I would like very much to use the baroque term "concertare") and then repeated through the fidelity, and lapses, of memory.

The present, largely tentative and scarcely conclusive writing has not achieved any positive result—not even regarding the four small pages of music by which it was occasioned. Yet, being in the mood for suggestions, I might repeat one here that I recently expressed only verbally,[22] i.e., that the kind of polyphony often called "archaic" or "peripheral" (although found in relatively recent and central sources) belongs to the normal practice of polyphony in most churches, large and small, of the Western world. On the other hand, the kind of artistic polyphony we have become used to considering standard for fourteenth- and fifteenth-century sacred music is but the valuable expression of a minority, the advancing standard of a special elite.

[22] On December 29, 1964, at Washington, D.C., in a short comment on the Cividale manuscripts concluding a session of the annual meeting of the American Musicological Society that had dealt with "Cathedral Repertories: Worcester and Cividale."

THE MOTETS OF LIONEL POWER

CHARLES HAMM

WITH certain composers of the fifteenth century it is possible and often desirable to distinguish between simple polyphonic settings of short liturgical works and more elaborate motets, but such a distinction is often difficult in the works of Lionel Power and is not at all necessary for the purposes of this paper. I am using the term "motet" here to designate settings of any liturgical texts other than sections of the ordinary of the Mass.

Table I lists all motets attributed to Power in at least one manuscript. There are eighteen of these, four with conflicting attributions to Dunstable.

TABLE I

MOTETS ATTRIBUTED TO LIONEL POWER*

1. *Alma redemptoris mater* I: Ao 212′ 214 (Leonelle); ModB 100-101 (Dunstable); Tr92 169′ 171 (Leonel)
2. *Alma redemptoris mater* II: Ao 187′ 188 (anon); BL 226 (Leonelle); ModB 134′ 135 (Dunstable); Tr93 361′ 363 (anon)
3. *Anima mea* I: BU 86 (Leonel); FM112 32′ 34 (anon); MuEm 150′ 151′ (Leonellus); ModB 117′ 118 (Leonel)
4. *Anima mea* II: ModB 110′ 111 (Leonel)
5. *Ave maris stella*: Tr92 97′ (Leonel?)
6. *Ave regina celorum* I: OH 36 (Leonel)
7. *Ave regina celorum* II: Ao 195′ 196 (anon); BL 303 (Leonel); SB 5′ 6 (anon); Tr92 132′ 133 (anon); Tr92 171′ 172 (anon)
8. *Beata progenies*: OH 38 (Leonel)
9. *Beata viscera*: Ao 10′ (Leonel)
10. *Gloriose virginis*: FM112 34′ 35 (Leonel); ModB 74 (Leonel)

---

* MANUSCRIPT ABBREVIATIONS
Ao   Aosta, Seminario, MS without signature
BL   Bologna, Liceo musicale, Q 15 (olim 37)
BU   Bologna, Bibl. Universitaria, 2216
FM112   Florence, Bibl. naz. Magliab., XIX, 112 bis
ModB   Modena, Bibl. Estense, lat. 471 ($\propto$ X, I, II)
MuEm   Munich, Staatsbibl., mus. 3232a (lat. 14274)
OH   Old Hall, St. Edmund's College, Old Hall Manuscript
SB   Oxford, Bodleian Library, Selden B26
Tr87   Trent, Castello del Buon Consiglio, MS 87
Tr90   Trent, Castello del Buon Consiglio, MS 90
Tr92   Trent, Castello del Buon Consiglio, MS 92
Tr93   Trent, Archivio Capitolare, MS 93

11. *Ibo michi ad montem*: ModB 98' 99 (Leonel)
12. *Mater ora*: ModB 110 (Leonel); Tr92 140' 141 (anon); Tr92 181' 182 (anon)
13. *Quam pulchra es*: ModB 111' 112 (Leonel)
14. *Regina celi*: Tr90 458' 459 (Leonell Anglicus); Tr92 142' 143 (anon)
15. *Salve mater salvatoris*: ModB 116' 117 (Dunstable); Tr92 193' 195 (Leonel); Tr92 215-215' (anon)
16. *Salve regina* I: BL 269 (Leonell Polbero)
17. *Salve regina* II: Ao 203' 206 (anon); ModB 86' 88 (Leonel); Tr90 366' 368' (Dunstable); Tr92 231' 233' (Dunstable)
18. *Salve sancta parens*: ModB 109' (Leonel); Tr92 102' (anon, with text "Virgo prudentissima")

A few general remarks, first. These motets are all settings of Marian texts. None is isorhythmic, though Power uses this technique in a few of his Mass sections. None makes use of canon or of systematic imitation, though fragments of imitative counterpoint are found in a handful of the pieces. Some are preserved in English manuscripts, some in Continental sources, some in both.

After locating these works, I next set about to group them in some logical way. In attempting to establish a chronology of the works of Dufay, I decided early that mensural usage alone would suffice;[1] but it took only a bit of work with the compositions of Power to see that such a technique would not work at all with this composer. My method has been, quite simply, to assume that pieces written at the same time share certain common characteristics. The number of motets being small, I decided to give myself a larger body of material by working with Mass music as well, after convincing myself that Power made use of similar compositional techniques in the two bodies of works. Table II lists these works in four groups, several further subdivided. Groupings were made not on the basis of a single criterion, but on general style of composition, manuscript location, cadence types, clefs, treatment of dissonance, disposition of voices and text, and whatever other evidence I could muster.

The group which I call Old Hall I is made up of all those works written in English descant style. All but one are found in the oldest layer of the Old Hall manuscript, in the hand of Scribe A.[2] Each is written for three voices clearly differentiated in range and notated

---

[1] Charles Hamm, *A Chronology of the Works of Guillaume Dufay, Based on a Study of Mensural Practice* (Princeton University Press, 1964).
[2] Rev. A. Ramsbotham, ed., *The Old Hall Manuscript*, Vol. 1 (1933), x-xi.

TABLE II

The Works of Lionel Power, by Groups

OLD HALL I
  Motets: *Beata progenies; Ave regina celorum* I; *Beata viscera*
  Mass music: Sanctus OH 81'; Sanctus OH 83' 84; Sanctus OH 88'; Agnus
      Dei OH 104'; Agnus Dei OH 105' 106; Agnus Dei OH 106;
      Sanctus OH 96' 97–Agnus Dei OH 107' 108

OLD HALL II[a]
  Motets: *Ave regina celorum* II
  Mass music: Et in terra OH 16' 17–Patrem OH 64' 65; Et in terra OH 18'
      19; Et in terra OH 20' 21; Patrem OH 71' 72

OLD HALL II[b]
  Motets: *Salve regina* I
  Mass music: Et in terra OH 19' 20; Patrem OH 69' 70; Patrem OH 68' 69;
      Patrem OH 70' 71; Sanctus OH 93' 94–Agnus Dei Ao 216' 217;
      Et in terra OH 17' 18; Et in terra Ao 231' 233; *Missa alma
      redemptoris*

OLD HALL II[c]
  Motets: *Ave maris stella* (?)
  Mass music: Patrem OH 61' (=Ao 238' 240); Sanctus OH 94' 95; Sanctus
      OH 95' 96; Agnus Dei OH 107 (=Ao 245' 246)

CONTINENTAL I[a]
  Motets: *Salve mater salvatoris; Regina celi; Anima mea* I; *Alma redemp-
      toris* I
  Mass music: *Missa rex seculorum*; Et in terra Tr92 44' 46; Et in terra Tr92
      8' 9; Et in terra Tr92 44' 45; Patrem Tr87 37' 39

CONTINENTAL I[b]
  Motets: *Salve sancta parens; Mater ora*

CONTINENTAL II
  Motets: *Gloriose virginis; Ibo michi ad montem; Anima mea* II; *Quam
      pulchra es*

---

with different clefs; chant is present in the middle voice, in a simple, almost unornamented fashion. The three basic mensurations of the time (¢, O, and C) are used, one for an entire composition or perhaps several of them in simple alternation, with movement in each in breves and semibreves and with the minim as the smallest note. The most characteristic cadence involves stepwise movement in the outer voices to an octave (Ex. 1). The range of each voice is usually an octave, possibly a ninth. Notation is in score, with text under the lowest voice.

Ex. 1

The second layer of works copied into Old Hall by Scribe A is much larger and has works of more variety; I have made three subgroups of these. The first, my Old Hall II^a, contains pieces which superficially resemble Continental motets of the late fourteenth and early fifteenth centuries. They are written for three, four, or five voices, the lower two without text, and there is often contrast in number of voices between sections. Voices are paired in range, often a fifth apart, and often all voices are written in modes transposed down a fourth or a fifth, resulting in an unusually low tessitura for the entire piece. There is no use of chant in any voice; the text is often telescoped in Mass sections; isorhythmic treatment is common. The three basic mensurations are used, with much more frequent alternation within a piece. Power has difficulty with four or five voices, particularly at cadences, where parallel perfect consonances, curious voice-leading, and odd dissonances are commonplace (Ex. 3). There is more dissonance than in the pieces in descant style, and a favorite cadence makes use of an unprepared dissonance (see Ex. 2).

Ex. 2

Though the tenor and contra move at times in larger note values than the upper voices, as in Continental motet style, they may also share similar movement. These works are all found in Old Hall, with no concordances.

The group Old Hall II^b contains all those pieces by Power which make use of perhaps his most characteristic device, which I call pseudo-augmentation. By this I mean the use of major prolation in the tenor (and sometimes the contra) against *tempus perfectum* in

Et in terra OH 16'17   *Ave regina celorum* II

Ex. 3

one or more of the upper voices, with a minim of the tenor equivalent to a semibreve of the other parts; this results, in Power, in a
faster beat on the semibreve in *tempus perfectum*, not in augmentation of the voice with major prolation as happens later in the
century.[3] Pieces brought together in this way have other common
characteristics: they are written for three voices (one, exceptionally,
has four); text is found in at least two voices; pitch is often quite
low; chant is sometimes traceable, now in the superius in highly
elaborated and often fragmentary form; and isorhythm is occasionally found. These are by far the most rhythmically complex of the
Power works, with extreme intricacies introduced by series of internal—often conflicting—mensurations and various sorts of coloration. A few semiminims are sprinkled among the predominant
semibreves and minims, and these are of the colored type rather than
the flagged sort found in works of the previous group. The so-called
"English figure," a cadential pattern characteristic of English music
of the second decade of the century and later, appears for the first
time (Ex. 4). What I take to be the earliest pieces in this group
are found only in the second layer of Old Hall, but several of the
later ones are concordant in Ao, BL, and Tr87.

Ex. 4

[3] Hamm, *A Chronology*, pp. 49-52.

The pieces which I have grouped as Old Hall II[c] have chant elaboration in the upper of three voices, all are transposed down to quite a low pitch level, there are few mensural complications, and there is no use of isorhythm. These are also found in the second layer of Old Hall, one in Hand C, with several concordances in Ao and one in Tr87.

My last two groups are called Continental I and II, not because of influence upon Power of continental music, but because the pieces brought together here are found in non-English sources. Stylistic influence clearly worked the other way, since Dufay, Binchois, and their contemporaries took over internal and external features of this style and continued to use them through the middle decades of the century. The works in Continental I[a] are all written for three voices, one rather high in pitch and the other two paired in range a fifth (or sometimes a seventh or an octave) below. Text is always in the top voice, and often in one of the lower ones as well. Structure is tripartite, with a mensural pattern of O C O ; movement is in semibreves and minims in O , but in breves and semibreves in C . An occasional shorter piece is bipartite, O , but otherwise identical. Duets, with text in both voices, relieve the three-part writing, and these are complete sections set off by strong cadences and barlines in the manuscript. A "drive to the cadence"—increased movement in all voices as a phrase nears an end—has become a characteristic device. The "English figure" is still used repeatedly, but a slightly more simple cadential figure, also involving a suspension, is equally common (Ex. 5). Tr92 is the main repository of these works, with concordances in Ao, Tr90, Tr93, MuEm, and ModB.

Ex. 5

Continental I[b] is a small subgroup of two motets quite similar in style to the works of the last group, differing only in that they are written in a single mensuration, *tempus perfectum*, throughout.

Four motets again different in style make up the last group, Continental II. These are written for three voices (one for four) with full text in all but one of the parts. There is complete equality

of voices, with much use of fragments of imitation among all parts.
The tenor and contra are paired in range a fifth below the superius,
and individual voices may have a range of as much as an eleventh.
The "English figure" has almost disappeared; the most typical cadence is now a simpler one with a suspended dissonance resolving
to the penultimate chord by direct stepwise motion (Ex. 6).

Ex. 6

Dissonance is limited to passing tones and suspensions. Text-music
relationships are carefully planned in declamatory sections, which
alternate with more melismatic writing; brief contrasting sections
for two voices relieve the three-voice texture. All pieces in this group
are *unica* in ModB with the exception of "Gloriose virginis," which
is preserved also in FM112.

I believe that these groups give us a rough chronological ordering
of the works of Power. There is undoubtedly some overlap from
group to group: I do not mean to suggest that all works in one group
were written before any of the works in the next group. Nor are all
works within a group identical in style. Unlike Dufay, who was
inclined to write clusters of pieces remarkably similar to one another,
Power manages to make each piece unique in at least some detail.
Within a group it is possible to trace a progression from the stylistic
features of the preceding group to those of the group following. My
arrangement of the works within each group is intended to be itself
chronological.

Thus in Old Hall II^b, the group made up of works in pseudo-
augmentation, the *Et in terra* OH 19′20 uses major prolation, in the
tenor and contra, only for the brief final section, the *Patrem* OH
69′70 has small sections in pseudo-augmentation alternating with
four-voice sections in which all voices are in major prolation, and
Salve regina has only the first of three large sections in pseudo-
augmentation. These three pieces must be the earliest ones in the
group, with characteristics pointing back to Old Hall II^a. The other
works in the group use pseudo-augmentation throughout, and the
Sanctus OH 93′94–*Agnus Dei* Ao 216′217 pair has taken on the

tripartite structure and the mensural simplicity of the following group, Continental I[a].

My groups Old Hall I and Old Hall II[a] must contain the oldest pieces by Power, and I believe that these two groups are roughly contemporary with one another. Old Hall I contains only motets and Sanctus and Agnus Dei settings, Old Hall II[a] only motets and Gloria and Credo settings. It seems likely that Power used one technique—descant style—for items with brief text and another—pseudo-motet style—for those with much more text. He died in 1445, at Canterbury. Assuming a full life span, his earliest works would have been written in the last years of the fourteenth century and the first decade of the fifteenth; the style of these works is perfectly consonant with such a suggestion.

Since most of the pieces in Old Hall II[b] and II[c] are found in the second layer added to the Old Hall manuscript by Scribe A, they must be contemporary with the pieces by Roy Henry. Manfred Bukofzer was convinced that the latter was Henry V (1413-22);[4] now Frank Harrison[5] and Andrew Hughes[6] argue that he was Henry IV (1399-1413). At any rate, these Power works must date from the first and second decades of the century, at a guess between 1410 and 1425.

Martin le Franc tells us in *Le Champion des dames* that Dufay and Binchois heard English musicians perform at the Burgundian court. Dufay came back to the north in 1433, after a long stay in Italy, and immediately after this journey his musical style changed dramatically, taking on many English characteristics. Unfortunately we have no record that Power was on the Continent at this time—or any other time, for that matter. But it is likely that his music was performed on this historic occasion, whether or not he was there himself. He was clearly the leader of the English school until Dunstable's ascendancy, and many stylistic details which became common property among British composers grew out of his individual practice. At any rate, the musical style which Dufay and other Continental musicians found so impressive in the early 1430's was the style of the Power works which I have grouped as Conti-

---

[4] Manfred Bukofzer, *Studies in Medieval and Renaissance Music* (New York, 1950), pp. 76-80.

[5] Frank L. Harrison, *Music in Medieval Britain* (London, 1958).

[6] Andrew Hughes, "English Sacred Music in Insular Sources, 1400- *ca.* 1450" (Doctoral thesis, Oxford, 1963).

nental II, and this style must have been well established by the time Dufay encountered it. These works by Power probably date from the decade 1425-35.

His last four motets would seem to have been written in the last decade of his life, 1435-45. If he had ever been on the Continent, he was back in England now; these pieces, though found only in Continental sources, resemble his earliest works in several curious ways.

Bukofzer printed *Alma redemptoris* II and *Salve regina* II, with conflicting attributions to Power and Dunstable, with the suggestion that the former is by Dunstable and the latter by Power.[7] I believe both are by Dunstable: both are atypical of Power's later works in that they go beyond tripartite structure in their alternation of O and ¢ ; and both make some use of paraphrase of chant in the superius. The other two motets with conflicting attribution, *Alma redemptoris* I and *Salve mater*, both of which Bukofzer credits to Power, are perfectly in his style, as I understand it. *Ave maris stella* is attributed to Power in the thematic index of the Trent codices,[8] but I cannot make out his name in the manuscript. *Beata viscera*, which I have as the last piece in Old Hall I, is found only in Aosta; if it is by Power, it is a somewhat later piece than the others in this group.[9]

A few words now about the implications of my suggested dating for the history of the cyclic Mass. The earliest pairs by Power are the Sanctus–Agnus Dei couple in Old Hall I (really a transitional piece between this group and the following one: the plainsong is in the tenor, with little elaboration, but the piece is for four voices with a textless contra and more alternation of mensuration patterns than is found in other pieces of this group), and the Gloria–Credo pair which I have as the first piece in Old Hall II[a]. Power was pairing two sections of the ordinary as early as the first decade of the century.

[7] Manfred Bukofzer, ed., *John Dunstable: Complete Works* (London, 1953), *Musica Britannica*, VIII.

[8] Guido Adler, "Sechs Trienter Codices. Erste Auswahl," *Denkmäler der Tonkunst in Oesterreich*, VII (Vienna, 1900), 77.

[9] Nanie Bridgman has recently discovered an additional source for several of the works of Power, Cod. AD. XIV. 49 in the Biblioteca Nazionale Braidense in Milan. *Alma redemptoris mater* II, with an attribution to Leonel, is found on 71'74, and the Sanctus and Agnus of the *Missa rex seculorum* are found on 74'80'. Madame Bridgman's report of her discovery is found in *Rivista Italiana di Musicologia*, Vol. I, 2 (1967), titled "Un manuscrit milanais."

Most interesting, if my dating is at all accurate, is the placing of the *Missa alma redemptoris* some time before 1425. The prolongation of the tenor in a cantus firmus Mass by notation in major prolation was a favorite trick of many composers later in the century, but when we group the Power Mass with motets and Mass sections written at about the same time, we see that this device was not something invented by Power especially for the tenor Mass, but was rather a compositional practice that he was currently using in various sorts of works. The other Power Mass, the *Missa rex seculorum*, apparently was written a decade after the earlier Mass. By this time he had outgrown his once-favorite device in his other works, and it did not occur to him to fall back on its use in this Mass.

Finally, among the several hundred anonymous motets found in manuscripts from the first half of the fifteenth century, about fifty are clearly by English composers. Some of these must be by Power, and if we could hit on some method for detecting these, our knowledge of this composer's art would be enriched.

We see in Power's motets stylistic changes perhaps greater than in the works of any other composer of the century, a progress from simple harmonizations of plainchant to complex, sophisticated works capable of exciting the admiration of such musicians as Dunstable, Dufay, and Binchois.

SOME AMBIGUITIES OF THE
MENSURAL SYSTEM

ARTHUR MENDEL

IN his Editorial Notes to *The Works of John Dunstable*, Manfred Bukofzer writes, ". . . editorial indications such as $\d. = \d$ . . . fix the relative tempo between the sections."[1] Since Bukofzer has explained earlier that "the original note values have been quartered in the transcription unless reduction by two is expressly stated,"[2] this means that he is suggesting that OⒽ = CⒽ in the original notation.

Is this true? In the Gloria from the Pembroke manuscript, Bukofzer's No. 2, is the 2/2 measure of the Qui tollis transcription twice as long as the 3/4 6/8 measure of the Et in terra and Cum sancto spiritu? And how does one determine this, in this instance or in any other where all the voices change signature at once? How was the transition managed in Dunstable's time? Bukofzer says that "in general $\d$ = c. 80-100, M. M. will be found appropriate." This suggests a beat on the $\d$ (= ◊); but he claims that it is the Ⓗ that remains constant, which means that the ◊ in C would be ⅔ as long as in O.

The only unambiguous evidence about the relation of the two signatures in Dunstable's own works must be where they occur in different voices simultaneously. The first such occurrence in the volume is in No. 15, the isorhythmic *Gloria super Jesu Christe Fili Dei*, at m. 69. Here the reduction in the tenor is only in the ratio 2:1, and the tempo-relation between the two signatures in the original notation is O◊ = C$\d$; but this is for a special reason (see II.1.1. in the table below). At m. 138, the reduction in the tenor, as in the other voices, is 4:1, and the relation of the values originally notated is O◊ = C◊, i.e., O$\overset{Ⓗ}{\underset{◊◊◊}{}}$ = C$\overset{Ⓗ◊}{\underset{◊◊◊}{}}$, not OⒽ = CⒽ. Similar situations occur in Nos. 16, 17, and 18.

[1] *Musica Britannica*, Vol. 8 (London, 1953), pp. xviif. It was Oliver Strunk who called my attention to Bukofzer's practice.

[2] He goes on to list certain exceptions to his normal reduction practice: the second section of Quam pulcra es (because the original notation has the signature Ȼ, which here implies augmentation); O rosa bella, relative to the notation in numerous sources but not to that in the Trent MSS.; and portions of the isorhythmic tenors, which must be read under changing time-signatures, and present a special problem.

Actually, any simultaneous occurrence of O and C in which O⊟ = C⊟ is extremely rare or nonexistent. There is at least one advocate of this relation, however, in the period of mensural notation: Giovanni Spataro.[3] Spataro attacks Gafurius for declaring that O◊ = C◊; such a view, he says, amounts to believing that three-thirds is more than two-halves. The "error" arises, he says, from the fact that Gafurius bases his reckoning on the (invariable) minim, rather than on the (invariable) breve and tempus. He prints a table with an ornate heading that reads: "Immutabile quantita del tempo." But in Chapter xvi he writes:

e questo si intende theorice: & non practice: perche li pratici: quali exercitano le figure de li predicti segni molto si alontanano de la verita: e de la prima intentione de li inventori di tali segni. . . .	and this, of course, speaking theoretically, and not practically. For the practical [musicians] who use the figures of the aforesaid signs are far from the truth and from the original intention of the inventors of such signs. . . .

In Chapter xi, too, Spataro refers scornfully to "li semidocti practici cantori."

So far as I know, Spataro is alone in his insistence on the equality of the breve in perfect and imperfect time. The fact that where they occur simultaneously it is the semibreve of one that is equal to the semibreve of the other does not prove, to be sure, that this is the relation when one succeeds the other. But it makes the "immutable quantity" of the semibreve or minim more likely than that of the breve, and nothing points to the latter except Spataro's assertions.

A similar question concerns the relation of the semibreve in major prolation to that in minor. Tinctoris reproves those who write the sign of major prolation when they mean a sesquialtera proportion of minims:

[3] *Tractato di musica nel quale si tracta de la perfectione de la sesqualtera producta in la musica mensurata exercitate*, 1531. Spataro was a pupil of Ramos de Pareia. But Ramos, in his *Musica Practica* of 1482 (reprinted by Johannes Wolf in the *Publikationen der Internationalen Musikgesellschaft*, Beihefte, 1901, Heft II), states that under any of the signs ☉, ℂ, O, or C, the "morula" (which he uses as equivalent to "mensura," which he relates to the pulse) falls on the semibreve, and goes on to say:

. . . et tunc brevis tres mensuras valebit in istis ☉ O, duas vero tantum in his ℂ C; . . .	. . . and then the breve will be equal to three *mensura*s [= semibreves] in ☉ and O, but only to two in ℂ and C; . . .

At quidam signo prolationis majoris et temporis perfecti vel imperfecti sesquialteram signant ut patet in sequenti:

But certain others signify sesquialtera by a sign of major prolation and tempus perfectum or imperfectum as is shown in the following:

112ᵛ

[D]iscan -   tus

Te -   nor

* The ligature is (erroneously) without coloration in the Brussels manuscript.

Ex. 1

Et alii eodem signo temporis imperfecti et prolationis majoris subsesquitertiam, ut hic:

And others show subsesquitertia by the same sign of tempus imperfectum and major prolation, as here:

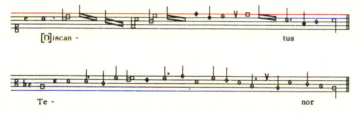

[n]iscan -   tus

Te -   nor

Ex. 2

Quod licet faciant Lerouge et Puyllois in Missis *Mon cuer pleure* et in quodam *Et in terra* plagalis autenti triti irregularis tamen est intolerabilis. Non enim sesquialtera vel subsesquitertia et haec prolatio equipollent, quoniam 1 semibrevis prolationis majoris 3 minimas valens non sit uni aut 2 semibrevibus minoris commensuranda, immo semibrevi et minimae, ut patet per Dufay in suo *Et in terra* de Sancto Anthonio, sic:[4]

That, however, which Lerouge and Puyllois do in their Masses *Mon cuer pleure* and in a particular *Et in terra* in an irregular plagal of the third authentic [sic] is intolerable, for sesquialtera or subsesquitertia and this prolation are not equivalent, since 1 semibreve of major prolation, worth 3 minimae, must not be measured with one or 2 semibreves of minor, but rather with a semibreve and a minim, as is shown by Dufay in his *Et in terra* from the Missa *Sancto Anthonio*, thus:

[4] Johannes Tinctoris, *Proportionale Musices*, reprinted in Coussemaker, *Scriptores*, IV (Paris, 1876), 171; translation by Albert Seay in *Journal of Music Theory*, I

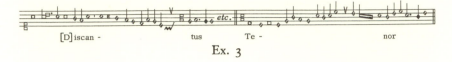

[D]iscan -   tus   Te -   nor

Ex. 3

Koswick, in his *Compendiaria Musice artis aeditio* (1518),[5] writes:

Similiter in his ⊙ ₵ cum circa omnes voces ponuntur, non est augmentatio, sed perfecta simplex prolatio qua tres minimae tactu mensurantur.	Similarly in the signs ⊙ and ₵, when they occur in all voices, there is no augmentation, but rather simple perfect prolation, in which three minimae are measured by the tactus.

Carl Dahlhaus[6] assumes that Koswick means that the perfect semibreve measured by the tactus is a minim longer, i.e., slower in the ratio 3:2, than the normal tactus to the imperfect semibreve of minor prolation, but Koswick is silent on this point. Agricola, who has often been quoted on these matters, sows considerable confusion. The most-quoted passage, from Chapter VI of the *Musica figuralis* (1532), is reproduced in facsimile[7] and translation on pages 142-145.

(1957), 41 and 68. The musical examples follow a careful copy of all of Tinctoris' examples in Brussels, Bibliothèque Royale, MS Fétis II, 4147, made in 1959 by John McKee; a photostatic copy of these is in the Princeton University Library: ML 96.5.T49q (SV). The examples have been compared with a microfilm of the Brussels manuscript. Ramos de Pareia is not entirely clear on this point. The same sentence quoted in n. 3 continues directly:

et sicut in aliis divisa fuit aequaliter in duas aut in tres semibreves, ita in istis [in] duas minimas aut in tres, prout signum perfectionem aut imperfectionem denotat, dividetur.	and just as in those [the breve] was divided equally into two or into three semibreves, so in these the division is into two minims or into three, accordingly as the sign denotes perfection or imperfection [i.e., perfect or imperfect prolation].

The grammar here is not clear; "dividetur" has no subject, since it is of course not the breve that is divided into two or three minims. One can read this passage as meaning ⊙ or ₵ = O or C , that is, as contradicting Tinctoris; but it is not clear that that is Ramos's meaning, particularly since in the analogous situation he so clearly states that O = C .

[5] *Pars* II, *Cap.* 5.

[6] "Zur Theorie des Tactus im 16. Jahrhundert," in *Archiv für Musikwissenschaft*, XVII (1960), 32.

[7] From the copy in the Library of Congress.

As if the ambiguities which are the principal subject of this discussion (i.e., those of the mensural symbols and numerals themselves) were not enough, the words the theorists use are often ambiguous, and at times it is possible to suspect that they did not have too clear an idea of their meaning themselves. Curt Sachs[8] claims that Georg Schünemann[9] misunderstands the words "noch so risch als." I have translated them "again as fast as" (i.e., "twice as fast as"), in agreement with Schünemann's interpretation. Sachs asserts that "in the archaic language of the sixteenth century" these words mean "just as fast as." But there are three reasons why Sachs cannot be right about this:

1. Agricola's example would make no sense if the whole tactus and the half tactus went at the same tempo.

2. In Chapter v, Agricola writes:

Den der gesang wird inn diesen zeichen O2.C2. noch so bald als inn den OC gesungen / darümb gilt eine semibre. inn den ersten zweien zeichen ein halben / und inn den andern ein ganzen Tact.	For the music is sung in the signs O2 and C2 again as fast [i.e., twice as fast] as in O and C, wherefore a semibreve in the first two signs receives a half tactus, and in the others a whole tactus.

Here again, to translate "noch so bald als"[10] as "just as fast as" would make nonsense of the passage.

---

[8] *Rhythm and Tempo* (New York, 1953), pp. 220f.

[9] "Zur Frage des Taktschlagens in der Mensuralmusik" in *Sammelbände der Internationalen Musikgesellschaft*, x (1908-1909), 73-114, and *Geschichte des Dirigierens* (Leipzig, 1913), pp. 48-49.

[10] Grimm's *Deutsches Wörterbuch*, viii, 869, says: "In earlier usage a simple *noch so* or *noch als* suffices for the meaning 'again as much as (*noch einmal so*).'" Two of Grimm's examples, unfortunately, can be used to support either meaning. But in two others—both from Logau, a contemporary of Agricola's—"noch so" clearly means "again as":

der kann bald ein Echo machen,
der nur redet was er wil,
als er etwa reden möchte
wird er hören noch so viel.

and

Kunst und Tugend machet Adel,
Adel machet auch das Blut;
wann sie beide sich vermählet,
ist der Adel noch so gut.

Der gantze Tact.

Ist/welcher eine vngeringerte Semibreuem odder eine Breuem in der helfft geringert/mit seiner be-
wegung/begreifft/wie im Exempel des 2. 3. 4. Ca-
pitels/vnd vberal wird gespürt.

Der halbe Tact.

Ist das halbe teil vom gantzen/Vnd wird auch
darũmb also genant/das er halb souiel/ als der gantze
Tact / das ist/ eine Semibreuem inn der helfft gerin-
gert / odder eine vngeringerte Minimã mit seiner be-
wegung/das ist/mit dem nidderschlagen vnd auffheben begreifft/wie im Exempel des 5. Capitels von der
Diminution odder geringerung/ vnd inn vielen an-
dern wird gesehen.

Vom gantzen vnd halben Tact
ein Figur.

Item/das nidderschlagen vnd das auffheben zu
hauff/macht allzeit einen Tact/Vnd wird der Halbe
noch so risch/als der gantz Tact/geschlagẽ /wie volgt.

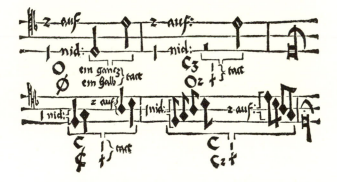

G ꜩꜩ   Der propor-

The Whole Tactus

is that which embraces by its motion an undiminished semi-breve, or a breve diminished by half, as can be seen in the example[s] of Chapters II, III, IV, and everywhere.

The Half Tactus

is one-half of the whole, and is called this because it embraces by its motion, i.e., with the down-stroke and the upward motion, half as much as the whole tactus, i.e., a semibreve diminished by half or an undiminished minim, as will be seen in the example of Chapter VIII, On Diminution, and in many others.

An Illustration of Whole and Half Tactus

The down-stroke and the upward motion together always make one tactus, and one beats the half [tactus] again as fast [NB] as the whole tactus, as follows:

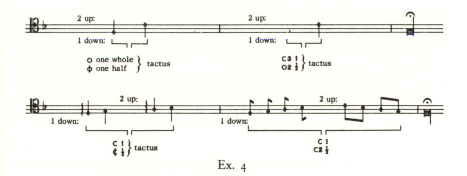

Ex. 4

Der Proporcien Tact.

Ist/welcher drey Semibre. als in Tripla / odder
drey Minimas als inn prolatione perfecta/begreifft.
Von diesem Tact sihe an das dritte vnd letzte Capitel
vnd volgends Exempel.

Vom Proporcien Tact ein vnter-
richtung.

Item/ alhie im Proporcien Tact/ wird eine Se-
mibreuis fast so risch/als sonst eine Minima im halben Tact ₵. die Minima wie eine Semini. die Se-
miminima wie eine Fusa gesungen/ wie volget.

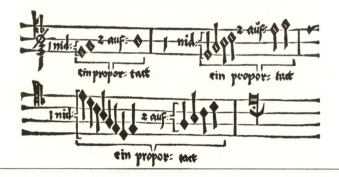

3. When Agricola means "[just] as fast as," he writes simply "so
risch als" (Chapter XII):

Auch ist zu wissen / wenn alle stymmen mit der Proportz zugleich / das ist / eine nicht rischer denn die ander gezeichnet wird / So wird alzeit der Proportien Tact / welcher drey Semibreves begreifft /geschlagen. Und also wird gemeinlich inn der masse eine Brevis so risch gesungen / als sonst eine minima inn solchen zeichen C ₵, wie oben im vi. Capitel vom Tact berürt.	It is also true that when all voices have the [triple] sign of proportion simultaneously, i.e., one not marked with a faster sign than another, one always beats the proportion tactus, which embraces three semibreves. And in this measure a breve is commonly sung as fast as a minim in the signs C and ₵, as discussed above in Chapter VI, On the Tactus.

The Proportion Tactus

is that which embraces three semibreves, in tripla, or three minims, in perfect prolation. About this tactus see the third and last chapters and the following example.

An Instruction Concerning the Proportion Tactus

Here, in the proportion tactus, one sings a semibreve almost [NB] as fast as one would ordinarily sing a minim in the half tactus ₵ , a minim as a semiminim, a semiminim as a fusa, as follows:

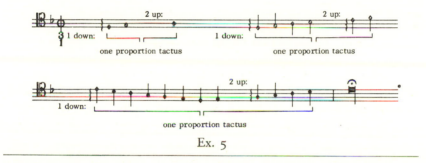

Ex. 5

In Chapter vi, Agricola has said that in the proportion tactus a semibreve goes "almost as fast as" a minim in the half tactus—that is, almost four times as fast as a semibreve in the whole tactus. If "almost four times as fast" means "three times as fast," this remark makes sense. In Chapter xii, he says that in triple proportion one beats the proportion tactus, and the breve is commonly sung as fast as a minim in C or ₵ . Two or three things seem to be wrong about this statement:

1. This time, Agricola says "as fast as," not "almost as fast as," as in Chapter vi.

2. This time, it is the breve of the proportion tactus that he equates with the minim of tempus imperfectum, whereas in Chapter VI it was the semibreve of the proportion tactus with the minim of the half tactus.

3. This time, he speaks as if the minim of ¢ were of the same duration as the minim of C , whereas in Chapter VI they were related as 1:2. Clearly there is at least one misprint in Chapter XII: either the word "breve" should be "semibreve" and the two signs for the minim should be Φ and ¢ ; or else the word "breve" is correct, and the two signs for the minim should be O and ç .

In Chapter VI, Agricola has said that "The proportion tactus is that which embraces three semibreves, in tripla, or three minims, in perfect prolation." His example shows only the tripla, which he notates:

Φ
3 . If the proportion tactus has a fixed tempo, as his "Instruction"
1

concerning it seems to imply, this would mean that

$$\frac{\Phi\boxminus}{3}\diamond\diamond\diamond = \odot \quad \text{or} \quad \mathsf{C}^{\diamond}_{\phi\phi\phi}$$
1

and that the minim of major prolation goes almost as fast as the minim of ¢ , i.e., perhaps three times as fast as C◊ , which would mean O or C◊◊ = ⊙ or ɛ◊◊◊ , and would make major prolation equal to a sesquialtera proportion of minims—the usage Tinctoris condemns.

In Chapter IV, "Von den dreien Gradibus" (i.e., modus, tempus, and prolatio), Agricola gives "ein Exempel von der volkomen Prolation und volko. Tempore," in which the discantus is notated in ɛ and the tenor and bass in ⊙ , and says of it:

Allhie werden drei Minimas odder eine volkomen Semibre. auff den Proportionirten Tact gesungen.	Here three minims or a perfect semibreve are sung to the Proportioned Tactus.

Presumably the proportioned tactus is the same as the proportion tactus, but, since all voices are in major prolation, the notation itself does not provide a key to the relations between major and minor prolation.

An indirect light is shed on the question, however, by his

ander schön Exempel von den dreien Gradibus zugleich / jedoch also das die Prolation zu der Augmentation oder grösserung des gesanges / wie das vii. Capitel ausweist / gebraucht wird.	another fine example of the three degrees at once / but so that prolation is used for the augmentation or enlarging of the music, as Chapter vii explains.

In this example Φ◊ = O2◊ = φ♩, and the three signatures are labeled: Φ "Tempus perfect, Prolationis imperfect," O2 "Modus minor pfectus, Tempus imperfect," and φ "Augmentatio Prolationis pfecte Temporis perfecti." Here the major prolation has semibreves which are three times as long as the semibreves of minor prolation; if the major prolation were not read in augmentation, its semibreve would be one and one-half times as long as that of minor prolation.

So Agricola can be read to mean either C◊◊ = C◊◊◊ or (less clearly) C♩ = C♩ or (and this is the only proportion that occurs commonly in the music of his period) C◊ = C♩. But the confusion does not end here. In Chapter vi he writes:

Gleich wie die beide Ciffern 3 und 2 in Proportione sesquial. zu hauff haben / also wird der Proporcien Tact wenn er langsam / gegen dem gantzen / odder gegen dem halben / so er risch geschlagen wird / geachtet und abgemessen / als ein Exempel. Der halbe Tact in diesem Zeichen ¢ begreifft solcher ♩♩ ii aber der Proportien Tact alzeit der ♩♩♩ iii. Darümb wird der Proportien Tact / soviel als eine Minima ♩ langsamer dann die andern beide gefüret / Und dieweil er nach der Art der sesquialtern / gegen den andern Tacten geschatzt / und sie anderthalb mal in ihm beschleust / mag er billich sesquialteratus oder Proportionatus Tactus (wie die Musici schreiben) genant werden. Auch braucht man ihn nicht überal / sondern allein in Prolatione perfecta / wie im 4. Cap. berürt / odder in Proportione Tripla / Hemiola / wenn sie alle Stymmen zu gleich	When the two figures 3 and 2 occur together in proportione sesquialtera, the proportion tactus is considered and measured against the whole tactus if one beats it slowly, or against the half tactus if one beats it fast; for example: the half tactus in this sign ¢ comprises two minims while the proportion tactus always comprises three minims. Therefore the proportion tactus is taken as much as one minim slower than the other two [i.e., than whole or half tactus]. And since it is valued in sesquialtera fashion in comparison with the other tactus, and contains them one-and-one-half times within itself, it may well be called sesquialteratus or proportionatus tactus (as the musicians write). Nor is it used everywhere, but only in prolatione perfecta, as mentioned in Chapter iv, or in proportione tripla or hemiola, when all the voices have the proportion at once, and here a semi-

haben / und so wird alzeit eine Semi- | breve is always sung according to the
bre. nach der Masse / wie sonst eine | measure that a minim otherwise has,
Minima gesungen / und ein solcher | and this tactus is always used in the
Tact wird alzeit gehalten inn den | melodies for dances having full jumps
Melodeyen / auff die vollsprüngige | in them, as in the old song *Hastu*
tentze zugerichtet wie inn den alten | *mich genommen,* etc.
liedlein / Hastu mich genommen etc.

In this passage a number of things are striking:

1. The proportion tactus does not have a fixed tempo; it can be taken either fast or slowly.

2. $\math0{C}\!\!\!|\; \flat = \frac{3}{2}\flat$; this is in conflict with what almost everyone else in the period says or does, be he theorist or composer.

3. The term "sesquialtera," normally used for the assigning of the same total duration to 3 notes that had previously (or "normally") been assigned to 2 notes of the same nominal value, thereby decreasing their duration, is here used for increasing the duration of the semibreve in the proportion 2:3. At first one wonders whether Agricola is not simply using the term "Proporcien Tact" here to mean "tactus inaequalis," i.e., a tactus of which two notes of the same value go to the down-stroke and a third to the up-stroke, irrespective of tempo. But then he confuses things completely again by saying that this Proporcien Tact is used in perfect prolation or in tripla or hemiola [sesquialtera] proportion, and that the semibreve in any one of them is to be sung "to the measure that a minim otherwise has."

And this is the man who is said to have commanded "das gesamte theoretische und technische Rüstzeug seiner Zeit in staunenswerter Vollkommenheit"![11]

The occurrence of major prolation in all voices simultaneously, with which Koswick and Agricola concern themselves, was rare if not completely obsolete by the time they wrote. I am indebted to Professor Lewis Lockwood for having pointed out the following example to me. Among Vincenzo Ruffo's *Capricci in Musica* (Milan, 1564), the twenty-second piece, *El Cromato*, is in ¢ in all voices, with flagged white semiminims. The fact that it contains a group of four crome (= fusae, here written as double-flagged white notes) suggests that its tempo may be slower than that of the pieces written in ¢3 (No. 13) or C3 (Nos. 21 and 23), which contain no such groups. Flagged white semiminims, too, are rare in the sixteenth century. Johannes Wolf did not know a single example occurring in

[11] Bernhard Engelke in the article "Agricola, Martinus" in *Die Musik in Geschichte und Gegenwart*, i (1949-51), 163.

actual music, although he pointed out that theorists continued to mention them as late as 1553 (Lusitano).[12] Ernst Praetorius[13] adds Zanger's *Practicae musicae Praecepta*, published a year later. Ruffo uses them, as they had often been used in major prolation (though long before his time) to avoid confusion between the semiminim and the colored minim, in such formations as: (C)♩ ♪♪♪♪♩♩•♩♩♩ etc.[14]

   Tinctoris, in the passage quoted earlier, agrees with the practice of the vast majority of composers; Spataro disagrees with what is probably an even more overwhelming majority. Agricola is on several sides of several questions. All three men were practising musicians as well as theorists. Spataro, as maestro di cappella at San Petronio, in Bologna, must have performed many works that did not follow his precepts (and perhaps none that did). Apparently he dismissed them as the products of "half-educated practising singers." The quotations from all three may serve as a reminder of the considerable caution with which "the theorists" must be approached for information on the performance of the music they write about, and on the intended meanings of its notation. We call a "theorist" everyone who ever set words on paper about music—whether he was putting together a primer for choirboys, describing the practice of his day as he understood it, prescribing a reform which he considered desirable, or indulging a bent for pure speculation. This last is what Spataro seems to have been doing when he wrote about the immutability of the tempus. His many pages on this subject seem to belong less to the history of music than to the history of (in this case not very interesting) ideas.

   Several attempts have been made in recent years to conjure away some of the complexities and ambiguities of the mensural system, as practised, or as described or constructed or reconstructed by theorists.

   Curt Sachs, in his *Rhythm and Tempo*, writes that "drowned in the superabundance of sources, neither the contemporary writers

---

[12] *Introdutione facilissima.*

[13] "Die Mensuraltheorie des Franchinus Gafurius," in *Publikationen der Internationalen Musikgesellschaft*, Beihefte, Zweite Folge, Heft II, p. 10.

[14] Cf. Charles Hamm, *A Chronology of the Works of Guillaume Dufay* (Princeton, 1964), pp. 53f, *et passim*. Tinctoris, in the first of his examples quoted above, near the end of the tenor, notates a semiminim and two colored minims without any difference in their visual form. Ockeghem, in the Et resurrexit of his *Missa L'homme armé*, makes the distinction (see the facsimiles in Apel's *Notation of Polyphonic Music*, p. 139, and in Plamenac's edition of Ockeghem's *Collected Works*, Vol. I, Plate IX). I am indebted to Professor Richard H. Hoppin for reminding me of this point.

nor their modern commentators have always seen how easy, consistent, and logical the tactus situation was."[15] But Sachs achieves a deceptively easy, consistent, and logical explanation largely by ignoring the difficulties, inconsistencies, and illogicalities in which "the tactus situation" and other parts of the mensural system abound, as well as by devoting a good deal of attention to such things as signatures consisting of a symbol followed by two or more numerals, which hardly ever occur in actual music.

Hans Otto Hiekel, in his article " 'Tactus' und Tempo" (1962),[16] follows Sachs's interpretation of "noch so risch als," attributing to Agricola (as does Sachs) the idea that the tempo of the tactus is invariable—this in the face of Agricola's words: ". . . der Proporcien Tact wenn er langsam / gegen dem gantzen / oder gegen dem halben / so er risch geschlagen wird. . . ." He claims that Agricola's example "Vom gantzen und halben Tact," reproduced in facsimile above, illustrates only the upper of the two lines of text below it, and that the first complete tactus in line 1 is to be considered only the down-half of the tactus for the signatures in line 2, and the second tactus of line 1 the up-half—this in the face of Agricola's description of "der halbe Tact" as embracing a diminished semibreve or an undiminished minim "mit seiner Bewegung / das ist / mit dem nidderschlagen und aufheben."

Franz Jochen Machatius, in 1955,[17] taking as his point of departure the often-discussed "Vi ricorda o bosch' ombrosi" from Monteverdi's *Orfeo*, tries to differentiate a tactus integer of the "Flemish epoch" and a "much faster accentuated form of motion, . . . the Canzonetta pulse, . . . [descended] from popular song forms . . . ." Machatius's thesis is that along with mensural (i.e., truly proportional) reduction there was a *sub rosa* "spielmännische Reduktion," in which when a section with a sign of triple (or sesquialtera, or sextuple) proportion follows one with a binary signature, one of the smaller values of the earlier section equals one of the smaller values of the later. In proportional reduction, a given duration is divided by 2 in the binary section and the same duration is divided by 3 in the sesquialtera; Machatius, basing himself partly on such usages as Agricola's, wants to make one-half of the binary duration equal one-third of the sesquialtera, so that the sesquialtera measure be-

[15] Page 220.

[16] *Bericht über den internationalen Musikwissenschaftlichen Kongress* (Kassel, 1962) (pub. 1963), pp. 145-47.

[17] "Über mensurale und spielmännische Reduktion," in *Die Musikforschung*, VIII (1955), 139-51.

comes one-and-one-half times as long as the binary. In the substitution of this "spielmännische Reduktion" for the proportion described
by most theorists, Machatius sees the essence of the *seconda pratica*.

His "proof" is involved. But it depends partly on such an example
as the following, from the third Laudate Dominum in Monteverdi's
Selva morale of 1640:[18]

Ex. 6

Here it is easy to jump to the conclusion, on "musical grounds,"
that $◦•◦◦ = ♪•♪♪$; i.e., $Φ\frac{3}{1}◦ = C♪$. But is this necessarily true?
Is not $Φ\frac{3}{1}⊟• = C♩$ at least as likely, on musical grounds? This
would mean that in modern transcription the piece would go:

Ex. 7

In the following example, too:

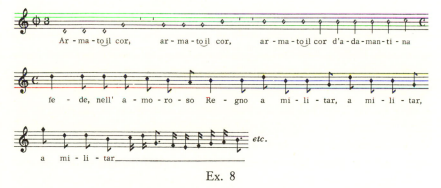

Ex. 8

Machatius would have $Φ3◦ = C♪$, which would make the
minims of "d'adamantina" equal to the coloratura semifusae of the
last syllable of "militar."[19] Machatius claims that "Vi ricorda o bosch'
ombrosi," being written in *note negre*, "has therefore, for example,
given up the possibility of coloration." But what is the ♦ that appears repeatedly in this aria, if not a colored semibreve? And, on
the other hand, if the black notes with stems are colored minims,
why is the equivalent rest written as a semiminim?

---

[18] *Tutte le opere*, ed. Malipiero, xv, 521-43.
[19] *Ibid.*, IX, 27. Doubtless Machatius means here ($Φ3♩ = C♪$), which is possible—
perhaps even likely.

Another attempt to exorcise the proportional relation 3:2, this time when ternary and binary divisions occur simultaneously, has been made by Michael Collins,[20] who claims that "hemiolia and sesquialtera proportions have no audible effect in 16th-century music," and later, somewhat more cautiously, that "Under no circumstances do sesquialtera and hemiolia under equal tactus [i.e., simultaneously with binary mensuration(s) in other voice(s)] imply triplets. . . . When sesquialtera or hemiolia appears in one or more but not in all the voices of a composition, the equal tactus of the voices in binary measure prevails. In this case the notes of the proportion fall . . . two on the downstroke and one on the upstroke of the [equal] tactus." This "squaring off" of triplets into binary rhythm had been known to Ernst Praetorius in 1905,[21] as well as to Bellermann in 1858.[22] They based their interpretations of it on Aron, Lusitano, and Vulpius; Collins cites additional theorists.

The trouble with all such *Eier des Columbus* as those of Sachs, Hiekel, Machatius, and Collins is not that the interpretations they favor never existed, but that these interpretations never had any such universal currency as is claimed for them. Proportions between binary and ternary mensurations have probably never been easy for choirboys or other insufficiently trained musicians. Doubtless in all periods means have been found to avoid them. (Even Carl Philipp Emanuel Bach calls the playing of eighth-note triplets against two even eighth-notes "oft unangenehm, allezeit aber schwer.")[23] Particularly when the binary and ternary divisions occur in succession, not simultaneously, it is impossible to be sure what happened to the tempo in the days before the metronome. But there is no reason to believe that the means described for avoiding "2 against 3" were always used, or that they were not sometimes mere makeshifts suggested for those who were incapable of performing the rhythms as notated.

In the attempt to understand the mensural system, it is natural to turn first to the theorists. To arrive at an understanding by induc-

---

[20] "The Performance of Sesquialtera and Hemiolia in the 16th Century," in *The Journal of the American Musicological Society*, XVII (1964), 5-28. In his doctoral dissertation and in a later article in *JAMS*, Collins has attempted to extend his exorcism of 3:2 up to 1750. One wonders when he thinks 3-against-2 performance began.

[21] Source listed in n. 13, above.

[22] Heinrich Bellermann, *Die Mensuralnoten und Taktzeichen des XV. und XVI. Jahrhunderts.*

[23] *Versuch über die wahre Art, das Clavier zu spielen*, I (1753), *Das dritte Hauptstück*, § 27.

tion from the vast body of musical works is a task of frightening size. But theorists frequently disagree; indeed, that is one of their principal pleasures. (What is left of a theorist's writings after one eliminates what he has copied from other theorists often consists largely of polemics against them.) It is frequently hard to determine which parts of their material are intended as descriptive and which prescriptive. Often only subordinate clauses, intended to set off the beauties of things as they should be by passing reference to the alleged evil of things as they are, give what may be an accurate glimpse of prevailing practice.

What is needed, it seems to me, is not more articles advocating this or that interpretation of this or that theorist, or of a group of theorists arbitrarily selected, but rather an orderly method of gathering and sorting evidence from both the theorists and (particularly) the music itself. We do not know for most composers how consistent they were in their own mensural practice.[24] We do not know what degree of consistency may have been imposed by publishers or copyists[25] on different composers. We need to gather evidence of the mensural practice of each of the principal composers, each of the principal publishers, perhaps each of the principal anthologies.

With a view to ordering this evidence, gathered from both the theorists and the music itself, in a useful and convenient way, I have, with the help of several groups of seminar students, put together the following outline. It classifies some of the features of the mensural system and gives to each of many possible alternative interpretations a number under which supporting and illustrative evidence can be assembled. For almost every interpretation, I have found evidence either in a theorist's dictum or in a piece of music. In a very few instances, I have included a category for the sake of symmetry, believing that I am not likely to have thought of an interpretation too far-fetched to have been advanced by some theorist somewhere, even though I have not yet encountered it.

In equations in this outline, the mensural signature before the equals sign is the one whose meaning is in question, and the one after the equals sign is used as a standard of comparison. The latter may occur in a piece of music either before or simultaneously with

---

[24] Hamm, in *A Chronology*, gives complete information on one composer. Robert L. Marshall, in an unpublished seminar paper, has shown that Binchois' practice was virtually identical with Dufay's.

[25] Hamm (*A Chronology*, pp. ix, 26) shows that for Dufay, at any rate, the copyists were remarkably faithful to their sources in the matter of mensural signatures and notation (apart from ligatures).

the sign whose meaning is to be determined, or, if it is O or C , it may be an implicit normal standard ("integer valor"). In actual music, when there is a change of signature, modern editors are not agreed as to how the relation between the time-values under the two signatures is to be indicated. In many instances there is no way of being sure what that relation is, on the basis of our present knowledge. I cannot see that anything is gained by presenting a "solution" to a problem that one has not in fact solved, unless it is made perfectly clear that this is a mere editorial suggestion. But if it is to be presented, care must be taken to make clear which value in the equation belongs to which signature.

In the following outline, the letters "a," "b," "c," etc., categorize the conditions under which the various mensural signs occur. In Categories I through VI, numerals from 1 to 10 categorize alternative interpretations of the sign in one respect, those from 11 to 20 in another respect, etc. So far as possible, the same numbers have been used to represent similar interpretations of the symbols categorized under III, IV, and V. In general, within each decade of numbers, the lower numbers represent the more common interpretations. Frequently, numbers are paired on this basis: e.g., II.1. occurs more commonly than II.2., and II.3. than II.4. To leave room for interpretations not encountered in the preparation of this table, a skip is made from the highest number needed in one group of alternatives to the first number of the next decade.

An Outline of Possible Alternative or Conflicting Interpretations of Features of the Mensural System

I. Tempus Perfectum
    a. O as initial signature in all voices
    b. O as medial signature in all voices
    c. O occurring simultaneously with other signature(s) in other voice(s)

      1. $O^{\boxminus}_{\diamond\diamond\diamond}$ = $C^{\boxminus}_{\diamond\diamond\diamond}$; i.e., O◊ = C◊
      2. $O^{\boxminus}_{\diamond\diamond\diamond}$ = $C^{\boxminus}_{\diamond\diamond}$; i.e., O⊟ = C⊟
      3. (*Cf.* II.1.1.)

II. Prolatio Maior
    a. ⊙ or ₡ as initial signature in all voices
    b. ⊙ or ₡ as medial signature in all voices
    c. ⊙ or ₡ occurring simultaneously with other signature(s) in other voice(s)

1. ☉ or ℂ𝅘 = ○ or ℂ◦ (simultaneous, preceding, or "normal")
    1. When a section in major prolation is followed by a section in minor prolation in the same voice, then 𝅘 = 𝅘 (i.e., the augmentation continues in effect after the change to minor prolation)
2. ☉ or ℂ𝅘 = ○ or ℂ𝅘 (simultaneous, preceding, or "normal")
3. ☉ or ℂ𝅘 = 𝇋 or ¢◦ (simultaneous or preceding)
4. ☉ or ℂ𝅘 = 𝇋 or ¢𝅘 (simultaneous or preceding)
5. ☉ or ℂ◦𝅘𝅘 = ○ or ℂ◦𝅘𝅘 (simultaneous, preceding, or "normal")
6. ☉ or ℂ◦𝅘𝅘 = ℂ◦◦𝅘𝅘𝅘 (simultaneous, preceding, or "normal")
7. ☉ or ℂ◦𝅘𝅘 = 𝇋 or ¢◦𝅘𝅘 (simultaneous or preceding)
8. ☉ or ℂ indicates a rather slow triple measure (i.e., augmentation in an undefined ratio)

III. A vertical or oblique stroke (virgule) cutting the signature-symbol, occurring
    a. as initial signature in all voices
    b. as medial signature in all voices
    c. simultaneously with other signature(s) in other voice(s)

    1. decreases the duration of all values
        1. in the ratio 2:1
        2. in the ratio 3:1
        3. in the ratio 3:2
        4. in some other definite ratio
        6. in an undefined ratio (i.e., indicates a "somewhat" faster tempo)
    2. if a prolation dot is present, cancels the augmentation which the dot would otherwise effect

    11. causes the tactus to be attached to the next higher value than if the stroke were not present
    12. does not change the value to which the tactus is attached

    21. does not affect the organization of modus, tempus, or prolation
    22. causes the symbol to refer to modus instead of tempus

    99. seems not to affect the significance of the symbol in any way

IV. A single numeral, occurring
    a. as initial signature in all voices
    b. as medial signature in all voices
    c. simultaneously with other signature(s) in other voice(s)
    d. with (repetition of) a signature-symbol
       m. numeral to right of symbol
       n. numeral below symbol
    e. without (repetition of) a signature-symbol

    1. decreases the duration of all values
    2. decreases the duration of some values only:
       1. ◊ and below
       2. ♩ and below
    3. decreases the duration as n:1 (calling the numeral n)
    4. decreases the duration as n:2 (when the numeral is 3)
    5. The numeral 3 or a multiple of 3 indicates a grouping in
       3's of one of the smaller values and an equality between
       this smaller value and one of the smaller values of the
       previous (or of "normal") mensuration, in which this
       value is grouped in 2's

    21. refers to the organization of the tempus, causing the sym-
       bol to refer to the organization of the modus
       1. with some decrease in duration:
          1. ◫ before numeral = ◫ after numeral
          2. ◫ before numeral = ◫ after numeral
          3. ◫ before numeral = ◫ after numeral
       2. without any decrease in duration
    22. refers to the organization of the modus, leaving the symbol
       to refer to the organization of the tempus
       1. the numeral 3 indicates perfection of both modus minor
          and modus maior
       2. the numeral 3 indicates perfection of modus minor only
    23. refers to the organization of the prolation, leaving the
       symbol to refer to the organization of the tempus
    24. indicates the number of
       1. ◊ per tactus
       2. ♩ per tactus
    26. is redundant, simply "annotating" coloration

    31. indicates that the rules of perfection and alteration apply
    32. indicates that the rules of perfection and alteration do not
       apply

41. indicates ternary notation of a passage to be "squared off" into binary rhythm
42. indicates ternary notation of a passage not to be "squared off" into binary rhythm

51. Each successive numeral indicates a comparison with the initial (or with a "normal") signature

52. Each successive numeral indicates a comparison with the preceding numeral or numeral-pair, if any, i.e., the effects of successive numerals and/or numeral-pairs are cumulative

V. Two numerals, one above the other, occurring
   a. as initial signature in all voices
   b. as medial signature in all voices
   c. simultaneously with other signature(s) in other voice(s)
   d. with (repetition of) a signature-symbol
      m. numerals to right of symbol
      n. numerals below symbol
   e. without (repetition of) a signature-symbol

1. establish between the duration of each value occurring before the numerals and that of the same (nominal) value after them the proportion of the upper numeral to the lower
2. establish this proportion as concerns some values only:
   1. ◊ and below
   2. ♩ and below
3. establish between the duration of each value occurring before the numerals and that of the same (nominal) value after them the proportion of the lower numeral to the upper
4. establish this proportion as concerns some values only:
   1. ◊ and below
   2. ♩ and below
5. The numeral 3 or a multiple of 3 indicates a grouping in 3's of one of the smaller values and an equality between this smaller value and one of the smaller values of the previous (or of "normal") mensuration, in which this value is grouped in 2's

24. Both numerals refer to the number of aliquot parts of the duration attached to the tactus before and after this signature respectively:
   1. in terms of ◊
   2. in terms of ♩

25. The lower numeral indicates a number of tactus, and the upper indicates the number of notes to this number of tactus:

1. ◊

2. ♩

26. are redundant, simply "annotating" coloration

31. indicate that the rules of perfection and alteration apply

32. indicate that the rules of perfection and alteration do not apply

41. indicate ternary notation of a passage to be "squared off" into binary rhythm

42. indicate ternary notation of a passage not to be "squared off" into binary rhythm

51. Each successive numeral-pair indicates a comparison with the initial (or with a "normal") signature

52. Each successive numeral-pair indicates a comparison with the preceding numeral, or numeral-pair, if any; i.e., the effects of successive numerals and/or numeral-pairs are cumulative

VI. Ɔ or ₵

    a. as initial signature in all voices

    b. as medial signature in all voices

    c. occurring simultaneously with other signature(s) in other voice(s)

    1. Ɔ decreases in the ratio 4:3, as compared with O or C (simultaneous, preceding, or "normal"), the duration of:

      1. ◊ and below

      2. ♩ and below

    2. ₵ decreases in the ratio 8:3, as compared with O or C (simultaneous, preceding, or "normal"), the duration of:

      1. ◊ and below

      2. ♩ and below

    3. ₵ decreases in the ratio 4:3, as compared with O or C (simultaneous, preceding, or "normal"), the duration of ⊟ and below

    4. Ɔ decreases the duration of all values, as compared with O or C (simultaneous, preceding, or "normal"), in the ratio 2:1

    5. ₵ decreases the duration of all values, as compared with

    O or C (simultaneous, preceding or "normal"), in the ratio 4:1

6. decreases the duration of all values, as compared with O or C , in an undefined ratio

VII. Tactus

1. conceived of as a bipartite signal, of which both up and down motions are significant: ↓↑ = 2 (or 3) beats—in the modern sense of the term "beat"
2. conceived of as a unitary beat, of which both up and down motions are mentioned only for the sake of (meticulous) completeness: ↓↑ = 1 beat
   1. described as audible
   2. described as inaudible

11. described as ↓↑
12. described as ↑↓

21. first motion and second motion always of equal duration
22. when the tactus is applied to three equal values or equivalent ("tactus inaequalis"), first motion embraces two of these, and second embraces one
23. when the tactus is applied to three equal values or equivalent, first motion embraces one of these, and second embraces two

31. roughly invariable in tempo, whether applied to ▤ , ◇ , or ♩
32. "invariability" refers only to steadiness of tempo throughout the performance of a single piece or section
33. variable in tempo:
   1. in definite ratio
   6. in an undefined ratio

41. "normally" ↓↑ = M.M. 60 to 80
42. "normally" ↓↑ = M.M. 30 to 40 or M.M. 20 to 27

51. ↓↑ always = ◇
52. ↓↑ applied to different values in different circumstances
53. O or C◇↓↑ called:

   1. "gantzer Tact" or equivalent
   2. "tactus generalis" or equivalent
   3. "tactus maior" or equivalent

4. "tactus minor" or equivalent

54. O or C◫ called:

    1. "tactus totalis seu integralis" or equivalent
    2. "tactus generalis" or equivalent
    3. "tactus maior" or equivalent
    4. "tactus minor" or equivalent

55. Ø or O2 or ¢ or C2◦ called:

    1. "halber Tact" or equivalent
    4. "tactus minor" or equivalent

56. "Proporcien Tact" or "Tactus proportionatus"
    1. faster than "normal" tactus:
        1. in ratio 3:1
        2. in ratio 3:2
        4. in some other definite ratio
        6. in an undefined ratio
    2. slower than "normal" tactus:

        1. ⊙ or ⊖ = O or C

    3. "tactus inaequalis" (VII. 22 or VII. 23 above) without specific tempo-implication

VIII. Coloration
    a. In perfect modus or tempus or major prolation
    b. In imperfect modus or tempus or minor prolation

    1. decreases the duration of values normally perfect only, 3:2
    2. decreases the duration of values normally imperfect:
        1. in the ratio 3:2
        2. in pairs of notes of adjacent value, or in groups consisting of one note of longer value and two or more notes totalling the next smaller value:
            the larger value 4:3, and
            the next smaller value 2:1
    3. decreases the duration of values normally perfect and/or imperfect in some ratio other than 2:1, 3:2, or 4:3

    41. indicates ternary notation of a passage to be "squared off" into binary rhythm
    42. indicates ternary notation of a passage not to be "squared off" into binary rhythm

A SAMPLE PROBLEM OF *MUSICA FICTA*: WILLAERT'S *PATER NOSTER*

LEWIS LOCKWOOD

A N IRONIC equation seems to dictate that as modern editions in ever-increasing numbers continue to widen our view of medieval and Renaissance music, the problem of unspecified accidentals becomes more ramified and more acute, and the need for the further creation of systematic knowledge in this field becomes steadily more critical for historians, theorists, and performers alike. To say this is not to minimize in the slightest either the formidable difficulties of this subject—one of the frontier problems of musicology—or the many significant contributions that have been made to it by such scholars as Riemann, Wolf, Dèzes, Apel, and, in particular, Edward Lowinsky. Yet how small an area of common ground has yet been established is only too clearly illustrated by such recent and far from isolated instances as one in which two modern editors of the same sixteenth-century piece present two widely different interpretations of its pitch-content,[1] and another in which the same editor, presenting the same pieces in successive editions, disagrees with himself as to the accidentals needed for various passages.[2] And equally indicative of the present state of this problem is the almost uniform absence, in modern editions of older music, of explicitly formulated hypotheses that might justify a particular interpretation. For, as has been recently pointed out,[3] whatever the editor's position—whether he adds no accidentals at all, or whether he distributes them generously to every part of the piece—some assumptions about the nature of the evidence and the ideal content of the piece must somewhere underlie his procedures. Admittedly, it is extremely difficult to state such assumptions with the clarity and precision that

---

[1] For example, the hymn *Veni creator spiritus* by Costanzo Festa, as edited by E. Dagnino in *Monumenta Polyphoniae Italicae*, II (1936), 78ff; and again by Glen Haydon in the same series, III (1958), 77ff. See my review of the Haydon edition in *Notes*, VIII (1960), 642-43.

[2] See Hermann Zenck's editions of the four-voice motets by Willaert, the full titles of which are listed later in this article as editions 1a and 1b. For a list of some discrepancies in accidentals, see the review of the second of these editions by Gustave Reese in *Notes*, VII (1951), 743-44.

[3] Arthur Mendel, "The Services of Musicology to the Practical Musician," in *Some Aspects of Musicology* (New York: Liberal Arts Press, 1957), p. 16.

we would like, whether for individual works, types of passages, repertoires, regions, periods, or groups of printed or manuscript sources. And these difficulties are still further compounded by the limited body of knowledge we now possess regarding such relevant phases of theory and practice as the history of solmization; the nature and meaning of transpositions; the determination of the "rules" of *musica ficta* that are relevant to a given repertoire; the relationship of accidentals in instrumental music to their use in vocal music; and the massive problems of obtaining, evaluating, and applying the writings of older theorists and commentators. Though none of these areas has lain uncultivated, much more remains to be harvested in all of them.

In the face of obstacles of this magnitude, comprehensive "solutions" to this network of problems are clearly beyond our present grasp, and the purpose of these remarks, far from suggesting that there is a single formula that would unravel the mystery, is essentially to reflect on the nature of the dilemma and on the character of some provisional conclusions that might be reached for a given composition. As a means of illustrating these considerations, specific comments center on the problems offered by one well-known motet of the earlier sixteenth century: Willaert's four-voice *Pater noster*. Yet in confining discussion to this piece I do not mean to imply that its particular problems can automatically be regarded as "representative" in any precise sense of the term, for neither our knowledge of the works of Willaert nor our knowledge of the period as a whole is sufficiently detailed to warrant such a claim. Nevertheless, it will be clear enough that the general character of the problem dealt with here is anything but unique, either for Willaert or for earlier sixteenth-century polyphony generally. Moreover, the example selected is a composition that was widely distributed in printed and manuscript sources in the second and third quarters of the century, and its aptness as a model for discussion is enhanced by the observation that its apparent harmonic structure is well within what we accept as roughly the basic diatonic boundaries of the period.

By way of further introduction to the problem we can begin with a remark by Willi Apel, who describes the present use of the term *musica ficta* as meaning "not so much the theory of early chromaticism, but the problems arising from the very scarce indications of chromatic tones in the musical sources prior to 1600, or, in other words, from the striking incongruity in this matter between the theoretical and the practical sources."[4] To this we are obliged to add that the problem entails not only the scarcity of accidentals but the conflicts in specification of them (whether scarce or plentiful) in the sources, and with this addition the problem can be seen to arise from two parallel inequalities—one lying in the interrelationships of contemporary sources, the other in the relationship of the pitch-notations in the sources to the pertinent theoretical literature. On the one hand, we are concerned with the accidentals themselves, whether explicit or fictive; on the other, with a body of doctrine that ought, ideally, to provide us with a system of procedure that should govern the use of these accidentals.

Obviously, this formulation also raises many difficulties. What precisely are the rules that should be applied to compositions of a given period, and in what order should they be invoked? To what degree are we justified in assuming that performers of a given period and place did, in fact, "tacitly understand" such rules and apply them in performance when the accidentals we (or some of us) think are needed were not specified (or were unequally specified) in sources we believe they used? What is the best of explanations we can offer for the incongruities of "authoritative" sources, and how can we determine, for a given piece, which sources are indeed authoritative, and to what degree? Since adequate consideration of any of these questions would expand this discussion far beyond reasonable limits, it will be necessary for the present to proceed on the basis of intuitive and provisional assumptions about the answers to some of them. Yet it seems essential to consider briefly, and again in general, not merely the problems inherent in constructing answers, but those inherent in the posing of the question itself; in short, to consider what it is that we are attempting to discover about the application of accidentals to those compositions we think may have required them. What, in other words, would a "solution" to a given piece look like, and how shall we know when we have reached it?

In a lucid note on this problem, Arthur Mendel outlined three "basic attitudes" which the modern scholar, editor, or performer may adopt: "1) that the accidentals in the sources are self-sufficient; 2) that more or less definite general principles for supplementing the explicit accidentals were systematically applied in performance

---

[4] *The Harvard Dictionary of Music*, 5th edn. (Cambridge, 1947), p. 466.

and should be applied in editing; 3) that the application of these principles was to a considerable extent a matter for the discretion and taste of the musician in charge of each performance."[5] To adopt the first of these views, as some scholars have done, is in effect to nullify the problem altogether, and by implication, to dismiss as irrelevant the mass of theoretical doctrine which led us to believe in the first place that there could ever have been accidentals which were not specified but which might have been understood; further, this view leaves us helpless to explain incongruities of notation in "the sources" (i.e., the musical sources) except as possible errors and oversights. The intuitive attraction of this view lies, of course, in its appeal to the modern musician's habitual instinct to perform "exactly what he sees"; nevertheless, it must be clear that unless we are dealing with a period in which pitch-notation had become satisfactorily consistent and complete in specifying accidentals (and exactly when this came about is another critical problem), only circular reasoning will justify appealing to such an "instinct."[6] Nevertheless, this view does reasonably apply to those early repertoires of which the notations *are* in principle complete with respect to pitch—namely, keyboard, lute, and other solo instrumental tablature notations. To adopt the second and third views, on the other hand, is to agree that needed accidentals could have been left unspecified, and those subscribing to one or the other differ only as to the way and degree in which these accidentals were employed. For medieval and Renaissance vocal literatures these distinctions admirably summarize the points of view that now seem to prevail. Yet even these offer a choice of alternatives so difficult as to border on the unknowable.

For, as matters stand, we do not have—and it seems to me unlikely

---

[5] A. Mendel, *loc.cit.*

[6] In the simplistic form in which it is often presented, this view often fails to take into account the two senses in which accidentals could be regarded as being fictive: 1) a "primary" sense in which an apparently plausible accidental is not found in a given source and is thus assumed to remain inapplicable; and 2) a "secondary" sense, supported by evidence from a number of early theorists, by virtue of which certain diatonic configurations (such as the neighbor-note progression A–G–A) are written without accidentals but are understood to require them, *yet without altering their diatonic solmization patterns* (e.g., A–G♯–A is sung La–Sol–La). The sharp is thus fictive in a dual sense: it is neither specified in the notation nor, when used, reflected in its hexachordal interpretation, but is "feigned" by the performer. On this point see the important but little-known dissertation by K. Dèzes, *Prinzipielle Fragen auf dem Gebiet des Fingierten Musik* (Berlin, 1922), pp. 69, 71.

that we are going to have—truly abundant and convincing evidence as to what the performers of vocal music in even a limited period and area (say, Venice, 1520-30, or Lyon, 1550-75) actually *did* when confronting this problem (if they confronted it) for any given composition. To be sure, we can and should amass the best and most relevant theoretical and practical evidence we can find; sift it, evaluate it, and apply it—but unless we can also procure even reasonably convincing documentary accounts as to what happened at particular performances at particular places over a given period, we shall not know precisely what the performers did.

Moreover, the few instances known to me in which contemporary writers tell us about the reactions of sixteenth-century performers to problems of accidentals tend strongly to suggest that the absence of accidentals, or their unequal specification, was more nearly a source of confusion and uncertainty than a stimulus to easy virtuosity in immediately supplying them. Several writers, all both theorists and practitioners, offer remarks that point unmistakably in this direction.

Pietro Aron, in the *Aggiunta* added to his *Toscanello* in its second edition of 1529, takes the position that the singer cannot be expected to know how to apply accidentals correctly and to understand the "intention and hidden purpose of the composer" in a piece he has never seen before, unless the accidentals are expressly written out. Indeed, the essential purpose of the *Aggiunta* is to exhibit the need for explicit accidentals and to cite a number of cases in which recent and contemporary composers (as Aron believes) had, in fact, stipulated accidentals in order to prevent misunderstanding. In the course of reading in the correspondence of the 1520's between Aron and the older Bolognese theorist, Giovanni Spataro,[7] I have found that the following significant passage, like some others in the *Aggiunta*, is in reality not Aron's own but is an almost verbatim plagiarism

---

[7] Codex Vat. lat. 5318, fol. 212, a letter from Spataro to Aron dated May 23, 1524. For an extensive account of this correspondence see Knud Jeppesen, "Eine Musiktheoretische Korrespondenz der früheren Cinquecento," *Acta Musicologica*, XIII (1941), 1-39, and especially p. 28. The reader can readily check the relationship between the second quotation given here from Aron's *Aggiunta* and the letter by Spataro, by consulting the facsimile of fol. 212 published by J. Levitan, "Adrian Willaert's Famous Duo *Quidnam Ebrietas*," *Tijdschrift voor Nederlandse Muziekgeschiedenis*, xv (1938), facing p. 176. The letter has long been noted for its reference to the puzzle duo, but its connection with the text of Aron's *Aggiunta* seems to have passed unnoticed.

from a letter written him by Spataro, one of several commenting critically on the first edition of the *Toscanello*. Yet although this unacknowledged borrowing scarcely bolsters our confidence in Aron, it does nothing whatever to diminish the force of the statement or to alter its meaning.

Hora si risponde se il cantore e ubligato o ueramente puo cantando uno canto non da lui piu uisto cognoscere, o intendere l'intento & secreto del compositore da lui pensato al primo moto, si conclude che no, se bene fussi quello che celebro la musica benche alcuni il contrario pensono, allegando la ragione dicono, Che ogni compositore fanno giuditio che gli loro canti habbino a essere intesi da gli dotti, & buoni pratichi, p[er] uno audito presto & repe[n]tino, massimamente quando occorreranno quinte, ottave, duodecime & quinte decime imperfette. Dico che a questo solo ne e maestro Iddio, & tale intelligenza muta, sola appartiene a lui, e non a huomo mortale, p[oi]che sara impossibile a ogni dotto & pratico poter sentire in uno subito una quinta, ottava, duodecima, o quintadecima imperfetta, che non commetta primamente lo errore di qualche poco di dissonanza, vero e, che piu presto sara sentito da uno che da l'altro, pur nondimeno non sara huomo che in questo non incappi. De laqual cosa dico, che coloro liquali non segnaranno il segno di ♭ molle dove naturalmente altro si vede, commetteranno non poco errore. . . .

Now we inquire whether the singer, performing a composition he has never seen before, is obliged to—or truly can—immediately understand the intention and hidden purpose of the composer; and we answer that he cannot. Even if I were one who heap praise upon music, while others think the contrary, alleging the reason that all composers think that their compositions ought to be understood by learned and able performers, and by a quick and skillful ear, above all when there occur diminished fifths, octaves, twelfths, and fifteenths. I say that only the Lord himself is the master of this, and that such tacit knowledge belongs only to Him, and not to mortal man. For it will be impossible for even a learned and practiced singer to hear, in a moment, a diminished fifth, octave, twelfth, or fifteenth, without his having first committed the error of perpetrating some small degree of dissonance. It is true that this will be more quickly heard by one than by another, but nonetheless there is no one to whom this will not happen. For this reason I say that those who do not indicate the flat sign where it is otherwise naturally used will commit no small error. . . .

And somewhat later:

Per tanto il Musico overo Compositore e ubbligato segnare lo intento suo, acio che il cantore non incorra in quello che dal detto compositore non

Thus, the musician or composer is obliged to indicate his intention, in order that the singer may not chance to do something that was never in-

fu mai pensato. Concludo adunque come ho detto che tal segno e cosi conveniente a gli dotti, come a gli indoti, & dico che il cantore non e tenuto nel primo moto, cantare le note ne gli luoghi dove tal segno puo accadere, se tal segno non appare, perche potrebbe errare, impero che puo stare, & non puo stare. . . . Et questo si intende ne gli concenti non prouisti, cioe non prima cantati, overamente considerati.[8]

tended by the composer. I conclude, therefore, as I have said, that such a sign is as useful to the skillful as to the unskillful; and I say that the singer is not to be expected, on first reading, to sing the proper notes in the places where this sign may occur, inasmuch as it may belong there, or may not belong there. . . . And this is intended with regard to pieces never seen before, that is, neither sung nor studied before.

In a treatise on music written about 1555 and preserved in manuscript in the Vallicelliana Library in Rome, the Papal singer Ghiselin Danckerts describes a dispute between two singers of the chapel of San Lorenzo in Damaso in Rome, about 1540, regarding the proper use of accidentals in the performance of a Lamentation by Scribano. I have attempted to deal with this anecdote and its implications elsewhere;[9] but it can be said here that the importance of the tale lies in its wealth of narrative detail, in the arguments advanced on either side, and in the insight it affords us into the practical problems that could arise in routine musical performance at this period.

Nicola Vicentino, in *L'Antica musica ridotta alla moderna prattica* of 1555, in the course of a discussion of the disposition of various intervals in composition, writes as follows:

. . . & quando si comporrà una compositione a cinque a sei et a sette voci, le Terze minori non si debbono molto usar nelle parti gravi perche faranno dubbiosi i cantanti di sustentar quelle, eccetto si non discenderanno. . . .[10]

. . . and when writing a composition for five, six, and seven voices, one should not make much use of minor thirds in the lower parts, because the singers will be in doubt as to whether these should be sharpened, unless they are descending. . . .

---

[8] Pietro Aron, *Aggiunta al Toscanello* . . . Venice, 1539, fols. H iv verso and I iv verso, respectively. The text of the 1539 edition is identical to that of 1529 except for its consistent expansion of the abbreviations of the earlier version.

[9] "A Dispute on Accidentals in 16th-Century Rome," *Analecta Musicologica*, II, 24-40. For a survey of Danckerts' life and works, see P. J. de Bruyn, "Ghisilinus Danckerts," *Tijdschrift voor Nederlandse Muziekgeschiedenis*, XVI (1946), 217-52, and XVII (1955), 128-57.

[10] *L'Antica musica ridotta alla moderna prattica*, fol. 82r. On the term *sustentar* as meaning "to make a chromatic alteration," see H. Riemann, *Geschichte der Musiktheorie* (2nd rev. edn., 1920), p. 373 *et passim*.

Praetorius, in his *Syntagma Musicum* (III, 1619) advances essentially the same point made by Spataro (and Aron) almost a century earlier. After observing at some length that many older and more modern composers have left the application of accidentals to the singers, he adds:

Ich aber bin gänzlich der Meynung/ dass es nicht allein sehr nütz unnd bequem/ sondern auch hochnötig sey/ nit allein vor die Sänger/ damit sie in jrem singen nit interturbiret werden: sondern auch vor einfältige Stadt Instrumentisten un[d] Organisten/ welche Musicam nit verstehen/ viel weniger recht singen können/ und dahero/ wie ich selbsten zum offtern gesehen und erfahren/ keinen unterscheyd hierinn zu machen wissen: Zu geschweigen/ dass der Componisten ihre Composition also beschaffen/ dass diese beyde Signa Chromatica an etlichen örtern gebrauchet/ an etlichen aber nicht in acht genommen werden dürffen: Darumb denn die beste Caution wehre/ wenn es die Componisten an allen örten; Da es von nöthen ist/ klärlich darbey schrieben / so hette man keines nachsinnens oder zweiffels von nöthen.[11]

I, however, am wholly of the opinion that it is not only very useful and convenient, but highly necessary, not only for singers, to prevent their being confused in their singing—but also for simple town players and organists, who do not understand music, still less how to sing, and thus, as I myself have often seen and experienced, do not know how to make any choice in this matter; not to mention that some compositions are made by their composers in such a way that in some places these two chromatic signs should be used, but in others should not be used. Therefore, the best precaution would be for composers, in all places in which they are needed, to write them out, so that there would be no doubt or uncertainty as to their being needed.

Like the singers of the period, then, we too are in doubt as to what the composer, in a given instance, truly intended. For of course all composers' autographs from this period have disappeared, except for a few fragmentary remnants; yet even if autographs were abundantly preserved, they would be enlightening only to the extent of our confidence that the composers, at least, made their intentions explicit, a view which the observations of Spataro-Aron and Praetorius scarcely encourage.

In the light of these considerations, I would propose another view: namely, that we can construe the problem not as an attempt to dis-

---

[11] Page 31. Praetorius continues with further comments and valuable examples.

cover what the musicians of the time, strictly speaking, did, but as an attempt to satisfy ourselves as to what they *might* have done—or, in a more restrictive sense, *should* have done; should have done, that is, if they had proceeded on the basis of theoretical doctrine and compositional practice which they could reasonably have known, and on which we can proceed to the extent that we know them. This difference in the posing of the question is, I think, no mere linguistic quibble, for it relieves us of the burden of attempting to show what the evidence for the most part will not reveal—namely, how the performers of earlier times actually selected alternative possibilities. Instead, it reduces the problem, for a given piece, to a set of more or less probable alternative hypotheses as to its pitch-content, based on the best evidence we can procure; and we can evaluate these as having greater or lesser plausibility, observing what conditions each satisfies. It can be suggested, therefore, that there may well be—and can have been—alternative readings not merely of some early compositions but of a vast number, and that our confidence in these readings will depend on our ability to develop theories of permissible content, the relative plausibility of which—again based on the best notational and theoretical evidence we can amass—may guide us in determining which reading we prefer.

With this brief outline of an approach to the problem in mind, we can turn to a consideration of the conflicting evidence for the notation of Willaert's four-voice *Pater noster*. In its complete form the motet consists of two sections, *Pater noster* and *Ave Maria*, and, as we should expect, both of these paraphrase their well-known plainsong antecedents. In many of the most important sources the two sections are, indeed, found in succession, but in some the second is not marked "secunda pars"; in others we find only the *Pater noster*, and in at least one manuscript source the two sections are present but are separated by three unrelated works by other composers.[12] Thus, as is frequently the case with sixteenth-century motets in two sections, either section, but especially the first, could circulate alone as a potentially independent piece. Partly in view of this tradition, and partly owing to considerations of space, the present remarks are confined

[12] The manuscript listed as No. 15 in the list of sources. See W. Brennecke, *Die Handschrift A. R. 940/41 der Proske-Bibliothek zu Regensburg* (Kassel, 1953), pp. 42-43 (Nos. 287 and 291 in the manuscript).

to the *Pater noster*, although they could be extended, on the basis of available evidence, to the *Ave Maria* as well.[13]

The piece is available in score in at least the following seven modern reprints:

1. (a) *Adrian Willaert, Sämtliche Werke*, ed. Hermann Zenck, Vol. I (*Publikationen Älterer Musik*, IX, 1937), 97ff.
   (b) *Adriani Willaert, Opera Omnia*, ed. Hermann Zenck, Vol. II (American Institute of Musicology, 1950), 11ff.
2. A. W. Ambros, *Geschichte der Musik*, V (1882), 538ff.
3. R. van Maldeghem, *Trésor Musical*, VIII, Année XII (1866), No. 38.
4. A. Smijers, ed., *Treize livres de motets parus chez . . . Attaingnant*, II, 1ff.
5. (a) *Jakob Obrecht: Werken*, ed. Johannes Wolf, *Motetten*, Bundel III, 131ff. (Attributed to Obrecht after Leipzig, Bibl. der Thomaskirche MS 49/50.)
   (b) W. Apel and A. T. Davison, *Historical Anthology of Music*; 1st edn. (Cambridge, 1946), No. 76 (*in this edition only*; attributed to Obrecht, following 5a).

Of these editions the most important for text-critical purposes are the two by Zenck, especially that in the *Sämtliche Werke*, which contains extensive critical notes listing variants from all the sources then known. But whatever modern edition is used, its essential background will consist of the earliest known sources, and of these Zenck listed seventeen, all from before 1600: seven printed editions, nine manuscript copies, and one intabulation for lute. In the absence of extensive bibliographies, we cannot be absolutely sure when such a group of sources is quite complete, and even now we can add to the seventeen sources listed by Zenck (Nos. 1-17 below) five more manuscripts (Nos. 18-22), of which Nos. 19, 20, and 21 may be among the most important we have for this composition. The following list is no doubt still incomplete, but on the basis of presently available evidence, it would appear to embody the primary source material for the motet. It should be noted that the first item in the list—the print designated as "E 1545c" (following Eitner)[14] is granted particular importance by Zenck, as by Ambros before him, because it is

[13] For observations on the *Ave Maria* as represented in the vihuela transcription by Pisador, see C. W. Fox, "Accidentals in Vihuela Tablatures," *Bulletin of the American Musicological Society* (September, 1940), pp. 22-24.

[14] R. Eitner, "Adrian Willaert," *Monatshefte für Musikgeschichte*, XIX (1887), 88ff.

the only *individual* collection of Willaert's motets produced during his lifetime (as opposed to anthologies) in which the *Pater noster* appeared. In the following list, the superscripts added to the dates for Nos. 2-8 are taken from RISM I in which the complete titles can be found.

Printed Sources

No.	Date	Publisher	Place	Title
1	1545	Gardane	Venice	Adriani Willaert . . . Motecta . . . Lib. II
2	1532[10]	Moderne	Lyon	Motetti del Fiore, Lib. I, 4 v.
3	1534[4]	Attaingnant	Paris	Liber II . . . quatuor vocum
4	1538[7]	Petreius	Nürnberg	Modulationes aliquot . . .
5	1539[12]	Gardane	Venice	Fior de motetti . . . Primus Liber, 4 v.
6	1545[4]	Gardane	Venice	Flos florum primus liber . . .
7	1564[6]	Rampazetto	Venice	Motetti del Fiore a 4 v.

Intabulations

8	1548[12]	Scotto	Venice	Intabolatura . . . Libro secondo . . . per . . . M. Julio Abondante

(Other intabulations not listed by Zenck: Mudarra, 1546; Valderrábano 1547[25]; Abondante 1548[12]; Pisador 1552[35].)

Manuscript Sources

9   Leiden, Stedelijk Museum MS 865, "E," ff. 99v-102.
10   Leipzig, Bibliothek der Thomaskirche MS 49/50, f. 196.
11   Leipzig, Bibliothek der Thomaskirche MS 51, f. 114v.
12   Munich, Universitäts-Bibliothek MS 326, f. 26v.
13   Regensburg, Bischöfliche Proske-Bibliothek, A. R. 772, f. 226v.
14   Regensburg, Bischöfliche Proske-Bibliothek, A. R. 875-877, II, No. 21.
15   Regensburg, Bischöfliche Proske-Bibliothek, A. R. 940-941, No. 287.
16   Toledo, Biblioteca Capitular, Cod. 21, f. 54.
17   Verona, Biblioteca Capitolare, Cod. DCCLX, f. 41v.
18   Vienna, Nationalbibliothek, MS Suppl. Mus. 15500, f. 199v.
19   Rome, Biblioteca Apostolica Vaticana, Palatini Latini MS 1976-1979, f. 1.
20   London, Royal College of Music, MS 2037, f. 5v.
21   Chicago, Newberry Library, MS Ry 14, 1st series, No. 4.
22   Rome, Biblioteca Musicale "Santa Cecilia," MSS 792-795, No. 1.

In classifying and evaluating sources from an age that has bequeathed us almost no autographs, our inevitable tendency is to attribute proportionately greater importance to those sources that most nearly approximate the autographs we lack. Thus, early and central sources will take precedence over later and more peripheral ones, and the more closely we can associate the origins of any given source with relevant circumstances of the composer's career, the greater its presumed authority in the hierarchy.

Since at least the main lines of Willaert's career have long been known, and since the provenance and dating of most of these sources can be fairly well established through external evidence, a preliminary sorting of the material can be made with some confidence. We have it on good authority that Willaert was born around 1490, in Bruges or in Roulaers; that he studied music under Jean Mouton at Paris, presumably around 1515; that he came to Italy around 1518, or perhaps slightly later; that from 1522 to 1527 he was a singer in the court chapel at Ferrara; and that in 1527 he was appointed *maestro di cappella* in the cathedral of San Marco at Venice, and held this distinguished post until his death in 1562. Apart from documents attesting to visits to Flanders in 1542 and 1556, there is no positive evidence to associate Willaert with any other areas than Venice during his long tenure at San Marco, and the only biographical detail that remains an unsolved puzzle is a reference to him in a chronicle of 1531 as "Cantor Regis Hungariae," which suggests a possible connection with the Hungarian court during his earlier years, and which has been neither confirmed nor satisfactorily explained away.[15] Against this background, the sources at our disposal range themselves into groups exhibiting greater or lesser degrees of proximity to the factual circumstances of his career, and I would provisionally group them as follows.

I a) Earliest positively dated sources: Prints: No. 2 (1532); MSS: No. 12 (1543)
  b) Presumably early sources: 17, 19, 20, 21
  c) Late or posthumous sources: 7, 9, 10, 11 (?), 14, 15, 18, 22
II a) Regionally peripheral sources: 2, 4, 10, 11, 12, 13, 14, 15, 16, 18, 22
  b) Perhaps regionally associated with the composer's career: 3, 9, 17, 19, 21
  c) Regionally associated with the composer's career: 1, 5, 6, 20

[15] The major biographical studies are those of E. Vander Straeten, *La Musique aux Pays-Bas*, I (Bruxelles, 1867), 248-62 and VI (Bruxelles, 1822), 174ff, and R. B. Lenaerts, "Voor de biographie van Adrian Willaert," *Hommage à Charles van den Borren* (1945), pp. 205ff.

Needless to say, this categorization is based on an elaborate chain of inferences from the evidence for the dating and provenance of all of these sources, evidence which is summarized in notes and at the end of this article. To the extent that these inferences are justified, they enable us to relegate to a low level of authority the sources that are definitely posthumous or late, and those emanating from areas with which we have no reason to believe that Willaert had any direct connection: Nürnberg, Regensburg, and other parts of Germany; Lyon; Toledo. At a somewhat higher level of importance are those whose associations are weak or distant: these include Nos. 3, 9, and 17.[16] Finally, we can isolate a small group of sources that would seem to represent the best tradition for the piece that we can now discern: Nos. 1, 19, and 20.[17]

[16] No. 3, Attaingnant's Liber II in his monumental series of motets, can be accorded some importance on the grounds that its place of origin is Paris, where Willaert had studied earlier; on the other hand, the publication date of the volume is some sixteen to nineteen years after the period to which we must assign Willaert's sojourn at Paris, and in the absence of evidence as to Attaingnant's sources, his edition cannot be considered to be directly associated with the composer at the time of publication. No. 9, the Leiden manuscript, is part of a series of indigenous manuscripts assembled at Leiden from about 1549 through the 1560's and 1570's (see *Die Musik in Geschichte und Gegenwart*, article "Leiden"). It is not an early source for this composition, but is at least from an area with which Willaert was at one time directly associated. No. 17 is also indigenous, contains a repertoire of motets by Josquin and his younger contemporaries, and may have been assembled around 1530. As a source emanating from Verona, it is at least geographically closer to the scenes of Willaert's Italian activities—Ferrara and Venice—than those stemming from outlying areas.

[17] No. 19 is among the manuscripts produced by the famous scribe Pierre Alamire; furthermore, it bears the inscription *Registrum dive Regine hungariae*, and has a series of coats of arms evidently belonging to members of the Hapsburg family. Walter Rubsamen (*Notes* [1950], p. 72), has suggested that the manuscript may have been compiled for Mary, Queen of Hungary, for whom Alamire is known to have made manuscripts in 1522 and 1530. Further studies on the manuscript are being undertaken by Herbert Kellman; for the present it can only be noticed that the manuscript inscription further suggests that the chronicler's reference to Willaert as "Cantor regis hungariae" may yet be corroborated by factual evidence—and that, if the date of the manuscript is "around 1530," it emerges as an early source for the *Pater noster*.

No. 20 is an as yet undescribed pair of part-books (superius and bassus) of an original set of four, for knowledge of which I am gratefully indebted to Herbert Kellman. These part-books appear to be of quite unusual interest, for their contents seem to point strongly toward origin at Ferrara. The composers represented include Willaert (at Ferrara 1522-27), his teacher Mouton, "Maistre Jan" (chapel master at Ferrara), and others associated with the court chapel. Moreover, the manuscript contains several pieces on texts associated with members of the House of Este, and alluding to events that occurred in Ferrara.

The importance of No. 1—Willaert's own Liber II, in its second edition of 1545—has been recognized ever since Ambros commented on the *Pater noster* a century ago and pointed out that its explicit accidentals are unusually extensive, particularly in comparison to the only other source at his disposal (No. 4).[18] Ambros was inclined to grant No. 1 far greater authority on the grounds that it was undoubtedly printed "under the master's eye." Admittedly, even a wider comparison of sources than Ambros could make shows that, except for Abondante's lute arrangement,[19] this version contains more explicit accidentals than any other printed source. But although it is tempting to suppose that these must have been products of the composer's supervision, the absence of all evidence reduces this to mere speculation. Furthermore, we should also grant some attention to the fact that the same piece was brought out by the same publisher, in the same city, and in the same year in another collection— Gardane's *Flos florum* of 1545—this being, in turn, a reprint of his *Fior de motetti* of 1539, and both of these representing selections from Moderne's *Motetti del Fiore* for the Italian market. And neither of these Venetian editions contain more than a small fraction of the accidentals found in Willaert's Liber II of 1545.

Beyond this, Willaert's Liber II of 1545 is, as mentioned earlier, a new selection culled from the two volumes of his motets that had been first published by Ottaviano Scotto in 1539; the *Pater noster*, though manifestly not a newly written composition, was inserted into this second edition of 1545 along with four other motets. Thus, the majority of the four-voice motets in these volumes provide an excellent opportunity to compare the number, type, and location of accidentals that were used for the two editions of 1539 and 1545; and on the basis of a close comparison, I can report a number of discrepancies between the two editions, enough to cast considerable doubt on the assumption that Gardane's versions were necessarily more reliable than those of his predecessor. Also, since Willaert was just as firmly established in Venice in 1539 as he was in 1545, there is no reason why the earlier editions should not also be regarded as potential products of his supervision, in which case the discrepancies

[18] *Geschichte der Musik,* iii, 110, 112, 120.

[19] Published in transcription (and transposed a major sixth upward from F—one flat to D—one sharp) by O. Chilesotti, "Il Pater Noster di Adriano Willaert," *Sammelbände der Internationalen Musik-Gesellschaft,* iii (1901-1902), 468-72.

between the two editions would suggest that if such supervision did take place, it was neither very careful nor very complete.

On the basis of even this cursory review of the sources, we come at last to that disturbing conclusion that could have been predicted from the outset, and that is so characteristic of the problem as a whole: despite our efforts to isolate a reasonably pure tradition for the piece, even the sources we regard as being most nearly reliable fail to agree in stipulation of accidentals. Admittedly two sources— Nos. 1 and 20—do contain a greater number of accidentals than any others, and to the extent that these sources carry even a modicum of authority, they suggest that the musical circles close to the composer—those of Venice and Ferrara—may have known the piece in a version involving not only extensive use of accidentals, but a preference for rendering them explicit. But what of the other, relatively early versions of presumably lesser authority, such as Petreius's edition of 1538 and the two other Gardane versions of 1539 and 1545, which contain very few of these accidentals? There is a strong temptation to assume that their diatonic readings of the piece can be—and could have been—merely peripheral alternatives to the more authoritative readings of Nos. 1 and 20. Yet, to sustain this view we ought to be able to show that it should have been improbable that their diatonic versions would have been converted into readings resembling those of Nos. 1 and 20 through the application of the rules of *musica ficta*. For, as noted earlier, to accept these diatonic versions at face value is to assume that they were truly self-sufficient, and it is precisely this assumption which the general theory of unstipulated accidentals effectively undermines. As is characteristic of the problem at this stage, we waver between the "tacit understanding" and "face-value" interpretations of the available versions.

Perhaps one means of escape from this condition of infinite regress is to scrutinize the relationship between the accidentals that *are* stipulated in authoritative sources and what we accept as the rules of *musica ficta*. In other words, if we accept the premise that those accidentals which *were* stipulated, were inserted by musicians closer than we to the practices of the time, and were probably included for reasons that a performer of the time could have understood, then, how likely does it seem that contemporary musicians might have recognized the relevance of the reasons we can adduce?

Unfortunately, this question also re-opens Pandora's box to reveal another host of problems, too extensive to be dealt with here, centering on the question as to what the rules of *musica ficta* are, and how they should be invoked.

For the present, in the absence of a systematic discussion and with full awareness of their extreme brevity, the following are offered, on the basis of an investigation of contemporary theorists and of summaries of the rules by Tucher, Riemann, Reese, and Lowinsky:[20] 1) a note above La is to be sung as Fa; 2) the linear tritone and diminished fifth are, wherever possible, to be converted into perfect intervals; 3) vertical tritones and diminished fifths and octaves are to be converted into perfect intervals; 4) in progressions from imperfect consonances to adjacent perfect consonances, the closer imperfect consonances are to be used (M3 $<$ P5; M6 $<$ P8; m3 $>$ unison; m6 $>$ P5, and similarly their replications beyond the span of an octave).

Assuming these rules, or indeed even others, there will be four categories of relationship between the rules and the accidentals that are either specified in the sources or are not specified but might be thought to be required:

A) Accidentals specified in at least one authoritative source and required by at least one known rule of *musica ficta*;

B) Accidentals specified in at least one authoritative source but *not* required by any known rule of *musica ficta*;

C) Accidentals not specified in any authoritative source but required by at least one known rule of *musica ficta*;

D) Accidentals not specified in any authoritative source and *not* required by any known rule of *musica ficta*.[21]

---

[20] G. von Tucher, "Zur Musikpraxis und Theorie des 16. Jahrhunderts," *Allgemeine Musikalische Zeitung* (1872/73), pp. 1, 17, 33, 49, 65, 81, 129, 161, 177, 193, 209.

H. Riemann, *Geschichte der Musiktheorie*, 3rd edn. (G. Olms, Hildesheim [1961]), pp. 378-88; G. Reese, *Music in The Middle Ages* (New York, 1940), pp. 380-82; Edward Lowinsky, preface to H. Colin Slim, *Musica Nova* (*Monuments of Renaissance Music*) (Chicago, 1964), pp. viii-xxi.

[21] Each element in this series calls for at least brief comment. Type D is, of course, merely included for the sake of completeness, for it is clearly trivial with respect both to the rules and the evidence; indeed, it would characterize only those accidentals suggested by modern editors which fit this category. Type A accidentals could be said to arise through the use of the accidental as some type of "warning-sign"; i.e., if it were truly assumed that the rules of *musica ficta* were tacitly

With these distinctions in mind it should be possible to establish at least a first categorization of the various contrapuntal configurations for which accidentals have been suggested, either by older scribes and printers or by modern editors, and to evaluate both the evidence and its effect on our interpretation of the content of the piece.

If we examine the broader tonal characteristics of the *Pater noster* as a framework for its internal procedures, we observe at once that the piece lies in the Fifth Mode with B♭ with respect to the range and activity of its tenor, and that this is confirmed early in the piece by means of its establishment of F as an initial area of tonal reference. Yet the establishment of F as a central region scarcely endures beyond the opening measures: the final harmony of the *Pater noster* (as of the *Ave Maria* following) is a complete triad on G; and although throughout the *Pater noster*, as in the plainsong antecedent on which it is based, there are a number of cadential formations in which the superius descends to a cadence on F; in all but two of these (mm. 32 and 79) a full cadence on F is evaded by the motion of the other voices. But if the harmonic organization of the piece only weakly substantiates its initial sense of F as center, its larger linear motion—if we may for the moment consider it independently—reinforces F somewhat more strongly: the basic melodic material of the piece is a close paraphrase of the plainsong *Pater noster*[22] (especially clearly preserved in Willaert's tenor), a melody dividing into two larger members with initial melodic parallels at "Pater noster" and "Panem nostram" (superius, m. 54). Yet this melodic parallel is not accorded a larger determining role in the harmonic scheme, as we see from the relative absence of confirmation of F; from the fact that the areas of cadential articulation are—as in much other pre-tonal polyphony—more or less equally, and weakly, established; and from the fact that all internal cadences have essentially the same duration.

---

understood by performers of the time, these accidentals should have been redundant and there should have been no need to write them out. Type B accidentals—inserted, as we assume, because no rule would require them—are the equivalent of those classes of accidentals generally discussed under the heading "causa pulchritudinis" by early theorists. Finally, Type C accidentals represent the normal class, on the assumption of the rules and of some degree of "tacit understanding."

[22] For comparative readings of a number of variants of the *Pater noster* plainsong formula, see *Die Musik in Geschichte und Gegenwart*, x, article "Pater noster" (by Bruno Stäblein).

As for the potential influence of the accidentals on the tonal organization, it should be noted at once that none of the apparent alternative means of applying them will serve to strengthen the sense of F as center, while at least one range of available accidentals would tend to settle the piece somewhat more firmly in the region of G.

As we have seen, the most authoritative sources differ widely in the number of accidentals they stipulate; nevertheless, we are now in a position to observe that those accidentals that *are* stipulated show a fairly high degree of uniformity with regard to the pitches affected. Moreover, the range of each voice is narrow enough to confine the problematic accidentals to a few notes, or even one, throughout the individual vocal part. Thus in the superius part the uniquely questionable note is f′ (f♯′ ?), to which the superius returns again and again as a melodic goal via the progression g′-f′ (f♯′ ?); and consistently supporting this upper line a tenth below is the bass, moving e (e♭)–d. For the bass, too, there is only one consistently questionable note, namely whether e is to be read as e♮ or e♭. The first appearance of this progression is at mm. 9-10, where it forms a model for subsequent repetitions:

Ex. 1. Willaert, *Pater Noster*, mm. 1-12 (after source No. 1)

Now, the f♯′ in the superius at m. 10/1 is stipulated only in the vocal sources labeled Nos. 1, 20, and 21 (it also appears in the lute version of No. 8, but as this is not a parallel to the vocal sources and, like other intabulations, involves the hand not merely of a transcriber but of an active musical agent other than the composer, its authority is here left open to question). This f♯′ represents an accidental of what I have called Type B—for it does not satisfy any presently known rule of *musica ficta*, but, rather its application results in a double violation of two otherwise unexceptionable linear intervals: it causes a diminished fourth with the preceding b♭' (m. 8/3) and a diminished fifth with the following c♮' (m. 11/3).[23] In other words, if the sharp at 10/1 were not introduced, no known rule of *musica ficta* would require it; and its stipulation here, and in other parallel progressions, confers a particular harmonic color and direction on the progressions in which it appears. Specifically it results in a D-major triad, with third in the highest voice, as local goal of the progression E♭$^{5\text{-}6}$–D, with both triads in root position and a motion in tenths between outer voices:

Ex. 2

This progression occurs *in this form* in the *Pater noster* no fewer than six times (mm. 9-10, 20-21 [g–f(♯?) in alto, with suspension in the tenor], 52-53, 57-58, 75-76, 110-11); and to this we can add three more instances in which the superius again moves g'–f(♯?)' with the bass supporting this line by descending g–d (mm. 35-36, 64-65, 104-105). Thus there emerges in the motet a cycle of nine progressions, spread out through the piece as a potentially linked chain of harmonic articulations, in which the superius moves from g' to f(♯?)', with five of these involving exactly the same linear pattern in the superius, the stepwise descent b♭'–a'–g'–f(♯?)'. Yet even in the vocal sources Nos. 1 and 20, the two most explicit in their accidentals, only seven of these nine progressions are assigned f♯'s. As for the bass e♭'s, the same sources provide a number of

---

[23] I assume here that the two notes in the superius at m. 10 should be treated identically (whether ♯ or ♮) for these reasons: first, where the sharp is stipulated it is characteristically below the two notes and may apply to both; second, because there is no reasonable basis for changing the hexachordal interpretation of the second f' with respect to the first. Tinctoris specifically tells us that an accidental endures as long as the same hexachord is maintained in a given linear combination: *Liber de Nat. et Prop. Tonorum*, Cap. VIII, p. 54. (This is the most important passage in Tinctoris's work for the discussion of accidentals, and the one most frequently misunderstood.) Ambros' interpretation of this measure is disputed by Kade; see Kade's remarks in the 3rd edition of Ambros' *Geschichte*, Vol. III (1893), 613 (*Nachtrag zu Seite* 112).

explicit flats for the above-listed measures and for others—but No. 1 omits the flat for one of these progressions (m. 52/3); while No. 20 omits the flat at 52/3, at 57/3, and at 110/3. Nor do any other vocal sources rival these in indicating sharps for the superius; while for the bass only No. 19 duplicates the flat indications of No. 20, while all the others offer fewer flats.

In summary, then, no vocal source indicates a sufficient number of accidentals to explicitly insure the parallelism of those progressions which are, in a potential or virtual sense, exactly parallel throughout the piece; and, if these *are* to be treated as parallelisms, at least a small minority will require editorial accidentals "derived" from those already stipulated in the best sources. Such "derivation" can of course be justified only by an assumption of harmonic consistency for the piece, indeed, a degree of consistency which its other points of cadential articulation will not supply by themselves, and which would confer on the piece a tighter plan of organization than any partial or literal application of the stipulated accidentals would provide. Whether we are justified in assuming such consistency is of course the paramount question that *we* shall have to decide, and it is here that we shall have to turn, in this or other cases, to the best knowledge we can amass of the theoretical presuppositions behind the composer's works; conceivably, too, an examination of parallel problems in other works by the same composer may shed further light on these. For the moment, however, we are obliged to fall back on the observation that the evidence of the best sources, though not thoroughly consistent, links a majority of these associative progressions within the work through explicit accidentals.

Yet one more consideration: it could be argued, on the other hand, that another, equally "consistent" reading of the piece could be constructed by simply following the version supplied by Petreius (No. 4), which lacks all f♯'s in the superius from beginning to end. This brings us back to the question raised before about this source, and we must again emphasize that the superius f♯'s in all the associative progressions mentioned earlier are accidentals of Type B—that is, there is at present no unequivocal reason to believe that singers following the rules should have supplied them. Yet even if the superius f♯'s were to disappear, the bass e♭'s would for the most part remain, since many of these are of Types A and C, and are clearly required in order to avoid forbidden linear and vertical intervals. Thus, the result would be an overall pattern of considerably less complexity and interest, removing the element of harmonic color established by the recurrent D major tried within an F–g context, and substituting for them d–minor triads throughout. Against this argument we can recall once again the low level of authority which we presently assign to the Petreius edition for this piece.

Yet in doing so we cannot truly eliminate the possibility that such alternative versions of the piece—one more authoritative, the other less so; one "central," the other "peripheral"—can be, and might have been, inferred from the existing sources. As matters stand, we have yet to establish any absolute basis for asserting that one of these versions is uniquely "correct," and even though the weight of the evidence supports the authority of the versions with extensive accidentals, this need not mean that the opposed interpretations are devoid of some possible historical and theoretical interest and validity. It means only that the versions with extensive accidentals can claim both a greater musical interest and a higher degree of legitimacy. For the present they stand closer to an ideal of "correctness" than any of the others.

The issue, admittedly, is not closed, and, as was predicted earlier, the conclusions are inevitably provisional. Yet perhaps these remarks may have served to emphasize once again how broad, difficult, and far-reaching this problem is; how much remains to be done within it; and, by implication, how fundamentally our view of this problem is bound to affect our entire conception of the structure and development of pre-tonal polyphony.

Postscript: A Note on the Manuscript Sources

The manuscript sources listed as Nos. 9, 17, 19, and 20 have been discussed earlier (see nn. 15 and 16). No. 10, Leipzig, Thomaskirche MS 49/50 is dated 1558; on this manuscript and No. 11 (not dated thus far) see Johannes Wolf, *Handbuch der Notationskunde*, I, 452; and Obrecht, *Werke, Motetten*, Bundel III, p. v.

No. 12, Munich, Univ.-Bibl. MS 326 is dated 1543, and its likely place of origin has been established as Augsburg; see Ludwig Finscher in *Die Musikforschung*, XI (1958), 189ff.

Of the Regensburg manuscripts, A. R. 772 is dated 1548 and is the work of the Regensburg chapel master Johann Stengel; see *Deutsches Musikgeschichtliches Archiv, Katalog Nr. 2* (Kassel, 1956), p. 48, and R. Eitner, *Quellenlexikon*, IX, 277. A. R. 875-77 is a late manuscript for the *Pater noster*, dated 1572 (see Zenck's critical remarks for the *Pater noster* in the Willaert *Sämtliche Werke*). A.R. 940/41 is dated 1557-60 by Wilfried Brennecke (see n. 12).

The Toledo choirbook (No. 16 in this list) belongs to an extensive series preserving the polyphonic repertoire of the Toledo cathedral; R. B. Lenaerts, in the *Report of the Fifth Congress of the I.M.S.* (Utrecht, 1952), p. 279, dates the manuscript 1549.

The Vienna MS Suppl. Mus. 15500 has been described by Winfried Kirsch in *Die Musikforschung*, XIV (1961), 290-302, who establishes its date as 1544 and its provenance as Germany.

ECHOES OF ADRIAN WILLAERT'S CHROMATIC "DUO" IN SIXTEENTH- AND SEVENTEENTH-CENTURY COMPOSITIONS

EDWARD E. LOWINSKY

ADRIAN WILLAERT's setting of Horace's verses from the fifth epistle, *Quid non ebrietas designat,* known as the chromatic "duo" (recently shown to have been conceived, and published about 1530, as a four-part composition)[1] is one of those

[1] Edward E. Lowinsky, "Adrian Willaert's Chromatic 'Duo' Re-Examined," *Tijdschrift voor Muziekwetenschap,* XVIII (1956), 1-36. As this book goes to press, the last issue of *Die Musik in Geschichte und Gegenwart* appeared with a comprehensive and up-to-date article on Adrian Willaert by Walter Gerstenberg (XIV, cols. 662-76). Surprisingly, the author raises doubts (col. 674) as to the authenticity of the "chromatic duo": "Should *Quid non ebrietas,* the experimental piece so much discussed until the present, indeed be authentic, as Spataro (1524) and Artusi (1600) believe, then it is surprising that it apparently remained unknown to Zarlino and Vicentino, Willaert's crown witnesses in the realm of the theory of music." It is true that neither Zarlino nor Vicentino ever alludes to Willaert's most controversial composition. Strange as this may seem, one may not conclude from this that the work was not known to them, much less that it was not written by Willaert.

There are good reasons why neither theorist mentions the work. Vicentino, in his *L'antica musica ridotta alla moderna prattica,* knows no one except himself. He quotes no compositions save his own; he does not even mention that great composer and chromaticist Cipriano de Rore, notwithstanding the common ties that bind him and Rore to Willaert and to the court of Ferrara. Since he never discusses Willaert's work, he cannot very well be considered a theoretical crown witness for the composer, whose disciple he claims to be in his first book of madrigals of 1546. One might on the same grounds question the authenticity of Rore's famous chromatic ode *Calami sonum,* which the author ignores just as he does Willaert's chromatic piece. Zarlino, as a decided anti-chromaticist (see Lowinsky, "Music of the Renaissance as Viewed by Renaissance Musicians," *The Renaissance Image of Man and the World,* ed. Bernard O'Kelly [Columbus, Ohio, 1966], p. 148 and n 104), was careful not to mention the youthful indiscretion of his master. Indeed, in his *Dimostrationi Harmoniche* of 1571 (pp. 236-37), he presents Willaert as a severe censor of the chromaticists. We must not forget that Willaert himself never published his experimental work in any of his Venetian prints, nor did he ever follow through on its implications in any of his later works.

Nevertheless, Willaert's authorship of the controversial work is uncontestable; it is confirmed not just by Spataro in 1524 and Artusi in 1600. It must be borne in mind that Spataro corresponded with a number of musicians in Venice; the constant mention of Willaert's name in connection with the work is proof that the belief in Willaert's authorship is shared by the correspondents. Spataro still refers to Willaert in a letter to Pietro Aron of 1533, which shows that he found no reason

rare works of art that provided generations of musicians with food for thought. When Hercole Bottrigari, in his *Desiderio* of 1594,[2] said that "this duo, which seemingly ends in a seventh, gave the musicians of those times so much to think and say and write," he did not foresee that the same work would still occupy musicians and thinkers in the generations ahead. Indeed, this small work of a mere forty measures may well be regarded as the fountainhead of the whole chromatic movement of the sixteenth century, and that means also of all following centuries. Its impact was incalculable. The present study is intended to illustrate its far-reaching influence through sixteenth- and seventeenth-century compositions modeled after it.

Willaert's composition was designed to demonstrate to a musical world standing under the ban of Pythagorean tradition the potentialities hidden in Aristoxenus' ideas. According to medieval tradition, each tone was divided into a major and a minor semitone. Aristoxenus, derided in the Middle Ages, but increasingly studied and accepted in the Renaissance,[3] taught the division of each tone into two equal semitones,[4] a doctrine that induced the Renaissance musician to think in terms of equal temperament. To demonstrate the Aristoxenian tenet, Willaert led one voice, the tenor, through the complete circle of fifths while keeping the other voice (or voices) strictly in the same mode. The last tone of the tenor, E-double flat, was then equal to D, the last note of the soprano (and bass).

I

Almost precisely one hundred years later a Roman composer, Romano Micheli, a virtuoso of counterpoint and of canon writing,

---

to change the attribution of the piece in the intervening years, and this is the more significant as Willaert from 1527 on resided in Venice as director of the Chapel of San Marco. Finally, the unique copy of the contemporaneous print of the *Libro Primo de la Fortuna* of ca. 1530 (see Lowinsky, "Adrian Willaert's Chromatic 'Duo' Re-Examined," pp. 28-29) assigns the work to "Adrien" in the index. In the centuries following at no point in the debates on the work—as will be seen in the quotations below—is Willaert's authorship ever questioned.

[2] *Il Desiderio overo de' concerti di varii strumenti musicali* (Venice, 1594), ed. Kathi Meyer, Veröffentlichungen der Musik-Bibliothek Paul Hirsch, Vol. 5 (Berlin, 1924), p. 21.

[3] Edward E. Lowinsky, *op.cit.*, pp. 7-22.

[4] For a presentation of Aristoxenus' temperament see Heinrich Husmann, *Grundlagen der antiken und orientalischen Musikkultur* (Berlin, 1961), pp. 38-50, chapter on "Die Temperatur des Aristoxenos."

published a canonic madrigal in which, according to the title of the print,[5] "the harmony by means of accidentals descends one tone and then ascends again." We offer the work in a transcription containing the original accidentals in the text, the necessary additional accidentals above the notes (Ex. 1).

Micheli writes a canon for six parts. The print contains only the first tenor. The key to the solution of the canon is given in the table of incipits showing the points of entrance and the pitches of the five canonic voices. Moreover, endings for all six parts have been provided. Micheli's six-part canon with its twofold modulation through the entire circle of fifths, once downward, once upward, is an extraordinary tour de force. "If it fails to equal the charm of other madrigals," writes the author in his dedication, "this will be excused because of the richness of its artifices."[6] In this one is tempted to agree with him. But when he goes on to characterize his composition as one the like of which musicians have never seen before,[7] we shall do well to reserve judgment.

How does Micheli achieve the feat of crossing twice through the circle of fifths in a six-part canon? The canonic voices follow the leader in unison (second tenor), in the octave (soprano), in the lower fifth (bass), and in the upper fourth (first and second altos). The entrances follow each other in the quick succession of semiminims so that the end of measure 1 sees four, the middle of measure 2 all six, voices assembled. The first modulation is set to the motive of a descending triad, in successive sequences downward, recalling, though in two different rhythmic forms, the initial triadic motive.

---

[5] *Madrigale | a sei voci in canone, | con la Resolutione delle parti, nel quale per mezo de gli accidenti l'armonia | discende un' tuono e di poi ascende il tuono già disceso, potendosi anco | cantare per i suoi riversi, come li Musici periti sanno: | studio curioso non più veduto. | Con un avviso à tutti li Signori Musici di Roma dato in luce da | Romano Micheli Romano | beneficiato nella metropoli | d'Aquileia. | All' Illustrissimo, e Reverendissimo Signore, il Signor Cardinal Ludovisio. | In Roma, appresso Luca Antonio Soldi. MDCXXI | Con Licenza de' Superiori.*

The sole surviving copy of this print, preserved at the library of the Accademia di Santa Cecilia in Rome, contains title page, dedicatory letter, the madrigal, two canons on the name of the Cardinal, addressee of the dedication, with the cardinal's coat of arms and the cardinal's hat, and, finally, an *avviso* addressed to "tutti li Signori Musici di Roma." The dedication carries the date of September 1, 1621.

[6] "[I]l quale se non fosse di quella vaghezza come gl'altri Madrigali, sarà scusabile per la pienezza de suoi artificij. . . ."

[7] "[P]oi che fin hora non è stato veduto da Musico alcuno altro Madrigale in tal similitudine."

O voi che sospirate

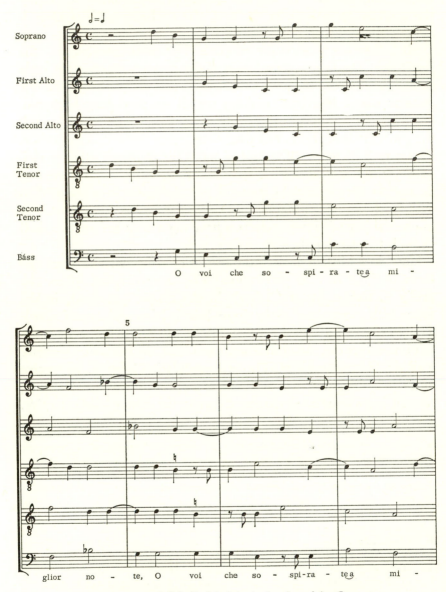

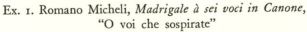

Ex. 1. Romano Micheli, *Madrigale à sei voci in Canone,*
"O voi che sospirate"

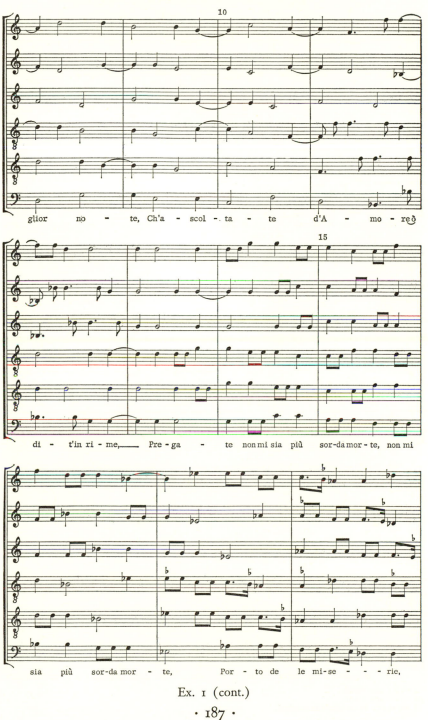

Ex. 1 (cont.)

Por - to de le mi-se - - - rie, Por - to de le mi-se - rie, e
fin del pian - to:____ Mu - tiu - na vol - ta quel suo an-ti - co
sti - le, Ch'ogn'huom at-tri - sta, Ch'ogn'huom at-tri - sta, Ch'ogn'-

1) Half a tone lower.
2) Whole tone lower.
3) All sharps are naturals in original.

Ex. 1 (cont.)

huom at-tri - sta e me, e me. può far si lie - to,___ Mu - ti u-na vol -

ta quel suo an-ti - co sti - le, Ch'ogn'huom at-tri - sta, Ch'ogn'huom at-

tri - sta, Ch'ogn'huom at-tri - sta e me, e me può

4) Half a tone lower.
5) Back to original pitch.

Ex. 1 (cont.)

Ex. 1 (cont.)

The descending modulation is prefaced by one measure of empty fifth-octave chords (m. 13). The particular canonic scheme combined with the descending triadic motive is designed to yield a harmonic sequence in which each major triad, before reaching the next chord at the lower fifth, goes through its relative minor, establishing the following chain of harmonies:[8] C–a–F–d–B♭–g–E♭–c–A♭–f–D♭, etc.

Micheli secures the safety of his modulatory course by indicating all accidentals from B♮ (m. 16) to C♮ and F♮ (mm. 20-21).[9] He stops short of writing double flats with the result that the critical measures (22-24) carrying the modulation to the point where the whole musical discourse falls one tone lower appear without any accidentals whatever. As soon as he reaches B-double flat and E-double flat, Micheli changes the motive of the descending triad to that of an ascending fourth and within a span of six measures (24-29), which traverse four successive motives of the fourth,[10] he has lifted the pitch level by one half tone. On this plateau he rests for three measures (30-32) before undertaking the last ascent, again

[8] Capitals designate major, small letters minor chords.
[9] Micheli, printing only the part of the first tenor, did not go beyond the notation of the F♮. In notating B-double flat in the score, we have followed the principle that all accidentals which flow with necessity from the canonic design of the work are to be treated as if Micheli had indicated them.
[10] B-double flat, E-double flat; C♮, F♮; D♭, G♭; E♭, A♭, to F♮.

with the help of the motive of the ascending fourth.[11] After another span of six measures (33-38) the canon has returned to its original pitch. Only now do sound and notation coincide again; the *inganno del occhio*, the double deception of the eye, is now complete.

How has this deception been accomplished? Once D had been reached as E-double flat and new tones such as B♮, E♮, C♯, etc. were needed, sharps had to be introduced to indicate the correct intervals by the relative means of marking the distances (mm. 25-28 and again mm. 35-38). The last note in measure 29 is the first note where the pitch level has been raised by half a tone, the last note in measure 38 marks the point where the return to the original pitch level has been effected.

The deception of the eye is fourfold. Notes appear a whole tone higher than they sound; sharps are used where flattened notes are sung; then notes appear half a tone higher than sounded, and sharps are used where naturals are sung.

But Micheli's bag of tricks is not emptied yet. In the loquacious title to this work, he mentions that the madrigal can also be sung *per i suoi riversi*. What this means we learn in Micheli's *Musiche pellegrine artificiose*,[12] where he explains, with the aid of music examples, the difference between "riversi" and "contrarij movimenti." "Riversi movimenti" are contrary motions that observe the precise intervals; "contrarij movimenti" are contrary motions that turn half to whole tones, major to minor intervals, and vice versa. In consequence, "riversi movimenti," with their precise observation of intervals, turn major harmonies to minor, minor to major, whereas contrary motions leave the modal character of the composition untouched. Applied to the present work this means that the whole composition can be performed in inversion and, being conceived in a major mode, will then emerge in a minor mode. Moreover, the modulations now move contrariwise, first ascending to the sharp region, returning to the natural, and then descending to the flat (Ex. 2).

What of Micheli's claim that never before had a madrigal like this been composed? Strictly speaking, this was true. A madrigal in six-part canon modulating twice through the circle of fifths and capable of being sung in precise inversion was a novelty. Micheli did not claim, however, that the work had no precedents in earlier,

---

[11] B♭, E♭; C, F; D, G; E, A to F♯.
[12] See n. 19.

O voi che sospirate

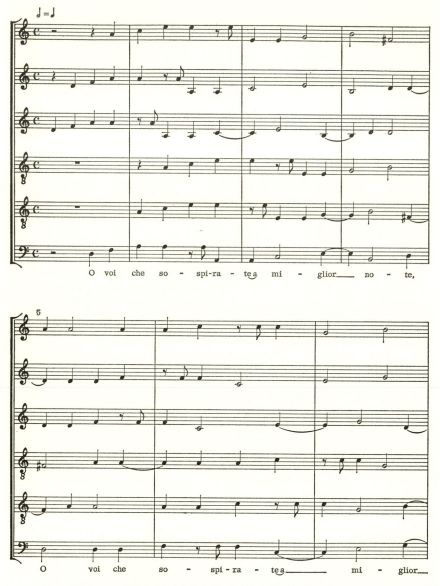

Ex. 2. Romano Micheli, *Madrigale à sei voci* (the reverse version),
"O voi che sospirate"

Ex. 2 (cont.)

Ex. 2 (cont.)

less comprehensive, experiments. Indeed, he pointed the way to historical precedent himself by the choice of his text. For the verses[13] from Petrarch's Canzoniere, on Laura's death, are the same ones that Luca Marenzio[14] used in the work from the second book of

[13] *O voi che sospirate* is the twelfth stanza from Petrarch's celebrated sestina *Mia benigna fortuna, e'l viver lieto.*

[14] Romano Micheli's interest in Luca Marenzio is not limited to the work presently under discussion. In his *Musica vaga et artificiosa* of 1615 (p. 39), he publishes a canon on the initial soggetto of Marenzio's *Liquide perle amor,* the work with which Marenzio opens the first book of five-part madrigals, his first publication (aside from an isolated madrigal in an anthology of 1577).

madrigals for five voices that contains the famous enharmonic modulation stretching from G major, C major, F major, through B♭, E♭, A♭, D♭, G♭ major (=F♯) to B minor and back to a cadence aiming at A minor but ending in A major.[15] This astonishing modulation, itself an echo of Willaert's "duo," accompanies the words addressed to Death: "Muti una volta quel suo antico stile" ("May he, for once, change his old style") (Ex. 3).

Romano Micheli takes a double cue from Marenzio. He chooses the same line expressing the wish for a change in Death's *antico stile* (applying it, in a *double entendre*, to the style of music), and he follows his predecessor in interpreting the "new style" as the new harmonic and modulatory freedom, the novel exploration of the circle of fifths, rendered possible through the rediscovery of equal temperament and the undaunted use of flats and sharps for all notes.[16] But whereas Marenzio limits this exploration to two-thirds of the circle in one direction, i.e., eight steps downward from G major to B minor, Micheli expands it to two full-length circulations in both directions. Could Micheli have been inspired by models older than Marenzio?

Certainly, the choice of a descending triadic motive in effecting the first modulation recalls similar, if more limited, modulations in the circle of fifths using the same motive—works such as Clemens non Papa's *Fremuit spiritu Jesu*[17] and Josquin's plaint of David, *Absalon fili mi.*[18] In going through the full circle of fifths could Micheli have been thinking of Willaert's "duo"?

The number of canonic works published by Romano Micheli is eloquent testimony that this native of Rome and disciple of Francesco Soriano and Giovanni Maria Nanino, luminaries of the Palestrina school, dedicated most of his life to the practical and theoretical exploration of the mysteries of canonic and other contra-

[15] See Luca Marenzio, *Sämtliche Werke*, ed. Alfred Einstein, Vol. 1, *Publikationen älterer Musik*, IV¹ (Leipzig, 1929), 69-70; see also Edward E. Lowinsky, "The Musical Avant-Garde of the Renaissance or: The Peril and Profit of Foresight," in *Art, Science, and History in the Renaissance*, ed. Charles S. Singleton (Baltimore, 1968), pp. 111-62, esp. pp. 145, 148-52.

[16] For autobiographical corroboration of the fact that Marenzio's madrigal served as model for Micheli's work, see Edward E. Lowinsky, "An Unknown Autograph Manuscript of Romano Micheli in Rome" (in preparation).

[17] See Edward E. Lowinsky, *Secret Chromatic Art in the Netherlands Motet* (New York, 1946; repr. 1967), pp. 23-24 and Ex. 22.

[18] *Ibid.*, p. 24 and Ex. 23.

Ex. 3. Luca Marenzio, "O voi che sospirate," from Einstein,
Luca Marenzio Sämtliche Werke, I, 69

puntal artifices.[19] He did so with missionary zeal, publishing invitations and challenges to musicians all over Italy and abroad to com-

[19] For a list of his works see Claude V. Palisca's bibliography in *MGG*, IX, cols.
273-74. To this list should be added the following publications: 1) *Avviso inviato
da me Romano Micheli Insieme col foglio reale del Canone musicale Fons signatus...*
In Roma, MDCL, Nella Stamperia di Lodovico Grignani. 2) *Musiche pellegrine
artificiose, et armoniose inventate da Romano Micheli Romano*, Opera Settima.
This work carries no date, but it must have been published after 1650, since reference is made to a print published in that year. The work carries the designation
*Opera settima. Opera sesta (Vivit Deus. Canones super plurium verborum vocali-
bus ...)* was published in Rome in the year 1644.

pete with him in the writing and in the solution of canonic enig-mas.[20] That he was acquainted with Willaert's chromatic "duo" is the more likely since he stayed in Venice where he published a work written on a canon by Willaert. This canon was published separately in the year 1618 and addressed, in Romano's best bravado manner, to "the most illustrious and very Reverend Gentlemen, the Gentle-men and most excellent musicians of the Chapel of the Pope and other Roman musicians."[21] It is accompanied by the following auto-biographical introduction:

Ritrovandomi in Venetia per il tempo concessomi della vacanza della mia residenza nella Chiesa Metropolitana d'Aquilea, li 19. del presente fui favo-rito dal Signor Luigi Grani Musico Eccellente de' Concerti di questa Sere-nissima Republica, del sottoscritto Canone in figura à sei voci, con un' altro à due, le quali cantano con quello à otto voci il restante delle parole, i quali Canoni meritamente sono stati sempre conservati con molta diligenza dalli Signori Musici di queste parti, essendo stati fatti già dall'antico, & famoso Musico Adriano

Finding myself in Venice during the time allowed me for vacation from my residence in the Metropolitan Church of Aquileia I was favored on the nine-teenth day of this month by Signor Luigi Grani, excellent director of the concerts of this most noble Republic, with the six-voice canon written be-low, with another for two voices, which sing the rest of the words, to-gether with the former, in eight parts. Deservedly, these canons have been preserved constantly, with much care, by the musicians living in these parts, since they were composed by the

[20] A story told by Giovanni Battista Doni illustrates Micheli's reputation as a famous contrapuntist, but a man without humanistic culture. In his *Discorso della ritmopeia de' versi Latini e della melodia de' cori tragichi (De' Trattati di Musica di Gio. Batista Doni . . .* , Vol. II [Florence, 1763], 203-25; 213) Doni tells of having composed some verses in the Asclepiadean meter on the occasion of the Pope's re-turn from Castel Gandolfo which began with the words "Salve sceptrigerum maxime Principum." He had them set first with, then without, observation of the meter. Then "I showed both compositions to the Rev. Romano Micheli, most experi-enced contrapuntist, and disciple in this profession of Soriani, without saying any-thing to him about this diversity, asking him merely which of the two he liked better. And he, without giving it much thought, gave preference to the one in which the meter was observed, although he did not recognize it as such." To Doni such unawareness was inexcusable ignorance and, in prefacing the story, he speaks of its protagonist as "uno di questi Contrappuntisti a dozzina," "one of these contra-puntists who are a dime a dozen." (On Doni's attitude to counterpoint and his judgment on Soriano, Palestrina's disciple and Micheli's teacher, see my article on "Musical Genius—Evolution and Origins of a Concept," *Musical Quarterly*, L [1964], 338-40.)

[21] The print, which has no title page, is addressed *Alli Molt'Illust.ri e Molto Rever.di Sig. li Sig. Eccellentiss.mi Musici della Cappella di N. S. et altri musici Romani miei Patroni osservandissimi* (Venice, Giacomo Vincenti, 1618).

Vuillaert, nel qual Canone à sei io conosco essere preso il soggetto dalle vocali di quella parola *Durate*: che dice ut, fa, re, & io per mostrare d'intendere quali sorti di studij siano, & che la Scuola Romana di questa professione è sempre stata non punto inferiore, mà più tosto delle altre Maestra, feci il medesimo giorno non solo, che il Canone à due fosse più elegante di figura; ma anche li aumentai di un'altro canone à quattro voci. . . .

Di Venetia li 24 Novembre 1618

ancient and famous musician Adriano Willaert. I know that the six-part canon was taken from the *soggetto dalle vocali* of the word *Durate* ("be persistent"), that is, from the solmization syllables *ut, fa, re*. To demonstrate my understanding of this kind of study and to prove the competence of the Roman school, which was never inferior in this profession, but rather the teacher of others, I wrote, on the same day, not only another more elegant two-part canon, but I also augmented it with another canon in four parts. . . .

Venice, November 24, 1618

Willaert's name, fame, and contrapuntal genius were well known to Romano Micheli. He deemed it an honor to pit his skill against that of the old Flemish-Venetian master. It is very likely then, particularly in view of the availability of Willaert's "duo" in Artusi's print of 1601, that Micheli knew the "duo" and had studied it with great care.

A later seventeenth-century composer and theorist corroborates this thesis indirectly. Angelo Berardi (born *ca.* 1630) deals with Willaert's "duo" in two of his treatises; he reprints it once in its entirety,[22] once in part.[23] His discussions are full of interest, and he confirms the result of our previous investigation[24] that Willaert was motivated by Aristoxenus' division of the tone into two equal semitones. More significantly, in this context, he places Romano Micheli's composition in that same tradition. In the *Miscellanea musicale* (pp. 59-61) he writes:

Aristosseno, sottilissimo Filosofo, divise il tuono in due semituoni eguali, sopra questo fondamento, Adriano

Aristoxenus, most subtle philosopher, divided the tone into two equal semitones. On this foundation Adrian

---

[22] *Documenti Armonici Di D. Angelo Berardi Da S. Agata Canonico nell'Insigne Collegiata di S. Angelo di Viterbo; Nelli quali con varij Discorsi, Regole, & Essempij si dimostrano gli studij arteficiosi della Musica* . . . (Bologna, 1687), p. 79.

[23] *Miscellanea Musicale di D. Angelo Berardi . . . Dove con dottrine si discorre delle materie più curiose della Musica: Con Regole, & Essempij si tratta di tutto il Contrapunto con l'intreccio di bellissimi secreti per li Professori Armonici* (Bologna, 1689), p. 60.

[24] Lowinsky, "Adrian Willaert's Chromatic 'Duo' Re-Examined," pp. 7-22.

Wilaert compose una cantilena à due voci Canto, e Tenore, l'intitolò: *Quid non ebrietas?* ove si vede che il Tenore cala un tuono intiero senza che il soprano si mova. Portarò solo quella parte di cantilena dove cala il tuono. Chi hà curiosità di considerarla intiera, veda i miei Documenti Armonici à car. 79. (Then follows the "Essempio d'Adriano.")

Con il medemo fondamento d'Aristosseno, Alfonso dal Violino compose una Sinfonia artificiosissima à 5. sopra ut, re, mi, fa, sol, la. D. Romano Micheli compose ancor lui un Madrigale à 6. in canone, che cala, e cresce un tuono con nobilissimo artificio: Rapportarò solo l'intervalli incompiti.

Willaert wrote a composition for two parts, soprano and tenor, which he entitled: *Quid non ebrietas?* Here one sees the tenor descend a whole tone without the soprano's participating in this modulation. I shall quote only that section of the composition where the tone level sinks. Whoever is curious to know the whole composition is referred to my *Documenti armonici* (page 79).

On the same foundation of Aristoxenus, Alfonso del Violino wrote a most artful sinfonia for five parts on the hexachord. The Reverend Romano Micheli, too, composed a six-part madrigal in canon which falls and rises one tone with most sublime art. I shall quote only the mere intervals.

Berardi leaves us entirely in the dark concerning the chromatic Sinfonia by Alfonso del Violino, but he quotes Micheli's canon in a skeletal outline devoid of rhythm, merely sketching the double course of the modulation (Ex. 4).

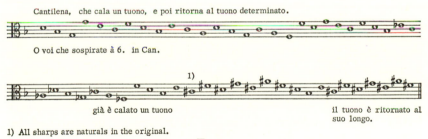

Cantilena, che cala un tuono, e poi ritorna al tuono determinato.

O voi che sospirate à 6. in Can.

1)

già è calato un tuono   il tuono è ritornato al suo longo.

1) All sharps are naturals in the original.

Ex. 4

Berardi returns to the idea of circulating modulation and the works illustrating it in his treatise entitled "Musical Mysteries Unveiled."[25] In this dialogue Martio, one of the interlocutors, referring to Berardi in the third person, says:

[25] *Arcani Musicali svelati dalla vera Amicitia Ne' quali appariscono diversi studij artificiosi, molte osservationi, e Regole concernenti alla tessitura de Componimenti Armonici, con un modo facilissimo per Sonare trasportato. Dialogo del Can. Angelo Berardi da S. Agata* (Bologna, 1690), p. 13.

Nella sua Miscellanea fà mentione di un Madrigale in canone à sei composto da D. Romano Micheli con nobilissimo artificio, che cala, e cresce un tuono, e d'una Sinfonia d'Alfonso del Violino, che camina conforme gl' insegnamenti d'Aristossero [sic], per mio amaestramento in questi secreti Musicali, prego V. S. farmi vedere questi componimenti distesi.

In his *Miscellanea* he mentions a madrigal in canon for six parts composed by the Rev. Romano Micheli with most sublime art, which falls and rises one tone, and a Sinfonia by Alfonso del Violino that follows the theories of Aristoxenus. For my instruction in these musical secrets I beg Your Excellency to let me see these compositions in their entirety.

To this Flavio replies:

Non solo di questi, mà di alcuni altri ancora nè quali apparisce manifestamente l'inganno dell'occhio, gle ne darò una piena cognitione, accio si conosca la verità del detto di Damone Ateniese, che *Musica est res profunda* etc.

Not only of these, but also of some other works in which the "deception of the eye" manifestly appears, I shall give you full notice so that the truth be known of that saying by Damon of Athens that music is a profound thing.[26]

Now Berardi prints the first tenor of Micheli's canon in full, with its correct rhythmic values and with text. He notes the entrance of the canonic parts with the customary *signa congruentiae*, but he fails to indicate the pitch level of these entries, and he gives the ending only for the tenor part, not for the other five voices.

II

Since Micheli's canonic madrigal has been preserved in full in the original print of 1621, nothing is lost. But an exciting gain accrues from Berardi's quotation of one section of the chromatic Sinfonia by Alfonso del Violino. We deal here, I believe, with a work of Alfonso della Viola, there being no records of a composer by the name of Alfonso del Violino. Moreover, in the course of the seventeenth century, the violin (*violino*) superseded the Renaissance viol (*viola*); the substitution of *violino* for *viola* is therefore easily understandable. Most importantly, the style of the excerpt—in particular the voice-leading and the counterpoint—would seem to point to the sixteenth century; and Alfonso della Viola was born in the early years of the Cinquecento and lived until about 1570.

---

[26] Damon of Athens is one of the earliest and most influential Greek theorists of music whose views on the ethical effects of the modes are reflected in Plato's and Aristides Quintilianus' writings (cf. Edward A. Lippman, *Musical Thought in Ancient Greece* [New York and London, 1964], p. 69).

"Viola's name," says Alfred Einstein, "is to be found in every history of music and every lexicon, as the chief composer for the tragedies, pastoral dramas, and comedies at the court of Ferrara; associated with him were M. Antonio dal Cornetto, who is wholly unknown,[27] and, as we shall see, Cipriano de Rore, the greatest master of the time."[28] Interestingly enough, in commenting upon Viola's compositions in his two madrigal books of 1539 and 1540, Einstein singles out his harmonic style: "Above all, however, Viola is much more colorful than Festa, Arcadelt, Verdelot, and most of the other musicians of the 'thirties."[29] In a series of well-selected examples he illustrates Alfonso's free use of chromaticism and modulatory harmony that had already attracted Kroyer's attention.[30] From Berardi we learn that Alfonso della Viola also participated in the more adventurous chromatic movement of the Cinquecento. Unfortunately, Berardi does not publish the whole work. But the fifteen measures that he offers and the accompanying remarks make it possible to assess the character and the significance of Viola's chromatic experiment.

"Alfonso's Sinfonia," writes Berardi, "is 230 measures long. You will content yourself with the study of that sole part in which the artifice and the deception of the eye are manifest."[31] Among the great chromatic experiments of the century it is the only one which

---

[27] Renato Lunelli, in his article "Contributi trentini alle relazioni musicali fra l'Italia e la Germania nel Rinascimento" (*Acta musicologica*, xxi [1949], 41-70), published a correspondence between Ercole II, Duke of Ferrara, and Cristoforo Madruzzo, Cardinal of Trent, between the years 1548 and 1551, from which it is evident that Antonio del Cornetto belonged to the Ferrarese court musicians. Lunelli assumes that Antonio was "maestro di cappella" in Ferrara in the year 1548, because in a letter of 1548 Ercole II refers to him as "capo," but "capo," I believe, means something like our "first violinist," or "concert master." As cornett player Antonio was "head" of the wind instruments and perhaps of the whole instrumental ensemble. From Walter Weyler ("Documenten betreffende de muziekkapel aan het hof van Ferrara," *Vlaamsch jaarboek voor muziekgeschiedenis*, i [1939], 81-113) we know that the Ferrarese musical establishment was divided into singers ("cantori") and instrumental musicians ("musici"), and an Antonio del Cornetto figures as early as 1533 in the Ferrarese account books (*ibid.*, p. 87).

[28] Alfred Einstein, *The Italian Madrigal*, 3 vols. (Princeton, 1949), i, 301.

[29] *Ibid.*, p. 305.

[30] See Theodor Kroyer, *Die Anfänge der Chromatik im italienischen Madrigal*, Publikationen der Internationalen Musikgesellschaft, Beiheft iv (Leipzig, 1902), 43-44.

[31] "La Sinfonia d'Alfonso è lunga 230. battute, si contentarà d'osservare solamente quella parte, nella quale consiste l'artificio e l'inganno dell'occhio" (*Arcani musicali*, p. 15).

is clearly conceived for instruments. This is evident from the absence of text or incipit, from the title Sinfonia, from the unvocal design of the voices, and from the lack of that thematic and rhythmic relationship between the single parts which is ordinarily engendered by their sharing one and the same text.

Obviously, the whole Sinfonia was written on an ostinato cantus firmus, the six notes of the hexachord, *ut re mi fa sol la*. In the section available to us, each note of the hexachord covers two measures and each hexachord is followed by a pause of one measure. If the hexachord began on G, we are now, with the hexachord on C♯, precisely in the middle. If every hexachord progression took 12 measures, the piece would come to 144 measures. If we add 12 measures for pauses, we reach the number 156. This would leave 74 measures unaccounted for. But 72 being 12 times 6, the possibility arises that either the series of hexachords was repeated, this time with only 1 measure per note, or it went downward in doubly accelerated tempo, and this time without pauses. This would result in a work of about 230 measures.

The boldest aspect of the work is the arrangement of the hexachords. The favorite route of sixteenth-century chromaticists is the circle of fifths. It is followed in the experiments of Willaert, Greiter,[32] Marenzio, even in Romano Micheli's canonic madrigal. It was adumbrated in Josquin's *Fortuna dun gran tempo*[33] and in his *Absalon fili mi*.[34] It became the chief modulatory device of motet and madrigal composers. But Alfonso della Viola, as may be seen from the D of the hexachord voice (m. 15), undertakes a much more difficult task when he arranges the hexachord ostinato in chromatically ascending (and perhaps also descending) patterns. The continual transitions from one hexachord to the next cause a harmonic shock, the absorption of which demands extraordinary skill. This is well demonstrated in the excerpt from Alfonso's Sinfonia (Ex. 5).

A sketch of the harmonic areas passed through in these fifteen measures leads us from B minor (m. 1), F♯ minor (m. 2), C♯ minor

[32] See Edward E. Lowinsky, "Matthaeus Greiter's *Fortuna*: An Experiment in Chromaticism and in Musical Iconography," *Musical Quarterly*, XLII (1956), 500-19, and XLIII (1957), 68-85.

[33] See Edward E. Lowinsky, "The Goddess Fortuna in Music," *Musical Quarterly*, XXIX (1943), 45-77.

[34] Lowinsky, *Secret Chromatic Art*, p. 24.

Sinfonia

Ex. 5. Alfonso del Violino, Sinfonia, from Berardi,
Arcani musicali, p. 15

1) Orig.:

Ex. 5 (cont.)

(m. 3), G♯ (= A♭) minor (mm. 4-5), B♭ minor (mm. 6-7), E♭ (= D♯) minor (mm. 8-9), A♭ (= G♯) minor (mm. 10-11), E♭ minor (mm. 12-15), to E♭ major, C minor (m. 14), and G major (m. 15). Needless to say, none of these harmonic areas is stabilized. Alfonso wanders from one to the other in a constant harmonic flux that has been well described by Giovanni Battista Doni (1594-1647) as the "tuono ambulatorio, o incerto."[35]

[35] Giovanni Battista Doni, *Compendio del trattato de' generi e de' modi della musica* (Rome, 1635), p. 89. Interestingly enough, Doni uses the term "circulation" in connection with such modulatory movements. He ascribes their use to the keyboard players of the archicembalo types with split keys:

Che la Circolatione usata da alcuni negl' istrumenti spezzati, con moltissimi tasti, non è altro, che una ricercata di tutte le voci di più tuoni connessi, e mescolati insieme; e per ciò potrebbesi chiamare in Greco ἀνακύκλησις τονικὴ.

Et ch'ella non è d'alcuna efficacia; ma serve solo per ostentare una grandissima pratica dell'Instrumento, & degl'intervalli. E che le divisioni del Monocordo Enarmonico secondo il Zarlino, e'l Salinas servono per questo: e di qui è che il Madrigale *O voi che sospirate* &c. di Luca Marentio, nel quale mette prima in ogni corda separatamente il diesi ✕, e poi il b molle si può chiamare d'un Tuono ambulatorio, ò incerto.

The "circulation" used by some on instruments with many and split keys is nothing else than a search of all tones of most keys connected and mixed together. One might therefore call it in Greek ἀνακύκλησις τονικὴ.

This circulation is devoid of any expressive power; it serves only for the display of an immense knowledge of the instruments and the intervals. This is also the purpose of Zarlino's and Salinas' divisions of the enharmonic monochord. This is the reason why Luca Marenzio's madrigal *O voi che sospirate* in which he first sharpens, then flattens each tone separately, may be said to be of an ambulatory, or uncertain, mode.

However keen Doni's observations are, he is not aware of the expressive potenti-

If the sequence of harmonies is astonishing, what is one to say of the melodic progressions? More unsingable lines would be hard to find in the middle of the Cinquecento; they point forward to Gesualdo da Venosa's late madrigals. But, as with Gesualdo, they receive their full justification from the harmonic context. Alfonso does not shy away from direct chromatic progressions (soprano, mm. 5-6; tenor, m. 5), or a diminished fourth (tenor, m. 1); cross relations abound, and there would be no way in which any of these lines could be solmized. One might say that the four contrapuntal voices poke fun at their cantus firmus, the old *ut, re, mi, fa, sol, la.* They are not, as it were, on speaking—or shall we say solmizating—terms with the ostinato.

The *inganno d'occhio* which Berardi attributes to the section from Alfonso della Viola's chromatic Sinfonia is of a different nature than the *inganni* created by Willaert and Micheli in their respective compositions, in which the tonal level differs from that apparent in the notation. In Alfonso's example we see the composer struggle with musical problems completely beyond the means of the notation available to him at his time. In experiments such as this each composer had to create his own notational methods in accordance with the contrapuntal and harmonic context designed by him. Alfonso, as a follower of Aristoxenus' doctrine that divided each tone into two equal semitones, and in view of the specific problems arising from the self-imposed task of writing a fantasia on a chromatically ascending hexachord, decided to designate each chromatic note either by a flat or by a sharp, whichever happened to be more convenient. Among the criteria for convenience were avoidance of double accidentals and the greatest possible coherence within the single phrases of each part. If, for our present purposes, we define a phrase as a melodic unit set off by a pause or pauses, we have seventeen phrases altogether. Of these no more than two (soprano, mm. 4-6; tenor, mm. 1-6) mix sharps and flats, if we leave aside the third phrase of the soprano in which only the first note deviates from the sharp construction of the phrase. This principle leads, however, to a merciless

---

alities nor of the deeper implications of the "circulation" for the development of harmony and the future of the tonal system—a future which he actually opposed since he was inimical to equal temperament and in favor of the highly complex keyboard instruments with multiple tone divisions.

clash of flats and sharps in the harmonic picture of the five-part composition, as confusing to a modern musician as it must have been to a contemporary of Alfonso's. It leads, moreover, to a few curious idiosyncrasies of notation. The flat not only lowers a note by half a tone, but also acts as a natural sign (see soprano, mm. 4 and 6). Whereas Alfonso does not mind writing a C♭, he avoids using an E♯; its necessity in the hexachord must be deduced from the context. In other places we have the bewildering sequence F♯, F♭ as mentioned above (soprano, mm. 5-6) to render the notation of an E♯ unnecessary. Except for the unorthodox uses of the flat, there is no "deception of the eye" and all that Berardi can have meant, it would seem, is the acoustical identity of tones appearing, say, as F♯ in one voice, as G♭ in another, i.e., what we call enharmonic change. Surely, performance of this work must have tested the mettle even of the instrumentalists of the court of Ferrara.

It is possible that Gesualdo heard this extraordinary work when he visited Ferrara in 1594. Alfred Einstein saw in this visit the most likely reason for the "radical change in Gesualdo,"[36] from the relative conventionality of the first two books of his madrigals to the fifth and sixth books with their extreme chromaticism, the third and fourth books taking a middle position. Obviously, Alfonso's Sinfonia was only one of many works that Gesualdo might have heard in Ferrara. Einstein underscores the importance of Luzzasco Luzzaschi for a proper understanding of Gesualdo's music. Hercole Bottrigari, in his account of the concerts at the court of Ferrara, published in 1594,[37] reported in particular about the celebrated *concerto grande* which the Duke of Ferrara reserved "for the entertainment of cardinals, dukes, princes, and other great people" and for which "all sorts of instruments" were used and which demanded "not one or two, but many rehearsals." Only two works, particularly composed for the purpose, were performed at these occasions, "one by the late Alfonso dalla Viuola [*sic*], the other by Luzzasco." Bottrigari's report proves that Alfonso's instrumental music was still cultivated in Ferrara at the end of the sixteenth century.

Einstein, in an attempt to determine why it is that after 1540 we hear so little of Alfonso della Viola, speculates that this may have been due to the arrival of Cipriano de Rore in Ferrara: "The tragic

---

[36] Alfred Einstein, *op.cit.*, II, 698.
[37] *Il Desiderio*, pp. 42-43 of the Meyer edition.

fate of being no longer able to keep up with a development suddenly accelerated by the appearance of a genius is one which Viola shares with many other musicians of his generation."[38] In view of the un-known *concerto grande* and the chromatic Sinfonia, the question arises whether we must necessarily equate Alfonso's lack of publications after 1540 with his ceasing to compose. Is it not possible, particularly if we consider Bottrigari's interesting division of Ferrarese music into "public, private, domestic, and secret," that Alfonso's music was kept as a "private reserve" for the use and enjoyment of the Ferrarese court and for the greater glory of the dukes of Este?

What might the date of Alfonso's chromatic hexachord fantasia be? We know of Cipriano de Rore's famous chromatic motet *Calami sonum*, set for four basses and beginning, in each voice, with an ascending chromatic tetrachord. Since Orlando di Lasso published the work in his first publication in Antwerp in the year 1555, having

---

[38] Alfred Einstein, *op.cit.*, I, 306. According to Weyler ("Documenten"), whose article was not known to Einstein, Alfonso's name is missing in the lists from 1535 to 1548 (the records for the years from 1536 until 1541 are lost). He returns, how-ever, in the lists of 1549. Lunelli's statement (also to be found in dictionaries of music) that Alfonso della Viola was *maestro di cappella* in Ferrara from 1534 till 1550, except for the year 1548, and that Cipriano de Rore took over as director of the Ferrarese court music in 1550, is not corroborated by archival documents. According to the lists published by Weyler, Rore is *maestro di cappella* from 1547 till 1558. An early seventeenth-century source of local Ferrarese history, overlooked by music historians, explains the huge gap in Alfonso's service. Marcantonio Guarini, in his *Compendio historico dell'origine, accrescimento e prerogative delle chiese e luoghi pij della città e diocesi di Ferrara* (Ferrara, 1621), p. 274, reports that "Francesco and Alfonso [both] nicknamed della Viola are also buried here [in the Cathedral of S. Francesco in Ferrara], the former chapelmaster of Ercole II and Alfonso II, dukes of Ferrara, and the latter chapelmaster of the Cathedral: uniquely gifted musicians, and rarely talented performers on all sorts of instruments, and in particular on the viola—which is why they were called della Viola." ("Giacciono quivi anche Francesco, ed Alfonso detti della Viola, l'uno Maestro di capella di Hercole, ed Alfonso ambi secondi Duchi di Ferrara, e l'altro della Cathedrale; soggetti nella musica singolari, e nel toccar ogni sorte d'istromenti rari, ed in particolare la Viola, che per ciò vennero detti della Viola.") It would seem therefore that Alfonso della Viola never left Ferrara—this explains why his name appears nowhere else during the years of his presumed absence—but that he simply changed positions. Having been part of the court music till 1534, he was then entrusted with the direction of church music at the cathedral, from which he returned to the court chapel sometime in 1548 or 1549—the account book of the year 1548 is missing. Perhaps he was recalled to the court chapel by the new *maestro di cappella*, Cipriano de Rore. That Rore's ascendancy did not diminish the esteem in which Alfonso was held at the court may be deduced from the fact that Rore had the highest salary save for Alfonso della Viola, who received one ducat more per month than the *maestro di cappella*.

left Italy the year before, it follows that it must have been composed in or before 1554. There is a strong possibility, both in view of Alfonso's harmonic freedom in his madrigal books of 1539 and 1540, and in view of Willaert's model of the early 1520's—and Willaert, too, had been at the court of Ferrara—that Alfonso della Viola's chromatic experiment preceded Rore's. After Willaert's "duo," which used for the first time the complete circle of fifths, and after Alfonso's fantasia on the hexachord arranged in chromatically ascending sequence, the only thing remaining to be done was to employ the chromatic scale itself. On the other hand, after the chromatic scale had been employed, the use of the diatonic hexachord, even in chromatically arranged sequences, was a step backward rather than one forward. Now Rore's stay at the court of Ferrara fell between the years 1547 and 1558. Presumably, Alfonso and Cipriano lived and worked together at Ferrara. Rore's chromatic ode may be dated as of the early 1550's, and I should assume that Alfonso's chromatic Sinfonia was written at the end of the 1540's. In fact, it might very well have been composed in 1549, when Alfonso rejoined the Ferrarese court musicians and the climate for chromatic experiments was extremely favorable. Surely this date is not too early in view of Matthaeus Greiter's *Fortuna*, written about 1550,[39] in which the tones *ut re mi re ut* appear as ostinato throughout the two *partes* of the composition systematically transposed in the circle of fifths from F to F♭, all notes explicitly indicated by written-in flats.

Such a date would also be supported by the development of Italian theory. In 1545 Pietro Aron published the *Lucidario in musica*, his last great treatise on music. He had always shown particular interest in questions of *musica ficta* and hexachord transpositions,[40]

---

[39] Lowinsky, "Matthaeus Greiter's *Fortuna*," p. 514.

[40] In the *Trattato della natura et cognitione di tutti gli tuoni* (Venice, 1525), Aron devotes Chapters xxv through xlv to a precise description of hexachord transpositions. Curiously enough, Aron treats only transpositions involving flats. For this he was criticized by Giovanni Spataro in a letter to Giovanni del Lago of October 30, 1527 (MS Vat. lat. 5318, fols. 139r to 140v). Referring first to Aron's *Toscanello* of 1523, Spataro continues as follows:

Ma a me pare che dapoi in quello suo tractato de tonis non poco sua ex(cellen)tia se sia alontonato de la mera verita: perche da uno solo signo de .b.	But it seems to me that later, in his treatise on modes, His Excellency has greatly strayed from the pure truth, for he derives two entirely different sets of

and in the *Lucidario* he summarized his teachings. He permits flat-
ting of A, B, D, E, G and raising of A, C, D, F, and G. This allows
for five hexachords with flats (F, B♭, E♭, A♭, D♭) and five hexachords with sharps (D, A, E, B, F♯). Although this number does
not exceed the system developed by John Hothby (d. 1487),[41] Aron
lifts the doctrine of transposition from the willful obscurity of
Hothby's enigmatic terminology to the clarity needed by the musician concerned with transposition from the performer's point of
view. Referring to works with unusual transpositions Aron says:

Conciosiache poche, o quasi niuna al presente se ne ritrovi, La qual cosa adiviene, perche poca quantità ne furono impresse.	If you find few of them at present, or hardly any at all, this happens because few of them are printed.[42]

In other words, works with extraordinary transpositions are being
composed, but hardly ever are they printed. Now this is a highly
interesting statement and one that squares with a number of well-
known facts. Willaert's *Quid non ebrietas* was not published in one
of the many editions printed in Venice under the master's supervision.[43] Cipriano de Rore's ode was published among his own works
only after his death in 1566. That it saw the light of the world in

---

molle signato in .D.sol.re. lui fa nascere dui exachordi inter se diversi: et differenti.	hexachords from one single accidental, the flat, added to D sol re.

Undoubtedly, Aron heard of this criticism from Lago with whom he, too, corresponded. For in a new edition of the treatise in Venice in 1531 he defends himself
against the contention "of some" that there are two schemes of transposition—one
with flats, the other with sharps—by saying that what he wrote in the first edition
was free of error ("senza errore alcuno"), but that he had limited himself to the
transposition by flats only, because, as Aristotle says, it is vain to demonstrate a
thing in many ways when it can be done in fewer. But in order to show that he
was not ignorant of the possibility of transposition by sharps, he was now going
to illustrate both schemes. In his demonstration Aron uses the flat for all tones
except C and F, the sharp for all tones except B and E.

[41] See A. W. Schmidt, *Die Calliopea Legale des Johannes Hothby* (Leipzig, 1897).

[42] *Lucidario In Musica di alcune oppenioni antiche, et moderne con le loro
oppositioni, & resolutioni, con molti altri secreti appresso, & questioni da altrui
anchora non dichiarati, composto dall'eccellente, & consumato Musico Pietro Aron
del Ordine de Crosachieri, & della citta di Firenze* (Venice, 1545), Book IV, chapter
11, "Della congionta del b, molle, & del b, quadro" ("On the Transpositions with
Flats and with Sharps"), fol. 38.

[43] See Lowinsky, "Adrian Willaert's Chromatic 'Duo' Re-Examined," pp. 29, 32.

1555 was due to the indiscretion of a fiery young genius. Orlando di Lasso himself never published his chromatic cycle on the twelve sibyls, a work of his youth. His sons published it posthumously in an edition of 1600.[44] Alfonso della Viola's chromatic Sinfonia was neither published nor referred to in the theoretical literature, as far as we know, throughout the sixteenth century. And when Nicola Vicentino taught the noblemen of Ferrara the subtleties of the Greek genera, he swore them to secrecy.[45] It seems a fair conclusion that the works of this kind available today are but a small remnant of a larger repertory.

Ten years after Aron's *Lucidario*, Nicola Vicentino published his *L'antica musica ridotta alla moderna prattica*, a publication provoked by his humiliating defeat in a public disputation.[46] In this treatise the expansion of the Guidonian system by way of transposition yields to the revival of Greek chromatic and enharmonic quarter-tone progressions produced on Vicentino's newly constructed *archicembalo* on which the octave could be divided into thirty-one tones. Whereas Rore's *Calami sonum* goes well with Vicentino's radical chromatic experiments, Alfonso della Viola's fantasia is more in tune with Aron's world. Alfonso expands the hexachord system by introducing F♭, C♭, B♯, and E♯, all declared impossible by Aron in diatonic music.[47] However, we should recall that in a preceding chapter of the same book Aron demonstrated the capability of the lute and other string instruments to produce transpositions inaccessible to the organ. The organ, with its stable keys, cannot produce tolerable sounding transpositions on E♭ or on B, but the players of string

[44] Modern edition, edited by H. J. Therstappen, *Das Chorwerk*, Vol. 48 (1937). On the date see Lowinsky, *Secret Chromatic Art*, pp. 92-93, and Wolfgang Boetticher, *Orlando di Lasso und seine Zeit* (Kassel, 1958), pp. 71-79.

[45] Ghiselin Danckerts, in his *Trattato . . . sopra una differentia musicale*, reports on the contract which Vicentino signed at the house of Cardinal Ridolfi in the year 1549 to teach five or six selected noblemen the mysteries of chromatic and enharmonic music, provided that they obliged themselves, under pain of paying a fine of 300 ducats, not to reveal to any living person anything of his teachings (see Adrien de la Fage, *Essais de diphthérographie musicale* [Paris, 1864], pp. 227-28).

[46] For the story see the facsimile edition by Edward E. Lowinsky, *Documenta Musicologica*, XVII (Kassel-Basel, 1959), Postface.

[47] In Chapter 7 of Book IV of the *Lucidario*, entitled "Question whether C and F can be flattened," Aron says that hexachords involving C♭, F♭, B♯, and E♯ are impossible "per via del genere Diatonico," or, as we would prefer to phrase it, "in the then prevailing tuning systems."

instruments can move their fingers to obtain any interval and trans-position.[48] Again, this fits Alfonso's Sinfonia, which unquestionably was written for five string instruments.

III

Design and structure of Alfonso's chromatic Sinfonia are strikingly similar to a well-known work of an entirely different repertory, John Bull's (*ca.* 1562-1628) celebrated four-part keyboard fantasia on the hexachord.[49] Bull also uses the hexachord as ostinato throughout his composition, transposing it to all twelve pitch levels and placing it alternately in each of the four parts. But he chooses shorter note values (semibreves), he uses the hexachord in ascending as well as descending order, and, most significantly, he reduces the shock of the transpositions by arranging them in whole-tone distance, the first series from G, A, B, C♯, E♭ to F, the second series from A♭, B♭, C, D, E, F♯ and back to G, point of departure, which is, at the end, confirmed in fourfold repetition. The piece, if one counts the final measure as two semibreves, is 227 semibreves long, almost precisely half of Alfonso's 230 breves.

[48] [H]avendo esso Organo le sue voci stabili, & ferme, & non essendo in lui spatio minore del semituono non potra reintegrare la prop[r]ia, & naturale sua forma delle sei sillabe, perche altro non puo rendere, che quello, che la corda per se rende, & suona, il che non aviene del Liutto, & d'altri simili stromenti, il qual Liutto puo essere aiutato col dito di colui, ch'el suona alla intensione, & re-missione di qualche spatio minuto per la reintegratione della sua consonanza, perche puo movere la mano, overo il dito in giu, & in su secondo che gli piace. (Chapter 5 of Book IV, fol. 35ᵛ)

Inasmuch as the said organ has stable and immovable tones and does not have an interval smaller than a half tone, it cannot preserve intact the proper and natural form of the six syllables [in all transpositions], for it cannot render any-thing else than what the key itself ren-ders and sounds. This is not the case with the lute and other similar instru-ments, for the lute can be aided by the fingers of the player with regard to raising or lowering [the tone] by some minute interval to effect the perfection of its harmony, for the player can move his hand and finger up and down as he pleases.

[49] See *The Fitzwilliam Virginal Book*, ed. J. A. Fuller Maitland and W. Barclay Squire, 2 vols. (London, 1894-99), I, 183-87; see also the recent edition of *John Bull, Keyboard Music: I* (*Musica Britannica*, XIV, London, 1960), pp. 53-55. Unfortunately, the latter edition normalizes Bull's notation; one must consult the edition of *The Fitzwilliam Virginal Book* to see the original notation which is a historical docu-ment of exceeding interest. Since both Alfonso della Viola and John Bull use sharps and flats interchangeably, their works are also related in the manner of their notation.

Bull's fantasia has long intrigued historians of keyboard music.[50] It is, both in his own *oeuvre* and among the rich output of keyboard fantasias in England and abroad, a rather isolated phenomenon. Did Bull know Alfonso della Viola's chromatic Sinfonia?

This question leads to a very curious discovery. Viola's work, unpublished in Italy, recorded, so it seems, only by Berardi, unknown to modern biographers of the Ferrarese master, forgotten in the chronicles of chromaticism, survives in a whole number of English manuscripts of the early seventeenth century—but under the name of Alfonso Ferrabosco.

In *The Musical Antiquary* of 1912,[51] in an article on "An Oxford Book of Fancies," Ernest Walker published a four-part fantasia by Alfonso Ferrabosco in which the hexachord appears on chromatically ascending degrees. In an edition of *Jacobean Consort Music*[52] appears, under the same name, a companion piece of this work, this time on the chromatically descending hexachord, again for four voices. The same publication also contains a five-part version of the fantasia on the chromatically descending hexachord, again with the same attribution. The four-part fantasia on the ascending hexachord also has a five-part version.[53] This work, the five-part companion of the fantasia on the descending hexachord, regrettably omitted in the *Musica Britannica* edition, contains the same fifteen measures printed in Berardi's treatise and ascribed there to Alfonso del Violino (Ex. 6). The transcription of Alfonso's hexachord fantasia has been made

[50] C. F. Weitzmann, *Geschichte des Klavierspiels und der Klavierlitteratur*, 3rd edn. by Max Seiffert (Leipzig, 1899), 1, 67, describes Bull's hexachord fantasia as a work in which the chromaticism of Italian vocal music is transferred to the keyboard, "enriching the music of the latter with expressive means of enormous potentialities." Charles van den Borren, in his book, *The Sources of Keyboard Music in England* (London, 1913), pp. 321-28, offers an interesting analysis of the work and concludes, similarly, after referring to the modulation of "the Italian 'chromatists,'" such as Marenzio, Gesualdo, and Monteverdi, that "with them these modulations were invariably called for by a poetic text, while in the piece by Bull they occur in the domain of pure music, and thus acquire an incalculable theoretic value." He underscores also the point already made by Fuller Maitland and Barclay Squire in the preface to their edition of *The Fitzwilliam Virginal Book* that John Bull must have used a keyboard instrument with equal temperament.

[51] Vol. III, 70-73.

[52] Edited by Thurston Dart and William Coates, *Musica Britannica*, IX (London, 1955), No. 23 (see also Critical Commentary to No. 23).

[53] See Lowinsky, "Matthaeus Greiter's *Fortuna*," p. 73 n 57.

Ut re mi fa sol la

Ex. 6. Alfonso della Viola, *Ut re mi fa sol la*, from London, B. M. Egerton 3665, pp. 999-1001 (attributed to Alfonso Ferabosco Jun.)

Ex. 6 (cont.)

Ex. 6 (cont.)

Ex. 6 (cont.)

Ex. 6 (cont.)

Ex. 6 (cont.)

from British Museum, MS Egerton 3665 (pp. 999-1001).[54] This huge
manuscript of 1040 pages written in score, previously entirely unknown, emerged in 1951 from the library of the Earl of Malmsley
and was acquired in that year by the British Museum. Thurston
Dart discovered that it was written by the same Francis Tregian, Jr.,
to whose stupendous industry and skill we owe the treasures of the
Fitzwilliam Virginal Book and the Sambrooke manuscript in the
New York Public Library (MS Drexel 4302).[55] Whereas the former
was devoted to keyboard music and the latter to motets and madrigals, the present manuscript contains chiefly a wealth of Italian vocal
secular music, but also a small, yet significant, collection of compositions for instrumental ensemble, forty compositions for five instruments,[56] among which appears our work with the title "Fantasie et
Pavano a. 5. di Alfonso Ferabosco il Sigmolo [*sic*]."[57] Contrary to
the impression created by this title, the pavan following the hexachord fantasia (we prefer to speak of the two parts of this work as
one fantasia) has nothing to do with it. The fantasia begins and
ends in C major; the pavan following is set in D Dorian.

[54] I am indebted to my former student, Mrs. Jane Troy Johnson, for sending me
a photocopy of the three pages containing the work from the microfilm at the Music
Library of the University of California in Berkeley. Almost at the same time the
complete microfilm of the manuscript arrived from the British Museum, where it
had been ordered many months ago.

[55] See Bertram Schofield and Thurston Dart, "Tregian's Anthology," *Music and
Letters*, XXXII (1951), 205-16.

[56] See Elizabeth Cole, "L'Anthologie de madrigaux et de musique instrumentale
pour ensembles de Francis Tregian," *La Musique instrumentale de la Renaissance*
(Paris, 1955), pp. 115-26.

[57] The original titles were cut off by an eighteenth-century book binder, who,
however, copied them carefully below the cut-off section (see Elizabeth Cole, *ibid.*,
p. 116). Mistakes occurred in that operation and "Sigmolo" is certainly a misreading
of "figliuolo," as "Pavano" must have been misread for "Pavana."

Francis Tregian's eminent musicianship is manifest in the care and accuracy with which he scored this perplexingly difficult work with its hundreds of sharps and flats. There are no mistakes. Throughout the manuscript, Tregian has ruled the pages beforehand so that he could not adjust the space available according to the number of accidentals required per bar. This is the reason why he supplemented the accidentals in the score with whole rows of flats and sharps below the notes. Since, in a work of this kind, the original notation is of historic importance, we reproduce Tregian's score without changes, except that we place all accidentals within the score. Accidentals placed above are our own; they are mostly cautionary or explanatory.

The four-part versions of the two hexachord fantasias, available in Walker's transcription and in the *Jacobean Consort Music* (No. 23), are later arrangements in which the treble viol is left out. But many of its passages are absorbed into the first tenor viol with octave transpositions wherever necessary, thus presenting a conflation of treble and first tenor parts. In particular, where the original first tenor pauses, it takes over the phrases of the treble viol. The result is that the four-part arrangement has a first tenor with very crowded and often jagged lines. The five-part version shows indisputable artistic superiority.

Before discovering Alfonso del Violino's Sinfonia in the hexachord fantasia published under Alfonso Ferrabosco's name, we had attempted a reconstruction of the design of the work. We can now compare hypothesis with reality: correct was the supposition of the chromatically ascending and descending hexachords, incorrect the number of hexachords and on which hexachord the piece began. Instead of twelve, Alfonso uses only eight hexachord transpositions (in this respect Bull, with his twelve transpositions, sought to surpass his model), and both ascending and descending hexachords move in slow breves. Indeed, the length of the two fantasias together ($121 + 112 = 233$ measures) is close enough to Berardi's 230 measures to lend strength to the supposition that, also from this point of view, the two works are merely two *partes* of one and the same composition. It would appear that Alfonso planned the Sinfonia so that the *prima pars* was based on the ascending and the *secunda pars* on the descending hexachord.

None of this answers the question as to who the composer of this extraordinary work is, Alfonso della Viola or Alfonso Ferrabosco II.

Although the question of authorship is not essential to our principal investigation, it is of sufficient interest to engage our attention. Moreover, it is a neat little problem in method, for the data available allow no clear conclusions based on indisputable facts; they allow no more than the formation of a hypothesis.

At first glance the evidence on the side of Alfonso Ferrabosco II appears overwhelming: four English manuscripts contain the five-part version of the work, nine the four-part version. If Ferrabosco is the composer, then the manuscripts harboring his work are notably contemporaneous with the author. Alfonso Ferrabosco II lived from about 1575 to 1628. The English manuscripts containing his works cannot be dated with certainty, but the music contained in them seems to belong to the period from 1599 to 1625.[58]

If the author were Alfonso Ferrabosco II, however, we would have to close our eyes to the Italian evidence. For it is hard to explain how Angelo Berardi, who never shows the slightest familiarity with English music or musicians, should have come into possession of an English fancy, and how, in the year 1690, the work of an English musician of around 1620 should have appeared in an Italian book. And what would be the reason for Berardi's not using the name Alfonso Ferrabosco? Why should he not have mentioned that this was the work of an English musician, working at the court of the King of England? When Mersenne, in his *Harmonie universelle* of 1636, publishes anonymously a five-part fantasia—recently discovered to be by Alfonso Ferrabosco II—he identifies the composer at least as "un excellent joueur de viole Anglois de Nation."[59]

[58] Thurston Dart and William Coates, in their introduction to *Jacobean Consort Music* (p. xvi), express themselves warily on the subject: "no-one can be certain that every piece in this volume was composed during the period enclosed by the dates 1599 and 1625—most of the music is preserved only in manuscript sources, and it is hazardous to attempt to date any of these with precision—but the editors hope that their guesses have not been ill-founded."

[59] See Raymond Vaught, "Mersenne's Unknown English Viol Player," *The Galpin Society Journal*, XVII (1964), 17-23. It should be added that Mersenne lived in Paris, Berardi in small towns—Viterbo, Tivoli, Spoleto; only at the end of his life did he come to Rome. Mersenne, preceding Berardi by half a century, was a contemporary of Ferrabosco; he was also, unlike Berardi, widely traveled and a figure of international renown, maintaining a formidable correspondence (of which ten volumes have been published so far) with scholars and musicians of many countries, including England; he knew personally, and had a high regard for, André Maugars, French violist who was, for several years in the early 1620's, a colleague of Alfonso Ferrabosco II at the court of the King of England. He might very well have brought

The chief reason for questioning the attribution to Alfonso della Viola lies in the great gap between the death of Alfonso della Viola (*ca.* 1570) and the publication of Berardi's work (1690). A minor reason lies in Berardi's changing the composer's name from Alfonso della Viola to Alfonso del Violino. The latter, in view of the traditional liberty taken with artists' names in centuries past (and in view of the point made before concerning the violin in the seventeenth century superseding the viola in the sixteenth), does not present serious difficulties; the former does.

However, Berardi's claim to reliability rests on a very solid foundation:

1. He transmits the fifteen most critical measures of the composition in an excellent and independent reading and in the superior five-part version which certainly constitutes the original. It is obvious that he had an excellent source at his disposal.

2. The gap between Viola's death and Berardi's publication is a less serious consideration if we take account of the fact that Berardi is above all the historian and theorist of sixteenth-century music.[60]

3. Berardi stands in a direct line of the musical tradition that leads back from Marco Scacchi through Giovanni Francesco Anerio to Palestrina, whom he considers the cornerstone of the art of counterpoint.[61]

---

with him the fantasia published by Mersenne when he returned to Paris in 1624. For Mersenne's opinion of Maugars see the introduction of Er. Thoinan to Maugars' *Response faite à un curieux sur le sentiment de la Musique d'Italie* (Paris, 1865; repr. London, 1965), p. 17.

[60] Berardi's intimate and comprehensive knowledge of the music of the past two centuries is manifest also in his wide reading of Quattrocento and Cinquecento writers on music. In his *Ragionamenti musicali* of 1681 he includes in his list of authors on music (pp. 177-82) the following (in an order governed by the alphabet of first names): "Andrea Ornito(parchus). Adriano Petit (Coclico). Bartolomeo Rami. Diruta nel Transilvano. Franchino Gafforo Laud(ense) prat(tica). Francesco Salina spec(ulativa). Giovanni Spadario Bolognese. Giovanni Spinosa. Giovanni Tinctoris. Gio. Maria Artusi prat(tica). Gio. Maria Lanfranco. Fr. Giovanni d'Avella prat(tica). Giuseppe Zarlino spec(ulativa) e prat(tica). Hermanno Finck prat(tica). Lodovico Fogliani da Modana [*sic*] spec(ulativa). Lodovico Zacconi da Pesaro, Agostiniano. D. Nicola Vicentino prat(tica). Othomano Luscino d'Argenta, La Musurgia. Oratio Tigrini prat(tica). Pietro Aron. Recaneto (by Stephanus Vanneus). Vincenzo Galilei.

[61] The famous division of church music into four different styles (see Friedrich Blume's article on Berardi in *MGG*, 1, cols. 1670-74, for a succinct summary) begins with the vocal polyphony of Masses and motets "in the old style," where he refers to Josquin, Mouton, Willaert, Morales, and the "divine" Palestrina (*Ragionamenti*

4. Berardi, the historian, places the Sinfonia into the tradition of Willaert's chromatic "duo" in one and the same breath with Romano Micheli's six-part madrigal, and in this order, suggesting thereby that Alfonso's Sinfonia precedes Micheli's madrigal.

5. Berardi's claim to reliability is furthermore strengthened by his transmission of the correct musical versions of three complex and sophisticated chromatic experiments of the past: Marco Scacchi's motet (to be discussed presently), Romano Micheli's madrigal of 1621, and Adrian Willaert's chromatic "duo" of about 1519.

To these arguments must be added the logic of historical circumstance. Chromaticism, after all, was the fruit of Italian developments, partly growing out of the Italian love of harmonic color and the abundant practice of *musica ficta*, partly the result of Italy's intense preoccupation with humanism and the intended revival of Greek music and the Greek genera. If Alfonso della Viola is the composer, there is no difficulty whatever in understanding the genesis of this bold composition. The theoretical background is defined by the treatises of Aron and Vicentino, the acoustical background by the recognition of Aristoxenus in the circle of Willaert and his pupils, the musical background by Alfonso's own madrigals and those by Cipriano de Rore as well as by the music of Nicola Vicentino; and both Rore and Vicentino were colleagues of Alfonso della Viola at the court of Ferrara.

Acceptance of Berardi's attribution imposes the obligation to explain the presence of the Italian Sinfonia in English manuscripts. This explanation is made easy by the presence of Italian musicians in England, and in particular, the Ferraboscos who gave England three generations of musicians. Alfonso Ferrabosco I, who had come to England to serve Queen Elizabeth in 1562, left the country for a journey to his homeland between the years 1569 and 1572, that is, toward the end of Alfonso della Viola's life. Whereas it might have been difficult for an Italian musician to wrest a copy of this work from the Ferrarese court famous for the jealousy with which it guarded its musical treasures, a musician in the service of the English Queen had uncommon advantages over Italian rivals. Thus it is

---

musicali, p. 133). In the *Documenti* he recommends for study Frescobaldi's "caprici" of 1624 and Soriano's, the Palestrina disciple's, "canoni sopra l'Ave Maris Stella" of 1610.

reasonable to assume that Alfonso Ferrabosco the Elder, upon his return from Italy to England in 1572, brought Italian music with him and among other scores that of Alfonso della Viola's Sinfonia.

However, do the English manuscripts really attribute the work to Alfonso Ferrabosco II? On this question the aforementioned edition by Dart and Coates leaves us completely in the dark, since ascriptions—or the lack of them—for the various sources are not indicated. The picture emerging from an examination of the different sources is highly interesting:

1. Christ Church, Oxford, MSS 404-408, consisting of part-books, transmits the work in its entirety without attribution. A. Ferrabosco's name appears, however, on the next piece, the "Dovehouse" Pavan.

2. Christ Church, MS 2. This score, usually ascribed to the hand of Dean Aldrich, carries no original attributions to Alfonso Ferrabosco II. His name appears in the modern index and over the music, written in pencil by a modern hand.

3. Christ Church, MSS 473-78. Both parts of the composition are in the four-voiced versions; the first is titled "Ut, re, mi," the following is marked "The second parte." The pieces are the fourth and fifth in a group of Ferrabosco four-part fantasias; both are ascribed to "Alphonso" in the original hand.

Here it should be observed that Alfonso Ferrabosco II might possibly have been responsible for editing the four-part version of this work.

4. Neither part of the fantasia occurs in Christ Church MS 472, which has twenty four-part fantasias by Ferrabosco, nor in Christ Church, MS 1004, which has a considerable Ferrabosco section.[62]

5. London, British Museum, MS Add. 29996, which contains the first part of the hexachord fantasia in condensed score (fol. 189^v), attributes it to "Alfonso."[63]

It should be remembered that many of these manuscripts contain Italian music. For example, Christ Church, MSS 404-408, from which

[62] The data under Nos. 1 through 4 have been assembled by Professor Frank Ll. Harrison, lecturer at Oxford University, and his student, Mr. David Chadd. I am grateful to both gentlemen for their kindness and the thoroughness of their research.

[63] I am greatly indebted to Miss P. J. Willetts, Assistant Keeper in the Department of Manuscripts of the British Museum, for her kind and prompt information on this manuscript. I should also like to express my gratitude to Mr. A. Hyatt King who with never-failing courtesy and speed directed my inquiry to the right place and person.

apparently the scores in MS 2 were transcribed, includes works by Marenzio, Monteverdi, Pallavicino, and Vecchi.[64] Surely, there is no reason why these manuscripts should not also contain a Sinfonia by Alfonso della Viola.

6. Royal College of Music, London, MS 1145, consisting of three part-books (Cantus, Altus, Tenor), contains the composition in its entirety with the attribution "Alfon: Ferra: Jun." Mr. Richard Townend, Assistant to the Reference Librarian of the Royal College of Music, at my request, investigated the handwriting of the attribution with the following result: a certain "Staresmore" collated MS 1145 with another source, the "Barnard score." He identifies himself at the end of each piece so compared in the following manner: "Exam. by Staresmore. Barnard score: B." The variants in the "Barnard score" are notated meticulously in the margin. The handwriting of the ascriptions in MS 1145 is the same as that of Staresmore. In other words, the attribution of the work to Ferrabosco is not part of the original manuscript, but has been added subsequently. Miss Pamela Willetts has tentatively—and, I think, persuasively—identified Staresmore with "the William Staresmore of Frolesworth in Leicestershire who compounded in March 1649."[65]

Concerning the handwriting of the attribution, I was able to confirm Mr. Townend's deductions from a study of the hexachord fantasia in MS 1145 made available to me in microfilm through his kind offices. I do not know what the "Barnard score" is. There is, of course, John Barnard, minor canon of St. Paul's Cathedral, who in 1641 published the *Selected Church Music*, a great collection of Anglican services by Tallis, Byrd, Ward, William Mundy, Parsons, Morley, Orlando Gibbons, and many others.[66] It is possible that the

[64] This information I owe to the kindness of Mrs. Jane Troy Johnson who is writing a dissertation on the English dances for string consort and who has studied the manuscripts of this literature at the libraries of Oxford.

[65] See P. Willetts, "Sir Nicholas Le Strange and John Jenkins," *Music and Letters*, 42 (1961), 40. I am indebted to Miss Willetts for her kindness in sending me an offprint of her essay and for answering a number of questions. I owe special thanks to Denis Stevens, Professor of Musicology at Columbia University, who referred me to Miss Willetts' article in the first place when I searched for information on Staresmore, and who explained in a letter of November 1, 1966, that "compounding has its usual legal meaning of concealing a felony, and was often applied to Royalists during the Commonwealth regime of Oliver Cromwell."

[66] See Ernest Walker, *A History of Music in England*, 3rd edn. rev. and enlarged by J. A. Westrup (Oxford, 1952), pp. 155-56; for further information see Denis Stevens, *Tudor Church Music* (London, 1961), p. 53 n 1.

same seventeenth-century musician was responsible for a collection of instrumental music. Indeed, this collection might conceivably be identical with one of the known manuscripts of fantasias. Perhaps one of our English colleagues can shed some light on this matter.

7. The manuscript of the British Museum, Egerton 3665, which ascribes the work to "Alfonso Ferabosco Jun.," was written by Francis Tregian, presumably while in prison, where he was kept from firsthand contact with musicians and sources. Indeed, it is possible to surmise the reason for Francis Tregian's error, if error it be, in ascribing the work, in contrast to so many other sources, to the younger Ferrabosco. As mentioned above, he gives it the following title: "Fantasie et Pavana a. 5. di Alfonso Ferabosco il figliuolo." Now the handwritten part-books of Christ Church, MSS 404-408, also contain the two *partes* of the fantasia followed by the same pavan,[67] but they carry neither a common title nor a common attribution. The pavan is ascribed to the younger Ferrabosco, the fantasia remains anonymous. Tregian, finding the three pieces together and the last one signed, might have thought they belonged together and consequently committed the honest error of ascribing the fantasia to the same author as the pavan. (Incidentally, "Tregian's Anthology," too, contains a wealth of Italian music, particularly madrigals.[68])

8. York Minster Library, MS M-3/1 S-4 S (three of four part-books), Nos. 9 and 10, "Alfonso Ferabosco" (in bass part only). The date "Dec. 7, 1667" appears in the bass part of No. 7.[69]

What seemed at first overwhelming documentary evidence has dwindled to the evidence of two sources. One is more than a generation later than all the other sources—it was written almost forty years after the death of Alfonso Ferrabosco and therefore should not be counted as a source with the authority of a contemporary document. The other is a contemporary source, but one written by a scribe who, owing to the limitations imposed upon his freedom of movement, was severely handicapped in verifying his ascriptions

---

[67] Here the piece appears with the title "Dovehouse Pavan"; in MS Egerton 3665 the same piece has the title "Pavane."

[68] See Bertram Schofield and Thurston Dart, "Tregian's Anthology."

[69] I owe the knowledge of this concordance to the kindness of Robert A. Warner, Professor of Music at the University of Michigan, who informs me that this manuscript chiefly contains fancies by John Jenkins (1592-1678). Professor Warner, in *The Music Review*, XXVIII (1967), 1-20, has published a study on a fancy by that composer containing an enharmonic modulation.

and cleansing them from errors. In all of this we must hold fast to the fact that the five-part version is the original version, that the four-part condensation may possibly be the handiwork of the younger Ferrabosco. The confusion in the attribution of the work may therefore have its origin in the existence of a four-part arrangement by Ferrabosco as well as in the name Alfonso, common to both della Viola and Ferrabosco Junior.[70]

There remains one question. We know that Alfonso Ferrabosco II composed instrumental music; what evidence is there, aside from Berardi's testimony, that Alfonso della Viola wrote fantasias for instrumental ensemble? There is circumstantial evidence in the account books of the court of Ferrara, excerpts of which were published by Weyler. Alfonso's cognomen, in the fashion of the time, points to his activities as a string instrument player. In the accounts of 1533, for example,[71] appear first the various singers followed by the designation "cantore"; then are listed:

> Jaches brumello organista
> Alfonso dala viola
> Frances[c]o dala viola
> hieron[ym]o graganello trombetta
> Jac[op]o graganello trombetta.

Luigi Dentice, in his *Duo dialoghi della musica*, published in Rome in 1553, has Serone, one of his interlocutors, refer to "Misser Alfonso della Viola" as "no less miraculous in counterpoint and composition than he is as a performer on the viola in ensemble playing."[72] And finally, there is the above-mentioned passage in Hercole Bottrigari's

---

[70] Professor Nino Pirrotta made the intriguing suggestion that the English sources might have been drawn from an Italian original which ascribed the piece to "Alfonso Ferra:"—a common abbreviation for Alfonso Ferrarese, that is, Alfonso of Ferrara alias Alfonso della Viola. What would have been more natural for an English copyist than to have interpreted this as "Alfonso Ferrabosco," to which he then would have added, for further distinction, "Junior" or "figliuolo"? (This tempting hypothesis would seem strengthened by the fact that the "Symon Ferra" of manuscripts Bologna Q 19, Bologna Q 23, and London, Royal College of Music, MS 2037 occurs in Peter Schoeffer's *Cantiones quinque vocum selectissimae* of 1539 [RISM 1539[8]] as "Simon Ferrariensis.")

[71] Weyler, "Documenten betreffende de muziekkapel aan het hof van Ferrara," pp. 86-87.

[72] "[N]on è meno miracoloso nel contrapunto & nel comporre, che nel sonare la Viola d'arco in conserto. . ." (fol. I 3[v]). On the term "conserto," see David D. Boyden, "When is a Concerto not a Concerto?," *Musical Quarterly*, XLIII (1957), 220-32, esp. 226-28.

Desiderio that establishes Alfonso della Viola as composer of a *concerto grande* of such quality that it is, in 1594, still heard at the splendid musical affairs of the court of Ferrara together with a similar composition by Luzzasco Luzzaschi.

The recent publication of the first print of ensemble music for four instruments, *Musica nova* of 1540 in Venice,[73] establishes Italy as the home of chamber music and Venice as the cradle of music for a quartet of instruments. The central figure in this movement is Adrian Willaert, who, in Ferrara, either preceded Alfonso della Viola, or—this is not quite clear—spent some time there together with him. At any rate, the artistic relations between Venice and Ferrara were of the liveliest sort throughout the whole century.

Were it not for the survival of one single part-book, we would not know of *Musica nova*. Were it not for the existence of one single, but fortunately complete, set of part-books—the concordant *Musicque de Joye*—the repertory of *Musica nova* would have been lost altogether. The existence of an Italian five-part Sinfonia in the repertory of English fancies would then be perhaps suspect. But against the background of Italian ensemble music (and Italian repertories in English manuscripts), Alfonso della Viola's appearance in England becomes less surprising. Della Viola's bold and beautiful composition, a work of the highest skill, may perhaps be thought of as a model in the repertory of English fantasias, a model that, as shown in its wide dissemination and in its four-part arrangement, attracted the attention of English consort players and writers as well as that of keyboard players—the latter proven by John Bull's chromatic hexachord fantasia. John Bull's work not only gains a new dimension, but also becomes more comprehensible: modeled most likely after the four-part keyboard version of the Viola work, the composition was written not for a well-tempered clavier (which probably did not exist; nor did England, as far as we know, boast the chromatic keyboards with split keys and microtone divisions known from contemporary Italy), but either as a condensed score for fretted string instruments capable of producing well-tempered harmony, or as a compositional experiment in "futurist" music.

The chances of establishing the identity of our hexachord fantasia on the basis of a stylistic analysis of the fantasias of the younger Ferrabosco are slight. None of the famous chromatic experiments

[73] *Monuments of Renaissance Music*, Vol. 1, ed. H. Colin Slim (Chicago, 1964).

from Willaert to Greiter, from Cipriano de Rore to Lasso's Sibyl cycle would ever have been attributed correctly, had they appeared anonymously, on the basis of stylistic analysis. Their very purpose was a search for new paths and novel sonorities, and thus comparison with the more conventional style of their composers could not convincingly lead to an unassailable attribution. Moreover, the presence of an Italian work on the English scene suggests that English composers may have learned from it—and there are many admirable traits that they could have borrowed from Viola's work aside from its astonishing chromaticism. And this may well explain certain similarities between the Italian model and other English works inspired by it in one way or another.

The discovery of Alfonso della Viola's chromatic Sinfonia in English sources restores a highly significant work to its rightful place in the history of Italian chromaticism. It also opens an intriguing perspective of Italian influence on the English fancy at the height of its development. For Alfonso's Sinfonia is not only an extraordinary piece for its daring design; it is a work of great intrinsic beauty as remarkable for its sweep of melody, its suppleness of rhythm, the dense weaving of its polyphony as for the freedom, imagination, and the utterly fantastic sound of its modulations.[74] The climax near the end (mm. 86-100), in the solemn, slow chordal passage with its emphatic syncopations and dissonances, with its ravishing modulation from G major to A♭ minor (resolving to major in the final chord) passing through E minor-major, touching the chords of C♯ minor, G♯ minor, D♯ minor, B major, F♯ major, and declining to the cadence in A♭ minor-major with the moving fall of a fifth in the soprano and a dominant seventh chord introducing the final chords, is an anticipation of Monteverdi's grandeur and eloquence, and an anticipation also of the *ligature e durezze* of the late sixteenth and early seventeenth centuries.

[74] Charles van den Borren (*The Sources of Keyboard Music in England*, p. 326 n 201), was the first scholar to connect Bull's hexachord fancy with the four-part fantasia by Alfonso Ferrabosco II published by Ernest Walker in *The Musical Antiquary*. He made the following observation: "The number of hexachords brought into play (8) is less than in the case of Bull, but the modulations are none the less of incredible boldness; they give occasion for the use of F-flat and E-sharp, which we do not find in Bull. The piece, written in four parts, sounds singularly well, and the modulations are made in an easier fashion than in the *Ut, re, mi, fa, sol, la* of Bull."

IV

How did Berardi come into possession of Viola's score? After all, he published the fragment about 120 years after the composer's death. Why was he so intensely interested in chromatic experiments? Time and again Berardi pays glowing tribute to his teacher Marco Scacchi, nowhere more feelingly than in the *Proemio* to his *Documenti armonici* of 1687.[75] Marco Scacchi retired to Gallese in 1649. The birthdate of Berardi is not known, but is assumed to be about 1630. If Berardi took up his studies with Scacchi around 1650 and if he continued them till the latter's death (between 1681 and 1687),[76] this association would have continued for three decades. Very possibly then, in view of so intimate and lengthy an association and of Berardi's own frequent testimonies that he was transmitting his master's teachings, he was left in possession of Scacchi's scores, writings, books, and works of other masters. Marco Scacchi himself was a pupil of Giovanni Francesco Anerio, by whom he was supposedly taken to Warsaw, where Anerio, probably in 1624, became director of the Royal Chapel.[77]

Now Giovanni Francesco Anerio, like his older brother Felice, had been associated as a singer with Palestrina and, as a composer, belonged to the school of the Roman master. It was from Scacchi that Berardi received the living tradition of the sixteenth-century school of counterpoint which was the central object of his theoretical studies. Scacchi himself, although a capable composer in the new *concertato* style, was a well-trained master of canon and counter-

[75] This is what Berardi writes: "In my most flourishing youth, notwithstanding that I was Canon and chapelmaster in a prominent city, I subjected myself completely to the discipline and guidance of the late Marco Scacchi, one-time director of the Royal Chapel of Poland, a post he held for thirty years. This famous artist retired to the city of Gallese, ancient home of his predecessors, because of his advanced age, and perhaps also so that he might enjoy that quiet and peace that is not so easily found in the bustle of courtly life and among the occupations and affairs of serious duties. These studies were our ordinary pastime, and since I believe they might be agreeable to the learned, and of use to the young students, I have undertaken to write these documents."

[76] See Claude V. Palisca in *MGG*, xi, cols. 1466-69.

[77] The erroneous biographic data in *MGG* and preceding dictionaries—according to which Giovanni Francesco Anerio in 1609 was Royal chapelmaster of Sigismund III of Poland, but returned to Italy in 1610 and died in 1621—have been corrected by Hellmuth Federhofer in two articles in *Die Musikforschung*, ii (1949), 210-13, and vi (1953), 346-47. Anerio died in 1630 in Graz on his return from Poland.

point; he entered into the theoretical controversy on the nature of the *stile antico* between K. Förster and P. Siefert with his *Cribrum musicum* of 1644.[78]

Scacchi's interest in the sixteenth-century tradition was broad enough to include the daring innovations of the chromaticists. Indeed, he composed a five-part motet in sixteenth-century style and in the purest tradition of Willaert's chromatic "duo," in which the second tenor, at one point, goes through the circle of fifths (Ex. 7). The work is published in Berardi's *Documenti armonici* (Book 1, Doc. xxviii) and the author prefaces it with the following note:

Motetto à 5. tessuto artificiosissimamente. Nel secondo Tenore le note appariscono tutte dissonanze dove si ritrova questo segno N. B., mà se saranno considerate con la ragione de' buoni fundamenti Musicali sono tutte consonanze. L'artificio in tutto consiste d'ingannar l'occhio.

Five-part motet designed with greatest art. The notes in the second tenor at the sign N. B. appear all to be dissonant, but when considered with the logic of sound musical foundations they are all consonant. The artifice consists entirely in the deception of the eye.

Scacchi could hardly have emphasized the connection with Willaert's "duo" in more unmistakable fashion. First of all, he singles out this passage of the five-part work for two-part treatment. (We must remember that Willaert's *Quid non ebrietas*, published *ca.* 1530 in a four-part version, entered the theoretical literature as a "duo" and was known in this form throughout the seventeenth century.) Secondly, Scacchi summarizes, as it were, Willaert's procedure by starting likewise from B♭ and going step for step to E-double flat. But he avoids all intermediary notes, limiting himself strictly to the tones of the circle of fifths. Thirdly, he too keeps the soprano in the home mode—at least in the critical two-part passage in which the second tenor modulates through the circle of fifths. Finally, Scacchi also follows Willaert in avoiding the notation of double flats and thereby creates the appearance of a chain of dissonances stretching from measure 25 to the end.

John Hawkins reprinted this piece from Berardi's treatise.[79] He resolved the puzzling notation of the second tenor without mentioning it, thereby destroying the "optical illusion" intended by the

[78] See Palisca, *loc.cit.*, for a summary of the controversy.

[79] *A General History of the Science and Practice of Music*, 2 vols. (London, 1776); 2nd revised edn. (London, 1853), in the reprint of Dover Publications (New York, 1963), II, 592-94.

Vobis datum est

Ex. 7. Marco Scacchi, *Vobis datum est*, from Berardi,
Documenti musicali, L.I, Documento XXVIII

Ex. 7 (cont.)

Ex. 7 (cont.)

Ex. 7 (cont.)

composer. Moreover, he gave the soprano in the two-part passage
an interpretation which I believe to be opposed to the one Scacchi
had in mind (Ex. 8). By flattening G and F in the soprano (mm. 24
and 25) he produced a dissonance on the first beat of measure 25,
violating the rules against skipping into and out of a dissonance,
and he created an unmelodious whole-tone sequence in the soprano
which is completely out of style. By leaving the soprano intact, we
run into one false relation between G♭ in the tenor and G♮ in the
soprano—small penalty for escaping Hawkins' harsh version.

Ex. 8

With great wit, Scacchi writes this composition to the words of
St. Luke 8:10, which is used in the liturgy as antiphon for the
Magnificat of Sexagesima Sunday (*Liber Usualis*, p. 510):

Vobis datum est noscere mysterium Regni Dei, caeteris autem in parabolis, ut videntes non videant, et audientes non intelligant.	Unto you it is given to know the mysteries of the Kingdom of God: but to others in parables; that seeing they might not see, and hearing they might not understand.

More than a century after Willaert, the circle of fifths is still considered a "mystery," comparable to the Kingdom of God which is known in its essence solely to the initiated, to the uninitiated only in parables. To underscore this point, Scacchi writes the critical two-part passage to the words "ut videntes non videant," marking thereby the *inganno d'occhio* of this passage.

It is astonishing that this piece, published in Berardi's *Documenti armonici* and reprinted by John Hawkins, should not, to my knowledge, have drawn a single commentary since Berardi's day—not even Hawkins himself, who praised Scacchi's compositions in general,[80] added an explanatory word to this extraordinary work, which, incidentally, he called "a madrigal." Berardi himself leaves no doubt that Scacchi followed Willaert. He adds the following commentary to his master's work (*Documenti*, p. 78):

L'inventione di calare un tuono, è antichissima. Il Primo Inventore fù Adriano Wilaert Musico rarissimo che ritrovò il modo di comporre à 2. Chori, che ciascuno da se stesso accordasse. Il sudetto compose un duo intitolato: *Quid non ebrietas*. L'artificio di questa cantilena consiste, che il Tenore cala un Tuono per mezo de gl'accidenti maggiori, & il Soprano resta nel suo luogo. Per curiosità degli studiosi ponerò in partitura il detto duo.

The invention of falling a whole tone is ancient. Its first inventor was Adrian Willaert, a musician of rare gifts, who discovered the technique of composing for two choirs so that each choir accorded within itself. The above-named composed a duo entitled *Quid non ebrietas*. The artifice of this composition consists in the tenor's falling one whole tone by means of major accidentals, while the soprano stays in its place. To satisfy the curiosity of the students I shall print the said duo in score.

Following the score of Willaert's "duo" Berardi remarks:

Quando uscì alla luce il sudetto duo, Gio. Spadaro fù d'opinione, che il finale concludesse in una comma antica, non bisogna maravigliarsi, dice l'Artusi poiche derivava dalla scuola di Boetio, conforme si legge in una sua lettera scritta à Don Pietro Aron l'Anno 1524. Io però sono di parere,

When the said duo appeared, Giovanni Spataro was of the opinion that the concluding interval exceeded its measure by one ancient comma. No wonder, commented Artusi, since Spataro followed the [Pythagorean] doctrine of Boethius, as one reads in a letter that he wrote to Pietro Aron in

[80] "The musical compositions of Scacchi are greatly esteemed by the Italians for the exceeding closeness of their contexture, and that ingenious and artificial contrivance, which manifests itself to the curious observer" (*ibid.*, p. 592).

che la divisione del tuono in due parti eguali secondo l'opinione d'Aristossero [*sic*], sia più propria per tessere Sinfonie per Istrumenti, che cantilene per voci.	the year 1524.[81] I, however, am persuaded that the division of the tone into two equal semitones [in other words, equal temperament] is more appropriate for instrumental than for vocal compositions.

This is indirect testimony for Berardi's belief that Alfonso della Viola's chromatic Sinfonia was written for string instruments adapted to equal temperament. Scacchi's ingenious five-part composition in imitation of Willaert's "duo" furnishes proof that he owned the latter work; it gives reason to believe that Berardi came into possession of Viola's work through his master, who in turn may have received it from Giovanni Francesco Anerio. Berardi received the Roman tradition from his master and never tired of praising it: "From Rome comes the true style of singing, playing, and composing,"[82] he exclaims; and again: "The Roman style of composition as well as of vocal and instrumental performance has always been applauded and embraced by all the world."[83]

Chance certainly plays a strange role in the way in which the old documents have come down to us to allow the reconstruction and evaluation of a movement that is of crucial significance to the evolution of the tonal-harmonic system and of the historical roots of twentieth-century music. Of Willaert's original four-part composition in the contemporary print of about 1530 there remains only one copy of one single part, the alto. Of Alfonso della Viola's role in the chromatic movement we would know nothing were it not for Berardi, writing more than a century after the event. Romano Micheli's canonic madrigal (aside from his autograph manuscript yet to be made known) comes down to us in only one copy at the library of Santa Cecilia in Rome. Berardi offers only an incomplete version. Marco Scacchi's virtuoso talent in rethinking and reconstructing Willaert's idea would have remained unknown were it not for his faithful disciple Angelo Berardi. Often it is out of such

[81] This is Spataro's letter to Aron of September 9, 1524; it is printed in the original and in translation in my article, "Adrian Willaert's Chromatic 'Duo' Re-Examined," pp. 22-26.

[82] *Ragionamenti Musicali composti dal Sig. D. Angelo Berardi . . .* (Bologna, 1681), p. 144.

[83] *Ibid.*, p. 143.

pebbles washed ashore from the ocean of human creativity that the historian must reconstruct the mosaic of the past.

Most of these precious pieces and fragments would never have reached us were it not for the emergence of a new sense of historical consciousness on the part of the Baroque musician. The Renaissance musician made short shrift of the medieval tradition.[84] He was not interested in understanding his own history but in overcoming it. He scanned new horizons in search of new shores. To realize his fresh vision he looked back with nostalgic reverence to ancient Greece. His attitude was neither historical nor critical; it was romantic. A monumental past was to be revived, not for the sake of understanding it, but for the sake of creating a new and exciting art for the present.

The fateful split between the *prima* and *seconda prattica* in the Baroque,[85] the coexistence of the old contrapuntal style for church music and for pedagogy with the new monodic style of the secular cantata and opera, caused a division of musical thinking. A split of this kind must lead to introspection; introspection leads to historical consciousness. In an effort to understand the "two souls in his breast," the Baroque musician explored the Renaissance tradi-

[84] See Edward E. Lowinsky, "Music of the Renaissance as Viewed by Renaissance Musicians," *The Renaissance Image of Man and the World,* ed. Bernard O'Kelly (Columbus, Ohio, 1966), pp. 129-77.

[85] Berardi himself gives an account of the two styles of music in his *Miscellanea musicale* of 1689, where he says (p. 39):

Duo sono le prattiche Musicali la prima è fondata nella dottrina di Platone dove dice, che l'armonia è Signora, e padrona dell'oratione. La seconda, che s'aspetta allo stile, e Musica moderna, è che l'oratione sia padrona, e Signora dell'armonia. Si chiama seconda prattica, essendo necessario di adoprare in questa le consonanze, e dissonanze differentemente di quello che l'hanno usate gl'antichi nella prima.	Two are the musical styles. The first is based on Plato's doctrine that harmony is lord and master of speech; the second, proper to modern music, is that the speech is lord and master of harmony. It is called second style, because in it consonances and dissonances must be handled differently from the way in which the old composers of the first style have used them.

Of course, Berardi has misread his Plato as well as his Zarlino (see Oliver Strunk, *Source Readings in Music History* [Princeton, 1950], pp. 4, 256), a mistake he tried to correct in his last treatise, *Il Perché Musicale* (Bologna, 1693), presented in the form of letters addressed to various musicians (see the letter *Al Sig. Antimo Liberati,* p. 14). But what matters is the clarity with which he, at the end of the seventeenth century, defines the beginnings of the Baroque style, which he then, in illuminating examples, illustrates and opposes to the *stile antico.*

tion. Again, this effort was neither historical in the strict sense of scientific inquiry nor was it critical. It was also suffused with romantic emotion which transformed the guild secrets of the old contrapuntal practitioners and their astonishing technical artifices into something akin to metaphysical mysteries. But this time the musician was preoccupied not with a remote past lacking in practical monuments, surrounded by the halo of ancient myth and the impenetrable thicket of theoretical complexities, but with his own immediate history, alive in an infinite number of compositions accompanied by numberless treatises, and present in the living tradition handed down from one generation to the next.

The interest of the Baroque musician in the history of music was, as it were, autobiographical.[86] The history of music was to him preeminently the history of *his* music. It is this new historical attitude, in addition to the revolutionary and indeed prophetic character of the work itself, that furnishes the explanation of why Willaert's "duo" continued to awaken new echoes which reverberated in compositions and in theoretical discussions for nearly two centuries.

[86] In illustrating the free dissonance treatment of the *stile moderno* with a quotation from Monteverdi's *Lamento d'Arianna*, Berardi traces the origins of the new expressive style and its novel attitude toward dissonance in the madrigals of Pomponio Nenna, Cipriano de Rore, Giaches Wert, and Luca Marenzio, and he contrasts their styles with that of Palestrina. He sees the chief difference between *prima* and *seconda prattica* in the uniformity of secular and ecclesiastical styles of the former and the distinctive differences not only between secular and sacred, but also between the various genres of secular and sacred music, of the latter. For the *prima prattica* he studies not only Palestrina but also the great chanson collections of the 1540's and 1550's; he enumerates their authors from "Jan Ochenheim" and "Jusquino" to "Adriano," "Crequilon," "Iandelatere," "Iaques Vaet," "Vulnerant" (Waelrant), and "Verdelot." He admits that some pieces like Janequin's and Verdelot's "Battaglia" avoid the uniformity of style, but finds that this is due to the gay character of the text, whereas in compositions set to serious texts there is hardly any difference between Mass, motet, and madrigal in style and dissonance treatment (*Miscellanea musicale*, pp. 39-40).

IV. ITALIAN OPERA

"VI SONO MOLT'ALTRE MEZZ'ARIE . . ."

STUART REINER

IN ROME, in the year 1626, the first performance was given of
a five-act *favola boschereccia* called *La catena d'Adone*. This
seems to have been the first stage piece with music by Domenico
Mazzocchi, and it is the only surviving opera attributed to him; yet,
on the basis of this one work, his name has been given a considerable
prominence in the history of opera. More precisely, Mazzocchi's fame
may be said to arise largely from a note that appears in the printed
score of *La catena d'Adone*, appended to a list of airs and choruses
belonging to that composition. The note reads:

<table>
<tr>
<td>Vi sono molt'altre mezz'Arie sparse per l'Opera, che rompono il tedio del recitatiuo, ma non son quì notate per non tediar chi legge, bastando hauer notate le più conte.[1]</td>
<td>There are many other semi-arias, scattered throughout the work, which break the tedium of the recitative; but they are not indicated here, in order not to weary the reader, it being sufficient to have indicated the more familiar ones.</td>
</tr>
</table>

The merit of recitative, which had been the primal principle of
operatic music, is not known to have been challenged in any previous
commentary. Consequently Mazzocchi's note, flatly associating recitative with "tedium," has come to be regarded as the announcement
of a fundamental departure in operatic esthetics: plainly, it implies
a repudiation of the Florentine "classical" ideal that had led, through
the essential creation of dramatic recitative, to the founding of opera
itself. Nor does the note merely disparage recitative; it informs us
that Mazzocchi had here resorted to a different genus—the "semi-
aria"—as offering greater musical interest. Unquestionably, the device
has enhanced the interest scholars have devoted to *La catena d'Adone*,
for their attentions generally have lighted upon this notable feature
of the work, its "many . . . semi-arias."

How influential, then, was this genus? And had Mazzocchi himself invented it? Really, we do not yet know the answer to either
of these questions. The name "mezz'aria," certainly, is not found in
any other known score; but of course it is the genus itself, under

[1] Domenico Mazzocchi, *La catena d'Adone* (Venetia: Alessandro Vincenti, 1626),
p. [127].

any name, that we should be interested in tracing, either in earlier or in later operas. Indeed, this interest has been expressed (and provoked) by more than one historian; nevertheless, the peculiar fact is that no history of the semi-aria, however sketchy, has yet been written. And the undoubted reason for this omission, more peculiar still, is that we do not yet know just what a semi-aria is. Mazzocchi himself did not define the term, and, as we have seen, he declined even to "weary the reader" with a complete list of the pieces he had in mind (which might have clarified his meaning).

To be sure, the note that calls our attention to these pieces also tells us that "the more familiar ones" have been indicated, apparently in the list to which the note itself is attached.[2] However, the examples in question evidently have been "indicated" merely in the sense that they are named somewhere within this list, for neither there nor in the body of the score is any piece actually labeled "mezz'aria."

Many pieces, though, are labeled "Aria." This seems helpful, for if we can discover from these pieces Mazzocchi's interpretation of the term "aria" we might deduce the meaning he attached to the dependent term "mezz'aria." Also, we may hope more easily to find in his list of musical numbers the examples of semi-arias ostensibly named there, if we may exclude those items marked "Aria." Thus, for our purposes the presence of this marking seems especially convenient.

Here, however, what seems a particularly appropriate source of evidence actually can be the most misleading—for Mazzocchi's own use of the designation "Aria" cannot properly be taken in all cases at its face value. The list he has furnished is headed "Racconto delle arie, e chori a varie voci," and only these two categories—"arie, e chori"—appear to be represented in it: of a total of twenty-seven pieces listed, seventeen are marked "Aria," seven are marked "Choro," two that are named without either marking are labeled "Aria" in the body of the score, and the single remaining piece, though not directly categorized, seems understood to be one of the "arie."[3] Even if we should surmise that the one piece not labeled has

---

[2] The list comprises thirty-four entries: of these, however, only twenty-seven are incipits of separate pieces; the remaining seven enumerate subordinate sections (e.g., second strophes) of the basic twenty-seven selections. (The seven dependent entries are marked as such, e.g., by the accompanying notation "la medema.")

[3] This piece ("Se l'occhio") is one of three that are named in the list without a

been left unclassified because it is a semi-aria, we cannot equate it with those "more familiar ones" we ought to find in the list. Where, then, are these semi-arias? Are they to be sought solely among the "chori"? This seems especially unlikely since Mazzocchi's note suggests that he had chosen to write semi-arias where he might have written recitative, a choice that would not arise in setting to music words assigned to the chorus; then too, his note refers to "many other [i.e., unlisted] semi-arias," whereas no choral piece in the opera has been omitted from the list. In short, it is most probable that the collection of "more familiar" semi-arias includes some items actually labeled "Aria": Mazzocchi must have applied this label, at least in some cases, with a license his note is meant to explain—that is, as a designation for pieces somehow resembling arias, but more accurately described by the modified term "semi-aria."

If Mazzocchi here used the word "aria" in an imprecise fashion, ought we to conclude that it had, for him, no precise meaning? In the usage of some of his contemporaries, certainly, the word appears at times to refer to no trait more definite than a general lyricism, implied by its literal, nontechnical meaning—"song," or "tune."[4] However, it is not reasonable to believe that Mazzocchi, like these writers, considered the term a catchall: his recourse to the name "semi-aria" would in that case have been senseless. As a self-evident refinement of terminology, this name presupposes a quite exact idea of what the basic term "aria," properly used, could and could not describe.[5]

---

marking of either "Aria" or "Choro." Unlike all the other entries, though, each of these three includes a specification of stanza structure (e.g., "per Ottaue"); two of the three pieces are labeled "Aria" in the body of the score, whence it can be supposed that such labeling was omitted in the list merely in favor of the stanzaic designation. Since all three of these pieces are solos, the marking "Aria" was in fact dispensable for all of them, inasmuch as they are named in a list confined to "arie, e chori." For these reasons, we may infer that "Se l'occhio" (a tenor solo "per Terzetti") was meant to be regarded as one of the "arie."

[4] Cf. e.g., Gaspari's comment on Domenico Maria Melli's two 1609 volumes of *Mvsiche . . . nelle quali si contengono . . . arie . . .* (Venetia: Giacomo Vincenti, 1609), pointing out that Melli had used the name "aria" for some of these pieces that "altre non sono che madrigali" (Gaetano Gaspari, *Catalogo della Biblioteca del Liceo Musicale di Bologna* [Bologna: Libreria Romagnoli Dall'Acqua], iii [1893], iii).

[5] In her analysis of *La catena d'Adone*, Anna Amalie Abert apparently was guided by an assumption that wherever Mazzocchi had marked a solo song "Aria,"

Therefore, it is relevant to observe that during Mazzocchi's lifetime, the word "aria" had been used with some frequency in a more technical connotation, that is, as a name for strophic songs or songs with strophic accompaniments.[6] There is excellent reason to think that Mazzocchi was among the composers who understood the term as having this implication: three pieces named in his list of "arie, e chori" actually are in no way distinguished from conventional recitative except in that each has a strophic accompaniment (see Ex. 1);[7] Mazzocchi labeled each of these three pieces "Aria," and it must be supposed that he did so in consideration of their strophicism.

Since it appears that Mazzocchi considered strophicism an attribute of the aria, we may attach some importance to the fact that ten other "arie" in his list have no strophic element. These ten, though, are not recitativic but distinctly lyrical (see Ex. 2);[8] in connection with them, Mazzocchi's marking "Aria" must be taken in its broader sense, as referring to this tuneful, song-like style.

---

he had meant the term literally—and, accordingly, that he had attached no very precise meaning to it (Abert, *Claudio Monteverdi und das musikalische Drama* [Lippstadt: Kistner & Siegel, 1954], p. 174). At the same time, Abert ignored the marking "Aria" wherever Mazzocchi had applied it to a piece for two or more voices (although this was a normal usage in Mazzocchi's time, and for roughly a century afterward); these pieces—which, we shall find, were labeled "Aria" in consideration of specific features independent of scoring—Abert classed merely as ensembles and choruses (Abert, p. 175). By thus disposing of all of Mazzocchi's "arie" (except the solo "Dunque in tanto," which she seems simply to have overlooked, in counting "sieben 'Arie'" [Abert, p. 174]), Abert eliminated all chance of discovering in Mazzocchi's list anything to justify his indication that some semi-arias are named there. (Indeed, Abert did not discuss this indication at all.) This handicap surely interfered with her calculations regarding Mazzocchi's semi-arias: the definition she proposed—"kurze, ariose Einschübe in das Rezitativ" (Abert, p. 174)—seems, on examination, too vague to be used with assurance in identifying particular examples, and Abert cited just one instance in which it might apply (Abert, p. 174). These shortcomings are especially regrettable since her discussion of semi-arias, although it is manifestly incidental to the subject of her book and consumes less than a single paragraph, is the most extensive treatment of the question hitherto published.

[6] Cf. August Wilhelm Ambros, *Geschichte der Musik*, ed. Hugo Leichtentritt, 3d edn. rev. (Leipzig: F. E. C. Leuckart), IV (1909), 360, 384-85, 836.

[7] The other two are "De' puri campi" and "Da re ch'ebbe di Cipro."

[8] The other nine are "Rida l'auretta amante," "Qua tra gioie gradite," "Se l'occhio," "Su dunque," "L'alme pure," "Su su dunque pastori," "Dunque liete e ridenti," "Florido nembo," and "Sì sì cara mia spene."

Ex. 1. Domenico Mazzocchi, *La catena d'Adone*
(Venetia: Alessandro Vincenti, 1626), pp. 81-82

Where either strophicism or lyricism was introduced, Mazzocchi might well have presumed that musical interest surpassed that of conventional recitative, for neither of these features was required or, ordinarily, adopted in recitative; rather, we see that for Mazzocchi both traits were associated with the aria. By the same token, though, Mazzocchi may have considered that where only one of these quali-

Ex. 2. Domenico Mazzocchi, *La catena d'Adone*
(Vincenti, 1626), p. 114

ties was present, the implications of the name "aria" were only partially fulfilled. Accordingly, such pieces as the ten non-strophic songs and the three strophic recitatives we have noted in *La catena d'Adone* may constitute the category Mazzocchi called "semi-arias"; these thirteen examples may in fact be those "more familiar ones" his list is supposed to include.

This hypothesis has considerable relevance to the suggestions of Mazzocchi's note, for we can see why either strophic, non-lyrical pieces or lyrical, non-strophic ones might be thought more interesting than ordinary recitative; we can see, too, why Mazzocchi might have called pieces of both these types "semi-arias"; and we find that the names of several such pieces are indicated in Mazzocchi's list.

But what of the "many other semi-arias, scattered throughout the work," which Mazzocchi omitted from his list "in order not to weary the reader"? Guided by the assumptions described above, we should find in *La catena d'Adone* just four unlisted pieces that we might consider semi-arias[9]—surely not enough to justify the apparent

[9] These are "La ragion perde" (III. i), "Nel gran regno d'amore" (IV. ii), "Noi dunque lieti in tanto" (V. iii), and "Lieto dopo l'errore" (V. iii). All four are lyrical, non-strophic songs; the first, though, which serves as a refrain for an extended recitative, appears four times, with varying embellishment.

sense of Mazzocchi's note. Indeed, the note itself required as much space and as much printers' ink as four titles would have done, and it is not demonstrably less wearisome to read. Unhappily, therefore, we must admit that the four pieces in question cannot be the "many other semi-arias" alluded to in the note. Have our inferences about the semi-aria been, after all, incorrect? Or should we suppose that Mazzocchi merely exaggerated in his note, calling four cases "many"?

Actually, neither conclusion is necessary. Some newly discovered evidence suggests a different reason why our search for Mazzocchi's "many other semi-arias" should yield only four specimens: others, once part of Mazzocchi's "many," may have been reduced long ago to ordinary recitative. This is not to propose that Mazzocchi revised his opinion of recitative before his score was published; rather, it appears that another composer revised, in some measure, the score itself—a composer whose attitude toward recitative happened to be precisely opposed to Mazzocchi's.

To be sure, the printed score of *La catena d'Adone* attributes the music to Mazzocchi alone, and so does the printed libretto;[10] indeed, no source hitherto known mentions Mazzocchi's having had assistance from another composer. The truth is that although he did receive such assistance, he had not sought it, nor in all probability did he welcome it; and he may have preferred not to have it publicly reported. We are able nevertheless to learn something of the episode, due to the following circumstances.

Approximately a year after the premiere of his opera—that is, sometime in 1627—Mazzocchi appears to have been considered for a commission to write some theater music for the Duke of Parma; the Duke was soon to be married, and the music was wanted in connection with the projected wedding festivities.[11] It is well known that the Parmesan court eventually hired Claudio Monteverdi for this service, but, as the present writer elsewhere has shown, other composers had actively sought the assignment.[12] Before the court

[10] Ottavio Tronsarelli, *La catena d'Adone, favola boschereccia* (Roma: Francesco Corbelletti, 1626), pp. 5-6.

[11] Emil Vogel guessed—correctly, as we shall see—that Mazzocchi must have been a contender for this commission, since Mazzocchi had dedicated his publication of *La catena d'Adone* to this same Duke (Vogel, "Claudio Monteverdi," *Vierteljahrsschrift für Musikwissenschaft*, III [1887], 385 n. 5).

[12] Stuart Reiner, "Preparations in Parma—1618, 1627-28," *The Music Review*, XXV (1964), 286-87.

had announced its selection, one of these aspirants, Sigismondo d'India, wrote to the impresario of the Duke's theater in a way that suggests he supposed Mazzocchi to be his principal rival; accordingly, he had some comments to offer about Mazzocchi's work. Here is the relevant portion of d'India's letter, which he wrote from Modena on September 2, 1627:

In Roma il principe aldobrandino mi diede l'opera de l'Adone a me benche si trouo poi ch'io ero amalato e non lo potei servire. Fui pero sforzato di rifare tutta la parte di Lorenzino il quale me la porto ch'io hero assediato de la febre in letto per [sic] doue ando tutta in limatura. di questo ella se ne potra informare da roma che sopra il tutto oltra ch'ella sa molto bene che chi compose l'adone non ha fatto altra opera sol che quella Pensi come potea riuscirne essendo tutta piene [sic] di canzonette non ui essendo proposito di stile recitatiuo anti lontanissimo sapendo lei che bisogna in simil opre esserli nato dentro.[13]

In Rome, the Prince Aldobrandino[14] gave the Adonis work to me, but it then turned out that I was ill and could not serve him. Nevertheless, I was forced to redo Lorenzino's entire part: he brought it to me, for I was in bed, besieged by fever; there, it got polished up completely—you may inform yourself about this from Rome. For above all (beyond the fact that you know very well that he who composed the *Adonis* has not written any other work but that one), think: how could he have succeeded with it, when it is all full of *canzonette*, there being no attempt at recitative style—rather, very far from it? For as you know, one must be born to such work.

For us, the chief point of d'India's remarks is that in claiming to have revised the music for "the Adonis work," he specified as an objectionable trait of the original setting that it had been "all full of *canzonette*," at the expense of recitative. We may reasonably suppose that d'India reversed this situation in the part he revised—that performed by the singer Lorenzino. Luckily, Lorenzino can be identified: almost certainly he was Lorenzo Sances, whose participation in the opera is indicated in a diary of the Sistine Chapel.[15]

[13] Sigismondo d'India, letter to [Enzo Bentivoglio], September 2, 1627 (Ferrara, Archivio di Stato: Archivio Bentivoglio, mazzo 209).

[14] The librettist of *La catena d'Adone* dedicated the text to Giovan Giorgio Aldobrandino, Prince of Rossano (Tronsarelli, *La catena d'Adone*, p. 3).

[15] The relevant entry, dated January 26, 1626, is quoted in Enrico Celani, "I cantori della cappella pontificia nei secoli XVI-XVIII," *Rivista musicale italiana*, XIV (1907), 779. (The notice refers to the performances with which Sances was involved as "le commedie delli Signori Conti"; this can be interpreted on the basis of a note in Tronsarelli's libretto [Tronsarelli, *La catena d'Adone*, p. 5] reporting that the opera had been presented at the home of the Marchese Evandro Conti.)

Sances was a contralto,[16] and there is only one contralto role in *La catena d'Adone*—the part of Adonis. D'India's letter, therefore, can be interpreted as notice that he had rewritten the entire title role of Mazzocchi's opera.

Can d'India's claim be trusted, though? His connection with *La catena d'Adone* is reported nowhere but in his own letter, which was written with an identifiable and strong motive; if he truly had reworked a leading role in the opera, how could Mazzocchi have neglected to acknowledge this in his publication of the score? Perhaps the answer is that Mazzocchi had a motive for silence as strong as d'India's motive for speaking out—more precisely, the same motive. For Mazzocchi seems in fact to have had some hope of securing the very desirable Parma commission,[17] and his chance of obtaining it must have rested largely on his achievement as the composer of *La catena d'Adone*—he had, according to d'India, "not written any other work but that one."[18] He may have foreseen that his prospects

[16] See Celani, "I cantori della cappella pontificia," p. 775.

[17] The Cardinal Aldobrandino, who was an uncle of the Duke Odoardo of Parma, was Mazzocchi's patron, and, in the summer of 1626, he had brought Mazzocchi to Parma; during that visit, there had been some discussion of the possibility of performing *La catena d'Adone* for the Duke: these facts all are mentioned in Mazzocchi's dedicatory preface to the score (Mazzocchi, *La catena d'Adone*, p. [iii]). From this, it appears that Mazzocchi had certain advantages as a candidate for employment by the Duke; it is possible in fact to suppose that Mazzocchi and his patron hoped that *La catena d'Adone*, as well as its composer, would serve in the Duke's approaching nuptial celebration.

Mazzocchi's allusion to what had taken place in Parma during his visit is so worded as to be susceptible of another interpretation. His dedication points out that the Duke "non ha . . . sdegnato di far segno di sentirla [i.e., the opera] volentieri taluolta cantare"; because the word "talvolta" can mean either "sometime" or "sometimes," this phrase may signify either that the Duke had shown his willingness to hear the work sung sometime, or that he had shown pleasure at hearing it sung on various occasions. The latter interpretation seems highly improbable: there is no other contemporary documentation indicating even one Parmesan performance of the work; and had there actually been several such performances, Mazzocchi would hardly have left the number, and the fact itself, so indefinite. It may have suited Mazzocchi's taste to let this ambiguous phrase suggest to the uninformed reader that the opera already had received an honor Mazzocchi actually was only hoping to obtain for it. If this was his intent, it has been fulfilled in recent times: the Parmesan scholar Nestore Pelicelli, quoting the two words "taluolta cantare" in a remodeled context (Pelicelli, "Musicisti in Parma nel secolo XVII," *Note d'archivio*, x [1933], 118), posited as a fact the probably imaginary series of Parmesan performances, which subsequently have been recorded as history in other studies.

[18] D'India's phrase "non ha fatto altra opera" may have concerned only the kind

would be seriously impaired if it could be supposed that in writing what was then his only well-known work, he had required the aid of another composer. (This could have been especially unfortunate since the other composer already had a considerable reputation: it might be imagined that Mazzocchi's status in the arrangement had been that of apprentice.) Thus, d'India's claim is not less credible because he was left to make it on his own behalf (and we observe, besides, that he counted on verification "from Rome," perhaps from Lorenzino). It can be presumed that d'India had, as he affirmed, rewritten Lorenzino's part.

But is this news relevant to the music we have in the printed score? Wishing to withhold the fact that d'India had been called upon to alter the work, would Mazzocchi have published the altered version—in which, moreover, a suppression of some "canzonette" presumably had augmented "the tedium of the recitative"? Actually, this is not so implausible as it seems, for we must bear in mind that copies of the printed score would go to persons who had attended the actual production, in which d'India's revisions apparently had been used. If these readers should discover in the score various songs they never had heard, touchy questions might be raised: Why had some songs been omitted, in performance? Had anyone objected to the music? Since Lorenzino evidently had objected, thereby bringing d'India into the matter,[19] it surely was better from Mazzocchi's point

---

of work directly relevant to his criticism—dramatic composition (or, in effect, "opera" in the current sense of the word); or Mazzocchi's earlier pieces may truly have been so little known as to have escaped d'India's notice, for few of these pieces seem to have been published, and none apparently had brought Mazzocchi's name onto a title page (his four-voice motet "Ecce crucem Domini," for example, had come into print as one of various *Sacri affetti . . . raccolti da Francesco Sammaruco . . .* [Sanctus Spiritus in Saxia (Rome): Luca Antonius Soldus, 1625]).

[19] D'India's letter does not say clearly what Lorenzino's objection had been; his own attitude toward Mazzocchi's "canzonette," and his treatment of them, may have been independent of that objection. However, it is not implausible that a singer in those times might have preferred recitative to "canzonette" in an operatic role: skill in performing recitative was then reckoned a distinguishing and valuable gift (cf. e.g., the letter of Girolamo Fioretti quoted in Reiner, "Preparations in Parma," pp. 276-77). Sances himself had in fact received special praise for his moving performance, in Vitali's *Aretusa*, of a climactic narration consisting of nine pages of recitative (Filippo Vitali, *L'Aretusa, favola in musica* [Roma: Luca Antonio Soldi, 1620], p. [iv]; the scene in question is on pp. 53-61); he may have felt that Mazzocchi's "canzonette" would not present to advantage his prized talent as a dramatic performer.

of view to see that such questions were not asked; and the surest way to avoid them was simply to print the work as it had been performed. It thus is a paradoxical fact that if Mazzocchi wished to conceal the embarrassing story of d'India's unlooked-for collaboration, his best chance lay not in discarding d'India's handiwork but in publishing it, as an ostensible part of his own composition.

That this is just what Mazzocchi did is most strongly and, for us, most pertinently suggested by the music of Adonis as we now have it. Stylistically, this role seems to reflect d'India's principles rather than Mazzocchi's: despite its great length, it consists almost entirely of conventional recitative.[20] The only solo song with which Adonis is permitted to "break the tedium" of his recitative,[21] moreover, is unlike any other song in the opera. The solo songs allotted to the other characters all are of the types we have recognized as semi-arias; Adonis' song, instead, is the one solo in the opera that fulfills both of the qualifications Mazzocchi seems to have attributed to the aria proper (see Ex. 3). The strophicism of the accompaniment in Adonis' song even has been emphasized, through the use of an instrumental ritornello,[22] just as the lyricism of the song has been emphasized through an extensive use of vocal embellishments. In short, this song can have no more connection with the concept of the semi-aria than can the many pages of recitative Adonis sings

[20] This cannot be attributed to the character of the text: the libretto provides, in the role of Adonis, some passages patently favoring formal song which, nevertheless, appear in the score as recitative—e.g., in III. ii:

> "Flebil ma forte Adone
> "Serba serba costante
> "A la Diva d'Amor la fede amante
> "E per lontane vie
> "Fuggi fuggi l'infido
> "D'amor furtivo ingiurioso nido."

In other roles, moreover, a single line of poetry sometimes is all the text used for a song of the type here presumed to be meant by the term "semi-aria" (i.e., "La ragion perde dove il senso abbonda" and "Nel gran regno d'amore arte ed inganno").

[21] In the final scene (V. iii) Adonis participates in two ensembles; since, however, d'India could not have made any significant changes at those points in the role without disarranging the other singers' parts, it is here presumed that only the solo utterances of Adonis can have been revised for Lorenzino.

[22] The accompaniment itself is in fact a fully strophic reworking of a bass pattern Alessandro Grandi had used in a less rigidly strophic arrangement: cf. the passages from Grandi's "Apre l'huomo" (*Cantade et arie a voce sola* [Venetia: Alessandro Vincenti, 1620], pp. 14-16) quoted in Manfred F. Bukofzer, *Music in the Baroque Era* (New York: W. W. Norton & Co., 1947), p. 32.

elsewhere. The song is stylistically exceptional in the opera, and the role of Adonis, in its entirety, is stylistically exceptional among the other parts. It can be inferred that what we now know as the music of Adonis is the version Sigismondo d'India made, and from which he eliminated all "canzonette"—which we may take to have been his deprecatory way of describing Mazzocchi's semi-arias.[23]

Ex. 3. Domenico Mazzocchi, *La catena d'Adone*
(Vincenti, 1626), pp. 16-17

[23] D'India need not be the author of Adonis' surviving aria; if in Mazzocchi's setting the piece already had its present unequivocal features, d'India may simply have let it alone, as something more substantial than a mere "canzonetta." Its presence, certainly, could offer no conflict with standard operatic practice, in which a single, clearly defined solo aria might be expected to occur in an otherwise straightforwardly recitativic role: cf., in Marco da Gagliano's *Dafne* (Firenze: Cristofano Marescotti, 1608), Apollo's "Non curi la mia pianta" (pp. 49-52) and Venus' "Chi da' lacci d'amor" (pp. 19-20)—the latter by an anonymous collaborator (see da Gagliano's foreword, *ibid.*, pp. [vii-viii]); in Stefano Landi's *Morte d'Orfeo* (Venetia: Bartolomeo Magni, 1619), Orpheus' "Gioit' al mio natal" (pp. 35-40) and Charon's "Bevi bevi" (p. 105); in Vitali's *Aretusa*, Diana's "Alma diletta" (pp. 80-81). D'India's contemptuous reference to "canzonette" might, according to its

This presumably is why we cannot now find the "many other semi-arias" Mazzocchi claimed to have written. Accordingly, our failure to find them need not mean that we have misunderstood what semi-arias are. Our interpretation of the term, and our identification of surviving specimens, need not await corroboration from those "many other" examples—that corroboration may have become forever unavailable in 1626, through Mazzocchi's deciding to publish his work with d'India's modifications.

Admittedly, such a decision must be regarded as extraordinary, and it cannot have been made lightly. We have considered what Mazzocchi might have hoped to gain by the expedient, but, of course, there was something he would risk as well; for if d'India should learn with displeasure that his work had been used without acknowledgment, his complaints could be damaging. (As we have seen, d'India did assert himself, and Mazzocchi did not receive either the Parma commission or, to our knowledge, any subsequent invitation to write another opera.)[24] Mazzocchi may well have hesitated before

context, more pertinently have been aimed at the other solo songs in Mazzocchi's opera, inasmuch as the hybrid character of these others genuinely undermined the integrity of "recitative style."

[24] We have no direct evidence that Mazzocchi's employment opportunities were decisively affected by the wagging of d'India's tongue and pen over the *Adonis* episode (as, for example, d'India's own fortunes had been altered by backbiting in Turin: see Federico Mompellio, "India, Sigismondo d'," *Die Musik in Geschichte und Gegenwart* [Kassel: Bärenreiter], VI [1957], col. 1136); however, a conjecture of the sort may be pertinent in explaining what otherwise seems puzzling—the peculiar stillbirth of Mazzocchi's operatic career. For with the inauguration of a theater in the Barberini palace in 1632, Rome became an especially important center of operatic activity; yet to Mazzocchi, who already had produced and published an opera of some interest, this local improvement brought no new opportunity, while commissions to write for the Barberini theater sometimes went to composers who appear to have had no prior operas to their credit. Regarding the kind of work in which he subsequently engaged, Mazzocchi wrote, "Il più ingegnoso studio, che habbia la Musica, . . . è quello de' Madrigali" (Mazzocchi, *Madrigali a cinqve voci* [Roma: Francesco Zannetti, 1638], p. [3]); but since he immediately added, "mà pochi hoggidì se ne compongono, e meno se ne cantano" (*ibid.*), his seeming expression of enthusiasm ends by assuming a defensive tone—if it carries any implication of aloofness toward more fashionable kinds of music (among which opera was prominent), the hint perhaps should be classed, as to spirit and accuracy, with the verdict of Aesop's fox concerning the high-hanging grapes. (Apparently under his own auspices, in fact, Mazzocchi soon afterward set to music for production in his home town, Civita Castellana, an opera libretto he himself had commissioned: see his preface to Tronsarelli, *Il martirio de' santi Abvndio . . . Abvndantio . . . Marciano, e Giovanni . . .* [Roma: Lodouico Grignani, 1641], p. 3.)

deciding whether to publish his own or d'India's version of Lo-renzino's part,[25] and it is possible that he drew up his incomplete list of "arie, e chori" before he had made the choice.

This might be the best way to account for the presence of his famous note. For the essential function of the note is to prepare the reader to expect incompleteness in the list, and perhaps it is no acci-dent that this expectation would make the list seem equally fitting no matter which version of the Adonis role were printed—if the printed version were "full of *canzonette*" not mentioned in the list, the dis-crepancy would occasion no surprise; whereas if some of these songs were left out of the score, they never would be missed on the basis of the list.[26] (Nor, of course, could they be missed on the basis of any reader's recollection of the opera as it had been heard; having never been publicly performed, the songs in question truly were, as the note suggests, not among "the more familiar ones.") Mazzocchi's asser-tion that he had curtailed the list merely "in order not to weary the reader" certainly is fatuous, for seven of the thirty-four entries in the list are plainly unnecessary: they are itemizations of subordinate strophes belonging to pieces already listed.[27]

Mazzocchi's note, then, may have been meant to limit rather than to increase the reader's supply of information—to mystify while seeming to enlighten. If so, it has had a signally enduring success, due largely to the unavailability heretofore of d'India's story, but due also, perhaps, to a certain artfulness in the note itself.[28] At this point, in-

[25] More than eight months elapsed between the premiere of the opera (which had taken place by February 13, 1626: see Alfredo Saviotti, "Feste e spettacoli nel seicento," *Giornale storico della letteratura italiana*, XLI [1903], 70) and publication of the score (in which the dedication is dated October 24, 1626: Mazzocchi, *La catena d'Adone*, p. [iii]). It may be relevant that during this interval d'India was away in Modena; his return to Rome—and to proximity with Mazzocchi's circle—was brought about unexpectedly by the death of Isabella d'Este in November of 1626 (see Mompellio, *loc.cit.*, col. 1137); by then, apparently, Mazzocchi had published the score of *La catena d'Adone*.

[26] Of course, if Mazzocchi were to publish d'India's version of the Adonis role (as it is here presumed that he ultimately did), some songs other than those of Adonis would have to have been left out of the list—if not, the omission of Adonis' "canzonette" from the score would leave no "other semi-arias" at all to which Mazzocchi's note could seem to refer. Perhaps Mazzocchi left unlisted the four "other" examples we now find in the score (see n. 9 above) to meet this contingency.

[27] See n. 2 above.

[28] This is not the only instance in which Mazzocchi can be suspected of using a verbal cunning. See n. 17 above.

deed, we may wonder how much of what the note suggests really is significant; for even its provocative reference to "semi-arias" may have been more novel than the kind of music thereby designated— strophic recitatives had had some use in opera from the very outset,[29] and non-strophic songs of course were familiar in various contexts and under various denominations. Perhaps the most noteworthy aspect of the name "semi-aria" is the distinction it indirectly reserved to the term "aria," as properly referring to a combination of lyricism and strophicism. (As we have seen, this distinction was not new, either; but Mazzocchi's implied emphasis of it may be historically interesting to the extent that it marks a particular concern with formal principles in opera, or with stabilization of the aria.) In any case, the term "semi-aria" seems to betoken semantic, rather than specifically musical, inventiveness.[30]

But if semi-arias were not in themselves an innovation, the importance Mazzocchi brought them may yet have been exceptional. He had used such pieces (as his note makes clear) at least partly out of a distaste for recitative and a corresponding wish to limit its influence in his own work. D'India's letter confirms that the result, in *La catena d'Adone*, had been appreciable: emphasis had there been displaced from the recitative style traditionally sovereign in opera to a more broadly musical idiom. Eventually, as we know, recitative decisively lost its former authority in opera; it is natural to wonder whether Mazzocchi's open resistance of that authority may have significantly encouraged the more widespread rejection of it that presently followed. Perhaps, indeed, we have a means of gauging Mazzocchi's influence, insofar as it may be reflected in the further fortunes of the semi-aria: for having arrived at a workable hypothesis regarding the nature of such pieces, we might plan in future to specify

[29] The prototypal operatic prologue, that of Peri's and Corsi's *Dafne*, is a strophic recitative (see Federico Ghisi, *Alle fonti della monodia* [Milano: F.lli Bocca, 1940], p. 33), and other composers, in writing prologues, followed the example Peri had set. So did Mazzocchi; accordingly, he included the prologue to *La catena d'Adone* in his aforementioned list, marking it "Aria."

[30] Mazzocchi's predilection for this sort of novelty is amply demonstrated in a four-page note in his *Dialoghi e sonetti posti in musica* (Roma: Francesco Zannetti, 1638, pp. 179-82). There, an explanation is offered of a musical sign he had used twice, in a single measure of one of those pieces, to represent the "Diesis Enarmonico" as distinct from the standard "Diesis Cromatico." In that note, high-flown as it is, Mazzocchi could not avoid pointing out what the music itself attests—that "questo . . . Diesis Enarmonico . . . è dell'istesso valore, che è quest'altro . . . detto Diesis Cromatico."

and to evaluate the degree of their prominence in opera after 1626.

In the light of d'India's testimony, though, such a plan may seem pointless, for his letter clearly suggests that Mazzocchi's methods were not considered successful—if this is true, they surely cannot have been imitated. D'India's views, of course, were not disinterested, and perhaps least so where the virtue of recitative was concerned. His own reputation appears to have been based largely on a specialization in the Florentine monodic style;[31] even in the 1620's, he had published five "laments" that are models of the strictly recitativic variety of dramatic monologue.[32]

With his letter about "the Adonis work," however, d'India sent along some other music he had written, including an apparently new lament that he hoped would demonstrate his own superiority as a dramatic composer; in the present context, this composition is especially interesting. D'India presented it in these words:

Mando a Vostra Signoria Illustrissima questa mia opera messa pur ora al luce quiui uedra a l'ultimo il Lamento di Armida composto da me in due ore a Tiuoli auanti al Signor Cardinale. da questo potra comprendere la mia maniera d'uscir in Scena la quale lei trouera ch'e [sic] è sola.[33]	I send Your Most Illustrious Lordship this work of mine, just now published. There, at the end, you will see the Lament of Armida, which I composed in two hours at Tivoli, in the presence of My Lord the Cardinal.[34] From this you will be able to comprehend my manner of coming forth upon the stage—which, you will find, is unique.

The one known work that d'India had "just ... published" in 1627 was his first (and only) book of four-voice motets;[35] among these sacred compositions, of course, there had been no "Lament of Armida." However, the present writer has located a copy of this motet

[31] See Mompellio, "D'India," *Enciclopedia dello spettacolo* (Roma: Le Maschere), IV (1957), cols. 711-12.

[32] These are: "Orfeo" and "L'Apollo" in d'India's *Mvsiche, libro qvarto* (Venetia: Alessandro Vincenti, 1621, pp. 10-13 and 24-28, respectively); and "Lamento di Didone," "Lamento di Giasone," and "Lamento di Olimpia" in his *Mvsiche, libro qvinto* (Venetia: Alessandro Vincenti, 1623, pp. 4-8, 11-14, and 17-21, respectively).

[33] D'India, letter to [Bentivoglio], September 2, 1627 (Archivio Bentivoglio, mazzo 209).

[34] The Cardinal Maurizio di Savoia had been d'India's patron for at least the preceding four years: he is named as such on the title pages of d'India's 1623 and 1627 publications, respectively, *Mvsiche, libro qvinto* and *Liber primvs motectorvm qvatvor vocibvs* (Venetiis: Alexandrum Vincentium, 1627).

[35] D'India, *Liber primvs motectorvm.*

publication in which, "at the end" (i.e., on the last pages of music), an additional piece is found, written in d'India's hand. This evidently is the lament in question.[36]

This piece (shown here as Ex. 4), for all that d'India may have

1) The bass note presumably should have been G.
2) This slur probably should have been placed one quaver later, so that the words would be articulated as in their previous appearance.

Ex. 4. Ms. in: Bologna, Biblioteca del Museo Civico, collocation AA122 (Sigismondo d'India, *Liber primvs motectorvm qvatvor vocibvs* [Venetiis: Alexandrum Vincentium, 1627]), *Bassvs pro organo,* pp. 21-22

[36] Bologna, Biblioteca del Museo Civico, collocation AA122. (This is not the only item in the Bologna collection that seems formerly to have belonged to the Bentivoglio family: see Reiner, "Preparations in Parma," p. [273] n. 4.) The piece is on pages 21 and 22 of the *Bassvs pro organo* volume: three printed staves had remained empty at the bottom of each of these pages; d'India added a fourth, handwritten staff on each page, and wrote the piece on the four resultant double-systems. That

meant it to prove, can readily be classified as a rather song-like solo madrigal of a type by no means unfamiliar in 1627. The only remarkable things about it, in fact, are its pronounced dissimilarity to d'India's five published laments (as, indeed, to other laments of the period) and its proportionate inconsistency with the apparent sense of his letter. For in the "Lament of Armida" declamatory values do not dominate, but are somewhat slighted in favor of lyrical ones—which is to say that although d'India offered the piece as a sample of his "unique" dramatic style, it actually has less in common with his own earlier dramatic monologues than with Mazzocchi's semi-arias. Accordingly, it might be wise to discount d'India's insinuation that Mazzocchi had failed as a stylist. The truth may be that response to *La catena d'Adone*—and, more precisely, to Mazzocchi's part of it— had been favorable enough seriously to call in question the pre-eminence of recitative, and to persuade even d'India that specifically musical values soon might, after all, prevail on the musical stage.

---

it is his autograph emerges from a comparison of the text with that of his letter. The verse, too, probably was his own. He had composed the texts of all five of his published laments, and the text of this one seems unlikely to have been sought farther afield, for it is plainly silly. (It may well have been part of what d'India had produced in those two fertile hours at Tivoli.) It is worth remarking that if the composition—and not merely the manuscript—originated after the motet book had been published, it is d'India's latest work now known, and may have been the last he completed. (The place and date of his death are uncertain; his letter quoted above is the last datable notice we now have concerning his activities.)

L'ERISMENA TRAVESTITA[1]

HAROLD S. POWERS

I

THE "favola seconda" of Aurelio Aureli is entitled *L'Erismena* after its principal heroine; the "travestita" is added here as mere caprice. It alludes to the fact that the heroine appears in masculine dress, like so many of her counterparts in opera of the time, and also to the fact that the work itself has survived not only in the musical dress provided by Francesco Cavalli for its original Venetian production at the Teatro San Apollinare in 1655, but also in a greatly altered version from fifteen or more years later.

Erismena had a life in production of at least eighteen years, and traveled all over north Italy. The last surviving dated libretto is from Forlì in 1673; in the intervening years there were productions attested by libretti in Bologna in 1661, Genoa in 1666, Bologna in 1668, and Lucca in the same year; there was a revival in Venice itself in 1670.[2] Allacci mentions a performance in Brescia as well, but gives no date for it.[3] Besides the libretti attesting the above per-

---

[1] I am indebted to the librarian of the Biblioteca Marciana in Venice for permission to have copies made of scores in the Contarini collection. I am likewise indebted to Mr. Stuart Reiner and Cav. Luigi D'Aurizio for searching for and providing films of libretti housed in Bologna libraries.

[2] The following printed libretti of Aurelio Aureli's *L'Erismena* have been used; the libraries indicated were the sources of the copies used here. Libretti are referred to in the text by place and year of the performance.

Venezia, 1655, Appresso Andrea Giuliani (Washington, Library of Congress)
Bologna, per l'Herede del Benacci, 1661 (Bologna, Biblioteca del Museo Civico) (*olim* Biblioteca del Conservatorio)
Genova, per Benedetto Celle, 1666 (Bologna, Biblioteca Universitaria)
Bologna, per l'Erede del Benacci, 1668 . . . "Rappresentata in Bologna nel Teatro Formagliari L'Anno 1668" (Bologna, Biblioteca del Museo Civico)
Bologna, Gio. Battista Ferroni, 1668 . . . "Da rappresentarsi in Lucca nel Teatro de' Borghi" (Bologna, Biblioteca del Museo Civico)
Venezia, 1670, Francesco Nicolini . . . "Ristampata per la recita nel Teatro Vendramino in S. Salvatore L'Anno M.DC.LXX." (Cambridge, Harvard College Library)
Forlì, per il Dandi e Saporetti, 1673 . . . "Recita nel Teatro Publico della Città di Forlì. Con l'agiunta degl'Intermezzi" (Bologna, Biblioteca del Museo Civico)

[3] Leone Allacci, *Drammaturgia*, 2nd edn.; (Venice, 1755), col. 299.

formances, there is also an undated scenario, and there are two scores in the Contarini collection of the Biblioteca Marciana, with call numbers Cod. It. IV.360 and Cod. It. IV.417.[4] Both scores are fair copies, in two quite different hands, neither of which is Cavalli's.[5]

Table I selects certain variant portions of the opera, indicating their presence or absence in each of the dated libretti, the two scores, and the scenario. The first column shows whether or not the source gives a Prologue, and if so, whether the Prologue is the one originally used for the opera *Ciro* (given in 1654 at SS. Giovanni e Paolo) or some other Prologue (which is different in each case—Aureli's own Prologue, printed in the Venice 1655 libretto, appears nowhere else).[6] The second column identifies the aria in a short recitative and aria scene sung by the minor character Diarte, if the scene is present. The third column refers to alternative *balli* after Act II; in some cases there is no mention of a *ballo* as such, but the text at the very end of the act itself is (except in score 360) that leading up to one or the other *ballo*. The fourth column shows the presence or absence of another recitative and aria scene for Diarte: the recitatives are the same, the arias differ. The penultimate column gives the first word of an aria for the secondary character Flerida. The final column marks the presence or absence of a pair of separate inter-act inter-mezzi, printed at the ends of two of the libretti. In Forlì 1673 the intermezzi are unrelated one to another; in Genoa 1666 they are mutually related and connected in theme with the Prologue, all three *aggiunte* having to do with newly weds (this libretto is dedicated to a Genoese bride).

Except with respect to Venice 1670, score 360, and of course the scenario, this table indicates all the textual differences among the sources except for a few cuts in the recitatives; there is no removal

[4] The scenario is bound in with the Venice 1655 libretto in the Library of Congress copy of that libretto. (There is no indication in any bibliographic reference or description that such is not the case with other copies of Venice 1655 and the scenario; and see the reference in n. 8 below.) The scores of *Erismena* will be referred to by the variable part of their call numbers, viz., 360 and 417.

[5] Cf. Henry Prunières, *Cavalli et l'opéra vénitien au XVIIᵉ siècle* (Paris, 1931), Pls. I-III.

[6] Egon Wellesz, "Cavalli und der Stil der Venezianischen Oper von 1640-1660," *Studien zur Musikwissenschaft*, I (1913), gives the entire *Ciro* prologue on pp. 79-91. The characters are Curiosità (Invidia in one or two of the later libretti), Architettura, Poesia, and Musica, who are putting the finishing touches to an opera about to be produced.

TABLE I

	Prol.	Diarte after I . 1	Ballo after Act II	Diarte after III . 1	Flerida after III . 1/III . 2	Intermezzi (printed last)
Ven. 55	other	——	*Mori e More*	——	*Amor* . . .	——
Bol. 61	*Ciro*	——	*Statue*	——	*Donne* . . .	——
Gen. 66	other	——	*Mori e More*	——	*Amor*; but *Donne* is substituted at the end of the libretto	yes
Bol. 68	*Ciro*	——	*Statue*	——	*Donne* . . .	——
Lucca 68	other	*Fiero fulmine*	Accademia (w. prep. speech for *Mori e More*)	——	*Donne* . . .	——
Ven. 70	——	*Per ripararsi*	(prep. speech for *Mori e More*)	rec *R*, aria *P*	(end of scene deleted)	——
Forlì 73	*Ciro*	*Fiero fulmine* (given at end before intermezzi)	(prep. speech for *Mori e More*)	——	*Donne* . . .	yes
360	——	*Per ripararsi*	——	rec *R*, aria *Q*	(no part for Flerida)	——
417	——	——	(prep. speech for *Mori e More*)	——	*Donne* . . .	——
*Scenario	*Ciro*	——	*Statue*	——	aria text cannot be inferred from scene summary	——

* III . 8 of the scenario is an interpolated machine scene—Fate and Fortune raising a storm—which appears in no other source.

of arias and no new or replaced material beyond what is shown. With respect to Venice 1655, Bologna 1661, and score 417, the table shows absolutely all the textual differences, beyond trivial matters of orthography, extra strophes for arias, and occasional substitution of synonymous or equivalent single words.

One cannot, of course, specify any details of text in the scenario, but it belongs with the early group of sources—Venice 1655, Bologna 1661, and score 417—which it follows exactly, except for a machine scene added in Act III. Very probably it represents the staged production in the first season, whereas the libretto of 1655 represents Aureli's drama as he wrote it. Though this particular scenario is not dated, many scenarii from earlier years are, and invariably the year given is the year of the printed libretto or the previous year. The fact that the scenario fits better with the Bologna 1661 libretto than with the Venice 1655 libretto, in the matter of the *Ciro* Prologue and the second Act *ballo*, suggests that the Bologna libretto more nearly represents the state of affairs at the first production. It may seem unlikely that the *Ciro* Prologue, having been used only a year earlier than the first *Erismena*—and at another theater at that— would have been substituted for Aureli's original Prologue; but there are several factors which would support the belief that the scenario represents the actual 1655 production. First, in bibliographical references to the scenario it is described as bound with the 1655 libretto (though it is separately paginated and has its own compositor's signatures). Second, the practice of printing scenarii in addition to libretti was virtually ended in Venice by 1655—in fact, the *Erismena* scenario is the last one in Groppo's list.[7] And third, not only is the actual text of the Prologue included with the scenario, as though it were needed while the rest of the text was available elsewhere—presumably in the printed libretto—but also the added Prologue text has neither page numbers nor compositor's signatures; it is simply bound in between the *interlocutori* on page 6 and the summary of the selfsame Prologue on page 7, as though it were a last-minute addition.

In any case, none of what must now be taken as the four early sources—Venice 1655, Contarini score 417, Bologna 1661, and the scenario—agrees precisely with any other. But they are so very close

[7] Antonio Groppo, *Catalogo di tutti i drammi per musica . . . all'anno presente 1745* (Venezia [1745]).

one to another, not merely in comparison with Venice 1670 or score 360, but even in comparison with the later out-of-town libretti which are directly modeled on them, that they must be taken as the closest we can get to an "original" version of *Erismena*. Thus score 417 is the "original" musical setting. Curiously, Wiel's catalogue of the Contarini scores says of 417

Le parole dello spartito corrispondono al libretto del 1670.
Quello del 1655 hà un prologo, che non hà l'altro, nè lo spartito....[8]

Evidently he did not go beyond the absence of prologues, for the words in 417 and Venice 1670 do not correspond well at all, whereas Venice 1655 corresponds very closely to 417. The corresponding pairing of scores 360 and Venice 1655 that is implied (though not specifically stated) in his entry for 360 works even less well.[9] The passing references to *Erismena* in the scholarly literature have followed Wiel's mistake here, except for Worsthorne.[10] Wiel himself, much later, contrasted the two *Erismena* scores, and the tone of his discussion could be taken to show that he had corrected the error.[11] Bjørn Hjelmborg's article on *Erismena* does not mention the fact that there are two scores, nor does the author identify which one he used. His musical examples show that he was using 360, and from a reference to the year 1655 one sees that he follows Wiel's catalogue on the dating.[12]

We are therefore left with three versions of the opera with significant differences in the body of the drama itself: 1) the "original" version, represented by the scenario, score 417, and Venice 1655; 2) the Venetian revival of 1670; 3) the version represented by score 360. The latter two versions each differ one from the other, as well as individually from 1655/417. They also have things in common which link them together and set them apart from the other post-1655 productions.

---

[8] Taddeo Wiel, *I Codici musicali Contariniani del secolo XVII nella R. Biblioteca di San Marco in Venezia* (Venice, 1888), p. 64.

[9] *Ibid.*, p. 10.

[10] S. T. Worsthorne, *Venetian Opera in the Seventeenth Century* (Oxford, 1954), pp. 108-109. Worsthorne's references to the tonalities of the sinfonie show that he has the scores in the right chronological order; the two versions are otherwise not discussed.

[11] Taddeo Wiel, "Francesco Cavalli," *The Musical Antiquary*, IV (1912-13), 17.

[12] Bjørn Hjelmborg, "Une partition de Cavalli," *Acta Musicologica*, XVI-XVII (1944-45), 39.

In the 1670 version all the *comparse* and two minor messenger roles are eliminated, the messages being assigned to secondary characters. There are many abbreviations in the dialogue, and a few changes made to be consistent with changes of setting and the reassignment of messages. There are additions, deletions, and replacements of arias. But no change is made in the order of events and speeches: all additions are interpolations only, and replacements are strictly *in situ* (with the one exception of a replacement by rearrangement shown in Table III below).

In Contarini score 360, on the other hand, not only are the minor roles omitted, but so is the long secondary role of the young court lady Flerida. Her plot functions are transferred to other characters, and her independent scenes or scene-sequences—comedy and lower-class love scenes, functioning as interludes before changes of set—disappear. But also much rearrangement and rewriting has taken place beyond that required by mechanics of casting and production. A characteristic place is shown in outline and summary paraphrase in Table II. This is the second of two action-segments in the opening set of Act I (by "set" is meant all that takes place between one change of setting and the next); it takes place on the battlefield where the army in which the disguised Erismena has been serving as a warrior has just been defeated by King Erimante and his ally Prince Orimeno. The essence of the action in this segment, which introduces Erismena, is that the "warrior" has fought admirably, has been wounded, is befriended by Prince Orimeno and his squire Argippo, and is sent by Orimeno under Argippo's escort back to King Erimante's court to have "his" wounded foot tended by the "slave-girl" Aldimira, with whom Orimeno is in love.

Table II shows the parts of this action-segment in parallel alignment. In the left column the parts are numbered 1 through 6, as they appear in the original version. In the right column, representing 360's version, the same numbers are preserved, equivalent or corresponding parts are horizontally aligned, and newly added parts are labeled A through D. As indicated in the Table, the 1670 libretto follows 1655/417 almost exactly, whereas 360 shows extensive rearrangement. Argippo's first encounter with the wounded "warrior" in 360 is an unfriendly one (B), to which the "warrior" responds with "Dispietato destino" (1), displaced from its original opening position and replaced there by a new monologue of similar import

TABLE II

Act I, Set 1, Segment 2*

1655/417 . I . 2 = 1670 . I . 3†	*360 . I . 3*
1. Eris: Dispietato destino . . .	Eris: Che averso iniquo fato . . . A.
2. Argi: Fatti appoggio, ò guerriero . . .	
Sento . . . la pietà . . . di farti carità . . .	
Eris: Cortese amico . . .	
Argi: . . . Troppo giovane tu sei . . .	
A voler incontrar punte di spade . . .	

1655/417 . I . 3 = 1670 . I . 4	*360 . I . 4*
3. Orim: Faville d'amore (aria)	Orim: Faville d'amore (aria) 3.
4. Argi: Signor . . . mira . . . quel guerriero . . .	
5a. Orim: Che rimiro? Piagato E'l Cavalier si prode? . . .	Ma che rimiro . . . 5a. Misero! Egli è piagato.
	Argi: . . . Renditi ò guerriero, o B. ch'io t'uccido . . . sei prigioniero.
	Eris: Dispietato destino . . . 1.
5b. Valoroso campione . . . M'obbliga il tuo valore à darti aita.	Orim: Valoroso campione . . . 5b. M'obbliga il tuo valore à darti aita.
6. Eris: . . . Gli humani tuoi favori Serviran di catene à l'alma mia.	Eris: . . . Gli humani tuoi favori 6. Serviran di catene à l'alma mia.
Orim: Servi Argippo al guerriero . . . Pietosa man dell'Idol mio Porgerà . . . Medicina e ristoro.	Orim: Servi Argippo al guerriero . . . Sanerà di tuoi piaghe il mio dolore/Idolo bel che m'ha ferito il core.
Argi: . . . Torno in corte à mirar chi mi ferì.	
	Ami chi vuol godere (aria) C.

TABLE II (Continued)

360 . 1 . 5

Argi:	Appoggiati, o guerriero . . .	2.
	Sento . . . la pietà . . . di farti carità.	
Eris:	Cortese amico . . .	
Argi:	. . . Troppo giovane sei A voler incontrar punte di spade.	
Eris:	Nume assistetemi (aria)	D.

---

* Text fragments as in 1655/417. Sections of dialogue are numbered consecutively for greater ease of comparison; completely new text portions in 360 are lettered.

† The 1670 version differs from 1655/417 only in that Argippo's two speeches in 2 end as they do here in 1670 (and 360), but run on for a few more lines each in 1655/417. Also, 1670 has "appoggiati" instead of "fatti appoggio" for his opening words, as does 360.

(A). Argippo's original friendly scene with the "warrior" (2) is now placed at the end of the action-segment, *after* he has received instructions from his master to take the "warrior" to Aldimira for treatment. From these and other rearrangements and additions, one can see that it is a matter not just of providing new arias (C and D) but of altering the motivation and character of the participants. For instance, Argippo in the original version is the initiator of the generous treatment of the "warrior"; in the revision, the aide-de-camp is deprived of his own generous motive and merely echoes his master's generosity.

Score 360 contains many places where matter is rearranged at least as radically as here, normally with similar effect or intention. In some places, bits and pieces of the action (with or without new text to fit) are even shifted to different portions of the opera. This happens even more with set pieces, which by their more generalized content are adaptable to varying dramatic circumstances. In the 1670 version, for instance, the role of the main heroine Erismena is reduced by the elimination of several big arias, and two new aria scenes are given to the other heroine, Aldimira. In score 360, Erismena gets her former arias back, while Aldimira's two extra aria scenes are moved to different places, being given to Idraspe and Diarte respectively. In fact, with a few exceptions (all but one of which are accountable in terms of cast changes), all of the material new in the 1670 version is found somewhere in score 360. At the same time, practically all of the pieces from 1655/417 which are *not* to be found in 1670 *do* occur in 360, often alongside the pieces which appeared in 1670 to have replaced them.

Table III outlines much of the second set of Act I, and it may serve as an illustration of some kinds of relationships among 1655/417, 1670, and score 360, where 1670 does not correspond precisely with the original.

This set is divided into three action-segments. In the first segment, before the portion shown in Table III begins, the "warrior" and Argippo, Prince Orimeno's squire, have arrived, with Orimeno himself one or two scenes behind. The "slave-girl" Aldimira welcomes her suitor Orimeno affectionately; but after he and his squire have departed, Aldimira feels herself falling in love with the "warrior" whose wounded foot she is tending. She excuses herself to the absent Orimeno and to her other suitor Idraspe for her inability to resist this new love.

Table III begins just after Aldimira and the "warrior" have left the stage, with the comments of Aldimira's companions (or companion) on her change of heart, and continues in outline and summary paraphrases until the end of the set. Where the character sings an aria, it is so indicated below the abbreviation of the character's name, in parentheses. Passages *al arioso* in common time are printed in italics, passages *al arioso* in triple time appear in small capital letters. Boundaries of action-segments—that is, places where there is a complete change of personnel on stage—are indicated by horizontal dividing lines.

At the end of the first action-segment, Aldimira's old nurse Alcesta and her companion Flerida are left on stage. As may be seen, all versions of this action-segment end with a solo scene for Alcesta, each with a different aria. In 360, where there is no Flerida, Alcesta's first comment is incorporated into the solo scene. (The Alcesta arias in this position from 1655/417 and 1670 are also found in 360, elsewhere in the opera.)

The second action-segment introduces Prince Idraspe, the other suitor of the "slave-girl" Aldimira. Unlike Orimeno, however, Idraspe is in disguise; he is serving as cup-bearer to King Erimante in order to further his pursuit of Aldimira. (He is also the faithless lover of Erismena, in whose pursuit Erismena has adopted her mili-

TABLE III

Act 1, Set 2, From Segment 1, End, to End of Set

	1655/417 . I . 8 (end)	*360 . I . 9 (all)*	*1670 . I . 9 (end)*
Alce:	Aldimira t'intendo . . . Spesso Amanti cangiar come fai tù.	Aldimira t'intendo . . . *Spess'Amanti cangiar come fai tù.*	Aldimira t'intendo . . . Spesso Amanti cangiar come fai tù.
Fler:	Di femina prudente . . . *Mutar pensier per appigliarsi al meglio.*		Di femina prudente . . . Mutar pensier per appigliarsi al meglio.
	1655/417 . I . 9	*360 . I . 9*	*1670 . I . 9*
Alce: (aria)	Maledetto sia del tempo . . . Imbiancar il crin mi fè.	Mirar hor questo hor quello . . . E satia d'uno, io dono il core all'altro. (Ogni bella, I . 23) (Maledetto, II . 16)	Ogni bella così fà.

	1655/417 . I . 10	*360 . I . 11*	*1670 . I . 11*
		(Idraspe's entrance aria "Caro albergo adorato," and his dialogue with his servant Clerio, in which Clerio reproaches his master for the betrayal of Erismena, and warns of impending danger, are the same in all.)	
Idra:	Amor Nume bendato . . . I perigli non vede . . . . . . all'amorose brame *Un cibo sol non trasse mai la fame.*	Amor nume bendato . . . I PERIGLI NON VEDE . . . . . . all'*amorose brame* *Un cibo sol non trasse mai la fame.*	
(aria)	Servire à più d'una Costuman gl'amanti . . .	Servire à più d'una Costuman gl'amanti . . .	Servire à più d'una Costuman gl'amanti . . .

TABLE III (Continued)

	1655/417.I.1.11	360.I.12	1670.I.12
Cler:		Che Protheo d'incostanza . . . *Più stabile è il suo cor che non è* *l'onda.*	
(aria)	Povere donne voi . . . Sono gl'affetti lor tutte bugie.	Povere donne voi . . . Sono gl'affetti lor tutte bugie.	Povere donne voi . . . Sono gl'affetti lor solo bugie.
	1655/417.I.1.12	*360.I.13*	*1670.I.13*
Eris: (aria)	Comincia à respirar . . . Ridi in mezo del duol, non penar più.	Comincia à respirar . . . Ridi in mezo del duol, non penar più.	
	1655.I.13	*360.I.14*	*1670.I.13*

(The opening of the dialogue of Orimeno and Erismena, in which Orimeno inquires after the "warrior's" wounds and learns that "he" pursues a faithless lover, is the same in all three texts.)

	1655/417.I.1.11	360.I.12	1670.I.12
Orim:	Non disperar amico . . . Cangiar vedrai la crudeltà severa *Ama costante, e spera.*	Non disperar amico . . . *Cangiar vedrai la crudeltà severa* AMA COSTANTE, E SPERA.	Non disperar amico . . . Cangiar vedrai la crudeltà severa Ama costante, e spera.
Eris: (aria)	La speranza . . . è un cibo amaro.	La speranza . . . è un cibo amaro.	Comincia à respirar . . . Ridi in mezo del duol, non pensar più.
		360.I.15	
Orim:		Quanto, quanto t'inganni . . . *La speranza è d'Amor* *dolce alimento.*	
(aria)		Senza speme . . . un cor non ama.	

tary disguise.) In 1655/417 Idraspe replies to a warning and a reproach from his servant Clerio in a speech beginning with love's
blindness to danger (in answer to the warning) and ending with
the need for more than one meal to satisfy love's hunger (in answer
to the reproach). In 360 this speech occurs and is followed by an
aria expanding on the concluding point of the speech; in 1670 the
aria replaces the speech. After his master's departure, Clerio reacts—
in both 1655 and 1670—with an aria of general good advice to the
ladies; in 360 the aria is preceded by a short monologue commenting
more directly on Idraspe's philosophy of love.

In the original conception, the third action-segment was framed
by two big arias for Erismena. In her re-entrance aria she expresses
relief; in the final aria she responds to Orimeno's friendly counsel
of hope with bitterness. In 360 the bitterness of the "warrior"
prompts Orimeno to a response of his own, contradicting "bitter
food" with his own description of hope as "sweet nourishment." In
1670 Erismena loses her bitter aria altogether, and her opening aria
of relief is placed *after* Orimeno's encouragement; thus her response
is changed from negative to positive, and the action-segment begins
without an aria.

In the portions covered by Table III it happens that the only items
new for 1670 are Idraspe's aria "Servire à più d'una," an addition,
and Alcesta's aria "Ogni bella così fà," a replacement. Idraspe's
"Amor Nume bendato" speech and Erismena's "La speranza" aria
are deleted. But 360 includes the original material, the replacing
material, and the additional material, all together and (in the
Idraspe-Clerio segment for instance) side by side, along with new
material found in no other version. From this situation, and many
similar ones, one can see that the verbal text of score 360 is far too
different from the 1670 libretto to allow 360 to be considered as the
Venetian revival.

Yet the two versions are closely related, and one of them obviously
was made with the help of the other. Certain trivial textual variants
in all four of the principal sources are suggestive of the relationship.
For instance, the second line of King Erimante's monologue ending
I. 1 reads "A consolar la Reggia" in all the libretti, including 1655
and 1670, while both scores read "A rallegrar la Reggia." As Ex. 1
shows, the *rifacimento* in 360 was made with the original setting in

mind and, as the textual variant shows, at hand.[13] At the same time, there is one set piece in the original, Orimeno's "Faville d'amore" (see Table II), which was completely reset in 360. There are two stanzas in each libretto, 1655 and 1670; in 1670 the closing line of the original second stanza, "Per vaga beltà," replaces the first stanza's original closing line "Ch'Amor gustar fà," and a much changed, independently rhymed second stanza is provided. The scores only show the respective first stanzas; but 417 gives 1655's final "Ch'Amor gustar fà," while 360 gives 1670's final "Per vaga beltà." This suggests that the music for the 1670 version was that of score 360, wherever the 360 music differs from 417.

In the absence of documentation for any production represented by score 360, however, the only question profitably to be asked is whether the version in score 360 as a whole antedates or postdates the 1670 production. That is, one can try to establish either that 360 was the source for the new material coming into the 1670 revival, or else that 360 was a conflation of material from both Venetian productions, the 1655 original and the 1670 revival. The internal evidence of the material itself and its disposition suggests that 360 was the later version. That is to say, one sees (in Tables II and III as well as elsewhere) that 1670 follows the original order of events exactly, merely adding, cutting, and replacing as it goes, while 360 rearranges drastically. While it is not inconceivable that 360 predates 1670, and that the material was then put back in its original order for the 1670 revival (while utilizing some 360 material), this is certainly a cumbersome hypothesis—contradicted by some strategic misprints showing that those portions of 1670 which retain original material were simply printed directly from a copy of 1655.

For instance, a binder's cue is carried over wrongly from 1655 into 1670, in a love scene for the characters Flerida and Argippo.[14] This place is the only one where a change in page coincides in both 1655 and 1670 with a point where new material is introduced. The version of 1655 continues over the page to a recitative for Argippo beginning "Al fin la ritrosetta"; 1670 continues (from the same point) over the page to a duet beginning "Venirai." But in 1670 the

---

[13] For other places where both scores have one wording and all the libretti have another, see footnotes to Exx. 2a, 8, and 9.

[14] Venice 1655. III. 13, p. 78 over to p. 79, and Venice 1670. III. 15, p. 58 over to p. 59. The existence of this and other strategic misprints in these two libretti was brought to my attention by Miss V. Ranganayaki Ayyangar.

binder's cue "Arg. Al" is mistakenly left on the first of the pages, instead of being replaced with the proper "Arg. Ven." That Aureli himself was directly concerned with the changes is indicated by the fact that the new dedicatory preface—which, amusingly enough, contains some hyperbole taken over word for word from the original preface—appears over his name in the 1670 libretto. The inference is that he provided the printer with a copy of the original libretto as well as handwritten pages containing the new material, with indications as to where it was to go and what was to be deleted. Therefore, whatever new text there is in 360 that corresponds to 1670 presumably was written by Aureli. To suppose, then, that 360 antedates 1670 would require us to suppose that Aureli also provided the 360 material *not* found in 1670, and the extensive rearrangement throughout the whole opera, and then went back to the original ordering of events in 1670 (including the restoration of Flerida to the cast), but used only 360 material for the new places. This too seems almost inexpressibly cumbersome, even if again it is not completely impossible.

In the absence of any documents beyond the score itself, one can say little more about the circumstances of score 360: for what purpose it was compiled, by whom, and more precisely when. Its presence in the Contarini collection, as a fair copy, might suggest that it was made for private performance at Marco Contarini's Piazzola villa; in any case, its presence in that collection, completely apart from musical style, allows a date no later than the middle 1680's.[15] Perhaps, as suggested by Professor Nino Pirrotta (in a private communication), it was aimed at Vienna. If the musical revisions and new settings were made by Cavalli himself, the compilation of the score was made by 1675 at the latest. In any case, the 360 musical material which also occurs in 1670 may be presumed to be from Cavalli's hand. The libretto of 1670 says nothing one way or the other, and the 360 score contains much of the original music from 1655 as well as settings of 1670 texts.

So we are safe in saying that score 360 postdates score 417, and probably safe in saying that much of its music was heard in 1670. And we are reasonably secure in postulating that in fact the whole of score 360 was put together after 1670, as a conflation and revision,

---

[15] For the dates and the nature of the Contarini collection in general, see the Preface to Wiel, *I Codici musicali*. On the specific points, see pp. viii and xii.

and that it was made in Venice. Perhaps we are a little less secure if we say that the score was made by Cavalli, and therefore before the end of 1675; but it is difficult to imagine who else could have wanted to go to the trouble which was taken, as we have seen and shall see, over many parts of the recomposition. At this time, contributions to an opera by a composer other than the original composer would be his own new compositions, not subtle recomposition of the originals.

II

The point in attempting to establish the credentials of score 360 is that the musical relationships between score 417 and score 360 are extremely interesting. They are of three kinds. First, much music in 360 is the same as in 417, or is merely transposed to fit different vocal ranges. Second, there is much new music: some represents settings of words found only in 360, some must have gone with the same words in 1670. Third, there is recomposition, both in recitative and in set pieces, of the 417 material. This recomposition ranges between the extremes of a completely fresh setting of an old aria text (Orimeno's "Faville d'amore," see Table II) and the mere transposition mentioned above. In many instances the recomposition may have been initially the result of having to provide for new vocal ranges in the cast—the two heroines, Erismena and Aldimira, and the servant Clerio are the only roles which have the same voice types (all soprano) in both 417 and 360. But much of the recomposing occurs in places where transposition alone would have done the job, and there are instances of recomposition of old material where the voices involved are the same as in 417.

As one might guess from the wide range of the reworking techniques, comparison of the two scores illuminates the changing conventions of opera in the third quarter of the seventeenth century with particular clarity. It illustrates a hundred fine points of craft, and furnishes many elegant demonstrations for the evolution of the design and treatment of dramatic music in a period during which it was undergoing fundamental and enduring changes.

1.

Example 1 may serve as an introduction to a comparison of the two scores. It is the conclusion of the opening scene in both settings: the elderly King Erimante, after awakening from a nightmare about an unknown warrior who will rob him of the kingdom he has just

* All libretti have "consolar."

Ex. 1

Ex. 1 (cont.)

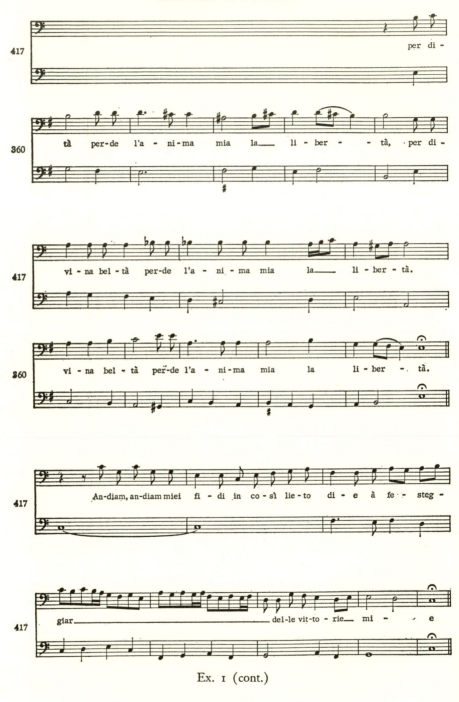

Ex. 1 (cont.)

conquered in battle, is now soliloquizing on his love for the "slave-girl" Aldimira. The versions are aligned, to show the corresponding placement of cadences at articulations in the text, the similarity and frequent identity of lines and contours, and such details as the corresponding placement of the colorful change of harmony at the word "ardo."

The significant difference between the two versions is in the overall plan. In the original setting, each of the four sections of the text (as marked by full cadences) receives about equal weight. The opening reference to the passage of time, the ensuing lines about the rising flames of love, the King's description of the object and effect of his love, and his abrupt return to the public world as he addresses his "fidi," are in balanced contrast in the original setting. If there is any special emphasis on a single part, it is on the rising of the flames of love. In 360, on the contrary, the monologue is directed toward an expressive climax at the end. The final call to the "fidi" is cut; but more significantly, the lines "Per divina beltà / Perde l'anima mia la libertà" are repeated in a sequential musical setting, and along with the preceding line are set in triple meter. What originally was merely one of three successive and brief common-time ariosi is now singled out and, by means of repetition and change of meter, made into a sixteen-measure "arietta" (as opposed to "arioso") with the characteristic *seicento* ABB design.

This revision of the opening scene of *Erismena* illustrates two structural levels of the development of musico-dramatic techniques. It provides a lyrical moment, a set piece, at the end of a whole scene; and at the same time it forces an unbalanced and dynamic motion toward that set piece onto a speech which was originally conceived as balanced and static.

2.

The next group of examples (Exx. 2a-6b, 8) is taken from the second set of Act I, from near the end of the first action-segment up to the end of the set. (An outline of this part of the opera is given above in Table III; the sequence of events is shown in this Table and rehearsed in the paragraphs above discussing the Table.)

Examples 2a and 2b show the sequence of musical events in the concluding portion of the *second* action-segment, the one involving Idraspe and Clerio (see Table III). Table IV gives the complete

TABLE IV

417 . I . 10 (end)	360 . I . 11 (end)
Idraspe	Idraspe

417 . I . 10 (end)	360 . I . 11 (end)
Amor Nume bendato,	Amor Nume bendato
Che di foco novel nutre mia speme,	che NUTRENDO MI VÀ DI DOLCE SPEME, (V/d)
I perigli non vede, non gli teme. (G)	I PERIGLI NON VEDE, E NON GLI TEME. (a)
De passati successi	DE PASSATI SUCESSI
La memoria hò perduta; e sappi amico	LA MEMORIA HO PERDUTA (F); e sappi amico
Ch'all'amorose brame	Ch'all'amorose brame
Un cibo sol non trasse mai la fame. (d)	Un cibo sol non trasse mai la fame. (d)
*RITORNELLO "non trasse mai . . ." (d)	RITORNELLO "non trasse mai . . ." (d)
Exit Idraspe	Idraspe (aria, 3/2, d)
	Servire à più d'una / Costuman gl'amanti.
	(Costuman gl'amanti) (d)
	De cori incostanti / Amica è fortuna.
	(Amica è fortuna) (a)
	Costuman gl'amanti / Servir à più d'una.
	(Costuman gl'amanti / Servir a più d'una) (d)
	RITORNELLO (aria—"costuman . . . servir . . .") (F, d)
	(one more stanza in 1670 libretto)
	Exit Idraspe

TABLE IV (Continued)

417.1.11

360.1.12

Clerio

Che Protheo d'incostanza!
E pur, sorte amorosa / Il suo genio seconda (a)
(*Più stabile è il suo cor*)
Più stabile è il suo cor che non è l'onda. (d)

*RITORNELLO "più stabile . . ." (d)

Clerio (aria, 3/2, d)

Clerio (aria, 3/2, d)

†Povere donne voi
Ch'a giovani tal'hor fede prestate (F)
Miserelle imparate (a)
A non far mai zerbinetti amanti
Amorose pazzie. (C)
Sono gl'affetti lor tutte bugie. (g)
(Sono gl'affetti lor tutte bugie) (d)

†Povere donne voi
Ch'a giovani tall'hor fede prestate (F)
Miserelle imparate (a)
A non far mai zerbinetti amanti
Amorose pazzie. (C)
Sono gl'affetti lor tutte bugie. (g)
(Sono gl'affetti lor tutte bugie) (d)

RITORNELLO (aria—"tutte bugie") (F, d)

RITORNELLO (aria—"tutte bugie") (F, d)

(second stanza, ritornello)

(second stanza, ritornello)

EXIT Clerio

EXIT Clerio

* Same music
† Same music
Letters in parentheses indicate the cadential harmonies.

text of the passage. Words in italics are set in common-time arioso, words in small capitals in triple-meter arioso; cadences are indicated by scale-degree letters in parentheses; the position of instrumental ritornelli and the text-settings echoed by their subjects are indicated; ritornelli which are musically identical are marked with an asterisk; identical aria-settings are marked with a dagger.

Each version of this action-segment concludes with the same "Povere donne" aria for Idraspe's servant Clerio, and the common-time ritornello preceding this aria is also the same in both versions. But this ritornello has nothing to do with the aria that follows, beyond being in the same key. It is, in both cases, made to echo the line of text which precedes it. In score 360 some new text is given to Clerio; his "Più stabile è il suo cor" is then musically set so as to "generate" the ritornello, that same ritornello which in 417 was "generated" by Idraspe's "un cibo sol non trasse mai la fame." This aphorism in turn has to have a new musical setting in 360, and hence a new following ritornello.

The funneling of a passage of recitative text toward an epitomizing, aphoristic final line such as "un cibo sol non trasse mai la fame," often formally pointed up by a rhyme, was frequently given musico-dramatic emphasis in mid-century operas by a setting *al arioso*, sometimes with sequential repetitions or echoing ritornelli or both. This device is found in *Giasone, Orontea,* and their successors, including of course the original *Erismena.* It was not new; such heightening of a hortatory, sententious, or moralizing epigram is perhaps most familiar to us in Busenello's and Monteverdi's character Seneca, but it appears as far back as 1626 in Mazzocchi's "La Catena d'Adone," as Pirrotta has pointed out, for the line "La ragion perde dove il senso abbonda."[16] In those earlier settings the device had appeared as an arioso refrain line following successive stanzas of recitative and was pompous rather than frivolous. In our examples the epigrammatic arioso is sung only once, and the comment, while sententious and pithy, is rather more immoral than moral. All the same, the position and function, and even perversely the character, of "Un cibo sol non trasse mai la fame" reveal its more respectable ancestry.

This device is paralleled in effect by the shaping of the preferred type of aria text and setting at mid-century. In the majority of arias,

[16] Nino Pirrotta, "Falsirena e la più antica delle cavatine," in *Collectanea Historiae Musicae,* II (Florence, 1956), 355-62.

Ex. 2a

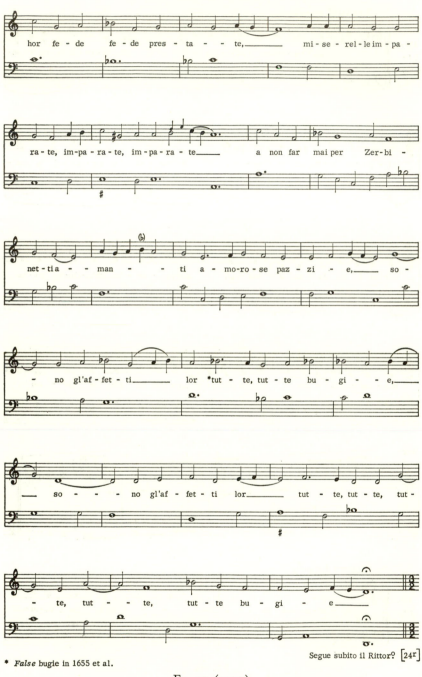

* *False* bugie in 1655 et al.

Segue subito il Rittor? [24r]

Ex. 2a (cont.)

Ex. 2a (cont.)

Ex. 2b

Ex. 2b (cont.)

Ex. 2b (cont.)

it is the *last* line which contains the main point, the *last* line which contains the most extensive word and phrase repetitions, the *last* line whose setting is repeated as a whole, sequentially, in two different tonalities. It so happens that Clerio's aria, "Povere donne," is an almost ideal specimen of one kind of ABB aria, so characteristically associated with the seicento (see Ex. 2a, Table IV). The way the ritornello echoes and further develops the figure for the words "tutte bugie," words which are the main and final point of the aria, is parallel to the way the "non trasse mai la fame" ritornello earlier in the segment echoes and develops the main and final point of Idraspe's speech.

Idraspe's little entrance aria "Caro albergo adorato," with which this action-segment opens, uses the ritornello in exactly the same way, to echo the final line (Ex. 3). But here the final line, set up by a rhyming line before it, is the same as the opening line; let us call it then a "reprise line." In the second strophe, the reprise line "Care soglie felici," is different in words but identical in affective meaning—just as, in Clerio's "Povere donne," the epitomizing final line of the second strophe has the semantically equivalent "tutti dipinti" in place of "tutte bugie" ("false bugie" in the libretti).

These examples show very well how both in arioso and in aria an important epitomizing verbal phrase may be connected with a clear-cut musical figure. They show further that such a short musical subject not only may be susceptible to extended vocal development with word or phrase repetition, but also may be abstracted from its verbal source and developed instrumentally without losing its connotation. Finally, the examples suggest that such a musical figure may be attached to some other verbal expression related in sense or in sentiment to the expression originally set by it. One can well suppose that the compiler of score 360 used Clerio's new line "più stabile è il suo cor che non è l'onda" (Ex. 2b) as a third-person equivalent, with a new metaphor, for Idraspe's "un cibo sol non trasse mai la fame" (Ex. 2a). In both versions it is Idraspe's inconstancy which is described in the arioso, recalled in the instrumental ritornello; and it is Idraspe's inconstancy which is generalized in the aria-text which follows immediately.

3.

It seems quite possible, in fact, that in score 417 the "non trasse mai la fame" ritornello was intended not only to echo Idraspe's sentiments at the end of this second action-segment but also to call attention to the fact that the identical sentiment had been expressed at the end of the first action-segment by Flerida. In the left-hand column of Table V, we can see that in 417 Flerida has an arioso-line (in italics) "mutar pensier per appigliarsi il meglio." Example 4a shows the setting of this line, whose subject and manner of accompaniment are strikingly similar to those of "non trasse mai."

* The 360 version is a fourth higher.

Ex. 3

TABLE V

417 . 1 . 8 (end)	360 . 1 . 10 (all)
Alcesta	Alcesta (new setting)
Aldimira t'intendo, Anco à me sempre piacque Nella mia gioventù	Aldimira t'intendo Anco à me sempre piacque Nella mia gioventu (*spess'Amanti cangiar*)
Spesso Amanti cangiar, come fai tù. (B♭)	*Spess'Amanti cangiar, come fai tù.* (G)
	RITORNELLO "cangiar . . ." (D, G)
Flerida	(aria, 4/4, G)
Di femina prudente E consiglio maturo e anch' io lo *scieglio:*	Mirar hor questo hor quello Ma scioglier il più bello Io sempre costumai con modo scaltro, (D)
Mutar pensier per appigliarsi il meglio. (B♭) (*Mutar pensier per appigliarsi il meglio*) (g)	E satia d'uno io dono il core all'altro. (a) (E satia d'uno io dono il core all'altro) (G)
Exit Flerida	*RITORNELLO (aria—"e satia d'uno . . .") (D, G)
417 . 1 . 9	
Alcesta (aria, 3/2, D)	(one more stanza, followed by ritor- nello)
Maledetto sia del tempo Quel momento / Che d'argento Imbiancar il crin mi fè. (D) E svanita già per me La speranza di godere Se non compri hoggi il piacere Che mi guardi alcun non v'è. (A) Maledetto sia del tempo Quel momento / Che d'argento Imbiancar il crin mi fè. (D)	Exit Alcesta
RITORNELLO (aria—"maledetto . . .") (A, D) (two more stanzas in 1655 libretto)	
Exit Alcesta	

* Same music
Letters in parentheses indicate the cadential harmonies.

In the later version of *Erismena,* the use of a single musical figure to set more than one verbal expression becomes a more-or-less routine device of construction for certain kinds of scenes. The scene for the old nurse Alcesta at the end of the first action-segment is a case in point. As set in 360, one and the same ritornello (as indicated by an asterisk in Table V) is originally made to echo the words "cangiar, come fai tù" of the arioso and subsequently to echo the similar sentiment expressed in the last line of the little ABB aria, "e satia d'uno io dono il core all'altro." As Ex. 4b shows, the ritornello fits the end of the aria much better than the end of the arioso, where its four-note subject is made to echo a rather contrived melisma on "cangiar." It would certainly seem as though the ritornello had been conceived in connection with the final line of the aria, and that only later was a setting of the speech from the original text somehow forced to provide a verbal impetus for the ritornello in the older fashion.

This equating of two independent but obviously similar older conventions, the post-*arioso* ritornello and the post-*aria* ritornello, seems intended to connect the formal aria with what leads up to it. Such a connection was by no means considered necessary at the time of the first *Erismena.* There the set pieces, as in other operas of the 1650's are for the most part pieces of musical and verbal décor. When they come at the ends of scenes, they function as interludes rather than as outgrowths of the dialogue.

The excerpt which appears in Table V and Exx. 4a and 4b, amounting to the end of the first action-segment of the set, illustrates both the change in function of set pieces and one mechanism through which it came about. In this humorous pendant to the action-segment, Aldimira has just left the stage with the unwitting latest object of her affections. Aldimira's companions comment upon her change of heart; in score 360, the absence of Flerida leaves the commentary entirely to Alcesta. At first glance the revision appears trivial: Flerida's "mutar pensier" speech is suppressed, and the scene for Alcesta goes directly from her "Aldimira t'intendo" speech to a substitute aria without further ado.

This is not at all what has happened. Although the stock aria of 417, "Maledetto sia del tempo," does not contradict the context, it really has nothing to do with what has just happened or what has just been said. The action of the set-segment concludes with Flerida's

Ex. 4a

Ex. 4a (cont.)

Ex. 4b

Ex. 4b (cont.)

comment on Alcesta's reaction to Aldimira's change of heart.
Alcesta's railing at old age in the aria is extra: it is an interlude. In
the 1670 libretto the scene is laid out identically (see Table III)
except that there is a substitute aria, beginning "Ogni bella così fà,"
and continuing in the same vein. The 1670 aria text, however, is
somewhat related to the specific circumstances, as its opening line

suggests. In the 360 version of the passage, the Alcesta aria is still more closely linked to the action; rather than an addition to Flerida's "Di femina prudente" speech, it is a paraphrase of it—only here, in the absence of Flerida, the "femina prudente" speaks for herself. Where in 417 Flerida continues Alcesta's "spess'amanti cangiar come fai tù" with "mutar pensier per appigliarsi il meglio," in 360 Alcesta amplifies her own remark, first with "mirar hor questo hor quello / ma sciogler il più bello," which has the same meaning, and then with "e satia d'uno io dono il core all'altro," which has the same kind of double setting. The actual words of the recitative and arioso in 417 and the aria in 360 are different, but the sense as well as the format are parallel. The fate of the aria "Maledetto sia del tempo," then, was not replacement but elimination (though it turns up elsewhere in score 360, as does the 1670 replacement). What Alcesta's "Mirar hor questo hor quello" replaces is not her "Maledetto" aria, but rather Flerida's speech, with its sententious and immoral epigrammatic epitome.

4.

To replace such an arioso with an aria serving the same purpose is not a very long step. In this case Alcesta's aria is only a measure and a half longer than Flerida's melismatic arioso, and the ABB formats of recitative-plus-repeated-arioso-line versus aria-beginning-plus-repeated-final-line are the same. A connection of the lyrical moment with the "Aldimira t'intendo" speech is not made musically in score 417; in 360 it is made through the ritornello, which echoes both the last line of the arioso and the last line of the aria.

A still closer connection between the parts of the scene would have been made if the last line of the aria stanza had been also its first line. Then the end of the arioso, the ritornello for the arioso, the beginning of the aria, the end of the aria, and the ritornello for the aria—in short, all the musical and verbal articulations—could have been linked through a common musical and ideological subject. Such a state of affairs is found at the very end of the 360 version of this set from Act I (see Ex. 5). This passage is discussed by Hjelmborg, who comments on its construction and on its resemblance to other places in the score.[17] But he does not show the music; and not only are the connections within the scene even tighter than he sug-

---

[17] Hjelmborg, "Une partition de Cavalli," pp. 49-50.

gests, but the scene as a whole is structurally parallel to the Alcesta scene, except in respect to the placement of the epitomizing line.

The parts of the scene are linked through the four-note motive "La speranza"/ "senza speme," which enters in most places as a cadence is being completed. It first appears in the bass under the word "tormento." Then it is heard in the violins—surely *over* the rhyming word "alimento," rather than after it, as the score seems to suggest. The numerals under the bass in the first measure of the ritornello are characteristically cadential, which suggests that the end of the arioso and the beginning of the ritornello as written would in fact be concurrent in performance. The same relationship of the parts appears later on, where the violins must enter as the voice completes the final cadence at the end of the first-stanza reprise-line.[18]

At the end of Ex. 5, the four-note motto-figure is shown entering at the beginning of the second stanza, with the reprise-line "Cara è à ogn'un se ben inganna." It becomes evident at this point that the composer had been thinking entirely in terms of the recitative and the first stanza, with reprise-line and motto-subject. Although the beginning of the second stanza is a perfectly reasonable setting of the text, there is no meaningful, properly stressed four-syllable sequence in the line to fit the motto-figure, and the words have to be adjusted to the music in quite a different way. The second stanza, though dutifully composed, is patently superfluous to the musico-dramatic conception of the scene.

One of the hypotheses about musico-dramatic development which is being considered here is that there are really only two basic types of situation which come to be used as preparation for set pieces. One of these is that in which a character expresses a personal feeling about his affairs; one instance has been noticed briefly already, in King Erimante's monologue in I. 1. The other basic situation that generates lyrical moments is what we have seen in the examples so far discussed from the second set of Act I: a character comments on what has taken place in a speech concluding with some sort of epigram. During the course of time, the natural final position of

---

[18] There are places in 417 (see Ex. 2a) and 360 (see Ex. 4b) where a ritornello overleaf from a sung passage is presaged "segue" or "subito." This would help to confirm the notion that a frequent, even normal, overlapping of the last tone of the vocal passage with the beginning of a separately written ritornello is to be presumed wherever otherwise possible. Where ritornello and preceding line are on the same page, no such reminder would be needed.

Ex. 5

Ex. 5 (cont.)

such an epigram, set *al arioso* at the end of a speech or scene, is taken over by somewhat more formalized lyric moments. The end result is the much later *opera seria* situation in which a scene or series of scenes concludes with a character singing a large aria which is more or less neutral "commentary" on what has gone before.

The first stanza of Orimeno's "Senze speme," with its epigrammatic reprise-line and melismatic middle, its thorough verbal and musical preparation in the recitative, its opening and closing ritornello, and its single plastic subject crystallizing the affect, is a good prototype for the "commentary" type of grand *da capo*. At the same time, it can be proposed as representative of an intermediate type in a longer evolution. It is equivalent in position and function to the

ABB aria "Mirar hor questo hor quello" from the end of the first action-segment of this set; the crucial difference is that the main verbal-musical idea appears at the beginning *as well as* at the end. But that aria of Alcesta's, as we have seen, had replaced Flerida's original scene-final arioso. One glimpses here several medial stages of a development from the sententious arioso of the second quarter of the century to a fundamental type of grand *da capo* scene of the much later *opera seria*.

5.

The solo scene for Orimeno which has just been examined was added to close the action before a change of set (360. I. 15). In the original version, the same action-segment had ended with Erismena's aria "La speranza è un non sò che." Examples 6a and 6b begin with part of the speech of Orimeno which motivates this aria; Table VI gives the text of the end of the scene in full.

This aria is Erismena's direct and bitter personal response to Orimeno's friendly counsel of hope. It is a most ingenious combination of affects and of functions. Though the overall design is a standard set piece pattern, an ABB with B as a refrain section, the settings of individual lines reflect the different character and function of those lines in terms of the mid-century conventions. The four-line stanza, beginning "La speranza è un non sò che / dove sia nessun lo sà," is in the sententious commentary vein and is accordingly set in common time with a moving bass. The first line of the refrain, "così misera imparo," is emotional reaction and accordingly is set in "heightened" recitative with an affective harmonization. The remaining line, "il viver di speranza è un cibo amaro," is another epigram; it is set, curiously enough, in 3/2. One might think this an attempt to infuse the line with one of the generalized emotions—love, joy, hope, grief, despair—associated with triple-meter aria style. But the fact that the meter changes back to common time at the emotive word "amaro" suggests that the 3/2 is intended to mock the triple-meter ethos, to use it ironically; the 3/2 belongs really only to the melismatic setting of "speranza" and its preparatory and connecting words. The ritornello confirms the mockery. It appears after the refrain, and there echoes the setting of "speranza," with the sequential figure now divided between the two violin parts. The sustained tone from the "speranza" flourish also appears in the

TABLE VI

417 . I . 12 (end)	360 . I . 14 (end)
Orimeno	Orimeno
Non disperar amico	Non disperar amico
Volubile è la sorte degl'amanti.	Volubile è la sorte degl'amanti. (B♭)
Ne suoi moti incostanti	Ne suoi moti incostanti
Varia sovente della *Rota i giri*, (F)	Varia soventi de la rota i giri.
Del bel per cui sospiri	Del bel per cui sospiri
Cangiar vedrai	*Cangiar vedrai (cangiar vedrai)*
la crudeltà severa:	*la crudeltà severa*: (d)
Ama costante e spera. (g)	AMA COSTANTE (AMA COSTANTE)E SPERA. (g)
†Erismena (aria, g)	†Erismena (aria, g)
RITORNELLO (3/2; d, g)	RITORNELLO (3/2; d, g)
4/4	4/4
La speranza è un non sò che (V/g)	La speranza è un certo che (V, g)
Dove sia nessun lo sà (V/d)	≠ Che ingannar il mondo sà (V/d)
Se tal volta corre à me	Se tal volta corre à me
Come vien poi se ne và. (F)	Come vien poi se ne và. (F)
(Rec: Cosi misera imparo	(Rec: Cosi misera imparo
3/2: Ch'il viver di speranza	3/2: Ch'il viver di speranza
è un cibo amaro) (d)	è un cibo amaro) (d)
Rec: Cosi misera imparo	Rec: Cosi misera imparo
3/2: Ch'il viver di speranza	3/2: Ch'il viver di speranza
è un cibo amaro. (g)	è un cibo amaro. (g)
RITORNELLO as above	RITORNELLO as above

(a second stanza, with the "cosi misera" refrain and the ritornello)

† Same music from here on, except for the second line of the stanza and some ornamental detail also in the stanza. Cf. Exx. 6a and 6b.

Letters in parentheses indicate the cadential harmonies.

ritornello and may be seen in Ex. 6a at the re-entry of the first violin near the beginning.

Hjelmborg pointed out the resemblance between the ritornello and the "speranza" melisma and also drew attention to the virtual identity of the bass line at the beginning of the ritornello and the bass line accompanying the first two lines of the aria.[19] But in fact

[19] Hjelmborg, "Une partition de Cavalli," p. 50. The whole aria, as it appears in 360, is printed on pp. 53-54 of his article.

Ex. 6a

Ex. 6a (cont.)

Ex. 6b

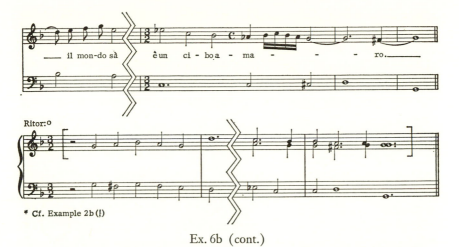

il mon-do sà   è un   ci - bo a - ma -   -   - ro.

Ritor:°

* Cf. Example 2b (♩)

Ex. 6b (cont.)

the relationship is closer still. Example 6b shows the aria opening
as it appears in score 360, the only score studied by Hjelmborg. In
the opening of the 417 setting, however, shown in Ex. 6a, the two
phrases of the vocal melody are in the same registers, respectively,
as the first and second violin parts at the beginning of the ritornello.
One sees there that the first two lines of the aria not only have the
same bass as the ritornello but the same melody, transformed to
duple meter and filled in. Beyond this, the opening ritornello in 417
is not an opening ritornello in the late seventeenth-century vein; it
is an arioso-echoing ritornello, like the "non trasse mai" ritornello
and others discussed above. It is an ironic transformation of the
setting of Orimeno's helpful "Ama costante e spera" just preceding
and shows just what Erismena thinks of his advice. Orimeno's
arioso is a familiar and conventional mid-century setting for the
idea of "costante," with its sustained tone over a walking bass.[20] The
first five notes of the arioso's bass plus the next four become the
sequential treble melody of the ritornello, followed then by the
sustained tone accompanied by the same motive. As the subject
moves through its version as "La speranza è un non sò che" to its
appearance with "speranza" in the 3/2 just before the final cadence,
the mockery becomes even clearer.

The resetting of Orimeno's "Ama costante" and the transposition

[20] For two characteristic earlier specimens, see Wellesz, "Cavalli und der Stil der
Venezianischen Oper," p. 24.

of the second line of the aria "La speranza" in 360—no doubt in the interests of a brighter sound for the new soprano—destroy the musical connection between the aria ritornello and what precedes it, and thereby considerably weaken the dramatic effect. The sarcastic ritornello of 417, with its play upon the arioso-echoing and aria-echoing ritornello conventions, has become an ordinary opening ritornello. The dramatic device has assimilated itself to a growing convention; it is beginning to become a habit.

We have supposed that there might be some sort of musical connection intended in 417 between Idraspe's "Un cibo sol non trasse mai la fame" in I. 10 and Flerida's "Mutar pensier per appigliarsi il meglio" in I. 8 (Exx. 2a and 4a). The subject of "La speranza è un non sò che," as it appears in the ritornello and the 3/2 melisma on "speranza," also seems to appear later in the opera. In 417, Erismena's "La speranza" aria ends the set; the third and final set of Act I deals with other matters, and she turns up there (with the one word "signor") only as a prop, so that the king can see that the captured "warrior" is in fact the one of whom he had dreamed at the beginning of the opera. Erismena reappears as a personage in her own right at the beginning of Act II, which begins in 417 with her aria "O fiere tempeste" (see Ex. 7). It will be observed that the ritornello for this aria has nothing to do with the aria itself, and also that its bass is identical with the melody of the "La speranza" ritornello and refrain (Ex. 6a). Since Erismena is making her first appearance after an absence, since her state of mind is similar, and since there is no evident connection musically between "O fiere tempeste" and its ritornello, one may well wonder if a connection is intended between the "O fiere tempeste" ritornello and the last thing heard before from Erismena, "La speranza è un non sò che."

It would be wrong, of course, to suggest a systematic and consistent use of "reminiscence motives" from the instances of "mutar pensier"/"non trasse mai" and "La speranza"/"O fiere tempeste." The ideas of "amorous inconstancy" and of "hope" are persistent themes in *seicento* opera, including *Erismena*, and there are many text phrases expressing each of the notions, with many different musical settings. But recurrence of single lines or phrases of text with the same musical setting, as refrain lines or as quotations from earlier scenes, is not unheard-of in operas of the 1650's and 1660's.

Ex. 7

Worsthorne prints one from Cesti's *La Dori*,[21] and they occur in earlier operas as well—Cesti's *Orontea* and Cavalli's *Giasone* each have one or two striking instances. The only thing new here is the possible association at some distance of a commonplace (but characteristic and recognizable) musical figure with a commonplace (but affective and familiar) concept or state of mind, rather than with the specific text that makes the concept or state of mind concrete.

6.

Returning to Erismena herself, at the end of the second set of Act I, we have seen that her aria "La speranza" is sung in direct response to Orimeno's well-meant "ama costante e spera." It is, there-

[21] Worsthorne, *Venetian Opera in the Seventeenth Century*, p. 77.

fore, a part of the drama itself, and the bitter feelings it expresses are motivated not merely by the general course of events to that point but quite specifically by the content of the preceding speech. It adumbrates the other principal type of set piece in Italian opera, in which direct emotional responses as well as sententious commentaries are set as arias and pushed to the end of scenes, taking the place of heightened declamation.

The aria with which Erismena begins the third action-segment, "Comincia à respirar," is representative of an older type (see Table III, and Ex. 8). Though the relief she expresses may be assumed to be some sort of euphoria resulting from the healing of her wounded foot, there has actually been no change in her position vis-à-vis the drama since she left the stage several scenes earlier with the newly enamored Aldimira. "Comincia à respirar," then, is a traditional entrance aria of the kind often seen in this period. In these arias, which are intended to set a point of departure for action to follow, the character expresses an emotional state arrived at *before* the particular action-segment opens. Such entrance arias are arias of generalized emotion—love, hope, joy, longing, sorrow, despair, and the like—and are not specifically tied to the immediate dramatic context. At mid-century, pieces which opened an action tended to be much more impressive and elaborate than the occasional arias which concluded an action. It was, in fact, the great musico-dramatic invention of the third quarter of the seventeenth century to have discovered how to set up a text in such a way as to allow the lyrical pause to follow and grow from the action, rather than precede the action or intervene between two actions.

"Comincia à respirar," like Clerio's "Povere donne" (Ex. 2a), is an ABB aria with two strophes; the principal difference in general design is that "Povere donne" has a separate (though very similarly constructed) final epitomizing single line for each of the two strophes, while "Comincia à respirar," like "La speranza," has the same pair of lines as refrain for each strophe. In large-scale pieces of this kind, where the epitomizing section contains two or more full lines, the section is normally set as a more-or-less independent part of a larger "aria pattern," as it is here. But just as in smaller medial and exit pieces the one-line epitome may come last ("Povere donne," Ex. 2a) or both first and last ("Caro albergo," Ex. 3), so also in the large pieces the independent refrain may appear either after, or

* Changes in ornamentation indicated with small notes.
† Con disperati *affetti* in 1655 et al.

Ex. 8

Ex. 8 (cont.)

both before and after, the strophes. In Erismena's entrance aria here, "Vivi lieto sù sù / Ridi in mezo del duol non pensar più" is a following refrain for each of two strophes; the ritornello is taken from the bass of the final endecasillabo line, minus the word-painting on "duol." "Comincia à respirar" has then the general design *SRR rit SRR rit*;[22] though both strophes and refrain are in triple meter, there is a perfectly evident rhythmic contrast, entailing also a faster tempo for "vivi lieto sù sù," matching the contrast in affect in the texts.

Another common pattern can be seen in an example recently published by Hjelmborg from Cavalli's *Doriclea* (1645).[23] This aria has the design *R' rit SR rit SR rit; R'* is the same as *R* musically but with two changes of wording in the text.[24] The significant formal difference between this and "Comincia à respirar" is the presence at the beginning of the *Doriclea* piece of an extra refrain and ritornello. But these are only two of many similar formal designs used in Roman cantatas or "canzone" of the mid-seventeenth century, though the Roman pieces seldom have concerting instruments and hence have shorter ritornelli or none.[25]

Omission of the second strophe and what follows it from the type of "canzona" that begins with its refrain section would leave *RSR*, that is, ABA. Often enough this musical format appears in the mid-century opera scores, though usually the libretti will provide some extra words. In *Erismena* the only large ABA of the "canzona" type for which there is no evidence of extra text in any source is Aldi-

---

[22] S=strophe (stanza), R=refrain (ripresa).

[23] Bjørn Hjelmborg, "Aspects of the Aria in the Early Operas of Francesco Cavalli," in *Natalicia Musicologica*, eds. B. Hjelmborg and S. Sørensen (Copenhagen, 1962), pp. 194-98.

[24] R and R' refer to the refrain and its variant. The middle section, as is common in large "aria patterns" of the time, is separately labeled "stanza" (sometimes the word "aria" was used, occasionally "strofa"); here, as in many other such pieces, the stanze are in common time, contrasting with the triple meter of the refrain. The stanze differ from strophe to strophe, the refrain is constant (R reads "Che dite voi, che dite / Tra le schiere d'amor / Si può trovar del mio più lieto cor," while R' has "Udite, amanti udite" for the first line and "non si" for "si può" in the third line).

[25] See for instance the "canzone" of Luigi Rossi and Carissimi in *Alte Meister des Bel Canto*, ed. Ludwig Landshoff (Frankfurt: Peters, n.d.), Vol. I, Nos. 8, 10, 11, 12.

mira's "Vaghe stelle" in Act II.[26] The overall design of this aria is *rit R rit SR rit*, i.e., *rit A rit B A rit*. In the middle section the instruments also echo individual phrases; the rhythm of text and music, though set in triple meter, is as noticeably different as the textual design. The most unusual feature is that the middle section does not cadence independently but rather makes its final cadence lead into "vaghe stelle" again, as though this were the first strophe of a reprise-line aria such as Idraspe's entrance aria in Act I (see Ex. 3).

But to say that "Vaghe stelle" "fait entrevoir le futur développement de l'opéra italien"[27] is to say too much, in spite of its generous proportions, its instruments, and its ABA format. Coincidence of formal design alone is not enough to warrant claiming this particular subclass of the "canzona" genre as an ancestor of the grand *da capo*. "Vaghe stelle" is not an exit aria; Aldimira is on stage both before and after she sings it in both versions of the opera. It is not an outcome of previous dialogue, but rather looks forward into the scene at whose head it stands (see Table VII, below). It is a constituent part of the action: Aldimira sings it, as a song, to arouse the "warrior" from a swoon. And it is just one of several possible designs for a large-scale aria pattern. Indeed, "Comincia à respirar" and "La speranza è un non sò che," with their ABB designs, are more typical for big arias than the ABA design of "Vaghe stelle."

The eventual emergence of the *da capo* design as a nearly universal feature of Italian opera arias must be attributed not merely to the prior existence of the ABA design but rather to some particular utility to the musical theater of the ABA design, during the time when it made itself apparent as the coming development. It was suggested earlier here, in connection with Alcesta's "Mirar hor questo hor quello" (Ex. 4b) and Orimeno's "Senza speme" (Ex. 5), that the traditional placement of an epitomizing line at the end of a speech was related to the traditional emphasis on the end of the aria, with its ABB format and sequentially repeated epitomizing final line. It was also suggested that the set pieces were coming more and more to take the place of speech-ending and scene-ending epitomes, traditionally often set *al arioso*. And it was finally suggested

[26] Printed in *La Flora*, ed. Knud Jeppeson (Copenhagen, 1949), Vol. III, 15-18. Hjelmborg discusses the aria in "Une partition de Cavalli," pp. 47-48, inexplicably describing it as "si bémol majeur." It is in G in both scores.

[27] Hjelmborg, "Une partition de Cavalli," p. 48.

that the new function of the set piece was more effectively prepared when the musical and verbal "motto" followed directly upon the heels of the preceding dialogue and was not delayed until the end of the aria verse; at the same time, the summing-up function could be preserved by retaining the final position of the epitomizing line as well. Whether this particular line of thought is reasonable or not, it is in considerations of this sort that one should seek for prototypes and premonitions of operatic devices such as the grand *da capo*, that is, not through *Formenlehre*, but through changes in dramatic function.

Once the concept that the main idea of the set-piece should come first as well as last is established as a fundamental musico-dramatic convention, *then* it becomes reasonable to suppose that development and changes in the *internal* structure of the two main parts—most notably the expansion of the prima parte and the corresponding contraction of the seconda parte—took place under primarily musical influences, though always bound to text in respect to motivic design and phrase structure. Indeed, given the invention of the basic device for encapsulating lyrical pauses right into the dramatic action, it would have been unthinkable that the lyrical pauses would not have been expanded and developed; all bounds imposed by the presumptive theatrical necessity to keep an action moving had been neatly removed. So the fact that the *da capo* aria as an operatic device was finally weakened and destroyed by gross musical abuses should not blind us to the possibility that it originated as a musico-dramatic, not a purely musical, necessity.

7.

The aria "Vaghe stelle" is sung by Aldimira in the middle of the first set of Act II. A summary of the preceding action, and the structure and paraphrase of the immediately following action, are shown in Table VII. The scene which "Vaghe stelle" opens, and the scene immediately following, present two further instances of the integration of a set piece more tightly into the action. Orimeno's aria "Amor ti giuro amor" and the duet "Occhi belli" are exit pieces for the characters in both versions of the opera. In the scene of Erismena and Aldimira, no significant revisions occur until the point at which the text summary begins in Table VII. In the revised version of the ensuing scene of Orimeno and Argippo, the music is transposed

TABLE VII

(In the first scenes of the opening set of Act II the "warrior" is told of Aldimira's affection
The next group of scenes brings Idraspe, Erismena's faithless lover, on in his role as the King
messenger, with a cup of poison which the captured "warrior" is ordered to drink. Acceptin
"his" fate stoically, the "warrior" agrees; but when Erismena recognizes her former lover
the messenger, she faints. The King, entering and seeing the prostrate "warrior," assumes th
poison has taken its effect, and cruelly turns what he supposes to be the "warrior's" corp
over to Aldimira, saying "here is your hero, asleep." The next episode begins with Aldimi
singing "Vaghe stelle" to the "warrior" in an attempt to awaken "him.")

1655/417.II.7-9	*360.II.8-10*	*1670.II.7-8*
Aldi: Vaghe stelle (aria)	*Vaghe stelle	Vaghe stelle

(In the ensuing dialogue between the awakening "warrior" and Aldimira, the tale of Idrasp
betrayal comes out, as though of the "warrior's" sister. Aldimira promises to hand the trait
over to the "warrior" if the "warrior" will yield to her love.)

Eris: Fingere mi conviene . . . Tuo consorte saro, ci unisca Amore.	Fingere mi conviene . . . *Quest'alma sara tua,* *(ci unisca)* *ci unisca Amore.* *(Quest'alma sara tua* *[ci unisca]* *ci unisca Amore.)*	Fingere mi conviene . . Tuo consorte saro, ci unisca Amore.
Aldi: O VOCI AMATE, E CARE . . . E come idolo mio t'amo, e t'adoro.	———	†"O voci amate, e care . "E come idolo mio t'ar "e t'adoro."
Duet: Occhi belli à voi mi dono. (Erismena begins)	Occhi belli à voi mi dono. (Erismena begins)	Occhi belli à voi mi do

Orim: Ah che vidi? ahi che intese? Mi tradisce Aldimira . . . Ah non t'havessi mai Conosciuto, o mirato.	Ah che vidi? ahi che intesi? Mi tradisce Aldimira . . . Ah non t'havessi mai Conosciuto, o mirato.	Ah che vidi? ahi che intesi? Mi tradisce Aldimira . Ah non t'havessi mai Conosciuto, o mirato.
Argi: Signor t'acqueta . . . Che delle Donne è già costume antico *Voler oltra l'amante* *(Voler oltra l'amante)* *anco l'amico.*	Signor t'acqueta . . . Che delle Donne è già costume antico *Voler oltra l'amante* *(Voler oltra l'amante)* *anco l'amico.*	Signor t'acqueta . . . Che delle Donne è già costume antico Voler oltra l'amante anco l'amico.

TABLE VII (Continued)

1655/417 . II . 7-9	360 . II . 8-10	1670 . II . 7-8
Orim: ——	Perfida dove fuggi? . . . Ah che l'empia infedele Porta ottuse l'orecchie à miei lamenti.	——
(aria) Amor, ti giuro Amor	Amor, ti giuro Amor	Amor, ti giuro Amor
Argi: Poveri innamorati (aria)	Donne quante sciochezze	——

* Published in *La Flora*, ed. Knud Jeppeson, III, 15-18.

† The quotation marks around this speech—the only such occurrence in Venice 1670—are a familiar convention of *seicento* libretti, and normally indicate that the poet's words were not set, i.e., not sung in performance.

throughout; otherwise the only change is the interpolation into score 360 of Orimeno's "Perfida, dove fuggi?" speech, which is set all in recitative, somewhat heightened chromatically in one or two spots.

As far as the placement of the set pieces is concerned, then, the differences between the versions are thus: in the case of the duet, the immediately preceding speech is deleted, in the case of the aria a speech for the character singing the aria is interpolated immediately before it. In both cases one can argue that the intent was to link the set pieces more directly to what preceded them.

In the Orimeno-Argippo scene, both versions open with a plastic and highly affectively declaimed speech by Orimeno, reacting to the love-scene he has just overheard and witnessed. The scene continues with Argippo's good counsel, which concludes with another rhyming, sententious aphorism set *al arioso*. Originally Orimeno followed this aphorism with his aria "Amor ti giuro amor" (see Ex. 9), a flexible, affective, instrumentally accompanied, multi-section aria with a two-line refrain. (The second section, still part of the strophe, is one of the earliest examples of what was to become *recitativo accompagnato*—again, not just in the formal sense, but quite specifically according to the text type and manner of the *accompagnato* of opera seria.) This aria, however, can hardly be construed as a response to Argippo's aphorism, or as a comment upon it; Orimeno clearly has not even heard Argippo. The aria is merely more of Orimeno's response to the previous scene of betrayal.

* The 360 version is a fourth lower; in the *accompagnato* the (violin) parts are sometimes inverted. There is a 2nd strophe with the "scioglier non posso" refrain. Bologna 1668 and Forli 1673 also have a 2nd strophe for this aria, but with words different from those of 360.

Ex. 9

cor la li-ber-ta-de io ten - to, per - do-na-mi, per-do-na-mi ò mia bel - la hor ch'io mi

pen - to.____ *Scio - - glier non pos - so, non pos - - so i

no - - - di, i no - di miei te - na - ci____

son.____ le.____ ca - - te -

*In 1655 *et al* the refrain text reads:
Spegner non posso gl'ardor miei voraci
Son le catene mie troppo tenaci.
360 has for the second line:
Vivi in catene, afflitto cor, e taci.

Ex. 9 (cont.)

Ex. 9 (cont.)

The abrupt shift in mood from Argippo's advice to Orimeno's emotions, combined with the shift from recitative-arioso to formal set piece, give the aria the character of an interlude. The addition of the "Perfida, dove fuggi?" speech in the 360 version leads the dramatic business away from Argippo and his aphorism back to Orimeno's response to Aldimira's betrayal of his love, without changing the style of the setting at the same time. The aria "Amor ti giuro amor" now becomes a smooth continuation and expansion of this new speech, and the pattern of recitative leading to aria which we have seen earlier in connection with one or two lighter moments is here forced into service at a more serious juncture.

8.

In the original version of the Aldimira-Erismena scene shown in Ex. 10a, the "warrior's" outward yielding to Aldimira's affections prompts an ecstatic outburst from Aldimira, in which joy and veneration are expressed in a plastic and flexible sequence of triple-meter arioso and common-time declamation. This passage discharges, so to speak, the emotional potential produced by the "warrior's" yielding; the duet begins with the "warrior" singing the words "Occhi belli," and the piece functions as an interlude, continuing and not at all inconsistent with what has gone before, but not growing directly out of it in any dramatic way.

In the revision (Ex. 10b) the removal of Aldimira's "O voci amate" speech has the effect of tying the duet directly into the action and making the duet itself serve as the expression of emotional response to the "warrior's" yielding.[28] Here the "warrior's" speech, ending "ci unisca Amore," is converted from its previous simple recitative into an arioso, using the basic cadential gesture of the original recitative as a subject, and the "warrior" continues on with the duet opening "Occhi belli." Though the text of the duet is as generalized as it was before, it is now forced to function as the expression of emotional response to the new turn of affairs.

From the purely musical point of view, the recomposition of the duet "Occhi belli" is the most interesting of all the revisions. In Exx.

---

[28] Venice 1655, 417, and Bologna 1661 all retain the "O voci amate" speech; 360 and the other libretti delete it. In Venice 1670 it is printed, but in quotation marks, which indicates that it was not heard in the performance; it is the only passage so marked in 1670.

10a and 10b the corresponding passages are lettered, for ease of comparison. The two settings appear at first to have nothing in common beyond the identical closing ritornelli, though it might appear curious that a new set piece in 3/4 would retain an old ritornello in 3/2. The ritornello bass echoes the bass of phrase Y in 417, which is a coda added on after the reprise (phrase X), which ends on a half-cadence. In 360 the original ritornello is made to echo a new phrase Y, which on second look is, after all, much like the original phrase Y. The other correspondences turn on characteristic features of 417's original settings—namely, the subject plus melisma in phrase A, the strong-beat setting of "non più, non più" in phrase B—as well as on similarities in the turns at the cadences and on the imitations moving harmonically by fifths in the compression of C and D. In 360 the setting is much shorter and much more tightly organized, in overall plan as well as in the handling of the original subjects of the sections. In 417 there are five full cadences and three half-cadences, each separately articulated. In 360 there are no half-cadences—phrase X is eliminated, and phrases C and D are combined—and of the five full cadences, the ones ending phrases A and B are elided into the beginnings of the subsequent phrases. The three separately articulated full cadences close the first appearance of the reprise section, precede the return of the reprise section, and close the reprise section before the ritornello. That is, the loose, broken-up, almost rambling structure of 417's setting, in which the reprise-line has no more formal and structural weight than any other section, is remodeled into what we might call an incipient *da capo*, with principal cadences at the end of each main section. The internal structure of the piece is tightened up, just as the piece as a whole is more tightly linked to the drama externally.

III

In the examples shown here, one is struck by the contrast, on many levels, between the aforementioned two basic types of musico-dramatic situation: 1) the situation in which a character is commenting, flippantly or otherwise, on something that has happened or has been said, without his being actually affected by it; 2) the situation in which a character responds directly and personally to a situation in which he is at that moment involved. This distinction between impersonal moralizing and personal emotion was traditional and

Ex. 10a

* T'honoro (1655 et al.).

Ex. 10a (cont.)

Ex. 10a (cont.)

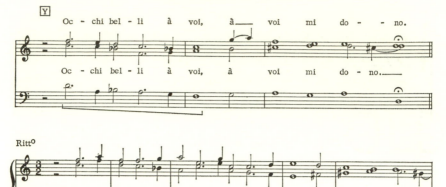

Ex. 10a (cont.)

was normally reflected in an ethos of meter as well. Generalized lyrical emotions—love, joy, hope, sorrow, despair—normally were expressed in triple-meter set pieces and freely distributed. Such emotions, arising as brief direct responses in dialogue, could then take on an aria-like metric ethos. The persistence past mid-century of the metric ethos is witnessed by the numerous almost mechanical changes from common time to triple-meter in 360 vis-à-vis 417 (Exx. 1, 2, and 6). Impersonal moralizing, too, had its traditional manner and placement, as we have seen; and a distinction of type, if no longer of meter, continued to be felt well after arias had come to be used in practice for comment and ariosi for emotional expressions, as shown by Mattheson's definitions:

... die Aria ... ein wohleingerichteter Gesang, der seine gewisse Ton-Art und Zeitmasse hat, sich gemeiniglich in zween Theile scheidet, und in einem kurzen Begriff einen grosse Gemüths-Bewegung ausdruckt. . . .

... the Aria ... a well-ordered song, which has its particular tonality and measure, is divided ordinarily into two sections, and expresses a grand emotion in a brief conceit. . . .

Ex. 10b

[etc., as in 417;]
[see Ex. 10a]

Ex. 10b (cont.)

Das Arioso ... kan eine blosse Erzeh-lung, oder sonst ein nachdencklicher lehrreicher Spruch, ohne sonderbare ausdrückliche Gemüths-Bewegung, darin enthalten und verfasset wer-den.[29]	The Arioso ... can be composed and contain in itself a plain narration, or else a contemplative instructive epi-gram without special expressive emo-tion.

The distinction of ethos and usage is clear, though since Mattheson is thinking in terms of *opera seria*, the scurrilous commentaries and scandalous situations of pre-Arcadian opera would not have come into question. But, in fact, such commentaries were of the utmost importance in the development of the standardized *opera seria* scene structure, even though at the time of the *Erismena*s they were often tied to wry, humorous, or indecent contexts, contexts of a sort which in fact ultimately disappeared from the "serious" musical theater.

The conversion of moral ariosi to immoral arias, during the period of the absorption of the pompous Arsetes and Senecas into the frivolous Idraspes and Alcestas, stabilized the position of commentary arias at the end of scenes. At the same time, more- or less-independently, the formerly freely distributed set pieces of *generalized* emotion came to be used for *specific* emotional responses arising from the events of the drama, in place of affective declamation; thus arias expressing emotions also came to occupy positions following turns of affairs in the play, rather than preceding them.

The *Erismena* versions illustrate the parallel developments of scene-final commentary set piece and scene-final emotional set piece from older traditions in several ways. They show how the association of musical subject not just with verbal phrases and verbal rhythm, but also with idea content, came to be used in voices and instruments alike to help provide links between a set piece and what leads up to it. They show that the traditional musico-dramatic emphasis on final lines of nonnarrative speeches was a factor in assisting arias—which had a similar emphasis—to usurp the functions of those speeches; and they illustrate linkage to preceding action being combined with emphasis on the final thought through an ever-greater reliance on the existing opening-line-refrain aria-type. They show traditional set pieces with general emotional content being used as expressions of specific emotional response rather than as interludes, sometimes through judicious adjustment of the

---

[29] Johann Mattheson, *Der Vollkommene Capellmeister* (Hamburg, 1739), p. 212.

preparatory material. And the revisions show these changes at a point where one can see the flexible older traditions of such operas as *Giasone* and *Orontea* side by side with the hardening conventions of the late seventeenth-century operas and their successors. One can see two distinct kinds of situation, with two distinct kinds of music, in the very process of their convergence into the single standard type of all-purpose recitative scene with a scene-ending set piece. One is able to see the so-called "motto" aria when its verbal subject was still a "motto"—that is, when it still had a clearly gnomic character—and before it had become a cliché. One can see a still flexible, mixed treatment of emotional response, in which recitative, common-time arioso, and triple-meter aria could all combine with instruments in a single composition whose conception as a whole is shown by the presence of a second strophe.

Finally—and it would seem, paradoxically—one can see that each of the changes, which in sum led to a conventionalizing and impoverishment of the musical drama, originated independently in the development of a specific technique for making traditional genres of theatrical music more integrally a part of the dramatic structure. But perhaps after all, in the light of what ensued, one should remove the paradox, take advantage of hindsight, and put the matter the other way around, in a more familiar way: each of these changes originated independently in the development of a specific technique for forcing the drama itself to provide occasion for formal music.

PLUS ÇA CHANGE

*Or, The Progress of Reform in Seventeenth- and
Eighteenth-Century Opera as Illustrated
in the Books of Three Operas*

NATHANIEL BURT

I

THE Italian intellectual of the seventeenth and early eighteenth centuries took it for granted that what we call "opera"
was a literary, rather than a musical form. This *dramma
per musica* was a modern version of the drama of the ancients. Music
was either the recitative, designed solely to heighten the effect of the
words, or the arietta, an interpolation designed to appeal to the crude
public. This is the basis for that change in taste, beginning in the
1690's, called the Arcadian Reform. It was a reform designed to
subordinate music to words and to restore to drama its ancient dignity. The end result of this successful revolution in taste was the
Metastasian *opera seria*—an ironic eventuality, since no opera was
so totally victimized by musicians and by vocalism. Like many reforms, the Arcadian Reform resulted in something precisely opposed
to the aims of the reformers.

One thing, however, the reform did effect. If it never succeeded
in subordinating music to words, at least it did chasten the style and
tone of the libretti. What had been in the seventeenth century a wild
licentiousness, became in the eighteenth century a severe if senti-
mental formalism. Bawdiness, confusion, improbabilities, irrelevan-
cies, all were tamed into elegance and refinement. The elegant
refinement was in itself as absurd as the Baroque confusion; but at
least it reflected a very real and obvious improvement in literary taste.

The progress of the Arcadian Reform is not to be here described.[1]
Three examples of libretti are merely to be exhibited to demonstrate
just what the reform meant in practical terms of literary organization. The demonstration involves three versions of what is essentially the same plot. The handling of this plot, and the variations in
tone and scene, should pretty much make the point. That this

[1] Nathaniel Burt, "Opera in Arcadia," *Musical Quarterly*, XLI, No. 2 (April 1955),
pp. 145-70.

change of taste may have been inevitable, a matter of fashion, no one can deny. But that the Arcadian Reform gave it intellectual backing and impetus is also obvious.

No one of these three operas is a specifically "reformist" one, like *La Forza del Virtù* of Domenico David.[2] *La Dori* (1663) by Appolonio Appoloni, the first of them, is a conspicuous example of unreformed opera. *Gl'Inganni Felici* (1695), a contemporary of *La Forza del Virtù*, is an early work of Apostolo Zeno, who became the chief exponent of Arcadian principles. *L'Olimpiade* (1733) is a mature work of Pietro Metastasio, who succeeded Zeno as court poet of Austria, and who represents the Arcadian Reform in its final flowering as *opera seria*. But it is the works, not the men, that concern us here.

The style, tone, characterization, and detailed working-out of the three pieces may be totally different. The basic pivot of plot is the same, and thus we can see, as though in the heredity of a family, the same bone structure covered with a singular variety of flesh. From this contrast one can, with some decent hesitation of course, project the difference between three periods of operatic-literary practice and tentatively chart a graph of development over a seventy-year period.

The essence of the shared plot is: A marriage contract has been made by parental authority. The youthful partners of this contract have met and fallen in love, but in a situation of disguise or confusion, so that they do not know themselves to be the officially betrothed ones. Instead, they believe the contract to involve a third party, an unknown stranger who stands between them. The action consists in unraveling this misapprehension by revealing the true identity of one of the characters. The contract then can be fulfilled, to universal rejoicing.

This essentially comic-romantic situation is in each case elaborated by an identical subplot. As in nearly every other Baroque opera, there is a "second pair." Also as usual, one member of this second pair is in love with a member of the first pair. This (of course eventually unsuccessful) lover is in turn loved and pursued by a temporarily rejected fourth party. In the end, with the happy union of the first pair, the second pair also resignedly weds. The final secret of identity, in at least two of these operas, is to be revealed by a faithful

[2] *Ibid.*, pp. 154-62.

old retainer who has been guarding the secret all along in preparation for the denouement.

The basic cast of characters in all three operas is the same: a father-figure, who must enforce the terms of the marriage contract; a first pair of lovers, who mistakenly believe themselves to be separated by the terms of the contract; a second pair, one of whom is in love with a member of the first pair, the other of whom (traveling in disguise), pursues and eventually wins the troublesome partner; an advisory character, tutor or courtier, who in *La Dori* and *L'Olimpiade* reveals all at the end; and a "facetious servant," who acts as newsbearer.

No one of these ingredients is obviously peculiar to just these three operas. It would be interesting to discover and catalogue, for instance, operas of the period that do *not* contain the formula of first and second pair. The father-figure (bass), the faithful retainer, the *servo faceto* are equally conventional. The marriage contract is, however conventional, a bit more special, and is what really links these three books. Though the identity of *La Dori* with *Gl'Inganni* is no doubt more or less coincidental, both authors drawing on a promiscuous stock of Baroque elements, the relationship between *Gl'Inganni* and *L'Olimpiade* can hardly be accidental. Metastasio was a disciple of Zeno and must have read his master's works. He could hardly have been unaware of Zeno's previous treatment of the Olympic theme. However, since he borrowed nothing but the framework, he probably felt no particular obligation. He at least never seems to have expressed any.

II

Notice of the background and reputation of *La Dori* can be found elsewhere.[3] The plot is so complicated and feckless that it would be hopeless to describe it in full. It will be enough to hint at the working-out of the formula and to give some impression of its quality.

Cast of Characters

Artaserse, satrap of Persia, regent of Oronte
Oronte, Prince of Persia, heir to the throne
Tolomeo (disguised as Celinda), Prince of Egypt
Dori (disguised as the male slave Ali), supposed Princess of Egypt
Arsinoe, Princess of Nicea, betrothed to Oronte

[3] *Ibid.*, pp. 164-67.

Arsete, courtier of Egypt, tutor of Dori and Tolomeo
Erasto, Captain of Persia, confidant of Oronte
Golo, servo faceto of Oronte
Dirce, old nurse of Arsinoe
Bagoa (in some editions, Erindo), eunuch of the harem

The Kings of Nicea and Persia have made a marriage contract, betrothing infant Dori of Nicea to Oronte of Persia. There is a legal document to that effect, signed and sealed.

Meanwhile, the King of Egypt has also had a daughter, also named Dori. This Dori dies accidentally and her guardian Arsete flees in guilt. In his exile he becomes a pirate and captures the other child-princess, Dori of Nicea. He then returns to Egypt, substitutes the Nicean Dori for the missing Egyptian princess—and no one discovers the difference.

TIME PASSES. Oronte is sent from Persia to Egypt to learn the art of war. There he falls in love with Dori. Unfortunately he has to return to Persia, to the bedside of his dying father. At that bedside, his father confides to Artaserse, future regent and guardian of Oronte, that the marriage contract with Nicea must be carried out, and if the Nicean Dori is still missing, Oronte must then marry her younger sister Arsinoe.

Dori disguises herself as a boy and leaves Egypt to follow her lover Oronte. She is accompanied by Erasto, a friend of Oronte whom he left behind in Egypt. They are separated by pirates. Erasto thinks Dori has been drowned, and when he finally arrives in Persia, he tells Oronte the sad news.

But in fact Dori has been washed ashore and sold as a slave—to none other than Arsinoe, Princess of Nicea. Under the name of Ali, Dori is now a favorite of her mistress who is, of course, really (a) her younger sister, (b) her rival for the love of Oronte. Arsinoe confides to her slave boy her passion for Oronte. The wedding plans proceed. Dori is distracted.

Tolomeo, Prince of Egypt, Dori's supposed brother, arrives in Babylon where the wedding is to be held. He is seeking vengeance on the faithless Oronte for deserting his sister. He disguises himself as a girl, Celinda by name, and manages to become part of the Nicean harem and a lady-in-waiting to Arsinoe. He falls in love with her and forgets all about revenge.

Finally Arsete, the old tutor, the original mixer-up of the Doris, also arrives in Babylon, sent out to look for both Dori and Tolomeo. He holds his guilty secret in reserve, fearful of being punished for his share in the *imbroglio*.

All this has happened *before* the curtain goes up! Obviously all that is required is for Arsete to reveal the whole truth: that Dori *Égyptienne* is really Dori *Nicienne*. Oronte can then marry her legally, Tolomeo can claim Arsinoe, and all's well. The three acts are spent avoiding the issue by means of various artificial subterfuges and complications and, above all, scenes of bizarre pruriency.

Delay in resolving the situation is achieved largely by means of disguises and consequent misunderstandings. Oronte does not see that the slave Ali is really his lost love. Virtuous Dori spends her time trying to get Oronte to do the right thing: marry Arsinoe, as per contract. Oronte, despite pressure from his guardian Artaserse, spends his time refusing. He exclaims, as a sort of leitmotif, "Dori, Dori, dove sei?" Meanwhile, Tolomeo, disguised as a girl, conceals his passion for Arsinoe, while Erasto, thinking Tolomeo really is a girl, declares his passion for her (him). A group of comic servants keep things moving between these romances.

We have, for instance, in Act I, Arsinoe and Celinda (Tolomeo) walking in the harem garden. Arsinoe is of course longing for Oronte, Tolomeo for Arsinoe. They compare their love troubles and Celinda is almost driven to blurting out his passion for Arsinoe. He sings an aria to her, and when Arsinoe becomes alarmed at his excitement, he says, "That is how I *would* sing to my lover if I could." Much badinage and misunderstanding ensues between Arsinoe and her disguised suitor.

Celinda is then left alone in the garden to bewail her fate. Bagoa, the eunuch in charge of the harem, then appears, and there follows a scene bizarre indeed. Bagoa orders Celinda back into the harem. What is she doing out here anyway? "Picking flowers," says Celinda. "Not picking flowers, but selling fruits maybe?" leers Bagoa. Celinda is thoroughly insulted. There ensues a short discussion of the modern laxity in morals; fruit is hardly worth selling nowadays, since it goes for nothing. Celinda insults and berates the eunuch. The eunuch bewails his fate; even the women act the man with him. *Ballet of Eunuchs*.

The oddity of this particular situation will be appreciated when it is realized that both Bagoa, the eunuch, and Celinda, the boy dressed as a girl, are parts in actual fact played by castrati. In other words, the *double-entendres* of this scene are quadrupled by having both performers *really* eunuchs.

Meanwhile all through Act I the action has been laced with adventitious—and very broad—comic scenes. Dirce, the lascivious old nurse of Arsinoe, pursues Golo, the loutish servant of Oronte. They quarrel furiously, hurling insults at each other. Similarly, in Act II we have Erasto's misguided passion for Celinda (Tolomeo). Celinda puts him off by saying, "Everything I *can* give, I give to you." Scenes such as these between a man in love with a boy dressed as a girl (both being in fact soprani and castrati) certainly make one wonder about mores and customs. But there is a curious superficial innocence about it all. That is to say, there is never a question, for instance, of perversion. A character is what he or she pretends to be, and one loves the woman of the costume as a woman. How the audience may have reacted to all this is another matter.

The main thread of the plot follows Ali (Dori) who contemplates suicide and tries to effect the marriage of Arsinoe and Oronte. She falls asleep, exhausted by her misfortunes, and is discovered by Oronte, who of course cannot penetrate her disguise. She awakens and tries to persuade Oronte to at least feign love for Arsinoe, but he refuses, though Artaserse continues to threaten him with loss of his kingdom if he persists in his mad infatuation for a girl supposedly drowned. Oronte is adamant. "Dori, Dori, dove sei?" he wails. (She is, of course, right on stage with him, but still determined to sacrifice herself for her friend and mistress and the good of Persia.)

Oronte falls asleep, exhausted by *his* misfortunes, and the ghost of his mother appears to him. (No opera of this time could afford to be without its *ombra* scene.) She tells him to be true both to his father's wishes *and* to Dori. But how can he?

The crestfallen Ali comes to tell Arsinoe that her efforts with Oronte have failed, that he will not love her. Arsinoe raves and works herself into such a passion that she faints in Ali's arms. Just at this point Oronte discovers them. He immediately assumes that they are guilty of adultery and condemns Arsinoe to death, without listening to their explanations and protestations. Of course this is a convenient way of disqualifying Arsinoe. Celinda throws off her disguise and emerges as the champion of Arsinoe. But he does not seem to recognize Ali as his sister (supposed sister). In any case, Oronte merely brushes him aside. *Ballet of Moors.* Comic scenes interspersed all the way through the act, of course.

Act III begins with Erasto quickly re-orienting himself to the sex metamorphosis of his beloved Celinda. He has obviously been deluded and that is that. Artaserse compliments him upon his philosophical approach, so different from Oronte.

Arsinoe is now desperate, unjustly condemned by the man she loves for an offense, indiscretion with a slave, that she obviously could never have committed. Ali, who is also desperate, has procured poison. She falls asleep, exhausted by *her* misfortunes. As she soliloquizes beforehand about her intention to commit suicide, Dirce overhears her. What a lovely boy! She would like to kiss him while he lies there in slumber, but somehow shame prevents her. He must not be allowed to destroy himself. Dirce has a potion to put Golo to sleep so that she can tear out his hair, etc. She substitutes her harmless soporific for Ali's poison and tiptoes off, but not before discovering that Ali is really a girl. Ali wakes and sends a farewell note to Oronte via the conveniently passing Arsete.

Meanwhile Oronte is desperate too. He definitely refuses to obey Artaserse's final command to marry Arsinoe. Artaserse, with the army behind him, deposes Oronte. He is no longer king. His servant Golo makes fun of him. "Even a vile servant disdains me," says the broken prince. Dirce decides that since he is no longer king, he might make a good lover for her. She puts the proposition to him, but he is still wrapped in dreams of Dori and does not even notice Dirce. He sings an impassioned love song, addressed anonymously to the missing Dori, but Dirce thinks he means it for her.

At last Oronte gives in; he can stand it no longer. He will marry Arsinoe. Everyone rejoices. But just at this moment Arsete arrives with the farewell message from Dori to Oronte. "Willingly do I slay myself that Arsinoe may marry you. Signed, Dori of Egypt." Consternation! Then Golo enters with the news that he has found the dying Ali, and while trying to save him, he discovered a piece of paper in his pocket. It is, of course, nothing less than the original contract between the Kings of Persia and Nicea betrothing Oronte and Dori! More consternation. Arsete is forced to explain everything.

But woe! Just when all is resolved, it seems that poor Dori is dead. Oronte bewails his fate. Tolomeo threatens to make him pay for his inconstancy to Dori. "Forgive me," says Oronte, "if Dori were still alive, I would still be faithful to her." At this moment, in walks Ali-Dori, alive. She has, of course, been merely temporarily stupefied by Dirce's potion. General rejoicing. Tolomeo and Arsinoe pair, lovers' quartet, finis.

This, needless to say, is merely a digest that does not follow every one of the ins and outs, turns and twists, recognitions and love complaints that lend such fascinating complexity to the original. I have merely tried to extricate what might pass for the main line, and such scenes as seem especially characteristic, omitting all but a few of the numerous comic scenes which are scattered quite irrelevantly throughout. Particularly charming are the interludes where Dirce gloats over Ali and Oronte in her forthright fashion; and any scene involving the eunuch Bagoa is sure to explore the further reaches of bad taste. Yet *La Dori* was the operatic paragon of its time. The Arcadian reformers did have a point.

III

Gl'Inganni Felici, though it may not have been intended to demonstrate reform, certainly does demonstrate an emendation of taste. It was produced in Venice in 1695 at the Teatro San Angelo and musicked by Carlo Polarolo, who also set David's *La Forza del Virtù*. It was Zeno's first work to appear on the stage.

Cast of Characters

Clistene, King of Siconia, father of Agarista
Armidoro (Demetrio), Prince of Athens, disguised as a tutor of painting, in love with Agarista
Sifalce (Orgonte), Prince of Thrace, disguised as a tutor of music, in love with Agarista
Agarista, daughter of Clistene, in love with Armidoro
Alceste (Oronta), Princess of Thessaly, disguised as a male astrologer employed at the court, in love with Sifalce
Arbante, henchman of Sifalce, posing as ambassador to Clistene from Thrace
Brenno, servo faceto of Clistene

The situation of the contract is here greatly simplified, requiring none of the elaborate offstage business of *La Dori*. Clistene, King of Siconia, is in charge of the Olympic games. He has promised his daughter Agarista to the winner. Meanwhile, he has kept her in conventual retirement, except that, in order to further her education, he has procured for her two tutors, Armidoro, a painter, and Sifalce, a musician. They are both handsome young men, and needless to say, princes in disguise. Armidoro is really Demetrio, Prince of Athens; Sifalce is Orgonte, Prince of Thrace. They both love Agarista and have assumed these base disguises to be near her. She loves Armidoro, but of course is prevented by her rank from admitting it. Another member of the ménage, Alceste the Astrologer, is really a woman, Oronta, Princess of Thessaly. She was formerly loved and betrayed by Orgonte-Sifalce, and is now here at court to keep her eye on him. Arbante, the confidant and henchman of Sifalce, is pretending to be the ambassador from the court of Thrace. Brenno is a comic servant of the court.

The Olympic games take place as scheduled. Both Sifalce and Armidoro, paragons of Baroque versatility, compete under their real names, and Armidoro wins. Agarista, informed that one Demetrio has won her hand, is grief-stricken. Using Alceste as go-between, the love of Agarista and Armidoro reveals itself; but when at last Agarista confesses to Armidoro and bewails the fact that she must marry the unknown Demetrio, Armidoro, instead of being grief-stricken too, is overjoyed. However he neglects to explain that he is Demetrio, since that would cut the plot off in the middle of Act II. Instead Agarista has a chance to spurn Armidoro, which she does.

Sifalce, meanwhile, has failed all around in his suit for Agarista. A formal request for her hand by the spurious ambassador Arbante has been turned down. Sifalce decides to abduct Agarista.

All this while, Alceste has been using her position as soothsayer to work on the conscience of Sifalce. She describes to him an appearance of the ghost of his deserted Oronto (herself) in a sort of fake *ombra* scene. But he merely laughs at her. She is desolate. He, of course, does not recognize her under her impenetrable disguise.

Alceste, overwhelmed by her misfortune, falls asleep. Fortunately, she talks in her sleep, and thus the whole story of her identity and desertion is revealed to the insomniac Agarista. She wakes, and the girls confide in one another, parting with a sisterly embrace. Unfortunately Armidoro sees them (compare *La Dori*, Act II); assuming that his friend Alceste is a man, he misconstrues the situation. "A spouse and a friend have so betrayed me," and he decides in despair to seek the asylum of the wilderness. *Arioso*: *"D'oscure foreste"* (III, 3). But Agarista meanwhile has discovered the identity of her lover and is now quite ready to fall into his arms.

A royal hunt—at which Agarista and Demetrio are to be officially introduced—is given to honor the forthcoming nuptials. The latter has retreated, however, to the "oscure foreste." During this hunt, Sifalce and his minions conceal themselves. Agarista and Alceste appear. Sifalce abducts Agarista, and wounds the protesting Alceste-Oronta, still without recognizing her. She is discovered by Clistene, and she tells him all.

SCENE BY THE DESOLATE SEASHORE. Armidoro wanders disconsolate. He bewails his fate. Enter Agarista pursued by Sifalce. She spurns him. Armidoro interferes. Fight. Sifalce is vanquished. Agarista falls into the arms of Armidoro. *He* spurns *her*. He won't tell her why (he still thinks she has betrayed him with Alceste), but offers to return her to her father. Alceste then appears and discovers the wounded Sifalce. They are reconciled. They return to the court of Siconia. There Alceste is finally revealed to Armidoro as Oronta. Armidoro understands and he and Agarista are reconciled; Clistene is satisfied, everyone is happy.

The family resemblance of this to *La Dori* is evident: the impenetrable disguises, the fragile misunderstandings, the convenient on-stage slumbers. The crux of the plot remains the same, but everywhere altered in detail. How much simpler the business of the contract now, without pirates, shipwrecks, slavery, substitutions of infants! The role of the sexes has been generally reversed. Now it is the heroine, not the hero, who is under parental duress and bound to a stranger; the hero now is the one who is a foreigner in disguise. In the same fashion, the second pair changes roles. Whereas Arsinoe loved Oronte, the hero of *La Dori*, now Sifalce loves Agarista, the heroine of *Gl'Inganni*. Whereas Tolomeo, in disguise (as the girl Celinda), pursued and eventually won Arsinoe, Oronta, in disguise (as the man Alceste), pursues and wins Sifalce.

The important differences, aside from those of scene and action, are more subtle and are largely a matter of attitude, taste, and treatment. For the wholehearted passionate gusto, and broad, rather obscene, comedy of *La Dori* has been substituted a sort of elegant trifling. At considerable risk of stylistic confusion, one might think of *La Dori* as Baroque, *Gl'Inganni* as Rococo. That at least helps define the difference between them. In the latter, the comedy is much less obtrusive and much less heavy-handed; the passions are not as serious somehow, and no one really wants to commit suicide. The high points of *Gl'Inganni* are to be found neither in the few comic scenes nor in the passionate ones, but in certain extraneous piquant businesses of gallantry.

For instance, much is made of the professional attributes of the intriguers. "Astri belli," sings Alceste, and avails herself of her mysterious avocation in her *ombra* scene.

There is a scene where Sifalce gives Agarista a music lesson, with clavier onstage. He sings classic love songs to her, substituting her name in them. Amorous confusion, interrupted ariettas, sweet misunderstandings. A mate to the musical scene is a painting scene, in which Armidoro passionately addresses the image of his love in the portrait he is painting of her. Agarista *in disparte* overhears him. Confusion, confessions, sweet misunderstandings.

Finally as pendant to these there is a Battle of the Arts, in which Sifalce and Armidoro defend their respective professions. Agarista awards the palm to music, simply in order to depress Armidoro. This is while she is still furious with him. They quarrel. Agarista says she'd even rather marry the unknown Demetrio, she hates Armidoro so. "What if Armidoro and Demetrio should be the same? Then she would hate Demetrio as much as she now hates Armidoro. He can't win.

IV

L'Olimpiade comes from the period of Metastasio's greatest fame, is one of his best-known pieces, familiar even now to Italian school children, and does not publicly admit to any plagiarism. It is not a reworking, but merely the use of the same plot and characters. How different it is, and how similar, may be seen in a cursory résumé of *L'Olimpiade*.

Cast of Characters

(Corresponding characters in "Gl'Inganni" in brackets.)

Clistene, King of Siconia [same as "Gl'Inganni"]

Megacle, Prince of Athens, in love with Aristea, friend of Licida [Armidoro]

Licida, supposed son of the King of Crete, in love with Aristea; former lover of Argene, bosom friend of Megacle [Sifalce]

Aristea, daughter of Clistene, in love with Megacle [Agarista]

Argene, lady of Crete, disguised as the shepherdess Licori, in love with Licida [Alceste]

Aminta, tutor of Licida [Arbante]

Alcandro, confidant of Clistene [Brenno]

The scene is the country of Elisis near the city of Olympia on the banks of the Alfeo.

The cast thus is identical to Zeno's *Gl'Inganni*. Arbante, the henchman of Sifalce, has been turned into a tutor (as in *La Dori*). Brenno has been elevated to councilor, but still acts as messenger and handyman. The only outright disguise is now that of Argene, involving no change of sex. However, the chief men, if not exactly disguised, are traveling under false pretenses.

The situation at the beginning is about the same. Clistene, as president of the Olympic games, is to give his daughter's hand to the winner. Licida, visitor to the games, falls in love with the daughter Aristea, wants to enter the contest; but since he is a Cretan, he is unacquainted with the athletic skills of Greece, the clytus and the discus. He sends for and persuades his dear friend Megacle, whose life he once saved, to take his place. Megacle is to pretend that he is Licida and win Aristea for his friend. But alas, having already promised, he then discovers that Aristea is none other than the girl he has loved for years. Aristea loves Megacle too, but her father will not permit her to marry an enemy Athenian. Aristea is desolate at the thought of giving her hand to another.

The fickle Licida, who now loves Aristea, was formerly affianced to Argene, Cretan of noble but not of royal blood. The families put a stop to the affair and commanded Argene to marry a foreigner— Megacle. Rather than submit, or die, she fled to Greece and now lives unknown as a simple shepherdess.

Megacle, true to his promise, wins the Olympic games under the name of Licida. At this point we have almost exactly the same situation as in Zeno. The king's daughter is loved by two suitors, one of whom she loves, but cannot marry, or so she believes. She has meanwhile been given to the winner of the games, without realizing that this winner is really her lover. But the development of *L'Olimpiade* proceeds somewhat differently and moves on an altogether more elevated plane.

Megacle encounters Aristea, but must repulse her in the interests of loyalty to Licida. He tries to commit suicide. Aristea, too, tries to commit suicide, thinking Megacle has already done so; in fact, both of them try simultaneously at one point, on opposite sides of a ruined hippodrome.

Licida recognizes Argene, they quarrel, and Argene in spite reveals Licida's and Megacle's real identity to the authorities. Licida is to be banished for his fraud. He pleads with Aristea who repulses him. He raves, and in his despair and fury tries to kill King Clistene. His impious hand is arrested by the majesty of the monarch, and he cannot do it. He is taken prisoner and is to be executed.

At this point begins a regular ballet of self-sacrifice. First Megacle sends Aristea to plead for the condemned Licida, but in vain. Then Megacle himself comes forward and offers to substitute himself, but in vain. Argene steps up and, claiming to be the wife of Licida, offers to take his place, but in vain. As proof of her wifehood, she shows Clistene a golden chain that Licida once gave her. It is the very chain that Clistene himself once placed years ago about the neck of his infant son Filinto, twin brother of Aristea. Clistene had been warned by an oracle that his son would one day try to kill him. He had ordered Alcandro to expose the child, but the soft-hearted man gave him instead to Aminta who happened to be passing by, and Aminta in turn gave him to the King of Crete to bring up as a substitute for his own dead son (compare *La Dori*). Alcandro and Aminta confess. General consternation.

Clistene is overwhelmed. Yet he must proceed with the sacrifice! Luckily a technicality saves him. He is King in Siconia, not in Olimpia. The day of his presidency and legal jurisdiction is now over, and he no longer has the power to condemn. Therefore, the fate of the prisoner must be decided by the populace and the priests of Elisis—and they very properly decide that the sin of the son shall not be visited on the suffering father. Licida is saved, Argene wins him, Aristea gets Megacle, and all's well.

Besides the change in the handling of the plot, the manner and attitude of *L'Olimpiade* is altogether different from that of its predecessors. There are still the basic artificialities of the plot, the disguises, the substitutions of children, the last-minute revelations. But as the Brenno of *Gl'Inganni* has been raised to councilor, so has the tone been universally moralized. The affair Sifalce-Alceste, formerly a case of mere desertion, is now true love thwarted by parents. The men are no longer mere rivals, but friends. Metastasio does not fail to intensify the potentialities of conflict in any way he can. The childhood substitution again furthers this end. And how much more serious is the love interest. No more of those pettish misunderstandings and transparent non-recognitions. Indeed, it is a relief to see how quickly everyone recognizes everyone else in *L'Olimpiade*. Here all is fire, melancholy, and conflict. The characters are torn between friendship and love, duty and love, past love and present love, duty and parental love.

The whole builds up cautiously but perfectly continuously—and above all without diversion—to the final sacrifice scene, where each character makes a bid for nobility. "How has everyone demonstrated his courage!" says the king. "Dare I be the only one guilty of weakness? Light the sacrificial fires!" How obviously the tone of the Arcadian Reform has been imposed upon the substance of *Gl'Inganni*.

It would seem superfluous here to underline the progress from the caprice of *La Dori* through the gallant artificialities of *Gl'Inganni* to the pseudo-classic high sentiment of *L'Olimpiade*. A footnote to the continuity and development of the three pieces is the just faintly comic character still retained by Alcandro in *L'Olimpiade* as lineal descendant of Brenno and further back of Golo, the *servo faceto*. In Act II, Scene 2 of *L'Olimpiade*, Alcandro, who comes to tell the ladies news about the winner of the Olympic games, tries their patience sorely with his attempts at a long-winded rhetoric. This is the only intentionally facetious moment in the piece. The whole progress of the Arcadian Reform can be traced in the heredity of this one personage, from a guffaw in *La Dori*, to a titter in *Gl'Inganni*, to the merest trace of a smile in Metastasio. Buffoons have been eliminated with a vengeance, and along with them almost every evidence of a sense of humor.

In three operas on the same foundations then, we can see demonstrated, over a period of seventy years, the progress of Italian *dramma per musica* from Baroque free-for-all to Metastasian stateliness. The reforms of the Arcadians were achieved. If they were sacrificed to the vanity of singers and the "bad taste" of the paying public, it was the fault of music, not of letters. In the long and bitter "Battle of the Arts," literature seemed at this point to have won; but the real victory went in the end to Sifalce, villainous musician.

APPENDIX I. CHART OF CHARACTERS

Position of Character in:	La Dori	Gl'Inganni	L'Olimpiade
I. Parental authority:	Artaserse	Clistene	Clistene
II. First pair (roles (a) and (b) reversed in later versions):			
Male:	(a) Oronte	(b) Armidoro (disguised)	Megacle (incognito)
Female:	(b) Dori (disguised)	(a) Agarista	Aristea
III. Second pair (roles (a) and (b) reversed in later versions):			
Male:	(a) Tolomeo (disguised)	(b) Sifalce (disguised)	Licida (incognito)
Female:	(b) Arsinoe	(a) Alceste (disguised)	Argene (disguised)
IV. Tutor: (knows the secret)	Arsete	Arbante (henchman only)	Aminta
V. Servo faceto:	Golo (Dirce) (Bagoa)	Brenno	Alcandro (courtier)
VI. Confidant:	Erasto	(eliminated)	——

Character (b) of first pair is a foreigner incognito or disguised.

Character (a) of second pair is a foreigner disguised so as to be near (b), who is unrequitedly in love with (a) of the first pair; change of sex in *La Dori* and *Gl'Inganni*.

L'Olimpiade shares with *La Dori*: story of substituted children, old tutor who knows all, attempted suicide of II (b), friendship of II (b) and III (b), life saved.

L'Olimpiade shares with *Gl'Inganni* the Olympic motif.

La Dori and *Gl'Inganni* share misunderstood embrace of females of first and second pairs.

Note elimination in *L'Olimpiade* and *Gl'Inganni* of confidant Erasto in interest of economy; also the extra comic characters of *La Dori*.

AGOSTINO STEFFANI'S
HANNOVER OPERAS
AND A REDISCOVERED CATALOGUE

PHILIP KEPPLER

SOME doubt still exists about the authorship of certain operas attributed to Agostino Steffani. There is no question about the operas written for and performed at the Munich court. The printed libretti for all these works name him specifically as the composer. The libretti for all the later operas, however, from 1689 on, lack this ascription.

It is generally assumed that Steffani wrote nine operas during his term as Kapellmeister at the court of Hannover. The autograph scores for six of these can now be identified. They are all in the Royal Music Library of the British Museum where they presumably found a home when the Elector of Hannover, Georg Ludwig, became George I of England and brought at least part of his magnificent library with him to London.[1] The autographs were obviously put to practical use. Each is bound in three volumes, one act per volume, probably for ease in handling at the cembalo during rehearsals and performances. The lower right-hand edges of the pages show evidence of extensive thumb wear, and there are markings in the scores showing alterations for subsequent performances. The volumes are bound in boards with a thin leather covering and distinctive gold-stamped pinwheel designs. The paper stock in every case but one (*Henrico Leone*) is the same. It is of durable, heavy quality, bearing a fleur-de-lis or shield watermark. The size varies slightly because of bindery trimming but is approximately 27.5 x 20.5 cms. The scores are without exception dated by the composer, and the title page of one of them (*La Liberta Contenta*) conceals a cleverly drawn monogram showing an "A" vertically linked to an "S."

The following table of Hannover operas, together with the dates of the printed libretti and autograph scores, and the British Museum shelf listings, will establish Steffani's authorship of these six operas beyond question:

---

[1] For an account of the provenance and associations of the Royal Music Library see A. Hyatt King, "The Royal Music Library," *The Book Collector*, VII (1958), 241-52.

Title	Libretto date	B.M. listing of autograph score	Autograph date
Henrico Leone	1689	R. M. 23. h. 7-9	1688
La Lotta d'Hercole con Acheloo	1689	—	—
La Superbia d'Alessandro	(a) 1690 (b) 1691*	R. M. 23. f. 12-14	1691
Orlando Generoso	(a) 1691 (b) 1692	R. M. 23. i. 13-15	1691
Le Rivali Concordi	(a) 1692 (b) n.d.	R. M. 23. k. 2-4	1692
La Liberta Contenta	1693	R. M. 23. h. 19-21	1693
Baccanali	1695	—	—
I Trionfi del Fato	(a) 1695 (b) 1695	R. M. 23. i. 3-5	1695
Briseide	1696	—	—

* This second version of the libretto was retitled *Il Zelo di Leonato*.

In attempting to verify the status of the three operas for which no autograph is known, one turns first of all to documentary sources in Hannover—primarily account books and correspondence—in hopes of finding at least a mention of Steffani as the composer. The Niedersächsisches Staatsarchiv in Hannover contains a ponderous hoard of documents from, to, and about Steffani the diplomat and Steffani the churchman—but precious little about Steffani the musician. It is impossible to discover precisely what his duties as Kapellmeister were or just how large the musical establishment was or how extensive its activities. Indeed, one cannot even find his address. Although a census of the city was taken in 1689 and the lodgings of everyone from the Oberhofmarschall to the lowliest tradesman recorded, Steffani's name is not on the list. The *Kammerrechnungen*, which make minute accountings for all court expenditures, give no hint of the elaborate and expensive opera productions there from 1689 to 1696, nor is Steffani's salary of 100 Taler per month recorded. The reason for this is frustratingly simple: Ernst August, Duke-Elector of Hannover from 1680 until his death in 1698, was also titular Bishop of Osnabrück and as such had at his disposal certain discretionary funds. He paid Steffani's salary and the expenses of

the glittering opera season out of his own pocket, and the corresponding account book has since been lost. Although there are several
marginal notations in the Hannover accounts referring to specific
pages in this so-called "Osnabrücksche Rechnung," no trace of it can
be found either in Osnabrück or in Hannover. After Ernst August's
death, the Hannover *Kammer* took over the payment of Steffani's
salary, but by this time the opera house had been shut down and
Steffani was engaged entirely on diplomatic missions.

It is evident that other vital documents have also disappeared,
especially in view of Georg Fischer's detailed description of the
Carneval season of 1696 and other events.[2] Hannover suffered extensive damage in World War II. One particularly heavy bombing raid
on October 9, 1943, ruined a large section of the Staatsarchiv, and a
flood in 1946 destroyed or rendered useless many more bundles of
documents that the bombs had spared. Especially distressing is the
loss of the records of the Oberhofmarschallsamt, which did contain
information about music and theater.

The first person to do archival research on the musical aspect of
Steffani's Hannover career was Friedrich Chrysander.[3] He investigated material at the Staatsarchiv, the Königliche und Provinzial-
bibliothek (now the Hannover Landesbibliothek), and the Hannover
Historischer Verein. His information came mainly from the printed
libretti of the operas—some of them handsomely bound private
copies belonging to the local nobility—and a rather unreliable history of the Hannover court by its illustrious Hofmarschall Carl Ernst
von Malortie.[4] Although the opera autographs and other scores were
available in the basement of Buckingham Palace while he was preparing his Handel biography, Chrysander did not see them. He knew
only two of the operas (*La Lotta* and *Le Rivali*) from copies in
Berlin and Heidelberg.

Chrysander's work was furthered by Georg Fischer, a leading
Hannover surgeon and local historian, who delved deeper into the
archival documents but whose access to the music was restricted to
say the least.[5] (To this day not a scrap of musical notation in

---

[2] Georg Fischer, *Musik in Hannover* (Hannover-Leipsig, 1903). This is the second
edition of his *Opern und Concerte im Hoftheater zu Hannover bis 1866* (Hannover,
1899).

[3] Friedrich Chrysander, *G. F. Handel* (Leipsig, 1858), I, 309-77.

[4] Carl Ernst von Malortie, *Der Hannoversche Hof unter dem Kurfürsten Ernst
August und der Kurfürstin Sophie* (Hannover, 1847).

[5] *Ibid.*, pp. 1-25.

Steffani's hand exists in Hannover.) But by far the most reliable exposition of Steffani's operatic activity is found in the monumental publication of Hugo Riemann, which brings together information from all sources available at the time.[6]

All three of these writers make reference to a manuscript catalogue of operas to which they give considerable weight. Chrysander and Fischer had obviously seen it, while Riemann refers to their printed reports. Neither Chrysander nor Fischer gives a description of the catalogue nor any indication of its provenance, date, or total contents. It is simply referred to as a "handschriftliches Verzeichnis" or "handschriftliches Blatt" and is called to account several times as the arbiter of the date or authorship of certain operas performed at Hannover.

Attempts to find the mysterious catalogue were at first unsuccessful. It was not in any of the library or archive lists of holdings. Its whereabouts was unknown to all staff members. Indeed, but for Chrysander and Fischer, there was no hint of there ever having been such a document. It came to light quite accidentally in a tiny, airless, and frigid anteroom on the top floor of the Hannover Landesbibliothek, where old libretti are stored in great disorder. Tucked behind them in a cardboard box labeled "Operntexte Braunschweig" were half a dozen libretti (none of them from Braunschweig) and two loose sheets of yellowed paper, the second one torn in half. This proved to be the missing "Verzeichnis." It has now been mended and bound and duly entered with the number IV 414a in the Landesbibliothek's catalogue of manuscript holdings.

The document itself is an inventory of the musico-dramatic events which took place in Hannover from 1679 to 1697, based primarily on information in the printed libretti then in the electoral library. At least three and possibly four scribes had a hand in it. The initial list must have been drawn up in 1698—that is, upon the death of Ernst August and the succession of his son, Georg Ludwig, to the electorate. An entry in the *Kammerrechnungen* for that year confirms that a certain Heinrich Tünningen of Lühde was paid 12 Taler "for inventory of operas ordered from here" ("so bey inventirung der Opern bey der anhero gefordert").[7] The complete list, with the handwritings separated, reads as follows:

---

[6] *Denkmäler der Tonkunst in Bayern*, XI² (1911), XII² (1912).
[7] Hannover State Archives, *Hann. Des. 76ᶜ, Ac. Calenberg, 1698/99*, p. 414.

incertae aetatis

1

Le Rivali concordi *diese opera ist obligatch Hortenseus*
1698 oder 97 ...
... Abate Steffani ...

Contrasto della honesta *...*
componierte
coi vitii

Per la sua Altezza Ser. il Sgr.
Duca di Hannover 3de ossequiosa del ca
valier Amalc

~~1695~~

Wenigstens eine particuliste Opera
wurd auch einen repraesentirt 1670

l'Alceste Drama per Musica Hortensio
da rappresentarsi per or
dine di Madama Benedetta
Henrietta l'anno 1379.

l'Alceste da rappresentarsi
di nuova l'anno 1681 alla
Maesta di Amalia Regina
di Danimarca.

l'Helena rapita da Paride da
rappresentarsi l'anno 1681 alla
Maesta di Sophia Amalia
Regina di Danimarca
Signor Valenti
de Sartorio le Madine.

2

- La Lotta d'Hercole con Achelos divertimento drammatico per il Teatro d'Hannovera nella Estate del 1689 von Steffani comp.

Hennico Leone dramma da recitarsi per l'anno 1689 nel nuovo Theatro d'Hannover von Steffani con un Elogio manuscritto di questo Prencipe.

f. Steffen Maur

- La superbia d'Alessandro Drama da recitarsi nel Theatro d'Hannover, l'Anno 1690

Steffen
Hort. Ma

- Il zelo di Leonato Drama per il Theatro d'Hannover 1691

f. Hort. Ma

= Orlando generoso drama per il Theatro d'Hannover 1691

B p 3
ef. M. Drama medesimo coll esplicazione Francese et tedesca.

f. Horte
Maur

- La Liberta contenta Drama per il Theatro di Hannover 1693

f. Horte
Maur

3.

Accademia per Musica cantata
alla corte Elettorale d'Hannover
per la funzione Sponsalizia di Ri
naldo e Carlotta. 1695.

= Baccanali celebrati nel picco
lo Teatro Elettorale d'Hannover
l'anno 1695.   Hort. Ma

- I Trionfi del fato o le
   Glorie d'Enea Drama
   da recitarsi nel Theatro
   Elettorale d'Hannover
   1695.   Hort. Chau

una altra Edizione per il
   Theatro El. d'Hannover
   con esempi. France. 1695.

- Briseide Dramma per Musica
   da recitarsi alla corte elet
   torale d'Hannover per il
   Carnevale dell'Anno 1695.

- Argument du poeme drama
   tique intitulé Briseide chan
   té en vers Italiens a la cour
   electoral d'Hannover. 1695.

4.

La Costanza nelle Selve favola
pastorale per Musica rappresentata alla corte Elettorale
d'Hannover negli ozzi dell'
Estate l'Anno 1697.   Ant. Mau

Scribe 1.	Scribe 2.	Scribe 3.
incertae aetatis [heading] [Very faint penciled notation in a different hand:] prima editio[ne] 1692 repetita 1694		
2. Le Rivali concordi	f. Hortensius	Diese opera ist ohngefähr 1698 oder 97 vorgestellet und vom Abate Steffani nachma[ls] Bishoff zu Spiga componirt

Contrasto della honesta
    coi vitii
Per la sua Altezza Ser. il Sgr.
  Duca di Hannover Ode
  ossequiosa
	del Ca
	valier Amalti	

1679 [struck out] Alceste in musicalischer Opera wird auffs neue repraesentiret 1679.		

l'Alceste Drama per Musica
  da rappresentarsi per or
  dine di Madama Benedetta
  Henrietta l'anno 1679.
	f
	Hortensio
	M[auro]	

l'Alceste da rapresentarsi
  di nuova l'anno 1681 alla
  Maesta di Amalia Regina
  di Danimarca.		

l'Helena rapita da Paride da
  rappresentarsi l'anno 1681 alla
  Maesta di Sophia Amalia
  Regina di Danimarca
    Signor Valenti
    H Sartorio le Machine.		

La Lotta d'Hercole con Acheloo
  divertimento drammatico per
  il Teatro d'Hannovera nella Estate
  del 1689
		von Steffani comp.

Henrico Leone Dramma da reci-
  tarsi per l'anno 1689 nel nuovo
  Theatro d'Hannover
	f.
	Hortensio
	Mauro
		von Steffani

con un Elogio manuscritto di questo Prencipe.		

Scribe 1.	Scribe 2.	Scribe 3.
La Superbia d'Alessandro Drama da recitarsi nel Theatro d' Hannover l'Anno 1690	Hort. Ma[uro]	Steffani
Il Zelo di Leonato Drama per il Theatro d'Hannover 1691.	f. Hort. Mau[ro]	
Orlando Generoso Drama per il Theatro d'Hannover 1691.		
Drama medesimo coll esplica zione Francese e Tedesca.	f. Hortens[io] Mauro	
La Liberta contenta Drama per il Theatro di Hannover 1693.	f. Horten[sio] Mauro	
Accademia per Musica cantata alla Corte Elettorale d'Hannover per la funzione sposalizia di Ri naldo e Carlotta. 1695.		
Baccanali celebrati nel piccio lo Teatro elettorale d'Hanover l'anno 1695.	f Hort. Mau[ro]	
I Trionfi del fato o le Glorie d'Enea Drama da recitarsi nel Theatro Elettorale d'Hannover 1695.	f Hort. Maur[o]	
una altra Edizione per il Theatro El. d'Hannover con esplic. Frances. 1695.		
Briseide Dramma per Musica da recitarsi alla corte elet torale d'Hannover per il Carnevale dell Anno 1696.		
Argument du poeme drama tique intitule Briseis chan te en vers Italiens a la cour electoral d'Hanover. 1696.		
La Costanza nelle Selve favola pastorale per Musica rappresen tata alla corte Elettorale d'Hannover negli ozzi dell Estate l'Anno 1697.	i Hort. Maur[o]	

—p. 3 mes. edit. [—p. 3 medesima editione]

Tünningen, the chief scribe, sets out to make a chronological list. Since two of the libretti bear no date, he therefore begins with them *incertae aetatis*, then continues systematically year by year. He makes no attempt to identify either the librettist or composer, since neither is printed on any of the title pages. In one case (*Helena Rapita*) he does supply the names Valenti and H. Sartorio, which he copied exactly from the title page where they had been inked in by an unknown hand. In the dedication, Valenti is identified as the librettist and (Hieronymus) Sartorio as the creator of decor and machinery. Tünningen missed other important information buried in the dedication of both editions of *Alceste*. He also missed the date of the second edition of *Orlando Generoso*, which is clearly printed. Hannover's first opera, the *Orontea* of 1678, and also *Paride in Ida* of 1687 are unaccountably lacking, although the libretti are still available and presumably were at the time of the inventory.

Scribe 2, in handwriting closely approximating that of the first, identifies the librettist where known. His entries are written into the right-hand margin with heavier pen strokes. All but one of his ascriptions are to the local court poet and friend of Steffani, Ortensio Mauro. In some of the libretti, Mauro's name is penned in on the title page—evidently after 1698—for Tünningen did not record it. In other cases these manuscript additions do not exist, and Scribe 2's ascriptions are our chief source for the authorship of the libretti in question.

Scribe 3 writes entirely in German and identifies the composer where known to him—in every case Steffani. He makes his remarks on any available space on the page. Judging from the handwriting and orthography, his additions were probably made about 1750. His one attempt to date one of the operas (*Le Rivali Concordi*) is way out of line, but for forgivable reasons, and is corrected on the page in pencil (*Silberstift*) by a faint but still legible (fourth?) hand. *Le Rivali*, according to Scribe 3, was "performed about 1698 or 97 and composed by the Abbot Steffani, later Bishop of Spiga." The penciled correction runs, "first edition 1692, repeated 1694." The score of *Le Rivali* was completed before the end of 1692, as Steffani's autograph attests. There is a printed libretto of the opera also dated 1692, although strangely enough no copy of this seems to have survived at Hannover. The opera was revised and presented again. A new score was made (not autograph) and a new libretto printed, this time without a date. Since Malortie declares that the opera took place on February 10 and 21, 1693, it is reasonable to assume that these were the first performances—that is, that the opera was written in 1692 but did not reach the stage until the Carneval season, which fell after the New Year. According to our catalogue, the opera, undoubtedly in its revised version, was brought out again the following year. Still a third score is available at the British Museum (R.M.23. i.17), which, although it is a clean copy bearing no marks of practical use, is nevertheless clearly dated 1697 *per il Theatro d'Hannover*, thus vindicating Scribe 3's late date. (One wonders, however, if the copyist did not simply misread the numeral 2 as 7.)

Of our three questionable operas only one (*La Lotta d'Hercole*) is here ascribed to Steffani. Indeed, Scribe 3 is reluctant to credit any operas at all to him after *Le Rivali*, although *I Trionfi del Fato* is known to be genuine, at least in part. In 1693, Steffani's diplomatic duties were stepped up enormously. He became a special envoy for Ernst August and was absent from Hannover much of the time. His name now begins to appear regularly in the *Kammerrechnungen* but always under the rubric for special foreign duty (Auf Commissionen und Verschickungen). He is referred to not as Kapellmeister, but as "Abbot Steffani, presently dispatched to Brussels" ("Abbé Steffani den ietzigen abgeordneten nach Brussel"), and there are numerous extra payments made to him for travel expenses and postage. The autograph of *I Trionfi* gives evidence of his haste and inattention to music at the time. The score was torn apart, revised, and put back together again before binding. At least two, perhaps three, different hands other than Steffani's are in evidence. One of them is unspeakably messy. It is possible to see where one scribe takes over from another, sometimes in the middle of a word, and the score is so full of cuts, emendations, and directions to turn to a different page that it is difficult to see how it could have been used as a performing score, although it certainly was.

La Lotta d'Hercole and *Baccanali* are minor, one-act works and both musically dull. *La Lotta* is dubbed a "divertimento drammatico," and even Chrysander noted its stylistic inferiority to the only other Hannover opera he knew. *Baccanali* was never performed in the big opera house at all. It was a summer trifle staged in the so-called "kleines Theater," a large converted room in the ducal residence, the Leineschloss, where operas were produced before the large theater was built.

Briseide has an especially suspect history. Fischer reports that

Pietro Torri was engaged for one year as Kapellmeister at Hannover, specifically for the Carneval season of 1696. His account is so detailed, including the names of singers employed, a gift of four medallions to Madame Torri, etc., that there must have been some documentary basis in fact.[8] It seems more likely that Torri would have been hired to write his own opera rather than to conduct someone else's. The working score of *Briseide* is not in London, but in Munich. Like the Steffani autographs, it is bound in three volumes with the same leather covering and gold stamping, and it shows evidence of practical use. The exterior looks precisely like that of the Steffani scores— it was undoubtedly bound by Rosenhagen, the Hannover bookbinder—but the handwriting is not Steffani's, nor is it that of the Vienna score or the other three scores in London, and one of these (B.M. Add. Ms. 32581) names Torri as the composer. Torri had close ties with both Steffani and Munich, and he took over the post of Kammerorganist there when Steffani left. He was appointed Kammermusikdirektor in 1703, Hofkapelldirektor in 1715, and Kapellmeister in 1732, and he died in Munich on July 6, 1737. It seems quite possible—to put it no more strongly—that he carried the manuscript of his one Hannover triumph with him.

To summarize: of the nine Hannover operas attributed to Steffani, six are definitely genuine and three must remain in doubt until the autographs or some other substantial proofs turn up. Of these three *La Lotta* must be awarded a "probable" on the basis of our manuscript catalogue, plus the fact that it was composed during Steffani's first year of residence as Kapellmeister and before he was swallowed up in politics, and also because Mattheson hints at Steffani as the composer of the opera when it was brought out in German translation at Hamburg in 1696. Mattheson's statement, however, is somewhat ambiguous.[9] *Baccanali* can be traced under a number of different titles: *La Festa d'Himeneo* (Berlin, 1700), with music by

---

[8] Fischer, *Musik in Hannover*, p. 22.

[9] Johann Mattheson, *Der Musikalische Patriot* (Hamburg, 1728), publishes a list of operas performed in Hamburg from 1678 to 1728. Entry No. 69 (p. 182), *Heinrich der Löwe* (i.e., *Henrico Leone*), indicates Steffani as the composer and Fideler (Fiedler) as the translator. The following entry reads: "Alcides. Wie vorhergehende" ("Alcides. Like the above"). The confusion arises over whether *Alcides* is identical with *La Lotta d'Hercole*—a Berlin score gives this as a subtitle to the work—and whether "*Wie vorhergehende*" refers to Steffani and Fiedler. In his private copy of the book, Mattheson continued the catalogue to 1751. This revised list was printed by Chrysander in the *Allgemeine Musikalische Zeitung*, XII (1877). The Steffani entries (p. 218) are the same.

Attilio Ariosti and Karl Friedrich Rieck; *Doppia Festa d'Himeneo* (Salzdahlum, 1718), with dedication signed by Georg Kaspar Schürmann; and *La Festa di Minerva* (Wolfenbüttel, 1719), are one and all the *Baccanali* text with minor alterations. The work was an occasional piece brought out for weddings and birthdays. There is no proof that Steffani was the composer of the original version. *Briseide*, because of the considerable circumstantial evidence against it, is very probably not by Steffani.

The lack of an autograph is certainly no proof of unauthenticity, but in the case of Steffani these scores seem to have been so carefully preserved, probably because of their royal ownership, that their absence casts a suspicious shadow over any assumptions. Not only the autographs of the originals, but also the scores of the revised versions of his operas were gathered into the royal library. The British Museum scores of *Orlando Generoso* (R.M.23.i.12) and *Le Rivali Concordi* (R.M.23.k.1), both written by the same copyist (not Steffani) and on the same paper stock as the autographs, match the second editions of their respective libretti. Like the autographs, they too were put to practical use. Although each is bound in one volume, they were both originally in three, since each act has its own pagination. They are thumb-worn, and there are occasional corrections ("a tone higher" ["un ton piu alto"], etc.) in the hand of the master himself. Steffani's own score of *La Superbia d'Alessandro* actually corresponds to the 1691 edition of the libretto, though without its new title, and is earlier in origin than the 1690 copy of the score (R.M.23.h.13), which contains not only the additional pieces for 1691, but also the last-minute revisions made in that autograph. As already mentioned, the autograph of *I Trionfi* served for both versions of the opera, the score having been ripped apart and reassembled to include the new music.

This hoarding instinct of the Hannover court brings us to a further observation on our manuscript catalogue. The list was evidently drawn up at the instigation of Georg Ludwig and was supposed to be a summary of the operatic performances at court. There are two known omissions, *Orontea* and *Paride in Ida*. But for these two, for which printed libretti exist, there is no reason to suspect that the list is otherwise incomplete. The Cesti-Cicognini *Orontea*, with a revised text, was Hannover's first opera. This is certified by an inventory of properties for *Alceste* made in 1679, which states that three of the chests contain "the stock of costumes belonging to the first opera, *Orontea*" ("den Vorrath zu kleidern so zur ersten opera, der Orontea gehörn").[10] The composer of *Paride in Ida*, according to the British Museum score (R.M.23.k.23), is "Signor Mancia," which probably means that Luigi Mancia's music was performed in Hannover to a text by Nicola Nicolini some nine years before its supposed premiere in Parma. The preface to the 1679 edition of the *Alceste* libretto states that the opera—originally titled *Antigona*, first performed in 1661 in Venice, reproduced there in 1670, and now "renewing itself every nine years like the phoenix" ("come la fenice")—has been readied for the Hannover stage. The music, originally by Pietro Andrea Ziani, has been renovated by Matthio Trento, the Hannover court organist. Our catalogue reveals that Mauro did the text revision. The phoenix rose out of season when *Alceste* was performed again only two years later. Valenti is named as inventor of the new prologue and Pier Antonio Fiocco its composer. The dedication of the 1681 libretto was signed by Nicolo Montalbano, court poet and central figure in one of the most fascinating detective stories in Hannover history. This "priest in a cavalier's coat" was the murderer of Count Philipp von Königsmarck, paramour of Georg Ludwig's wife, and one good reason why there was no new opera in Hannover in 1694![11]

The other non-Steffani entries in the catalogue need not overly concern us. Montalbano also signed the dedication of *Helena Rapita*, but the libretto does not inform us who the composer was—in all likelihood it was Giovanni Domenico Freschi, whose opera by the same name had been performed in Venice four years earlier. There is a libretto of the *Contrasto della Honesta coi Vitii*, but neither the date nor the composer is given. It is a short allegorical work in one act involving the characters Honestà, Bellezza, Inganno, Prodigalità, and Amore. The librettist, Cavalier Amalti, was probably one of the horde of Italian noblemen, or pseudo-noblemen, who choked the payrolls of the Hannover court in the seventeenth century. The *Elogio Manuscritto* is a fulsome essay lauding the exploits of King Henry the Lion and inferring a comparison between him and Duke

---

[10] Hannover State Archives, *K.G.Cal.Br. Arch. 22/XII 10.* The author is indebted to the present Prince of Hannover, Ernst August, for permission to use his private archives.

[11] See Georg Schnath, "Der Fall Königsmarck," *Hannoversche Geschichtsblätter,* Neue Folge VI, 179-341.

Ernst August, who was so enlightened as to construct a magnificent opera house to perpetuate the Lion's memory.[12] The text, and probably the music, for the *Accademia per Musica* was written by Count Francesco Palmieri, the librettist for *Briseide*. The work has disappeared, but it apparently made a good impression on the court librarian, the famous Gottfried Wilhelm Leibniz, who wrote to Palmieri on November 12, 1695: "Your *Accademia per Musica* combines the beauties of music and ideas. This is what is needed for such a great ceremony." ("Vostre *Academia per Musica* joint les beautés de la Musique à celles des pensées. C'est ce qu'il faut pour une si grande ceremonie.")[13] It also made an unfavorable impression on Mauro, who injured Palmieri's pride by writing a stern criticism of it. A libretto for the last entry on the list, Mauro's *La Costanza nelle Selve*, is still extant in the Landesbibliothek. At the bottom of the title page is clearly penned: "Manza hat die Music gemacht" ("Manza [i.e., Luigi Mancia] composed the music").

All things considered, the opera repertory at Hannover was decidedly small, much smaller than that of the neighboring houses at Braunschweig and Wolfenbüttel, to say nothing of the renowned establishment at Hamburg. It was certainly smaller than the twenty-two items recorded in Fischer. All of his entries before 1678 can be discounted. Although scores for some of these exist, there is no indication that they were ever performed at Hannover. By correlating the known printed libretti, the London scores, and the manuscript catalogue, one can correct the mistakes and omissions in both Chrysander and Fischer and arrive at a more accurate schedule of what probably took place.

At the beginning of his reign, Ernst August was ascetic, not to say miserly, in his expenditures for music. One of his first actions was to dismiss all the Italian musicians. Kapellmeister Vincenzo de Grandis simply disappears from the books altogether, and the post remained vacant for eight years. In the *Kammerrechnungen* the accounts for music were no longer carried under the rubric *Bey der Hofcapelle*, but simply *Denen Musicanten*, and on the rolls there were only a handful of musicians, mostly French. Only two operas

---

[12] Hannover Landesbibliothek MS XXIII, 331. Catalogue by Eduard Bodemann, *Die Handschriften der königlichen öffentlichen Bibliothek zu Hannover* (Hannover, 1867).

[13] Hannover Landesbibliothek Leibniz Correspondence, MS 708.

took place in the first two years, both in 1681. *Alceste* was a repeat from 1679; *Helena Rapita* may well have been arranged for by Ernst August's brother, the former Duke Johann Friedrich, before his death. There were no more operas for six years. In his intense and often clever maneuvers to have Hannover named as the Ninth Electorate in the Holy Roman Empire, Ernst August discovered that costly display and lavish spectacle were a sure way of winning support. He must have decided with the production of *Paride in Ida* that the "kleines Theater" was entirely too small and unimpressive a house to serve his purposes. He thereupon purchased land adjoining the Leineschloss, erected in an incredibly short time a splendid opera house whose reputation soon rivaled that of Versailles, and hired Steffani, whose political acumen as well as musical gifts were already known to him, as Kapellmeister. He opened his private purse strings, the opera house was inaugurated on January 30, 1689, with *Henrico Leone*, and for seven brief years Hannover experienced operatic glory.[14] The seasons were short and the operas few, but the productions were the talk of the Continent.

At some undetermined time a professional copyist was called in to make clean copies of the opera scores, beginning with *Paride in Ida*. These scores are now to be found in the Royal Music Library of the British Museum. They are handsomely bound in heavy leather covers with a gold imprint of a rearing horse, the "springendes Pferd" emblem of Lower Saxony, on the front. The quality of the paper is superb and the handwriting a work of art. Like the autographs, they may have come over to London with George I. At all events they were at one time in the possession of Queen Caroline, wife of George II, whose library was inventoried in 1743.[15] Unfortunately there are many mistakes in music and text, some of them caused by the copyist's unfamiliarity with Italian (*spanentoso* for *spaventoso*, etc.), but a comparison of the volumes of this set with our manuscript catalogue will reveal the thoroughness with which these works were preserved:

[14] The date of the opening of the Hannover opera house is proved by E. I. Luin in "Antonio Giannettini e la musica a Modena alla fine del secolo XVII," *Atti e Memorie della R. Deputazione di Storia Patria per le Provincie Modenesi*, Serie VII, Vol. 7 (1931), 145-230.

[15] *A Catalogue of the Royal Library of Her Late Majesty Queen Caroline Distributed into Faculties.* The author thanks Mr. A. Hyatt King for making a photostat copy of this manuscript available.

Paride in Ida	R.M.23.k.23
Henrico Leone	R.M.23.h.11
La Lotta d'Hercole	R.M.23.h.15
La Superbia d'Alessandro	R.M.23.h.13
Le Rivali Concordi	R.M.23.i.17
La Liberta Contenta	R.M.23.h.16
Baccanali	R.M.23.f.16
I Trionfi del Fato	R.M.23.i.1
Briseide	R.M.23.g.21
La Costanza nelle Selve	R.M.23.h.1
Amor Vien dal Destino	R.M.23.h.2

Amor Vien dal Destino is by Steffani. Although not performed until 1709 in Dusseldorf, it was undoubtedly written many years earlier while he was still in service at Hannover.[16] The autographs of this work (R.M.23.h.3-5) and one of Steffani's Munich operas, *Marco Aurelio* (R.M.23.i.7-9), are also in the British Museum.

It will be noted that *Orlando Generoso* is missing from the set. It was tempting to equate the score of this opera recently acquired by the Hannover Stadtbibliothek with the missing *Orlando*.[17] However, a comparison of a photographed page with the London scores reveals that the handwriting is not the same, and information by letter from the Stadtbibliothek confirms that size and binding are different. Steffani once loaned a score of *Orlando* to Sophie Charlotte, daughter of Ernst August, Queen of Prussia, and by far the most musically sophisticated lady in the Hannover circle. On November 21, 1702, less than three years before her death, she wrote to Steffani that she still had it.[18] Whether this was the copy in question and whether it was ever returned there is no way of knowing; but since Sophie Charlotte's residence and library were in what is now Charlottenburg, it is sad to contemplate that her *Orlando* may have perished in the ashes of Hitler's Third Reich.

[16] See Gerhard Croll, "Zur Chronologie der Düsseldorfer Opern Agostino Steffanis," *Festschrift K.G. Fellerer* (Regensburg, 1962), pp. 82-83.

[17] Heinrich Sievers, *Die Musik in Hannover* (Hannover, 1961), p. 53. A facsimile page of the score appears opposite p. 61.

[18] Richard Doebner, *Briefe der Königin Sophie Charlotte von Preussen und der Kurfürstin Sophie von Hannover an hannoversche Diplomaten*, in *Publikationen aus den Königlichen Preussischen Staatsarchiven*, Vol. 79 (Leipzig, 1905), pp. 79-80.

THE TRAVELS OF *PARTENOPE*

ROBERT FREEMAN

ACCORDING to a favorite theme of early eighteenth-century critics of Italian opera, viable musical drama had become impossible sometime during the seventeenth century, partly because librettists had allowed themselves to become subjugated to the whims of the singers, the composers, the set designers, and the impresarios.[1] Additional evidence that the dramatic ideas of late seventeenth- and early eighteenth-century librettists were normally given little consideration by their colleagues in the theater can be found in the correspondence of both Zeno and Metastasio,[2] as well as in the allusions of countless libretto prefaces to changes ". . . introduced, not out of disrespect for the work's author, but rather to satisfy the wishes of our highly honored singers . . . ," or in order to accommodate a work to unstated peculiarities of theatrical taste in the town where it was to be staged. It is my purpose here to examine, with respect to Silvio Stampiglia's libretto, *Partenope* (Naples, 1699), and twelve of its earliest reworkings for productions in Rovigo (1699), Mantua (1701), Florence (1701), Venice (1708), Ferrara (1709), Bologna (1710), Brescia (1710), Milan (1713), Livorno (1713), Trent (1713), Rimini (1715), and Modena (1720), several unexplored questions suggested by the view just indicated of the early eighteenth-century Italian opera house. What sorts of

---

[1] Andrea Perrucci, *Dell'arte rappresentativa premeditata ed all' improviso* (Naples, 1699), p. 59; Giovanni Maria Crescimbeni, *La bellezza della volgar poesia* (Rome, 1700), reprinted in Venice, 1730, pp. 106-108; Crescimbeni, *Comentarii intorno alla sua istoria della volgar poesia* (Rome, 1702), I, 234-35; Ludovico Antonio Muratori, *Della perfetta poesia italiana* (Modena, 1706), II, 35-54; Giovanni Vincenzo Gravina, *Della ragion poetica* (Rome, 1708), reprinted in Gravina's *Opere scelte italiane* (Milan, 1819), pp. 136-40; Pier Jacopo Martello, *Della tragedia antica e moderna* (Rome, 1715), reprinted in *Scrittori d'Italia*, ccxxv, esp. 294-95; Benedetto Marcello, *Il teatro alla moda* (Venice, 1720), English translation by R. Pauly in *MQ*, xxxiv, esp. 372-80; Scipione Maffei, *Teatro italiano* (Verona, 1723), I, vi-vii. For another translation of the sections from Marcello's essay entitled "To the Poets" and "To the Composers of Music," see Oliver Strunk's *Source Readings in Music History* (New York, 1950), pp. 518-31.

[2] Apostolo Zeno, *Lettere di Apostolo Zeno* (Venice, 1785), I, 143, 154; II, 213, 284, 406; III, 198, 315; IV, 264-65, 332-33; VI, 93-96, 100-101; Pietro Metastasio, *Tutte le opere di Pietro Metastasio*, ed. B. Brunelli (Milan, 1943-54), III, 230, 510, 700, 790, 905, 1151, 1166-67; IV, 273-74; V, 91, 259, 303, 308, 478.

changes were forced upon the unwilling poet, normally present for the original production but usually absent from the inevitable revisions for productions in other cities? Who made these changes and at whose behest were they made? What were the reasons for the changes, and what regard, if any, was taken for preserving whatever dramatic coherence existed in the original? Were the changes indicative of local traditions, as often suggested in libretto prefaces, or should these allusions be taken more as window dressing intended to flatter local audiences or to conceal local deficiencies? To what extent, finally, do the changes reflect those trends in the history of the printed libretto sometimes associated with the reforming influence of the Arcadian Academy: an increasing seriousness of moral tone, a reduction in the proportion of musical numbers to dramatic dialogue, the elimination of arias at places other than the ends of scenes, a reduction in the number of set changes, and an increasing attention to the *liaison des scènes*—an effort to avoid a succession of discontinuous scenes achieved by retaining at least one character in successive scenes between set changes.[3]

We shall begin the comparison of the thirteen *Partenope* libretti on which this study is based[4] with a scene-by-scene plot summary of the 1699 Naples original, accompanied by a synoptic view of the order of scenes in all thirteen libretti. The following symbols will be in use:

1. *Dramatis Personae*
   A—Partenope, Queen of Partenope, present-day Naples
   B—Rosmira, Cypriote Princess disguised as an Armenian named Eurimene, in love with Arsace

[3] Max Fehr, *Apostolo Zeno und seine Reform des Operntextes* (Zurich, 1912); Nathaniel Burt, "Opera in Arcadia," *MQ*, XLI; Harold Powers's "Il Serse trasformato" (*MQ*, XLVII-XLVIII) rightly stresses the degree to which these trends reflect the increasing experience of impresarios and their employees with a still relatively new genre.

[4] The libretti concerned (identified, as are other source materials in this article, according to the RISM code) are the following: Naples (1699)—I-Bc 6904; Rovigo (1699)—I-Bu.A.VIII K.11.64.2; Mantua (1701)—I-Bc 6906; Florence (1701)—I-Bc 6905; Venice (1708)—I-Bc 6907; Ferrara (1709)—I-Bc 737; Bologna (1710)—I-Bc 6908; Brescia (1710)—B-Bc 21.335; Milan (1713)—I-Bc 6909; Livorno (1713)—I-Rsc Carvallhaes 11.868; Trent (1713)—I-Bc 4491; Rimini (1715)—I-Bu A.III.caps. 100.16; Modena (1720)—I-MOe 83.I.16. The libretti for the productions in Brescia, Livorno, Rimini, and Modena were generously brought to my attention by Charles Troy.

C—Arsace, Prince of Corinth, former lover of Rosmira
D—Armindo, Prince of Rhodes, in love with Partenope
E—Emilio, Prince of Cuma and a suitor of Partenope
F—Ormonte, captain of Partenope's guard
G—Anfrisa, Partenope's elderly nurse
H—Beltramme, Rosmira's manservant (named Niso in the Milan and Trent versions)
I —Deidamia, Princess of Samos; appears in Rovigo and Trent versions only
J —Climene, Princess of Rhodes, sister to Armindo; appears in Mantua version only

2. / : new scene
// : set change
} : interruption in the *liaison des scènes*
+ : character enters after scene has begun
( ): character on stage, asleep
▽ : character opens scene by singing an aria
△ : character sings an aria in mid-scene, but does not exit
○ : character exits in mid-scene, after singing an aria
□ : character exits after singing scene-ending aria
[ ]: character sings scene-ending aria, but does not exit

Act I. /1. In a scene before her subjects, Partenope asks the gods to protect her newly founded city, naming it after herself. Animal sacrifices are offered. /2. Eurimene, claiming to have been washed ashore by a storm, requests and receives Partenope's hospitality. In an aside, Arsace remarks on the resemblance between Eurimene and his former lover, Rosmira. /3. Ormonte announces that Partenope is threatened by the Cumians and their leader, Emilio. Arsace is now almost certain that Eurimene and Rosmira are the same person. /4. Rosmira orders Beltramme not to disclose her identity. Armindo, for no apparent reason, tells Rosmira of his secret passion for Partenope, whom he identifies as the lover of Arsace. Rosmira, in love with Arsace herself, is clearly upset, and tries to persuade Armindo to inform Partenope of his feelings towards her. //5. Beltramme misleads Partenope's elderly nurse, Anfrisa, into thinking that he finds her attractive. /6. Rosmira discloses herself to Arsace, then forces him to swear not to disclose her identity, threatening him with the revelation to Partenope of Rosmira's former relationship with Arsace. Arsace admits in a monologue that he is still attracted by Rosmira. //7. Ormonte and Partenope discuss the military threat posed by Emilio. /8. Armindo nearly succeeds in telling Partenope that he loves her. Partenope's intuition tells her of Armindo's feelings, but she swears eternal devotion to Arsace. /9. A love scene between Partenope and Arsace is interrupted by the entrance of Eurimene. /10. Eurimene (Rosmira) now feigns love for Partenope, maintaining that his (her) love is more enduring than Arsace's. When Partenope reaffirms her love for Arsace, Eurimene threatens Arsace with eternal mental torment. Left alone at scene's end, Arsace confesses that he is torn between Partenope and Rosmira. /11. Beltramme continues to mislead Anfrisa. //12. Emilio offers Partenope peace through love. Turned down, he threatens a Cumian attack. /13. Partenope appoints Arsace general of her armies, then, goaded by jealous remarks directed at Arsace by Armindo and Eurimene, removes Arsace from his command and decides to join the battle herself. /14. Arsace tries to keep Rosmira from joining Partenope's army. Armindo is upset when he learns what has happened in Scene 10. /15. Rosmira tries to persuade Armindo that he need not fear her competition for Partenope's affections. Armindo resolves to impress Partenope by his courage in battle.

TABLE 1

Act I								
Naples	[A] CDG	BHACD G	FBH Ⓐ [C] DG	[D] Ⓑ H	☒Ⓥ + Ⓖ	[C] + Ⓐ(Ⓑ)	[A] F	[A] △
Rovigo	[A] CD I	BHACD [I]	BH Ⓐ [C] D	[D] Ⓑ H	☒Ⓥ	[C] + Ⓐ(Ⓑ)	[A] I	[A] △
Mantua	[A] CD	BHACD	FBH Ⓐ [C] D	[D] Ⓑ H	☒Ⓥ + (Ⓕ)	[C] + Ⓐ(Ⓑ)	A F	A △
Florence	A CD	BHACD	FBH Ⓐ [C] D	[D] Ⓑ H		[C] + Ⓐ(Ⓑ)	A F	[A] △
Venice	[A] CD	BHACD	FBH Ⓐ [C] D	[D] Ⓑ H		[V] C + Ⓐ(Ⓑ)	A F	[A] D
Ferrara	[A] CD	B ACD	FB Ⓐ [C] D	[D] Ⓑ H		[C] + Ⓐ(Ⓑ)	A F	A D
Bologna	[A] CD	B ACD	FB Ⓐ c D	[D] Ⓑ H		[C] + Ⓐ(Ⓑ)	A F	A Ⓓ
Brescia	A CDG	BHACD G	FBH [A] c DG	[D] Ⓑ H		[C] Ⓐ(Ⓑ)	A F	[A] △
Milan	[A] CD	BHACD	FBH Ⓐ [C] D	[D] Ⓑ H		[C] + (Ⓑ)	A F	A Ⓓ
Livorno	[A] CD	BHACD	FBH Ⓐ [C] D	[D] Ⓑ H		[C] + Ⓐ(Ⓑ)	A F	[A] D
Trent	[A] CD I	BHACD [I]	BH Ⓐ [C] D	[D] Ⓑ H	☒Ⓥ	[C] + Ⓐ(Ⓑ)	A I	A Ⓓ
Rimini	[A] CD	B ACD	FB Ⓐ c D	D Ⓑ		[C] + B	A F	A Ⓓ
Modena	[A] CD	B ACD	FB [A] c D	[D] B		B + c [C] ∑ A F	C ∑ A F	A D

TABLE 1 (cont.)

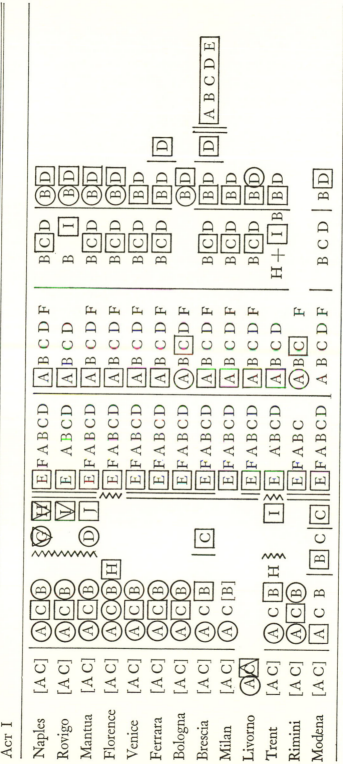

Act II. /1. The forces of Partenope defeat the Cumians; Arsace and Eurimene subdue Emilio. //2. Beltramme, who has fled the battlefield in fright, tries to convince Anfrisa that he is acting as a military messenger. The subject turns to a discussion of the latest fashions in amorous intrigue. /3. Partenope gives the captured Emilio his liberty. After an argument between Eurimene and Arsace about the credit for capturing Emilio, Eurimene challenges Arsace to a duel. Partenope, angered at Eurimene's accusations against Arsace, swears eternal devotion to Arsace and orders Eurimene arrested. /4. While Eurimene and Arsace continue their argument, Armindo and Emilio remark on Eurimene's valor, striking in a person of such unimpressive physical stature. /5. Emilio and Armindo both criticize Arsace for his attacks on Eurimene. General amazement follows Eurimene's unexpected defense of Arsace's character. /6. Beltramme and Rosmira discuss the latter's amorous problems. Beltramme ends the scene with a long aria questioning modern woman's preference of lap dogs to men. //7. After Arsace has persuaded Partenope to release Eurimene from prison, he repeats in private that he is still unable to decide between Partenope and Rosmira. /8. Armindo finally brings himself to tell Partenope of his feelings for her. After his exit, Partenope admits that she is drawn to Armindo, but reasserts her fidelity to Arsace. Anfrisa, left alone on stage, asserts that it is better to choose one's mate than to have one imposed. /9. Ormonte tries to persuade Eurimene to leave the area, now that his freedom has been granted, but Eurimene refuses. /10. Eurimene persuades Armindo to tell Partenope that Eurimene wishes to speak with her. /11. Arsace asks Rosmira for pity and swears his newly discovered devotion for her. In the act's final aria, he warns the audience of the anguish which awaits those who change lovers.

Act III. /1. When Partenope agrees to an interview with Eurimene, Arsace fears the worst. /2. Eurimene, claiming to be in the employ of Rosmira, whom Partenope apparently knows and admires, forces Arsace to tell Partenope that he has betrayed Rosmira. Par-

TABLE 2

Aст II

Naples	[ABCDF] E		A + G ⟩ W BCDEF	[B][C]DE	B[DE]
Rovigo	[ABCD] E		(I)+[H] ⟩ W BCDEI	[B][C]I E	B[I E]
Mantua	[ABCDF][A]		[X]+[H] ⟩ W BCDEF	[B][C]DE	B[DE]
Florence			W BCDEF	[B][C]DE	B[DE]
Venice	[ABCDF] E	‖[E]	W BCDEF	[B][C]DE	B[DE]
Ferrara	E + [ABCDF]	‖[E]	W BCDEF	[B][C]DE	[B]DE
Bologna	BCE ∣ ADBCE ‖[ABCDF] E∣ E		W BCDEF	[B][C]DE	[B]DE
Brescia			W BCDEF	[B][C]DE	B[DE]
Milan	[F] ∣ [ABCDF]E	‖[E]	W BCDEF	[B][C]DE	B D E
Livorno	E + [ABCDF]	∣E	W BCDEF	[B][C]DE	B D E
Trent	E + [ABCDH]	E[I]H	W BCDE	B[C] H	B[I E]
Rimini	BCE ∣ ABCDE ‖[ABCDF] E∣ E		W BCDEF	[B][C]DE	[B]DE
Modena	B E+C ∣ ABCDE ‖[ABCDF] E∣[E]		W BCDEF	[B][C]DE	[B]DE

Naples	(B)[H]	‖A[C]G	(A)(D)G ⟩ B[F]	B D	(B)C	
Rovigo	(B)[H]		[A]D ⟩	B I	(B)C	
Mantua	(B)[H]	A C	[A]D ⟩ B F	B D	(B)C	
Florence	(B)[H]	A C	[A](D) ⟩ B F	B D	(B)C	
Venice	B H	A[C]	[A](D) ⟩ B F	B D	(B)C	
Ferrara	[B]	A[C]	[A](D) ⟩ B[F]	B D	(B)C	
Bologna		A[C]	[A](D) ⟩ B[F]∣ B D	B D	(B)C	
Brescia	[B]	A C	A D ∣[A] ⟩ B D	B C	[C]
Milan	B H	A[C]	[A](D) ⟩ B[F]	B D	(B)C	
Livorno	B H	A[C]	[A](D) ⟩ B[F]	B D	(B)C	
Trent	(B)[H]		[A](D) ⟩	.B[I]	(B)C	
Rimini		‖A[C]	[A](D) ⟩ B[F]	B D	(B)C	
Modena	⟩A C	A[D]	⟩B[F]	B D	(B)C	

tenope dismisses Arsace forthwith and turns her attentions to the
eager Armindo. Arsace is relieved to have had the choice between
Rosmira and Partenope made for him, until Rosmira tells him that
her motive was not love but vengeance. /3. Eurimene challenges
Arsace to mortal combat for a second time, but Arsace refuses for
reasons which, because of his oath in I/6, he is unable to disclose.
In order to impress Partenope with his valor, Emilio offers his services as Arsace's champion. /4. Arsace engages in verbal parrying
with a Rosmira clearly torn between love and revenge. //5. Ormonte
is appointed referee for the forthcoming duel between Emilio and
Armindo, who has meanwhile agreed to substitute for Eurimene.
/6. Beltramme tells Anfrisa that he has heard of cases similar to
Arsace's. When he informs her that he himself has had more than
one lover, Anfrisa declaims in mock-heroic fashion about woman's
wretched fate. /7. Arsace, alone, now complains of his own fate, but
is put to sleep after only ten lines of recitative by some incidental
"armonia di varii stromenti." /8. Rosmira and Beltramme watch
Arsace's slumber. Rosmira hopes that Arsace will not break his oath
of I/6, for that, she feels, will be a sign that he has made himself
worthy of her renewed trust. /9. Rosmira, now in Partenope's presence, awakens Arsace, who, still lamenting his evil fate, breaks his
oath by asserting that Rosmira and Eurimene are the same person.
/10. Emilio and Armindo prepare for the duel, while discussing
their motivations for becoming involved in the feud between Eurimene and Arsace. /11. Beltramme takes artful leave of his senses,
claiming to see strange beings in the heavens and to be pregnant,
singing bits from several arias previously used by the other singers
and finally making Anfrisa believe he is about to marry her.
//12. Just as the duel is about to begin, Arsace finally hits upon a
way of forcing Rosmira to admit herself what he has, albeit in the
act of awakening, already disclosed in III/9. He will fight Eurimene,
but the combatants are to be bare-chested. When Eurimene claims
that Arsace has insulted him (her) by implying that he (she) might
be wearing a metal vest, Emilio and Armindo become offended and
refuse to fight. To avoid the bare-chested combat, Rosmira is obliged
to confess her identity. Marriages are arranged between Partenope
and Armindo, Rosmira and Arsace, Beltramme and Anfrisa; Emilio
is given his freedom. The work ends with a chorus in praise of
Partenope and the newly founded city which bears her name.

TABLE 3

Act III

Naples	[▽ + A D E]	Ⓑ C Ⓐ D E	B C Ⓓ E	Ⓒ + Ⓑ	Ⓐ Ⓓ F G ⌇ G ⒶⒽ ⌇[C]
Rovigo	[▽ + A D E]	Ⓑ C Ⓐ D E	B C D E I	Ⓒ Ⓑ	⌇ Ⓓ Ⓘ ⌇[C]
Mantua	[▽ + A D E]	Ⓑ C Ⓐ D E	B C Ⓓ E	Ⓒ + Ⓑ	Ⓐ Ⓓ F	[C]
Florence	[▽ + A D E]	Ⓑ C Ⓐ D E	B C Ⓓ E	Ⓒ + Ⓑ	Ⓐ Ⓓ F	[C]
Venice	[▽ + A D E]	Ⓑ C Ⓐ D E	B C Ⓓ E	Ⓒ + B	A Ⓓ F	[C]
Ferrara	[▽ + A D E]	Ⓑ C Ⓐ D E	B C Ⓓ E	Ⓒ + B	Ⓐ Ⓓ F	[C]
Bologna	[C + A D E]	Ⓐ C Ⓐ D E	B C Ⓓ E	Ⓒ B	⌇Ⓐ Ⓓ F	[C]
Brescia	▽ + A D E	Ⓑ C Ⓐ D E	B C Ⓓ E	Ⓒ + B	A D F	⎡D⎤ ⌇[C]
Milan	[▽ + A D E]	Ⓑ C Ⓐ D E	B C Ⓓ E	Ⓒ + B	A DⒻ	[C]
Livorno	C A D E	Ⓑ C Ⓐ D E	B C Ⓓ E	Ⓒ + B	A D F	[C]
Trent	[C] + A D E	Ⓑ CH Ⓐ D E	B CH Ⓓ E I	Ⓒ + B	Ⓓ Ⓘ ⌇[C]
Rimini	[C] + A E	Ⓑ C Ⓐ D E	B C Ⓓ E	Ⓒ B	⌇Ⓐ Ⓓ F	[C]
Modena	C A D E	B C Ⓐ D E	B C D E	C B ⎡B⎤⌇Ⓐ Ⓓ F	C

Naples	(C) [B] H	Ⓐ Ⓑ Ⓐ H ⌇ Ⓓ Ⓔ Ⓕ ⌇ G H	A F + B C D E + G H
Rovigo	(C) [B] H	Ⓐ Ⓑ Ⓐ H	A B C D E I H
Mantua	(C) [B] H	Ⓐ Ⓑ Ⓐ H ⌇ Ⓓ Ⓔ Ⓐ ⌇ Ⓘ + Ⓕ	A F + B C D E J H
Florence	(C) [B] H	Ⓐ Ⓑ Ⓐ H ‖ Ⓓ Ⓔ Ⓕ ⌇ H	A F + B C D E + H
Venice	(C) [B] H	Ⓐ Ⓑ Ⓐ H ⌇ D E	A F + B C D E
Ferrara	(C) [B]	Ⓐ Ⓑ Ⓐ ⌇ D E ⌇ Ⓓ	A F + B C D E
Bologna	Ⓐ	Ⓐ Ⓑ A ⌇ D E F	A F B C D E
Brescia	(C) [B] H	Ⓐ Ⓑ Ⓐ H	A F + B C D E G H
Milan	(C) [B] H	Ⓐ Ⓑ Ⓐ H ⌇ D E	A F + B C D E
Livorno	(C) [B] H	Ⓐ Ⓑ C H ⌇ D E	A F + B C D E
Trent [H] (C)	(C) [B] H	Ⓐ B C H	A + B Ⓐ D E I H
Rimini	Ⓐ Ⓑ + A ⌇ D E F	A F + B C D E
Modena	⎡C B + A⎤ ⌇ D Ⓔ	A F + B C D E

Let us turn our attention first to those features of the revisions which would have attracted the attention of the early Arcadians. The five comic scenes for Beltramme and Anfrisa, peculiar to the Naples original[5] and responsible there for five of the eight breaks in the *liaison des scènes*, are replaced in the Rovigo and Trent versions by four scenes for Beltramme and/or Deidamia (princess of Samos in love with Eurimene), a new character who appears in the Rovigo and Trent versions only. The Rovigo Beltramme is, like his Neapolitan counterpart, a cowardly and sometimes dull-witted miser who privately ridicules the pathetic affections of the aristocrats with whom he shares the stage; but the scurrilous mode of expression which characterizes his part in the Naples original is carefully bowdlerized for Rovigo. Although the four new scenes for Beltramme and for Deidamia, all peculiar to the Rovigo and Trent versions, are less episodic than the scenes which they replace in the Naples original, in both Rovigo and Trent they account, nonetheless, for four of the five breaks in the *liaison des scènes*. The Beltramme of the Florence revision is as bumbling and cowardly as his predecessors but so coarse that a line of the aria in his only solo scene (III/10) seems to have been eliminated from the printed libretto by the censors:

> Certe donzelle
> Perchè son belle
> Fanno l'ardite.
> Ma botto botto
>
> . . . . . .
>
> Restan ferite.

The Mantuan Beltramme, now acting only as messenger between Rosmira and Climene (a princess from Rhodes who, like Rovigo's Deidamia,[6] is in love with Eurimene, but whose recitatives and arias

---

[5] I-Nc 32.2.3, the only extant score for the Naples production of 1699, cuts a dozen lines of recitative and a Beltramme aria in III/6, eighteen lines of recitative in III/11 (eliminating not only the ribald scene of Beltramme's feigned pregnancy but also, unfortunately, his mimicry of serious arias sung by other singers in the cast), and all of I/11. These cuts are precisely the same as those in D-Dl Mus. I/F/39, a two-volume manuscript of uncertain provenance comprising *scene buffe* from eighteen Neapolitan productions from just before and after the turn of the century.

[6] The addition of Deidamia and Climene to the Rovigo-Trent and Mantua versions respectively made possible not only the inclusion of an additional virtuoso

are altogether distinct from the Rovigo version), no longer has any scenes of his own, but manages a duet with Climene and an innocuous solo aria in II/6. Beltramme's entirely humorless role in Venice is cut to two dozen lines of recitative in four scenes with Rosmira, the carrying out of whose orders is Beltramme's only activity in the libretto. His only speech of more than three lines (eight lines in II/6) is necessary only by way of preparation for Rosmira's scene-ending exit aria. The Beltramme part for Milan and Livorno is precisely the same as in the Venetian version, except that the Milanese servant is called Niso, a name which is later taken over for the otherwise Rovigo-oriented servant role of the Trent revision. An additional peculiarity in the servant role of the Trent libretto concerns the interjection of recitatives and arias for Niso at moments (I/14, II/1, II/5, III/2, III/3, III/7) which, in all the other *Partenope* libretti, involve no servant: most of the comic interpolations in Trent concern Niso's efforts to appear valorous while avoiding battle, but none of them is indecorous. Hardly necessary in either the Venice or Milan revision, the servant role is cut altogether for the productions in Ferrara, Bologna, Rimini, and Modena. The Brescia revision is the only one of the twelve which retains both of the comic characters from the Neapolitan original, albeit in functionless, vestigial roles that between them do not amount to twenty lines of recitative. It should be noted, of course, that although the *Partenope* revisions show a clear decrease in the importance of the comic characters, there is no concomitant attempt to imitate the more gradual and logical method of plot development which characterizes the libretti of Zeno. Arsace is as unable in Modena as he was in Naples to decide between Partenope and Rosmira, while Rosmira's vacillation between love and vengeance for Arsace is resolved in all thirteen versions through that monument to seventeenth-century impropriety, Arsace's challenge to a bare-chested duel.

---

in both libretti but also the use of endings which involve symmetrical pairings off of all the principal singers. Opera-ending marriages vary from production to production as follows: Naples and Brescia—Partenope and Armindo, Rosmira and Arsace, Anfrisa and Beltramme; Rovigo and Trent—Partenope and Emilio, Rosmira and Arsace, Deidamia and Armindo; Mantua—Partenope and Armindo, Rosmira and Arsace, Climene and Ormonte; Florence, Venice, Ferrara, Bologna, Milan, Livorno, Rimini, and Modena—Partenope and Armindo, Rosmira and Arsace.

Table 4 shows a general decrease in the proportion of musical numbers to numbers of scenes, and hence, because of the relatively constant numbers of recitative lines among analogous versions of the same scene, a general falling off in the proportion of musical numbers to recitative dialogue, at least with respect to the libretti.

TABLE 4

	No. of scenes	No. of musical numbers	Ratio
Naples	38	65	1.7
Rovigo	33	53	1.6
Mantua	37	61	1.6
Florence	33	51	1.5
Venice	34	45	1.3
Ferrara	36	50	1.4
Bologna	33	43	1.3
Brescia	35	43	1.2
Milan	35	45	1.3
Livorno	33	40	1.2
Trent	35	52	1.5
Rimini	32	38	1.2
Modena	38	30	.8

Table 5 indicates that this was at first the result of reductions in the shares of the comic roles and of the secondary singers, later of general cuts in the principal roles. There is a decline in the number of entrance-, medial-, and medial-exit arias, but only in the Brescia, Livorno, and Modena versions is there any notable increase in the percentage of scene-ending exit arias, as is shown in Table 6.[7]

Although the number of sets varies from ten in the Naples and Rovigo productions to six in the Modena version, there is no evi-

[7] Although a "medial-exit aria" and a "scene-ending exit aria" may often have been indistinguishable in actual performance, they would not have seemed so to many of the more literary librettists of the period. Anxious to impress their Arcadian colleagues with the degree to which an operatic libretto might follow precepts proper to classical tragedy, poets like Zeno resented the interruption of aria verses, especially those occurring in the midst of scenes. (Considerations such as these may lie behind a characteristic shared among the *Partenope*s by the Brescia [I/8-9, I/13-14, II/6-7, II/9-10, III/5-6] and Modena [I/5-6, I/10-12, III/4-5] libretti but observable in many libretto families of the period: the tendency to rearrange divisions between scenes so that, through the creation of additional scenes but without other significant changes in recitatives or arias, arias not previously of the scene-ending exit variety are transformed so as to become such arias.)

TABLE 5

	A	B	C	D	E	F	G	H	I	J	Chorus	Totals by city	Minus ensemble duplications	No. of musical numbers
Naples	14	13	15	11	4	4	9	10			1	81	16	65
Rovigo	13	13	13	8	3			4	9		1	64	11	53
Mantua	13	13	15	12	5	6		2		6	1	73	12	61
Florence	12	12	14	10	4	3		3			1	59	8	51
Venice	13	13	16	7	6	1		0			1	57	12	45
Ferrara	13	14	15	10	6	3					2	63	13	50
Bologna	13	13	13	9	3	2					1	54	11	43
Brescia	12	13	13	9	2	1	0	0			2	52	9	43
Milan	12	12	15	7	5	4		0			1	56	11	45
Livorno	12	11	12	5	3	3		0			1	47	7	40
Trent	11	12	11	6	3			5	8		1	57	5	52
Rimini	12	10	13	5	3	2					1	46	8	38
Modena	10	8	8	5	3	3					1	38	8	30

TABLE 6

	Total musical numbers	Entrance arias	Medial arias	Medial-exit arias	Scene-ending arias	Scene-ending exit #	Scene-ending arias %
Naples	65	4	7	17	7	30	46
Rovigo	53	4	4	13	6	26	49
Mantua	61	4	5	17	6	29	48
Florence	51	2	4	15	6	24	47
Venice	45	3	2	10	9	21	47
Ferrara	50	3	2	11	8	26	52
Bologna	43	1	3	13	5	21	49
Brescia	43	2	3	5	5	28	65
Milan	45	4	1	10	7	23	51
Livorno	40	1	0	10	5	24	60
Trent	52	2	1	15	6	28	54
Rimini	38	1	1	12	5	19	50
Modena	30	1	0	2	3	24	80

dence that the reduction in number resulted directly from Arcadian influence. None of the libretti boasts about any effort at emulating Aristotle's well-known unity of place; both the Bologna and Rimini libretti actually apologize for the limited number of sets used in those productions by blaming the restricted facilities. Significant is

the degree of freedom with which set changes were added and sub-
tracted and the extent to which especially the Mantua, Venice, and
Ferrara productions ignore the scenic specifications of the Naples
original. In Naples and Florence, for example, the opening set is
described as "part of the city near the sea" and "in the country near
the city," but in Mantua it takes place in "an entrance of the royal
palace" and in Ferrara in "a vestibule of the great temple of Apollo."
Similarly, Naples' Act III opens in a large gallery and Florence's in
a courtyard, but Mantua's begins in indoor apartments, Ferrara's in
a garden across from the palace, and Venice's in a location mysteri-
ously identified only with the adjective "grottesco." It would appear
that Italian audiences continued to expect several stage sets per act;
but since *Partenope*, like most other such works of the period, could
be equally well represented before a considerable variety of stage
sets, local impresarios probably paid more attention to the tastes of
local audiences, to the specific abilities of the local set painter and
machinist, and no doubt to the use of expensive sets in storage from
previous productions than they did to the manner in which the work
had been staged originally.

Tables 1 through 3 show a drop from the eight breaks in the
Naples *liaison des scènes* to the three breaks in the Brescia revision,
but this decrease results more often from the elimination of comic
scenes than from the rearrangement of material that is actually
retained. That new breaks in the *liaison des scènes* not present in
the Neapolitan original result *only* from the elimination of stage sets,
and that scenes added for new characters (Deidamia in the Rovigo
and Trent versions and Climene in the Mantuan) occur *only* at spots
where breaks had already occurred in the Neapolitan *liaison des
scènes* as the result of comic scenes, suggests that continuity of stage
action was a meaningful but by no means decisive consideration to
those responsible for the revisions.[8]

Although there are uncounted eighteenth-century libretti whose
identical or similar titles suggest a family relationship not borne out
by actual comparison, the thirteen libretti under study here are
related not only through the similarity of their sequences of scenes,
but also through their almost exactly identical lines of recitative. The
same five lines of recitative are cut from I/1 in all revisions except

---

[8] For a discussion of some artistic and practical problems which result from ignoring the *liaison des scènes*, see Perrucci, *Dell'arte rappresentativa*, pp. 148-50.

those for Venice, Milan, and Livorno, apparently because a number of theaters preferred not to represent the flight of numerous swans and eagles to which the cut lines refer. The combat scene which originally opened Act II is cut in Florence,[9] while additional material for Emilio, including a new solo scene, is supplied in Venice and retained in all subsequent cities except Brescia, though in a somewhat reorganized form in the Bologna, Rimini, and Modena libretti—a group which, as we shall see, bears other family resemblances. Otherwise, such minor changes as occur in the recitatives appear only in connection with the dropping of old characters and the adding of new ones, and in connection with short passages of recitative that are cut or added because of arias that are cut or added, or because of arias whose positioning has been changed.

This is not a statement which can be made with respect to the arias. From Tables 1 through 3 we have already seen the extent to which the revisions, while eliminating many arias without replacing them, add other arias in positions where none were present originally. Table 7 indicates the number of occasions in which an aria text is replaced, in the same position, by an apparently new aria text

TABLE 7
NUMBER OF SUBSTITUTED ARIA TEXTS—BY ROLE

	A	B	C	D	E	F	H	I	*Total per revision*
Rovigo	1	2		1		2			6
Mantua	3	2	6			1	1		13
Florence		1		1					2
Venice	3	5	3	duet					12
Ferrara	3	2	2	5	3	2			17
Bologna	2	4	4	6					16
Brescia		1	2	2					5
Milan		1	2	1		3			7
Livorno	5	2	1	2	2	2			15
	duet								
Trent	1	2	2	3			3	3	14
Rimini[10]		1		1					2
Modena	5	5	4	3	3	2			22

[9] In Brescia the scene is transferred to the end of Act I.

[10] An appendix following the final scene of the Rimini libretto contains aria texts which do not appear in the body of the libretto: for Rosmira (I/5), Emilio (II/2, II/4), Armindo (II/9), and Ormonte (II/10).

for the same character. The relatively high number of aria substitutions in specific revisions and in specific roles suggests that impresarios yielded to the wishes of the most importunate singers, and that some impresarios yielded more easily than did others. We know from Benedetto Marcello's *Teatro alla moda* and from the less famous operatic criticism of Marcello's Bolognese contemporary, Pier Jacopo Martello, that the librettists of the period were often obliged to do the bidding of the singers. I quote from the harangue against contemporary operatic practices which Martello addresses to himself through the person of an old hunchback who claims to be Aristotle, miraculously preserved over the centuries through the use of a secret elixir:

La professione del compor melodrammi, Martello mio, è una scuola per voi di morale che più di ogni altra insegna a' poeti il vincer se stressi, rinunciando al proprio desiderio. Fatti ben animo a cangiar l'arie non cattive in cattive; se un musico o se una musica vorranno al piè di un tuo recitativo conficcarne una che abbia guadagnato loro l'applauso in Milano, in Vinegia, in Genova, o altrove, e sia pur lontana dal sentimento, lo quale dovrebbe ivi esprimersi, che importa? Lasciala lor metter dentro, altrimenti te li vedrai tutti addosso trafiggerti le tempie con soprani e contralti rimproveri. Il meglio che ti possa accadere sarà il ridurli a capitolare che ti si permetta lo stirare su quelle note parole men discordanti dal tuo sentimento, nel qual caso t'intralcerai in un impegno spinoso. Non conto per niente l'eguaglianza de' versi e delle sillabe, conto il conservare nelle parole quelle vocali su cui dee passeggiare la voce del musico. L'A potrà cangiarsi nella E, non nella I, perché nitrirebbe, e abbaierebbe nella U. Déi conservare ancora gli accenti, altrimenti le brevi sillable ti pronunzieran lunghe, e

Martello, my friend, the profession of writing libretti is a school of morals which, more than any other, teaches poets how to conquer themselves by renouncing their own wishes. Take heart, and change arias that are not bad into those that are. If a singer would like to nail to the foot of one of your recitatives an aria which has won the public's applause in Milan, Venice, Genoa, or elsewhere, even though the aria in question is far from the sentiment which ought to be expressed at the place where it occurs, what does it matter? Let the singer insert the new aria, otherwise you will see yourself attacked on all sides, your head splitting with reproaches of sopranos and contraltos. The best that can befall you will lie in forcing the singers to agree that for the already-composed music you be permitted to write words that are less discordant to your original sentiment; but in this case you entangle yourself in a thorny obligation. That the new verses be equal to the old in the number of both lines and syllables is not a matter that can be neglected; of special importance is the preservation in your new

lunghe le brevi. Ma dimmi, e qual ripiego troverai tu se in luogo di un' aria di sdegno, che vi era già collocata, un'altra vi si dee porre che era d'amore e che di sdegnose parole vuol rivertirsi? Se non è stato un gaglioffo il compositore di quella musica, avrà adattate le note a quella prima espressione tal che non riusciran poi adattabili alla seconda. Io dunque stimerei sempre meglio il permettere che i musici a loro talento cacciassero l'arie, ove vogliono, che il farmi complice del lor mancamento col caricarle. E basta bene che non discordino nella tessitura musicale, della qual cosa lascia tutto il pensiero al maestro di cappella.[11]

text of those vowels on which the voice of the singer can make rapid melismas. An "A" can be changed to an "E" but not to an "I," since this would produce a neighing effect and would bark itself into a "U." In addition, you must preserve the accents, otherwise the short syllables would be produced long and the long short. But tell me, what solution will you find if, in the position of an aria of scorn and disdain, already established in its niche, you have to use another whose text *was* love but which has now to be reclothed with a scornful text? Unless he was a lout, the composer of the original setting will have adapted his notes to the expression of the original text, so that the music can no longer be successfully adapted to the new text. In such a case I would always deem it better to allow the singers to insinuate their own talents into the arias wherever they wish, rather than make myself an accomplice to their mistakes in overloading the notes. It is enough that the new arias do not clash with the music of those already present, a concern which you should leave entirely to the composer.

In arriving at the substitute aria texts whose distribution is summarized in Table 7, the anonymous poets probably followed a variety of procedures. If a singer were to insist on performing the music of some aria "x," not originally part of the opera being staged, the poet might write a new text for "x," reversifying the poetic ideas involved in the text of aria "y," previously used in this position, according to principles something like those outlined by Martello. The Mantuan revision of Arsace's aria at the end of I/3 will serve as an illustration of the discernible tendency in the revisions toward a reduction in the number of lines and syllables.

[11] Martello, *Della tragedia*, pp. 290-91.

Naples	Mantua
O Eurimene ha l'idea di Rosmira	Mie pupille, o m'ingannate
O Rosmira si finge Eurimene.	O mirate il primo amor;
Più lo sguardo in quel volto s'aggira	Veggio ben sue luci vaghe
Più confusa quest'alma diviene.	Da le piaghe del mio cor.

Sometimes the poet was able in his revision to preserve not only the ideas of the original text but many of the actual words as well. An example from the Bologna revision of Arsace's aria at the end of I/6:

Naples	Bologna
Sempre il più dolce strale	Sento amor con nuovi dardi
E' il primo stral d'amore,	Ma il più dolce è il primo strale,
A mille nuovi dardi	E fra cento accesi sguardi
Il primo sol prevale,	Il primiero al fin prevale.
Che fanno i primi sguardi	
Di due pupille vaghe	
Eterne piaghe al core.	

In the absence of musical remains for any of the post-Naples productions under study here, we have no trace of the original texts for the substitute arias. Hence, we are unable to determine the degree to which the poets of the revisions followed Martello's advice about preserving those texts' poetic structure in reversifying ideas that had been the bases for earlier *Partenope* arias. But the substitute aria texts leave no doubt about the sensitivity of most contemporary operatic poets to the demand for singable texts whose sentences end with words involving open A's and O's.

Martello seems to suggest that a singer working for a company whose poet was too proud, too stupid, too lazy, or too overworked to write verses for already-existing music was sometimes allowed to perform both the music and the text of an aria already in his repertory, without any revision of the text. Given the present state of our bibliographic resources for the repertory to which *Partenope* belongs, the only means for recognizing such instances lies in detecting the inappropriateness of a substitute text to the dramatic situation in which it appears. But *Partenope*, like many another early eighteenth-century libretto, abounds in situations where one could easily imagine a considerable variety of aria texts; and, although many of the substitute aria texts used in the *Partenope* revisions are quite different from the texts they replace, not one seems sufficiently inappropriate to the position where it occurs to suggest recourse to the procedure just outlined. For example, in describing his love for Partenope toward the end of Act III, Armindo is permitted the use of all three of the following texts:

NAPLES AND MANTUA	FLORENCE
Destommi amore	Vezzose pupillette
Tempeste al core,	Co' lampi e con saette
E fu quest'alma	Voi m'accendete il cor,
La Navicella.	A i raggi di due faci
Al fin su'l lido	Si belle e si vivaci
Gioisco, e rido,	Fenice io son d'amor.
Cangiossi in calma	
La mia procella.	

FERRARA
La viola a rai del sole
Mesta langue, e il soffre, e tace
Che quel raggio è sua beltà;
Il mio core al vivo raggio,
Langue e tace,
E al suo duol spera pietà.

These texts are as different from each other as any used in the thirteen libretti on which this study is based, but the essentials of semantics and metaphor are sufficiently alike so that the dramatic situation which motivated the one could well have motivated the others. If a singer in any of the *Partenope* revisions was allowed to substitute both text and music of an aria used previously in another work, his choice of aria was circumscribed by dramatic considerations. Perhaps Martello's permission that the singers ". . . cacciassero l'arie ove vogliono" was intended more as humorous exaggeration than as serious advice. The creation of characters clearly enough drawn in the recitatives as to discourage the use of such contrasting substitute arias as the above is one of the unrecognized achievements of Apostolo Zeno.[12] A natural consequence of this achievement is the apparent disappearance, later in the century, of such phenomena as the Rovigo production's role for Deidamia, a centonate role comprising five new arias (three of them in positions previously taken by the comedians of the intermediary scenes)[13] and three arias which

[12] For more information on this development, see my Princeton University dissertation (1967), "Opera without Drama; Currents of Change in Italian Opera, 1675 to 1725, and the Roles Played Therein by Zeno, Caldara, and Others."
[13] In the preface to the libretto for the Venice production these scenes are actually called "intermezzi"!

had actually belonged in the Naples production to the roles of Arsace and Armindo.

The appearance in a libretto revision of a substitute aria more appropriate than the original to the dramatic situation in which it occurs, suggests either that the poet responsible for the revision was very skillful or that he was able to complete his new aria text before passing it on to the composer who set it. The aria which Partenope addresses to Arsace in I/10 of the Naples original could, for example, be used in a variety of circumstances, but the aria which she uses in the Mantuan revision has, though Partenope does not yet realize it herself at the time she is singing it, a particular relevance which the Neapolitan original lacks.

NAPLES	MANTUA
Solo per te ben mio	Per te solo, amato bene
Solo per te vogl'io	Vo saper, che cosa è amar;
Languir d'amore,	La beltà d'un caro amore
Altri non vuo, che sia	Perde assai del suo splendore
Alma de l'alma mia,	Quando è facile a cangiar.
Cor del mio core.	

It should be mentioned, finally, that in studying substitute arias from libretti, in this case the only available sources, there is no way of detecting those frequent changes which affect the music performed without leaving any visible trace in the libretto—changes in the music made to accommodate the varying abilities of a role's successive performers.

That singers' previous "hits" were not the only source for substitute arias and that singers' whims were not the only determinative force in the substitution of new arias for old is suggested by several provocative results of our comparative study of the thirteen *Partenope* libretti. The similarity of Rosmira's substitute aria text in Venice I/13 to a text sung by an altogether different soprano in *Gli equivoci del sembiante*, another libretto set five years earlier by the composer of the Venetian *Partenope*, Antonio Caldara,[14] suggests that singer and composer may well have paged together through the latter's old scores in a search for substitute arias.

[14] *Gli equivoci del sembiante*, dramma per musica da rappresentarsi nel Teatro Novo di Casale l'anno 1703 (libretto I-Bc 732). That it was Caldara who set this libretto is certified on page 4, after the *argomento*.

NAPLES—I/15
Rosmira's aria
S'havessi un altro core
Saprei cangiar desio;
Se ti scoprisse amore
Quel ben, che l'alma adora
Tu scorgeresti al'ora
Quanto fedel son'io.

VENICE—I/13
Rosmira's aria
La mia fè vivace e bella
Per te sempre splenderà;
Che s'ho al cor qualche facella,
Mai la tua non turberà.

GLI EQUIVOCI—I/10
Ortano's aria
La mia fè vivace e bella
Anche in ombre splenderà;
E nel ciel fatta una stella
Al suo sol s'aggirerà.

Another striking substitution involving Rosmira's last aria in Act I concerns the Rovigo production, where the part of Rosmira was taken by the Signora Maria Maddalena Manfredi, a soprano of the Duke of Savoy and the only singer in the Rovigo cast who had participated in the original Naples production; there too she had sung the part of Rosmira. Although the Naples and Rovigo performances were separated by less than a year and although all of the other principals in the Rovigo cast used nothing but aria texts sung earlier in the year at Naples, Signora Manfredi's Rovigo role included a substitute aria in I/15. It is possible that her substitute aria in Rovigo was the reversification of an aria with which she had had unusual success during the months between the Naples and Rovigo productions or the result of her dissatisfaction with an aria she had sung in Naples.[15] The only other instance in the thirteen *Partenopes* where we know that the same singer performed the same part on two separate occasions[16] involves a substitute aria that did not originate with the singer in question. Antonio Archi, a castrato in the service of the Duke of Mantua before the collapse of Gonzagan rule in 1707, sang the role of Arsace in the Florence production of 1701 and again in the Ferrara production of 1709. Of the fifteen non-

[15] The substitution in II/6 of I-Nc 32.2.3 of a new aria for Signora Manfredi on a text that appears subsequently in the Rovigo libretto supports such an interpretation.

[16] The Mantua, Milan, and Rimini libretti are the only *Partenopes* studied which do not indicate the singers for those productions.

choral numbers in which Archi participated in Ferrara, eleven were on texts that he had sung earlier in Florence, one was part of an ensemble common to Naples and Ferrara that had been cut in Florence, and two were substitute arias introduced in Ferrara and peculiar to that version. One, however, was a substitute aria introduced in the Venice production of 1708, where it had been sung, not by Archi, but by Nicola Grimaldi. This is the only detectable instance in the thirteen *Partenope* libretti where a singer, performing the same role for a second time, used a text invented on a previous occasion for another singer. But it is by no means the only instance of an aria text which, substituted in one production of the work, then reappeared in some of the subsequent revisions. Table 8 summarizes these cases, indicating the previous *Partenope* libretti in which each of the migrating substitute arias had already appeared. The names of cities are replaced in the table by the following lower-case letters: Rovigo—k; Mantua—l; Venice—m; Ferrara—n; Bologna—o; Brescia—p; Milan—q; Livorno—r; Trent—s; Rimini—t. Capital letters represent the characters, as listed above.

Unless one is prepared to believe that the libretti for the post-Venice productions were wholly the result of local collations of previously printed libretti,[17] it would appear that some body (or bodies) of printed and manuscript material must have accompanied *Partenope* from town to town. Table 9 shows what the evidence of Tables 1, 2, 3 and 8 indicates as the apparent genealogy of the thirteen *Partenopes*. That the exact relationship of the individual libretti cannot be stated with certainty results from the lack of musical remains for all but the Naples production, from the absence of source material of any kind for productions in Genoa (1704), Vicenza (1714), and Bologna (1719),[18] and from the distinct possibility that there were still other productions between 1699 and 1720 that have disappeared without a trace.

[17] That eighteenth-century librettists were sometimes avid collectors of other poets' libretti indicates that one cannot discount the possibility of such collations. See, for example, Apostolo Zeno's personal libretto library, among the holdings of the Biblioteca Marciana, Venice.

[18] The evidence for the Genoa production consists of an entry in an eighteenth-century manuscript chronology of Genoese opera, part of the basis for a catalogue of opera produced in Genoa between 1652 and 1771 that forms an appendix to Remo Giazotto's *La musica a Genova* (Genoa, 1951).

TABLE 8

	A	B	C	D	E	I	Chorus
Florence		II/4 (k)	II/7 (m)				
Ferrara	I/9 (m)	I/9 (m), III/7 (m)	III/4 (m)	III/3 (m)			
Bologna	III/2 (m)	I/9 (mn), II/7 (m)	II/5 (m)				
Brescia	I/8 (mn), II/1 (n) III/2 (m)	I/8 (mn), III/4 (m)	III/4 (m)				I/1 (n)
Milan	I/9 (mnp), I/11 (o) III/2 (mop)	I/9 (mnop), III/4 (mp) I/13 (m), III/7 (mn)	I/5 (m), III/4 (mp) II/8 (mn)	I/7 (o)	II/3 (m)		
Livorno	III/2 (mopq)	I/12 (m), II/6 (mo), III/4 (mpq), III/7 (mnq)	II/7 (mnpq) III/4 (mpq) III/8 (m)		III/9 (moq)		
Trent	I/13 (oq) III/2 (mopqr)	II/7 (mor) III/4 (mpqr)	I/3 (q) III/4 (mpqr) III/9 (q)	I/4 (k) I/8 (oq)	II/2 (mq)		
Rimini	I/9 (o) I/11 (oqs) III/2 (mopqrs)	I/4 (o), I/9 (mnopq) II/7 (mors), III/4 (o) III/7 (o)	I/5 (o) II/8 (mnpqr) III/4 (o) III/7 (o)	I/7 (oqs) II/9 (o) III/5 (o)	III/8 (moqr)	I/2 (k) I/11 (k) III/5 (k)	
Modena	III/2 (mopqrst)						

TABLE 9

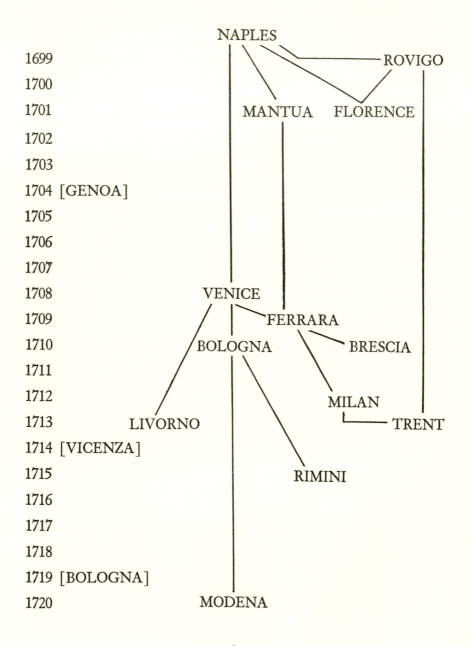

1699

1700

1701

1702

1703

1704 [GENOA]

1705

1706

1707

1708

1709

1710

1711

1712

1713

1714 [VICENZA]

1715

1716

1717

1718

1719 [BOLOGNA]

1720

Of special interest are the focal position occupied in the genealogy by Venice and the fact that productions as late as those in Ferrara and Trent—while drawing on many of the substitute aria texts apparently introduced in Venice—nonetheless include elements otherwise peculiar to the early productions of Mantua and Rovigo. Table 8, taken together with the lists of participating singers that are prefatory to several of the libretti, indicates the unlikelihood that any of the *Partenope* materials were carried from one production to another by a singer.

Sesini's attribution of the music for the productions in Naples, Mantua, Florence, Venice, and Milan (and of some of the music for the Ferrara production) to Antonio Caldara[19] suggests yet another possible means of transmission for the *Partenope* materials. Sesini's attributions, based on manuscript entries on the title pages of the Bologna Conservatory's copies of the libretti for the productions just listed, are supported for the Venetian production by contemporary catalogues of operatic productions.[20] But the appearance of other manuscript entries in the same anonymous hands on the title pages of other libretti in the Bologna Conservatory Library indicates that such attributions were probably made too long after the fact to be reliable,[21] especially in the face of conflicting and apparently more contemporary evidence. The conflicting evidence consists in this case of attributions in I-Nc 32.2.3 and in D-Dl Mus. I/F/39/II (scores stemming from the original Naples production of *Partenope*) and in the libretti from the Rovigo and Brescia productions to a shadowy

[19] *Catalogo della Biblioteca del Liceo Musicale di Bologna*, v (ed. Ugo Sesini) (Bologna, 1943), I, 81.

[20] *Le glorie della poesia e della musica contenute nell'esatta notitia de'teatri della città di Venezia*, published anonymously by Giovanni Carlo Bonlini (Venice, 1730), p. 154; *Drammaturgia di Lione Allacci accresciuta* (Venice, 1755), p. 600. The following attribution appears in print on page 11 of the Ferrara libretto: "La musica è parte del Sig. Antonio Caldara e parte del Sig. Giuseppe Beniventi." Other composers who seem to have contributed to the first twenty years of *Partenope* productions include Luca Antonio Predieri, identified in a manuscript entry on the title page of I-Bc 6908 as the composer of the 1710 Bologna production, and Antonio Quintavalle, identified on page iv of the Trent libretto as "Maestro di Cappella di Sua Altezza Reverendiss., e di questa Insigne Cattedrale," and credited in the same place with having sustained the production at Trent through his "virtuosissima composizione."

[21] Prof. Nino Pirrotta suggests that the manuscript attributions to Caldara probably result from that variety of uncritical inference (often based on catalogues like those of Groppo, Bonlini, and Allacci) which bedevils so much of early operatic history.

composer whose name appears variously in the earliest of the four sources as Luiggi Manzo, Luigi Mancia, and Sig. Mancia.[22] That Caldara and Mancia were not one and the same composer, operating in different cities under different names, is indicated by a comparison of the Neapolitan score for *Partenope* with the chronologically closest of Caldara's many extant composing scores, the *Opera Pastorale* of 1701.[23] The arias of the Neapolitan *Partenope* score, predominantly syllabic and seldom involving word repetition or the twofold presentation of the first section of aria text which characterizes the main section of most *da capo* arias of the period between 1700 and 1750, are considerably shorter than the average Caldara aria of 1701. Striking, too, in a comparison of the two scores is the much more elaborate and specific instrumentation of the Naples score, in which divided viola parts are a frequent feature of a typically five- or six-voice texture. "Continuo arias," much less frequent in the Naples score than in the Caldara autograph of 1701, are normally accompanied in the earlier score by lute and violoncello. The average rate of harmonic change in the dramatically more convincing recitatives of the Naples score is considerably slower than in the Caldara score; and the cadential formula which, beginning on any of the twelve pitch classes and in a variety of rhythmic patterns, occurs so often in Caldara's recitatives that it becomes a reliable means of distinguishing his operatic scores from those of his early eighteenth-century contemporaries, hardly appears in I-Nc 32.2.3.

But if Caldara was not the composer of the *Partenope* score performed in Naples in 1699, there is reason, beyond the apparently unreliable manuscript attributions on the title pages of the Bologna Conservatory libretti, for believing that he had already written music for *Partenope* before the 1708 production in Venice. As *Maestro di cappella* of the Mantuan court for two years before the production of *Partenope* planned there for the spring of 1701, Caldara would normally have been responsible for whatever new music had to be

---

[22] For more information on this composer, see the "Mancia" articles in *MGG* and in the recently completed *Enciclopedia della musica*; and especially Claudio Sartori, "Il dilettante Luigi Mancia, dignitario dell'Imperatore," *RMI*, LV, 404-25. In his *MGG* article, Sartori mentions other orthographic variants that have appeared in musical lexicons: Luigi Manza and Carlo Manza.

[23] A-Wgm Caldara autograph 37.

written for that occasion.[24] That the two concluding lines of recitative in Mantua I/8 and in Ferrara I/7 are the only element
peculiar to those two libretti and that Caldara is listed in an eighteenth-century manuscript chronology of Genoese opera as the composer of the *Partenope* staged in Genoa during 1704,[25] are two additional indications that Caldara may have participated in the Mantuan
production of 1701. On the other hand, it seems unlikely that Caldara
was involved in the Florence production during the fall of 1701 for,
although the libretto for that production lists three Mantuan singers,
it contains none of the eighteen added or substituted arias which
differentiate the Mantuan libretto from the Naples libretto.[26]

In investigating an apparently popular libretto and its reworkings
all over northern Italy during a brief but critical period in the
history of Italian opera, we have observed a notable lack of interest
in several of the directions toward which the most progressive
librettists of the period were working. This lack of interest, except
in the case of the Neapolitan original itself (the work of Silvio
Stampiglia, one of the fourteen founding members of the Arcadian
Academy),[27] is not surprising, for one does not expect to find the
most recent literary tendencies manifested in the labors of hacks
charged with the pasting together of the poetic odds and ends to
which Martello alludes. The assertion put forward in so many
Venetian libretto prefaces that the audiences of that city were particularly fond of brevity is fully borne out in the number of arias
replaced in the Venetian *Partenope* by two or three lines of recitative each. But the thirteen libretti studied here form too small a part
of the larger picture to tell us what we seek to know about the local
traditions (except perhaps for Neapolitan coarseness) that must have
determined many of the revisions.

[24] The evidence summarized by Ursula Kirkendale in her recent article, "The
War of the Spanish Succession Reflected in Works of Antonio Caldara," *Acta*, xxxvi,
223, is supplemented by newly discovered documents in a forthcoming article of my
own.

[25] Giazotto, *La musica a Genova*, p. 327.

[26] It is puzzling why the post-Mantua revisions fail to use even a single one of
the fourteen substitute texts introduced in Mantua, especially since Caldara was
not the only Mantuan composer involved with *Partenope*. Antonio Quintavalle, the
composer mentioned in the preface of the Trent libretto, had been the organist
of the Mantuan court chapel during Caldara's tenure there as *maestro di cappella*.

[27] Michele Maylender, *Storia delle accademie d'Italia* (Bologna, 1926), I, 247.

We have learned something of the procedures in use for the adaptation of an old libretto to changing circumstances in a number of different cities. But our observations are too much the result of inference from specifically limited source materials[28] to provide satisfactory answers for the questions raised in the first paragraph of this paper. The following tools—not now in existence but, partly because of recent strides in the application of the computer to humanistic studies, within the realm of the possible—would help to provide some of those answers.

1. Alphabetic indices of the first lines of operatic arias used over specific periods of time and within specific geographical areas, or drawn up on the basis of the holdings of specific libraries rich in the requisite scores and libretti.

[28] Just as this paper was ready for the press, I discovered two important additional musical sources: US-Wc M1500.S26P3 and US-Wc M1500.V64P4, copy scores of originals in the Gesellschaft der Musikfreunde (Vienna) and in the British Museum, attributed to Domenico Sarro and to Leonardo Vinci, respectively. These two scores, which seem to stem from productions of *Partenope* staged during 1722 in Naples and during 1724 in Rome, share not only fourteen substitute aria texts found in none of the other *Partenope*s studied, but also a great deal of musical material (none of which appears in the "Mancia" score of 1699): short snippets of instrumental music, two choruses, and almost all of the recitative. That the "Vinci" score in the British Museum is a Vinci autograph which suggests nothing of Vinci's indebtedness to Sarro, is an additional indication of the pitfalls awaiting those too ready to take even contemporary attributions on eighteenth-century operatic scores at face value. Frank Walker's demonstration (*MQ*, xxxviii, 369-83) that an early eighteenth-century *opera buffa*, after circulating for several years, might end as a mélange containing material by several composers—an unadvertised pasticcio—is shown by our study of the *Partenope*s to apply equally to an opera of the so-called *seria* variety.

Other points concerning both the "Sarro" and "Vinci" scores as well as Handel's autograph score (GB-Lbm R.M.20.6.11) for the London *Partenope* of 1730 are summarized below:

1. The "Sarro" score includes comic "intermezzi" for Beltramme and Eurilla between Acts I and II, at the end of Act II, and as the penultimate scene in Act III. None of the three is taken from the only other known *Partenope* production containing such scenes, the Naples original of 1699.
2. The libretto used by Handel contains substitute aria texts introduced earlier in the productions of Venice, Bologna, and Modena as well as half a dozen texts that were apparently new in 1730; but it also shares eighteen aria texts with the Naples original of 1699, a conservatively high number for a production so distant in time from 1699.
3. The Handel autograph, prepared for a production which involved three singers who had already performed in the Ferrara and "Sarro" productions, albeit in different roles, contains no musical borrowings from "Mancia," "Sarro," or "Vinci."

2. Thematic indices of aria incipits.
3. Biographies of individual singers, based wherever possible on archival materials from the libraries of patrons and impresarios, and concentrating on the kinds of musical and dramatic material specific to the repertories of individual performers.[29]

[29] I am at work now on such a biography of the well-known castrato, Farinelli.

V. STUDIES OF THE GREAT COMPOSERS

HANDEL'S *GIULIO CESARE IN EGITTO*

J. MERRILL KNAPP

OF ALL Handel's operas, *Giulio Cesare in Egitto*, first performed in London on February 20, 1724, is probably the
best known; it has probably also had the most performances since the composer's death. There were thirteen performances
the first season in February, March, and April 1724; ten in January
and February, 1725; eleven in January, February, March 1730, and
four in February, 1732.[1] Loewenberg[2] lists productions in Brunswick,
Hamburg, and Vienna during Handel's lifetime, and a planned one
in Paris in 1724. Dr. Arnold put on a 1787 London performance
under this title, but an examination of the libretto shows the work
was an adaptation of the original, utilizing arias from other Handel
works as well as from *Giulio Cesare in Egitto*.

Modern revivals started with Oskar Hagen in Göttingen in 1922
and continued up to the present in Germany and the rest of the
Continent, as well as in America and England. It is the one Handel
opera which can presently be said to have found a place in the
modern German operatic repertory. Today, there are even three
recordings of the work, though all are considerably abridged.[3]

Reasons for this popularity are not hard to find. The work is one
of the most richly scored of all Handel's operas; it contains a goodly
number of splendid arias and dramatic situations; and the subject
is relatively familiar. Moreover, the so-called monotonous succession
of *opera seria* recitative and aria is broken up in each act by three
of Handel's best accompanied recitatives, three brief choruses, instrumental music, a duet in Act I, and several cavatinas and ariosos.

The subject of the libretto (whose title is seldom given complete
and is the key to the plot) is Caesar's adventures in Egypt after he
vanquished Pompey. Winton Dean has summarized the story well:

---

[1] *The London Stage* (1660-1800), Part 2: 1700-1729, ed. Emmett L. Avery, 2 Vols.
(Carbondale, Illinois: Southern Illinois University Press, 1960), and *The London
Stage*, Part 3: 1729-1747, ed. Arthur H. Scouten, 2 Vols. (1961).

[2] Alfred Loewenberg, *Annals of Opera* (Geneva: Societas Bibliographica, 1955),
p. 150.

[3] Handel Society (HDL-18) (deleted). Handel Society Chorus and Orchestra,
Walter Goehr, conductor. Vox (VUX-2011) (formerly PL8012). Vienna Akade-
miechor and Pro Musica Chamber Orchestra, Hans Swarowsky, conductor. Victor
(LSC 6182). New York City Opera Co., Julius Rudel, conductor. [Many excerpts.]

Caesar has defeated Pompey at the battle of Pharsalia and pursued him to Egypt, where Cleopatra and her brother Ptolemy are engaged in a fratricidal struggle for the throne. Ptolemy, a self-indulgent and treacherous character, tries to win Caesar's favour by murdering Pompey and sending his head as a present. Cleopatra employs subtler means; disguising herself as Lydia, a woman wronged by Ptolemy, she soon fascinates Caesar. Pompey's widow Cornelia and her son Sextus are also in Egypt, and Cornelia's charms are almost as overwhelming as Cleopatra's. During the opera she is the object of indecent advances from three different characters—Ptolemy (who employs her as an under-gardener in his seraglio), his general Achillas, who is as dishonourable as his master, and Caesar's general, Curius. Each time she is rescued at the last minute, generally by Sextus, who in the end disposes of Ptolemy. At intervals mother and son also save each other from suicide and reconsecrate themselves to vengeance. In Act 2 Caesar narrowly evades death at the hands of Ptolemy's assassins and escapes by swimming Alexandria Harbour. In Act 3 Achillas changes sides after a quarrel with Ptolemy over the possession of Cornelia, but is killed in a battle in which Cleopatra is captured. Finally Caesar reasserts his power and is proclaimed Lord of the World, whereupon Cleopatra offers herself (in more than one sense) as a "tributary Queen to Rome's great Emperor."[4]

Nicola Haym, who is generally listed as the author of the libretto,[5] merely appropriated his text (with alterations) from G. F. Bussani's *Giulio Cesare in Egitto*, first set by Antonio Sartorio for Venice in 1677. This was the case for most of Handel's libretti: practically all of the London operas were based on Italian originals of the late seventeenth and early eighteenth centuries. Haym very probably used a later version of this libretto for his source—his aria texts differ from Bussani's—but the recitative is practically the same. A great battle by water and land which takes place on the stage in Bussani is relegated to a position behind the scenes in 1724. Also with Haym, Sextus becomes much more an avenger of his father's death, and Cornelia grieves more. Moreover, the scene at Pompey's

[4] Winton Dean, "Handel's 'Giulio Cesare,'" *The Musical Times*, Vol. 104, No. 1444 (June 1963), p. 402.

[5] Alfred Loewenberg, *Annals of Opera*, p. 150. William C. Smith, "Catalogue of Works" in *Handel a Symposium*, ed. Gerald Abraham (London: Oxford University Press, 1954), p. 289, says Haym is the author, but Edward J. Dent in his chapter, "The Operas" (p. 30 in the same book) gives the correct source.

memorial and Caesar rising from the sea have been added. The cast of characters in Bussani is the same as that given in Haym's 1724 libretto, with the exception of Rodispe, who appears as a nurse of Cleopatra's. Two of the minor parts in 1724—Nireno, Cleopatra's eunuch and Curio, Caesar's general—are much more prominent in this earlier libretto than they are in Haym's. Wolff thinks Handel may have known Bussani's libretto in Germany.[6] It was given in Brunswick in 1691 under the title of *Cleopatra*, with music by J. S. Cousser and the German translation by Friedrich Christian Bressand.

Libretti (which are often the only good source for what was actually heard at a given performance) survive for the first three productions of *Giulio Cesare in Egitto* in London—those of 1724,[7] 1725,[8] and 1730[9]—but no libretto has been found for the 1732 production. These word books also help to sort out the music which Chrysander prints in the Appendix of his *Händelgesellschaft* score.[10]

The first two libretti are the only ones which list singers; the casts for the third and fourth productions (1730 and 1732) must be conjectures. The characters (in their Italian form) and singers with designation of voice range are given below. The 1730 and 1732 casts can be fairly well established by reference to the singers who were on the King's Theatre (Haymarket) roster for the 1729-30 and 1731-32 seasons.

[6] Hellmuth Christian Wolff, *Die Venezianische Oper in der zweiten Hälfte des 17 Jahrhunderts* (Berlin: Elsner, 1937), p. 53.

[7] Giulio Cesare / In Egitto. / Drama / Da Rappresentarsi / Nel Regio Teatro / di Hay-Market. / Per / La Reale Accademia di Musica. // In Londra: Per Tomaso Wood nella Piccola Bretagna. M.DCC.XXIV Quarto. 85 pp. (Copies in British Museum; National Library of Scotland; Bibliothèque du Conservatoire, Paris; Princeton University Library; Rowe Library [2], Kings College, Cambridge; William Andrews Clark Library (University of California at Los Angeles).

[8] Giulio Cesare / In Egitto. / Drama / Da Rappresentarsi / Nel Regio Teatro / di Hay-Market / Per / La Reale Accademia di Musica: // The Second Edition, with alterations. N. B. the Alterations have this " Mark before them. // London; Printed and Sold at the Opera-office in the Hay-Market. M.DCC.XXV. Quarto, 79 pp. (Copies in British Museum [2]; National Library of Scotland; Princeton University Library; Library of Congress, Washington, D. C.)

[9] Giulio Cesare / In Egitto. / Drama. / Da Rappresentarsi / Nel Regio Teatro / di Haymarket. // The Third Edition. // London: / Printed and sold by T. Wood in *Little Britain*. M.DCC.XXX. Quarto. 75 pp. (Copies in Huntington Library, Pasadena, California; Newberry Library, Chicago.)

[10] *Giulio Cesare* (G. F. Händel Werke), ed. Friedrich Chrysander (Leipzig: Deutsche Händelgesellschaft, 1875).

INTERLOCUTORI ROMANI
Giulio Cesare, Imperator de' Romani
Curio, Tribuno di Roma

Cornelia, Moglie di Pompeo

Sesto Pompeo, Figlio di Pompeo e Cornelia

INTERLOCUTORI EGIZZI
Cleopatra, Regina d' Egitto
Tolomeo, Re d' Egitto, Fratello di Cleopatra
Achilla, Generale dell' Armi e Consigliere di Tolomeo
Nireno, Confidente di Cleopatra

FEBRUARY, MARCH, APRIL 1724
Giulio Cesare—Senesino, alto castrato
Curio—Lagarde, bass
Cornelia—Anastasia Robinson, contralto
Sesto—Margherita Durastanti, soprano
Cleopatra—Francesca Cuzzoni, soprano
Tolomeo—Gaetano Berenstadt, alto castrato
Achilla—Giuseppe Boschi, bass
Nireno—Bigonsi, alto castrato

JANUARY, FEBRUARY 1725
Senesino

Anna Dotti, contralto
Francesco Borosini, tenor
Cuzzoni
Andrea Pacini, alto castrato
Boschi

JANUARY, FEBRUARY, MARCH 1730
Giulio Cesare—(Antonio Bernacchi, alto castrato)
Cornelia—(Antonia Merighi, contralto)
Sesto—(Annibale Fabri, tenor)
Cleopatra—(Anna Strada, soprano)
Tolomeo—(Francesca Bertolli, contralto)
Achilla—(Johann Riemschneider, bass)

FEBRUARY 1732
(Senesino)

(Anna Bagnolesi, contralto)
(Giovanni Pinacci, tenor)
(Anna Strada)
(Francesca Bertolli)
(Antonio Montagnana, bass)

After the first season, the parts of Curio and Nireno were cut—their lines being absorbed by the other characters or omitted entirely. Since neither had any arias to sing in the original production, the adjustment came only in the recitative. There is some mystery about Nireno in the 1725 season, which will be discussed subsequently. The only major change in voice range was in Sesto's part—from soprano to tenor in 1725 (and tenor in 1730 and 1732). Tolomeo was probably sung by a woman in 1730 and 1732—Francesca Bertolli—who excelled in taking male parts; but the voice range remained the same as it was in 1724 and 1725.

The stars of the original production were Senesino and Cuzzoni, particularly the latter who was given some of the finest music in the opera. Anastasia Robinson's voice had sunk from soprano to contralto several years earlier, and this was to be her last season with the Royal Academy. Durastanti, who also specialized in male roles and had been a bulwark of the company, left London after the 1724 season. Boschi, the dependable bass-baritone, had his usual villain role. The most we know about Berenstadt is that he was "an *evirato* of a huge, unwieldy figure."[11] The finest addition in the 1724-25 season was the tenor, Francesco Borosini, who took the leading role in *Tamerlano* and sang Sesto in *Giulio Cesare in Egitto*. Quantz called him a splendid singer and a fine actor with a voice that was "ausserordentlich biegsam und lebhaft."

Handel's autograph of the opera (R.M.20.b.3) is worthy of a study in itself. It is really a series of sketches, many of which were reworked or discarded before the first performance. Burney originally thought the autograph was a copy for the 1725 production, but the absence of any of the new arias sung by Borosini indicates this is hardly possible. Handel started off originally by having Cornelia a soprano and Sesto, an alto. He also writes for a Berenice, who later turns out to be Nireno. In Handel's Act I autograph, she is a much more important character—Cleopatra's confidante and cousin as well as the mastermind behind Cleopatra's pursuit of Cesare. As the opera was altered, her part was drastically cut and her arias, if Handel wanted to keep them, were reassigned to Cleopatra or Cesare.[12] There are some seven or eight other arias in the work which have never been published. Two or three of them have genuine merit and deserve to see the light of day (see Appendix A).

What Chrysander printed in his *Händelgesellschaft* volume of *Giulio Cesare in Egitto* was a close musical equivalent of the 1724 libretto. He also presents six other arias in an appendix but gives little clue as to where they belong and when they were performed. The Smith-Hamburg score was, as usual, his primary source for the music. The last folios (ff. 148-66) of this copy have the appendix arias exactly as printed in *HG*.

A comparison of the 1724 libretto with Chrysander's score shows that, with the exception of some scene numbers here and there and a few lines of recitative and stage directions, they are textually virtually the same. Sesto's "Cara speme" (Act I, 8) does not appear in

[11] Charles Burney, *A General History of Music*, ed. Frank Mercer, 2 Vols. (New York: Harcourt, 1935), II, 719.

[12] One of Berenice's original arias for contralto was the famous "Va tacito e nascosta" for horn and strings (Act I, 9) which is a wonderful piece of music but textually just a simile aria about the crafty huntsman stalking his prey in silence. It was given to Cesare with a subsequent loss of dramatic verity at that point in the opera where Cesare meets Tolomeo for the first time.

its proper place, however, but at the end of the libretto as an after-thought. It was evidently interpolated for Durastanti for this season only, since it does not appear in either the 1725 or 1730 libretti.

In Act II, Chrysander includes an arioso for Tolomeo, "Belle dee" (Scene 9) which appears only in the Hamburg score and in neither the autograph or any libretto. There is considerable question as to whether it was sung in 1724 or at any other time. Conceivably, it was inserted for Berenstadt, who may have felt the music assigned to him was not sufficient in quantity. *Opera seria* singers were very jealous about the number of arias each sang, and often their position in the hierarchy of a cast was determined by this count and not the intrinsic importance of the character they assumed in the plot. Although Berenstadt was classified in the second rank after Senesino and Cuzzoni, he had reason to expect his totals would equal those of Durastanti or Anastasia Robinson—and without this arioso, it was considerably less (Durastanti—five arias, one duet; Robinson—three arias, two ariosi, one duet; Berenstadt—three arias) (see Appendix B).

In 1725, as mentioned, Nireno and Curio do not appear in the printed cast; Borosini, the tenor, took Sesto's role; and Dotti and Pacini, an Italian contralto and alto castrato respectively, replaced Anastasia Robinson and Berenstadt. In Act I, the libretto omits "Cara speme," originally written for soprano, but includes at the end in Scene 11 a recitative and an aria for Sesto as tenor, "S'armi a miei danni," which appears on pages 143-45 in the Appendix of *HG*. Sesto and Cornelia's duet, "Son nata a lagrimar," which concluded the act in 1724, is not in this libretto and was evidently omitted, since it was written for Sesto as a soprano with the vocal part on top in the score. This excision makes sense in that any attempt to have had this line transposed down an octave for tenor would have altered the relationship between the two voices.

The matter of octave transposition brings up an interesting point concerning Sesto's two arias ("Svegliatevi nel core"—Act I, 4; and "L'angue offeso"—Act II, 6) which remain in the 1725 libretto and were presumably sung by Borosini an octave lower than written. The main argument against allowing Handel's castrati parts to be trans-posed down an octave for tenors and baritones (generally, the latter, since most castrati were altos), is the damage it does to the balance of orchestral accompaniment and voice. Obviously, the gain for contemporary audiences is dramatic verity, but should that out-weigh musical considerations? In this case, Handel presumably countenanced the transposition. Therefore, say some, it can be done on other occasions. The generalization, drawn from particular music, may not be quite apt in this instance. Both arias are in C minor; both have vocal lines which, after transposition, do not go lower than the continuo (often not the case with the change from alto to bass register); and the string parts do not go so high that they create an enormous gap between their tessitura and the vocal line. The arias may also have been retained because they emphasize Sesto, the avenger of his father's death, who will eventually dispatch the tyrant.

In Act II (1725), the end of Scene 10 (Scene 8 in the libretto) contains an added aria for Tolomeo, "Dal mio brando," which is the same as "Dal mio cenno" (page 148 of *HG* Appendix), except for some textual changes. Perhaps, the addition was inserted to please Pacini who was not offered "Belle dee," as his predecessor had been. The text is sufficiently general to have been substituted almost anywhere (another eighteenth-century operatic practice which often makes hash out of dramatic continuity and the story's original intention).

Sesto's final aria in Act II, Scene 11 (Scene 9 in the libretto) is "Scorte siate" for tenor, not "L'aure che spira" as given in *HG*, p. 89. It cannot be found in the Appendix of Chrysander's score nor in Handel's autograph, but it does appear in three manuscript copies—the first, a full score (British Museum, R.M.19.c.7f.147 as an "additional Song Sung by Sig^r. Borossini"; British Museum, R.M.18.c.3f.5, Aylesford Collection; and British Museum Additional MSS 31, 571, f. 102).

In Act III, Scene 6 is changed for Sesto as a tenor. It is found in its entirety on pages 154-56 of the *HG* Appendix. The new aria is "Sperai ne m'inganni." (The libretto says "Saprai" instead of "Sperai.") "La giustizia" is cut. The rest of the act is much the same as 1724 except for the omission of Nireno and Curio.

Royal Music 19.c.7 (the manuscript copy of the full score) has a series of additional songs given at the end of the score. They are divided in three groups as songs for: 1) "Sig^r Borossini" (one has already been mentioned), 2) "Sig^ra Sorrosina," and 3) a single song for "Sigr. Baccini" (Pacini). The first and third groups can be accounted for in previous remarks about the 1725 production. The second is somewhat of a mystery. No Signora Sorrosina is listed in any of the casts, but the two arias assigned to her in this manuscript are found on pages 139 and 146 of the *HG* Appendix. They are "La speranza all' alma mia" and "Chi perde un momento"—both for soprano. The first, according to Chrysander, was sung by Cleopatra (in the soprano version) and the second by Nireno. Yet in the *Giulio Cesare* sketches (30 H 6, in the Fitzwilliam Museum, Cambridge) which are in Handel's hand, "La speranza" is given to Nireno also. Although the lady who evidently sang these songs is not named in the librettos, she is listed in the roster of King's Theatre (Haymarket) singers for the 1724-25 season as Signora Sorosini. This may have been the stage name of Leonora d'Ambreville, Borosini's wife—a singer of French origin. But Loewenberg[13] thinks otherwise. There was an Italian singer, Benedetta Sorosina, who appeared in Venice in 1722-23 and again in 1727-28. She was probably the Signora Sorosini who was in London in 1724-25. Yet, if Nireno's part was cut out of the opera in 1725, how could Sorosina have sung these two arias? It is conceivable that Nireno might have been reintroduced into some later 1725 performance (there were three February performances after a long run in January) for this purpose. Only the discovery of an amended libretto would verify the supposition (see Appendix C).

With the 1730 production, the problems are somewhat simpler. In Act I, Scene 3, Cesare's "Empio, diro, tu sei" is cut. (It may not have been to Bernacchi's liking.) In Scene 8, after Sesto's last line of recitative, he leaves the stage, and Cornelia sings "La speranza all' alma mia" in place of "Cara speme." This version of the aria (for *contralto*) appears on pages 141-42 of the *HG* Appendix. It was probably substituted to give Antonia Merighi (if she was the singer) a chance to do something different. At the end of the act the situation is the same as it was in the 1725 libretto, i.e., the duet, "Son nata a lagrimar" is cut, and in its place Sesto sings "S'armi a mio danni." In Act II, Scene 4, Achilla's "Se a me non sei crudele" is cut (Riemschneider was a minor singer), and at the end of the act (Scene 11), "L'aure che spira" returns as in the 1724 libretto, but this time it is sung by *Cornelia*—not Sesto. This version for contralto is found on

[13] Alfred Loewenberg in an article on "Borosini," *Grove's Dictionary of Music and Musicians* (5th ed.) (1954).

pages 150-54 of the *HG* Appendix. In Act III, Scene 2, "Domerò la tua fierezza" for Tolomeo is cut and in its place appears "Dal mio cenno," which in 1725 was found in Act II, Scene 10. Scene 6 of Act III is the same as it was in 1725—"La giustizia" is cut and the scene is for Sesto as tenor with the aria "Sperai ne m'inganni" (see Appendix D).

No copy of a 1732 libretto has come to light. The presumption is that because the parts did not change in voice (although the singers did), and there were so few performances, the 1730 version of the opera was used and no further editing was necessary. (Tabulations of all these changes which the librettos and scores document appear at the end of this article.)

Handel's changes and rearrangements to accommodate different singers after the original season were not always in the best interests of the work, and most of the time, the opera suffered. The arias which appear in Chrysander's Appendix of the *Giulio Cesare in Egitto* volume are, in general, inferior to the originals. Handel was in too much of a hurry. Often he took arias from other operas or, in some cases, let singers substitute songs they liked by other composers (the texts were sufficiently general for the moods they portrayed—love, vengeance, jealousy—and could be interchanged without much difficulty).

The glory of *Giulio Cesare* remains in its superb accompanied recitative (particularly "Alma del gran Pompeo," which has often been singled out as one of Handel's great musical soliloquies and was fortunately never tampered with, and "Dall' ondoso periglio," where recitative and arioso mingle in a manner which is almost Mozartean); in the beautiful "V'adoro, pupille" at the opening of Act II, with its accompaniment of alternating orchestras (one on the stage) of harp, theorbo, viola da gamba, plus the usual strings and winds; in Cleopatra's "Se pieta" for violin 1, 2, viola, separate bassoons, and continuo—a moving lament which Leichtentritt[14] thinks is one of the finest baroque pieces ever written. For all these and a good deal more, we are very grateful.

[14] Hugo Leichtentritt, *Händel* (Berlin: Deutsche Verlags-Anstalt, 1924), p. 668.

APPENDIX A
Original Plan of Act I as found in the Autograph
(R.M.20.b.3)

(Acts II and III are substantially the same as Handel's 1724 version of the opera, although there are a number of sketches and arias which were never printed because they were presumably not used in a performance. See listing below.)

Scene   *Act I*

1.		Coro	Viva il nostro Alcide
	Giulio Cesare	Aria	Presti omai (1724: revised and used in Act II, 9 as Belle dee for Tolomeo in D major.)
2.		Recit.	
3.	Giulio Cesare	Aria	Empio, dirò
4.	Sesto-Cornelia	Duet	Son nata a lagrimar (for Sesto as alto; Cornelia as soprano in f♯ minor; 1724: transferred to Act I, 11 and transposed to e minor for Sesto as soprano and Cornelia, alto.)
	Cornelia	Aria	Priva son
	Sesto	Aria	Svegliatevi nel core

5. Text differs from that of 1724.

	*Berenice	Aria	Tutto può donna (G major. Even before first performance, transferred to Cleopatra I, 13 and put in A major. 1724: transferred to I, 7 for Cleopatra.)

6. 1724: remains part of Scene 5

	Cleopatra	Aria	Non disperar in D major (1724: revised and transposed to E major.) Different setting here. *Unpublished.*

7. 1724: Scene 6 — No aria for Tolomeo (1724: L'empio sleale for Tolomeo placed in this scene.)

8. 1724: Scene 7. Text differs here from that of 1724.

	Giulio Cesare	Acc. Recit.	Alma del gran Pompeo
	Giulio Cesare	Aria	Non è si vago in F major (1724: transposed to E major. Cleopatra's Tutto può ends this scene.)

* Substituted for Berenice in I, 5 either:
    a) Nobil cor non può mirare (1724: revised for II, 5 as Si spietata for Tolomeo).
    b) Di te compagna fide (1724: revised for I, 8 as Tu la mia stella sei for Cleopatra).

9. 1724: Scene 8

Cornelia	Aria	Nel tuo seno for alto, f minor. *Unpublished.* (1724: different setting of text in g minor. Aria for Sesto [Cara speme] added in this scene. Opening ritornello later used to introduce Cleopatra's Voi che mie fide in III, 7.)
Cleopatra	Aria	Speranza mi dice in B flat major (1724: discarded. Tu la mia stella replaces it.) *Unpublished.*

10. 1724: Scene 9

Giulio Cesare	Aria	Questo core incatenato in D major (1724: discarded. Va tacito replaces it.) *Unpublished.*

11. 1724: Scenes 10 and 11

Achilla	Aria	Se a me non sei in G major (1724: transferred to II, 4 and replaced in this scene by Tu sel il cor.)
Cornelia	Aria	Priva son d'ogni conforto in E major (1724: transposed to D major and transferred to I, 4. Son nata [duet], substituted here, concludes the act.)

12. Deleted in 1724.

Berenice	Aria	Va tacito (1724: transferred to Giulio Cesare in I, 9 with slight alteration of text but not of music.)

13. Deleted in 1724.

Cleopatra	Aria	Handel began an aria but did not complete it.

Act II

In this act there is an early version of Venere bella, which is almost a sketch for the aria later printed in *HG* (Händelgesellschaft volume).

Act III

Scene 3 contains an aria for Cleopatra, Troppo crudele siete (Largo in f minor), which was later discarded in favor of Piangerò la sorte mia. It is a fine piece of music which has remained unpublished.

APPENDIX B[1]

Giulio Cesare in Egitto
(1724 Version)

Cast

Giulio Cesare	Senesino, alto castrato
Curio	Lagarde, bass
Cornelia	Anastasia Robinson, contralto
Sesto	Durastanti, soprano
Cleopatra	Cuzzoni, soprano
Tolomeo	Berenstadt, alto castrato
Achilla	Boschi, bass-baritone
Nireno	Bigonsi, alto castrato

Scene		Act I		Key
1.		Coro	Viva il nostro Alcide	A
	Giulio Cesare	Aria	Presto omai	D
2.		Recit.		
3.	Giulio Cesare	Aria	Empio, dirò	c
4.	Cornelia	Aria	Privà son	D
	Sesto	Aria	Svegliatevi nel core	c
5.	Cleopatra	Aria	Non disperar	E
6.	Tolomeo	Aria	L'empio, sleale	E flat
7.	Giulio Cesare	Acc. Recit.	Alma del gran Pompeo	
	Giulio Cesare	Aria	Non è si vago	E
	Cleopatra	Aria	Tutto può donna	A
8.	Cornelia	Cavatina	Nel tuo seno	g
	*Sesto	Aria	Cara speme	E flat
	Cleopatra	Aria	Tu la mia stella	B flat
9.	Giulio Cesare	Aria	Va tacito	F
10.		Recit.		
11.	Achilla	Aria	Tu sei il cor	d
	Sesto-Cornelia	Duet	Son nata a lagrimar	e

* Printed at end of 1724 libretto. Not in 1725 or 1730 libretti. Included in most of the Printed Songs (see William C. Smith, *Handel: A Descriptive Catalogue of the Early Editions* [London; Cassell, 1960] under "Giulio Cesare," editions 1 and 8). Probably was sung in 1724 only, as a last-minute addition for Durastanti.

[1] *Secco* recitative is not indicated unless a scene consists of it alone. Cavatina is a one-part aria. All the other arias are *da capo*. No keys are given for recitative. Lower case keys are minor; capitals are major. R.M. is Royal Music in the British Museum. Scene numbers in parentheses in Act III are the libretto scenes which differ in order from the musical ones.

Scene			Act II	Key
1.		Recit.		
2.		Sinfonia		F
	Cleopatra	Aria	V'adoro, pupille	F
	Giulio Cesare	Aria	Se in fiorito	G
3.	Cornelia	Cavatina	Deh piangete	d
4.	Achilla	Aria	Se a me non sei crudele	G
	Tolomeo	Aria	Sì spietata	C
5.		Recit.		
6.	Cornelia	Aria	Cessa omai	F
	Sesto	Aria	L'angue offeso	c
7.	Cleopatra	Aria	Venere bella	A
8.	Giulio Cesare	Aria	Al lampo dell'armi	B flat
	Cleopatra	Acc. Recit.	Che sento, oh Dio	
	Cleopatra	Aria	Se pieta	f sharp
9.**Tolomeo		Cavatina	Belle dee	D
10.		Recit.		
11.	Sesto	Aria	L'aure che spira	e

Scene			Act III	Key
1.	Achilla	Aria	Dal fulgor	B flat
2.		Sinfonia		D
	Tolomeo	Aria	Domerò la tua fierezza	e
3.	Cleopatra	Aria	Piangerò la sorte mia	E
4.	Giulio Cesare	Acc. Recit.	Dall'ondoso periglio	
		Cavatina	Aure, deh per pietà	F
		Acc. Recit.	Dite, dov'e	
		Cavatina	Aure, deh per pietà	F
5.(4)Giulio Cesare		Aria	Quel torrente	C
6.(5)Sesto		Aria	La giustizia	g
7.(6)Cleopatra		Acc. Recit.	Voi, che mie fide ancelle	
	Cleopatra	Aria	Da tempeste	E
8.(7)		Recit.		
9.(8)Cornelia		Aria	Non ha più che temere	D
Last		Sinfonia		G
	Cleopatra-Cesare	Duet	Caro, bella	G
		Coro	Ritorni omai	G

** Not in any libretto. Text only in autograph (R.M.20.b.3). Text and music in Hamburg score and R.M.18.c.10 (Aylesford). Not in any Printed Songs because it runs on into recitative. May have been sung in 1724.

APPENDIX C

Giulio Cesare in Egitto
(1725 version)

Cast

Giulio Cesare	Senesino
Curio	Part cut
Cornelia	Anna Dotti, contralto
Sesto	Francesco Borosini, *tenor*
Cleopatra	Cuzzoni
Tolomeo	Andrea Pacini, alto castrato
Achilla	Boschi
Nireno	? (See below)

Scene		*Act I*		*Key*

(Same as 1724 except for cuts and rearrangement
of recitative and also the following)

4.	Sesto	Aria	Svegliatevi nel core	c
		(Probably sung an octave lower)		
5.	*Nireno	Aria	La speranza	G
8.	Sesto	Aria	Cara speme *omitted*	
11.	Sesto-Cornelia	Duet	Son nata *omitted*	
	Sesto	Aria	S'armi a miei danni	B flat

Act II

(Same as 1724 except for cuts and rearrangement
of recitative and also the following)

1.	*Nireno	Aria	Che perde un momento	E flat
6.	Sesto	Aria	L'angue offeso	c
		(Sung an octave lower with alterations)		
9.	Tolomeo	Cavatina	Belle dee *omitted*	
10.(8)	Tolomeo	Aria	Dal mio brando	F
11.(9)	Sesto	Aria	Scorta siate	a

Act III

(Same as 1724 except for cuts and rearrangement
of recitative and also the following)

6.(5)	Sesto	Aria	La giustizia *omitted*	
	Sesto	Aria	Sperai ne m'inganni	A
9.		*La Marche* instead of Sinfonia (See *HG*, 126)		

* These arias were probably sung in 1725 when Sorosina took part in the opera. Although the texts do not appear in the printed libretto, the arias are found in other musical sources and can be placed in the given scenes with the altered recitative.

APPENDIX D

Giulio Cesare in Egitto
(1730 version)

(*Note*: Based on 1725 revival. Parts of Curio and Nireno are cut. Sesto is a tenor. No cast is given in the printed libretto, but it can be surmised. Version is far less effective dramatically because of further cuts.)

Cast

Giulio Cesare (Antonio Bernacchi, alto castrato)
Cornelia (Antonio Merighi, contralto)
Sesto (Annibale Fabri, tenor)
Cleopatra (Anna Strada, soprano)
Tolomeo (Francesca Bertolli, contralto)
Achilla (Johann Riemschneider, bass)

Scene			Act I	Key
			(Same as 1725 except for the following)	
3.	Giulio Cesare	Aria	Empio, dirò *omitted*	
8.	Cornelia	Aria	La speranza	F
9.	Giulio Cesare	Aria	Va tacito (text of B part is changed)	

Scene			Act II	Key
			(Same as 1725 except for the following)	
1.	This scene is cut entirely			
4.	Achilla	Aria	Se a me non sei crudele *omitted*	
11.	Sesto	Aria	Scorte siate *omitted*	
	Cornelia	Aria	L'aure che spira	d

Scene			Act III	Key
			(Same as 1725 except for the following)	
2.	Tolomeo	Aria	Domerò la tua fierezza *omitted*	
	Tolomeo	Aria	Dal mio cenno (brando)	F
4.	Giulio Cesare	Cavatina	Aure deh per pietà (2nd time) (*omitted*)	

Comment:

On March 21, 1730, there was a benefit performance of *Giulio Cesare in Egitto* for Anna Strada, at which time additional arias were added for her. One of these was presumably "Io vo di duolo," published by Walsh in the fourth volume of *Apollo's Feast* as "An Additional Song in Julius Caesar sung by Sigᵃ Strada." It also appears in R.M.18.c.9 as "Additional Song in Julius Caesar" and was printed by Chrysander with the recitative that precedes Piangerò (Act III, 3) among the additions to *Tolomeo* (*HG*, 76, p. 90) since it later appeared in that opera.

"Parmi che giunta" (*Tolomeo*, Appendix, p. 92) may also have been sung since it is in B flat and could follow the altered recitative for Cleopatra on p. 89. See also the note by Barclay Squire, *King's Music Library*, 1: *The Handel MSS*, p. 123.

MUSICAL SKETCHES IN J. S. BACH'S CANTATA AUTOGRAPHS

ROBERT L. MARSHALL

WHEN one considers that present-day Bach research has subjected the available source material to an intensive philological scrutiny epitomized by a new edition of the complete works[1] and the establishment of a new chronology of the vocal compositions,[2] it seems particularly surprising that there has been no study of J. S. Bach's musical sketches and drafts for over thirty years. Georg Schünemann's essay, "Bachs Verbesserungen und Entwürfe,"[3] though managing to provide an idea of the nature of this material, is marred by generality, incorrect identifications, and inaccurate transcriptions (all perhaps inevitable in an initial attempt), making it evident that a new comprehensive and systematic investigation, taking advantage of the latest philological and style-critical research, is in order. The following essay is intended to serve as an outline for such a study.[4]

The sketches present on the whole few problems of identification. The great majority seem to be memory aids written at the bottom of a recto to record the immediate continuation of the music on the next page while the ink was drying. Similarly, tentative marginal notations of the opening themes for later movements of the same work, and more rarely, for works to be composed in the near future, usually resemble the final versions enough to be recognized easily. Rejected drafts for the beginnings of movements and sections (also

---

[1] *Johann Sebastian Bach. Neue Ausgabe Sämtlicher Werke* . . . (Kassel, Leipzig, 1954ff), henceforth cited as NBA. The volumes of critical reports will be cited as NBA Kr. Bericht.

[2] See Georg von Dadelsen, *Beiträge zur Chronologie der Werke Johann Sebastian Bachs* (Trossingen, 1958) and Alfred Dürr, "Zur Chronologie der Leipziger Vokalwerke J. S. Bachs," *Bach-Jahrbuch 1957*, pp. 5-162. Dürr's earlier *Studien über die frühen Kantaten J. S. Bachs* (Leipzig, 1951) should also be mentioned, although his methods for establishing the chronology of the pre-Leipzig cantatas were not based primarily on a study of the manuscripts. A summary of all this research appears in Arthur Mendel, "Recent Developments in Bach Chronology," *The Musical Quarterly*, XLVI (1960), 283-300.

[3] *Bach-Jahrbuch 1935*, pp. 1-32.

[4] A more complete treatment, including transcriptions of all extant Bach sketches and drafts forms a major part of the present writer's dissertation on the autographs of J. S. Bach's vocal works.

to be considered here) are hardly problematic when found directly before or above the final version. If the draft began a new sheet, however, Bach often turned the sheet around and started writing again, or he temporarily laid it aside, so that a rejected version for a movement can appear in a much later portion of the same manuscript (as is the case for Fig. 1)[5] or even in the manuscript of another work. In the latter case the drafts can usually be readily identified either through an autograph title or the presence of a text, and sometimes they provide traces of otherwise lost or presumably lost compositions. It is clear, for example, from the title above the draft, BWV Anhang 2 (Fig. 2), on the last page of the autograph score to the motet *Der Geist hilft unser Schwachheit auf* that Bach at least planned to write a new cantata for the 19th Sunday after Trinity, 1729;[6] and Alfred Dürr demonstrated that Bach probably composed the cantata *Ich bin ein Pilgrim auf der Welt* by identifying the text in a copyist's sketch, found in the autograph score to Cantata 120a, *Herr Gott, Beherrscher aller Dinge*.[7] The Bach manuscripts, however, have already been finely combed many times, and it is not likely that there will be many more discoveries of this kind.

Identification of handwriting creates in general a less troublesome problem than would at first appear. Although many sketches are so short and written so hastily that it is impossible to state with absolute certainty whether or not they are autograph, the musical nature of these sketches usually enables a reasonably probable attribution.

[5] In Cantata No. 117, *Sei Lob und Ehr' dem höchsten Gut*, for example, the rejected draft for the first movement appears upside down on the last page of the autograph (which is now in private possession). Facsimiles of the first and last pages of the manuscript are printed in Wolfgang Schmieder, *Musikerhandschriften in drei Jahrhunderten* (Leipzig [1939]), pp. 6-7; Fig. 1 is reproduced from this anthology. See also the transcription in the foreword to the Bach-Gesellschaft complete edition, Jahrgang 24, p. xxxvii.

[6] For the dating see A. Dürr, "Zur Chronologie," pp. 98-99. The autograph is in the Staatsbibliothek, Berlin-Dahlem (West Berlin), *Mus. ms. Bach P 36/1*; Fig. 2 is reproduced from the facsimile edition, edited by Konrad Ameln (Kassel, 1964). The call numbers of the Bach manuscripts belonging to the former Berlin Staatsbibliothek will be cited henceforth simply as P. . . , or P. . . WB to indicate that the manuscript is at present in the Deutsche Staatsbibliothek, Berlin, or the Staatsbibliothek, Berlin-Dahlem (West Berlin). The writer wishes to express his appreciation to the custodians of these collections for their continually friendly assistance.

[7] P 670 WB. See A. Dürr, " 'Ich bin ein Pilgrim auf der Welt,' eine verschollene Kantate J. S. Bachs," *Die Musikforschung*, xi (1958), 422-27. A facsimile of this page of the manuscript appears also in NBA Kr. Bericht 1/33, opposite p. 58.

There is hardly reason to assume, for example, that anyone other than Bach would have troubled to write preliminary sketches for later movements or for the following measures in an autograph score, and it is almost exclusively in such cases that there is really any uncertainty about the hand. A number of sketch-like entries written to clarify illegible passages are almost always easily recognizable as non-autograph and can often be positively identified as being in Zelter's or Philipp Emanuel Bach's hand. This encourages the assumption that other sketches of this type written in an ambiguous hand are likewise non-autograph.

A unique combination of problems concerning the identity of both the handwriting and the musical passage is posed by a pencil sketch, presumably of a fugue subject, written on the back of a cello part bound together with the autograph score to Cantata No. 49 (P III). While the cello part is in the hand of Anna Magdalena Bach, the sketch may be autograph.[8] A certain identification of the hand is not possible, however, since the notation is quite faded. (This unfortunately also made it impossible to obtain a legible photograph of the sketch to reproduce here.) But the general features of the text script and the form of the C-clefs recall J. S. Bach's handwriting, even though the pencil and ink script of the same person can vary considerably. The theme, given here in Ex. 1 in its presumably final reading, *post correcturam*, and the text, Psalm 121, 2, could not be located among the extant cantatas, so that, if the sketch is autograph, we apparently have a trace of another lost or planned composition.[9]

[8] The handwriting of the cello part is identified in G. Dadelsen, *Bemerkungen zur Handschrift Johann Sebastian Bachs, seiner Familie und seines Kreises* (Trossingen, 1957), p. 34. Paul Kast, *Die Bach-Handschriften der Berliner Staatsbibliothek* (Trossingen, 1958), p. 8, attributes the pencil sketch to an unknown copyist. The pencil, incidentally, was invented long before Bach's time.

[9] Professor Werner Neumann of the Bach-Archiv, Leipzig, writes that the psalm was part of the service for the Sunday after New Year in the Leipzig liturgy of the time. Since there are only two extant Bach cantatas for this feast—BWV 58 and 153 (excluding Part 5 of the Christmas Oratorio)—it is particularly tempting to reckon with lost cantatas for this Sunday. It must be pointed out, however, that this liturgy for the Sunday after New Year did not fall in every liturgical year, so that the three extant works may have been adequate for Bach's needs.

A word about the musical examples. The transcriptions of sketches attempt to reproduce any corrections found in the original manuscript unless the contrary is stated. The original readings appear in normal engraving; corrections in small or shaded notes. Corrections of time signatures are given in larger type. It is hoped

Ex. 1. P 111, f.13r: sketch for a fugue subject? Final reading

The value of the sketches, of course, is not primarily the evidence they may occasionally afford of lost compositions, but what they reveal about Bach's composing practices.[10] Before turning to an analysis of individual sketches, however, a few words about the character of the autograph manuscripts are necessary.

Almost all extant sketches and drafts are found in the "composing" scores of the Leipzig cantatas. Through the often large number of formative corrections, the character of the handwriting, and the presence of sketches and drafts for opening themes, the manuscripts reveal that Bach wrote down these compositions while he composed them. It is therefore doubtful that he kept many, if any, separate sketch books or sheets at this stage of his career. This is easily understandable when we recall that Bach not only wrote the great majority of the Leipzig vocal compositions at the rate of one cantata per week during his first three years as Thomas-Cantor,[11] but also that the later festival cantatas for state visits of the Saxon royalty and funeral music often had to be prepared on a few days' notice.[12]

In the manuscripts of the pre-Leipzig cantatas, on the other hand, the complete absence of sketches, the comparatively few, mostly

---

that this method draws the reader's attention first to the original reading and thereafter to the correction, thereby encouraging him to reconstruct the genesis of the passage. Musical examples devoted to the final readings only, however, are based on the complete editions, unless the heading specifically refers to the original manuscript.

[10] The question whether the Bach autographs can contribute to an understanding of his "creative process" was raised and briefly discussed at the Leipzig Bach festival of 1950 at the inception of the current philological activity, but the problem has apparently not been seriously investigated since. See the discussion following Wolfgang Schmieder's essay "Bemerkungen zur Bachquellenforschung," *Bericht über die wissenschaftliche Bachtagung . . . Leipzig, 1950*, pp. 229-30.

[11] See the literature cited in n. 2 above.

[12] The royal visit, for example, for which Bach composed *Preise dein Glücke* (BWV 215) was announced three days in advance. See NBA Kr. Bericht I/37, p. 66.

minor or technical corrections (e.g., of voice-leading), and the normally relaxed appearance of the handwriting strongly suggest that
at this time Bach worked a great deal from preliminary drafts which
probably were subsequently destroyed. The autographs of most
Weimar church cantatas can perhaps best be described as "revision
copies"—an intermediate stage between the "composing scores" of
the Leipzig cantatas and the famous calligraphic *Reinschriften* of
many instrumental works.[13] The invention of themes and the overall
design of the formal movements were presumably worked out in
advance, the final touches then added in the revision copy. In at
least two instances—Cantata No. 61 (P 45/6) and 185 (P 59 WB)—
the preliminary drafts were apparently so complete that Bach had a
copyist write out large portions of the final manuscripts. Bach's
slower production tempo in Weimar—the church cantatas were
mostly written at four-week intervals between 1714 and 1716[14]—
presumably encouraged this more leisurely routine.

Single-voiced sketches for the beginnings of movements testify
that Bach first wrote down a melodic idea—a motif, phrase, or complete ritornello theme.[15] But this first written gesture was surely
preceded by a careful "pre-compositional" analysis of the given ma-

[13] It is clear that we have to reckon with the loss—presumably with the destruc-
tion by Bach himself—of the initial manuscripts of such works as the *Well-Tempered Clavier*, the Brandenburg Concertos, and the sonatas for unaccompanied
violin. Since this paper (and the writer) is concerned primarily with the cantata
autographs, the manuscripts for instrumental works will for the most part not be
considered here.

[14] A. Dürr, *Studien*, pp. 52-57.

[15] It is tempting to speculate whether Bach's well-known rejection of Rameau's
theories cannot perhaps best be explained from this point of view. We know from
the obituary written by Philipp Emanuel Bach and J. F. Agricola that ". . . Bach
did not engage in deep theoretical reflections about music . . ." (reprinted in *Bach-
Jahrbuch 1920*, pp. 25-26), and since there was no German translation of Rameau's
theoretical writings during his lifetime, it is improbable that Bach was familiar at
first hand with the details of Rameau's doctrines. It is quite conceivable, however,
that Bach had heard Rameau's tenet: "it is harmony . . . that is generated first"
(translated in Oliver Strunk, *Source Readings in Music History* [New York, 1950],
p. 571), and that he shared Mattheson's opinion that "We consider the Melody as
the basis of the entire art of composition, and cannot understand it . . . when for
example it is maintained counter to all reason that the melody is derived from the
harmony⁺ . . . . ⁺ See *Traité de l'Harmonie* par M. *Rameau*, L. II Ch. 19 p. 139,
Ch. 21 p. 147. Most astonishing, it is maintained that the harmony is engendered
first. I submit: what is engendered must have parents." Johann Mattheson, *Der
vollkommene Capellmeister* (Hamburg, 1739), p. 133. Facsimile edition, Margarete
Reimann, ed. (Kassel, 1954).

terial—for vocal music, the text, sometimes also a chorale cantus firmus.

The text must have been analyzed from two points of view: its structure and its "affect." The form and the prosody of the poem clearly influenced not only the composer's choice of form and meter, but also more specific decisions regarding the rhythm of the theme and the placement of tonic accents, i.e., the choice of pitches. It is well known also that the *Affektenlehre* played an enormous role in Baroque musical aesthetics, and Bach's endorsement of this doctrine is documented.[16] The composer's understanding of the affect influenced his choice of mode (perhaps of tonality as well), tempo, orchestration, texture, style, and the employment of rhetorical "figures."[17] Of course external circumstances—the singers and instrumentalists at his disposal, and their abilities—also played a significant role in Bach's preliminary considerations. The extant tentative marginal sketches for opening themes can often be regarded as first, rough translations of the text into musical terms which had then to be refined into more idiomatic, convincing musical statements. In comparing these sketches with the final versions it is possible, by observing the elements retained and those reworked or rejected, to determine what the constants were and what the variables in Bach's conception, and in turn what was probably the generating idea of the theme.

A draft for the opening motif of the aria "Kann ich nur Jesum mir zum Freunde machen" from Cantata No. 105, *Herr, gehe nicht ins Gericht*, reveals, for example, Bach's interest in designing a ritornello theme that would later bear the first line of the text. A neutral rhythmic and melodic contour (repeated f′, repeated eighth-notes) was to prepare an "exclamatio"—a large upward melodic leap[18]—emphasizing the word "Jesum," after which the rhythmic and melodic flow would be released (Ex. 2). This germinal idea was preserved in the final version but refined in accordance with purely

[16] See the statement of Bach's pupil Johann Gottfried Ziegler, quoted in Philipp Spitta, *Johann Sebastian Bach* (Leipzig, 1873-80), I, 519.

[17] Bach's historical connection with the *Figurenlehre* and the use of rhetorical figures in his music have been investigated primarily by Arnold Schmitz, *Die Bildlichkeit der wortgebundenen Musik Johann Sebastian Bachs* (Mainz, 1950).

[18] See Hans-Heinrich Unger, "Die Beziehungen zwischen Musik und Rhetorik im 16.-18. Jahrhundert" (Berlin dissertation, 1941), p. 77, and Johann Gottfried Walther, *Musicalisches Lexikon* (Leipzig, 1732), p. 233. Facsimile edition, Richard Schaal, ed. (Kassel, 1953).

Ex. 2. P 99, f.3v: BWV 105, Movement 5; sketch for ritornello theme

musical considerations. By omitting the fourth-beat figure of the first measure of the original conception, the weak double skip of a sixth plus a fourth was avoided and the melody made more concise and tonally focused (Ex. 3).

Ex. 3. BWV 105, Movement 5, mm. 1-3, Violin 1 and Horn, final version

Bach's first draft of the "Pleni" theme for the Sanctus of the *B minor Mass*, written on the bottom of the first page of the autograph (P 13/1, f.1r),[19] indicates that here again the primary consideration was to achieve a proper declamation and representation of the text. The words "coeli" and "terra" suggested an upward octave leap followed by a descending seventh, while "gloria" inspired a melisma. The dactylic structure of the text was directly translated into a straightforward triple meter. Bach wrote down the complete subject to the cadence with no apparent concern at the moment about contrapuntal problems. The conception was exclusively text-engendered and purely melodic (Ex. 4).[20]

pleni sunt coeli & terra glo —— ria

Ex. 4. P 13/1, f.1r: *B minor Mass*; first sketch for "Pleni" theme

[19] In several manuscripts thematic sketches for later movements appear on the bottom of the first page of the score, but it would be rash to assume that Bach got the initial idea for the Pleni while working on the opening measures of the Sanctus, or, in a similar case, that he interrupted his work on the first movement of Cantata No. 57 (P 144, f.1r-1v) to jot down the ritornello theme for Movement 7. While these are of course possibilities, it is equally likely, if not more likely, that the completed first page lay uppermost on the composer's desk and within his reach. The only reasonable certainty is that Bach wrote down such sketches—there are about a half-dozen—some time before beginning actual work on the movement concerned.

[20] As the transcription shows, Bach began to draft the theme in the alto clef but changed his mind after writing the clef and the first note. See n. 9 above.

While retaining the essential melodic and rhythmic contour elicited from the text in the first sketch for the "Pleni" theme, Bach turned his attention in a second preliminary draft (f.4v) again to purely musical problems (Ex. 5). The text is not only absent here

Ex. 5. P 13/1, f.4v: Sanctus, mm. 46bff; second sketch for "Pleni"

but was apparently neglected entirely. (The beaming of the eighth-note passage in the third measure of the theme overlooks the syllabic requirements of the text.) The opening interval has been sharpened from an octave to a sixth, probably not only to increase the "kinetic energy" of the melody, but for tonal reasons as well. The new tone f'♯ serves a pivotal function in the transition from the end of the Sanctus section in f♯ minor to the D major beginning of the Pleni. The first two melodic and harmonic intervals

$$
\begin{array}{cc}
\text{a} & \text{f'♯} \\
\text{F♯} & \text{d}
\end{array}
$$

were to negotiate between the two tonalities via the ambiguous a-F♯, while the entire configuration formed a D major chord. (This perhaps explains why the continuo part accompanying the fugue subject was entered in this draft.) The final version (Ex. 6) repre-

Ex. 6. P 13/1, f.5r: Sanctus, mm. 46bff; tenor and continuo, final version

sents a synthesis of the two tentative sketches, combining the opening
motif of the second sketch with the continuation of the first version.
After writing down the third measure (or perhaps the fourth) of
the Pleni, Bach changed the meter from 3/4 to 3/8, probably to
clarify the tempo relation between the two sections.[21]

Although, as the preceding examples indicate, the rhythm and
meter originally suggested by the text structure were often generating and constant factors in Bach's conception of the theme, he did
on occasion recast the musical realization of the text meter. A rejected
draft (Ex. 7) found upside down on the last page of the autograph
score to Cantata No. 29, *Wir danken dir, Gott, wir danken dir*
(P 166, f.9v) is presumably the first version of Movement 3 of the
cantata—"Halleluia, Stärk' und Macht"—which like the draft is a
tenor aria in A major and begins a new sheet in the manuscript
(f.6r).[22] Apparently Bach originally intended a basically agogic
treatment of the trochaic text in triple meter. If the ritornello theme

Ex. 7. P 166, f.9v: BWV 29, rejected draft for Movement 3?

[21] Exactly what this tempo relation is has been a matter of dispute. See the
exchange between Bernard Rose and Arthur Mendel in *The Musical Times* (1959),
pp. 385, 683f., and *ibid.* (1960), pp. 107, 251.

[22] See the comments above, in the second paragraph of this essay. The draft is
catalogued in W. Schmeider, *Bach-Werke-Verzeichnis* (Leipzig, 1950), p. xiv, as
an unidentified sketch, presumably after Schünemann, "Bachs Verbesserungen,"
pp. 25-26.

was conceived as a setting for the first line of the text, the planned underlaying may have been:

Ex. 8. BWV 29, Movement 3: draft, hypothetical text-underlaying

The final alla breve setting (Ex. 9) relies primarily on dynamic and tonic accentuation to insure a convincing musical declamation of the text.

Ex. 9. BWV 29, Movement 3, mm. 20-24, tenor, final version

Similar reconsiderations probably motivated the abandonment of the first draft (Fig. 3) of Movement 31, "Schliesse, mein Herze" of the Christmas Oratorio (P 32 WB f.31v).[23] Here too the ritornello theme was probably text-engendered and designed to declaim the dactylic text in a strict and straightforward syllabic style (Ex. 10), but then Bach decided on a heavily emphasized agogic declamation in duple meter (Ex. 11):

Ex. 10. P 32 WB f.31v: Draft for Movement 31, mm. 1-4:
theme with hypothetical text-underlaying

Ex. 11. BWV 248, Movement 31, mm. 25-28: alto, final version

The original conception of the affect was retained, however, in the tonality, voice (alto), and phrase structure (2 + 2 measures). A number of characteristic melodic formulae are also common to both versions. Compare m. 2 of the first with m. 1 of the final version,

[23] Figure 3 is reprinted from the facsimile edition of the Christmas Oratorio, A. Dürr, ed. (Kassel, 1960). A facsimile of f.31v appears also in NBA ii/6, p. x. The most accurate and complete transcription is in NBA Kr. Bericht ii/6, pp. 50-51.

Fig. 1. BWV 117, draft for first movement from the autograph score
(in private possession), f.10v

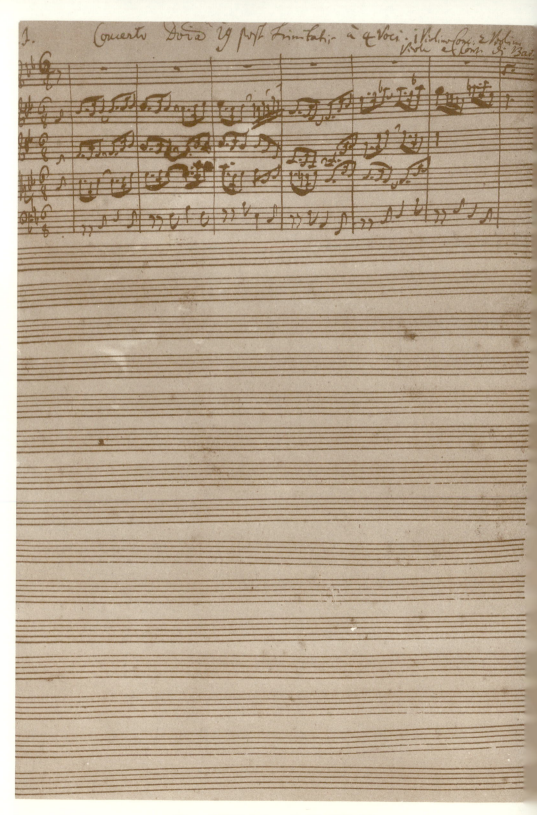

Fig. 2. BWV Anh. 2, P 36/1 WB, f.8v

Fig. 3. Draft for Movement 31, "Schliesse, mein Herze," from
the Christmas Oratorio, P 32 WB, f.31v

Fig. 4. Drafts for BWV 65, Movement 1, mm 19-23a, P 120, f.7r

m. 1 of the first with m. 2 of the final reading, and m. 3-4 in both versions.

The sketches and drafts testify overwhelmingly, as do the composing scores in general, that Bach's initial melodic ideas were normally completely formed by the time he set them to paper, although he often corrected or rejected them subsequently. There is no evidence that he ever *deliberately* first wrote down preconceived contrapuntal, melodic, or numerical schemes which were to be elaborated afterwards. The following rejected draft for Cantata No. 183, *Sie werden euch in den Bann thun* (Ex. 12)[24] reveals no traces of the two-voiced contrary motion model from which it is presumably derived (Ex. 13).[25]

Ex. 12. P 89, f.10v: first draft for Cantata No. 183, Movement 1

[24] The draft is found upside down in the autograph to Cantata No. 79, *Gott, der Herr, ist Sonn' und Schild* (P 89, f.10v). Although the Reformation cantata was probably written for October 31, 1725, and BWV 183 for Exaudi; May 13, 1725, the key, the instrumentation, and the watermark of the paper of the draft are the same as that found in the original sources for the Exaudi cantata (see A. Dürr, "Zur Chronologie," pp. 81, 83) so that it is clear—as Spitta pointed out (II, 831-33)—that the draft indeed belongs to BWV 183 and not to a third setting of this text (besides BWV 183 and 44). The draft is not mentioned however in the critical report to this cantata in NBA Kr. Bericht I/12, pp. 294-318.

[25] The writer is indebted to Dr. Ulrich Siegele, Tübingen, for pointing out this model to him. See also Siegele's "Die musiktheoretische Lehre einer Bachschen Gigue," *Archiv für Musikforschung*, XVII (1960), 152-67, for a discussion of a similar contrary motion model underlying the Gigue of the sixth English Suite (BWV 811).

Ex. 12 (cont.)

Ex. 13. Two-voice contrary motion model

In countless instances, however, Bach later added figuration to the original melody. When writing movements in motet style, he often composed to some extent in half-note values, "dissolving" the individual lines subsequently.[26] A similar technique can be observed in the following draft for an unfinished chorale-prelude in the *Orgelbüchlein* (P 283, f.18r) (Ex. 14).[27]

Ex. 14. P 283, f.18r: *Orgelbüchlein*

[26] The evidence for this is not provided by any extant sketches and therefore will not be presented here, it is discussed in my dissertation.

[27] The sketch illustrates primarily Bach's manner of writing cantus firmus compo-

As mentioned earlier, the greatest number of sketches, found almost exclusively on rectos, record the continuation of the music to be written, after the ink dried, on the following verso. One can consider such sketches extended *custodes*, usually found on the bottom of the page on any spare staff or staffs. If no staffs were available, the sketches were entered below the score in tablature notation. Reaching the end of a recto probably caused a considerable interruption, for the composer had not only to wait until the ink dried, but also to write down the brackets, clefs, signatures—perhaps even rule the staffs[28]—on the new page before being able to begin composing again.

Since there are only about a hundred continuation sketches in the Bach autographs, they are obviously not found on every recto page of every composing score. They were usually necessary only when Bach was interrupted at the page-turn *during the free invention of new musical material*. Therefore, they do not occur in recitatives or in simple four-part chorales. In the chorale settings the melodic material, rhythm, and texture were predetermined, while the recitatives are so completely bound to the text that there was hardly a danger of a musical thought being lost during the interruption. The absence of continuation sketches in recitatives suggests that they were not thought out at all in any detail in advance, but composed note by note, or rather syllable for syllable, governed only by the affective and prosodic character of the text, and presumably by a general conception of the tonal design of the movement. But also in the freer forms—choruses and arias—there are relatively few continuation sketches. If a page ended during a major repetition of an earlier passage, usually a quotation of ritornello material, they were rarely necessary, for one can hardly speak here of "free" invention. Such passages for the most part involved literal copying, or per-

---

sitions in the style of the *Orgelbüchlein*. See the discussion below on the order in which parts were written down.

[28] Bach probably ruled the staffs for an entire sheet—all four pages—in advance, before beginning to write on it. Therefore, the need to rule staffs in the middle of work on a composition occurred only when Bach completed one sheet and took a new one, assuming he had not ruled enough paper beforehand for the whole composition. Presumably, however, he usually had an adequate supply of ruled sheets on hand, for continuation sketches on the last page—verso—of a sheet are exceedingly rare. The second sketch (Ex. 6) to the "Pleni" theme of the *B minor Mass* is such an instance—particularly the sketch of the continuo part for the final measures of the Sanctus section. See the discussion below of this sketch.

haps mechanical or nearly mechanical transposition of "pre-existent," i.e., earlier material. The manuscripts here then cease to be *composing* scores in any real sense and take on a much cleaner appearance reminiscent of the autographs of "parody" compositions and arrangements of earlier works. Similarly the tight organization of choral fugues, their use of permutation and combination of a limited number of musical elements, reduces the role of free invention even more than the techniques of ritornello repetition in the arias and free choruses and explains the rarity of such memory supports in these movements.[29]

The continuation sketches when present, however, reveal significantly not only what part or parts in a particular musical genre and situation were conceived, i.e., written down first, but also how far in advance they were thought out. They confirm, particularly in arias, the impression gained from observation of opening drafts that Bach usually wrote down the principal melodic part first in a given context. The great majority of these marginal notations, varying in length from two notes to fourteen measures, lead a new melodic unit, begun shortly before the end of the page to the next significant cadence or caesura. Bach rarely sketched the beginning of a completely new passage when the page ended together with a major articulation, suggesting strongly that he normally thought in complete melodic phrases, one at a time.

The sketches occur, as one would conclude from the preceding remarks, predominantly for the leading instrumental part of opening ritornelli or for the voice part of later freely composed passages, i.e., sections essentially independent of major quotations of earlier material. Vocal sketches usually include the text, but otherwise carefully notate the beaming, testifying once more to Bach's meticulous concern with problems of declamation and to the text-engendered character of his melodic invention. The following passage from the aria, "Höchster, was ich habe" from Cantata No. 39, *Brich dem Hungrigen dein Brot*, may serve as a typical example. The sketch concludes the final vocal episode of the movement before the closing ritornello.[30]

[29] The most complete analysis of the compositional designs of Bach's arias is found in A. Dürr, *Studien*, pp. 104-51. The choral fugues are analyzed in Werner Neumann, *J. S. Bachs Chorfuge* (Leipzig, 1938).

[30] The placement of the syllable "-fer" at the beginning of m. 59 in the sketch, suggests, as the transcription illustrates, that the text was written down before the

doch kein Opfer wil - tu doch wiltu doch kein Opfer n[icht]

Ex. 15. P 62, f.10r: BWV 39, Movement 5, continuation sketch
for soprano, mm. 56-59

Occasionally Bach did not complete the melodic phrase but sketched only the essential contour, the conclusion presumably regarded then as inevitable. There are numerous sketches, for example, in which the sketched phrase is complete except for the last few cadential tones. Similarly in the following continuation sketch for the bass part (mm. 134-35) of the aria "Rase nur, verweg'ner Schwarm" from the cantata *Preise dein Glücke* (BWV 215) Bach was content to note only two of the remaining four measures of the phrase begun in m. 133 probably since the third measure is a literal

Ex. 16. P 139, f.15r: BWV 215, Movement 5, continuation sketch
for bass, mm. 134-35

repetition of the second and the final measure an "inevitable" stepwise fall to the cadence tone.

Weil das Gift und der Grimm von dei – nem Nei - de

Ex. 17. BWV 215, Movement 5, mm. 133-37, bass, final version

At times continuation sketches reveal that the harmonic progression represented by the continuo part was initially drafted. In such passages the upper parts embellish the harmonic framework defined by the continuo rather than develop an individual melodic character. This technique is especially typical of Bach's homophonic choruses and elaborately orchestrated movements, wherein the upper parts can usually be regarded as written-out thoroughbass realizations characterized by scale and arpeggio figures, broken chords, and similar rhythmic and melodic diminutions of the fundamental chord

music in this instance. The beaming here, however, makes the underlaying unambiguous. See the final version of the passage in the Bach-Gesellschaft complete edition, Jahrgang 7, p. 345, mm. 6-9.

tones. The sketch for the concluding measures of the Sanctus of the *B minor Mass* preceding the "Pleni" section illustrates this technique (see Ex. 6 above). One could perhaps maintain that the continuo (and bass) line here was sketched as the principal bearer of the melody, developing the dominant triplet motif of the movement. But its primary function is clearly to spin out via this motif the harmonic sequence of fifths initiated in m. 41 in b minor to the final f♯ minor cadence. The violins move essentially in parallel with the continuo, while the upper voices of the chorus and the doubling instrumental parts provide a realization of the thoroughbass rhythmicized to accommodate the syllables of the text.

In arias, on the other hand, the principal melodic parts rarely relinquish their primacy in freely composed passages. The few extant marginal sketches for the continuo line in aria movements are confined to passages based on ritornello material. The sketches here usually indicate any modifications of the harmonic structure of the ritornello that may be necessary for the immediate tonal development of the music. In the autograph (P 41/1) to the funeral ode *Lass Fürstin, lass noch einen Strahl* (BWV 198), Bach wrote the following tablature sketch for the continuo part of m. 30a of the aria "Wie starb die Heldin so vergnügt" (f.12r)

A   a   G   F   E

apparently to remind himself that this measure of the instrumental interlude was to have the same harmonic and melodic function as the original statement in m. 5—transposed down a fourth—in contrast to m. 21 where the harmonic rhythm had been retarded (Ex. 18).

Ex. 18. BWV 198, Movement 5, continuo

Here again, however, the continuo part is also melodically the most significant, for the two gambas have held chord tones.

On occasion, Bach sketched a purely melodic part on the bottom of a recto within a literal repetition of earlier material which entailed, properly speaking, no "free" invention. Here too, however, it is usually possible to reconstruct his deliberations. Emil Platen[31] has demonstrated that the instrumental interludes in many of Bach's chorale fantasias for chorus and orchestra are comprised exclusively of elements extracted literally from the opening orchestral ritornello, but shortened and spliced into new configurations as well as transposed if necessary to prepare the entrance of the next line of the chorale strophe. The following tablature sketch appears on the bottom of f.2r of the autograph (P 1215) of Cantata No. 133, *Ich freue mich in dir*, noting presumably the continuation of the violin 1 part for m. 52 of the first movement:

Ex. 19

The final version, however, written directly on the new page without any traces of correction, reads (Ex. 20):

Ex. 20. P 1215, f.2v: BWV 133, Movement 1, m. 52,
Violin 1, final version

The measure belongs to the fourth interlude of the movement and is constructed from the following measures of the opening ritornello (the exponent $^{-3}$ refers to the interval of transposition—down a minor third; the absence of an exponent indicates a non-transposed repetition of the corresponding measure of the ritornello):

Fourth interlude: m. 47b 48   49   50   51   52 53 54 55 56 57
Opening ritornello: m. 0^{-3} 1^{-3} 2^{-3} 3^{-3} 4^{-3} 6   7   9 10 11 12.

[31] Emil Platen, "Untersuchungen zur Struktur der chorischen Choralbearbeitung Johann Sebastian Bachs" (Bonn dissertation, 1959), especially pp. 164-204.

The tonal function of the interlude, beginning in b minor, is to prepare the entrance of the fifth line of the chorale in A major. According to the sketch, Bach had initially planned to continue the interlude after m. 51 by joining mm. 15-17 of the opening ritornello, rather than mm. 6-7 + 9-12 onto the first four transposed measures of the interlude. The original combination would have effected the desired harmonic progression through E to A major more quickly (Ex. 21a), but would not have permitted a natural *Einbau* of the chorale into the subsequent measures of the ritornello (mm. 57-58 = mm. 12-13a) and was consequently abandoned (Ex. 21b).

Ex. 21a. BWV 133, Movement 1, Violin 1, fourth interlude,
original plan, mm. 48ff

Ex. 21b. BWV 133, Movement 1, Violin 1, mm. 51-57

The various stages of incompleteness represented in the 45 extant drafts and sketches for the beginnings of movements invite an attempt to reconstruct the sequence of steps in which Bach set down the individual parts in a specific musical context. The available evidence, while admittedly sparse, is sufficient to indicate that Bach composed, even within one musical style, in different ways on different occasions. One is tempted to maintain from one chain of evidence that Bach composed homophonic ritornelli as follows:

1) wrote down the melody for the first phrase (Exx. 2 and 3);
2) composed the continuo part to this phrase (Ex. 7);
3) filled in the inner parts for the first phrase (Fig. 2);
4) drafted the melody for the following phrase (Ex. 12);
5) wrote the continuo for the second phrase (Plate 1);

and so on until the ritornello was completed.

This hypothesis, considered from the point of view of musical logic, is quite appealing. But as early as the second stage it rests on an assumption—from the fact that there are no extant single-voiced opening sketches of accompanimental continuo parts above which the upper melodic part was later composed[32]—that the melody in this particular instance was also written down before the continuo part. By the third stage the number of different possibilities has further increased, for it is now also possible that Bach composed the continuo in BWV Anhang 2 (Fig. 2), for example, after having written down all the upper homophonic parts. Indeed, there are sketches that show that Bach did occasionally write down the middle parts of a homophonic texture before the continuo when his interest in textural detail apparently took precedence over the establishment of the outer-voice harmonic structure. Consider the following two-voiced unidentified sketch appearing on the same page with the draft to BWV 183 (P 89, f.10v).

Ex. 22. P 89, f.10v: unidentified sketch

By the fourth stage, we must also reckon with the possibility that Bach first wrote down the two melodic phrases of the ritornello

---

[32] There are several sketches for the continuo ritornelli of quasi basso-ostinato movements, but here of course the continuo is the principal, indeed only, melodic part of the ritornello. See the sketch for Movement 4 of Cantata No. 62, transcribed in NBA Kr. Bericht 1/1, p. 80.

before returning to the beginning to compose the continuo—or the inner parts—for the first phrase.[33] The following diagram attempts to illustrate a few of the various possible combinations of stages:

The Genesis of Homophonic Aria Ritornelli

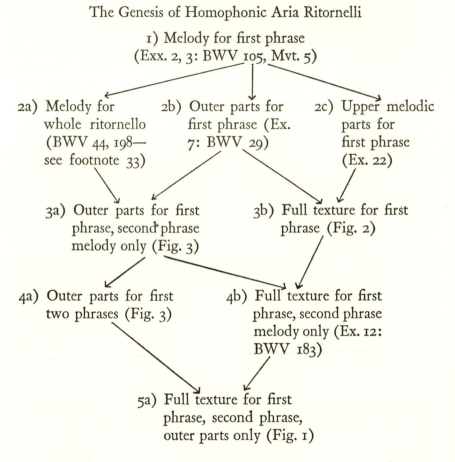

1) Melody for first phrase
(Exx. 2, 3: BWV 105, Mvt. 5)

2a) Melody for whole ritornello (BWV 44, 198— see footnote 33)

2b) Outer parts for first phrase (Ex. 7: BWV 29)

2c) Upper melodic parts for first phrase (Ex. 22)

3a) Outer parts for first phrase, second phrase melody only (Fig. 3)

3b) Full texture for first phrase (Fig. 2)

4a) Outer parts for first two phrases (Fig. 3)

4b) Full texture for first phrase, second phrase melody only (Ex. 12: BWV 183)

5a) Full texture for first phrase, second phrase, outer parts only (Fig. 1)

A careful examination of the manuscripts may help at times to eliminate some of these possibilities in a particular instance. One can regard

    1. the position of the barlines: a) what part or parts are most naturally accommodated by the barline, b) what part or parts

---

[33] Bach often sketched the melody for the entire ritornello theme. See the sketches of the (almost) complete ritornello themes of Movement 10 of BWV 198 (P 41/1, f.1r) transcribed in NBA Kr. Bericht I/38, p. 100, and BWV 44, Movement 6 (P 148, f.6v) transcribed in NBA Kr. Bericht I/12, p. 260.

are obviously uncomfortably squeezed into the available resultant space or even go over the barline, c) what parts have
"too much" room (see, for example, the facsimile of BWV
Anh. 2, Fig. 2);

2. the vertical alignment of the parts: a) the alignment of notes
to be sounded together within the bar, b) the evidence of notes
placed to avoid clashing with another part which had been
previously written down (for example, a note on a leger line
above the staff may have been set to avoid clashing with a low
note on the staff above. See the facsimile of BWV 117 (Fig. 1).
The position of m. 9, note 6 of the flute part in relation to m. 2,
note 1 of the continuo implies that the continuo for the first
phrase was composed before the melody of the second phrase.);

3. variations in the color of the ink; this, however, is rarely a
reliable index.

An analysis, finally, of any corrections present may yield valuable
clues concerning the order in which the parts were composed.[34]

The extant sketches and drafts for choral fugues allow a rather
more certain reconstruction of Bach's usual procedures in this form.
After deriving from the text a satisfactory subject (see Exx. 2, 3,
4-6), Bach apparently then wrote in the statements of answers and
subjects in the remaining voices, thereby establishing the order of
successive voice entries as well as the pitch and time intervals between
them. Thereupon he worked out the shape of the countersubject in
the first voice and entered it afterwards in the other parts, and so on.
There is no evidence that Bach *in fact* composed choral-fugue
expositions in homophonic "blocks" to work out the details of the
necessary invertible counterpoint in advance.[35] His procedures, after
inventing the subject, accord with traditional notions about how one
goes about writing a fugue. The foregoing remarks can be illustrated
with a facsimile (Fig. 4) of two drafts for mm. 19-23 of the first

[34] See A. Mendel, "Recent Developments," pp. 292-93, for such an analysis of
the opening exposition of the fugue subject in the autograph (P 103 WB) to Cantata
No. 182, *Himmelskönig, sei willkommen.*

[35] This seems to be implied in W. Neumann, *Chorfuge,* pp. 14-52. Neumann does
not expressly suggest that Bach initially composed homophonic *Stimmtausch* blocks
of invertible counterpoints as the starting point of his compositional activity, but
the reader is likely to have this impression from the style of the argumentation.

movement of Cantata No. 65, *Sie werden aus Saba alle kommen* (P 120, f.7r).[36]

It is possible, by separating the individual layers of corrections, to distinguish at least ten stages in the evolution of this fugue exposition. While considerations of space prohibit a complete analysis, a number of observations are relevant here.[37] The original one-measure subject (Ex. 23) had been written down in all voices before the countersubject was entered in any part. This is evident from the vertical alignment of the voices in mm. 2 and 3, and from the low swing of the abbreviation hook of "werden" in m. 4.

Ex. 23. P 120, f.7r: BWV 65, Movement 1, m. 19, bass, original fugue subject

(In the second draft on staffs 17 and 18 the space left in m. 3 of the bass part illustrates the point quite emphatically.) Thereafter, Bach wrote in the first version of the countersubject in the bass and tenor lines. The opening motif of the subject was now altered to the present reading in all four voices (as in Ex. 24b), perhaps to obtain a closer melodic relationship with the opening theme of the movement (as in Example 24a). Perhaps simultaneously, Bach revised

[36] The drafts are found in the autograph to Cantata No. 81, *Jesus schläft, was soll ich hoffen,* below the concluding chorale, leading one to suppose at first—as Schünemann seems to do ("Bachs Verbesserungen," p. 22)—that Bach wrote the draft to the middle section of the Epiphany cantata, BWV 65 (first performed January 6, 1724) after completing the cantata for the fourth Sunday after Epiphany, BWV 81 (first performed January 30, 1724; see the datings in A. Dürr, "Zur Chronologie," pp. 65-66). This would clearly have wide-ranging consequences for our notions of Bach's work rhythm in the first Leipzig years. A closer examination of both manuscripts reveals at once, however, that Movement 1, m. 19 of BWV 65 begins a new sheet in the autograph (P 147, f.3r). Bach, then, had taken a new sheet, left the upper nine staffs free for the instrumental parts and had begun to draft the fugue exposition on staffs 10 to 14. After discarding the draft, he laid the sheet aside until beginning to compose BWV 81. The case is completely analogous to those discussed earlier—see notes 5 and 24 above, and p. 413—except that this time Bach did not turn the sheet upside down before re-using it.

[37] Schünemann's discussions and transcriptions of this sketch, both in "Bachs Verbesserungen," pp. 23-25, and in *Musikerhandschriften von Bach bis Schumann* (Berlin, 1936), pp. 15-17 (from which Fig. 4 is reproduced), are considerably oversimplified.

Ex. 24. BWV 65, Movement 1

the countersubject—before the original reading had been entered in the alto—presumably to shift the tonal orientation of the exposition from G to C major.

Bach decided now to increase the length of the subject from one to two measures, and this obliged him to begin a new system. This fundamental change presumably had a twofold purpose: to offer a contrast to the stretto-like entrances of the first theme (m. 9), and to lend a formal symmetry to the movement which in its final reading has the following proportions:[38]

$$
\begin{array}{ccc}
A & B & A' \\
\text{Mm. 1-18(19)} & \text{19-45} & \text{45-53} \quad \text{or} \\
18 \quad + & 27 \quad + & 9 \quad \text{measures} \\
& 27 &
\end{array}
$$

The remaining strata of corrections are devoted to relatively minor details and need not concern us here.

There has been no attempt here to consider any of the broader questions implicit in this kind of study regarding, for example, the psychology of the creative process or the relevance of biographical knowledge for an understanding of works of art. This study has been limited rather to the more immediate problems posed by the extant musical sketches of J. S. Bach. However, it is hoped that the examples selected for consideration have succeeded in illustrating not only the questions this material raises but also the kinds of questions it helps to answer.[39]

---

[38] See also the analysis of the dovetailing in m. 45 in W. Neumann, *Chorfuge*, p. 58.

[39] The author is indebted to Professor Arthur Mendel for valuable criticisms and suggestions regarding this paper.

HAYDN'S *CREATION* REVISITED: AN INTRODUCTORY ESSAY

VERNON GOTWALS

Time's gloomy force will overcome the flesh;
What *thou* hast wrought will evermore be fresh. . . .
So will the future's sons come at the call
Of thy Creation's high and heavenly song.

HEINRICH VON COLLIN

P RESENT-DAY performances of *The Creation* do not always reveal the "wondrous unity of Haydn's oratorios" claimed for them by Paul Henry Lang. Is this for want of the "positive, virtuoso singing and playing" demanded by the "plainly dramatic music [of] most 18th-century oratorios"? Has "romantic sanctimoniousness"[1] concealed the true nature of Haydn's oratorio? Is it in fact a wonderfully whole work?

A close study of the score uncovers many things hidden in the average performance. This essay makes bold to claim *The Creation* as a living masterpiece of invention, of economy and restraint, of originality and inspiration. Three factors serve today to darken the original lustrous picture: a miscalculation in the libretto,[2] the patina of a century and a half of subsequent musical practice, and the unimaginative and heavy-handed performances of the work still mounted (and occasionally recorded) today—when such treatment of Handel or of Bach is widely frowned upon. Before these areas can be dealt with, however, the origin and early history of the work and the question of an authentic English-language performing score must receive some attention.

One had best begin a study of *The Creation* with Griesinger's report on its origins.

---

[1] All three quotations are from a review by Professor Lang of a recorded performance of Beethoven's *Christ on the Mount of Olives* in *The Musical Quarterly*, L (1964), 544.

[2] A miscalculation that admittedly has Biblical sanction. The first Genesis account of creation introduced man and woman (verse 27) *before* the seventh day of rest; but surely the librettist would have done well to reserve the human animals for Part III. Many have sensed the problem involved, but not even Tovey's solution is satisfactory. (See Donald Tovey, *Essays in Musical Analysis*, v, *Vocal Music*, London, 1937, pp. 114-46.) Attempts to remodel old masterworks usually fail; we must accept the work as it stands.

The first idea for the oratorio *The Creation* belongs to an Englishman, Lidley by name, and Haydn was to have composed Lidley's text for Salomon. He soon saw, however, that his understanding of the English language was insufficient for this undertaking; also the text was so long that the oratorio would have lasted close to four hours. Haydn meanwhile took the text with him to Germany. He showed it to Baron van Swieten, the royal librarian in Vienna, who arranged it as it now stands. . . . Swieten was the life secretary of a musical society in Vienna whose members . . . were accustomed to arrange several concerts a year. Only classical compositions were performed in these concerts, and the oratorio *The Creation* was likewise intended for them. Haydn composed *The Creation* in 1797, thus in his sixty-fifth year, with a fire that usually animates only a young man's breast.[3]

A "public" dress rehearsal took place on April 29, 1798, the first performance itself on April 30, in the hall of Prince Schwarzenberg, one of the noble patrons. His palace then stood in the Neuer Markt square.[4]

It was without doubt *The Creation* that finally sealed Haydn's reputation as one of the world's great composers (and probably *The Creation* that kept that reputation alive during decades of eclipse for his instrumental and operatic music, an eclipse from which they have by no means yet emerged).

"Copies of *The Creation*," Dies tells us, "soon spread throughout Europe." He continues:

In Paris in view of this interest, they sought to outdo other cities, and the first [foreign] performance in fact took place there, although with some alterations. . . . The masterwork was heard with amazement everywhere. Poets, aesthetes, and critics took

[3] See Vernon Gotwals, *Joseph Haydn: Eighteenth-Century Gentleman and Genius* (Madison, Wis., 1963), pp. 37-38. This work, hereafter referred to as "Gotwals" contains annotated translations of the Haydn biographies by G. A. Griesinger and by A. C. Dies.

[4] The structure was demolished in 1893, and the site is now occupied by a hotel. These were really private occasions. *The Creation* was not performed for the general public until March 19, 1799, in the Burgtheater. An announcement of the event, reproduced in facsimile in Naumann's *History of Music*, gives the hour as 7 P.M., offers free libretti at the box office, and in a very flowery paragraph states that no individual number will be encored lest the effect of continuity be lost. See Emil Naumann, *The History of Music*, tr. F. Praeger (London, n. d.), II, facing p. 864.

occasion to express themselves thereon in all sorts of ways (Got-wals, pp. 183, 185).

Dies and Griesinger give many details of this unquestionable popular success of *The Creation* and of its companion work *The Seasons*.[5]

Haydn's last public appearance and the last music he ever heard performed by another involved *The Creation*. The famous stories of the University Hall performance on March 27, 1808 (at which Beethoven is supposed to have been present and from which Haydn had to be carried away early in tears of triumph), and of the visit on May 17, 1809, of a French (and thus enemy!) officer who sang to Haydn "In Native Worth" need not be retold here. They under-line the fame of the work and its brilliant reflection on its author.

None of this *réclame* seems to have turned Haydn's head. The simplicity of his religious outlook, his modesty, his accurate self-appraisal are nicely connected with the masterwork by Griesinger:

> His patriarchal, devout spirit is particularly expressed in *The Creation*, and hence he was bound to be more successful in this composition than a hundred other masters. "Only when I had reached the half-way mark in my composition did I perceive that it was succeeding, and I was never so devout as during the time that I was working on *The Creation*. Every day I fell to my knees and prayed God to grant me the strength for a happy completion of this work." . . . In all modesty Haydn did not fail to perceive his own worth. . . . "If a master has produced one or two superior works, his reputation is established." His *Creation* would endure, and probably *The Seasons*, too (Gotwals, pp. 54-56).

Haydn's *Creation* is a work, like Handel's *Messiah*, that has had a continuous performance tradition since its first appearance. Haydn himself acknowledged his debt to Handel. Thus we find Giuseppe Carpani, another earlier biographer, claiming that without his extensive experience of Handel's music in England in the 1790's

---

[5] One of the most interesting is Michael Haydn's opinion, cited by Dies: "You may receive this oratorio with awe and devotion:—The inserted slips of paper mark places that specially pleased me. You will find none at the arias, and so on, other-wise the score would have looked like a hedgehog. The spot *Und Liebe girrt das zarte Taubenpaar* particularly seems to me to be very successful. Here and there you will be surprised; and what my brother manages in his choruses on eternity is something extraordinary, and so on" (Gotwals, p. 186).

Haydn would not have composed his prodigious work *The Creation* in which is heard Handel's great eloquence instilled in
Haydn's mind and wonderfully allied to his own richness of
instrumentation. And I know that I happened to be near Haydn
in the Schwarzenberg palace when Handel's *Messiah* was being
performed, and when I expressed admiration for one of those
magnificent choruses, Haydn told me, He is the father of us all
(Gotwals, p. 235).

One also may well suppose, however, that when Haydn's own operas
are better known, it will be seen that they too are a not inconsidera-
ble source of the *Creation* manner. Certainly Haydn's vast experience
in operatic production contributed much.

The Creation, again like *Messiah*, began at once to earn money
for its composer. Griesinger tells us that

> Haydn's fortune was significantly increased by the oratorio.
> [Prince Schwarzenberg and company] made him a present of five
> hundred ducats. A benefit concert and the authorized edition of
> the score yielded him something like twelve thousand gulden
> (Gotwals, p. 39).

And Dies adds some details:

> Haydn's oratorios were turned to charitable purposes. He spoke
> with visible joy of the profit that for several years flowed into so
> many cashboxes from the performance of his works. He showed
> me an extract of the accounts of the musical society whose *Assessor
> perpetuus* he was for over eight and a quarter years (until 1805)
> which showed that the net balance at that time amounted already
> to 3,369 florins. The first performance of *The Creation* brought to
> the benefit of this society, after expenses, 4,162 florins; that of *The
> Seasons* 3,209 florins (Gotwals, p. 192).

Although money values in Haydn's time became complicated (I
have elsewhere devoted an entire article to the attempt to unravel
them),[6] it can be said here that the terms "gulden" and "florin" are
interchangeable, that a ducat is four to five gulden, and that if one
thinks of 500 ducats as 2500 to 5000 present-day dollars and 12,000

[6] "Joseph Haydn's Last Will and Testament" in *The Musical Quarterly*, XLVII
(1961), 331-53.

gulden as 15,000 to 25,000 dollars, he will not be hopelessly wrong.[7]

Thus the sibling oratorios not only helped to ensure Haydn's comfort in old age but, like *Messiah*, contributed largely to contemporary charitable undertakings.

Haydn was already at work on *The Creation* when he visited Albrechtsberger on December 14, 1796, for the latter wrote next day to Beethoven that Haydn "was here yesterday [and] is busy with the idea of a big oratorio which he wants to call *The Creation*; he played through some of his ideas for it and I think it will be very good."[8]

The autograph is lost. Dies thought it was stolen from a drawer in Baron van Swieten's desk after his death. But Haydn had written to Griesinger in 1801 that "the autograph . . . of the *Creation* is to remain in the hands of Baron von [!] Swieten, inasmuch as, after the Baron's death, both works, together with his own beautiful collection, will be left as mementos to the Imperial and Royal Library."[9] This did not happen. Larsen concludes, "It is not at all impossible but certainly improbable that both manuscripts should suddenly turn up."[10] As Eusebius Mandyczewski tells us in the Breitkopf & Härtel Gesamtausgabe volume (xvi/5, 1924), the only source is the original edition, seen to by Haydn himself. The folio score is 301 pages plus separate trombone and contrafagotto parts "for which there was no room in the score."

Haydn's correspondence tells the story of this first edition which van Swieten thought Haydn should handle himself to avoid dishonoring the work by business negotiations! For the *Allgemeine Musikalische Zeitung* of June 15, 1799, Haydn wrote an advertisement describing the work "to appear in three or four months, neatly and correctly engraved and printed on good paper, with German

[7] One wonders if Haydn perhaps exaggerated when he wrote to George Thomson in Edinburgh on October 17, 1804, "With . . . the *Creation* and the *Four Seasons*, I have made, here in Vienna over a period of three years, forty-thousand florins for our poor widows of musicians" (H. C. Robbins Landon, *The Collected Correspondence and London Notebooks of Joseph Haydn*, London, 1959, p. 234). In any case, he is certainly reckoning in paper money, so the sum is something like 16,000 florins hard currency.

[8] Quoted in Rosemary Hughes, *Haydn* (London, 1950), pp. 99-100n.

[9] Landon, *Correspondence*, p. 184.

[10] Jens Peter Larsen, *Die Haydn-Überlieferung* (Copenhagen, 1939), p. 58. See also Gotwals, pp. 260-61.

and English texts; and in full score. . . . The price of the Oratorio, which will consist of some 300 pages, is to be 3 ducats, or 13 Fl. 30 Kr. in Viennese currency" (*Collected Correspondence*, p. 155). Haydn then set about getting a list of notable subscribers, including, he hoped, the Queen of England.[11] He corresponded with Burney about other English subscribers. By November 1, 1799, he was able to write to C. G. Breitkopf in Leipzig, "Perhaps no work has ever been published with as many different subscribers as this one" (*Collected Correspondence*, p. 168). He told Breitkopf in the same letter that "since the *Creation* will be engraved and printed here in Vienna, I was obliged to give Herr Artaria the principal commission. But as far as the pianoforte arrangement is concerned, lack of time prevents me from doing this myself. Anyone is free to do it." The work appeared on February 26, 1800, followed on March 8 by a piano-vocal score arranged by Sigismund Neukomm and a quintet arrangement (2 violins, 2 violas, and cello) by Anton Wranitzky.[12] But the production of copies was slow. On July 1, 1800, Haydn wrote to Härtel, "Between ourselves, I am really to be pitied that I entrusted my costly *Creation* to the sleepy Herr Artaria, the more so since I let them have the piano score, and some other small things, at no cost" (*Collected Correspondence*, p. 171). Still, the venture was a success. On October 16, 1800, Haydn wrote from Eisenstadt to Artaria & Co., "I should like to know if in the meantime some more copies [of the *Creation*] have been printed or not, and if not, I would ask you once again to press the matter through Baron von Swieten . . . for yesterday I received a letter from Dr. Burney in

[11] He secured the Queen *and* the King. See Karl Geiringer, *Haydn*, 2nd edn. (New York, 1963), p. 179. The index of subscribers, six and a half pages long, is a fascinating list. The King and Queen of England together with the Prince and Princess of Wales, the Duchess of York, and the Princesses Augusta, Elizabeth, Maria, Sophia, and Amalia of England, are sandwiched in the middle of an introductory list, set in large type, that begins with Ihre Majestät die Kayserinn Königinn and ends with Die K. K. Hofbibliothek (Her Majesty the Imperial Queen; The Imperial and Royal Court Library). The less august subscribers are listed alphabetically. Their number, 386 in all, includes many old friends such as Dr. Burney, Cannabich, Dr. Herschel, Magdalena von Kurzbeck, Count Razumowski, Haydn's great and good friend in London M^{ris}. Schroeter, and Charles Wesley. Most of the familiar Viennese nobility are present and most of Haydn's London friends and musical acquaintances. Thirty-six subscribers are down for more than one copy, Haydn's London sponsor Salomon taking twelve, an unknown Heinrich Reinsdorf ten, Longman, Clementi et Comp. seven, Princess Esterházy six, and so on.

[12] Franz Artaria and Hugo Botstiber, *Joseph Haydn und das Verlagshaus Artaria* (Vienna, 1909), p. 76.

London, in which he asks for 40 copies more to be sent to him as soon as possible" (*Collected Correspondence*, p. 177). And on April 28, 1801, he wrote to Hyde & Clementi in London, "You received through Herr Artaria and Comp. two hundred and twelve (IN FIGURES: 212) copies [of the *Creation*]" (*Collected Correspondence*, p. 179). In the meantime, *The Seasons* had been performed; but Haydn, fending off importunate offers from Hoffmeister in Leipzig and from André in Offenbach, entrusted its publication to Breitkopf & Härtel, for whom Griesinger was now acting as agent. Haydn eventually (1803) turned over to Breitkopf & Härtel the plates (and the responsibility for the sale) of *The Creation* as well.

Haydn's complaints about Artaria's somnolence are balanced by the beauty of this first edition. The engraving is clear, and the accuracy is very high. The title page, like the text throughout, is bilingual:

DIE SCHOEPFUNG/ Ein/ Oratorium/ In Musik gesetzt/ von/ Joseph Haydn/ Doctor der Tonkunst, der königl. Schwedischen Academie der/ Musik Mitglied und Kapellmeister in wirklichen Diensten/ seiner Durchlaucht des Herrn Fürsten von Esterhazy./

THE CREATION/ An/ Oratorio/ Composed/ by/ Joseph Haydn/ Doctor of Musik, and Member of the royal Society of/ Musik in Sweden, in actuel Service of his highness/ the Prince of Esterhazy./ Vienna/ 1800.

In the lower right is a circular colophon containing the initials J. H.

In the 1803 Breitkopf edition, the words "Vienna, 1800" are replaced by "Leipzig./ Bey Breitkopf & Härtel/ 1803," and Haydn's seal disappears. The first few plates may be altered or new; from the first recitative on, they are clearly identical with the original edition. According to Hermann von Hase (*Joseph Haydn und Breitkopf & Härtel*, Leipzig, 1909, p. 16), "The plates, 303 in number, were still used until 1871; then a new engraving took their place."

"The sketches for the 'Creation,'" which have been examined and reported on by Karl Geiringer, "show that the spontaneous freedom of expression which stamps the final draft of the work was the product of extraordinarily intense labor. Of that easy reliance on sure instinct which Haydn's youthful works so often reveal, there is here not a trace."[13] The sketches also reveal by indirection how good the finished product is. If one compares what Haydn (and many a lesser composer) might have settled for with what he finally wrought, the simplicity so often found in late works of truly great composers will be revealed. One example must suffice here. What appears in the original edition as

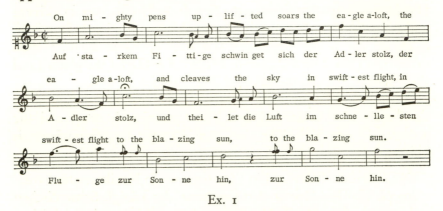

Ex. 1

was first sketched by Haydn as follows (Geiringer, p. 304):

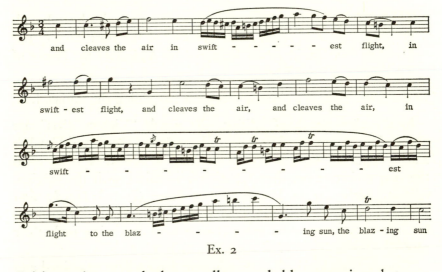

Ex. 2

Geiringer cites several other equally remarkable comparisons between first thought and final inspiration.

The libretto of *The Creation* has been from the start as controversial as certain aspects of the music. Dies's initial account says:

[13] Geiringer, "Haydn's Sketches for 'The Creation,'" *The Musical Quarterly*, XVIII (1932), 299-308.

The German text of *The Creation* was received with approval at that time, but this approval decreased in the future, and criticism at last ventured to find the text unworthy of Haydn's music and wished aloud to fit a better to it. *The Seasons* suffered the same fate. Haydn was too much obliged by both texts to quit the sphere of music and to wander around in the region of painting (Gotwals, p. 175).

The matter of translation has also been problematical. Vincent Novello began very early to make improvements in van Swieten's English. Tovey in his well-known essay uses a translation he calls "the new Oxford text" (by Messrs. Fox Strangways and Steuart Wilson). There are other modern translations by the late Henry S. Drinker and by Robert Shaw and Alice Parker. Apparently, problems in declamation and dissatisfaction with van Swieten's unidiomatic English will continue to produce "new" English versions of the libretto. In my opinion, it would be better to provide the German and English texts as van Swieten and Haydn delivered them to the engraver for the first edition, and thus allow conductor and singers to make what few adjustments may be inescapable. Haydn, after all, spoke not only German but fluent Italian, some French, and certainly quite a bit of English. He made the necessary musical accommodations. They are legion. Here is a pair of examples, the first ones that occur in the score of Biblical and of non-Biblical words:

Ex. 3

One might argue that what is changed here has little or no musical significance. But consider the following examples:

From "Rolling in foaming billows":

Ex. 4

Or the beginning of the chorus:

[The adjustment for the notes in brackets admittedly must be deduced.]

Ex. 5

Or in the trio "Most beautiful appear":

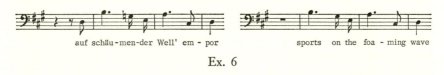

Ex. 6

A text as carefully prepared as this by its composer need not be "improved" by anyone, however crafty his use of his native tongue compared with the van Swieten-Haydn English.

An Italian version came soon after the first edition. It was published by Artaria as "La Creazione del mondo del Celebre Signor Maestro Haydn per il Clavicembalo e Canto recata in versi italiani sotto le stesse note da Giuseppe de Carpani" in March 1801.[14]

It is one thing to agree that the original edition provides the best performance source of the work and another to use it for an actual performance. The Breitkopf & Härtel Gesamtausgabe unaccountably contains only the German text. The Peters Edition full score is for practical purposes a reprint of the original that comes close to reproducing the Haydn-van Swieten version. Where differences occur, they are slight. One example will suffice:

[14] Artaria and Botstiber, *Joseph Haydn*, p. 99.

Original Edition	Peters Edition
Most beautyfull appear,	Most beautyful appear,
with verdure young adorn'd. . . .	with verdure young adorn'd. . . .
Their narrow sinuous veins	Their narrow sinuous veins
distil in crystal [later "crystall"] drops. . . .	distil in cristal drops. . . .
The chearful [later "chearfull"] host of birds.	the cheerful host of birds.
And in the flying whirl	And in the flying whirl
the glitt'ring plumes are died.	the glitt'ring plumes are dy'd.

Most English-language editions, however, employ Novello's retouched translation. Comparison of Novello's edition with Haydn's original yields some fifty-odd lines with alterations. A few examples follow:

VAN SWIETEN	NOVELLO

"Now vanish, before the holy beams"

Down they sink in the deep of abyss	Down they sink in the deep abyss

"With verdure clad"

Here vent their fumes the fragrant herbs. . . .	Here fragrant herbs their odours shed. . . .
By load of fruits th'expanded boughs are press'd;	With copious fruit the expanded boughs are hung;
to shady vaults are bent the tufty groves;	In leafy arches twine the shady groves;
the mountains brow is crown'd with closed wood.	O'er lofty hills majestic forests wave.

"In native worth"

To heav'n erect and tall, he stands	Erect, with front serene, He stands
a man, the Lord and King of nature all.	A Man, the lord and king of nature all.
The large and arched front sublime	His large and arched brow sublime,

The final recitative

if not, misled by false conceit,	If not, misled by false conceit,
ye strive at more, as granted is,	Ye strive at more than granted is;
and more to know, as know ye should!	And more desire to know, than know ye should.

These examples, chosen more or less at random, suggest that declamation is less the point at issue than whether an unselfconscious original should be tampered with. It should be preserved in all its linguistic innocence.

The Lidley (or in Tovey's emendation, Linley) text that Haydn turned over to van Swieten is usually said to be based on the first chapter of Genesis and on Book VII of Milton's *Paradise Lost* (1667, 2nd ed. 1674).[15] In fact, of the 32 verses of Genesis 1 plus 2:7, 15½ are used verbatim by the librettist, a bit less than half of this famous passage. The Biblical words occur only in recitative passages, though by no means all of the recitative text is Biblical. The version is essentially the King James translation.[16] There are echoes of Genesis in the Miltonic and Lidley/Linley verses alike. The surviving Miltonic echoes in Lidley-van Swieten are sparse but unmistakable. A few examples will do:

PARADISE LOST (Book VII)	CREATION (Original Edition)
Immediately the Mountains huge appeer	Mountains and rocks now emerge, their tops into the clouds ascend.
Emergent, and thir broad bare backs upheave	
Into the Clouds, thir tops ascend the Skie: (285-87)	("Rolling in foaming billows")
Brought forth the tender Grass, whose verdure clad . . .	With verdure clad the fields appear . . .
Thir branches hung with copious Fruit: or gemm'd	By load of fruits th'expanded boughs are press'd;
Thir Blossoms: with high Woods the Hills were crownd. . . . (315, 325-26)	. . . the mountains brow is crown'd with closed wood.
They summ'd thir Penns, and soaring th' air sublime (421)	On mighty pens uplifted soars
The Earth obey'd, and strait Op'ning her fertil Woomb teem'd at a Birth	Strait opening her fertile womb, the earth obey'd the word, and teem'd creatures numberless,
Innumerous living Creatures, perfet formes, (453-55)	in perfect forms and fully grown.

The "tawny lion" and the stag's "branching head" are pure Miltonic epithets, too. If van Swieten really translated Lidley into German,

[15] Milton's *Argument* for Book VII is as follows: "*Raphael* at the request of *Adam* relates how and wherefore this world was first created; that God, after the expelling of *Satan* and his Angels out of Heaven, declar'd his pleasure to create another World and other Creatures to dwell therein; sends his Son with Glory and attendance of Angels to perform the work of Creation in six days: the Angels celebrate with Hymns the performance thereof, and his reascention into Heaven."

[16] But not verbatim; in verse 14, for instance, we find one omission and two insertions: "And God said, Let there be lights in the firmament of [the] heaven, to divide the day from the night" [and to give light upon the earth]; "and let them be for signs and for seasons and for days and [for] years."

and then translated the German as set by Haydn back into English, we must be astonished to find this much of Milton surviving the sea change.

There is a good bit of evidence floating about to suggest that Haydn's *Creation* is a flawed masterpiece. Even Tovey, whose essay is essentially restorative, finds surgery necessary: "That some cutting is advisable I do not deny . . ." (*Essays . . .*, v, 122).

In 1939, Wallace Brockway and Herbert Weinstock, writing in *Men of Music: their Lives, Times, and Achievements* (New York), found that "time has not been kind to *The Creation*: it has been all but crowded out of the repertoire." They thought the choruses mostly feeble, the descriptive passages "a kind of sublime journalism." And they concluded, "The fine things in *The Creation* are scattered too sparingly to prevent a performance of the whole oratorio from being a chore to the listener. He rises from his seat with the paradoxical feeling that he has heard a masterpiece—but a very dull one" (p. 120).

Forty years earlier, John F. Runciman wrote in *Old Scores and New Readings* (London, 1899; 2nd ed. 1901), in a remarkably captious essay entitled "Haydn and his 'Creation,'" that "the work is singularly deficient in strong sustained choruses." He liked "Awake the harp" but considered the finale "light opera." He thought the arias a bit better; Haydn's attempts at humor he called "practical jokes."

> It is hard to sum up the "Creation," unless one is prepared to call it great and never go to hear it. It is not a sublime oratorio, nor yet a frankly comic oratorio, nor entirely a dull oratorio. After considering the songs, the recitatives, the choruses, in detail, it really seems to contain very little. Perhaps it may be described as a third-rate oratorio, whose interest is largely historic and literary (pp. 91-92).

But already in 1801, a sober appraisal appeared in the *Allgemeine Musikalische Zeitung*; its author considered the oratorio "a natural history or geogony set to music, where the objects pass before us as in a magic lantern." He thought the author of the Biblical account would have been astonished to find his story "such a great hit again at the end of the 18th century, decked out in all the display of modern music!" While "the exceptionally beautiful, masterly choruses may compensate us for the aesthetic mistakes of most of the other sections," the work was really fit only for "the English, who are still accustomed to Handel's rain and snow paintings, and who . . . must find in this *Creation* one of the greatest masterpieces that they have ever heard" (Gotwals, p. 200).[17]

I shall reserve judgment until the survey of the score is completed,[18] but one answer to the vexed question of picture-making in a sacred work may be found in Oliver Strunk's dry observation: "Written for the concerts of the 'Society of Noble Amateurs,' *The Creation* and *The Seasons* speak to the plain man."[19]

Haydn himself should perhaps have the last word:

> It will not displease my readers [writes Dies] to learn Haydn's own view in a few words. The Emperor Francis [II] asked him on the occasion of a performance of *The Seasons* to which of his works he himself gave the first place, to *The Creation* or to *The Seasons*? "To *The Creation*," Haydn replied. And why? "In *The Creation* angels speak and tell of God; but in *The Seasons* it is only Simon talking" (Gotwals, p. 188).

[17] Not all critics have been so obtuse. Arnold Schering, for instance, in his *Geschichte des Oratoriums* (Leipzig, 1911), writes a fine appreciation, noting among other things, the "working hand in hand of orchestra and singers, of tone-painting and fantasy," and "the fascinating melodic style, the energy of the choruses, the abundance of new formal patterns" (pp. 384-85).

[18] In a planned monograph of which this is the introductory chapter.

[19] In his chapter on Haydn, in David Ewen, *From Bach to Stravinsky* (New York, 1933), p. 82.

SOME MUSICAL JOKES IN MOZART'S
LE NOZZE DI FIGARO

DAVID LEWIN

MUCH has been written concerning wit in this wittiest of operas. I should like, in the sequel, to focus attention upon what seems to me one of its most characteristic features, namely, the quite extraordinary nature and extent of the involvement of textual connotation in the total fabric of that humor.

One finds, to be sure, brilliant effects dependent simply upon what might be called "standard" techniques of operatic comedy. One would include in this category the use of thematic material with conventional connotations inappropriate to the immediate text, as at the entrance of the military band music in "Non più andrai" over the word "fango," or in the use of the descending chromatic figure conventionally associated with suffering as Figaro invents his injury in the second act finale (mm. 602-605). Such devices are, nevertheless, a stock in trade of comic opera composers.

More unusual and sophisticated is the joke at m. 30 of Bartolo's aria ("La vendetta"): "Coll' astuzia" hardly describes the manner or compositional placement of the Doctor's embarkation on an extended tonicization of V. As in the previous examples, the music functions ironically with respect to the text; here, in addition, the irony advances a point of characterization. Further, the (violated) conventional expectation of material in the tonic key at this point is supplemented by and dependent upon expectations inherent in the musical structure itself—that is, Bartolo's "modulation" is not simply unexpected and clumsy, it "sounds wrong."[1]

Mozart's felicitous use of climax, agogic accent, and other straightforward text-setting devices brings out, at times, jokes only latent in the libretto. "Ti vo' la fronte incoronar," for example, sings Suzanna to her hiding husband ("Deh vieni," mm. 38ff), and we may imagine his reactions as she lingers on this thought in her vocal line before casually adding "di rose." One might presume that Suzanna, per-

---

[1] The "fango" joke was brought to the author's attention in reading Siegmund Levarie's *Mozart's Le Nozze di Figaro*. Levarie also comments on the "Coll' astuzia" passage. I have heard the "suffering" allusion mentioned by several sources and cannot trace the origin of the observation.

ceiving the effect she has produced, sings the repetition of this line of text directly at the concealed Figaro. "Rose spinose" indeed!

The next example again illustrates the use of a textual connotation (this time as a pun) in connection with a point of tonal structure. The duet between the count and the countess which opens the second act finale is cast, more or less, in sonata form. Perhaps its most atypical formal aspect is the absence of any thematic reprise of the opening subject. Instead, the count returns to the opening key at the beginning of a "development section" ("Quà la chiave!") and, again, for a tonal reprise ("Mora, mora"), but with fresh thematic material on each occasion. That is, he is unable, at this point in the action, to formulate and stick with any one thematic idea (the dramatic significance of this is evident); he does, however, insist upon the tonic key.[2] The joke here lies in the punning emphasis of this fact in "Quà la chiave!" at the count's first return to the tonic.[3]

One can hardly omit, in discussing textual-musical wit in *Figaro*, reference to the famous "Cinque" of the opening number. This is generally cited as an isolated, "throw-away" joke; on closer inspection, however, it turns out to be only one part of an elaborate comic *agon* involving librettist and composer.

The opening of *Le Mariage de Figaro* reads as follows:

Figaro. Dix-neuf pieds sur vingt-six.
Suzanne. Tiens, Figaro, voilà mon petit chapeau. . . . (etc.)[4]

The extended computation in the opera libretto ("Cinque—dieci—venti—trenta—trenta sei—quarantatre") was then (presumably) conceived by Da Ponte. It is in the nature of one of the *lazzi* typically introduced freely into *commedia* situations, and the point, I think, is this: Figaro measures "5, 10, 20, 30." At this juncture, the audience is evidently to infer that his measuring instrument is ruled

[2] The fact that the count insists specifically on the key of E♭ at this moment also seems dramatically significant to the author, in view of the tonal spectrum and associations set up so far in the opera. There is, of course, not space to argue the point here.

[3] "Chiave" no longer signifies "key" in this sense; the latter is currently translated by "tonalità." "Tonalità," however, was only introduced into Italian in 1838 (Carlo Battisti and Giovanni Alessio, *Dizionario Etimologico Italiano* [G. Barbèra: Florence, 1957]); prior to that date, "chiave" was in fact employed, as reference to an earlier dictionary will show (Joseph Baretti, *English and Italian Dictionary* [Tipografia Cardinali: Florence 1832]).

[4] Maurice Rat, ed., *Théatre de Beaumarchais* (Garnier Frères: Paris, 1950).

in multiples of five units. Hence the following odd announcement of "36" (6 more units) can be interpreted logically only as the estimated final measurement. The latter inference, however, is then controverted by "43," which, advancing 7 more units, is completely nonsensical in this little arithmetic system. One imagines some sort of burlesque stage business broadly pointing the joke, as for instance Figaro's holding up a ruler or tape of exactly the same length to the audience after each announced measurement. The little piece of text serves quite nicely as a thematic preparation for the entire drama, which is itself permeated by obsessive calculations that "go haywire," and which contrasts to these the less absorbing but more viable human contexts represented, in the opening number, by Suzanna with her hat.

Mozart's addition (or comeback) to this textual joke is his "computing" motif, which measures off, from the point of reference of the repeated low d in the melody, successive intervals of a fifth, sixth, and seventh. After this, the referent low d is lost and the motif itself soon liquidated. The musical invention mirrors exactly the arithmetic breakdown of the measurements in multiples of five units via the introduction of subsequent lengths of six and seven units. The generally inapposite aspect of Figaro's calculations is, of course, much highlighted by the apparent irrelevance, after "Cinque" sung to the fifth in the accompanying melody, of "dieci" under the sixth, and "venti" under the seventh.

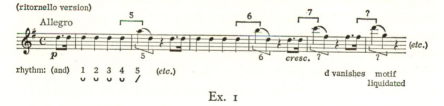

Ex. 1

Finally, I should like to point out Mozart's frequent use, particularly in the later numbers of the opera, of a technique which I should call "oblique textual reference": the employment of a motivic or thematic reminiscence which not only recalls the situation in which the music was previously heard but also carries a specific ironic allusion to the earlier text. The curious reader will find many instances for himself (Basilio's aria is full of them, for example); I shall here, for purposes of illustration, cite only the little e minor figure which accompanies the count's presentation of the jewel to "Suzanna" in the fourth act finale ("Oltre la dote, o cara!", m. 82). The reference, via musical association, to Figaro's "poco contante!" (Non più andrai, mm. 55-56) is, I feel, unmistakable. Without doing the count the injustice of imagining the gem to be of inferior quality, we may still feel, along with the spying Figaro, that "Suzanna's" reward is pretty meager, considering what she has to endure to obtain it.

This technique can be adapted easily to attain ironic effects that are more sardonic than humorous, and it is interesting to note its uses, in this connection, in *Don Giovanni*. A spectacularly chilling example is the derivation of the Don's "Ah! già cade il sciagurato" in the moonlight trio at the end of the opening scene from Donna Anna's earlier "Come furia disperata ti saprò perseguitar" (mm. 102-105). The effect of the Don's (unconscious? self-conscious?) musical quotation at this point is enormously enhanced by his prior lack of initiative, either on the stage or thematically, through the entire scene: we are all the more curious to obtain some definitive statement from him at this juncture, and his continued inability (refusal?) to initiate new thematic material here is all the more striking. One notes, however, that the irony invokes not so much Donna Anna's precise words as their general sense in the context of the earlier situation.

As in the above example, one senses in the later opera a turning away from the sharpness with which the ironic verbal-musical relations are so brilliantly etched in *Figaro*. To be sure, one still finds more than a trace of the earlier attitude remaining: the connotative plays on "Cosa Rara," "Come un Agnello," "I Due Litiganti," and "Non più andrai" in the second act finale need only be adduced to support the point (although even these are inspirations of a more literary than musical character). On the other hand, I do not think one could find any ironic musical effects in *Figaro* so essentially independent of any verbal component as are several in *Don Giovanni*. Among the latter, I think particularly of the breathtaking recurrence of the little F major anacrustic triplet figure with which Leporello, waiting without, impatiently attends the Don's appearance in the opening measures of the first scene: in the second act finale, the same figure is used to represent the impatient knocking of the statue at the door ... this time experienced "from within."

Figaro remains the *ne plus ultra* of a certain attitude toward the synthesis and interaction of textual connotation and music in comic opera; in that respect, perhaps only *Falstaff* can be compared with it. This is, I would think, one reason for the special fondness with which the work is regarded by all those who enjoy words and word-play.

"STÜRZET NIEDER, MILLIONEN"

ELLIOT FORBES

IN HIS book, *Der junge Beethoven*,[1] Ludwig Schiedermair calls
attention to Beethoven's two Imperial Cantatas and the prophe-
cies to be found there of the three giants in vocal music to come:
Fidelio, Missa Solemnis, and the Ninth Symphony. These two cantatas were written in 1790; the first, *Cantata on the Death of
Emperor Joseph II*, in the spring following the death of the emperor
on February 20, and the second, *Cantata on the Elevation of Leopold
II to the Imperial Dignity*, at the time of the new emperor's election
and coronation, September 30 and October 9, respectively. It is not
surprising that Beethoven felt obliged to set these two cantata texts—
both presumably by the Bonn poet Severin Anton Averdonk—since
his employer, Elector Max Franz, was a younger brother to both
monarchs.

As one would expect, Schiedermair devotes most of his attention
to what is clearly the finer work, the Funeral Cantata. The author
discusses the influences upon this music from operas that Beethoven
had helped to perform at court as a member of the orchestra. Then
he cites the direct borrowing from this cantata for the great
"humanity" theme in *Fidelio*: the setting of "O Gott! welch' ein
Augenblick!" in the finale of the second act. The evolution of this
melody in F from the Funeral Cantata through the three versions
of *Fidelio* of 1805, 1806, and 1814 has been thoroughly analyzed by
Willi Hess in his *Beethovens Oper Fidelio*.[2] However, Schiedermair
does make reference to a relation between the Elevation Cantata
and the *Missa Solemnis* and the Ninth Symphony. It is the purpose
of this article to investigate this relationship in more detail.

The cantata opens with a long recitative for soprano,[3] ending in
C, which is followed by a big aria in G; two short recitatives for
bass and tenor respectively lead to a trio for the three soloists in A;
the concluding movement is for four-part chorus in D. It is interesting to compare the texts of the two cantatas. They are both

---

[1] Leipzig, 1925, pp. 398-410.

[2] Zurich, 1953, pp. 158-64.

[3] After the soprano's first three measures, Beethoven has a corresponding answer
for chorus and then curiously abandons the chorus for the rest of the section.

primarily bombastic. The first, however, gave the composer a variety of moods upon which he capitalized with music that always transcends the text: 1) chorus of woe, modulating from minor to the relative major; 2) recitative for bass concerning the evil of the world (the spirit of the music is not unlike that of Pizzaro's aria, "Ha! welch ein Augenblick!"); 3) aria concerning Joseph, the savior of mankind; 4) the aria for soprano and chorus, which was revived in *Fidelio*, depicting the effect of his reign on mankind; 5) soprano recitative and aria, contemplating the sleeping hero; and 6) repeat of the chorus of woe, ending this time in the minor, the key of the cantata as a whole.[4] With the exception of the first part of the opening recitative of the Elevation Cantata, in which the text reminisces over the state of slumber and sadness at the time of Joseph's death, Averdonk's poetry evokes with deadly consistency but one mood: the hailing of the new ruler. A sampling: recitative—"Er ist's Leopold"; aria—"Hörst du nicht der Engel Grüsse über dir? Germania!"; recitative—"Sehet, er kömmt"; recitative—"Völker, weint nicht mehr! Ich sah ihn lächeln"; trio—"Ihr, die Joseph ihren Vater nannten, weint nicht mehr!"; and final chorus—"Heil! Heil!" It is small wonder that after the initial change of mood Beethoven seemed to have little inspiration for his creative task. There is reason to believe that Beethoven had feelings about Joseph II from firsthand experience; according to Schindler, on Beethoven's visit to Vienna in 1787, "two persons only were deeply impressed upon the lifelong memory of the youth of sixteen years: the Emperor Joseph and Mozart."[5] On the other hand, Beethoven was unlikely to have had any feelings at all about the new emperor.

Against this background we may consider the final chorus. The temptation to compare it with the finale of the Ninth Symphony becomes irresistible when one discovers that after "Heil! Heil!" the text continues: "Stürzet nieder, Millionen." What a vast difference in the object before whom millions are called to bow down! The first stanza of the cantata shows that this is not an evocation to a ruler beyond the stars:

---

[4] Compare the opening to both choruses with the opening to the second act of *Fidelio*.

[5] Anton Schindler, *Biographie von Ludwig van Beethoven*, 3rd edn. (Munster, 1860), Vol. 1, pp. 14-15.

Stürzet nieder, Millionen
an den rauchenden Altar
Blicket auf zum Herrn der Thronen
der euch dieses Heil gebar!

Schiller's *An die Freude* of course ends:

Ihr stürzt nieder, Millionen?
Ahnest du den Schöpfer, Welt?
Such' ihn über'n Sternenzelt!
Über Sternen muss er wohnen.

In both cases the text calls for music which evokes on a large scale. Here the comparison may safely end. The fact that there is such a great difference in the quality of the two musical settings, composed more than thirty years apart, comes as no surprise. Yet here are hints of the noble simplicity of expression to which Beethoven was to return at the end of his life. The Ninth Symphony was the voluntary preoccupation of a great deal of a lifetime. The cantata was composed in a hurry, probably to the Elector's order and lacks the stamp of workmanship that characterizes all of Beethoven's great works, that is, a series of ideas hammered out first in sketch form until they were ready to be developed.

The final chorus begins with a nine-measure gesture, *un poco allegro e maestoso*, which implies convincingly the 223 measures which are to follow. Up to this point the hand is sure and the expectation great. The first four measures (Ex. 1) show how the strings in triplets drive from D to F♯ in anticipation of the first two chords for chorus. Example 2 shows the last five measures of the introduction and the start of the allegro section. The rise to A in the chorus is combined with a descending sweep in the strings; this falling figure and the opening instrumental idea reappear in the coda, as we shall see, to make a basic unifying element in the chorus as a whole. What is interesting here is the relationship between the two. The opening figure sets up the rhythmic momentum which releases, as it were, the descending answer: the objective, D to F♯, has been expanded to D to A.

Ex. 1. *Beethovens Werke, Kritische Gesamtausgabe*, Ser. 25 (Leipzig: Breitkopf and Härtel, 1888), p. 95; hereafter referred to as *GA*.

Schiedermair's reference to the *Missa Solemnis* can easily be explained at this point. He likens the thematic setting of "Stürzet nieder, Millionen" (Ex. 2) to the opening idea of the Credo. To us, however, it sounds like a typical start to a fugal section in eighteenth-century style. What follows is the major disappointment of the cantata. One cannot help comparing the potential of half-note relationships here (D–C♯, G–F♯, G♯–A) and their lack of development to the great treatments of these melodic cells in his later music. Example 3 recalls how Beethoven set the Schiller words in the Ninth Symphony.

Ex. 2. *GA*, p. 96

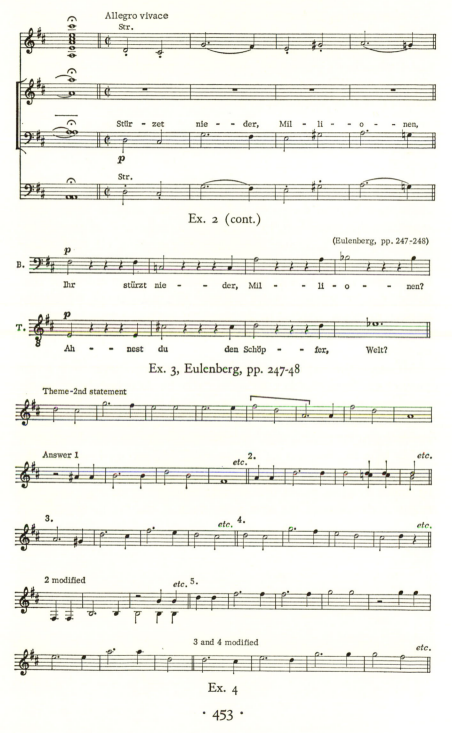

Ex. 2 (cont.)

Ex. 3, Eulenberg, pp. 247-48

Ex. 4

Unfortunately, the cantata theme does not grow but rather is stated monotonously during the next 150 measures in alternation with 5 stereotype answers (Ex. 4). The falling arpeggio of number one (in brackets) is reflected by intermittent statements in the winds, rising and falling on the triadic degrees. The plan of the main section might be diagrammed as follows:

A				A₁		theme in	Codetta	
	answers							
theme 1	2	3	4	theme 1	2 modified	imitation	5	3 and 4 modified
10	21	29	47	65 73	85 93	109	125	143 161
D: I	V	iii	V	V I	V iii	V	I	I I

The feeling of emptiness is caused both by the absence of tonal elaboration beyond the poles of I and V (the stops on iii are mere steppingstones from V to I) and by the anticlimactic answer of the theme expressed in answer five, where the semitone G♯ to A of the original theme receives the inevitable answer, C♯ to D, in such unimaginative terms. The tension and hence the grandeur of Beethoven's later works revolve around the manner in which the musical question, implicit in the opening phrase or section, does not receive its fulfilling answer until a culminating point later in the movement.

Although the last seventy measures, marked *Allegro non tanto*, journey no further afield, either tonally or thematically, than the preceding, they are rather more interesting as sound. At the outset, Beethoven develops an ostinato figure for the first violins which consists of a fluctuating scale over the dominant seventh. Example 5 shows how the figure is set against itself in contrary motion in the third measure by the entrance of the second violins. Beethoven was to make frequent use of this device; a poignant example comes to mind at the close of the first movement of the Ninth Symphony:

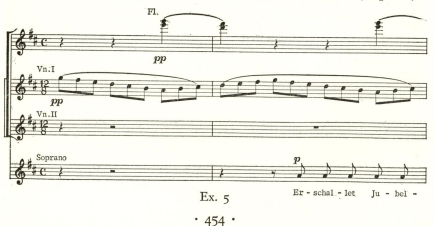

Ex. 5

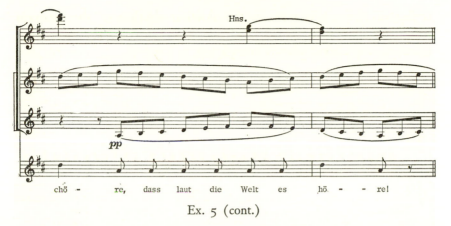

Ex. 5 (cont.)

at m. 513 the chromatic descent and return from D to A is given
to the lower instruments, which soon becomes the bass to a diatonic
theme above, rising and falling in contrary motion. But the sound
here is bright. Twice there is a start of the figure pianissimo in order
to work up to a forte climax. This sound befits the final mood of
the cantata text:

> Erschallet Jubelchöre,
> dass laut die Welt es höre!
> er gab uns Jubel und Heil,
> er gab uns Frieden und Heil!
> gross ist er!

The vocal writing is not and does not need to be involved or
significant. The voices in effect are supplying harmony notes for
this all-encompassing instrumental figure, which, as the tension and
dynamics grow, is taken up by the full orchestra against dominant
pedals in the inner voices and alternations between A and D in the
timpani. After a fourteen-measure build-up, an answer in block
chords for four measures sets the stage for a repeat of the effect.
For contrast the first eight measures this time are set for four solo
voices with six measures tutti. The answer this time is ten measures
long and leads into a final section lasting twenty-nine measures.

If there is no need at this point for tonal resolution, there is an
opportunity for thematic recall which Beethoven grasps convincingly. The original instrumental figure (Ex. 1) has more forward
drive now since it starts on the second rather than the first eighth-
note of the measure. The text, "gross ist er!", is set to the original
rising figure on the triadic notes, and the descending scale in the

orchestra (Ex. 2) is now in the flowing rhythm of the ostinato figure (Ex. 5) with its fall and rise (see Ex. 6). After seventeen measures the choral part is completed.

Ex. 6

With the setting of the empty text completed, Beethoven seems liberated; the orchestral writing of the last twelve measures reveals a clear form of thematic combination and resolution, which at last raises the level of musical thought from the commonplace. The scale descent in its original rhythm is now introduced on the tonic

and achieves the effect, so common in Beethoven, of slowing the
momentum for a last contemplative moment before the final rush
of notes. After six measures, this lilting figure receives its answer
in a final combination of three ideas. Above the ostinato figure in
the lower strings, the violins state the rising triadic idea in the
rhythm of the opening instrumental figure (Ex. 7). For the first
time the listener experiences that focus and conciseness of musical
invention in the working-out of ideas that the introduction had led
him to expect. This expectation would not exist if this element were
not the hallmark of all the composer's significant works.

Ex. 7

It is one of the measures of Beethoven's greatness as an artist that
any clues to this greatness, such as the humble ones discussed here,
can be of concern to all who revere his art.

WAGNER'S MUSICAL SKETCHES
FOR *SIEGFRIEDS TOD**

ROBERT BAILEY

WAGNER originally planned to make just one opera
from the Nibelung material with which he had become
familiar during his years in Dresden. In 1848, according
to his usual habit, he wrote an elaborate prose scenario and then a
complete libretto for a "grand heroic opera in three acts" (and a
prologue) called *Siegfrieds Tod*.[1] Later on, he expanded his material
into a tremendous cycle for three days and a preliminary evening,
and *Siegfrieds Tod*, after careful revision, assumed its position as
the final opera in *Der Ring des Nibelungen*. The structure of the
whole cycle thus parallels that of the first dramatic conception,
eventually called *Götterdämmerung*,[2] which serves as "a recapitula-

* I appreciate this opportunity to offer my sincere gratitude to Professor Strunk
who drew this subject to my attention and who, with characteristic generosity,
turned over to me his own transcriptions and notes on the problem. Transcriptions
from Wagner's sketches are printed here with the gracious permission of Mme
Winifred Wagner, Bayreuth. Portions of this essay were delivered as a lecture at
the annual meeting of the American Musicological Society in Washington, D.C.,
December 26-29, 1964.

[1] The scenario was published by Otto Strobel in *Richard Wagner: Skizzen und
Entwürfe zur Ring-Dichtung, mit der Dichtung "Der junge Siegfried"* (Munich,
1930), pp. 38-55. This scenario, dated October 20, 1848, at the end, lacks the prologue for which Wagner later made an undated prose sketch, published *ibid.*, pp.
56-58. The poem, complete with prologue, was written between November 12 and
28, 1848, according to the dates at the beginning and end of the manuscript; it was
revised during the first weeks of 1849 and, in this form, was incorporated into the
German edition of Wagner's collected writings: *Sämtliche Schriften und Dich-
tungen*, 5th edn. (Leipzig, n.d.), II, 167-228. (The pagination is the same in the
6th edition.)

[2] The title remained *Siegfrieds Tod*, even in the cycle, for some time. Wagner
changed it because of the conclusion of the work, which was not given its final
form until after a considerable portion of the music had been composed. The first
documented mention of the new title occurs in a letter to Franz Müller of Weimar,
dated June 22, 1856, i.e., several months after *Die Walküre* was complete in full
score. For the important passages of this letter and for further information on the
problem of the ending, see Strobel, *Skizzen*, pp. 258-61, and his supplementary
article, "Zur Entstehungsgeschichte der Götterdämmerung: Unbekannte Dokumente
aus Wagners Dichterwerkstatt," in *Die Musik*, xxv/5 (February 1933), 336-41.
Ernest Newman has summarized the essential facts in *The Life of Richard Wagner*,
II (New York, 1937), 354-56.

tion of the whole, a prologue and three pieces."[3] It is now possible to trace almost every step of that complicated evolution of the poem to its completion at the end of 1852, thanks to the excellent publications of Otto Strobel,[4] archivist to House Wahnfried until his untimely death in 1953.

Shortly after Wagner had finished the initial revision of *Siegfrieds Tod*—during the first weeks of 1849[5]—he became involved with the revolutionary forces in the Dresden uprising and ultimately was forced to flee German territory. He devoted most of his time during the ensuing years to literary activity: this is the period not only of the *Ring* poem, but also of his longest and most famous prose treatises—*Art and Revolution, The Artwork of the Future, Opera and Drama*, and *A Communication to My Friends*. But he also began sketching music for *Siegfrieds Tod* in the summer of 1850. Accordingly, not only are these the first musical sketches connected with the *Ring* in any way,[6] but also they constitute Wagner's only dramatic music between the completion of *Lohengrin* in the spring of 1848 and the beginning of work on *Das Rheingold* in the late autumn of 1853. As far as *Siegfrieds Tod* was concerned, Wagner himself later wrote about this period as follows:

> During that period, in the autumn of 1848, I did not even think about the possibility of performing *Siegfrieds Tod*, but regarded the technical completion of its poem and isolated attempts at setting it to music as nothing more than a private satisfaction to which I treated myself at that time of disgust with public affairs and of withdrawal from them.[7]

[3] ". . . *eine Wiederholung des Ganzen, ein Vorspiel und drei Stücke*." From the entry in Cosima Wagner's diary for September 9, 1876, published in *Bayreuther Blätter*, LIX/1 (Winter 1936), 5.

[4] For an English summary of Strobel's publications with critical commentary, see Ernest Newman, *Life*, II, 24-31 and 325-61, and "The Nibelung's Ring" in *The Wagner Operas* (New York, 1949), pp. 393-450.

[5] Strobel, *Skizzen*, pp. 59-60, and Newman, *Life*, II, 31.

[6] The first draft of the poem contains a musical fragment in the margin on the page with Siegfried's monologue and death in the second scene of Act III. This page was first published in facsimile by Houston Stewart Chamberlain, *Richard Wagner* (Munich, 1896), following p. 266. Chamberlain assumed that this fragment was related to *Siegfrieds Tod* even though it has the appearance of trombone parts for something else as yet unidentified. The page is also reproduced in Erich Engel, *Richard Wagners Leben und Werke im Bilde* (Vienna, 1913), p. 169.

[7] *Eine Mitteilung an meine Freunde*, in *Schriften*, IV, 331.

He had also been encouraged to proceed with the music by Liszt, who by the spring of 1850 was reporting favorably on the preparations under way at Weimar for the forthcoming production of *Lohengrin*. Liszt promised to use his influence to persuade the Grand Duke to commission *Siegfrieds Tod* for Weimar and to give Wagner a grant which would enable him to finish the opera within a year.

The commission never materialized, but Wagner nonetheless set to work with enthusiasm. As he tells us in his autobiography,

> I now felt very much attracted to accepting the Weimar proposal. Still worn out by my strenuous labor on *Opera and Drama* and exhausted by so much which weighed sorrowfully upon my heart, I sat down again—for the first time in a long while—at my Haertel piano which had been recovered from the Dresden catastrophe, in order to see how I might get started on the composition of my weighty epic drama. In a hasty sketch, I drafted music for the Norns' scene which had only been outlined in that first version [of the poem]; just as I was setting Brünnhilde's first address to Siegfried to music, however, all my courage failed me since I could not refrain from asking myself which singer should bring this heroine to life the following year.[8]

Wagner's reference to *Opera and Drama* is incorrect, for he did not begin work on the treatise until after he had abandoned his attempts to write the music for *Siegfrieds Tod*. He was indeed exhausted by a great deal which weighed sorrowfully upon his heart at that time, but it was not the strenuous labor of writing *Opera and Drama*; rather it was the disastrous love affair with Jessie Laussot in Bordeaux,[9] which Wagner apparently felt obliged to smooth over for the benefit of Cosima to whom he dictated the autobiography in later years. In *A Communication to My Friends*, written only a year or so after these events, his chronology is more accurate:

> After I had returned [to Zurich], I deceived myself once more with the thought of carrying out the musical setting of *Siegfrieds Tod*: half-despair was still at the root of this decision, for I knew I should now be writing this music only for paper. The intolerably

[8] *Mein Leben* ("Erste authentische Veröffentlichung," Munich, 1963), p. 541.
[9] For further biographical information on this episode, see Newman, *Life*, II, 136-58.

clear knowledge of this disgusted me once more with my project; in consciousness of the fact that in any case I should, for the most part, be ever so completely misunderstood in my endeavor, I again had recourse to literary work and wrote my book on *Opera and Drama*.[10]

In short, Wagner made sketches for the music of *Siegfrieds Tod* before he had written *Opera and Drama*, and the treatise is thus to some extent the result of at least some practical experience in working out a new manner of writing musical drama, rather than purely a presentation of theoretical ideas in advance, as we have always supposed. The two passages just quoted indicate some of the reasons why he gave up the project before completing even the prologue. But he must also have felt the need to organize his new ideas more concretely before attempting to apply them on a grand scale.

In 1933, an extended musical sketch for the prologue of this work was published in facsimile.[11] At the beginning, it bears the date August 12, 1850, and it contains a careful draft in ink of the Norns' scene and continues through the second speech in the ensuing duet of Brünnhilde and Siegfried. While Newman and Westernhagen both referred to it as a "Composition Sketch," Strobel[12] called it an "Orchestral Sketch," implying in his use of this term that there must also have been an earlier and less elaborate sketch for the same material.[13] The published sketch, in addition to being carefully

[10] *Schriften*, IV, 337.

[11] In *L'Illustration* (February 11, 1933), pp. 166-68. This sketch has been discussed by Newman in *Life*, II, 159-61, and in *Wagner Operas*, pp. 412-14, and also by Curt von Westernhagen, *Vom Holländer zum Parsifal: Neue Wagner-Studien* (Zurich, 1962), pp. 38-54, and "Die Kompositions-Skizze zu 'Siegfrieds Tod' aus dem Jahre 1850" in *Neue Zeitschrift für Musik*, 124/5 (May 1963), pp. 178-82. For a long time the sketch was in the possession of M. Louis Barthou, who left it to the Bibliothèque Nationale in Paris. It has since been sold and is now in France in private hands.

[12] *Richard Wagner. Leben und Schaffen: Eine Zeittafel* (Bayreuth, 1952), p. 41.

[13] Wagner's procedure in working out the music for a dramatic work perhaps requires some explanation. He ordinarily made at least two complete drafts: first, a very hasty and sketchy one in pencil, and secondly, a more detailed and elaborate one in ink. Strobel, in an attempt to put all the treasures of the Bayreuth archives into some kind of order, categorized these drafts with the names *Kompositions-skizzen* and *Orchesterskizzen*, and through the writings of Newman the terms have become familiar to English-speaking readers as "Composition Sketch" and "Orchestral Sketch." Wagner never referred to these drafts in any consistent way, and the terms are misleading, for the function and degree of elaboration of the drafts

written in ink with a minimum of corrections, contains detailed dynamic indications, tempo indications, and some stage directions, elements usually lacking in a Composition Sketch. Strobel's assumption was, of course, entirely correct: the Composition Sketch for *Siegfrieds Tod* is now in the Library of Congress, Gertrude Clarke Whittall Foundation.[14]

We can recognize at a glance that this sketch was made before August 12, when Wagner began the Orchestral Sketch, and we may assume that it was written some time after July 27, on which date

---

changed drastically during his career. As the orchestral fabric became more complicated, he naturally found it necessary to work out things more extensively in advance of the full score, so that the first draft of *Tristan*, for example, represents in many passages as advanced a stage as the second draft for *Tannhäuser*. And, similarly, for the last works of all, the first draft is nearly as complete as the more bare passages of the Orchestral Sketch of *Tristan*. The orchestral part gradually requires more staves, occasionally using as many as four in the latest works. The term "Orchestral Sketch" is particularly misleading because these drafts do not in any way approximate an orchestral score, and indications for the instrumentation are minimal. We must always bear in mind that anything actually noted down was much more meaningful to Wagner than it would be to us without our preliminary knowledge of the final version. In any event, all Composition Sketches have in common an emphasis upon the setting of the text, with the accompaniment for the moment relegated to the background; and the Orchestral Sketches have in common their attempt to bring the most essential details of the accompaniment into final focus. Once the Orchestral Sketch was complete, Wagner could consider his creative task at an end, for it sufficed to remind him of the music in detail, and all that remained for him was to work out the specific instrumentation in the definitive full score.

[14] The manuscript was formerly in the possession of a certain Gustav Herrmann of Leipzig. In 1913, he allowed it to appear in an exhibition whose catalogue contains the first known description. The entry begins as follows: "*Musical Sketches for 'Siegfrieds Tod,'* Wagner's first Nibelung drama, for which he worked out the libretto in November, 1848. It was to contain three acts and a prologue. The present musical sketches, made in 1849 [*sic*], are the sole evidence for the fact that Wagner in these early years was already thinking of even the musical realization of the Nibelung material, and at the same time proof that he found the main motives for the music of the Nibelung trilogy at that time." *Richard Wagner Gedächtnis-Ausstellung, aus Anlass des hundertjährigen Geburtstages Richard Wagners*, veranstaltet vom Komitee für das Leipziger Richard-Wagner-Denkmal und dem Stadtgeschichtlichen Museum zu Leipzig (Leipzig, May 1913), pp. 22-23. There follows a short paragraph (paraphrased in Westernhagen, *Wagner-Studien*, p. 39n) describing the sheet sufficiently well to identify it as the one now in the Library of Congress, which acquired it from an intermediate owner, Jerome Stonborough. Meanwhile, the first two lines of this sketch had been published in quasi-facsimile by Julius Kapp in *Richard Wagner: Sein Leben, sein Werk, seine Welt in 260 Bildern* (Berlin-Schöneberg, 1933), p. 50.

he made it clear in a letter to his friend, Theodor Uhlig, that he had not yet started composing the music for *Siegfrieds Tod* but was about to do so and that for this purpose he had procured a *Rastral* (a device for drawing musical staves).[15] The Washington Sketch is actually written on paper with staves drawn by such a device, and Wagner consistently uses lower case letters for the initial letters of common nouns,[16] a habit which he does not seem to have picked up until the winter of 1849-50. Like the published sketch, the earlier one is a single large sheet written on both sides. It, too, contains a setting of the prologue—the entire Norns' scene, with a few omissions which are added in the Orchestral Sketch, and the first part of the duet, which continues for an additional eleven lines beyond the later version. There are also sketches for music associated with the Valkyries. The lower portion of the second side of this sheet has been published in reduced facsimile.[17]

At this time, Wagner had not even thought of an opera which would correspond to the one we know today as *Die Walküre*, but the presence on this sheet of music for the Valkyries is not surprising. In the original versions of *Siegfrieds Tod*, he had planned to have all the Valkyries come to Brünnhilde in the third scene of Act I to plead with her to give up the ring which Siegfried had entrusted to her keeping during the duet. In the final poem for the *Ring*, however, it is only Waltraute who steals away from Valhalla on the hopeless mission. Wagner's first conception was a melody in two complementary phrases:

[15] *Richard Wagner's Briefe an Theodor Uhlig, Wilhelm Fischer, Ferdinand Heine* (Leipzig, 1888), Letter No. 14, p. 45. This publication gives no date for the letter since there is none on the original document. Glasenapp, in *Das Leben Richard Wagners*, II, 5th edn. (Leipzig, 1910), 434 dates it July 27 without a word of explanation. Nevertheless, this date proves to be correct, as can be seen in the dated letter of the same day to Julie Ritter, in which Wagner says that he has had "a rather lengthy letter to write to Uhlig" that very day. This letter to Julie Ritter leaves no doubt that the letter in question is the one to which Wagner refers. See Siegmund von Hausegger, ed., *Richard Wagners Briefe an Frau Julie Ritter* (Munich, 1920), Letter No. VI, p. 45.

[16] Wagner had planned to publish the poem in the spring of 1850, but this idiosyncrasy, together with his insistence upon the use of Roman type, had made the printer refuse his manuscript. For the projected publication, he wrote a preface which was published for the first time in Edgar Istel, "König Ludwigs 'Wagner-Buch,'" in *Die Musik*, X/1 (1910-11), 15-23. That preface was later incorporated into the 6th edition of *Schriften*, XVI, 84-85.

[17] Emanuel Winternitz, *Musical Autographs from Monteverdi to Hindemith* (Princeton, 1955), II, Plate 131.

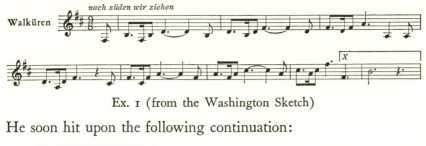

Ex. 1 (from the Washington Sketch)

He soon hit upon the following continuation:

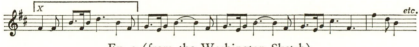

Ex. 2 (from the Washington Sketch)

The section marked *x* replaces the section so marked in Ex. 1. Because Wagner evidently wrote out the label "Walküren" before he noted down the theme, we are safe in assuming that he conceived the theme with the Valkyries in mind but without any specific textual association. Afterwards, he probably looked through the text of this scene and found that the lines of the concluding chorus could be adapted to the melody, and then wrote out the *incipit* above the first measure.[18]

As it stands, the melody differs rhythmically from its final form, in that the note on the second beat in each measure is sustained through most of the third. The second four-measure phrase begins in the dominant minor here and returns directly to the tonic, so that the melody as a whole lacks the vibrant color it later assumed. Wagner's next step was to elaborate a revised form of the melody *in ink*:

Nach sü - den wir zie - hen,   sie - ge zu zeu - gen   kämp-fen-den hee - ren zu

Ex. 3 (from the Washington Sketch)

[18] This kind of situation occurred frequently. See, for example, Wagner's letter of July 9, 1859, to Mathilde Wesendonk (Wolfgang Golther, ed., *Richard Wagner an Mathilde Wesendonk: Tagebuchblätter und Briefe, 1853-1871* [Berlin, 1908], p. 161), regarding a melody which he did not even know belonged in the final scene of *Siegfried* until after he had searched through the text!

Ex. 3 (cont.)

The first measure of the accompaniment is worked out, and Wagner has transposed the second phrase so that it now begins in the relative major, evidently in order to avoid the square feeling given by the immediate return to the tonic and to postpone the high f-sharp until the end. He has carefully adapted the text, and in addition, we find the call of "Hoiho!" associated with the Valkyries in the later work, but not part of the *Siegfrieds Tod* poem at all—a feature which has grown directly out of the *musical* conception. On the other hand, the adaptation of the text has necessitated some rhythmic changes in the earlier part of the melody.

The last two lines of this portion of the manuscript show the whole melody in B major and written out in octaves, presumably to indicate fuller instrumentation. Once again the third phrase is repeated, and except for two further details—the up-beat into the seventh measure and the c♮ (Neapolitan) in the eleventh—the melody has now assumed the final form in which it is used in *Die Walküre* and in the concert excerpt known as the "Ride of the Valkyries."[19]

[19] The instrumental selection known as the "Ride of the Valkyries" is not simply the orchestral accompaniment of the beginning of the third act of *Die Walküre* with an appended "concert ending," but a new composition based on the material of that scene. Wagner made the excerpt in Biebrich during the autumn of 1862 for a series of concerts projected for the coming winter in Vienna. On October 14, he wrote to Wendelin Weissheimer, who was responsible for the preparation of the parts in Leipzig: "It was difficult to prepare the piece properly; I had to rearrange the order of various passages in the score ["musste in der Partitur bald vor, bald rückwärts greifen"]. Yet, as you will find, everything is unerringly put in order; I have even attached a special set of instructions." The text of the entire letter is printed in W. Weissheimer, *Erlebnisse mit Richard Wagner . . .* , 2nd edn. (Stuttgart and Leipzig, 1898), pp. 182-84. Glasenapp quotes only the first of these two sentences, and his ensuing account of the situation (in *Leben*, III, 4th edn., Leipzig, 1905, 397) is misleading in its implication that Wagner himself wrote out a full score of the new piece, from which Weissheimer could then get the parts copied. A later passage in Weissheimer's memoirs (pp. 209-210) makes it clear that this was not the case: "According to agreement I had remained in Leipzig in order to keep the copyists under my eye and to assist them with advice in their huge and very complicated task of writing out Wagner's scores. This was especially necessary in the case of the 'Ride of the Valkyries,' which had to be written out in an order different from that in which it stood in the score, because for concert use Wagner had excluded the vocal parts and had therefore undertaken changes in the arrangement of the piece. Close attention had to be paid to this and other circumstances so that nothing would go wrong." In other words, the parts were copied from the full score of the *third act of the opera*, Wagner having indicated the new ordering and supplied instructions about the ending and other necessary changes.

He conducted the premiere of the new piece at the first of the Vienna concerts

Newman has discussed two later drafts of this melody, the earliest known versions at the time he was writing.[20] The first, dated July 23, 1851, contains only the first four bars shown above in Ex. 3, and Newman correctly assumed that the motive had been conceived much earlier. The second sketch, made for an autograph album, is dated November 12, 1852, and continues for eight measures with a change in text in the last line, which eliminates the up-beat into the seventh measure. Detailed examination of the various versions of the last line of this quatrain illustrates Wagner's procedure in gradually working out text and music, each in relation to the other. The various versions of the text may be summarized as follows:

Prose Sketch (1848): nach Walhall erschlagene Sieger zu geleiten

Poem (1848/9): nach Walhall zu führen erschlagene Sieger

Washington Sketch (1850): zu führen nach Walhall erschlagene Sieger

Autograph Album (1852): wehrliche Sieger zu senden nach Walhall

---

on December 26, 1862, where it was an immediate and extraordinary success. He conducted it again at a concert in Munich given at the command of Ludwig II on December 11, 1864. In spite of the public's continuing interest in the work, however, Wagner was never satisfied with it. Several years later, the following notice—inspired, if not actually written by the composer—appeared in the *Musikalisches Wochenblatt* (II/44, October 27, 1871, p. 700): "For the purpose of settling various enquiries about the means of obtaining the score of the so-called 'Ride of the Valkyries' by R. Wagner, we herewith inform our readers that as yet, such a composition does not even exist, as there is no score at all for it from Wagner's hand. The orchestral parts for this piece were put together at one time by a capable Viennese copyist,—to be sure, according to Wagner's delineation of certain passages of the *Walküre* score (brought about, however, by special circumstances),—copied at some time or other, and later bought and used by B. Bilse, among others, behind Wagner's back and without his consent. Richard Wagner protests categorically against such a patchwork being presented to a concert audience as an actual piece of music,—a patchwork which he sanctioned only at a time of distress in making up a really 'attractive' concert program." The reference to a copyist in Vienna, rather than in Leipzig, undoubtedly resulted from a confusion in Wagner's mind later on, since the parts for most of the other selections played in the Vienna concerts had indeed been copied there. An interesting sidelight on this problem is the fact that among the copyists in Vienna was none other than Johannes Brahms! (See *Mein Leben*, p. 817.)

[20] *Life*, II, 240-42.

In Ex. 3, double alliteration is paralleled by rhythmic similarity in the first and second measures, and again in the fifth and sixth:

nach *s*üden wir *z*iehen   für *h*elden zu *f*echten
     *s*iege zu *z*eugen   and   *h*elden zu *f*ällen

If the version of the poem had been followed in the last line, the first syllable of the word "führen" would occur on the second beat in alliteration with "fechten" and "fällen," whereas no such alliterative parallel exists between the first two lines. Wagner therefore reversed the order of the first two phrases of the last line. The parallel structure is heightened by the new text of 1852: the initial "f" is eliminated altogether, as is the weak syllable at the beginning of the line, thus making the two couplets of the text and the two phrases of accompanying music exactly complementary in rhythm and placement of alliterative syllables.

When Wagner wrote *Die Walküre* later on, he used this melody only as an instrumental motive, and it is a striking characteristic of his unique imagination that this melody should have lingered in his memory in a form conditioned and changed by the gradual adaptation of texts with which it is nowhere associated in the opera. With this early conception in 1850 of an important musical motive, Wagner has established the tonality of a whole scene (*Die Walküre,* III/1) in advance of the composition of any of the music for the present *Ring*. This is also true of the Norns' scene, as has been pointed out by Newman.[21] The opening portion of that scene in *Götterdämmerung* is in E♭ minor, just as it is in these sketches for *Siegfrieds Tod*, made some nineteen years before, even though the two versions of that scene have entirely different texts.

A complete composite transcription of the music for the prologue is appended to this study. I have followed the reading of the Orchestral Sketch (the *L'Illustration* Sketch) as far as it goes (up through m. 166) and taken the remaining material from the earlier Composition Sketch (the Washington Sketch), supplying the text and a detail of the accompaniment in the last nine measures. The prologue does not run straight on from beginning to end in the earlier sketch, but the order of Wagner's procedure is not difficult to determine. He began in ink at the top of the sheet with the opening of the pro-

[21] *Ibid.*, p. 160.

logue; the use of ink may indicate that he was copying or elaborating a still earlier sketch of some kind. After making quite a few corrections, he broke off at m. 20. The remainder of the prologue is written in pencil and is thus probably the first draft. The passage in ink (see Ex. 4) extends onto the fourth staff. Beginning at the end of the fourth staff, Wagner continued in pencil through m. 41. He then turned the sheet over and started at the top with m. 56, continued through m. 77, and switched back to the first side to complete the Norns' scene (through the first major cadence of the instrumental epilogue at m. 108). The last four staves on the first side contain the beginning of the duet without the orchestral introduction, through the fourth line of Siegfried's first speech (m. 157). The duet continues at the bottom of the second side, the sketches for the music of the Valkyries having intervened, probably before Wagner began composing the duet. His work with the Washington fragment may be summarized as follows (measure numbers as in my composite transcription):

I. Recto, staves 1-4	Ink	(Mm. 1-20: elaborated version?)	Prologue/ Scene 1
II. Recto, staves 4-6	Pencil	(29-41: first draft, no text)	
III. Verso, staves 1-5	Pencil	(56-77: first draft)	
IV. Recto, staves 6-9	Pencil	(77-108: first draft)	
V. Verso, single staves 6 and 7	Pencil	(Valkyries: first draft; textual incipit only)	Act I/ Scene 3
VI. Verso, staves 8-11	Ink	(Valkyries: elaborated version; includes text)	
VII. Recto, staves 10-13	Pencil	(122-57: first draft)	Prologue/ Scene 2
VIII. Verso, staves 12-14	Pencil	(158-92: first draft)	

The declamatory style of the vocal lines and the harmonic style of the accompaniment are reminiscent of *Lohengrin*. But in some respects, Wagner has tried to get away from the more "regular" structure and the effect of squareness in his earlier works. In the

Norns' scene, for example, he has hit upon a new technique of tripartite organization. First of all, there are the three characters who sing of the past, the present, and the future. There are three occurrences of a refrain and three major narrative sections. Throughout, Wagner has consistently avoided traditional phrase lengths of four and eight measures. The overall tonal organization, with E minor used as the tonality contrasting with E♭ minor, is also a distinctly new feature. The formal structure of the scene may be diagrammed as follows:

Measures		First Norn (PAST)	Second Norn (PRESENT)	Third Norn (FUTURE)
1-9	*REFRAIN* 3 mm. (instrumental) + 6 mm. (vocal) ───── 6/4 e♭ minor			
10-20	SECTION I: *Alberich and the Rheingold* 6/4 e♭ minor	3 mm.	3 mm.	5 mm.
21-29	*REFRAIN*			
30-47	SECTION II: *Gods and Giants: Grief of the Gods* **C** e minor	6 mm.	6 mm.	6 mm.
48-56	*REFRAIN*			
56-77	SECTION III: *Siegfried and Brünnhilde* **C** e♭ minor→E♭ major	6 mm.	6 mm.	9 mm.
78-80	*MODIFIED REFRAIN* 3 mm. (vocal) ───── 6/4 E♭ major			
81-93	CODA (vocal) 6/4 E♭ major	2 mm.	2 mm.	2 mm. + 6 mm. à 3
94-108	*Instrumental epilogue* 6/4→ **C** E♭ major			

The sketch in ink at the top of the first side of the Composition Sketch represents a version of the first twenty measures (Refrain and Section I) even earlier than that shown in the complete transcription:

* For the sake of clarity, Wagner's corrections are not indicated.

Ex. 4

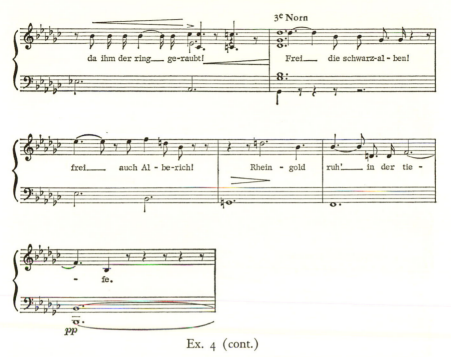

Ex. 4 (cont.)

Wagner must have seen that 6/4 would permit a less forced and more natural manner of declamation, and he proceeded accordingly from this point. When working out this section in the Orchestral Sketch, he not only made the necessary change in the meter, but also wrote a simpler bass figure in eighth notes, and introduced a change to duple meter at the end of the section. In this context, it is enlightening to glance at the beginning of the Composition Sketch for *Das Rheingold*, in which Wagner again used a bass figure in sixteenth notes, evidently planning already at this early stage to have similar openings for the first and fourth operas of the cycle.

Ex. 5. *Das Rheingold*, Composition Sketch (original in the Archiv des Hauses Wahnfried)

Ex. 5 (cont.)

Section II follows in pencil with no text, and the music for the third Norn's speech is missing. Wagner turned the sheet over to begin the music for Section III, and on the first staff is the following motive:

Ex. 6

The application of this material to the speeches of the first and second Norns follows, and it corresponds to mm. 56 through 68 in the transcription. Wagner expanded each of the first two measures of the original motive into a two-measure phrase for the first and second of the three lines, and then wrote a two-measure concluding phrase for the final line, which is similar in its scalar descent to the last two measures of the original motive. He then repeated the whole of the new phrase a third higher for the speech of the second Norn. In each of these speeches, the first two lines make one sentence, the third line a contrasting sentence, and this is reflected in his sequential setting of the first two lines in each case. Once again, as noted in the development of the theme of the Valkyries, the adaptation of the text has brought about changes in the initial musical conception: in this case, a conventional phrase of four measures has been expanded to six.

The most revealing section of the Norns' scene in the Composition Sketch is the setting of the first part of the third Norn's speech which follows immediately, for Wagner has two versions of it, with a correction in the fourth measure of the later version (see Ex. 7). Except for the word "treu," Wagner did not even bother to write out the text in the first version, but crossed out the whole passage and continued immediately with the new idea. In correcting the fourth measure of the latter, however, he wrote on top of his original thought, and this may have occurred at some later time, after he had tried it out at the piano.

Sequential treatment of this passage is present already in the earlier version. The sequential unit has two measures here, but only one in the corrected version, so that the musical line divides accord-

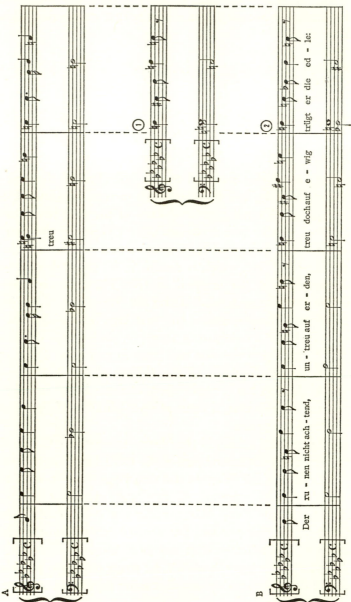

Ex. 7

ing to the structure of the text and thus follows the sense of the line. In addition, Wagner has eliminated the *Lohengrin*-like dotted rhythm in the second and fourth measures. The next two measures were originally alike in the later version, except for the contrast of the f♯ and f♮, this similarity evidently growing out of the double alliteration on the first and third beats:

*tr*eu doch auf *e*wig
and
*tr*ügt er die *e*dle.

But Wagner evidently felt that the sense of the line was improved if the whole of these two measures ran on as one melodic unit rather than being divided in half, since the two lines made a continuous clause. The juxtaposition of major and minor forms of a short phrase is a feature of Wagner's earlier style, and we see here a stage in its disappearance.

The poem of *Siegfrieds Tod* underwent extensive revision in 1852 so that it could serve as the final drama in the cycle. At that time, Wagner wrote an entirely new text for the Norns' scene, which he later considered "only outlined" in the earlier version.[22] But he left the text of the duet for Brünnhilde and Siegfried essentially unaltered. He did not begin composing the music for *Götterdämmerung* until the autumn of 1869, by which time he had written many of his most important works—*Tristan*, the new scenes of *Tannhäuser* for the ill-fated production in Paris, and the *Meistersinger*, in addition to the first three operas of the *Ring*—and his musical style had changed drastically. This is the only text for which Wagner made two independent settings, and they are separated by a crucial interval of nineteen years. As material for comparative study of stylistic change, they are as revealing as Alban Berg's two settings of Theodor Storm's *Schliesse mir die Augen beide* in 1900 and 1925.

Wagner's fundamental concern during the years following the completion of *Lohengrin* was the construction of a dramatic text that would be specifically and uniquely suitable for musical elaboration—a text constructed in such a way that, as Wagner later expressed it, the musical form is already completely prepared in the poem.[23]

[22] See the above quotation from *Mein Leben*.
[23] "*Zukunftsmusik*," in *Schriften*, VII, 123.

We have already seen some evidence of this concern in the Norns' scene, with its threefold refrain and three-part structure growing directly out of the dramatic material. In addition, however, Wagner wanted to find means of avoiding long stretches of recitative-like declamation in narrative texts, such as Telramund's accusation in the first act of *Lohengrin*, or in most of the speeches of the king. Part of the trouble lay in Wagner's almost complete avoidance of triple meter, the central flaw in the music of *Lohengrin*: the only passage in triple meter in the entire work is the short section in the first act extending from the king's prayer to the duel.[24] This shortcoming in the music was undoubtedly a direct outgrowth of writing poetic texts almost exclusively in iambs and trochees, also a characteristic of much German literary poetry of the early nineteenth century in spite of tentative experiments in the direction of poetic prose by men like Novalis.

Wagner's solution for the time being lay in *Stabreim*, or alliterative verse, and Westernhagen[25] has pointed out that this device permitted a freer alternation of duple and triple meter. But there is more to it than that. Wagner uses it to create a constantly shifting pattern of stressed syllables, above and beyond the ordinary metrical accentuation. Further, it enabled him to set up symmetries between lines or groups of lines without using the same number of syllables. And finally, there is the effective euphony of the device when the lines are *sung*.[26] That Wagner found texts constructed along these

[24] The use of triple meter, particularly of the 3/4 signature, is an important characteristic of Wagner's later musical style, for he seems to have avoided it altogether before 1850. It is rare enough in *Rienzi*, and in *The Flying Dutchman* it is used only for a short section in the choral scene of Act III. In *Tannhäuser*, Wagner employs it only for the Pilgrims' Chorus in Act III and at the beginning of the overture. It is hardly surprising that when he revised the first two scenes for Paris in 1860-61, he used 3/4 for one of the newly composed speeches of Venus and also for her big speech in the middle of the scene, taken over almost literally from the Dresden version where he had composed it in 4/4. On a passage in the poem of *Der junge Siegfried*, conceived originally for 2/4 meter but later (in the final *Siegfried*) actually written in 3/4, see Newman, *Wagner Operas*, pp. 407-410.

[25] *Wagner-Studien*, p. 50.

[26] We must constantly bear in mind that these are texts to be *sung*. As poems designed exclusively for *music*, they are unsurpassed, and nothing could represent greater misunderstanding of Wagner's intentions or do him greater injustice than to consider them apart from the music which accompanies them. In short, arguments back and forth about their *"literary"* quality are both uninformed and irrelevant. The fact that Wagner published the texts separately in no way negates this: he often enough had cause to regret his action. On April 15, 1859, for example, he wrote to Mathilde Wesendonk: "It occurred to me on that occasion [of reading

lines ideal for music, is indicated by the following passage of his letter to Theodor Uhlig of September 2, 1851, concerning *Der junge Siegfried* (later called simply *Siegfried*):

> I am now beginning the music, with which I really propose to enjoy myself. That which you cannot even imagine is happening quite of its own accord. I tell you, the musical phrases make themselves for these stanzas and periods, without my even having to take pains with them; it all grows out of the ground as if it were wild. I already have the beginning in mind, also some plastic motives such as Fafner.[27]

We have already seen some of these principles at work in his sketches for the music associated with the Valkyries, and we may now proceed to the duet itself. The earlier sketch is especially important here because it continues for eleven lines beyond the Orchestral Sketch. (It would be quite wrong to assume that Wagner had these sketches in his possession when he set to work at the composition of *Götterdämmerung* in 1869; in all likelihood, he had long since lost track of them, but they would have been of no use to him in any case.)[28]

Brünnhilde's first speech is organized in three stanzas and printed in this fashion in the final edition of the complete *Ring* libretto.[29] This permits yet another kind of tripartite musical organization

---

Goethe's *Tasso*] that it was ill-advised of me to publish [the poem of] *Tristan* after all. Between a poem entirely designed for music and a purely poetic stage-play, the distinction in design and realization must be so fundamentally different that the former, viewed with the same eye as the latter, must remain almost wholly incomprehensible as regards its essential meaning,—until it is completed by the music" (Golther, *Wagner an Mathilde Wesendonk*, p. 125).

[27] *Briefe an Uhlig, Fischer, Heine*, Letter No. 30, p. 99. This publication again has no date for the letter, but it is supplied, presumably from the envelope surviving with the copy made by Uhlig's widow, in John N. Burk, ed., *Letters of Richard Wagner: The Burrell Collection* (London, 1951), p. 620. It sounds as if Wagner may have made some musical sketches for *Der junge Siegfried* around this time, but aside from a few jottings in the margin of the poem, nothing of the kind has come to light so far. His statement about the beginning of the work seems sufficient evidence that he had at least decided upon the tonality of B-flat minor for the Nibelungs before the composition of the *Ring*, just as he had done in the case of B minor for the Valkyries.

[28] The very fact that these sketches survive but are not at Wahnfried is an indication that Wagner did *not* have them in his possession after 1864, from which time he gave all his musical manuscripts either to Cosima or to Ludwig II. The ones in Cosima's possession are at Wahnfried, while those given to Ludwig have been lost. On the latter group, see *Sänger-Zeitung*, xxxiv/10 (October 1958), p. 6.

[29] *Schriften*, vi, 182-83.

from that found in the Norns' scene. Both settings of the duet follow the same tonal plan: the first stanza begins in the tonic (A♭ major in 1850, E♭ major in 1869) and ends in the dominant, and both the second and third stanzas end in the tonic. In addition, the last lines of the first and third stanzas have the same metrical pattern, with the alliterative syllables in the same position. In 1850, Wagner gave each pair of lines approximately equivalent rhythmic patterns, arranged in such a way that the alliterative syllables always occur on the strong beat of a measure:

Ein ein - zig Sor - gen macht mich säu - men,

mög'st du die Ar - me nicht ver - ach - ten,

dass dir zu we - nig mein Werth ge - wann.

die dir nur gön - nen, nicht ge - ben mehr kann.

Ex. 8

In the later version, the phrase structure is much freer and thus the phrases for the two lines of each couplet are not of the same length. The important syllables now invariably coincide with the first beat of a measure:

Ein ein - zig Sor - gen lässt mich säu - men,

mög'st du die Ar - me nicht ver - ach - ten,

dass dir zu we - - nig mein Werth ge - wann.

die dir nur gön - - nen, nicht ge - - - ben mehr kann.

Ex. 9

Wagner has also emphasized the rhythmical similarity of "Ein einzig Sorgen" and "macht mich säumen" by setting each phrase to the same vocal line, a parallel which had not appeared in the earlier setting. And in the last line of each stanza, he has greatly increased the duration of the alliterative syllables, apparently to draw attention to the cadential function of these lines by setting them apart from the rest in style.

Westernhagen[30] has drawn attention to the similarity in treatment of "wie liebt' ich dich" in the two settings, with the rhythmic extension of the first word and the drop of a sixth in the melody; in addition, the melodic idea is the same in both settings of "liess' ich dich nicht." Each time, Wagner gave special treatment to this line, undoubtedly because of the symmetry of "liebt' ich dich" and "liess' ich dich."

In the second stanza, "heiliger Runen reichen Hort" stands in apposition with "Was Götter mich wiesen." In the earlier setting, Wagner has used the same rhythmic pattern on e-flat for the beginning of each line and supplied a different continuation. In 1869, however, he used sequence rather than simple repetition to enforce the grammatical relationship, and the melody of the entire first line is used again, continuation and all, for the second line, but a minor third higher. In both settings, the vocal line for "Was Götter mich wiesen" is the same, with the drop of a perfect fifth at the end. We encounter a similar situation in the third line of this stanza, "doch meiner Stärke magdlichen Stamm": Wagner seems to have felt on both occasions that the phrase "magdlichen Stamm" merited special treatment, and curiously, he devised the same melodic configuration, in spite of the different musical context, in each setting. The same figure, a third higher, is used for the first phrase of the following line, "nahm mir der Held," in 1850; in the later version, however, Wagner separated the two lines with a quarter rest and wrote a new figure for the phrase in question.

The first two lines of the third stanza are set up symmetrically; in 1850, Wagner gave the first half of each line, "des Wissens bar" and "an Liebe reich," the same figure, a third higher the second time. In addition, he used the same bass line for the second line as he had used for the first line, but a sixth lower. In 1869, however, he reinforced only the parallel between the two halves of the first line, "des Wissens bar" and "doch des Wunsches voll," by using the

30 *Wagner-Studien*, pp. 46-47.

same figure a perfect fifth higher for the second phrase as he used for the first—and ignored the parallel situation in the second line.

Every line in the text of Brünnhilde's speech is divided into two phrases, each of which has two metrical feet, and alliteration connects the two halves of each line.[31] In Siegfried's speech, on the other hand, there are three feet to the line, and the alliteration serves to link two successive lines into couplets. This fundamental change in the structure of the text is reflected in the music of 1850 by a change to triple meter and by a change of key to C major. In 1869, the rhythmic structure of the music is so complicated that a change in meter is not necessary, and the modulation (also to C major) is postponed until the final couplet.

The first two couplets of this speech have essentially the same melodic lines in the 1850 setting, whereas in the later version melodic repetition is used only to support the parallel in the text between "Lehren" in the third line and "-lehret" in the fourth, a parallel which had received no consideration in the earlier setting. The last two couplets also have essentially the same settings in 1850, with a one-measure change of meter in the latter line of each couplet. Thus, in 1850, Wagner had set the speech in triple meter but had made an effort to contrast its duple structure with the three-part structure of Brünnhilde's preceding speech by using a twofold statement of one melodic line for the first two couplets and a twofold statement of another melodic line for the last two couplets. In the later setting, however, sequential treatment once again replaces repetition in the last two couplets, and the first line of each one has the same melody, but a semitone higher the second time. The second line of each couplet has a different vocal line, but the accompaniment continues the sequential parallel established in the first line of each couplet.

The last line of the speech serves, with a change in the verb, as a refrain after the next two speeches of Brünnhilde. The second and third occurrences of this refrain are essentially the same in the first setting, including the one-measure change to duple meter, but with the first syllable of the word "Brünnhilde" extended the second and third times. In the 1869 version, the parallel in the melodic lines is

---

[31] These remarks apply to the text of *Siegfrieds Tod* as printed in *Schriften*, II, 170. In the later text of the complete *Ring* (*Schriften*, VI, 182-83), however, each phrase is printed as a separate line.

less exact, though here the first syllable of the word "Brünnhilde" is also lengthened in the second and third occurrences of the refrain. No metric change enforces the identification; instead, the orchestral accompaniment clarifies the function of this line as refrain.

Brünnhilde's next two speeches are organized in tercets, representing a return to the idea of tripartite structure in contrast to the duple structure of the intervening speech of Siegfried. The second and third lines both begin with the words "gedenke deiner," and Wagner has used a sequence in the vocal line in 1850. Later, however, he used the sequential idea only in the accompaniment, where it is carried one line further to support the parallel with the first line of the second tercet (also beginning with "Gedenke"). This symmetry had been ignored in 1850.

The second tercet has the same construction as the next speech, and each of the six lines uses the letter "f" as the alliterative consonant. Each tercet is followed by Siegfried's refrain. In 1850, the two units are set sequentially, refrain and all. In the 1869 version, the first lines and third lines correspond, but in different ways: the first are simply set to a repeated note a whole tone apart, while the third lines correspond in their use of the same characteristic motive, varied rhythmically and melodically the second time.

Wagner's setting of these lines in *Götterdämmerung* runs to 110 measures, whereas his earlier sketch contains only 71, so that the final version is half again as long as the earlier one. In several passages, he improved the declamation; by 1869, he had become a master of that art. In setting "Willst du mir Minne schenken," for example, he had placed the word "mir" on the first beat of m. 168, whereas the important stress of the line is placed more correctly and naturally on the first syllable of "Minne" in the later version.

In general, the vocal writing in 1850 emphasizes the smaller intervals except at a few important points, representing a continuation of the ingratiating lyrical style of such a passage as the bridal chamber scene in *Lohengrin*. The vocal lines are relatively independent, and one still has the feeling of melody plus accompaniment. In the later style, larger and more "characteristic" sixths, sevenths, and even octaves are regular features of the vocal writing. The role of the orchestra is expanded considerably, so that the vocal lines are overlaid on a more complicated orchestral fabric and thus serve as isolated strands of a richer polyphonic texture. And Wagner's harmonic vocabulary in 1869 naturally represents a considerable advance beyond that of 1850.

We have seen that Wagner favored sequential treatment of various kinds to the mere repetition he had used in 1850. And where he had used sequences to underscore textual parallels in the earlier version, he found different means to do this later on. The two settings of the duet, in short, are alike more in their overall structural plan than in specific melodic, harmonic, or rhythmic details. The structure is certainly the important feature conditioned by the text, in which Wagner was careful to set up refrains and corresponding or contrasting lines and groups of lines, all of which might be reflected in the music.

By now it will be apparent that the central interest of the 1850 sketches does not lie in the more or less coincidental resemblance of an early turn of phrase to one in the later *Ring*. Rather, they are invaluable for the light they shed on the problem of what Wagner had formulated before he began composing the music for *Das Rheingold*, and in the insights they provide about his compositional methods. In recent years, it has become a commonplace among students of Wagner's works to speak of the "simultaneous conception of words and music," yet careful comparison of the two versions of the duet provides convincing evidence that this idea needs modification. While at work on the music for the second act of *Siegfried*, Wagner summed up his own view of the matter in a revealing passage of his letter to Liszt on December 6, 1856: "Strange! Only during the act of composition does the real essence of my poem reveal itself to me: everywhere I discover secrets which had hitherto remained hidden even from me."[32] Wagner certainly wrote his libretto with a view to making it suitable for musical realization, but insofar as the libretto foreshadows the music at all, it foreshadows two decidedly different settings equally well.

[32] Erich Kloss, ed., *Briefwechsel zwischen Wagner und Liszt* (Leipzig, 1910), Part ii, Letter No. 223, p. 138.

APPENDIX

Wagner's 1850 Setting of the Prologue to *Siegfrieds Tod*

Ex. 10

Brünn-hild ge-wann der held, brach der Wal-kü-re schlaf!

lie-bend lernt sie ihm ru-nen. Der ru-nen nicht ach-tend,

un-treu auf er-den, treu doch auf e-wig trügt er die ed-le;

doch sei-ne that taugt sie zu deu-ten, frei zu voll-en-den, was

froh er be-gann. Win-dest du noch im wes-ten? We-best du

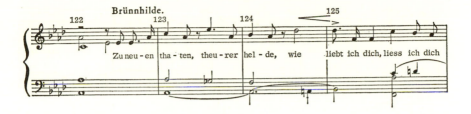

Brünnhilde.

Zu neu-en tha-ten, theu-rer hel-de, wie liebt ich dich, liess ich dich

nicht? Ein ein-zig sor-gen macht mich säu-men: dass dir zu we-nig mein werth ge-

wann. Was göt-ter mir wie-sen, gab ich dir, hei - li-ger ru-nen

rei - chen hort; doch mei-ner stär - ke magd-li-chen stamm nahm mir der

held, dem ich nun mich nei - ge: des wis-sens baar, doch des

wun-sches voll, an lie - be reich, doch le - dig der kraft: mögst du die

(langs.)

ar - me nicht ver - ach - ten, die dir nur gön - nen, nicht ge - ben mehr

(lebhafter) Siegfried

kann! Mehr gabst du, wun - der-frau, als ich zu wah - ren

weiss! Nicht zür - ne, wenn dein leh - - ren mich un - be-leh - - ret

liess! Ein wis - sen doch wahr ich wohl: dass mir Brünn - hil - de

VERDI'S USE OF RECURRING THEMES[1]

JOSEPH KERMAN

IN THE last act of *Otello*, at Otello's entrance *di una porta segreta* and again at his suicide, the orchestra plays music that was first heard at the high point of his love-duet with Desdemona in Act I. It is a famous dramatic stroke; many listeners, I believe, would have to search hard in their memory of Verdi's operas or of anyone else's to match its extraordinary feeling of summation, poignancy, and catharsis. One's sense of this masterstroke can be clarified by study of the "interior context," analyzing the musical and dramatic structure of *Otello*; it can also be clarified by study of the "exterior context," tracing outside the work the tradition to which the device belongs. For manifestly the idea of recalling earlier music in an opera did not come new to Verdi's mind in 1887. Everyone will think of thematic recurrences in many of the earlier operas—in *Rigoletto* and in *Aïda*—without perhaps realizing how widely, indeed how indiscriminately, Verdi employed this means throughout his career. This essay will trace some aspects of Verdi's use of recurring themes, or recurring passages, with special attention to the type that reaches its culmination in *Otello*.

This type has been given the name of *Erinnerungsmotiv*, or "reminiscence theme": "the introduction of a previously heard theme when there is in the action an obvious reminiscence of the earlier situation with which the theme is associated."[2] I think we would do a little better with the term "recalling theme," since opera is a form of drama, and of all memory verbs "to reminisce" seems the most undramatic. Notice that the above definition speaks of recalling a dramatic situation, not a person or a notion. It is both possible and helpful to discriminate between "recalling themes" and "identifying themes"—the latter being associated in a general way with groups of people (armies and priests in *Nabucco*, monks in *Don Carlo*), or with persons (Aïda, Tom, and Sam), or with ideas (the force of

[1] The material of this essay was first put together in 1955, at the instigation of Oliver Strunk, who was then heading the Program Committee for the Twenty-First Annual Meeting of the American Musicological Society, at Princeton. Some of the points were rapidly covered in my *Opera as Drama* (New York, 1956), pp. 154-58.
[2] Donald Jay Grout, *A Short History of Opera* (New York, 1947), p. 349.

destiny). Identifying themes are sung or played when the group, person, or idea is strongly in evidence, like a sonorous or "hermeneutic" extension of its physical or psychological presence. They are not used to link one stage of the drama to another, but simply to identify or make vivid. They serve to remind the audience rather than to remind the people in the play.

That the greatest subtleties are possible in the use of such themes we know from Wagner's practice, within which it would certainly be reckless to try to draw a hard line between functions of identification and recall. But surprisingly or not, with Verdi the distinction can be drawn rather cleanly. His use of identifying themes is with a few exceptions very uncomplicated. As an artistic device, the recalling theme interested him much more.

And in this area, a number of types are worth distinguishing, roughly graded on a scale of dramatic usage running from literalness to imaginativeness. Sometimes a libretto furnishes occasion for what may be termed "literal recall": a character is reminded in so many words of something said at an earlier juncture in the opera. In *Ernani*, Silva taunts Ernani in Act IV by quoting to his face the words and music of his pledge in Act II. In *Rigoletto*, however, when Rigoletto remembers Monterone's curse, he does so without Monterone talking to him; the musical recollection is motivated psychologically, not literally. To be sure, the librettist still pointed the way by having Rigoletto say to himself "Quel vecchio maledivami!" In the last act of *La Traviata*, a more imaginative stage yet is reached. When Violetta is reading Germont's letter, and then again later when she expires, the orchestra plays the music of Alfredo's original declaration of love in Act I even though no words in the libretto specifically refer to that act or that occasion. The composer has taken it on himself to interpret her memory.

An interesting and historically not unimportant middle stage between literal recall and more imaginative types comes up with persons in abnormal states of consciousness. When someone is mad, or dreaming, or in prophetic fervor, he may be supposed to "hear things." So recurring music for such a character really amounts to a literal representation of his abnormal state. The *gran scena* of *delirio* or *sogno* or *sonnambulismo* or *profezia* emerges as a regular cliché from the time of Bellini and Donizetti on. Often the character hears music from earlier in the opera—preferably from an earlier love-duet; and he or she may very well be restored to sanity by the right tune. The popularity of these scenes must have been due in part to the opportunities provided for musical recall.

When Verdi began writing for La Scala, around 1840, the thematic recurrences in the operas he heard[3] were almost all of the literal kinds. Identifying marches, choruses of priests, and so on, formed a part of every composer's stock in trade. "Recalling themes" tended to be concentrated in dream scenes and mad scenes—literal representations of unusual states of mind. Thus Bellini in *La Sonnambula* and *I Puritani*, and Donizetti in *Lucia di Lammermoor, Maria Padilla*, and *Linda di Chamounix*, to mention some of the more important works. *Linda* (1842), an especially extreme case, scored a particular success at La Scala at the time of *Ernani*, right after *Nabucco* and *I Lombardi*. Abandoned in Act II, Linda goes mad, singing part of the cabaletta of her previous love-duet (later we are informed that in her madness she sings it all the time). When the repentant Carlo returns to her, she refuses to credit him until *he* sings the cabaletta, which done, she regains her wits and all ends happily. In addition there are several appearances of a melancholy ballata (descended from Rossini's *La Cenerentola*) having to do with a girl who was unable to follow her mother's good advice about sexual prudence. Thus the two recurring themes symbolize the central dramatic conflict of the opera, such as it is.

On the other hand, some important works managed perfectly well without recurring themes. Mercadante's *Il Giuramento* and *Il Bravo*, the great successes at La Scala just prior to Verdi's run with *Nabucco, Lombardi*, and *Ernani*, involve none at all.

In French opera, recurring themes had a considerable tradition. Meyerbeer made the most of this with the repetitions of Rimbault's ballade in *Robert le diable*, and of "Ein' feste Burg" in *Les Huguénots*; the fashion seems to be reflected in the Parisian work of Bellini and Donizetti—scattered thematic recurrences of one sort or another may be noted in *I Puritani, Le Duc d'Albe, La Favorite, Les Martyrs*, and *Dom Sébastien*, as well as in Verdi's French under-

---

[3] Repertory is listed in Pompeo Cambiasi, *Teatro alla Scala, 1778-1881* (Milan, 1881), and Luigi Romani, *Teatro alla Scala: Cronologia* (Milan, 1862). For a note on Rossini's practice, see Alfredo Bonnacorsi, "Il Leitmotiv," *Bolletino del Centro Rossiniano di Studi*, IV, No. 1 (1958), 1-4 (I am grateful to Professor Marvin Tartak for this reference).

takings. Most interesting in this respect is *Le Prophète*, the toast of Paris while Verdi was there with Giuseppina in 1849. In this opera—it has been characterized as "hysterical and disheveled"[4]—Meyerbeer seems to have cast around for musical repetitions of all kinds and descriptions. The most obvious, the recurring *prêche* of the Anabaptists, will be cited later. The hero Jean's first major piece, in which he relates his prophetic dream, looks forward thematically not only to the famous Coronation March:

Ex. 1

but also to the big chorus on the occasion of his investiture in Act IV. Prior to this, when on two separate occasions he has qualms about joining the Anabaptists, the orchestra cites arias associated with his mother Fidès or his sweetheart Berthe. And at the start of the prison scene in Act V, Fidès almost absent-mindedly recalls a few bars of the cabaletta that ended Act IV.

Abramo Basevi, a Florentine physician, opera composer, and music critic who wrote a detailed study of Verdi's early operas in 1859—a study that is still better than most—considered that recurring themes in opera were first introduced and best used by Meyerbeer, run into the ground by Wagner, and not too well handled by Verdi: "Il *Verdi* veramente non fu mai molto felice nella ripresa dei *motivi*; nella quale industria il *Meyerbeer* fu tanto eccellente, e forse unico."[5] With which we cannot agree. However, it is clear that Verdi's heritage in this matter can be traced quite simply to Donizetti and Meyerbeer. (Wagner is, of course, not in the picture.) That a real tradition existed in Italy until shortly prior to Verdi's career is not so clear, though the reader may amuse himself by thinking of recurring themes in considerably older operas.

For the first dozen years of Verdi's career, his operas contain many recurring themes, used in a thoroughly haphazard fashion. So it was

[4] Wallace Brockway and Herbert Weinstock, *The World of Opera* (New York, 1962), p. 219.
[5] A. Basevi, *Studio sulle Opere di Giuseppe Verdi* (Florence, 1859), p. 71.

with his contemporaries. Only rarely in the 1840's does Verdi go beyond what is called for—shouted for—in the libretto. Identifying choruses and marches recur in *Nabucco* (1842), *I Lombardi* (1843), *I due Foscari* (1844), *Stiffelio* (1850), and especially in *La Battaglia di Legnano* (1848), which displays something of the grim system of *Les Huguénots*. In *I due Foscari*, Verdi experimented rather surprisingly with a full network of identifying themes for each of the three principals, the Council of Ten, and even the people of Venice; each has a musical "calling card," which serves not to recall previous dramatic situations but simply to identify. I am unable to say whether Verdi copied this scheme from any other opera. In any case he did not follow it again until *Aïda*.

As for "recalling themes," an instance occurs as early as *Oberto* (1839), Verdi's rather unassuming first work for the stage. At the beginning of Act II, the *seconda donna* recalls some music from her earlier love-duet with the hero: "Riccardo! . . . Oh! soavi memorie! . . ." In *Nabucco* (1842), the monologue of the mad King Nebuchadnezzar involves several past themes as well as a future funeral march; when he repents, prays to the God of Israel, and is miraculously cured, the distinctive solo cello is heard from the previous *preghiera* of the Israelite High Priest. The heroine of *Giovanna d'Arco* (1845), as an "inspired" character, hears a recurring chorus of angels and also one of devils. She also hears, in Act I, six bars of what is to be an important military march in Act III (this is oddly prophetic of the prophetic *rêve* in *Le Prophète*). In *Attila* (1846), the vision which presently becomes a reality was specifically set up in the libretto, like the repetition of the pledge in *Ernani* (1844).

In these years there is little consistency and little art in Verdi's use of recurring themes. A third of the early operas do not employ the means at all. We are doubtless sufficiently grateful for not having to suffer a procession of tired recalling themes during the *gran scena di sonnambulismo* for Lady Macbeth (or during the *sogno* for Francesco in *I Masnadieri*). Verdi too may have felt that the evocative dream or mad scene had seen its day.

Musical recall on a more imaginative level, however, was another proposition. It was in the course of composing *Rigoletto*, in 1850-51, that Verdi seems to have been struck by the immediate theatrical force of this device, and perhaps also by its congeniality to his personality, musical style, and conception of drama.

Thanks to the full-length composition draft of *Rigoletto* published in facsimile by Carlo Gatti,[6] we are able to see something of the evolution of Verdi's idea here. As is well known, the original title was to have been *La Maledizione*, and from the first, Verdi followed the obvious course of providing parallel music for Rigoletto's parallel exclamations at the end of Acts I and III, "Ah! la maledizione!!" At the time of the draft, however, he did not yet intend to use a single musical setting for the recurring words "Quel vecchio maledivami!" in Act I, Scene 2—even though the librettist Piave set them up for him, almost literally, no fewer than four times during the scene. In the draft, the four remarks are set to different declamatory patterns, the first three (evidently) to be sung unaccompanied, *cupo voce*, and the last to be supported by a diminished seventh chord:

Ex. 2

[6] *L'Abbozzo del Rigoletto di Giuseppe Verdi*, with an introduction by Carlo Gatti (Milan, 1941).

Within the next months, Verdi changed this to the greatly superior German sixth that we know, altered the other three places to agree with it, and then composed the Prelude to the opera out of this material. (The draft contains no indications for a prelude. In *Ernani*, too, the recurring pledge music appears in the Prelude.) It is noteworthy that the figure for "Quel vecchio maledivami!" is not precisely equivalent to any of the actual curse music of Monterone, similar as it may be on account of the monotone C and the rhythmic profile. The non-identity is a relic of Verdi's original reluctance, as it seems, to provide obvious relationships.

In any case, the recollection of Monterone's curse is suitably gripping—one is tempted to think, the more so for not consisting of a precise quotation. As for "La donna è mobile," that was an item handed on a silver platter from Hugo to Piave to Verdi. One might attempt to describe it as an "identifying canzone" handled ironically and climactically, but the piece seems safely *hors de classification*.

And after *Rigoletto*, Verdi would appear to have tried to work recalling themes of the imaginative variety into all or almost all his operas. To be sure, in *Il Trovatore* (1853), a retrospective work, the character who does the remembering is again half-mad: Azucena twice recalls the burning of her mother through the spectral canzone "Stride la vampa!" It will be granted that this refines the treatment of people "hearing things" past the stage represented by *Nabucco*. In his next forward-looking work, *La Traviata* (1853), Verdi used imaginative recall even more extensively than in *Rigoletto*. As mentioned above, Alfredo's declaration from Act I, "Di quell' amor," reappears in the orchestra two acts later as Violetta reads the letter, and again as she dies; on the latter occasion the theme is developed simply, but movingly, by means of a modulating sequential extension. But this theme of Alfredo's had already been sung by Violetta during the aria "Ah, fors' è lui," at the end of Act I, when she is debating whether to devote herself to *amor* or to *gioia*. Then, in order to dramatize her conflict, Verdi actually has "Di quell' amor" sung again by Alfredo off stage during her cabaletta "Sempre libera." Alfredo is said to be serenading outside *sotto al balcone*, but it is possible that the whole thing is a figment of Violetta's excellently fertile dramatic imagination.[7]

[7] Verdi, not Piave, must be responsible for this idea. It does not figure in the libretto.

In *Rigoletto* and *La Traviata*, the recalling theme becomes what Gino Roncaglia calls a "tema-cardine," a recurring theme around which the entire drama is made to hinge.[8] It spans the total action, from the first act to the last, and it is contrived so as to touch on the central dramatic idea: Monterone's curse, the love of Alfredo. Viewing Verdi's *œuvre* as a whole, I could not quite agree that the "tema-cardine" functions as systematically, as consciously, or always as artistically as Roncaglia implies, but his point is certainly well taken in reference to *Rigoletto* and *La Traviata*. These recurring themes do more than recall or identify: they provide, in a single musical gesture, a compelling particular focus for the dramatic action.

Between *La Traviata* and *Otello*, Verdi experimented restlessly with recurring music of all varieties. The results are never as convincing as in *Rigoletto* and *La Traviata*, and indeed, by comparison with those works on the one hand and *Otello* on the other, none of the middle operas makes a satisfactory dramatic totality (not even *Aïda*, in the present writer's judgment, for all its ostentatious smoothness of technique). In *Simon Boccanegra* (1857), Verdi repeated music only along the most conventional lines: for the chorus and for the fevered dream or *sogno* of the Doge. In *Un Ballo in maschera* (1859), a number of fragments recur. Amelia arrives on the heath in Act II to the strains of her prayer from Act I; Riccardo, preparing to renounce Amelia, recalls his earlier love-song about her;[9] Tom and Sam are identified by a rather unfortunate recurring theme in fugato. *La Forza del destino* (1862, 1869) features an even more unfortunate identifying theme for the force of destiny, which pries its way into many arias and other numbers. Then Leonora's prayer from the beginning of the Monastery Scene is sounded just before her formal induction into the hermitage at the end of the scene. (Music and treatment are modeled on those of Amelia in *Ballo*.) *Don Carlos* contains a large number of recollections—too many,

---

[8] Gino Roncaglia, "Il 'Tema-cardine' nell' opera di Giuseppe Verdi," *Rivista Musicale Italiana*, XLVII (1943), 220-22.

[9] This case is interesting from another point of view. After his meditative slow aria, the receipt of urgent news gives Riccardo every excuse to embark upon a cabaletta, but instead of this he simply sings an ecstatic epitome of his earlier piece. Did Verdi hope to achieve in this way something of the force of the traditional cabaletta without its tedium and banality? Ponchielli obtains a similar effect after the "Suicidio" aria in *La Gioconda*.

even in the original version for Paris (1867). The cabaletta in which Carlos and Rodrigue pledge friendship, "Dieu, tu semas dans nos âmes," is recalled several times, generally with pathetic overtones. Elisabeth brings to memory during her great last-act aria excerpts from her love-duets with Carlos in Act I (Fontainebleau) and Act II. The Fontainebleau love-duet theme also occurs to Carlos in prison (Act IV, Scene 2). An identifying monks' chorus, etc., links Acts I and V.

Rather curiously, *Aïda* (1871) works with a regular scheme of identifying themes for persons and groups, like *I due Foscari* of thirty years before. While in general the dramatic use of these themes is stiff and uninteresting, there are some highly imaginative exceptions: notably the bleak development of the Priests' fugato during Aïda's reply to Amonasro's tongue-lashing ("Padre! a costoro schiava non sono," Act III):

Ex. 3

Once again the most emphatic recalling theme is a prayer, Aïda's "Numi, pietà."

For fifteen years following *Aïda*, Verdi composed no new operas, but he did revise *Simon Boccanegra* and *Don Carlos* for La Scala (1881 and 1884). The revisions show little solicitude for the recurring themes. In *Simon*, some melodic details were improved in the cabaletta "Figlia! al tal nome io palpito" (Act II), but when during his *sogno* Simon dreams this piece, the orchestra coolly recalls something very much like the earlier, inferior version (Act III):

Ex. 4

SOGNO (1857 = 1881)
Andante

Ex. 4 (cont.)

In *Don Carlo*, that Fontainebleau love-duet theme which is recalled twice in later acts was in real jeopardy, for Verdi's decision was to cut out the Fontainebleau episode altogether. The new version salvages no more than six bars of music from the duet, played cryptically by the orchestra during the course of Carlo's opening scene in the new Act I, some time before Elisabetta makes her first entrance:

Ex. 5

Still, in Act IV Elisabetta remembers a full *ten* bars of the tune—which in the new version of the opera she had never even heard. As though to make up for this, Verdi threw in recollections of two more love themes, bringing the total number of these to four. The effect is rather disheveled. One thinks of *Le Prophète*.

A detail of Verdi's revision of *La Traviata* for Paris in 1866 makes one think of *Tosca* and *La Bohème*: the second-act curtain was rung down to an orchestral statement of "Amami, Alfredo."[10] Fortunately, this revision, like the Paris revision of *Otello*, has not been allowed to stand.

With *Otello*, however, nothing is careless and nothing is diffuse. As impressive as the force and centrality of the recalling themes in this opera is the economy with which they are handled, especially by contrast with *Don Carlo* and *Aïda*. There are only two such themes. The lesser of them, Iago's unctuous phrase warning Otello of the "green-ey'd monster," forms the substance of the Prelude to

[10] According to Francis Toye, *Giuseppe Verdi: His Life and Works* (New York, 1959), p. 323. This score I have not seen.

Act III—a phrase which, as the late Francis Toye observed, "fortunately did not become a 'jealousy-motif.' "[11] In the Prelude the general *Stimmung* somewhat resembles that of the passage cited above
from *Aïda* and also resembles the opening of Act V of *Le Prophète*:

Ex. 6

The modal *unisono* theme that appears here in the bass recurs
several times in the course of the opera. It is the Anabaptists' sermon
"Ad nos, ad salutarem undam" (known also as the subject of
Liszt's fugue). The differences between the two act-openings doubtless interest us more than their similarities. Not only does Verdi
build an appreciable piece of music out of the theme, as against
Meyerbeer's single period, but he also furthers the drama very subtly
by seeming to conclude with a deceptive cadence and then returning

[11] *Ibid.*, p. 417.

to it and completing it after the first recitative, the Herald's speech. What the Prelude records is the relentless working of the *veleno* of jealousy in Otello's mind between the acts—something that Shakespeare indicates in quite a different way by opening his Act IV in the midst of a shattering exchange:

> *Iago.* Will you think so?
> *Oth.*   Think so, Iago?
> *Iago.*   What,
>   To kiss in private?
> *Oth.*   An unauthoriz'd kiss.
> *Iago.* Or to be naked with her friend in bed
>   An hour, or more, not meaning any harm?

The operatic Moor of Venice is distracted momentarily, by a deceptive cadence and a Herald announcing important affairs of the Signory. But only momentarily; Otello dismisses the Herald at once and returns to his obsession. Verdi's direction is exactly appropriate: *Come prima.* So is Otello's next word: "Continua"—to Iago, whose characteristic snarling trill has now invaded the cadence.

The other recurring theme, the orchestral music for the kiss at the height of the love-duet in Act I, returns in Act IV when Otello enters to kill Desdemona and then again when he stabs himself. As in *La Traviata*, this deserves to be called a true "tema-cardine"; and now Verdi seems more conscious than ever of the full power latent in the device. The recalling theme spans the opera from first to last and touches on the fundamental tragic issue:

> I kiss'd thee ere I kill'd thee. No way but this—
> Killing myself, to die upon a kiss.

It can be argued that as a dramaturgical instrument, Verdi's recurring music does considerably more than Shakespeare's couplet. Otello's love for Desdemona, but particularly the crux of "kiss and kill," is central to Shakespeare's dramatic conception and also to Verdi's. Verdi's use of musical recall here reaches its ultimate dramatic refinement.

And in technical terms, this recalling of the kiss can be seen to follow a certain procedure developed in *Traviata, Ballo, Forza,* and *Aïda*: reserving for purposes of recurrence the expansive *maggiore*

Ex. 7

conclusion to a composite piece of a kind that moves very emphatically from the minor to the major mode. Arias of this kind abound in Verdi's work: "Tacea la notte," "Il lacerato spirito," "Me pellegrina ed orfana," etc. After *La Traviata*, he had the good instinct to use the concluding *maggiore* part sometimes as a recurring theme. The paradigm in Ex. 7 will perhaps make the point clear.

The novelty in *Otello* is, of course, that the recurring *maggiore* phrase is not a prayer or declaration but a purely orchestral fragment, to which Otello merely adds some broken words the first and last times. However, its emotional quality, and its surging appoggiaturas, 6/4 chords, and string tremolo show a definite kinship with the earlier compositions. (A primitive instance of the same technique may be pointed out in *Jérusalem*, the revision of *I Lombardi* for Paris in 1847. At the start of Act II, Roger [Pagano], as the repentant hermit, prays in a composite aria which comes directly from *Lombardi*—and which in *Lombardi* is heard this once and never again. But for Paris, Verdi made it recur. Presently a starving pilgrim staggers in to tell of a group of his comrades in straits, and Roger, deciding to go to their aid, briefly sings the words "Fais ô mon Dieu que je sauve leurs jours" to the climax of the *maggiore* strain:

Ex. 8

Ultimately Roger returns, and as the chorus whispers that this must indeed be the holy man, the *maggiore* phrase sounds again, now in the orchestra. The phrase serves, then, as a primitive and rather aimless identifying theme. It never turns up in the later acts.)

The expansive *maggiore* phrase used as a recurring theme—we have pursued it tenuously from Jerusalem to Cyprus, from Boston to Memphis—seems to come home to roost at last in Windsor. With just such a phrase, the merry wives read Sir John's outrageous twin love letters: "e il viso tuo su me risplenderà . . ."—and burst into laughter; later on, after considerable byplay and scheming, they recall the letters, the music, and the laughter:

Ex. 9

(The *minore* antecedent, already transformed in *Otello*, has entirely withered away.) A love theme, again—but in a rather special light. It is beautifully characteristic of *Falstaff* that the case should involve parody, and a double parody at that: the merry wives mocking Falstaff's grandiloquence, and the old composer mocking his own emotionalism in one of his own favorite operatic devices.

But a discussion of *Falstaff* would have to move on to new ground: for whereas *Otello* can still be treated as a culmination (however astonishing) of the old tradition, this is not true of *Falstaff* in the matter of recurring themes or anything else. Recurring themes now serve as much for musical organization as for identification or recall, as witness the famous "Dalle due alle tre." Furthermore, thematic relationships on a much subtler level than simple recurrence seem to be constantly, and slyly, at work. These aspects of thematic treatment have been skirted in the present essay, because although they are not altogether absent from the early operas, they are less important there than blunter effects. But our rough scaffold of "recalling" and "identifying" themes will no longer support the "buon corpo di Sir John," the density and brilliance of Verdi's new musical technique in *Falstaff*.

The one completely straightforward use of recurring themes is the love-music of Nannetta and Fenton, which shines luminously and clearly within each of the three acts. Its dramatic purpose would be to articulate or illuminate the dualism that grounds Verdi's conception here—as Edward T. Cone has pointed out:

> What is not usually mentioned is that the complete content involves a basic contrast. On the one hand is the world of fighting and clowning, of appetites and revulsions, of plots and counter-plots. Its depths are indicated by the darkness of Ford's jealousy; but its true representative is Falstaff himself. . . . But there is another world: that of Fenton and Nannetta, which they create for themselves. Its symbol is Nannetta's fairyland, and into its unreality the lovers are able, for a little while, to escape. . . .[12]

The constancy and separateness of this charmed vision is determined in part by the constancy of the music that identifies it, and by the very simple way in which it recurs. So in addition to its numerous very amusing details of recollection—"Reverenza," "Va, vecchio John," "Caro Signor Fontana"—*Falstaff* has its real "tema-cardine," as Signor Roncaglia would doubtless allow. The innocence of the technique itself, by contrast with the high style of thematic activity around it, reflects the contrast between fairyland and Windsor jungle.

The technique is not only innocent but old, old and blunt. Verdi had touched on it in *Oberto, Conte di San Bonifacio*. The study of a composer's development is often the study of his growing sensitivity to means known to him, but known imperfectly, from the beginning.

[12] Edward T. Cone, "The Old Man's Toys: Verdi's Last Operas," *Perspectives USA*, 6 (1954), 132-33.

BIBLIOGRAPHY OF THE WRITINGS
OF OLIVER STRUNK*

COMPILED BY THOR WOOD

BOOKS AND ARTICLES

"Vergil in Music," *Musical Quarterly*, Vol. 16 (1930), pp. 482-97.

Program notes, 1930-1934, in *National Symphony Orchestra Magazine* [Washington, D.C., 1930—].

"Haydn's Divertimenti for Baryton, Viola, and Bass (After Manuscripts in the Library of Congress)," *Musical Quarterly*, Vol. 18 (1932), pp. 216-51.

State and Resources of Musicology in the United States; a Survey Made for the American Council of Learned Societies. Washington, D.C., 1932. 76 pp. (American Council of Learned Societies Bulletin, 19).

"Sources and Problems for Graduate Study in Musicology," *Volume of Proceedings of the Music Teachers National Association, 28th Series . . . 1933*, pp. [105]-116.

"Haydn," in *From Bach to Stravinsky, the History of Music by Its Foremost Critics*, edited by David Ewen. New York: W. W. Norton [© 1933], pp. 77-87. Reprinted in *The World of Great Composers*, edited by David Ewen. Englewood Cliffs: Prentice-Hall [© 1962], pp. 91-102.

"Notes on a Haydn Autograph," *Musical Quarterly*, Vol. 20 (1934), pp. 192-205.

Reports of the Chief of the Music Division, in *Report of the Librarian of Congress for the Fiscal Year Ending June 30, 1935*, pp. 131-56; *Report of the Librarian of Congress . . . 1936*, pp. 128-46. Also separately reprinted.

"Zeuner, Charles," in *Dictionary of American Biography*. New York: Charles Scribner's Sons, 1936, Vol. 20, pp. 651-52. Reprint ed., Vol. 10, Pt. 2, pp. 651-52.

"The Historical Aspect of Musicology," *Volume of Proceedings of the Music Teachers National Association, 31st Series . . . 1936*, pp. [218]-20. Reprinted in *Papers Read at the Annual Meeting*

* The compiler gratefully acknowledges the generous assistance of Professor Kenneth Levy, and, in the final stages of preparation, of Professor Strunk himself.

of the American Musicological Society, December 29, 1936, Chicago, Ill., pp. [14]-16.

"Origins of the 'L'homme armé' Mass," abstract in *Bulletin of the American Musicological Society*, No. 2 (1937), pp. 25-26.

"Early Music Publishing in the United States," *Papers of the Bibliographic Society of America*, Vol. 31 (1937), pp. 176-79. Read December 30, 1937, at a meeting of the Society held in Philadelphia.

"Some Motet-types of the 16th Century," *Papers Read at the International Congress of Musicology, Held at New York, September 11th to 16th, 1939*. New York: published by the Music Educators' National Conference for the American Musicological Society [© 1944], pp. 155-60.

"The Tonal System of Byzantine Music," *Musical Quarterly*, Vol. 28 (1942), pp. 190-204. Originally titled, "The Mode in Byzantine Music," and read at a meeting of the Greater New York Chapter, American Musicological Society, May 17, 1940.

"Carl Engel (July 21, 1883-May 6, 1944)," *Bulletin of the American Musicological Society*, No. 8 (1945), pp. [1]-2. Nominally, but not actually, a committee report: Resolutions Committee, Oliver Strunk, chairman.

"Intonations and Signatures of the Byzantine Modes," *Musical Quarterly*, Vol. 31 (1945), pp. 339-55. Originally titled, "The Intonation Formulas and Modal Signatures in Byzantine Music," and read at a meeting of the Greater New York Chapter, American Musicological Society, October 23, 1944.

"Guglielmo Gonzaga and Palestrina's *Missa Dominicalis*," *Musical Quarterly*, Vol. 33 (1947), pp. 228-39. Read at the annual meeting of the American Musicological Society, February 23, 1946.

"Byzantine Psalmody and Its Possible Connection with Hebraic Cantillation," abstract in *Bulletin of the American Musicological Society*, No. 11/13 (1948), pp. 19-21. Read at "Symposium on Ancient Hebrew and Early Christian Melody" at Temple Emanu-El in New York City in connection with the tenth anniversary of Lazare Saminsky's Three Choir Festival, March 24, 1946.

"An Editorial," *Journal of the American Musicological Society*, Vol. 1, No. 1 (1948), p. 3.

"The Music of the Old Hall Manuscript—a Postscript," *Musical*

Quarterly, Vol. 35 (1949), pp. 244-49. Reprinted in *Studies in Medieval and Renaissance Music* by Manfred Bukofzer (New York: W. W. Norton [© 1950], pp. 80-85) with minor changes and additions.

"Relative Sonority as a Factor in Style-critical Analysis (1450-1550)," read at the annual meeting of the American Musicological Society, December 28, 1949.

"Intorno a Marchetto da Padova," *Rassegna musicale*, Vol. 20 (1950), pp. 312-[315].

Source Readings in Music History, from Classical Antiquity through the Romantic Era, selected and annotated by Oliver Strunk. New York: W. W. Norton [© 1950]; London: Faber, 1952. xxi, 919 pp. Paper-bound ed.: W. W. Norton, 1965. 5 v.

"The Classification and Development of the Early Byzantine Notations," *Atti del Congresso Internazionale di Musica Sacra, organizzato dal Pontificio Istituto di Musica Sacra e dalla Commissione di Musica Sacra per l'Anno Santo (Roma, 25-30 Maggio 1950)*, edited by Igino Anglès. Tournai: Desclée, 1952. Pp. [111]-13.

"S. Salvatore di Messina and the Musical Tradition of Magna Graecia," abstract in Πεπραγμένα τοῦ θ' Διεθνοῦς Βυζαντινολογικοῦ Συνεδρίου Θεσσαλονίκης. Athens: Vol. 2 (1956), p. [274]. Written for the ninth Congrès international d'études byzantines, Thessalonika, 1953.

"The Alleluia-cycle in Byzantine Chant," read at a meeting of the Greater New York Chapter, American Musicological Society, April 16, 1955.

"The Notation of the Chartres Fragment," *Annales musicologiques*, Vol. 3 (1955), pp. [7]-37.

Report to the Dumbarton Oaks Research Library and Collection of Harvard University on two Slavic manuscripts in the library of the Chilandar Monastery, August 28-29, 1955. Published (in excerpt) as part of Roman Jakobson's preface to *Fragmenta Chiliandarica Palaeoslavica, A. Sticherarium*, pp. 8, 9. (Monumenta musicae byzantinae; [principal series], Vol. 5.)

"St. Gregory Nazianzus and the Proper Hymns for Easter," *Late Classical and Mediaeval Studies in Honor of Albert Mathias Friend, Jr.*, edited by Kurt Weitzmann and others. Princeton: Princeton University Press, 1955. Pp. 82-87.

"The Byzantine Office at Hagia Sophia," *Dumbarton Oaks Papers*, No. 9/10 (1956), pp. [175]-202.

"Two Stichera on the Death of the Emperor Nicephorus Phocas," abstract in *X. Milletlerarasi Bizans tetkikleri kongresi tebligleri; Actes du X. Congrès international d'études byzantines. (Istanbul, 15-21.IX.1955)*. Istanbul, 1957, p. [294].

"Influsso del canto liturgico orientale su quello della chiesa occidentale," *L'enciclica 'Musicae sacrae disciplina' di Sua Santità Pio XII; testo e commento, a cura dell'Associazione Italiana S. Cecilia*. Roma: Associazione Italiana S. Cecilia per la Musica Sacra [1957], pp. 343-48.

"Some Observations on the Music of the Kontakion," read at a private conference on Byzantine music, Copenhagen, August 1958.

"The Antiphons of the Oktoechos," *Journal of the American Musicological Society*, Vol. 13 (1960), pp. 50-67.

"A Further Note on the Proper Hymns for Easter," *Classica et mediaevalia*, Vol. 22 (1961), pp. 176-81.

"Melody Construction in Byzantine Chant," supplementary paper, published originally in *Résumés des rapports complémentaires, XIIe Congrès international d'études byzantines*. Beograd, 1961, pp. 73-75. Published in amplified form in *Actes du XIIe Congrès international d'études byzantines, Ochride, 10-16 septembre 1961*. Beograd: Vol. 1 (1963), pp. [365]-73.

"A Cypriote in Venice," *Natalicia musicologica Knud Jeppesen, septuagenario collegis oblata*, edited by Bjørn Hjelmborg and Søren Sørensen. Hafniae: Wilhelm Hansen, 1962. Pp. 101-13.

"The Latin Antiphons for the Octave of the Epiphany," in *Recueil de travaux de l'Institut d'études byzantines no. VIII₂; Mélanges Georges Ostrogorsky*. Beograd: Vol. 2 (1964), pp. [417]-26. (Srpska Akademija Nauka i Umetnosti, Belgrad. Vizantološki Institut. Zbornik radova. No. 8.)

"Two Chilandari Choir-books," read at the Dumbarton Oaks symposium, "The Byzantine Mission to the Slavs," May 1964. A reduced version of the paper, "Zwei chilandari Chorbücher," was read at the Bratislava symposium, "Anfänge der slavischen Musik," August 1964; the papers of the symposium were published under that title, edited by Ladislav Mokrý. Bratislava: Verlag der Slowakischen Akademie der Wissenschaft, 1966. Pp.

65-76. (Slowakische Akademie der Wissenschaft. Institut für Musikwissenschaft. Symposia I.)

"Erich Hertzmann (December 14, 1902-March 3, 1963)," *Acta musicologica*, Vol. 36 (1964), pp. [47]-48.

"Strunk, Oliver," in *Die Musik in Geschichte und Gegenwart.* Kassel: Bärenreiter, 1949— . Vol. 12, cols. 1626-27.

"H. J. W. Tillyard and the Recovery of a Lost Fragment," *Studies in Eastern Chant.* General editors, Egon Wellesz and Miloš Velimirović. London, New York: Oxford University Press. Vol. 1 (1966), pp. 95-103.

Specimina notationum antiquiorum . . . . Folia selecta ex variis codicibus saec. x, xi, & xii phototypice depicta, edited by Oliver Strunk. Hauniae: Munksgaard, 1966. Pars principalis, 187 plates; pars suppletoria, xiii, 40 pp. (Monumenta musicae byzantinae; [principal series], Vol. 7.)

"Byzantine Music in the Light of Recent Research and Publication," read at the Thirteenth International Congress of Byzantine Studies, Oxford, 1966. Separately published (Oxford, 1966) as Main Papers, VIII (pp. [1]-10); reprinted in the same form *Proceedings of the XIIIth International Congress of Byzantine Studies.* London, New York: Oxford University Press, 1967, pp. 245-54.

"Verdiana alla Library of Congress," read at the Primo congresso internazionale di studi Verdiani, Venice, July 31-August 2, 1966. To be published in the proceedings of the congress.

"P. Lorenzo Tardo and His *Ottoeco nei mss. melurgici*; Some Observations on the Stichera Dogmatika," published in Italian in *Bollettino della Badia greca di Grottaferrata*, Nuova ser. Vol. 21 (1967), pp. [21-34], as "Padre Lorenzo Tardo ed il suo Ottoeco nei mss. melurgici: Alcune osservazioni sugli Stichera Dogmatika." Reprinted in the same form in *Proceedings of the XIIIth International Congress of Byzantine Studies.* London, New York: Oxford University Press, 1967, pp. [243]-64.

MISCELLANEOUS

Six Preludes for Piano (7/23-5/24). Manuscript given to the Library of Congress, January 1931.

"Quarterly Book-list," *Musical Quarterly*, Vol. 15, No. 2 (April 1929) until Vol. 20, No. 3 (July 1934).

"Works of Horatio W. Parker," compiled by W. Oliver Strunk, pp. 164-69 of "A Study of Horatio Parker," by David Stanley Smith, *Musical Quarterly*, Vol. 16 (1930), pp. 153-69. Published also in *Horatio Parker; a Memoir for His Grandchildren*, by Isabel Parker Semler. New York: G. P. Putnam's Sons [© 1942], pp. 318-30.

Music from the Days of George Washington, collected and provided with an introduction by Carl Engel, the music edited by W. Oliver Strunk. Washington, D.C.: U.S. George Washington Bicentennial Commission [1931; 2nd edn., 1932], ix, 61 pp. Holograph scores in the Library of Congress, copied and edited by Mr. Strunk. "A collection of patriotic and military tunes, piano and dance music, songs and operatic airs."

Music Library Association. *A Provisional List of Subject Headings for Music, Based on the Library of Congress Classification.* [Rochester], 1933. 69l. "The actual preparation of the list for publication was undertaken by Mr. W. Oliver Strunk of the Division of Music" of the Library of Congress.

Program of mediaeval music, under the direction of and accompanied by comments by Oliver Strunk. Meeting of the Mediaeval Academy of America at Princeton University, April 1941; meeting of the Greater New York Chapter, American Musicological Society, December 8, 1941.

"A Comparison between the French and Italian Music," by François Raguenet. Text of an English translation of *Parallèle des Italiens et des Français*, edited for publication in *Musical Quarterly*, Vol. 32 (1946), pp. 411-36.

"Index of Incipits of the Hirmologion Manuscript in the Library of Congress, Washington, D.C.," unpublished manuscript, written with Erich Hertzmann. Cited by Miloš Velimirović in *Byzantine Elements in Early Slavic Chant*. Copenhagen: Munksgaard, 1960, main vol., p. 135.

REVIEWS

Music in Ancient Arabia and Spain, being La Música de las Cantigas, by Julian Ribera; translated by Eleanor Hague (London and Stanford, 1930 [1929]). In *Art and Archaeology*, Vol. 29 (1930), p. 143.

Documenta polyphoniae liturgicae. . . . Serie I. 1. Guillaume Dufay,

Fragmentum missae. 2. Leonel Power, Missa super "Alma Re-demptoris Mater," edited by Laurence Feininger (Rome, 1947, 2 vols.). In *Journal of the American Musicological Society*, Vol. 2 (1949), pp. 107-10.

La Musica, sotto la direzione di Guido M. Gatti, a cura di Alberto Basso. Parte prima: Enciclopedia storica. (Torino, 1966, 4 vols.) In *Rivista italiana di musicologia*, Vol. 2 (1967), pp. 183-86.

TRANSLATIONS

"Musical Life in Paris (1817-1848); a Chapter from the Memoirs of Sophie Augustine Leo," translated and annotated by W. Oliver Strunk, *Musical Quarterly*, Vol. 17 (1931), pp. 259-71, 389-403.

"August Wilhelm Ambros (November 17, 1816-June 28, 1876)," by Guido Adler, *Musical Quarterly*, Vol. 17 (1931), pp. 360-73.

"Haydn and the Viennese Classical School," by Guido Adler, *Musical Quarterly*, Vol. 18 (1932), pp. 191-207.

"Ludwig Thuille (November 30, 1861-February 5, 1907)," by Edgar Istel, *Musical Quarterly*, Vol. 18 (1932), pp. 463-70.

"Richard Wagner in Vienna," by Alfred Orel, *Musical Quarterly*, Vol. 19 (1933), pp. 29-37.

"Johannes Brahms, His Achievement, His Personality, and His Position," by Guido Adler, *Musical Quarterly*, Vol. 19 (1933), pp. 113-42.

"Brahms, Choral Conductor," by Maria Komorn, *Musical Quarterly*, Vol. 19 (1933), pp. 151-57.

"Was Mendelssohn Indebted to Weber?; an Attempted Solution of an Old Controversy," by Georg Kinsky, *Musical Quarterly*, Vol. 19 (1933), pp. 178-86.

"Style-criticism," by Guido Adler, *Musical Quarterly*, Vol. 20 (1934), pp. 172-76.

"Peter Cornelius," by Edgar Istel, *Musical Quarterly*, Vol. 20 (1934), pp. 334-43.

L'Isola disabitata, by Metastasio, prepared for the performance of Joseph Haydn's setting in the auditorium of the Library of Congress on March 9, 1936; unpublished; in the Library of Congress.

The Italian Madrigal, by Alfred Einstein; translated by Alexander H. Krappe, Roger H. Sessions, and Oliver Strunk. Princeton: Princeton University Press, 1949. 3 Vols.

INDEX